Karl Barth's Critically Realistic Dialectical Theology

Karl Barth's Critically Realistic Dialectical Theology

Its Genesis and Development
1909–1936

BRUCE L. McCORMACK

CLARENDON PRESS · OXFORD

Oxford University Press, Great Clarendon Street, Oxford OX2 6DP

Oxford New York
Athens Auckland Bangkok Bogota Bombay
Buenos Aires Calcutta Cape Town Dar es Salaam
Delhi Florence Hong Kong Istanbul Karachi
Kuala Lumpur Madras Madrid Melbourne
Mexico City Nairobi Paris Singapore
Taipei Tokyo Toronto
and associated companies in
Berlin Ibadan

Oxford is a trade mark of Oxford University Press

Published in the United States
by Oxford University Press Inc., New York

British Library Cataloguing in Publication Data
Data available

Library of Congress Cataloging in Publication Data
Karl Barth's critically realistic dialectical theology:
its genesis and development, 1909–1936 / Bruce McCormack
Revision and expansion of the author's thesis (doctoral)—
Princeton Theological Seminary, 1989
Includes bibliographical references and Index.
1. Barth, Karl, 1886–1968. 2. Theologians—Switzerland—
Biography. 3. Reformed Church—Switzerland—Clergy—Biography
I. Title.
BX4827.B3M37   1995   230'.044'092—dc20   94-19487[B]
ISBN 0-19-826956-0

1 3 5 7 9 10 8 6 4 2

Printed in Great Britain on acid-free paper by
Bookcraft (Bath) Ltd., Midsomer Norton

. . . For
Mary Schmitt McCormack

PREFACE 1997

The response to the first edition of this book has been gratifying, to say the least. Given the natural tendency we all have stubbornly to resist challenges to long accepted paradigms, the readiness on the part of many to embrace the new interpretive scheme set forth in these pages has been a pleasant surprise to me. Equally surprising, however, has been the tendency of some (while praising the book highly) to find in it an exercise in historical theology and nothing more. Thus far, it has been the rare reviewer (Clive Marsh comes immediately to mind) who has fully appreciated what I was trying to achieve on a constructive level and has raised the necessary question about what this implies for theology *after* Barth. Two books have appeared since I completed work on this one which confirm its findings at many points: Thies Gundlach's *Selbstbegrenzung Gottes und die Autonomie des Menschen* and Johann Friedrich Lohmann's *Karl Barth und der Neukantianismus*. Such differences as remain between their conclusions and my own are debating points between interpreters thinking largely along the same lines.

25 September 1997

PREFACE

The present work constitutes the first instalment in a two-volume project on Karl Barth's theology. Both volumes are intended in differing ways to challenge the view which has dominated the historiography of twentieth-century theology in the English-speaking world: namely, that Karl Barth was the leading representative of the "neo-orthodoxy" which was dominant in the period 1930–60. The first volume will lay the foundation for revision through a genetic-historical interpretation of Barth's theological development. The central goal here will be to demonstrate that the "turn" to a "neo-orthodox" form of theology which is usually thought to have taken place with the *Church Dogmatics* in 1931–2 is a chimera. There was no such turn. Subsequent to his break with "liberalism" in 1915, Barth became what we shall call a critically realistic dialectical theologian—and that is what he remained throughout his life. The second volume will examine Barth's relationship to the Reformed tradition on the one hand and modernity on the other, through a systematic analysis of the doctrines set forth in his Göttingen lectures on dogmatics (1924/5).

This first volume, then, is an exercise in intellectual biography. As such, it seeks to fill a rather significant gap in the literature on Karl Barth, locating itself between the attempts which have been made to describe the development of Barth's theology without much attention to the biographical and historical factors which conditioned it on the one side and a work like Eberhard Busch's on the other, which sets forth the life of Barth on the basis of autobiographical reminiscences and letters while keeping critical judgements about Barth's theological development to a bare minimum.

Of works of the first type, there is no lack in the literature. The best of them have been written by theologians (Hans Urs von Balthasar, Hans Frei, T. F. Torrance, Eberhard Jüngel, and Christofer Frey)—which helps in some measure, I think, to account for their shortcomings. Each of these interpreters had a

tendency to stand outside the development and to ask (consciously or unconsciously): what is the most significant result of
this development from the standpoint of systematic theology?
Having identified a shift in theological method as the most significant result, they then scrutinized Barth's early writings with a
view to locating the point where "dialectical thinking" gave way
to "analogical thinking". Such an approach, in my view, had a
decided tendency to give to methodological questions a prominence that they simply did not have in Barth's development
when that development is viewed genetically—that is, from a
standpoint within the development itself.

The distortion produced by such an approach could go unnoticed so long as the material needed to produce a more truly
genetic-historical account of Barth's development was lacking.
But now the situation has changed dramatically. A veritable flood
of material has come into print in recent years in the framework
of the Karl Barth *Gesamtausgabe*: catechetical lessons; occasional
contributions to socialist newspapers in which Barth reflected on
the political, social, and religious problems of the day; early lectures to students (which tended to speak more directly "to the
situation" than did many of the theological books and treatises
which Barth prepared for publication in those days); and working papers, drawn up for discussions with close friends and opponents.

In recent years there have been a significant number of out-
standing studies written by a new generation of German scholars
who have been much more sensitive to the requirements of a
genuinely genetic approach to the problem of Barth's development. I am thinking here especially of the books by Ingrid
Spieckermann, Michael Beintker, Werner Ruschke, and Herbert
Anzinger—scholars whose influence upon my own reflections
will be evident on every page of the present work. The success
of these scholars in correcting a number of the errors which have
surrounded Barth interpretation from the 1920s to the present
day, however, was the result of an intense concentration on particular phases within Barth's overall development or on tracing
the fortunes of a single theme or problem (for example, "dialectic") through a couple of phases of that development. None of
them have tried to "put it all together"; to assess the significance
of recent contributions for an understanding of Barth's develop-

ment as a whole. What is offered here, then, is the first truly genetic-historical treatment of the whole of Karl Barth's theological development, from his earliest "liberal" days to the mature perspective which emerges in the second volume of the *Church Dogmatics* (the Doctrine of God). The reader will find in this book the first attempt in English to trace thoroughly Barth's development prior to the second edition of his commentary on *Romans*. Pre-war sermons are mined to show that Barth's "break" with "liberalism" in 1915 had been prepared for some time earlier in certain material dogmatic decisions made between 1911 and 1914. The precise nature of the "break" is then explained and the first-fruit of that "break", the first edition of *Romans*, is fully explicated (for the first time in a published English-language work). Finally, the nature of the revision between the two versions of *Romans* is considered against the background of the influences and conditions which helped bring it about.

Of even greater importance, however, is the new paradigm which is here offered for understanding Barth's development in the 1920s. Although there were others before me (most notably Ingrid Spieckermann) who challenged the adequacy of the von Balthasarian formula of a "turn from dialectic to analogy", no one has yet seen fit to question the periodization of Barth's development to which that formula gave rise—a periodization which attached immense significance to Barth's 1931 book on Anselm, *Fides quaerens intellectum*. The second half of this book will set forth a thoroughly revised periodization, one which arises out of the recognition that material decisions in dogmatics were of vastly greater importance for furthering Barth's development than were methodological modifications (methodological modifications being themselves the reflex of material decisions). It thereby challenges the usual assumption that the book on Anselm constituted something of a watershed in the development.

The fruit of this genetic-historical work is nothing less than a completely new way of reading Karl Barth's theology. Barth's development, I will argue, did not entail the abandonment or even the weakening of his early commitment to "dialectical theology". His mature theology is best understood as a distinctive form of "dialectical theology" which I will refer to throughout as "critically realistic dialectical theology" (to distinguish it from the more nearly idealistic form set forth by Rudolf Bultmann, for example). Where that has not been grasped, virtually the whole of Barth's theology has been read in the wrong light.

A brief word is in order about the use of sources for this study. With the exception of some of the citations from the *Church Dogmatics* (which, on the whole, I have found to be reliable), all of the translations from German texts are my own. I have, none the less, sought to provide parallel citations from available English translations in the footnotes. The only exceptions to the latter practice are to be found in those cases where the translations were actually abridgements or, in some instances, where the translations were sufficiently questionable that I simply could not recommend them.

The present volume is a lightly revised but greatly expanded version of my 1989 doctoral dissertation, written for Princeton Theological Seminary. The crucial thesis regarding the negligible importance of Barth's book on Anselm (from a genetic point of view) was already fully developed there. But the dissertation was only able to treat the development from 1921 to 1931. Here, a much more comprehensive interpretation has been undertaken.

During the nine years devoted to this project, a number of debts have been incurred which should be acknowledged. The study began with a year's research in Basle, Switzerland, in 1984/5. The funds for this research were provided by a Fulbright/Swiss Government Grant. I wish to thank Prof. T. A. Freyvogel, then President of the Swiss Federal Stipend Commission and his able assistant, Frau Heidi Dannegger, for their help in making our year in Basle a most memorable one.

A number of people in Basle gave unselfishly of their time to offer advice and encouragement. I think above all in this connection of Professors Markus Barth, the late Christoph Barth, and Jan M. Lochman. Most importantly, a special word of thanks is due to the Director of the Karl Barth-Archiv, Dr Hinrich Stoevesandt, and his wife Elisabeth. Not only did Dr Stoevesandt provide me with valuable unpublished materials which were necessary to proving my thesis, but he opened his home to my wife and me on many occasions. In the years subsequent to the completion of the dissertation, he has continued to support me with wise counsel and encouragement. For the richest possible Christian fellowship, I offer to the Stoevesandts my sincere thanks. A vital contribution to my work in this period came from a most congenial colleague and friend, Ingrid Spieckermann. Her brilliant 1985 Göttingen dissertation was the first demonstration to me that there were others who were working along lines similar to my own and her encouragement in several memorable conversations kept me going at a time when I doubted the wisdom of taking on a paradigm which had dominated Barth research for over forty years. The impact of Spieckermann's own work on my reading of Barth makes itself felt most noticeably in the interpretation which is offered here of the second edition of *Romans*. A last important influence on my work at the stage of my dissertation research was made by my *Doktorvater*, Edward A. Dowey, Jr. It was Prof. Dowey who first taught me the value of a genetic study for understanding a great theologian such as Barth. For his faith in me and his willingness to allow me to try out a completely new paradigm for interpreting Barth's development, I shall always be grateful.

My good friends Dr Niklaus Peter (the University of Basle) and Prof. George Hunsinger (Bangor Theological Seminary) read the whole of my dissertation and offered invaluable advice. Any mistakes in interpretation which may still remain are entirely my own and are not to be attributed to them. My colleague Elsie McKee (Princeton Theological Seminary) interrupted her Zurich sabbatical in 1990/1 to track down some hard-to-obtain editorials written by Karl Barth for socialist newspapers which provided the material basis for the thesis advanced in Chapter 4 of this book.

A Princeton Theological Seminary Research Grant provided me with funds needed for a sabbatical semester in Tübingen in the spring and summer of 1992, during which the lion's share of the first four chapters were written. Dietrich Korsch (University of Passau) proved to be an important stimulus to further reflection during this time. I am grateful for his friendship and encouragement.

In the last months of revising and editing, Princeton Theological Seminary provided me with a research assistant. Without the help of Mr D. Paul La Montagne, the book would not have been completed when it was. In addition to ensuring that the citations practice in the footnotes was consistent, Mr La Montagne also prepared the indices to be found at the end of this volume. Beyond that, his quick and sympathetic understanding of what I was trying to achieve made him an excellent sounding-board for thinking through some difficult decisions in the final stages of the project.

Finally, I wish to thank my wife Mary. What I wrote in the preface to my dissertation remains true: her willingness to see her life turned upside down by moves to various countries (Switzerland, Scotland, and Germany) in pursuit of my life's work is a never-ending source of amazement to me. In gratitude for her love and patience, I dedicate this book to her.

B.L.M.
Princeton, New Jersey
13 October 1993

ACKNOWLEDGEMENTS

The author gratefully acknowledges receipt of the following:

Theologischer Verlag Zurich (Zurich, Switzerland): permission to cite from Bernd Jaspert, ed., *Karl Barth-Rudolf Bultmann Briefwechsel*; Eduard Thurneysen, ed., *Karl Barth-Eduard Thurneysen Briefwechsel, Band 1, 1913–1921*; Eduard Thurneysen, ed., *Karl Barth-Eduard Thurneysen Briefwechsel, Band 2, 1921–30*; Karl Barth, *Die christliche Dogmatik im Entwurf*, ed. by Gerhard Sauter; Karl Barth, *Fides quaerens intellectum: Anselms Beweis der Existenz Gottes im Zusammenhang seines theologischen Programms*; Karl Barth, *Predigten 1913*, ed. by Nelly Barth and Gerhard Sauter; Karl Barth, *Predigten 1914*, ed. by Ursula and Jochen Fähler; Karl Barth, *Der Römerbrief (Erste Fassung) 1919*, ed. by Hermann Schmidt; Karl Barth, "Schicksal und Idee in der Theologie" in idem, *Theologische Fragen und Antworten*.

Gütersloher Verlagshaus / Chr. Kaiser (Gütersloh, Germany): permission to cite from Karl Barth, *Das Wort Gottes und die Theologie*; Karl Barth, *Die Theologie und die Kirche*; Jürgen Moltmann, hg. *Anfänge der dialektischen Theologie* Teil 1 und 2.

William B. Eerdmans Publishing Co. (Grand Rapids, MI): permission to cite from Karl Barth, *The Göttingen Dogmatics*; Karl Barth, *The Theology of Calvin, 1922*.

Oxford University Press (Oxford, England): permission to cite from Karl Barth, *The Epistle to the Romans*, trans. by Edwyn C. Hoskyns.

The Karl Barth-*Stiftung* (Basle, Switzerland): permission to cite from the following unpublished material: Karl Barth, "Religion und Sozialismus" (Baden, 7 December 1915); Karl Barth, "Unterricht in der christlichen Religion", ¶ 28: "Christus Jesus: Seine Person"; Karl Barth to Paul Althaus (Postcard, late summer 1924?); Karl Barth to Paul Althaus (letter, 30 May 1928); Karl Barth to Paul Althaus (letter, 14 September 1929); Karl Barth to Hans Asmussen (letter, 14 January 1932); Karl Barth to Emil Brunner (letter, 26 January 1924); Karl Barth to Eduard Thurneysen (letter, 9 January 1931).

The Emil Brunner-*Stiftung* (Zurich, Switzerland): permission to cite from the following unpublished material: Emil Brunner to Karl Barth (letter, 23 January 1924); Emil Brunner to Karl Barth (letter, late summer 1924?).

CONTENTS

Contents

ABBREVIATIONS

B–B Br.	*Karl Barth–Rudolf Bultmann: Briefwechsel, 1922–1966*
B–R Br.	*Karl Barth–Martin Rade: Ein Briefwechsel*
B–Th. Br. I	*Karl Barth–Eduard Thurneysen: Briefwechsel, 1913–1921*
B–Th. Br. II	*Karl Barth–Eduard Thurneysen: Briefwechsel, 1921–1930*
CD	Karl Barth, *Church Dogmatics* (4 volumes, 13 parts)
ET	English Translation
KD	Karl Barth, *Kirchliche Dogmatik* (4 volumes, 13 parts)
NSDAP	*Nationalsozialistische Deutsche Arbeiterpartei* (National Socialist German Workers' Party)
Romans I	Karl Barth, *Der Römerbrief (Erste Fassung) 1919*
Romans II	Karl Barth, *Der Römerbrief, 1922*
SP	*Sozialdemokratische Partei* (Social Democratic Party of Switzerland)
SPD	*Sozialdemokratische Partei Deutschlands* (Social Democratic Party of Germany)
USPD	*Unabhängige Sozialdemokratische Partei Deutschlands* (Independent Social Democratic Party of Germany)

Homeless in this world, not yet at home in the next, we human beings are wanderers between two worlds. But precisely as wanderers, we are also children of God in Christ. The mystery of our life is *God's* mystery. Moved by Him, we must sigh, be ashamed of ourselves, be shocked and die. Moved by Him, we may be joyful and courageous, hope and live. *He* is the Origin. Therefore, we persist in the movement and call: 'Hallowed be Thy name! Thy Kingdom come! Thy will be done, on earth as it is in heaven!'

(Karl Barth, *Konfirmandenunterricht, 1909–1921*, 372-3.)

How good were those years, when the great significance of all of 'our' insights, or lack of insights, manifested themselves only in our hurried walking back and forth on the Friesenweg [between Safenwil and Leutwil], and neither Jülicher nor even Harnack but at most the inhabitants of Holziken and Schöftland could shake their heads at the sight on the street of two strange wanderers between two worlds.

(Eduard Thurneysen to Karl Barth, 6 Oct. 1921, *B–Th. Br.* I. 524.)

Introduction

THE VON BALTHASAR THESIS AND THE MYTH OF THE NEO-ORTHODOX BARTH

I. THE REIGNING PARADIGM

For over forty years now, interpretation of Karl Barth's theological development has stood beneath the massive shadow cast by Hans Urs von Balthasar's 1951 book, *Karl Barth: Darstellung und Deutung seiner Theologie*. The thesis advanced by von Balthasar was this:

Just as Augustine underwent two conversions (the one from crass error to the true God and to Christianity and the other, much later, from the religious, Neoplatonizing philosophy of his youthful writings to true theology), so too in the development of Karl Barth there are two decisive turning-points. The first, the turn from liberalism to Christian radicalism took place during the First World War and found expression in the *Römerbrief*. The second is the end-point of his liberation from the shackles of philosophy in order to arrive at a truly independent theology. This second turning-point took place after a nearly ten-year struggle, sometime around 1930. 'The real document of this farewell . . . from the remnants of a philosophical or anthropological . . . grounding and exposition of Christian doctrine . . . is not the widely read little brochure *Nein!*, directed against Brunner in 1934, but rather the book on Anselm of Canterbury's proof for the existence of God, which appeared in 1931.'[1]

---

[1] Hans Urs von Balthasar, *Karl Barth: Darstellung und Deutung seiner Theologie* (4th edn.; Einsiedeln: Johannes Verlag, 1976), 101. Von Balthasar took his clue for locating the second 'turning-point' from Barth himself—as the quotation at the end of the passage demonstrates. The quotation comes from Barth's contribution to the 'How my Mind Has Changed' series published by *The Christian Century* in 1939. Missing from von Balthasar's quotation is the larger context—which might have turned the interpretation in a very different direction from the one von Balthasar actually took. In context, the passage reads: 'If I now attempt to judge how far I have actually changed in these last years with regard to my work, then it seems possible to put the case in a formula: I have been occupied

Von Balthasar did not concern himself with explaining the nature of the first 'break'. It was the second 'break' which he was most interested in; the one which he said occurred sometime during the writing of Barth's little book on Anselm. And as von Balthasar described it, it was indeed a 'break'. Amongst the words he chose to describe it was *Umbruch* or "radical change".[2] The content of this shift was then described in terms of a 'turn from dialectic to analogy'—a formula which has exercised a tremendous influence in scholarly reflection on Barth's development. We will return to a consideration of the meaning of the formula in the next section. For now, it is important to note that what is suggested by this paradigm is that discontinuity far outweighs continuity in the development which occurred between the second edition of the commentary on *Romans*, which appeared in 1922, and the first part-volume of the *Church Dogmatics*, published in 1932. Barth's first effort at a prolegomena to dogmatics—the *Christliche Dogmatik im Entwurf* of 1927—was simply a 'false start'.[3] It was Barth's study of Anselm which made it necessary for him to begin his dogmatics anew as *Church Dogmatics*. Consistent with this view, the 'classical' formulation of the *analogia fidei* was to be found, according to von Balthasar, in *Church Dogmatics* I/1.[4]

Interestingly enough, however, von Balthasar's understanding of Barth's development was not nearly so tidy as the picture just drawn would seem to indicate. The truth is that von Balthasar also had a second model for interpreting Barth's development which was not altogether compatible with the first. We first catch sight of the second model when he says that the *Christliche Dogmatik im Entwurf* represented 'immense progress' over against

approximately equally with the *deepening* and the *application* of that knowledge which, in its main channels, I had gained before . . . The *deepening* consists in this: in these years I have had to rid myself of the last remnants, etc.' Karl Barth, *How I Changed my Mind* (Edinburgh: The Saint Andrew Press, 1969), 42. Now a 'deepening' of a knowledge already acquired is hardly the same thing as a decisive turning-point. Little wonder that when Charles Clayton Morrison, the editor of *The Christian Century*, turned to the task of interpreting the results of his literary symposium, he numbered Barth amongst those who had testified to 'no change'. See Charles Clayton Morrison, 'How their Minds Have Changed', *The Christian Century*, 51 (4 Oct. 1939), 1197–8.

    [2] Ibid.
    [3] The description of the *Christliche Dogmatik* as a 'false start' comes from Barth himself. See Barth, *KD* III/4, p. viii; *CD* III/4, p. xii.
    [4] Von Balthasar, *Karl Barth*, 117.

the theology of *Romans* II and that it was 'completely oriented towards that which was to come'.[5] On this view, the *Christliche Dogmatik* is made to be the first document of a gradual and evolutionary 'turn to analogy'. The 'turn' is not to be conceived of as occurring quite suddenly with the book on Anselm. Nor is it completed with the appearance of that book.

The replacement of the principle of dialectic by that of analogy did not occur suddenly . . . It occurred slowly, imperceptibly in the first volumes of the *Kirchliche Dogmatik* and can be seen as having definitively taken place in the third [part-] volume [*KD* II/1, 1940], whereas the second volume [*KD* I/2, 1938] catches sight of the principles without having opportunity to make use of them . . . Whoever does not pay attention to this development and seeks the finished formula already in the first volume [*KD* I/1, 1932] will seek it in vain. To be sure, this volume energetically overcomes the existential-anthropological starting-point of the *Christliche Dogmatik* in order to set forth a purely theological doctrine of the Word of God . . . but Christology remains in the background. In the first volume, the concept of the *analogia fidei* appears without the least connection to Christology.[6]

The second model then, sees the 'turn to analogy' as occurring gradually from 1927 to 1938, at which point analogy emerges in its 'fully developed form'.[7] Decisive for von Balthasar in locating the final emergence of analogical thinking in 1938 is its Christological grounding. As he put it in another passage, 'In the *Church Dogmatics*, there occurs imperceptibly but irresistibly the replacement of the central concept "Word of God" by the central concept "Jesus Christ, God and man." '[8] It was the emergence of this Christological concentration in *Church Dogmatics* II/1 which allowed analogy to come to its full expression.

The two models could be reconciled *if* the 'turn to analogy' were said to begin with the Anselm book and to continue until the emergence of the 'fully developed form of analogy'. Then the beginning, at least, of what is conceived to be a gradual 'turn' would be identical with the second 'conversion' of the first model. But it is not at all clear that this is what von Balthasar intended. The beginning of the phase labelled 'turn to analogy' is said to begin with the *Christliche Dogmatik* of 1927. Seen in the light of the second model, the significance of the Anselm book is

---

[5] Ibid. 3.   [6] Ibid. 116–17.   [7] Ibid. 124.
[8] Von Balthasar, *Karl Barth*, 124.

considerably diminished. Most striking of all, perhaps, is the fact that the distance separating the two versions of the prolegomena (the *Christliche Dogmatik* and *Church Dogmatics* I/1 and I/2) is greatly reduced. The two versions of the prolegomena are now knit closely together and are thought to belong together in the same phase of development.

Thus, the periodization which emerges from the first model is this: 'dialectical theology' (1918–31) and 'analogical theology' (1931 and following). On the second model, the periodization is a bit more nuanced: 'dialectical theology' (1918–27), the 'turn to analogy' (1927–38), and 'analogy in its fully developed form' (1938 and following). What this tells us above all, I think, is that von Balthasar was really not at all sure where to place the *Christliche Dogmatik* in a periodization of Barth's development. If a guess were to be hazarded as to which of these two models lay closest to von Balthasar's intentions, it would have to be that the second more closely approximated what he wanted to say. Unfortunately, it is the first model which has exercised the greater influence, especially in the English-speaking world. This influence was unfortunate because (as will be demonstrated in this book) the second model actually lay closer to the truth.

Where von Balthasar was at least tempted to see the *Christliche Dogmatik* as initiating Barth's turn to analogy, for Hans Frei that volume belonged without question to the dialectical period and the shift which was thought to take place with the Anselm book was seen to be dramatic in character—in Frei's word, it represented a 'revolution' in Barth's thought.[9] T. F. Torrance, in his influential study published in 1962, displayed some of von Balthasar's hesitance as to where to locate the *Christliche Dogmatik* in his scheme of Barth's development, but like Frei, he finally placed it in a second period of 'dialectical thinking', with the decisive turn coming with the Anselm book.[10] Since the appear-

[9] Hans Frei, 'The Doctrine of Revelation in the Thought of Karl Barth, 1909 to 1922', Ph.D. dissertation (Yale University, 1956), 194.

[10] T. F. Torrance, *Karl Barth: An Introduction to his Early Theology, 1910–31* (London: SCM Press, 1962), 133, 182. That Professor Torrance's reading of Barth's development was shaped from a very early date by von Balthasar's first model is made clear by a 1952 article he contributed to the *Scotsman*. There Torrance wrote, 'In his recent work, *Karl Barth. Deutung und Darstellung seiner Theologie*, von Balthasar takes careful account of the development of Barth's theology, which falls into three main stages: 1. The early period, reaching its climax with the first edition of his *Romans* in 1918, when he was still under the influence of the idealist philosophy; 2. the nineteen twenties, which saw a thorough

ance of Torrance's book, the idea that Barth's Anselm book represented a more-or-less radical departure from the dialectical theology of the second *Romans* commentary has been taken to be one of the most assured results in Barth research by English-speaking scholars.[11]

In recent years however, three scholars especially have done a great deal to undermine the received paradigm (i.e. von Balthasar's first model). The first study deserving mention here is Eberhard Jüngel's 'Von der Dialektik zur Analogie' which appeared in 1982.[12] For Jüngel, there was only one 'break' in the development of Barth's theology—namely, the break with the "liberal" theology of his student years which occurred sometime during the First World War. What unfolded thereafter is, in Jüngel's view, most accurately described as a 'theology of the

revision of his *Romans* and the first volume of his projected Dogmatics when Barth had come under the influence of Kierkegaard and his theology became dialectical and realist; 3. at the end of that decade, however, came the really decisive change when, in his study of Anselm, Barth swept aside the language of Kierkegaard and existentialism and emerged, as he said, out of his egg-shells. Ever since then the theology of Barth has been the theology of analogy in which Christology plays the dominant role.' See T. F. Torrance, 'Theology of Karl Barth', the *Scotsman* (14 Apr. 1952), 4.

[11] Among recent examples of this tendency the following should be noted. Steven G. Smith interprets Barth's development along the lines of a shift from a 'mainly negative to a mainly positive conception of the otherness of God'. The point at which this shift is seen to occur is once again the Anselm book where the 'otherness of God' is said to be related for the first time to the 'analogy of faith'. Thus, Smith's analysis moves entirely within the well-worn path first trodden by von Balthasar (in his first model). See Smith, *The Argument to the Other: Reason beyond Reason in the Thought of Karl Barth and Emmanuel Levinas* (Chico, Calif.: Scholars Press, 1983), 162, 160. Still more recently, Stephen H. Webb has tried to chart Barth's development in the 1920s through clues drawn from a rhetorical analysis of *Romans* II and the later dogmatic writings. The results are surprisingly conventional; the 'turning-point' in Barth's development of a 'realistic theology' is said to occur with the Anselm book. Webb, *Re-figuring Theology: The Rhetoric of Karl Barth* (Albany NY: State University of New York Press, 1991), 157. Webb's book amply demonstrates the limited value of rhetorical analysis for interpreting what is, after all, a *theological* development. The shift in style in which Webb is interested (a shift from an 'expressionistic' to a 'realistic' style) took place in 1921 when Barth left the pastorate for a teaching post in Göttingen. Why then suddenly introduce the Anselm book as the turning-point in the emergence of a realistic theology? The answer clearly has nothing to do with rhetorical analysis, since on rhetorical grounds alone the shift would have to have been located in 1921. At the crucial point, Webb simply takes for granted the validity of the received paradigm (which was developed on the basis of a theological analysis of the *content* of Barth's thought, not on the basis of rhetorical analysis). In the final analysis, Webb's book contributes nothing new to an understanding of how Barth's *theology* developed in the 1920s.

[12] Eberhard Jüngel, 'Von der Dialektik zur Analogie: Die Schule Kierkegaards und der Einspruch Petersons', in idem, *Barth-Studien* (Zurich and Cologne: Benziger Verlag, and Gütersloh: Gütersloher Verlagshaus Gerd Mohn, 1982), 127–79.

Word of God'. 'This expression is . . . better suited [than the
alternative "dialectical theology"] to describe the continuity in
the path which Barth followed after the break with the theology
of his teachers—though it was, to be sure, a winding path with
several turns.'[13] Jüngel did think it proper to speak of a dialectical
phase and he was able to offer a *terminus a quo* and a *terminus ad
quem* for it. The starting-point is provided by the second edition
of Barth's commentary on *Romans*. To find the end-point, it is
first necessary to define carefully that which made the second
Romans to be "dialectical". Jüngel took his clue from Barth's
description of his task in the preface to the second edition. There
Barth spoke of the need to penetrate through the Bible to the
'inner dialectic of the *Sache*' to which the Bible witnesses.[14]

> The phrase 'the inner dialectic of the *Sache*' is intended to express the
> idea that not only speech about the *Sache* but also the *Sache* itself should
> be conceived of as dialectical. Accordingly, we are dealing here not
> simply with a dialectical knowing of a being which in itself is undialec-
> tical; rather, the dialectic in human knowing corresponds to a dialectic
> in the being to be known. The being to be known is itself dialectical.[15]

According to Jüngel, the end-point of the dialectical phase will
be found at that point where Barth abandoned the thought that
the being to be known was itself dialectically structured.

Jüngel's thesis is that it was a critical pamphlet written by Erik
Peterson against the 'dialectical theology' which forced Barth to
take this step.[16] In Barth's article-length response to Peterson, he
had written, 'The Revelation of which theology speaks is not
dialectical; it is no paradox . . . That scarcely needs to be said.'[17]

---

[13] Eberhard Jüngel, 'Von der Dialektik zur Analogie: Die Schule Kierkegaards und der
Einspruch Petersons' 128.

[14] Barth, *Der Römerbrief, 1922* (Zurich: TVZ, 1940), p. xiii. The German word *Sache*
can mean 'object' or 'subject' or 'subject-matter'. None of these definitions however, is
particularly apt for translating the word as Barth tends to use it. Certainly, Barth intends
the word to carry the sense of something objectively real. Yet he is not referring to an
empirical object either. Here, he is using it to speak of the divine–human relation. At
other times, he will use it to speak of the objectivity of God in revelation.

[15] Jüngel, 'Von der Dialektik zur Analogie', in idem, *Barth-Studien*, 143.

[16] Erik Peterson, 'Was ist Theologie?', reprinted in idem, *Theologische Traktate*
(Munich: Kösel Verlag, 1951), 11–43. Peterson's pamphlet will occupy us at some length
further on, so we will not provide an exposition of his argument here. See below, Ch. 8,
Sect. 7.

[17] Barth, 'Kirche und Theologie', in idem, *Die Theologie und die Kirche* (Munich: Chr.
Kaiser Verlag, 1928), 319; ET 'Church and Theology', in *Theology and Church: Shorter
Writings 1920–28* (London: SCM Press, 1962), 299.

Barth then had gone on to define "dialectic" in theology strictly in terms of a *Dialektik der menschlichen Erkenntnis*—a dialectic of human knowing. With the 'shift' entailed in this statement, according to Jüngel, it then became possible for Barth to move on to a theology of an (in itself) undialectical Word of God and to bid farewell to a merely dialectical theology. From this point on, Barth began to develop his doctrine of the *analogia fidei*.[18]

The picture which emerges from Jüngel's essay is one of a dialectical phase stretching from 1921/2 to 1925 (or 1927 at the latest). He was happy to retain the language of a 'turn from dialectic to analogy' as the most apt description of Barth's development, but he tended to regard the 'turn to analogy' as something which occurred only gradually between 1927 and 1931.[19] The *Denkbewegung* which found expression in the book on Anselm is said by Jüngel to be 'already observable in the *Christliche Dogmatik*'.[20] In the final analysis, Jüngel's model for interpreting Barth's development corresponds most closely to von Balthasar's second model, not the first.[21]

Jüngel's analysis was important in that it had the effect of calling into question the decisive significance normally accorded to the Anselm book; yet it was not without problems of its own. As we shall see, Jüngel was right in sensing that a significant development had occurred sometime around 1925, though the explanation he offered for this development was flawed. Barth's doctrine of revelation was never simply "undialectical", not even in the *Church Dogmatics*. Therefore, a more carefully worked-out explanation of the development will have to be provided.

---

[18] Jüngel, 'Von der Dialektik zur Analogie', in idem, *Barth-Studien*, 135–6.

[19] Ibid. 129. It should be pointed out that although Jüngel cited von Balthasar's formula with approval, the two men did not mean the same thing by it. When von Balthasar spoke of "dialectic", he had chiefly in mind Barth's so-called "dialectical method" of pitting theological statement over against counter-statement (thesis against antithesis) without allowing a synthesis of the two to emerge. See von Balthasar, *Karl Barth*, 79–93. What Jüngel saw as most basic to Barth's "dialectical theology" on the other hand, was not a method but a *Realdialektik* in the being to be known. Therefore, although Jüngel has retained the formula of a 'turn from dialectic to analogy', he has done so only by altering its meaning.

[20] Eberhard Jüngel, 'Einführung in Leben und Werk Karl Barths', in idem, *Barth-Studien*, 47.

[21] Jüngel even accepts von Balthasar's contention that the category of the "Word" is supplanted in *CD* II/1 from its position of prominence and replaced by the category "Jesus Christ". In line with this, he speaks (again as von Balthasar did) of analogy as attaining predominance within the *Church Dogmatics* in a progressive fashion. Jüngel, 'Von der Dialektik zur Analogie', in idem, *Barth-Studien*, 128, 179.

In 1985, a book appeared which for the first time successfully challenged the validity of the 'dialectic to analogy' formula. Ingrid Spieckermann's *Gotteserkenntnis* concentrated its attention on Barth's break with liberalism and the problem of identifying in detail wherein the truly new element in Barth's 'post-liberal' theology lay.[22] Spieckermann traced the development of Barth's 'new' theology only through the year 1924, but that did not prevent her from making a major contribution to resolving the question of how Barth's theology developed in the 1920s.

Spieckermann's contribution lay above all in her remarkable discovery of a form of analogy in *Romans* II which belongs to the same structural type as that which Barth would later refer to as the *analogia fidei*. Her thesis is that the 'analogy of the cross', which emerges already in the phase of *Romans* II, provided the 'ground and limit' of all dialectically constructed theological witness to God in His Self-revelation.[23] Though Spieckermann's thesis is indeed startling, I believe that it is correct. The *Urgestalt* of the *analogia fidei* is indeed to be found in *Romans* II—as will be thoroughly demonstrated in the course of our exposition of that commentary.

Spieckermann also deserves credit for bringing one other significant consideration to light which had heretofore been lost to view. Though it was not always realized by previous interpreters, Barth gave two complete cycles of lectures on dogmatics (covering everything from the doctrine of God to eschatology) before beginning his monumental *Church Dogmatics*. The first cycle was given at the University of Göttingen over three semesters (summer semester 1924 to summer semester 1925) and was completed at the University of Münster with lectures on eschatology in the winter semester 1925/6.[24] The second cycle was given in

[22] Ingrid Spieckermann, *Gotteserkenntnis: Ein Beitrag zur Grundfrage der neuen Theologie Karl Barths* (Munich: Chr. Kaiser Verlag, 1985).

[23] Ibid. 143.

[24] These lectures are now being published within the framework of the Karl Barth Gesamtausgabe. To date, the first two of what will be a three-volume work have appeared in German. See Barth, '*Unterricht in der christlichen Religion*', i. *Prolegomena*, ed. Hannelotte Reifen (Zurich: TVZ, 1985) and '*Unterricht in der christlichen Religion*', ii. *Die Lehre von Gott/Die Lehre vom Menschen, 1924/125*, ed. by Hinrich Stoevesandt (Zurich: TVZ, 1990). The first eighteen paragraphs (covering prolegomena and the doctrine of God) have been translated into English. See Barth, *The Göttingen Dogmatics: Instruction in the Christian Religion*, vol. i, trans. Geoffrey Bromiley (Grand Rapids: Wm. B. Eerdmans, 1991).

Münster over three semesters stretching from the winter semester 1926/7 to the winter semester 1927/8. The *Christliche Dogmatik im Entwurf* of 1927 set forth in published form the 'Münster Prolegomena': the revised, second version of the lectures on prolegomena to dogmatics which Barth had already given in Göttingen. Spieckermann was the first scholar to have access to the Göttingen lectures—though her access was limited to the first eighteen paragraphs (the lectures on prolegomena to dogmatics given in Göttingen in the summer semester of 1924 as well as four paragraphs of the lectures given on 'Dogmatics I' in the winter semester 1924/5). What she saw, however, was sufficient to convince her that the differences between the first and second versions of the prolegomena were quite small.[25] Thus, where interpreters in the past had at times been tempted to see the *Christliche Dogmatik* as the starting-point of a new phase in Barth's development, Spieckermann now saw clearly that any such new phase would have to be adjusted back in time, to begin in 1924 with Barth's first lectures on prolegomena.[26]

With this adjustment in mind, Spieckermann interpreted Barth's development as follows. She saw the development after the break with liberal theology (which she located in the summer of 1915) as a more or less continuous unfolding of a single material insight or intention.[27] That intention was to ground theology in the objectively real Self-speaking of God in revelation. Barth advanced four different models for explicating that intention, thus giving rise to four phases in his development. The first phase began with the break with liberalism and ended in January 1920; the second stretched from January 1920 to (roughly) 1924; the third, from 1924 to the Anselm book in 1931; the fourth comprised the *Church Dogmatics*.

The one weakness in Spieckermann's otherwise brilliant analysis lies in her understanding of the role played by the Anselm book in Barth's development. In fact, Spieckermann can speak of her four phases as together constituting two 'stages'; the first three phases belonging to the first 'stage' and the last phase being

---

[25] That view has been confirmed by Michael Beintker in a review of the prolegomena volume of the Göttingen Dogmatics. See Beintker, 'Unterricht in der christlichen Religion', in Gerhard Sauter (ed.), *Verkündigung und Forschung: Beihefte zur 'Evangelische Theologie'*, 2 (Munich: Chr. Kaiser Verlag, 1985), 46.

[26] Spieckermann, *Gotteserkenntnis*, 140–3, 227.   [27] Ibid. 72–82.

itself identical with the second and last 'stage'.[28] Such a move, of
course, grants a very high degree of significance to the book on
Anselm. But if *Fides quaerens intellectum* is not connected in some
way with the emergence of so-called "analogical thinking"
(because the 'turn to analogy' occurred at a much earlier point in
time), then the logical question to ask is: why continue to attach
so much importance to it? Spieckermann's answer is that the
Anselm book sets forth a 'revision of method' based upon a clear
distinction between the 'ontic' and the 'noetic' rationality of the
object of theology (and the priority of the former over the
latter).[29] But that answer, as we shall see, is a problematic one
because such a distinction was presupposed earlier (though it was
not set forth in those precise terms).

Spieckermann's discovery of the presence of a form of analogy
within what had usually been thought of as Barth's 'dialectical
phase' found independent confirmation two years later in
Michael Beintker's *Die Dialektik in der 'dialektischen Theologie' Karl
Barths*.[30] Beintker's book is without doubt the most important
work to date on the period 1922–31 and deserves very close
study. Beintker too, found distinct evidence of 'analogical
moments' in Barth's early theology, emerging first in the famous
Tambach lecture of September 1919 and surfacing here and there
throughout the 1920s.[31] Like Spieckermann, he was able to find
something like an 'analogy of the cross' in *Romans* II, as well as
an example of what he calls an 'analogy of relations' (that is,
Barth's assertion that love of the neighbour should and can mirror the love which God has for us).[32] The first instance of the
analogia fidei in the strict sense is located by Beintker in the
Christliche Dogmatik of 1927, where an analogical relation
between God's speech (*Deus dixit*) and human knowing of it is
affirmed.[33] Thus, Beintker concludes that the concept of analogy

[28] Spieckermann, *Gotteserkenntnis*, 19.   [29] Ibid. 228–9.

[30] Michael Beintker, *Die Dialektik in der 'dialektischen Theologie' Karl Barths* (Munich:
Chr. Kaiser Verlag, 1987). Beintker had not read Spieckermann's book before finishing
his own.

[31] Ibid. 259–79.

[32] Ibid. 261–2. Cf. 280, where Beintker says, 'the *Denkform* of the *analogia relationis sive
proportionalitatis*, which sets forth a correspondence between the God–human relation and
the human–human relation, forms a constant in Barth's work from the time of the
Tambach lecture on.'

[33] Ibid. 263. The crucial passage appealed to in order to confirm this view is this: 'The
human being does indeed do something corresponding, parallel, analogical in her own

in the *Christliche Dogmatik* is 'on the way' to the later, more fully developed doctrine of analogy.

Beintker's major contribution to a proper understanding of Barth's theology in the twenties did not lie in tracing the emergence of analogy however. It lay rather in his searching analysis of the meaning of "dialectic" in the so-called "dialectical theology" of Karl Barth. Beintker was able to identify no less than four distinguishable dialectics at work in *Romans* II and the occasional lectures and essays of that phase.

The first dialectic is referred to by Beintker as a 'noetic' dialectic; a dialectical structuring of human thinking and speaking in theology.[34] The *locus classicus* of this form of dialectic is to be found in Barth's famous 1922 lecture 'The Word of God as the Task of Theology'. In this lecture Barth set forth for the first time (in a well-considered theoretical form at least) what came to be known as his "dialectical method": that is, a method which calls for every theological statement to be placed over against a counter-statement, without allowing the dialectical tension between the two to be resolved in a higher synthesis.

But 'dialectic for Barth was more than a "*Denkform*"'[35]. The 'noetic' dialectic is preceded by and has its ground in a *Realdialektik*—a dialectic in objectively real relations. The *locus classicus* in this case is to be found in Barth's famous words from the preface to *Romans* II:

But what do I mean when I call the *inner dialectic of the Sache* and its recognition in the words of the text the decisive factor in understanding and exposition? . . . If I have a "system", it consists in that which Kierkegaard called the 'infinite qualitative difference' between time and

creaturely sphere of being in view of that which God does in His, in that He reveals Himself.' See Barth, *Die christliche Dogmatik im Entwurf*, ed. Gerhard Sauter (Zurich: TVZ, 1982), 138. What is at stake in this passage is indeed an analogical relation between divine speaking in the act of revelation and human knowing in the act of faith. Beintker is right to see in this an example of what Barth would later call the *analogia fidei*. It must be pointed out that the Göttingen Prolegomena only came into Beintker's possession as he was correcting the final draft of his book for publication. Had he had the earlier version of the prolegomena, he would have had to adjust his thesis slightly, placing the first instance of the *analogia fidei* in 1924 rather than 1927—as he himself implicitly acknowledges through the provision (in the final draft) of the parallel passage in *Unterricht* to the one just quoted. See Barth, '*Unterricht in der christlichen Religion*', i. *Prolegomena*, 114; ET *The Göttingen Dogmatics*, 94.

[34] Beintker, *Die Dialektik in der 'dialektischen Theologie' Karl Barths*, 25–31.
[35] Ibid. 31.

eternity; in keeping that difference constantly in view in both its negative and positive significance. 'God is in heaven and you are on earth.'
The relation of *this* God to *this* human being, the relation of *this* human
being to *this* God, is for me both the theme of the Bible and the sum of
philosophy.[36]

It is this *Realdialektik* (not the noetic dialectic) which is predominant in *Romans* II and Beintker shows that it takes two principal
forms (which constitute the second and third kinds of dialectic
analysed). In both cases, the dialectic of time and eternity is
employed as a conceptual apparatus for bearing witness to what is
in fact a soteriological theme.[37] The first of these forms has as its
focus the relation of an eschatologically conceived revelation to
the events which occurred in AD 1–30 in the life of Christ.[38] The
second form focuses on the relation of an eschatologically conceived new humanity to the believer who exists in time.[39] The
fourth and final dialectic identified by Beintker is what Barth
referred to in the phase of *Romans* II as 'the dialectic of life'.
What is in view here is the common human experience of the
contradictory nature of existence (the continuous tension
between pleasure and suffering, etc.).[40]

The significance of Beintker's examination of the various
forms of dialectic at work in the phase of *Romans* II is this: in the
light of this illuminating analysis, it will no longer be possible to
speak simply of a 'turn from dialectic to analogy' without at least
making clear which dialectic is thought to be left behind and
which—if any—continue to make themselves felt at later stages.

How then do these advances finally impact on Beintker's own
understanding of the overall picture of Barth's development?
Beintker wants to retain the von Balthasarian language of a 'turn
from dialectic to analogy'. Yet he emphasizes that just as analogy

---

[36] Barth, *Der Römerbrief, 1922*, p. xiii.

[37] It is Beintker's great merit to have shown convincingly that the oft-discussed
time–eternity dialectic functions in the theology of *Romans* II *not* to set forth a metaphysical dualism (as has often been thought), but rather to serve the purpose of witnessing to
the dialectic of judgement and grace in the 'crisis' brought about by revelation. Thus, the
time–eternity dialectic—so far from setting forth a metaphysic—has its home within the
framework of soteriology. See e.g. Beintker, *Die Dialektik in der 'dialektischen Theologie'
Karl Barths*, 33. That Beintker is absolutely correct in this analysis is in my view beyond
doubt. Rightly understood, *Romans* II was everywhere governed by an antimetaphysical
outlook, as will be demonstrated at the appropriate point in our exposition. See below,
Ch. 6, Sect. 3.

[38] Ibid. 31–40.   [39] Ibid. 40–55.   [40] Ibid. 55–9.

could already be found as early as the Tambach lecture, so also dialectic continues to be found in the *Church Dogmatics*.[41] Therefore, the 'turn' in question has to be regarded along the lines of a shift in emphasis and not simply as the replacement of one form of thought by another. Beintker expresses it this way:

The thesis of a turn from the "thought-form" (*Denkform*) of dialectic to the "thought-form" of analogy . . . is correct insofar as it seeks to comprehend Barth's thought from the point of view of which "thought-form" was dominant at any given time. Dialectic was *dominant* in the twenties; analogy was *dominant* for the period after *Fides quaerens intellectum*.[42]

The view described advances beyond von Balthasar's first (and more influential) model only to the extent that it abandons the thought of a second 'conversion', a second watershed in Barth's development. Dialectic and analogy are seen by Beintker to coexist throughout the 1920s (and they continue to do so in the *Church Dogmatics*). Therefore, the 'shift' is a shift in emphasis, not a qualitative leap forward. But Beintker still follows von Balthasar in associating the 'turn' with the book on Anselm in 1931.

Like von Balthasar before him, however, Beintker gives evidence of not being wholly satisfied with this interpretation. Beintker too, has another scheme for interpreting Barth's development.

Strictly speaking, one can speak of *the* "dialectic theology" of Karl Barth or (alternatively) of a clear predominance of dialectical "thought-forms" and argumentation only with reference to *Romans* II and the essays grouped around it . . . the publications which appeared in 1922 form Barth's dialectical period in the strict sense. . . . In the works appearing after *Romans* II, dialectic increasingly loses significance.[43]

Clearly, the assertion here that the dialectical *Denkform* is dominant only during the phase of *Romans* II stands in direct contra-

---

[41] The coexistence of dialectic and analogy was already demonstrated in 1974 in Eberhard Mechels, *Analogie bei Erich Przywara und Karl Barth: Das Verhältnis von Offenbarungstheologie und Metaphysik* (Neukirchen-Vluyn: Neukirchener Verlag, 1974), 199 ff. Cf. Beintker, *Die Dialektik in der 'dialektischen Theologie' Karl Barths*, 251–9.

[42] Beintker, *Die Dialektik in der 'dialektischen Theologie' Karl Barths*, 280.

[43] Ibid. 18. Cf. 278, where Beintker makes Barth's January 1923 debate with Adolf von Harnack belong to the phase of *Romans* II, only then to speak of a rapid change occurring shortly thereafter which made possible the emergence of a form of analogy corresponding to that which dominates the *Church Dogmatics*.

diction to Beintker's contention noted above, namely that dialectic is the dominant *Denkform* throughout the 1920s. In the final analysis, Beintker was as stumped as von Balthasar had been in his efforts to integrate the *Christliche Dogmatik* (or its predecessor, the Göttingen prolegomena lectures) coherently into a scheme of Barth's development.

Michael Beintker's work represents the last and greatest effort to interpret Barth's development along the lines first laid down by Hans Urs von Balthasar. One can clearly see in it, however, all the problems which have plagued that line of interpretation from the very beginning. As long as scholars seek to explain Barth's development in terms of dialectic and analogy, the vacillation between locating the more significant 'turning-point' at the point where the *analogia fidei* first emerges and locating it at the point where it receives its final 'deepening and clarification' will continue. The riddle of how Barth's theology developed will not be solved along this line. Fortunately, there is a better way.

2. WHERE DO WE STAND NOW?

If there is one point on which all recent Barth scholarship agrees, it is that von Balthasar's belief in a second 'break' in Barth's development cannot be sustained. Ingrid Spieckermann's description of a continuous unfolding of a single material intention through different models of explication can be regarded as the best formulation of a conviction now widely held. Beyond this shared conclusion, however, considerable disagreement and ambivalence remain.

There are two problems which have been left unresolved by research in this field to date. The first has to do with the degree of significance assigned to Barth's 1931 book on Anselm. Here great ambivalence prevails. Recent scholarship has tended to suggest that the emergence of forms of the *analogia fidei* took place much earlier than was once thought. The effect of this discovery has been to force Michael Beintker to reduce the significance of the Anselm book to that of a signpost marking a modest shift from the predominance (though not exclusivity) of a dialectical "thought-form" to the predominance (though not exclusivity) of an analogical "thought-form". Consistent with that position,

Beintker can then speak of the significance of the Anselm book in terms of a 'deepening' of a starting-point in thought which had dominated Barth's theology for some time (probably since 1924).[44] But such an answer would hardly justify continuing to speak of a 'turn' with *Anselm*. Understandably, Ingrid Spiecker-mann has abandoned the von Balthasarian formula altogether in favour of seeking a different explanation for the importance of the book on Anselm in a developmental scheme.

In the light of these efforts, it is only reasonable to ask, why has the book on Anselm enjoyed such a fierce hold on the minds of interpreters of Barth's development? The answer is actually quite simple. The book on Anselm comes between the *Christliche Dogmatik* (which Barth later judged a 'false start') and the 'new beginning' with the *Church Dogmatics*. Scholars have felt con-strained (and rightly so) to provide some explanation for why Barth would start his dogmatics again from the beginning rather than simply revising the existing book. The most obvious answer seemed to be the one which Barth himself offered: a break-through of some sort had occurred with the Anselm book which not only made possible but actually *necessitated* starting again from the very beginning. The contention of this book will be that the reason Barth began his dogmatics again had very little to do with the theological learning-process which occurred between 1927 and 1931. The differences between the *Christliche Dogmatik* and *Church Dogmatics* I/1 and I/2 are simply not great enough to require beginning anew. I will argue that it was above all the his-torical coincidence of the disintegration of relations between Barth and his erstwhile theological comrades (Friedrich Gogarten, Rudolf Bultmann, and Emil Brunner) with the dra-matic change of political fortunes in Germany which occurred at the parliamentary elections of September 1930 which moved Barth to distance himself in as public a way as possible from his former friends. What better way than to exaggerate the distance separating his own theology in the present moment of 1931 from the theological way he had followed throughout the twenties (and thereby from the theology which he had promoted together with Gogarten *et al.*)? If this view is sustained (and I think the evidence is overwhelmingly convincing), then the importance of

---

[44] Beintker, *Die Dialektik in der 'dialektischen Theologie' Karl Barths*, 283.

the Anselm book from a genetic standpoint will at the very least be called into question and will need to be reassessed.

The second problem has to do with the viability of the von Balthasarian formula itself. In the light of the foregoing contention that the importance of the book on Anselm has been exaggerated, the most logical solution might seem to be to simply alter the periodization while retaining the formula. So, for example, one might wish to speak of a 'turn from dialectic to analogy' in 1924. Although there would be a certain amount of truth in such a position, it would not resolve all the difficulties. Periodization alone is not the problem. The problem is that the formula itself is finally inadequate for describing Barth's development.

There are four principal problems with the von Balthasarian formula which argue for its abandonment.

1. The first problem with the formula has to do with the indefiniteness of the first term. Beintker's careful study of the range of possible meanings of the word "dialectic" in the phase of *Romans* II has helped to make clearer what ought to have been clear all along: that the repetition of the formula by scholars after von Balthasar all too easily serves to conceal important differences of opinion. What von Balthasar meant by 'turn from dialectic' was a turn from a particular *Denkform* (by which he meant especially "dialectical method"); what Jüngel means by it, however, is a turn from a theology which has its ground in a particular kind of *Realdialektik*. Already, on this most basic level, the formula easily gives rise to misunderstanding.

2. The second problem is far more weighty. The *analogia fidei* is itself an *inherently dialectical concept*. Far from representing the abandonment of dialectic, the 'analogy of faith' is grounded in what I will refer to here as the 'dialectic of veiling and unveiling' in revelation. To understand the significance of this claim, we must first set forth in a provisional way Barth's understanding of analogy.[45]

The 'analogy of faith' refers most fundamentally to a relation of correspondence between an *act* of God and an *act* of a human

---

[45] On Barth's doctrine of analogy, the following are relevant: Joachim Track, 'Analogie', *Theologische Realenzyklopädie*, ii. 625–50; Horst Georg Pöhlmann, *Analogia entis oder Analogia fidei?: Die Frage der Analogie bei Karl Barth* (Göttingen: Vandenhoeck & Ruprecht, 1965); and Eberhard Mechels, *Analogie bei Erich Przywara und Karl Barth*.

subject; the act of divine Self-revelation and the human act of faith in which that revelation is acknowledged. More specifically, the analogy which is established in a revelation event is an analogy between God's knowledge of Himself and human knowledge of Him in and through human concepts and words. There are three aspects of this analogy which need to be highlighted. First, the analogy in question is not posited with creation. It is not an analogy between the *being* of the Creator and the *being* of the creature—which Barth refers to as an *analogia entis* in contrast to an *analogia fidei*. The focus here is not being but rather a highly concrete event: the event of revelation. Second, there is nothing in the being or knowing of the human subject which helps to bring this event about—no capacity or pre-understanding which might be seen as a necessary precondition to its occurrence. The only capacity needed for the analogy is one which God Himself graciously provides in the event itself as a gift, namely faith. In the event of revelation, human knowledge is made by grace to conform to its divine object. Thus (the reader will forgive an overused metaphor, but it is good Barthian language), the direction in which the analogy works is always 'above to below'. That is to say, God's Self-knowledge does not become analogically related to a prior human knowledge of Him in revelation; rather, human knowledge is conformed to His. God's act is the analogue, ours is the analogate; His the archetype, ours the ectype. Third, the 'analogy of faith' is to be understood 'actualistically', that is, strictly as an event. The relation of correspondence which is established in the revelation-event does not become a predicate of the human subject. To put it another way, the "being" of the human subject is not altered through the experience of faith's knowledge of revelation. The analogy endures only so long as the revelation-event endures. Thus, the 'analogy of faith', once realized, does not pass over into human control. It must continue to be effected moment by moment by the sovereign action of the divine freedom if it is to be effected at all.

The central area of theological reflection to which this understanding of analogy was applied by Barth is that of the relation of the content of revelation to human language (concepts and words). Barth's view is that human language in itself has no capacity for bearing adequate witness to God. If human language is nevertheless able to bear witness, it will only be because a capacity not intrinsic to it has been brought to it from without. But that is grace, not nature. In a gracious and sovereign act, God takes up the language of human witnesses and makes it to conform to Himself. God must therefore speak when spoken of by human witnesses if such witness is to reach its goal. He must reveal Himself in and through the 'veil' of human language. It is at this point that the *inherently dialectical* character of the *analogia fidei* is clearly seen.

The dialectic of 'veiling and unveiling' in revelation which (as we shall see) was so characteristic of Barth's thought in the phase of *Romans* II was taken up into his doctrine of analogy and preserved in it as its first moment. The establishment of an analogical relation between revelation and human language as the second moment depends entirely on the *Realdialektik* of the divine veiling and unveiling as the first moment. God unveils Himself by veiling Himself in human language. In truth, the *Realdialektik* of veiling and unveiling is the motor which drives Barth's doctrine of analogy and makes it possible.

The great weakness of the formula of a 'turn *from* . . . *to* . . .' is now clearly seen. Dialectic was never simply left behind as the formula implies. To be sure, the so-called "dialectical method" gradually took a back seat to a dogmatic method—a fact which no doubt led to the formula in the first place. But as will be shown, "dialectical method" was never the principal form of dialectic in the first place. Like "analogy", it too had its ground in the *Realdialektik* of the divine movement in revelation and was simply a conceptual tool for bearing witness to it. "Dialectical method" *could* have been abandoned altogether—in truth, it was not, but it could have been—without in the least requiring the abandonment of the vastly more important *Realdialektik*. The great weakness of the von Balthasarian formula is that it conceals from view the extent to which Karl Barth remained—even in the *Church Dogmatics!*—a *dialectical theologian*. Where this has not been recognized, the temptation to view Barth's mature theology in an all-too positive light (as, e.g., a "neo-orthodox" theology) has rarely been avoided.

3. The third major weakness in the received formula is that— in its original usage at any rate—it brings two concepts together on the same plane of theological discourse which actually belong to different planes, and thereby commits a category error. The

reason is this: von Balthasar used the phrase a 'turn from dialectic to analogy' to speak of a turn away from "dialectical method". But if one were to speak intelligibly of a 'turn from dialectic to analogy' (where the dialectic in question is "dialectical method"), the 'analogy of faith' too would have to be a theological method. But it is not. The 'analogy of faith' refers to the result of a divine act over which human beings have no control. "Method" on the other hand, is a procedure, a conceptual tool which enables human thinking to perform certain tasks, to accomplish certain goals. In other words, "method" is something humans do. Viewed in this way, the difference between the 'analogy of faith' and "dialectic method" is as great as that between heaven and earth. To be sure, the 'analogy of faith' had methodological *implications*. Barth's conception of analogy belonged to those fundamental decisions which made his "dogmatic method" possible (a method which was first employed in Göttingen in 1924 and received final clarification in *Fides quaerens intellectum*). But it was not itself a method.

It should be noted that no privileged claim is being made here for Barth's doctrine of analogy. It was a *doctrine* like any other. It did not fall down from heaven; it was constructed by a human being. So, to say that the difference between "analogy" and "dialectical method" is as great as that between heaven and earth is not to say that one of them had its origins in heaven. It is simply to point out the categorial difference between human speech about an act of God and human speech about the actions of human beings.

4. The fourth and ultimately conclusive argument against the continuation of the practice of interpreting Barth's development by means of a concentration on "dialectic" and "analogy" is that it fails to penetrate deeply enough into the *material* theological conditions in Barth's theology which gave rise to "dialectic" and "analogy" in the first place. In *Romans* I and II, the central theological theme was that of the Kingdom of God. In 1924 concentration on the theme of the Kingdom gave way to the centrality of an incarnational Christology. The argument here will be that it was Barth's adoption of the ancient anhypostatic-enhypostatic model of Christology in May 1924 (together with his elaboration of a doctrine of the immanent Trinity) which provided the material conditions needed to set free the elaboration of the *analogia*

fidei. All further adjustments which took place on the level of what might properly be called method flowed from this material decision and were a reflex of it.

What this suggests, among other things, is that the riddle of how Barth's theology developed in the 1920s will only finally be solved by taking up a standpoint within that development and viewing the matter genetically. For too long the procedure has been anything but genetic. Interpreters have stood at the end of the development and asked themselves: what is the most significant fruit of this development from the standpoint of systematic theology? Having answered this question in terms of the elaboration of the *analogia fidei,* they have then conceived of their task as consisting in tracing the emergence of that conception. In other words, they have made their own primary concern to be Barth's as well and read it back into the development. Viewed genetically however, from a standpoint *within* the development itself, everything looks different. It was as Barth concentrated his attention on the material problems of Trinity and Christology in 1924 that solutions to methodological questions also began to emerge—something which Barth himself was only gradually aware of.

3 . A NEW PARADIGM

What will be offered here is nothing less than a *Gesamtdeutung* covering the years 1909 to 1936. To set forth the development as a whole (rather than concentrating solely on the years 1921 and following) offers the following advantages: 1. It will make much clearer the extent to which Barth's development was indeed the unfolding of a single material insight through several differing models of explication, thereby emphasizing the continuity which prevailed in that development from the first emergence of the new starting-point in 1915; 2. It will also make it clear that at every point, shifts in Barth's models of explication had their roots in material decisions in dogmatic theology, thereby underscoring the fact that Barth was from first to last a theologian (and not a philosopher turned theologian as von Balthasar and those who followed in his wake seemed to imply); and 3. It will for the first time draw together in a single volume a critical reflection on the fruits of recent German studies into aspects of the development for a proper understanding of the development as a whole.

The new paradigm for interpreting Barth's development which will be advanced in this book is as follows:

1. Dialectical Theology in the Shadow of a Process Eschatology (1915–January 1920).

Barth's break with liberalism will be located in the summer of 1915. What emerged over the next five years was a form of dialectical theology whose fundamental shape was controlled and determined by a 'process eschatology' which preserved a tension between present realization and future fulfilment in its conception of the Kingdom of God. The great document of this early form of dialectical theology is *Romans* I.

2. Dialectical Theology in the Shadow of a Consistent Eschatology (January 1920–May 1924).

As a result especially of the influence of Franz Overbeck and Heinrich Barth, Karl Barth's conception of the Kingdom was fundamentally altered in early 1920, thereby necessitating the revision of his commentary on *Romans*. *Romans* II therefore was stamped by a 'consistent' or thoroughgoing eschatology which allowed for very little present realization (even to the point of making the incarnation itself most problematic).[46]

3. Dialectical Theology in the Shadow of an Anhypostatic-Enhypostatic Christology (First Stage: Pneumatocentrism, May 1924–September 1936).

In May 1924, the relation of the Kingdom of God to history set forth in Barth's 'consistent eschatology' was modified by the adoption of an anhypostatic-enhypostatic Christology which enabled him to conceptualize how revelation can be fully present *in* history without becoming a predicate *of* history. Thus he was able to affirm the incarnation in a coherent way without surrendering the critical gains of *Romans* II. It should be noted that although Christology provided the ground of Barth's theology in this phase, it cannot yet be said that his theology was governed by a 'christocentric concentration'. If anything, it was a theology concentrated on the actualization of revelation by the Holy Spirit

---

[46] The language of 'process eschatology' and 'consistent eschatology' are taken over from Beintker. See Beintker, *Die Dialektik in der 'dialektischen Theologie' Karl Barths*, 45, 110–11.

in the present and therefore was more nearly pneumatocentric than christocentric. To put it another way, the *locus* of the *Realdialektik* which absorbed Barth's attention in this phase was not so much the incarnation itself as it was the revelation event in the present moment. This concentration is seen most clearly in the highly actualistic conception of election and reprobation which was set forth in the Göttingen Dogmatics and continued to hold sway on into *Church Dogmatics* I/1 and I/2.

4. Dialectical Theology in the Shadow of an Anhypostatic-Enhypostatic Christology (Second Stage: Christocentrism, September 1936 and following).

In June 1936, Barth heard a lecture given by Pierre Maury in Geneva on the subject of election. As a result of the influence which this lecture had upon him, Barth modified his doctrine of election by making its central focus to be the election of Christ as Mediator (and of individuals *in Him*) rather than the election of individuals as the effect of a revelation–event in the present. The document of this modification was the lectures which he gave on election in Debrecen, Hungary, in September 1936. The effect which this had on his theology as a whole was to shift its focus from a pneumatocentric concentration to a christocentric concentration; in other words, from a concentration on the present actualization of revelation to a concentration on the *Deus dixit* in the strict sense. This final 'shift' first makes itself felt in the treatment of the doctrine of God in *Church Dogmatics* II/1 (upon which Barth began to lecture in the summer semester of 1937). Thus, there is a truth contained in von Balthasar's talk of a shift from concentration on 'the Word' to a concentration on 'Jesus Christ'—though his way of describing it was hardly satisfactory.[47]

Three observations are in order with respect to the new elements in this interpretive scheme. First, although scholars have always been inclined to regard *Romans* I as "pre-dialectical", that practice will be abandoned here for the following reason. The fact that *Romans* I is generally regarded as "pre-dialectical" rests upon a historical accident, not careful interpretation of the contents of the book itself. The element of historical contingency lies in the fact

---

[47] George Hunsinger is right to object to von Balthasar's language, but that should not prevent us from seeing that von Balthasar was right to sense a shift somewhere around 1936–8. See Hunsinger, *How to Read Karl Barth: The Shape of his Theology* (New York: Oxford University Press, 1991), 7.

that the first book was not widely known in Germany when the second edition appeared. It was the second edition therefore which first elicited the tag "dialectical theology", sometime in 1923. Since that time the second edition has been allowed to define what is dialectical theology and what is not.[48] The effect of this bit of largely accidental historiography is that *Romans* I has scarcely ever been allowed to command attention in its own right. It has repeatedly been interpreted through the lens provided by the second edition, with a view to highlighting differences between the two. In the process, significant elements of continuity have been lost to view. A careful reading of *Romans* I will show that it too sets forth a form of dialectical theology. There is, therefore, no good reason to continue to allow that fact to be concealed by the perpetuation of the old, accidental historiography. Second, conspicuous by its absence in this scheme is any reference to the book on Anselm. The decisive 'turn' from the theology of *Romans* II occurred in 1924 and when it did the major influence was not Anselm of Canterbury but Heinrich Heppe's *Reformed Dogmatics*. However significant the book on Anselm may be from a systematic theological point of view, from a genetic-historical point of view it cannot be accorded the status of a turning-point. All three versions of the prolegomena therefore belong to the same phase. Third, material questions in dogmatics are seen to control and determine the shape of the development. Whatever changes occurred in Barth's method were simply a reflex of decisions made in the areas of eschatology, Christology, and the doctrine of election. From a genetic point of view, those material questions have to be regarded as having decisive importance.

4. SYSTEMATIC RELEVANCE OF THE DEVELOPMENTAL PROBLEM

The relevance of the developmental question for interpreting Barth's theology as a whole is not far to seek. The popularity of

[48] Michael Beintker has contributed more than any other scholar to identifying a particular kind of "dialectical theology" in *Romans* I. See Beintker, *Die Dialektik in der 'dialektischen Theologie' Karl Barths*, 109–27. Yet he continues to refer to the theology set forth in that book as "pre-dialectical" precisely because it falls short of the kind of 'tension-filled dialectic' found in *Romans* II. Ibid. 18. But that of course, is to read the first edition in the light of the second, a practice which will not be followed here.

von Balthasar's first model (with its suggestion of a second 'break' after the break with liberalism) has most certainly contributed to the perpetuation of the Anglo-American reading of Barth's later theology as "neo-orthodox".

It has long been recognized that America and England never provided fertile soil for a thoroughgoing reception of Barth's theology. But the evidence is slowly mounting that even within that very small minority which could be counted as Barth's followers in the English-speaking world during the twenties and thirties, Barth's theology was only partially accepted. Many of the central themes of his early theology (for example the 'infinite qualitative distinction' between God and humankind, the sole normativity of God's Self-revelation in Christ, the rejection of natural theology, the love of paradoxes and dialectic) simply proved unacceptable. A tremendous amount of cultural translation was required to make Barth's theology assimilable. As Richard Roberts has put it, a 'process of normalization' took place which adjusted and reformed Barth's theology in accordance with more traditional norms.

This process of normalization became the easier as the distance in Barth's own work from the earlier dialectical extremity seemed to grow greater both in time and actual content . . . In the American literature, the observation of the apparent, gradual estrangement of Barth himself from his dialectical phase and the emergence of the strongly systematic thrust of the *Christliche Dogmatik* in 1927 and then the *Kirchliche Dogmatik* proper from 1932 onwards, provided the opportunity for commentators to relate Barth's later work to their own presuppositions without excessive compromise. Barth was thus assimilable into given critical expectations once the dialectical origin had been distanced.[49]

Thus, the Barth who was received in the Anglo-American world was to a large extent a Barth stripped of his dialectical origins. The Barth who belonged to the sources of "neo-orthodoxy" in the Anglo-American world was himself a product of a "neo-orthodox" reading. This "neo-orthodox" reading was simply reinforced in the 1950s by the assimilation of von Balthasar's thesis of a second 'conversion' in Barth's development. To this day,

---

[49] Richard Roberts, 'The Reception of the Theology of Karl Barth in the Anglo-Saxon World: History, Typology and Prospect', in Stephen W. Sykes (ed.), *Karl Barth: Centenary Essays* (Cambridge: Cambridge University Press, 1989), 125, 137.

the "neo-orthodox" reading of Barth remains the predominant one in the English-speaking world.

In Germany the situation is rather different. To be sure, the "neo-orthodox" reading is not unknown there. The charge had already arisen with respect to the first edition of *Romans*, as Barth himself attested in the preface to the second edition.[50] Originally, the phrase referred no doubt to Barth's supposedly pre-scientific pneumatic exegesis or, alternatively expressed, to his alleged enmity to historical criticism. The appearance of *Die christliche Dogmatik* in 1927 gave critics new reason for using the phrase. Reviewers were quick to notice the prominence given a medieval scholastic like Anselm of Canterbury and the role played by seventeenth-century Reformed scholasticism. The perception was widespread among liberals that Barth was a theological reactionary who wanted to overthrow the fruits of scientific theology acquired since the 1780s (or thereabouts) in order to return to the theology of a former age. Ferdinand Kattenbusch gave expression to this view when he wrote in 1934,

[Barth] wants to be "orthodox", to adhere to the line which theology followed until the dawn of the "Enlightenment", of "Rationalism". On this line, he wants to insert into theology that which the Reformed and Lutheran orthodox did not allow to come into its own with respect to Bible, confession and dogma. Therefore, "medieval" and "patristic" elements, so far as a Luther and a Calvin continued them, should remain and be reappropriated.[51]

Or again,

[Barth] thinks *"juristisch-bekenntnismäßig"* ["in legal conformity to the confessions"], like the *orthodoxy* which grew out of the Reformation, which "heard" the Word of God in the Bible as mediated by the Book of Concord or the Heidelberg Catechism or some textbook about the gospel declared to be binding.[52]

The criticism implied by the term was given renewed force in the 1950s through the translation into German of the first volume of Paul Tillich's *Systematic Theology*. Tillich saw in Barth the spectre of a 'kerygmatic theologian' who wanted to derive the

---

[50] Barth, *Der Römerbrief, 1922*, p. vi.
[51] Ferdinand Kattenbusch, *Die deutsche evangelische Theologie seit Schleiermacher* (Gießen: Verlag von Alfred Töpelmann, 1934), ii. 46.
[52] Ibid. 48.

contents of his theology solely from the Bible (and perhaps the confessions) without regard for the 'situation'. To the extent that the 'situation' was not systematically integrated into Barth's method, it became a "neo-orthodox" method which served the cause of *repristination*.[53]

In 1972 however, a process of revision began which has led to the demise of the "neo-orthodox" reading of Barth in Germany. Friedrich-Wilhelm Marquardt set forth the controversial thesis that Barth's theology was the product of influences which had their origin not in the peculiar problems of the pastor as he/she mounts the pulpit Sunday after Sunday,[54] not in Barth's rediscovery of the Bible and of Paul, but in his political activity on behalf of the working classes in his Safenwil parish; in other words, in his socialist engagement. Indeed, Marquardt could go so far as to argue that Barth's later Christological concentration represented no 'break' in Barth's thought but was merely tacked on to an already developed concept of God drawn in large measure from reflection on socialist praxis.[55] Marquardt's book was indeed controversial and even his most ardent defenders hesitated to commit themselves fully to his daring thesis regarding the development of Barth's doctrine of God. Marquardt's questions, however, were much more important than the answers he himself gave to them. For the first time, a scholar had made the question of the impact of Barth's historical (social, political, and cultural) context upon his theology to be of central significance for interpreting that theology as a whole. The great merit of Marquardt's book (and the further research into the socio-political determinants of Barth's theology which it spawned[56]) was its insistence that Barth's theol-

---

[53] Paul Tillich, *Systematic Theology* (Chicago: University of Chicago Press, 1951), i. 5.

[54] This was Barth's own explanation of the impulse which first moved him to abandon the theology which he had received from his teachers and to seek something new. See Barth, 'Not und Verheißung der christlichen Verkündigung', in idem, *Das Wort Gottes und Die Theologie* (Munich: Chr. Kaiser Verlag, 1925), 101–2.

[55] Friedrich-Wilhelm Marquardt, *Theologie und Sozialismus: Das Beispiel Karl Barths* (3rd edn.; Munich: Chr. Kaiser Verlag, 1985), 21–5.

[56] The literature on the interrelation of Barth's socialist political activities and the development of his theology is by now quite extensive. The following may be considered a sampling of the most important contributions. Helmut Gollwitzer, *Reich Gottes und Sozialismus bei Karl Barth* (Munich: Chr. Kaiser Verlag, 1972); Ulrich Dannemann, *Theologie und Politik im Denken Karl Barths* (Munich and Mainz: Chr. Kaiser Verlag and Matthias-Grünewald Verlag, 1977); Friedrich-Wilhelm Marquardt, *Der Christ in der Gesellschaft, 1919–1979: Geschichte, Analyse und aktuelle Bedeutung von Karl Barths Tambacher Vortrag* (Theologische Existenz heute, 206; Munich: Chr. Kaiser Verlag, 1980); Peter

ogy was always *zeitgemäß*; that is, it was always directed to a particular situation and really had no intention of being 'timeless'.[57]

A second major stimulus towards revision was provided by Trutz Rendtorff in the same year in which Marquardt's book first appeared. In a provocative essay entitled 'Radikale Autonomie Gottes', Rendtorff advanced the thesis that Barth's 'revolution' in theology had consisted in initiating a 'new Enlightenment' whose major concern lay in securing the freedom and autonomy of God (rather than the freedom and autonomy of human beings as had been the case with the 'first Enlightenment').[58] This concern by no means represented a simple repudiation of the Enlightenment. Barth shared with the Enlightenment a self-consciousness which was critically disposed towards traditional authorities.[59] And the standpoint from which he subjected traditional authorities to critical scrutiny (i.e. that of the freedom and autonomy of God) would itself have been

Winzeler, *Widerstehende Theologie: Karl Barth 1920–35* (Stuttgart: Alektor Verlag, 1982); Friedrich-Wilhelm Marquardt, Dieter Schellong and Michael Weinrich (eds.), 'Karl Barth: Der Störenfried?', *Einwürfe*, vol. iii (Munich: Chr. Kaiser Verlag, 1986); Peter Winzeler, 'Der Sozialismus Karl Barths in der neuesten Kritik', *Evangelische Theologie*, 48 (1988): 262–72. The early literature generated by Marquardt's 1972 book was evaluated in English in George Hunsinger (ed.), *Karl Barth and Radical Politics* (Philadelphia: Westminster Press, 1976).

[57] That the "situation" was indeed granted a constitutive role in Barth's methodological reflections is easily demonstrated. Consider e.g. the following statement taken from Barth's treatment of the "dogmatic norm"(!) in theology: 'In its testing of the Church's proclamation, dogmatics must orient itself to the concrete situation towards which Church proclamation itself must today be geared . . . i.e. to the Word of God as it is spoken in the present and is to be proclaimed by the Church. Dogmatics must therefore locate itself with the teaching Church in this concrete situation, making the place and task of the teaching Church its own, trying to hear with its own ears the Word of God which is spoken in the present to the present . . . An ecclesial attitude excludes the possibility of a dogmatics which thinks and speaks in a *timeless* way.' Barth, *KD* I/2, 939–40; ET *CD* I/2, 840. Cf. the parallel passage in the Göttingen Dogmatics where Barth says, 'Dogmatics may not turn its back on the *present*, the moment. As a dogmatician, I may not think and speak timelessly as if I were a person living in the fourth or sixteenth centuries.' See Barth, '*Unterricht in der christlichen Religion*', i. *Prolegomena*, 357; ET *The Göttingen Dogmatics*, i. 295. A careful comparison of Barth's method with Tillich's would show that Barth was not altogether lacking in what Tillich called a 'method of correlation'. The major difference between the two lay in the fact that Tillich's method of correlation was built upon a foundation laid by the Lutheran understanding of the relation of law and gospel, while Barth's was erected on the soil of a Reformed view of the priority of gospel over law.

[58] Trutz Rendtorff, 'Radikale Autonomie Gottes: Zum Verständnis der Theologie Karl Barths und ihre Folgen', in idem, *Theorie des Christentums* (Gütersloh: Gütersloher Verlagshaus Gerd Mohn, 1972), 164.

[59] Ibid. 165–6.

impossible without building upon the conception of human freedom and autonomy already present in the Enlightenment. For Rendtorff, Barth could with all propriety be regarded as an 'exponent of liberal theology'[60] and deserved to be protected from those admirers who wanted to see in his theology a 'repristination of pre-modern theology'.[61]

Twenty years after its publication, Rendtorff's essay continues to arouse scholarly debate. Certainly his thesis has not found universal acceptance in all of its points. Still, the great value of the essay lay in the stimulus it provided to reopening the question of Karl Barth's relationship to "modernity". Although opinions continue to vary, the one point generally agreed upon today is that Barth's stance *vis-à-vis* the world of modern thought cannot be adequately described solely in terms of repudiation and opposition; elements of continuity can be found in the midst of discontinuity.[62]

To a large extent, this work of revision has gone unnoticed by theologians in the Anglo-American world who by and large continue to dismiss Barth as the foremost exemplar of that most lamentable of twentieth-century aberrations: the "neo-orthodox" theologian. The present study is offered in the hope that through a reconsideration of Barth's development, the "neo-orthodox" misreading of his theology will at last be seen for what it is and be set aside in the historiography of twentieth-century theology. This book will be followed by a sequel which will be more systematic in nature. It will seek to clarify Barth's complex relationship to tradition and the modern world through a theological analysis of the Göttingen Dogmatics.

---

[60] Trutz Rendtorff, 'Radikale Autonomie Gottes: Zum Verständnis der Theologie Karl Barths und ihre Folgen', in idem, *Theorie des Christentums*, 164.

[61] Ibid. 174.

[62] Among the contributions to an analysis of Barth's relationship to "modernity" (in its various facets), the following should be noted. K. G. Steck and Dieter Schellong, *Karl Barth und die Neuzeit* (Munich: Chr. Kaiser Verlag, 1973); Trutz Rendtorff (ed.), *Die Realisierung der Freiheit* (Gütersloh: Gütersloher Verlagshaus Gerd Mohn, 1975); Dieter Schellong, *Bürgertum und christliche Religion* (Munich: Chr. Kaiser Verlag, 1975); Wilfried Groll, *Ernst Troeltsch und Karl Barth—Kontinuität im Widerspruch* (Munich: Chr. Kaiser Verlag, 1976); Christof Gestrich, *Neuzeitliches Denken und die Spaltung der dialektischen Theologie: Zur Frage der natürlichen Theologie* (Tübingen: J. C. B. Mohr, 1977); Dietrich Korsch, 'Christologie und Autonomie: Zu einem Interpretationsversuch der Theologie Karl Barths', *Evangelische Theologie*, 41 (1981), 142–70; Trutz Rendtorff, 'Karl Barth und die Neuzeit: Fragen zur Barth-Forschung', *Evangelische Theologie*, 46 (1986), 298–314; John Macken, *The Autonomy Theme in the 'Church Dogmatics': Karl Barth and his Critics* (Cambridge: Cambridge University Press, 1990).

PROLOGUE
The Making of an Outsider . . .

We may not expect that life leads to sitting and possessing; in no sense, at no moment. We cannot remain standing; we may not, and we ought not even once wish to do so. Whatever awaits us on our way . . . is under no circumstances our goal. Even the most important, the beautiful, the tragic moments of our lives are only stations on the way, nothing more . . . Saying farewell! that is the great rule of this life. Woe to us if we reject this rule, if we want to remain standing, calling a halt and attaching ourselves to a particular station. . . . There is nothing left for us but to acknowledge this 'Saying farewell!', becoming obedient to it . . . here we have no lasting city.

(Karl Barth, sermon, 28 December 1913)

1
The Marburg Background

I. THE CULTURAL CONTEXT OF BARTH'S EARLIEST DIALECTICAL THEOLOGY

In a provocative essay published on the occasion of the centennial celebrations of Karl Barth's birth, Dieter Schellong raised an intriguing question. What was it that drove Barth? What was it that sustained him through over a half-century of intensive theological work? Schellong's answer was 'expectation'.[1] Expectation joined with an eschatologically conditioned longing describes not only a fundamental constant in Barth's personality over the years; it provides an important point of access to comprehending the significance of his theology.

It was Barth himself who provided Schellong with this clue. In July 1922, Barth delivered an address to a group of ministers at Schulpforta in Saxony. He had been asked to give an introduction to his theology. But he opened with a disclaimer.

It always embarrasses me a little to hear 'my theology' spoken of so seriously . . . because I then have to ask myself with some perplexity, in what might my theology consist? Where could the cathedral or fortress be which deserves this name and which one could be introduced to, by means of a ground-plan perhaps? . . . I must openly confess to you that that which I can in any case call 'my theology' consists finally—when I examine it closely—in a single point. And it is not a *stand*point, as one might demand as the most minimal requirement of a proper theology. Rather, it is a *mathematical* point on which one cannot stand. It is merely a *view*point.[2]

What is that viewpoint which, if seen and understood, would constitute an introduction to Barth's theology? Finally, it reduces

[1] Dieter Schellong, 'Barth Lesen', in Marquardt, Schellong, and Weinrich (eds.), 'Karl Barth: Der Störenfried?', 6.
[2] Karl Barth, 'Not und Verheißung der christlichen Verkündigung', in idem, *Das Wort Gottes und die Theologie*, 99.

to this: 'To sigh: *Veni creator spiritus* is, according to Romans 8, an act more full of hope than the triumphalism which acts as if it already had Him. You have been introduced to "my theology" when you have heard this sigh.'[3] This statement, filled as it is with longing and hope for the coming of God, a new world, and a new humanity, and at the same time containing a decisive protest against all human attainments and possessions, everything which now exists and lies ready to hand, is the best single introduction not only to the early theology of Barth but even to his later, mature theology.

Move ahead a number of years in time, to the lectures with which Barth concluded his teaching career in 1962. In these lectures, Barth sounded once again this early theme.

Veni creator spiritus! 'Come, O come, thou Spirit of life!' Even the best theology cannot be anything more or better than this petition made in the form of resolute work. Theology can ultimately only take the position of one of those children who *have* neither bread nor fish, but doubtless a father who has both and will give them these when they ask him. In its total *poverty* evangelical theology is rich, sustained and upheld by its total lack of presuppositions. It is rich, sustained and upheld since it lays hold of God's promise . . .[4]

In Barth's sigh '*Veni creator spiritus*' we do indeed catch sight of an enduring element in Barth's theology: a point of integration which sustained that theology through all the years. The prayer which is uttered in that sigh is the prayer of a person who *possesses* nothing which might provide a precondition for doing theology. It is the expression of an anti-bourgeois spirit on the soil of theology. It is the eschatological reservation which Karl Barth understood as circumscribing the whole of his life's work.

The roots of Barth's sigh are to be found in the years prior to the outbreak of the First World War, in the subterranean currents of the counter-culture which was beginning to emerge in German-speaking countries during those years. In Germany itself, the runaway arms race of the years 1905–14 and the financial burdens which they placed on governments, the deep-lying social problems which went largely ignored while military spend-

    [3] Karl Barth, 'Not und Verheißung der christlichen Verkündigung', in idem, *Das Wort Gottes und die Theologie*, 123.
    [4] Karl Barth, *Evangelical Theology: An Introduction*, trans. Grover Foley (Grand Rapids: Wm. B. Eerdmans, 1979), 58.

ing increased, and the ostentatious and heroic art forms favoured by the ruling classes provided the conditions necessary to produce significant movements of opposition to the values of the ruling classes: various forms of socialism, the *Wandervogel* (or "Youth Movement"), and most eloquently perhaps, expressionism.

Expressionism was first of all an artistic movement but it found spokespersons in drama and literature as well. To call expressionism a movement, however, is to use the term loosely. It had no single programme or philosophy.[5] While most expressionists located themselves on the political left, some could be found on the right as well. Most of the artists and thinkers associated with this movement were united, however, by a deep-seated *Angst* before the spectre of modernity. Wilhelminian culture was seen as decadent and banal, the vehicle of propaganda and lies.

In Wilhelminian Germany, the expressionists were the "outsiders" who fed on the opposition with which they were met by the privileged classes; people given if not by nature, then at least by weight of circumstances, to swimming against the stream. As the expressionist poet Ernst Blass was later to put it, 'what I was engaged in . . . was a literary movement, a war on the gigantic philistinism of those days . . . a spirited battle against the soullessness, the deadness, laziness, and meanness of the philistine world . . . We were definitely the opposition. There were two camps. There was the enemy and the opposition.'[6] Though deeply cynical about things as they were, most expressionists were none the less optimistic about the possibility of creating a better future. They saw themselves (in the pre-war years at least) as standing in the vanguard of a movement which would lead to the creation of a new humanity, and if ideas as to what that new humanity would look like varied from person to person, the hope for the future was nevertheless their common property. The militancy, yearning, and hopefulness which permeated the movement were nicely captured in the single-word names given to the two radical journals which, in pre-war Berlin, acted as a forum for advancing the new counter-culture: Herwarth Walden's artistic

---

[5] Peter Gay, *Weimar Culture: The Outsider as Insider* (New York: Harper Torchbooks, 1968), 105.
[6] Ernst Blass, 'The Old Cafe des Westens', in Paul Raabe (ed.), *The Era of German Expressionism* (Woodstock, NY: The Overlook Press, 1985), 29–30.

journal *Der Sturm* and Franz Pfemfert's literary magazine *Die
Aktion*. As Lothar Schreyer, a member of Walden's inner circle,
would later recall, 'The storm [*Der Sturm*] purifies, uproots,
destroys. But it also roars through the world like the Holy Ghost.
It is the never-ending transformation, the renewal from the
ground up, the cypher under which the spiritual truth of the
Absolute meets the frailty and hope of temporal existence.'[7]

While expressionism was largely a German movement, it had
its adherents in most European countries. In Switzerland, the
decade of the nineties had seen the emergence of an official state
art, promoted by the federal government to strengthen patriotic
feeling in the populace.[8] Such a *Kulturpolitik* was bound to produce a reaction. Expressionism itself was brought to Switzerland
through the self-imposed exile of many German expressionists in
Zurich during the First World War.[9] In any case, it is in this
broad cultural context that the roots of Barth's sigh—and in a
very real sense, of his dialectical theology—are to be found.

For all of its variety, the expressionist spirit could not be better
captured than by the following words with which Eduard
Thurneysen opened a sermon in 1917.

We have already spoken often of the great perplexity [*Ratlosigkeit*] and
longing [*Sehnsucht*] by which our entire time and world has been
grasped. There will scarcely be any among us who have not been
touched and moved by it. We are all different from our fathers in that
we are conscious of a strange unrest [*Unruhe*] in ourselves and around us
which can no longer be suppressed by any means; which rather grows
constantly and swells like a powerful flood. We sense simply that much,
much, perhaps everything which we have thought and done up to this
point no longer suffices because it does not bring us forward; does not,
in any case, liberate us from the deep embarrassments, disturbances and
needs under which we suffer and we look longingly for a new thinking
and doing which would bring us real liberation. We sense that we are at
the end of our strength and wisdom and that a new beginning has to
take place. We find ourselves in a deep dissatisfaction with everything
hitherto [*allem Bisherigen*] and ready to hand [*Vorhandenen*]. Like an under-

[7] Lothar Schreyer, 'What is *Der Sturm?*', in Raabe (ed.), *The Era of German
Expressionism*, 194.

[8] Hans Ulrich Jost, 'Bedrohung und Enge (1914–1945)', in Beatrix Mesmer (ed.),
Geschichte der Schweiz und der Schweizer (Basle: Helbing & Lichtenhahn, 1986), 751.

[9] Ibid. 753.

ground stream, this unrest and longing goes through the life of our day and moves humankind inwardly and shakes violently external things and relationships.[10]

Unrest, longing, a fundamental opposition to everything now in existence—all of these words and phrases which coloured Thurneysen's speech could and did find frequent expression in the literature of other outsiders of the period. Such shared language gives evidence of the strong cultural undercurrents which pervaded a thought-world in which Barth and his friend Thurneysen also lived.

In the years prior to the First World War Barth already carried within himself many of the attitudes just described. To be sure, he was not yet an outsider. He was part of the theological establishment; a favoured son of the liberal theological world and its ardent defender. Still, the longing for a new humanity already dominated his theological and political writings. All that was yet required for the transformation was a catalyst, a spark, something which would stimulate further growth of the seeds of opposition which were already at work within him and would eventually cause him to break his remaining ties with the cultured theological world he had known. The spark came with the outbreak of the First World War.

In Barth's pre-war writings, it is possible to trace the collision of two worlds: one that was passing away, the other struggling to be born. In this chapter, the focus will be on the first of these worlds—the gracious and comfortable world of late-Wilhelminian academic theology. In the next chapter, we will concentrate our attention on those elements which speak of another world, the coming world, and which show Barth in the process of becoming an outsider. The goal of this Prologue is to make clear why Barth reacted as he did to the outbreak of the war and why he then moved in the direction he did in his new theology.

[10] Karl Barth and Eduard Thurneysen, *Suchet Gott, so werdet ihr leben!* (2nd edn.; Munich: Chr. Kaiser Verlag, 1928), 133.

2. UPBRINGING AND STUDENT YEARS

Karl Barth was born in Basle, Switzerland, on 10 May 1886 to a family steeped in a moderate Pietism.[11] His father, Johann Friedrich ('Fritz') Barth, was a teacher at the local College of Preachers. In the spring of 1889, Fritz Barth received a call to the University of Bern where eventually he became an *Ordinarius* Professor of Early and Medieval Church History. Fritz Barth's theology leaned in the direction of what was called at the time a "positive" theology (i.e. a mild conservatism). The leading influence upon him during his university days had been that of the Swabian Pietist, Johann Tobias Beck, at the University of Tübingen. Although he would remain a "positive" theologian all of his life, the Pietist influence made Fritz Barth value Christian experience over doctrine, so much so that he could regard orthodoxy as the 'ossification of the Church's life, against which Pietism successfully protested'.[12]

Karl spent his growing-up years in Bern. It was there that he underwent confirmation instruction under Robert Aeschbacher in 1901/2. Aeschbacher was a charismatic preacher and teacher and it was during the course of these classes that Karl made the decision to study theology. Two years later, upon completing his schooling, he began his studies at the University of Bern.

Bern at that time was something of a theological backwater. Little took place there that was exciting and innovative. Even the liberals on the faculty seemed out of step with the times. They all adhered to the old speculative (Hegelian) line in theology which followed F. C. Baur and regarded the advent of Ritschlianism with horror. Karl dutifully completed his first four semesters at Bern and then did as many Swiss theological students did; he proposed to continue his studies in Germany, where the truly important developments were taking place. He wanted very much to go to Marburg, but his father was opposed to the idea. Theology at Marburg stood on the extreme left wing of the

---

[11] The subject of Barth's relationship to Pietism has been thoroughly examined by Eberhard Busch. See Busch, *Karl Barth und die Pietisten: Die Pietismuskritik des jungen Karl Barth und ihre Erwiderung* (Munich: Chr. Kaiser Verlag, 1978).

[12] Fritz Barth, *Christus unsere Hoffnung: Sammlung von religiösen Reden und Vorträgen* (1913), 401. Cited by Busch, *Karl Barth und die Pietisten*, 19.

Ritschlian movement. Fritz Barth would have preferred that his son go to Halle or Greifswald, which were the centres of conservative theology in Germany. In the end, they compromised. Karl went to Berlin, where he avoided Reinhold Seeberg (his father's theologian of choice) and heard instead Adolf von Harnack, Julius Kaftan, and Hermann Gunkel. It was Harnack who made the greatest impression. During that semester in Berlin, he studied Immanuel Kant's *Critique of Pure Reason*, Friedrich Schleiermacher's *Speeches on Religion to its Cultured Despisers*, and Wilhelm Herrmann's *Ethics*. From his first reading of the *Ethics*, Barth knew himself to be a devoted disciple of Herrmann.

Herrmann was *the* theological teacher of my student years. The day almost twenty years ago in Berlin when I first read his *Ethik* (Ethics) I remember as though it were today. If I had the temperament of Klaus Harms, I could speak of Herrmann in the way in which he spoke of Schleiermacher, or I could say as Stilling did of Herder, 'From this book I received the push into perpetual motion.' I would like more reservedly, though no less gratefully, to say: on that day I believe my own independent interest in theology began.[13]

Barth was more determined than ever to go to Marburg but his father was unyielding. The next semester was spent back at Bern. Then, at the insistence of his father, Karl spent the winter semester of 1907/8 at Tübingen. Fritz Barth was quite concerned that his son should hear some soundly conservative theology. But the semester in Tübingen was a disaster. Listening to Adolf Schlatter and Theodore Häring (a right-wing Ritschlian friend of his father's) only convinced Karl that the truth was not to be found along this line. With his final semester of university studies looming before him, Barth's father finally relented and gave permission for him to go to Marburg. It was there that he finally found his home.

Barth listened avidly as Herrmann lectured on Dogmatics I (Prolegomena) as well as on ethics. He also heard Adolf Jülicher, Wilhelm Heitmüller, and the inimitable Martin Rade. In addition to being a professor of theology, Rade was also the editor of *Die Christliche Welt*, perhaps the most influential theological

---

[13] Karl Barth, 'Die dogmatische Prinzipienlehre bei Wilhelm Herrmann', in idem, *Die Theologie und die Kirche* (Munich: Chr. Kaiser 1928), 240; ET, 'The Principles of Dogmatics According to Wilhelm Herrmann', in *Theology and Church*, trans. Louise Pettibone Smith (London: SCM Press, 1962), 238.

journal in Germany at the time. Rade was unique among German professors at that time for his congeniality and accessibility to students. Barth spent many a happy hour at the open evenings for students which were held in Rade's home on a regular basis. The young Swiss student must have made a good impression on Rade as well, for at the end of the year he was chosen to be the editorial assistant of *Die Christliche Welt*. And so, after completing his final theological examinations in Switzerland during the late summer of 1908, he returned to his beloved Marburg for a further year, to serve as Rade's assistant and to breathe the academic air one more time before entering the pastorate.

The happiness of the three semesters which Barth spent in Marburg was increased by the acquisition of a small group of friends with whom he would remain quite close for life. Among them was Eduard Thurneysen (whose father had served as best man at Fritz and Anna Barth's wedding). Thurneysen was at that time a disciple of Ernst Troeltsch. Barth also made the acquaintance of Rudolf Bultmann. Looking back on this period of his life from the vantage point of later years, Barth wrote,

Everything which I saw and heard in those surroundings had such a self-evident splendour. This world, represented by so many clever and gifted people, went on its way in a manner so certain of itself, that I would have laughed at anyone who would have predicted to me at that time that my own future could lie in any other direction than in some kind of extension of the Marburger, and especially, the *Christliche Welt* theology . . .[14]

It was the self-certitude of this theological world especially, which would soon become most questionable to him. But for now, he could only revel in it.

3. THE THEOLOGICAL SITUATION AT THE TURN OF THE CENTURY

By the early 1890s, theology in German university circles—if not in the churches—was dominated by the members of the Ritschlian school. To be sure, their reign was not a peaceful one. Throughout the last years of his life, Albrecht Ritschl (d. 1889)

---

[14] Karl Barth to Johannes Rathje, 27 Apr. 1947, in Diether Koch (ed.), *Karl Barth: Offene Briefe, 1945–68* (Zurich: TVZ, 1984), 120.

had been the subject of harsh criticism at the hands of conservative theologians like Hermann Cremer, C. E. Luthardt, and F. H. R. Frank as well as liberal (speculative rationalist) theologians like R. A. Lipsius and Otto Pfleiderer. Still, the number of theologians who counted themselves members of Ritschl's school was impressive and included such luminaries as Wilhelm Herrmann, Adolf von Harnack, Ferdinand Kattenbusch, Johannes Gottschick, Julius Kaftan, Friedrich Loofs, Theodore Häring, and Martin Rade. It also had at its disposal a very powerful journal to disseminate its views (*Die Christliche Welt*). The hallmark of this theological movement was its commitment to a churchly theology, oriented towards God's Self-revelation in the historical person of Jesus Christ. It is significant that Ritschl himself had been a church historian and a historian of dogma before he became a dogmatic theologian; historical enquiry lay at the heart of the concerns of most of the Ritschlians. When the most serious challenge to this theology came, it came from within, from a group of younger Ritschlians who took the demand for honesty in historical enquiry to lengths that made the older members of the school shudder.

It is a sign of how fast things could change at that time that in 1892, at the time of the so-called "Apostles' Creed controversy", Adolf von Harnack could be the symbol of liberal Protestantism in the minds of many[15] and just five years later could be regarded as belonging to the older, more conservative faction within Ritschlianism. The source of this dramatic change in fortunes was the explosive emergence in the mid-1890s of the

---

[15] In 1892, a little-known Baden-Württemberg pastor named Christoph Schrempf was deposed from his pastoral office for refusing to require that those bringing their children for baptism recite the Apostles' Creed as a public demonstration of their faith. Understandably, a number of students training for the ministry were upset by this. A group of students at Berlin approached Harnack for advice. His response was to publish an essay in *Die Christliche Welt* which, while not advocating the discontinuation of the use of the Apostles' Creed in worship services, noted that acknowledgement of the Creed was scarcely an adequate test for the theological maturity of ministers and laity. On the contrary, the truly mature would have to take offence at certain statements in the Creed (especially those touching upon the Virgin Birth). At the same time, Harnack held that the 'essential content' of the Creed lay at the heart of Evangelical confession (viz. the communion of the saints, the forgiveness of sins, and eternal life) and that the theologically mature should be able to acquire a positive relation to its basic thoughts. For his trouble, Harnack was vilified in the right-wing press for subverting the foundations of the Christian faith. See Johannes Rathje, *Die Welt des freien Protestantismus: Ein Beitrag zur deutsch-evangelischen Geistesgeschichte, dargestellt an Leben und Werk von Martin Rade* (Stuttgart: Ehrenfried Klotz Verlag, 1952), 64–74.

Religionsgeschichtliche Schule ("history of religions school") led by Ernst Troeltsch.

Troeltsch had at one time been a student of Albrecht Ritschl and could still be counted among his followers as late as 1894.[16] But he very quickly became convinced that the attempt to provide theology with a historical-critical foundation—if it were to be carried through with radical consistency—had to lead to the abandonment of the dogmatic assumptions which had governed the investigations into the history of earliest Christianity carried out by members of the Ritschlian school. The central assumption that Troeltsch focused upon was the belief in the absoluteness or finality of Christianity. Such an assumption was evidence of a residual commitment to a supranatural conception of revelation on the part of the Ritschlians—a thing which Troeltsch felt had been rendered impossible by the modern understanding of the historical-critical method. Given that the discipline of history was properly governed by the principles of analogy and correlation, any appeal to a supranatural revelation was ruled out of court. Furthermore, strict adherence to historical method laid upon theology the demand that it understand the emergence of Christianity within the widest possible context of the historical development of religion generally considered. This meant, in practice, comparative studies of early Christianity and other religions contemporary to it. The value (or "truth") of Christianity (or of any other religion) must emerge from historical study. It could not be presupposed. And the criteria by which to assess such value must be elicited by the historian from the historical process. The net effect of these views was that Christianity could at best be considered relatively superior to other alternatives. It could be understood as the highest stage in the development of human religion *to date*. But the possibility that future development might lead to a form of religion superior to Christianity could not be excluded. No historical form of religion could be judged "absolute". Historical study by itself was incapable of coming to such a conclusion.[17]

[16] Hans-Georg Drescher, 'Ernst Troeltsch's Intellectual Development', in John Powell Clayton (ed.), *Ernst Troeltsch and the Future of Theology* (Cambridge: Cambridge University Press, 1976), 6–7.

[17] See esp. Ernst Troeltsch, 'Über historische und dogmatische Methode in der Theologie', in idem, *Gesammelte Schriften* (Tübingen: J. C. B. Mohr, 1913), ii. 729–53.

By 1897 the split between the "older", ecclesially oriented, dogmatic Ritschlians and the "younger", scientifically oriented, history of religions school was complete and was documented in that same year by Gustav Ecke in his book, *Die theologische Schule Albrecht Ritschls*.[18] This split had a profound impact on the course of *Die Christliche Welt*. In the late 1890s, Rade took the fateful step of opening the doors of his journal to the young radicals of the history of religions school. One by one, his closest friends who had helped to found the journal in the mid-eighties (Friedrich Loofs, Paul Drews, and Wilhelm Bornemann) withdrew their support. What had been a journal promoting the views of classical Ritschlianism became, by the turn of the century, a journal whose editorial policy was oriented in the direction of liberalism.[19]

By the first decade of the twentieth century, Troeltsch's programme had become the most important factor in defining the theological situation. No doubt, the older Ritschlians continued to exercise considerable influence and were attractive to many students. But there were other students for whom the only real option left was between Troeltsch and a theology which offered the promise of overcoming all historicism in theology—namely, the theology of Wilhelm Herrmann. Such a student was Karl Barth. By the time he studied in Marburg, Herrmann seemed to be the only viable alternative for combating Troeltsch. 'The name of Troeltsch, then at the heart of our discussions, signified the limit beyond which I thought I must refuse to follow the dominant theology of the age. In all else I was its resolute disciple . . .'[20]

What then was the shape of the theology which Barth learned in Marburg? And how did it address itself to the leading questions of the day? The answers to these questions will be found through a consideration of the theology of Wilhelm Herrmann. Before turning to Herrmann, however, it would be helpful first

---

[18] Gustav Ecke, *Die theologische Schule Albrecht Ritschls und die Evangelische Kirche der Gegenwart* (Berlin: Reuther & Reichard, 1897).

[19] Rathje, *Die Welt des freien Protestantismus*, 103.

[20] Karl Barth, 'Autobiographische Skizzen Karl Barths aus den Fakultätsalben der Ev.-Theol. Fakultät in Münster (1927)', *Karl Barth–Rudolf Bultmann: Briefwechsel, 1922–1966*, ed. Bernd Jaspert (Zurich: TVZ, 1971), 305 (hereafter *B–B Br.*); ET. *Karl Barth–Rudolf Bultmann Letters, 1922–1966*, trans. Geoffrey Bromiley (Grand Rapids: Wm. B. Eerdmans, 1981), 153.

to take a slight detour. The significance of Marburg for Barth's earliest theology was not exhausted by Herrmann's influence. Theology at Marburg was conducted in close conversation with the resident philosophers, Hermann Cohen (1842–1918) and Paul Natorp (1854–1924), both of whom had a considerable interest in the question of the nature of religion and its place in modern culture. The Marburg "neo-Kantianism" of Cohen and Natorp exercised a good deal of influence on Herrmann and through him on the young Barth. Even after Barth's break with Marburg theology, the philosophical categories of Cohen and Natorp continued to play an important role in the earliest phase of his dialectical theology. Whether these categories could be retained without undergoing a significant alteration in content is a question which we will have to return to further on. It is clear, however, that no exposition of Barth's earliest theology can afford to overlook the impact of Marburg neo-Kantianism.

Nevertheless, it must be pointed out that although Marburg philosophy will be treated here first, this should in no way be taken to mean that philosophy was more significant for Barth than was the theology of Herrmann. Barth had no desire to be a philosopher. He was first, last, and always a theologian. Like Herrmann before him, Barth was willing to take for granted the validity of certain aspects of Marburg neo-Kantianism, where to do so strengthened the case he wanted to make theologically—or at least, did not infringe upon that theology. Where he agreed with Cohen and Natorp, he did so without ever having troubled himself to test their philosophy on philosophical grounds; where he disagreed with them, he did so for theological reasons.[21] At every point, his theological concerns governed his use of philosophy. Herrmann's theology was much more significant for Barth than was the philosophy of the neo-Kantians. If then we consider neo-Kantianism first, it is only because to do so will help to make the significance of Herrmann's theological programme that much clearer.

[21] This point has been established nicely by the very fine recent work of Simon Fisher, *Revelatory Positivism? Barth's Earliest Theology and the Marburg School* (Oxford: Oxford University Press, 1988), 185–94. The following sketch of Marburg neo-Kantianism owes much to Fisher's detailed and lucid treatment of the subject. In addition, the following have also been helpful: Roger Johnson, *The Origins of Demythologizing* (Leiden: E. J. Brill, 1974) and Lewis White Beck, 'Neokantianism', in *The Encyclopedia of Philosophy*, v. 468–73.

4. MARBURG NEO-KANTIANISM

"Neo-Kantianism" was in some respects a misnomer as a description of the project being carried out by Cohen and Natorp. Like Kant, Cohen was extremely interested in establishing the epistemological foundations of modern science. But science had not stood still in the intervening years. Whereas Kant understood science in terms of Newtonian physics, Cohen was fascinated by developments in mathematical physics. Such a science was far more "pure" than the science Kant knew, in that it interested itself in the relations of mathematical concepts and not in empirical data. With this science as his model, Cohen undertook to criticize Kant for inconsistency in carrying out his transcendental enquiry.

According to Kant, theoretical or scientific knowledge is constituted by two factors: 1. intuition (*Anschauung*) or the awareness of data perceived by the senses (*Empfindung*), and 2. the categories of the understanding (*Verstand*) by which that which has been intuited is assembled, so to speak, to form what we normally think of as the objects of our knowledge. The categories are basically rules for organizing the data supplied by the senses. Both factors are necessary for knowing to occur and each requires the other. As Kant put it, 'Thoughts without content are empty, intuitions without concepts are blind.'[22] In other words, the content of our knowledge is provided by the senses (intuition) and the form of our knowledge is provided by thought itself. Intuition without the form given to it by the understanding is just a meaningless jumble of data; it is blind. On the other hand, the categories of the understanding without a content given to them to work on are purely formal and therefore, empty. The restriction implied by this account of knowing is clear: what is known is not things-in-themselves (*Dinge an sich*) but things as they appear to us, as they are given to our senses and formed into objects by the categories. Kant called things as they appear to us *phenomena*; things as they are in themselves he referred to as *noumena*. It is important to add that although Kant introduced a split between the noumenal and phenomenal

[22] Immanuel Kant, *Critique of Pure Reason*, trans. Norman Kemp Smith (New York: St Martin's Press, 1965), 93.

worlds and restricted knowledge to phenomena, he had no doubts himself about the existence of noumena. Indeed, in a very real sense, it is the thing–in–itself which, by forcing itself upon us from without, gives rise to our knowing. This is implicit in the thought that the phenomena are *given* for our intuition. And it is this point which Cohen found so objectionable.

The focal point of Cohen's critique of Kant was the role played by *Empfindung*. Cohen saw Kant's talk of a manifold of sensed data which comes to the knower from without as the residue of a pre–critical ontology. Kant had not yet become sufficiently critical. Had he done so, he would have recognized that there is nothing *given* to thought which is not itself the creation of thought. There is no thing–in–itself in Kant's sense. Thought provides not only the form of the objects known (through the categories), it also *generates* the contents of its objects. Cohen's epistemology was thus a far more radical idealism than anything envisioned by Kant. There is no being which does not have its origin in thought. To "be" is, in a word, to be known.

Cohen could not simply deny the existence of sensation. It is, after all, a fundamental feature of human experience. He did allow for it to the extent that he saw sensation as providing the occasion for the generative activity of cognition. But sensation was seen as nothing more than a question mark without value for cognition. Furthermore, because Cohen regarded being as the product of thought, he tended to see the being of the empirical world as somehow unreal, deficient being. The only being which is truly real is that which thought itself generates.[23] It is not surprising that Ernst Cassirer, one of Cohen's most brilliant students, described Cohen as 'one of the most resolute Platonists that has ever appeared in the history of philosophy'.[24]

A corollary of Cohen's attempt to purify epistemology from all external factors is that the "subject" of the knowing process described is not to be confused with any existing individual. His subject is, in Simon Fisher's phrase, the 'ideal epistemological subject'.[25]

The idealism of neo–Kantianism is transcendental, not subjective. The knowing subject is not that consciousness which constitutes the object

---

[23] Fisher, *Revelatory Positivism?*, 39.

[24] Beck, 'Neokantianism', 471.

[25] Fisher, *Revelatory Positivism?*, 47.

of psychological inquiry. All that belongs to the body, to the particularity of the self is excluded. What remains is consciousness pure and simple, which has no more reality than a mathematical point.[26]

Cohen's description of the way in which thought generates its objects does not, therefore, refer to a process which occurs in the subjective awareness of any individual. It refers to that 'objective consciousness' (Barth's most characteristic way of referring to it) from which all subjective elements have been filtered out. This highly abstract process of reasoning does create difficulties of course, chief of which is whether the ideal epistemological subject has any reality at all. What is its relation to existing human beings? How could Marburg neo-Kantianism take account of the individual? Natorp especially, was sensitive to this problem and sought to provide an answer to it which would not create asymmetries for the Marburg system, but to treat it here would prolong our consideration of neo-Kantianism unduly. Of greater significance for our purposes will be Herrmann's attempt to exploit this difficulty lying at the heart of neo-Kantianism.

Cohen's insistence that the stuff of sensed experience cannot be considered a source of the content of knowledge found its most pointed expression in his notion of 'origin' (*Ursprung*). In so far as this category would have an interesting career in the early phase of Barth's dialectical theology, its original meaning merits comment. Cohen's use of the term is quite straightforward in the light of the foregoing exposition. Thought cannot have its 'origin' in anything outside of itself. It is, so to speak, self-originating. Fisher delineates three meanings of the word *Ursprung* in Cohen's thought. The first and most obvious is that origin refers to a point of commencement, the beginning of cognition in thought itself. Secondly, Cohen's use of the term does not envision a spatial or temporal origin. It is purely a question of *logical* origin. The third and final aspect of Cohen's usage has to do with the potency of thought to produce its content autonomously. In this sense, *Ursprung* means 'originary' or 'originative'.[27] The net effect of Cohen's doctrine of *Ursprung* is that the ideal epistemological subject is credited with a kind of knowledge which traditionally had been attributed to God alone.

[26] M. Bochenski, *Contemporary European Philosophy* (Berkeley, Calif.: University of California Press, 1956), 92; cited by Johnson, *The Origins of Demythologizing*, 49.

[27] Fisher, *Revelatory Positivism?*, 40–1.

Perhaps it is easier to grasp this nuance of potency in Cohen's understanding of origin by recalling Kant's hypothetical Archetypal Knower
(the Divinity). In several writings Kant contrasted human cognition
with the sort of intellectual cognition which, according to the rationalist schools, characterizes the mind of the maker. The former was called
by Kant *intuitus derivativus*, since human knowledge depends upon there
being something in existence for it to discover and, by implication,
upon empirical intuition. Divine intuition, being *intuitus originarius*, is
not so dependent. It is *originarius* because it creates the objects of its
knowledge either *ex nihilo* or from its own thought. With Cohen's philosophy human thought becomes *originarius* in that it is creative and
productive.[28]

Clearly for Cohen, the ideal epistemological subject has been
dressed out in attributes of the divine. But there is nothing to
prevent a later theological realist from taking up this description
of originary thinking and using it to describe the creative functions of an objectively existing God.

Cohen's account of the epistemological foundations of science
was intended to be valid for any field of knowledge whatsoever.
No mode of cognition was allowed to exist which would not
conform to the rules laid down in the generative model. Cohen's
goal was to show the unitary character of all human knowledge.
For him, there were only three validly recognized patterns of
cognition: logic, ethics, and aesthetics. Taken together, these
three modes of consciousness were thought to exhaust that
which can be known scientifically. Logic concerns itself with
being or that which is true, ethics with that which ought to be or
the good, and aesthetics with beauty. Of the three, logic was
considered to be primary, for it was in this sphere that Cohen
developed the model of generation which was asserted to be
valid for all scientific knowledge. To understand the implications
of this assertion, it is sufficient to point out that ethical ideals are
no more given to knowledge than being is. The good is an ideal
that is generated by the 'pure will' in response to some problem.
"Purity" of will here means an ideal will, untouched by psychological and sensual pressures and freed from all external authority.
Cohen was insistent that only that will is ethically pure which is
truly autonomous. To sum up, in each recognized branch of
knowledge objects are produced in accordance with rules for

[28] Fisher, *Revelatory Positivism?*, 41–2.

generation which are valid for that sphere. The products of the three modes of consciousness taken together at any given moment are identical with the achievements of culture at that point in history. And so, when Cohen spoke of that objective consciousness of which these three patterns of cognition were the only possible modes, he most typically called it *Kulturbewußtsein* ("culture-consciousness").

The most pressing problem raised by the Marburg neo-Kantian reduction of knowledge to the three branches of logic, ethics, and aesthetics was where to place religion. This was not only a problem for a theologian like Herrmann (who accepted with little reservation the neo-Kantian epistemology), but also for Cohen and Natorp. Neither of the Marburg philosophers had any room for a God who stood outside of the being generated by thought, but both were religious humanists who were deeply committed to the idea that religion was a most significant force in the formation of culture.

The most obvious solution to the question of where to locate religion was to treat it in terms of one of the three acknowledged branches of knowledge. This was indeed the route taken by Cohen and we will return to it in a moment. Natorp's solution was more complex. It involved a modification of Friedrich Schleiermacher's understanding of religion as "feeling" (*Gefühl*). For Natorp, feeling is a most fundamental inwardness or self-consciousness which accompanies and, indeed, vivifies all cognitive striving of whatever kind (scientific, ethical, etc.). One can sense in this description Natorp's attempt to finally relate the ideal epistemological subject to the concretely existing human individual who experiences herself as a self. As Fisher rightly points out,

It is obvious here that Natorp is attempting to combine two fundamentally contrary conceptions of *Bewußtsein*: one of which is an abstract epistemological category and another which refers to a subject's active awareness of meaningful and vivid experience. In his writings on *Religionsphilosophie* the latter gains explicit priority over the former as its objectless, non-cognitive, but fecund *Grund*.[29]

Religion is non-cognitive in that it is incapable of generating an object. It is, therefore, without an object. This means of course,

[29] Ibid. 76.

that for Natorp, there is no God. The value of religion lies strictly in its power to animate thinking, willing, and aesthetic feeling.[30]

Herrmann Cohen was a deeply pious—albeit quite liberal— Jew. For him, the place to accommodate religion within the Marburg system was under the heading of ethics. His views on religion prior to the war are to be found in his *Ethik des reinen Willens*. For Cohen, the self (like the objects known by science) is not a given so much as it is an ongoing task. The self is realized through a lifetime of fidelity to the moral law. As noted above, however, the moral law is itself generated by thought. It is not given in advance by the deity. This meant too, that only those choices are moral which are made in complete freedom and this includes freedom from coercion or even gracious assistance from God. Furthermore, Cohen was confident that history is teleologically ordered. The collective realization of the good by society as a whole results in a moral progress of the human race. This has as its consequence the progressive unfolding of the ideal ordering of human relationships, which Cohen construed in socialist terms. Cohen was far from being a Marxist; he believed that human beings would establish a socialist society through progress in moral development.

What then, is the role played by God? Cohen brings God into his reflection on ethics at the end of his system, not at the beginning. He held that the unfolding of ideal ends was an eternal process which would never be perfectly realized in history. God is brought in as the guarantee that there will always be a world in which moral goals are progressively attained. God also has the function of assuring that the various parts of Cohen's system (logic, ethics, and aesthetics) cohere in a single, unified whole. God is the idea of unity.

It is clear that God has only ideal existence. God does not exist as things and people exist. To attribute existence to God would mean to confuse God with the world. When Cohen wished to speak of God's relation to the world, he used his logical term *Ursprung*, showing thereby that the God–world relation is a purely logical one, not a personal one. Indeed, it goes without saying that God is not personal. God is like the mathematical

---

[30] Natorp distinguishes the religious feeling of inwardness from aesthetic feeling terminologically by using *Gefühl* for the former and *Fühlen* for the latter. Ibid. 78.

concept zero: a very important place-holder in the system but completely without content; featureless and colourless.

Marburg neo-Kantianism was a typical product of that world which passed away with the First World War. A system which had been consciously set forth as a scientific ground for explaining the advance of German culture would no longer find acceptance with the near collapse of that culture after the war. Talk of an ideal epistemological subject would seem strangely irrelevant in a world where the identity of the individual had become a question of pressing existential concern. If idealism were to survive after the war, it would have to become self-critical.

5. WILHELM HERRMANN'S THEOLOGY OF RELIGIOUS EXPERIENCE

(i) *Between Ritschl and Schleiermacher. An Overview of Herrmann's Life and Work*

To describe Herrmann's theology as Ritschlian is correct as far as it goes, but Ritschlianism was scarcely a monolithic movement and, in any case, Herrmann was an independent thinker. Certainly, it is an adequate description of the origins of Herrmann's thought, since it was Albrecht Ritschl who provided the first important stimulus in his development. But by the time Karl Barth studied with him, Herrmann's relationship to Ritschlian modes of thought had been stretched to the breaking-point.

Wilhelm Herrmann was born on 6 December 1846 in Melchow (in Altmark). His father was a free-thinking pastor, who proudly displayed a bust of Schleiermacher on his desk. Herrmann was a very fine student; as a schoolboy he had already read with understanding Kant's First Critique. From 1866 to 1871, he studied theology at Halle, where he served as a secretary to the great Revival preacher/theologian, August Tholuck (with whom he also lived for some two and a half years). On the whole, he did not find the Pietistic atmosphere at Halle to his liking, but its influence on him could still be detected long after his encounter with Ritschl in the mid-1870s. It was not a peripheral matter when Herrmann later chose to entitle the central

chapters of his *Ethik*, 'Die Wiedergeburt' ('Rebirth') and 'Die
Bekehrung' ('Conversion'); the renewal of the inner person lay
very much at the heart of his concerns.[31] It must also be said,
however, that his mature understanding of religious experience
owed a great deal to the early Schleiermacher of the *Speeches*.

The turning-point in the young Herrmann's theological
development occurred very shortly after the completion of his
Habilitationsschrift (on Gregory of Nyssa) in January 1875. It was
then that he read the recently published three volumes of
Ritschl's magisterial work *Justification and Reconciliation* (1870–4).
It is important to note what Herrmann received from Ritschl,
for the seeds of the differences which would later divide him
from other Ritschlians were already sown here. The great contribution of Ritschl, from the point of view of a good many later
Ritschlians, was that he called theology back from the subjec-
tivistic turn it had taken in Schleiermacher as well as from the
speculative rationalism of the followers of Hegel.[32] He did so in
favour of a more objective theology, grounded in historical facts.
Such a theology was to be thoroughly modern; it would embrace
with open arms the necessity of critical study of the Bible. But it
would offer a serious alternative to the prevailing liberal theology—an alternative which would have far more to offer to the
churches. Herrmann too, in his way, placed a high premium on
the importance of the historical foundations of the Christian
faith. But from the very beginning, what attracted him most
about Ritschl was the latter's insistence upon the independence
of religion from the natural sciences and philosophy. Already in
his earliest essays, Herrmann strove to distinguish faith from
knowledge and to oppose every attempt to ground the former in

[31] Wilhelm Herrmann, *Ethik* (5th edn.; Tübingen: J. C. B. Mohr, 1913).

[32] In his very influential historical sketch of 19th-c. theology, Ferdinand Kattenbusch
summed up the significance of Ritschl this way: 'To the extent that I have been able to
clarify for myself the significance of this man, it rests in the fact that he really broke with
Schleiermacher's method more completely and cheerfully than anyone else.' Kattenbusch,
Von Schleiermacher zu Ritschl (3rd fully revised edn., Gießen: J. Ricker'sche
Verlagsbuchhandlung, 1903), 55. Similarly, Julius Kaftan saw Ritschl's achievement to lie
in taking up the basic tendency of Schleiermacher's thought (viz. the belief that dogmatics
has as its task the setting-forth of the knowledge of faith in independence from all philosophy) while avoiding his errors. The errors were two: first, Schleiermacher failed to see
that statements of faith contain and set forth real knowledge (*Erkenntnis*) and second, he
failed to ground dogmatics in the historical revelation of God in the person of Jesus
Christ. Julius Kaftan, *Dogmatik* (7th and 8th improved edn.; Tübingen: J. C. B. Mohr,
1920), 110–11.

the latter. He saw in Ritschl a return to a truly Lutheran conception of faith.[33]

Herrmann was probably the first significant thinker to commit himself to Ritschl. To that extent, Martin Rade's judgement that it was Herrmann who founded the Ritschlian school contains more than a grain of truth.[34] Certainly, he was its charter member. Even more significantly perhaps, it is not always clear who led and who followed in the relationship between the master and the young theologian who was twenty-four years his junior. It was Herrmann who, even more forcibly than Ritschl, made it his goal to exclude every last vestige of metaphysics from theology.[35] This was already made clear in Herrmann's programmatic essay of 1876, 'Die Metaphysik in der Theologie' as well as in his 1879 book, *Die Religion im Verhältnis zum Welterkennen und zur Sittlichkeit*. It was the latter which secured for Herrmann his call to a professorship in theology in Marburg that same year. Ritschl's lengthy essay, 'Theology and Metaphysics', followed in 1881.[36] Other converts to the Ritschlian programme were quickly added.

Herrmann's attachment to the Ritschlian school remained steadfast throughout the last years of the nineteenth century. The question which preoccupied him during these years was nicely captured in the title of an essay written in 1884, 'Why Does our Faith Need Historical Facts?'[37] The problem of the relation of faith to history finally found its answer for Herrmann in a very strict concentration on the inner life of Jesus (summarized as a life of pure surrender and devotion to the will of His Father—

[33] See Wilhelm Herrmann, 'Der evangelische Glaube und die Theologie Albrecht Ritschls', in idem, *Gesammelte Schriften*, ed. Friedrich Wilhelm Schmidt (Tübingen: J. C. B. Mohr, 1923), 1–25.

[34] Martin Rade, 'Adademische Gedächtnisrede auf Wilhelm Herrmann', in Wilhelm Herrmann, *Dogmatik* (Gotha and Stuttgart: Verlag Friedrich Andres Perthes, 1925), xii.

[35] In the year of Ritschl's death (1889), Herrmann wrote an essay in which he said that Ritschl 'never completely divorced religious knowing from cognition of the world and thereby from metaphysics'. Herrmann saw this as his particular contribution; Ritschl only imperfectly followed him in this. Wilhelm Herrmann, 'Der Streitpunkt in betreff des Glaubens', in idem, *Gesammelte Schriften*, 256. The influence which Herrmann exercised over Ritschl has been confirmed by George Rupp, *Culture-Protestantism: German Liberal Theology at the Turn of the Twentieth Century* (Missoula, Mon.: Scholars Press, 1977), 33–4.

[36] Albrecht Ritschl, 'Theology and Metaphysics', in Philip Hefner (ed.), *Albrecht Ritschl: Three Essays* (Philadelphia: Fortress Press, 1972), 151–217.

[37] Wilhelm Herrmann, 'Warum bedarf unser Glaube geschichtlicher Tatsachen?', in idem, *Gesammelte Schriften*, 214–38.

which is also the essence of religion) to the exclusion of the traditions in the New Testament which record His teachings and
actions. *The* historical fact upon which faith is grounded is the
inner life of Jesus. That is the point of view which found expression in Herrmann's celebrated book *The Communion of the
Christian with God*, the first edition of which was written in 1886.
Already however, this concentration on the inner life of Jesus
brought Herrmann's position into a tension with that of Ritschl
(and with a number of his more historically oriented followers)
who placed highest value on the life and teachings of Jesus. To
ground theology historically meant for them to ground it by
means of the discipline of historical enquiry. Not so for
Herrmann; for him, "historically grounded" meant grounded in
that communion with God which only comes about in history.

Around the turn of the century, several events conspired
together to move Herrmann even further away from the other
Ritschlians. The first was the growing split within the Ritschlian
school between the "older", more orthodox Ritschlians and the
"younger", more radical "history of religions" school, led by
Troeltsch. The second was the centennial republication of
Schleiermacher's *Speeches*, a book which had a deep impact on
Herrmann.[38] The third was the publication of Hermann Cohen's
Logik der reinen Erkenntnis (1902) and his *Ethik des reinen Willens*
(1904). Christology—with its attendant problem of the relation
of faith and history—faded into the background. The question
which now dominated Herrmann's attention was that of the
condition for the possibility of religion.[39] From that point on,
the needle indicating Herrmann's deepest-lying commitments
swung from Ritschl back in the direction of Schleiermacher. To
be sure, residual elements of Ritschlianism could still be found in
his thinking. And he remained a Ritschlian in the sense that all of
his closest friends were associated with that school; his ties with
them remained externally unbroken. But henceforth, his theology acquired a far greater independence. It was a kind of existentialized Schleiermacherianism belonging to no existing school.

[38] Barth would later recall that Herrmann had told his students that the first four of the
Speeches 'were the most important pieces of writing to have appeared before the public
since the closing of the canon of the New Testament'. See Eberhard Busch, *Karl Barth:
His Life from Letters and Autobiographical Texts* (Philadelphia: Fortress Press, 1976), 44.

[39] Peter Fischer-Appelt, 'Einleitung', in Wilhelm Herrmann, *Schriften zur Grundlegung
der Theologie* (Munich: Chr. Kaiser Verlag, 1966), xxxii.

It should be noted that the shift away from Ritschl was smooth and gradual. It involved no real "break" in Herrmann's thinking. It simply represented the elaboration and further clarification of ideas which had been present in his thought from the beginning—but their elaboration under the new conditions which prevailed in theology and Church after the turn of the century.

The last public comment which Herrmann made on Ritschl betrayed a certain amount of bitterness. Ritschl, Herrmann said, 'wanted to be the head of a school and expected to be respected as such by those who attached themselves to him. He could fly into a rage when one of us, whose adherence was especially important to him, confronted him with proof that he had made a mistake in a simple historical question.'[40] Herrmann recalled that when his *Communion of the Christian with God* had first appeared, Ritschl could scarcely find himself in it. He had found it necessary to read it several times before he could convince himself that there was something valuable in it. By contrast, Herrmann added, Ritschl once told Johannes Gottschick (a more classical Ritschlian) that he had the greatest joy in him (Gottschick) because he encountered nothing in him which did not accord with his own conception of piety. Ritschl's significance, Herrmann concluded, should in no way be compared with the greatness of Schleiermacher. Ritschl's greatest achievement had been to save Luther's work from passing into oblivion. Schleiermacher on the other hand, had begun something which never would have occurred to Luther—to trace the rise of religion in the consciousness of the individual. The implication was clear: Schleiermacher's greatness lay in the originality of his contribution to the development of Christian theology. By comparison, Ritschl's theology was epigonous.[41]

---

[40] Wilhelm Herrmann, 'Albrecht Ritschl, seine Größe und seine Schranke', in Karl Holl (ed.), *Festgabe von Fachgenossen und Freunden A. von Harnack zum siebzigsten Geburtstag dargebracht* (Tübingen: J. C. B. Mohr, 1921), 405–6.

[41] It is perhaps appropriate to point out here that even an ardent admirer of Ritschl's like Ferdinand Kattenbusch could say, 'As a theologian, as a dogmatician, Schleiermacher drew upon everything and achieved an original, comprehensive work as no one else among the "scientific" representatives of evangelical Christianity before him or since. He dared to attempt a new direction in theology and carried it off as those do who make *epochs*. Ritschl is not to be compared to him in this sense. But he did initiate a new *phase* within the epoch which was established through Schleiermacher.' Kattenbusch, *Von Schleiermacher zu Ritschl*, 56. It is impossible not to hear in judgements like these Barth's

It is not our task here to enquire into the justness of
Herrmann's final pronouncement on Ritschl. We are concerned
here only to establish how Barth himself understood his earliest
theology. The crucial point for our purposes is this: by the time
Barth studied with Herrmann, the latter's relationship with
Ritschlianism had become attenuated. However much residual
Ritschlianism might still have existed in Herrmann, that was not
the element which attracted Barth to him. What Barth was com-
mitting himself to was a Herrmannian/Schleiermacherian form
of theology and not Ritschlianism (at least not in its classical
form). The significance of this claim will be made clearer by a
brief examination of the shape of Herrmann's theology in the
decisive period when Barth studied in Marburg.

(ii) *The Independence of Religion from Science and Ethics*

Herrmann's theology can best be set forth by focusing upon its
central theme: the 'way to religion'.[42] The fundamental concern
reflected in this theme was to show that religious knowing—the
knowledge of faith—is a special kind of knowing which is inde-

later description of the significance of Ritschl: 'Ritschl has the significance of an episode
in more recent theology, and not, indeed not, that of an epoch.' See Barth, *Die protestantische Theologie im 19. Jahrhundert* (5th edn.; Zurich: TVZ, 1985), 598; ET *Protestant
Theology in the Nineteenth Century* (Valley Forge, Pa.: Judson Press, 1973), 654. I mention
this because of the extremely hostile criticism which Barth has received in recent years for
making this judgement. James Richmond would like to explain the source for the 'very
potent, quasi-personal dislike entertained by Barth for Ritschl' as rooted in the rough ride
which Barth's Ritschlian colleagues at Göttingen gave him during the early 1920s.
Richmond, *Ritschl: A Reappraisal* (London: Collins, 1978), 33–4. The truth is that Barth's
assessment of Ritschl's stature had nothing to do with his troubles in Göttingen (a subject
to which we will give close attention further on). It was an assessment which he could
have written any time after 1910 and the reason for this lies in the simple fact that *there
was little or nothing in it which he had not learned as a student from the Ritschlians themselves.*
That Barth became exceedingly hostile towards Ritschlianism in the 1920s is, of course,
not to be denied. But the source of that hostility did not lie where Richmond placed it—
as we will show at the appropriate place (see below, Ch. 7, Sect. 2).

[42] This is the title given to a pivotal paragraph of Herrmann's lectures in dogmatics. See
Wilhelm Herrmann, *Dogmatik*, para. 11; ET *Systematic Theology*, trans. Nathaniel
Mickelem and Kenneth Saunders (London: George Allen & Unwin, 1927). These lec-
tures were published after Herrmann's death by his old friend and colleague, Martin
Rade. The lectures were printed in the form in which Herrmann gave them in the winter
semester of 1915/16, the last time he lectured on the subject. But they had not changed
in any essential way since Barth heard them as a student in the winter semester of 1907/8.
See Barth, 'Die dogmatische Prinzipienlehre bei Wilhelm Herrmann', in idem, *Die
Theologie und die Kirche*; ET 'The Principles of Dogmatics According to Wilhelm
Herrmann', in idem, *Theology and Church*.

pendent of all other forms of cognition and therefore cannot be reduced to any branch of scientific knowledge that was acknowledged by the neo-Kantians. The reason for this lies first of all in the fact that the reality known by faith (i.e. God) lies beyond the reality to which science has access. God, for Herrmann, was a unique, transcendent, supramundane being, not to be confused with the world which science knows.

For me, the elimination of metaphysics from theology signifies the clear insight that the methodical knowing of the real in science absolutely does not reach to the reality of our God. It lays hold of nature and the eternal ground of nature, the natural law, and therefore that which we recognize in faith as the work and expression of God, but it does not lay hold of the supranatural God Himself. When we therefore eliminate metaphysics from the theological presentation of faith, we confess thereby that we can only come to God because He has come to us in history . . .[43]

Given that science has no access to God, Herrmann had nothing but contempt for those philosophies of religion which sought support for faith in some kind of scientific demonstration.

God's reality lies beyond all of that which science can prove. If we understand that, then our faith will not be weakened thereby but will rather be reminded of the hidden element which is its strength. On the other hand, this understanding will overthrow that lame science which lives from the prejudice that it is necessary for the protection of faith. When this science, which dares to call itself *Religionsphilosophie*, dies, then faith will be made to stand on its own feet.[44]

Herrmann had a deep-lying suspicion of natural theology, believing that only those could see traces of God in nature who had already, without recourse to nature, experienced revelation in their souls.[45] Faith is made to stand on its own feet when religion lives from revelation alone.

The second reason why religion cannot be reduced to patterns of scientific knowing is that the Self-revelation of God in which religion takes its rise was understood by Herrmann to be a miracle (something which he defined in supranaturalist terms as an

---

[43] Wilhelm Herrmann, 'Zur theologischen Darstellung der christlichen Erfahrung', in idem, *Gesammelte Schriften*, 245.

[44] Wilhelm Herrmann, 'Die Wirklichkeit Gottes', in idem, *Schriften zur Grundlegung der Theologie*, ed. Peter Fischer-Appelt (Munich: Chr. Kaiser Verlag, 1967), ii. 292.

[45] Herrmann, *Dogmatik*, para. 6; ET *Systematic Theology*.

event occurring *supra et contra naturam*[46]). Knowledge of God is a gift—a divine creation of faith in an individual. It is something that comes to us from without; it is a given and not something we create. Herrmann was quite happy to grant the validity of the neo-Kantian epistemology in so far as it touched upon the knowledge gained in natural science, ethics, etc. But he could not allow religion to be incorporated into an epistemology which treated being as a function of thinking. For that idea, applied to religion, would mean that if religion has an object at all, it is an object of the mind's creating.

Behind Herrmann's debate with Cohen and Natorp over the nature of religion—a debate which reached its peak during Barth's student days in Marburg—lay his concern that religion not be seen to be illusory. Herrmann was keenly aware of the burden laid on theology by the anthropological reduction carried out by Ludwig Feuerbach. He was, for example, quite critical of the move made by Julius Kaftan, to make religion the product of the human *desire* for fulfilment of life, for he saw in such a conception a failure to vindicate religion from Feuerbach's critique.[47] The essence of religion did not lie for Herrmann in a universally experienced desire but rather, in something already actualized. And, as we shall see, religion is not something which is objectively observable in those who experience it. Hence Kaftan's desire to demonstrate its existence must end in failure. All Kaftan could demonstrate was the universal desire for religion, not the actual presence of it. The way to counter Feuerbach did not lie on this path. In any case, Herrmann's preoccupation with vindicating the reality of religion in the face of the Feuerbachian critique helps to account for the passion with which he carried out his debate with Cohen and Natorp. The neo-Kantian constructivist epistemology had the effect of making "God" an object of the mind's creating, like any other. What was at stake in this debate was nothing less than the reality of God. Herrmann wanted to articulate a vision of the origin of faith which would provide an alternative to Cohen's reduction of religion to ethics and Natorp's characterization of religion as an objectless feeling.

The third and final reason why religion cannot be reduced to

[46] Herrmann, *Dogmatik*, para. 31, p. 51; ET *Systematic Theology*, para. 31, p. 83.
[47] Ibid. para. 7, p. 9; ET 25.

any form of scientific knowing is that it is a historical fact, not a natural one. By historical fact, Herrmann meant first of all that religion is not a trait of human nature *per se*. It is something which is found only in particular individuals. Herrmann was quite critical here of the later Schleiermacher of the *Glaubenslehre* who made religion to be a constituent part of every human consciousness in that he defined religion as the feeling of absolute dependence. That such a feeling was an essential part of consciousness, Herrmann did not deny. But such a feeling was not itself religion. Moreover, the object of that feeling was not the God of religious faith; it was rather the world and its life-forces on which our biological lives are dependent. The name of this object is fate, not God.[48] On the other hand, Herrmann could approve of the early Schleiermacher of the *Speeches*, for this Schleiermacher treated religion as a historical phenomenon which is to be found only in particular, actually existing individuals.[49]

To speak of religion as historical fact meant in the second place that it was hidden in nature. A natural fact is one which is known by the processes so well described by Neo-Kantian epistemology. A historical fact on the other hand, is not so governed because it is hidden from direct observation. Clearly, Herrmann was using the word 'historical' in a highly specialized sense. History as the study of what took place would deal with external events which are open to investigation by any interested party and such an investigation would, by definition, be governed by the general epistemology set forth by Cohen and Natorp. No, what Herrmann meant by 'historical' was something like the spiritual cause of historical events lying hidden from view. 'Historical' then, refers to a kind of spiritual reality which has the power to make history. The significance of this lay in the view that only that person could understand such a spiritual reality who actually participated in its effects. This distinction of what might be called "outer" history from "inner" history will be of great significance further on when we look at Herrmann's Christology. For now, it is important to see that by defining religion as something 'historical' (i.e. as particular and hidden), Herrmann had succeeded in putting it beyond the reach of neo-Kantian epistemology.

[48] Ibid. para. 9, p. 12; ET 29. [49] Ibid. paras. 9 and 10, pp. 11–15; ET 28–33.

It remains for us only to make clear what religion was for Herrmann in positive terms. Religion is a God-given ability to see the working of God in all the events of one's life.[50] This definition was, by intention, a very brief and general one. Since religion was thought to take its rise in special experiences which are peculiar to the individual, Herrmann believed that it could take as many different forms as there were men and women in whom it could be found. But this definition was felt to be sufficient to describe the common element in all religious experience.

(iii) *The Way to Religion*

In his published *Auseinandersetzungen* with Cohen and Natorp, Herrmann described the way to religion in *religionsphilosophischen* terms.[51] His defence of religion sought to exploit the weakness he detected in Cohen's philosophy: the failure to address the problem of the experience of the self as a self. Herrmann held that we first become aware of ourselves as selves when confronted with other things or people. It is the sense of our otherness from the world of experience which gives rise to the notion of selfhood. No matter how "purified" (in Cohen's sense of the term) our knowledge of the world becomes, we still want to relate that which we know to our experienced self. But the claim to be a self or to have a self is an audacious one, for it lacks that scientific demonstrability which accrues to all the objects generated by the mind's knowing activity. The self is something hidden, inward, completely personal and individual. We have our selves for ourselves alone. Therefore, it is impossible to demonstrate to another that the thought of one's self is a true thought. When this is fully understood, when the notion of a self is compared with the ideas generated lawfully by science and ethics, belief in selfhood is severely threatened. For how can we continue to believe in something whose existence lacks the kind of certainty which attaches to the objects of science and ethics?

Human life under these conditions is a life of perplexity and even anguish. The fundamental demand of ethics is that one be truthful and in this context that meant for Herrmann that one

---

[50] Herrmann, *Dogmatik*, para. 4, p. 5; ET *Systematic Theology*, 20.
[51] For the account which follows, see esp. Wilhelm Herrmann, 'Hermann Cohen's Ethik (1907)', in Herrmann, *Schriften zur Grundlegung der Theologie*, ii. 88–113.

cannot hold to something without a sufficient justification. But the justification for the belief in self can obviously not be a scientific one. That is excluded from the outset. But what then is the alternative? A person can continue to hold on to the thought of herself as a self without justification but to do so would be to be untruthful. To refuse to allow the longing for truthfulness to be suppressed is to be on the way to religion, for this longing is a longing for God.

What is required is the encounter with a Reality so overwhelming, a power so great, that the experience of it cannot be doubted. And that is precisely what happens in the encounter with God. In that encounter, a Reality is experienced to which science has no access but whose existence cannot be doubted. In the light of the existence of that Reality, the existence of the self who experiences it can also not be doubted. The division of self against self created by the longing to be truthful on the one hand and the uncertainty of belief in the self on the other, is overcome and healed. This experience of God in the hidden depths of individual life is again, not something which can be demonstrated to others. It is a *self-authenticating* experience. But since the Reality known in this experience is more real than the reality known by any science, it is more than sufficient for freeing the individual from uncertainty and doubt.

Herrmann could also describe this same experience in far more theological terms.[52] He was at one with Cohen in the belief that the good is something that is autonomously generated by the will. But what Cohen failed to appreciate was the extent to which we are unable to do the good that we will. When we come to an awareness of the radicality of human evil, we are crushed by a sense of guilt.[53] Ethics can do nothing to answer the fundamental need of the human heart for forgiveness. Religion alone can do that. Religion is the answer to a question which arises in connection with ethics but which ethics is powerless to answer. In the encounter with the gracious Self-revelation of God, the individual experiences forgiveness and freedom from

[52] For what follows here, see esp. Herrmann, *Ethik*, paras. 18, 19, 21, 22.

[53] Herrmann was somewhat unique among Ritschlians in the emphasis which he placed upon the radicality of human sinfulness. It was this perception which also led him to be highly critical of culture-optimism, as Horst Stephan has pointed out. See Horst Stephan and Martin Schmidt, *Geschichte der evangelischen Theologie in Deutschland seit dem Idealismus* (3rd. edn.; Berlin: Walter de Gruyter, 1973), 315.

the guilt of sin. The sinner is justified. It is clear now why religion cannot be reduced to ethics. Ethics does have an important role to play in relation to religion; it can be a *praeparatio evangelica*. But religion arises on the other side of the boundary of what ethics is able to accomplish.[54] It should be clear what Herrmann has accomplished here. He has used the Neo-Kantian epistemology to help set the limits of ethics in order then to create a space for religion at a point lying outside those limits, thereby overcoming the Neo-Kantian treatment of religion from within.[55]

The experience of God, it should be noted, does not arise with necessity from the longing for God. For Herrmann, the longing to be truthful provides at best a "point of contact". But the living God alone determines when and if He places Himself in our way. God is a life-giving power which renews the inner person, whether he/she wills or not. This transformation or renewal of the inner person is described in Christian terms as redemption, being made a new creature or being born again.

To his credit, Herrmann did not allow the experience of rebirth to be isolated from its ground in Christ, thereby becoming a subject of interest in its own right.[56] The certainty that we have been born again will not be found through a psychological investigation of a process of renewal which is supposed to be somehow normative for all. The certainty of this experience will only be had by continuous concentration on Christ. Herrmann was quite critical of the Pietist attempt to provide a genetic account of how faith arises. Such attempts overlook the pure individuality of religious experience.[57] Moreover, Herrmann did

---

[54] The influence of Luther's conception of the relation of law and gospel is very noticeable in a statement like the following: 'The experiences out of which a person acquires the power of real life or becomes religious are called "revelations". Such experiences can only come to the person who has been shaken and rendered desperate by the fact that her own life is without truth, and therefore impotent and null. In the longing to escape from this condition of despair, from the untruth of the idea (which sways her whole existence) that she has a life of her own—here lies for us the way to God.' Herrmann, *Dogmatik*, para. 12, p. 16; ET *Systematic Theology*, pp. 34–5.

[55] This point has been well made by Horst Stephan, *Geschichte der evangelischen Theologie*, 315.

[56] Wilhelm Herrmann, *The Communion of the Christian with God*, trans. J. Sandys Stanyon and R. W. Stewart (Philadelphia: Fortress Press, 1971), 342–53.

[57] Cf. Herrmann, *Dogmatik*, para. 10, p. 14; ET *Systematic Theology*, 32: 'the peculiarity of religion consists in the very fact that it cannot be reduced to the knowledge of something universally valid, but simply to the secret life of the soul which the individual alone

not think of regeneration as something which is completed in a moment in time but rather as something which continues throughout life.

If the Christian could look upon her new birth from God as the spiritual riches now in her possession, then she might be called a fruit fallen from the tree of life, but not a branch of Christ the Vine.[58]

Herrmann's understanding of religious experience was thus individual and dynamic. It could not be frozen for examination as are dead facts and, in any case, religious experience was understood to have its home in the hiddenness of the individual's personal life.

(iv) *The Historical Jesus as the Ground of Faith*

How is the experience of revelation in which new life is bestowed upon a person related to the historical person called Jesus of Nazareth? For Herrmann, the historical Jesus is the revelation of God, the uncontestable saving fact in which our faith in God is grounded.[59] But of course, when Herrmann spoke of the "historical" Jesus, he did not mean Jesus as he might be known with the tools of historical-critical research. Historians, in so far as they seek to reconstruct what really happened, work merely with external features: with events and teachings, with facts and forces. Historians deal only with external history. To that extent, the "object" of their scrutiny falls under the generative laws which govern all theoretical knowing (as described by Cohen). But for Herrmann, there is also an internal history—a history of spiritual effects to which the historian *qua* historian has no access. The *locus* of divine revelation in Jesus lies not so much in what he did or said as it does in his "inner life", which is hidden to view. The incomparable moral purity of that inner life exercised a redemptive power on Christ's first disciples by which their lives were transformed. The effectiveness of their witness in turn, lay not so much in what they said but in who they were; in the lives they led. And so it comes about that, two thousand

can recognize in each case as a reality. It must, therefore, have in everyone its own special history. There is no religion which can be identical in all men and women. Religion exists only in individuals.'

[58] Herrmann, *The Communion of the Christian with God*, 345.
[59] For what follows, see ibid. 57–111, as well as Herrmann, *Dogmatik*, paras. 15–19.

years later, we first catch a glimpse of that inner life of Jesus through the effect it has had on other believers in the Church. They become to us a source of revelation, helping us to see that it is possible to live a truthful, authentic existence. Through their witness, we are enabled to come to the Gospel accounts with eyes that have been opened to the reality which lies hidden there. We see the picture of a man who lived in perfect surrender to God, who was able to love all people without exception, and who knew himself to be without sin. We are so startled by this incomparable phenomenon that we are only able to attribute it to the power of God. In that we do so, we too experience that power which Jesus experienced. We come to understand that His Father will not reject us in spite of our failures, but rather, accepts us as children. It is for this reason that Jesus alone is the revelation which grounds our faith in God.

It should be clear that the problem of how a contingent and accidental event could have universal and eternal significance (a problem much discussed at the time) is completely dissolved by Herrmann's Christology. The inner life of Jesus is not something which lies in the past alone. It is a reality which is always contemporaneous through its impact on the lives of other believers in the Church. Lessing's 'wide ugly ditch' was therefore no problem for Herrmann. The difficulty which this solution posed for the historical critic is obvious: it is highly questionable whether the Jesus who stood on the plane of history is really necessary to the whole proceeding. In so far as Herrmann already knew the content of Christ's inner life *before* coming to the text of the Gospels, he had a key with which to unlock the secrets of the narratives which the historian as historian lacks. But he was thoroughly convinced that no one could rightly understand the Gospel accounts who did not share in the experiences which gave rise to them. The Gospels are expressions of faith. If the expressions are abstracted from the faith-experience which gave rise to them, they become incomprehensible (or wrongly comprehensible). For Herrmann, there was no such thing as a *theologia irregenitorum*.

It was precisely because he insisted that the power of the inner life of Jesus was a present reality that Herrmann could be content to let the fires of historical criticism rage. He felt quite certain that no matter how much doubt was cast on the authenticity of the narratives, enough of a reliable picture would remain to allow him to validate his understanding of the moral purity of the inner life of Jesus. A cynic might be tempted to say that Herrmann's flight from history to a "storm-free" inner reality was carried out in the interests of protecting himself against results of historical study which might not fit his picture of Jesus. However, Horst Stephan was probably correct in suggesting that Herrmann's motivation was centred far more in his concern for the personal (one might even say, existential) reality of the individual.[60] To put it this way is to suggest that Herrmann was influenced less by the problems created by radical historical critics like Ernst Troeltsch than he was by his desire to resolve the problems posed for him by Hermann Cohen.

Be that as it may, Herrmann's attempt to separate faith from knowledge (which had been his guiding idea since the late 1870s) led him to insist that genuine faith does not strive for objective supports, not even in the Gospel narratives which set forth the teaching of Jesus. This was the ultimate significance of Luther's insistence on justification by faith alone. Herrmann had a marked antipathy to the orthodox conception of faith which included an element of assent to doctrines as true. Faith for him was trust or pure surrender. Doctrines cannot be made the object of such confidence because they are at best only the imperfect articulation of the contents of inner experience—an experience that was always personal and individual, never universal. Nothing roused Herrmann to wrath more quickly than the spectre of doctrine which is presented as *Lehrgesetz*—a law to which belief must subscribe. If anything was normative for Herrmann, it was the experience of faith itself prior to being conceptualized. Not even the teachings of the Bible could be made a *Lehrgesetz*.[61]

---

[60] Stephan and Schmidt, *Geschichte der evangelischen Theologie*, 316.

[61] In an essay published in 1907 (a year before Barth's arrival in Marburg), Herrmann characterized Ritschl as 'the last great representative of orthodox dogmatics'. Ritschl never fully succeeded in overcoming the orthodox conception of the dogmatic task (viz. to set forth the content of that faith which is to be believed). He fell back into this conception of the dogmatic task to the extent that he made Holy Scripture a source of ideas of faith which ought to be believed. See Herrmann, 'Die Lage und Aufgabe der evangelischen Dogmatik in der Gegenwart', in idem, *Gesammelte Schriften*, 117–19.

(v) *The Weaknesses in Herrmann's Thought*

Herrmann carried on a running controversy with Ernst Troeltsch throughout the first decade of the twentieth century and most of his weaknesses emerged with clarity during the course of it. Troeltsch saw in Herrmann the final and most radical example of what he called 'the agnostic theory of religious knowledge'.[62] As such, he belonged to a line which began with the later, ecclesiastical Schleiermacher (Troeltsch wanted to retain the mantle of the early Schleiermacher's authority for himself) and was continued by Ritschl. Dogmatic agnosticism means the abandonment of all that can properly be called "knowledge" in the sphere of religion. It does not lay claim to real knowledge of its object; the basis for what it (improperly) calls knowledge lies in feeling and all dogmatic statements are said to be inadequate and symbolic. Such a theology 'has everywhere abandoned the demonstration of scientifically valid general truths in favour of personal, subjective convictions of a confessional sort'.[63] Religious "knowledge" has been made completely independent of rational knowledge on the assumption (and it can only be that) that its object is completely different from the objects known by the sciences.[64]

Furthermore, in spite of all the talk about how the personality of Jesus provides the ground and goal of all Christian religious experience, it is demonstrably clear that no inner connection between Jesus and the believer is necessary at all. For the most part Herrmann had surrendered the idea that redemption is a historical act, something achieved by Jesus which believers must then appropriate in the present. 'A real miracle of redemption effected by a historical act is transformed into a redemption that is continually new and achieved by the knowledge of God in faith.'[65] Yet in spite of this, Herrmann wanted to insist that present experience was in some way tied to the historical personality of Christ. But the connection he sought to establish was hardly convincing.

---

[62] Ernst Troeltsch, 'Half a Century of Theology: A Review', in *Ernst Troeltsch*: *Writings on Theology and Religion*, ed. Robert Morgan and Michael Pye (Atlanta: John Knox Press, 1977), 58.

[63] Ibid.   [64] Ibid. 59–60.

[65] Ernst Troeltsch, 'The Significance of the Historical Existence of Jesus for Faith', in *Ernst Troeltsch*: *Writings on Theology and Religion*, ed. Morgan and Pye, 187.

It is anything but obvious that the religious personality of Jesus can be fully and clearly known and made directly and personally effective, just like the immediately operative influence of one man upon another . . . If instead one stresses the mediation through the community and the living effect by means of subsequent Christian personalities, one is then dealing not with the historical fact but with its infinitely modified and enriched continuing effects, and it is impossible to say for certain what comes from Jesus and what from the later period and the present.[66]

Herrmann never bothered to answer these substantial objections. He simply ridiculed Troeltsch for lapsing back into the orthodox confusion of faith with knowledge.

Troeltsch was certainly right in pointing to a basic agnosticism in Herrmann's conception of the relation of faith to its object. The problem in Herrmann's thought was not the notion that faith has a unique object; that was the element of truth in his conception. The flaw lay in the complete disjunction between faith and knowledge. Barth's later departure from Herrmann would entail an emphatic insistence that God is really and truly *known*—that *Gotteserkenntnis* is possible.

Troeltsch was also right in his belief that in Herrmann all tangible connection with the Jesus of history had been severed. He was right to point out that the attempt to establish a connection to the historical personality of Christ through subsequent Christian personalities made it impossible to know what in present experience was original to Jesus and what was subsequent. This impossibility made the agnosticism running through Herrmann's thought all the more pointed. On the other hand, it has to be said that Herrmann's recognition that the historian as historian has no access to the object of theology belonged to his strengths. Historians have access only to those events and figures which are themselves products of the historical process. But revelation is not produced by history. The normal rules of historical explanation (analogy, correlation, etc.) do not apply to events whose origin is supernatural. Thus far, Herrmann was right. But his strength could become a weakness if history and historical study were ignored altogether. If revelation is not *of* history, it is nevertheless true that revelation is *in* history. Troeltsch's historicism could not be overcome in Herrmann's way—by simply ignoring everything connected with the historical life, teachings, and death of Jesus. A better answer would have to be found, one which would establish more clearly the relation of revelation and history.

There was one final problem in Herrmann's thought which is of the greatest importance here because it marks the point where Barth would finally have to depart from the theology of his teacher. In spite of the realistic overtones in Herrmann's talk of a divine Reality lying beyond all that to which science (and for that matter, ethics and aesthetics) has access and in spite of his stress on the need for faith to be grounded in the Self-revelation of God alone, at the crucial point in his debate with Hermann Cohen, he reverted to an idealistic attempt to justify belief in God. He posited God as the answer to the existential and ethical problem of how one can be truthful while believing in the existence of one's self. The effect of this move was to reduce "God" to an Idea, postulated in order to account for a particular human experience. This fundamental commitment to idealistic modes of thought was only further exacerbated by the agnosticism pointed to by Troeltsch. Where God is thought to be finally beyond rational knowing, the tendency to reduce the reality of God to an idealistic postulate is strengthened. That Herrmann wanted a more realistic theology is clear. But he was unable finally to achieve it because he took as his starting-point an 'ethical-anthropological pre-understanding'[67] which would only allow for an idealistic conception of God.

(vi) *Conclusion: The Influence of Herrmann on Barth's Theology*

This then was Wilhelm Herrmann: religious individualist and anti-historicist, a stern opponent of metaphysics and apologetics in theology, and the leading influence on the earliest theology of Karl Barth. When Barth's break with Herrmannian theology would finally come, the focal point would be the latter's idealism. The idealistic theology of Barth's youth would be replaced

---

[67] Michael Beintker, *Die Gottesfrage in der Theologie Wilhelm Herrmanns* (Berlin: Evangelische Verlagsanstalt, 1976), 117. Beintker's work is important for pointing to the conflict which existed between the more or less realistic "intention" of Herrmann's doctrine of God and the idealistic "modality" in which he sought to set forth that intention. See *Die Gottesfrage*, 114–27.

by what will here be described as a "critical realism".[68] The word "critical" is meant to suggest that Barth never simply abandoned his idealistic inheritance. Idealism would prove to be a valuable ally in establishing the limits of human knowing. Barth would continue to acknowledge the general validity of the idealistic point of view where knowledge of the "given" was concerned. The "given" (or what we customarily think of as the "real") is the product of the knowing activity of the human subject. The word "realism" is meant to suggest, however, that after the break Barth would always insist that the divine being was real, whole, and complete in itself apart from the knowing activity of the human subject; indeed, the reality of God precedes all human knowing. But the only way to secure this theological realism against idealistic constructivism was by *consistently* starting with it, rather than with (for example), an account of the gap between ethical ideal and human life. The result would be a completely new framework for theological thinking. Barth would seek to ground theological reflection in the objectively real 'self-presupposing divine subjectivity'[69] in revelation; i.e. to start from the reality of God. All the other differences between Barth and Herrmann would flow from this difference in starting-point: differences in how the nature and function of rationality in theology are viewed, differences in how doctrine is valued, differences in Christology, etc.[70]

[68] See below, Ch. 3, Sect. 1.   [69] Spieckermann, *Gotteserkenntnis*, 72–82.

[70] Hans Frei has described Barth's break from liberalism as a break from "relationalism": i.e. the notion that revelation is an internalized content of human experience, something directly given to religious experience so that a relational nexus between God and the human individual is established in the revelation event—an *Ineinanderstellung* ("co-inherence") of revelation and experience. See Frei, 'The Doctrine of Revelation in the Thought of Karl Barth', 27, 33, 140, 361. There is a great deal of truth in this way of describing Barth's break, but it is a truth whose significance for Barth's development cannot be fully realized without close attention to Barth's "critical realism". It was Barth's critically realistic starting-point which enabled him from 1915 on to overcome an idealistically grounded "relationalism". Therefore, "critical realism" provided the larger framework in which the break with "relationalism" took place. Frei himself was not sensitive to the larger framework of Barth's new theology in the period 1915–19; indeed, Frei thought that in *Romans* I, Barth had simply 'thrown together' idealist and 'Biblical realist' thought-forms in an indiscriminate manner (p. 149). The truth is—as we shall see—that Barth's new realistic starting-point was worked out much more carefully and thoroughly in the period of *Romans* I than Frei thought. Frei's failure to come to terms with Barth's shift in starting-point and framework of thought provides at least a partial explanation for his (mistaken) belief that Barth's break with liberalism was not really complete until sometime between the two editions of *Romans* (around 1920). For a more complete explanation of the shortcomings in Frei's analysis, see below, Ch. 3 n. 64.

Virtually all of the themes and tendencies which we have seen in Herrmann (the definition of revelation as *Self*-revelation and the insistence on its self-authenticating character, the opposition to natural theology, apologetics, etc.) would survive Barth's break with the theology of his teacher and would remain enduring elements in his dialectical theology as well. And yet all of these themes and tendencies would be brought into the service of a very different theological programme. Here, if anywhere in Barth's life, it would be entirely just to claim that not one stone would be left standing on another once the break was complete.[71]

6. KARL BARTH'S EARLIEST THEOLOGICAL WRITINGS (MARBURG AND GENEVA, JULY 1909–JULY 1911)

Barth's earliest published essays in theology showed him to be a very enthusiastic follower of Wilhelm Herrmann. They also made clear his strong attachment to the general epistemological theory of Cohen and Natorp. It is above all two essays which need to be considered here.

The first of these essays was written during the last days which Barth spent in Marburg as assistant editor of *Die Christliche Welt* (therefore, around the end of July or early August 1909). The essay was quite brief; it was entitled 'Modern Theology and Work for the Kingdom of God' and it appeared in a section of 'Theses and Antitheses' which was a regular feature of the *Zeitschrift für Theologie und Kirche* at that time.[72] The essay was occasioned by a recent discussion amongst students as to why so few graduates of the more "modern" theological faculties were applying for work in foreign missions. The "thesis" which Barth set forth was that it was indeed 'incomparably more difficult' for students educated by the more "modern" theological faculties of Marburg and Heidelberg to make the transition into pastoral activity than it was for students from more conservative places

---

[71] Hendrikus Berkhof's description of the later dialectical Barth as a 'Herrmannian of a higher order' is good; in fact, it is very good. See Berkhof, *Two Hundred Years of Theology* (Grand Rapids: Wm. B. Eerdmans, 1989), 201.

[72] Karl Barth, 'Moderne Theologie und Reichgottesarbeit', *Zeitschrift für Theologie und Kirche*, 19 (1909), 317–21.

like Halle and Greifswald.[73] The reason for this, he argued, was
not hard to find. Conservative students, when called upon to testify to their faith, had at their disposal a whole host of authoritative doctrines which they could, with good conscience, set forth
as normative for the faith of others. The "modern" theological
student had no such normative statements of faith. The reason
for this was quite simple; it lay in the very nature of the modern
understanding of religious life.

The essence of modern theology, Barth said, lies in religious
individualism. Strictly individual, first of all, are the ethics which
provide the presupposition of the religious life. There are no
generally valid ethical norms which are brought to an individual
from without; rather such norms are generated by the willing
activity of the individual. The awakening to the religious life
which follows is equally individual in nature. Where a person has
come to the awareness that the ethical demand is one that is
impossible to fulfil, there the possibility arises that she will
encounter a Power so overwhelming that she can only bow in
obedience and trust. The source of the revelation of this Power
will vary. It could be occasioned by reflection upon the Christian
tradition; but it could just as well come about through the
impression created by contemporary forms of the life of the
Church. There is no generally valid *ordo salutis*, there are no
'generally valid sources of revelation which one can demonstrate
to another'.[74]

A further characteristic of modern theology flows from the
first. Barth calls it 'historical relativism'. Because religion rests
upon personal rather than generally valid grounds, theology is
free—nay, compelled, for the sake of truthfulness—to submit the
New Testament to investigation by means of historical science. It
recognizes that for such a science, there are no absolute magnitudes. All things are relative. But because its trust and confidence
are grounded elsewhere than in the factual reliability of these
writings, it is willing to treat them with the same methods of
study with which it also treats Zoroastrianism, etc.

Given that these two elements—religious individualism and
historical relativism—constitute the content of the satchel which
a student of modern theology takes with him from the university,

---

[73] Ibid. 317.   [74] Ibid. 318.

he must appear severely disadvantaged when compared with graduates of the more conservative schools. Faced with this situation, those who have been mere 'schoolboys' and not serious students of Herrmann and Harnack will frequently just cast their school satchels overboard when they enter the pastorate and conform to the expectations of their parishioners. They will conduct themselves as the conservatives do. Barth has only contempt for such a solution. "Modern" theological students should simply be realistic about the difficulties they will face and press forward with their tasks. Theirs is not an easy road, but it is the only viable one.[75]

The essay was written in a highly provocative form. There were gaps in Barth's argument which did not help to further understanding among readers. There can also be little doubt that Barth set out to shock people, and he succeeded. His "thesis" quickly called forth "antitheses" from two distinguished Ritschlian professors of practical theology, Ernst Christian Achelis of Marburg and Paul Drews of Halle.[76] Of the two, Achelis demonstrated greater sympathy for Barth's ideas. Drews was clearly upset, in large measure because he (mistakenly) understood Barth to be saying that "modern" theology made a student useless from the point of view of practical pastoral activity.[77] The exchange was completed by a further response from Barth to his two critics.[78]

---

[75] Barth has been interpreted by Hans Frei as giving expression in this essay to a certain wistfulness—almost as if he really envied the conservative students who seemed so much more sure of themselves. See Frei, 'The Doctrine of Revelation in the Thought of Karl Barth', 14. If correct, that would mean that Barth was never fully committed to a liberal perspective. While such a reading is understandable, it is none the less misguided. As Barth noted in a letter to Martin Rade, 'the picture of the perplexed candidate who [stands] at the edge of despair . . . does not fit me.' Karl Barth to Martin Rade, 14 Nov. 1909 in *Karl Barth–Martin Rade: Ein Briefwechsel*, ed. Christoph Schwöbel (Gutersloh: Gutersloher Verlagshaus Gerd Mohn, 1981), 70 (hereafter *B–R Br.*). Properly understood, the essay fairly bristles with Barth's sense of superiority to both those on the theological right (whose wealth of doctrinal norms only conceals the poverty of their personal religious experience) and those modern students on the left who jump ship at the first available opportunity. This essay is the typical product of the youthful enthusiasm of a recent graduate who writes out of a sense of tribal loyalty to his mentor.

[76] Ernst Christian Achelis, 'Noch einmal: Moderne Theologie und Reichgottesarbeit', *Zeitschrift für Theologie und Kirche*, 19 (1909), 406–10; Paul Drews, 'Zum dritten Mal: Moderne Theologie und Reichgottesarbeit', *Zeitschrift für Theologie und Kirche*, 19 (1909), 475–9.

[77] That both Drews and Achelis misunderstood Barth's point has been recently demonstrated by Herbert Anzinger, *Glaube und kommunikative Praxis: Eine Studie zur 'vordialekti-*

At the heart of the debate stood the critics' concern that Barth had opened the door to a thoroughgoing subjectivism in his description of the essence of modern theology. Achelis asked,

Am I wrong in thinking that Barth wants to leave to individual judgement what the individual wants to acknowledge as liberating revelation in the Christian tradition or in the life-expressions of contemporary religion? Is there, then, an innumerable multitude of possibilities for the revelation which liberates and forces us to yield? For evangelical theology and piety, there is only *one* revelation worthy of the name, in which 'God has poured out His heart toward us', and this revelation is named Jesus Christ. Only *that* side of the Christian tradition and *that* living expression of contemporary religion can help us to faith and strengthen us in faith, in which *the* revelation encounters us. Christ alone is the source of revelation which is valid for us . . .[79]

Put in this way, there was nothing Barth could disagree with. For him too, there was ultimately one source of revelation. But the question at least had the virtue of forcing him to clarify his understanding of the objective moment in revelation, as well as providing further elucidation of his suspicions about doctrine and its role in the genesis of faith.

In his response, Barth noted that for him too, religious individualism finds its limit in the fact that it is bound to Jesus Christ as its norm and authority. The question is, how is that to be understood? *How is Christ presented to us?* Is Christ made present to us by an authoritative teaching about him? Or is it not rather the case that a doctrine brought to us from without is simply an expression of someone else's faith which at best provides the occasion for our own personal encounter with revelation—an encounter which takes place not in the conceptual realm of ideas but in the depths of the soul? At this point, Barth appealed to Schleiermacher's account of the origin of doctrine in an attempt to explain his concern more fully.

The revelation of the glory of Christ is given nowhere other

schen' Theologie Karl Barths (Munich: Chr. Kaiser Verlag, 1991), 23–32. The clash between Drews and Achelis on the one hand and Barth on the other is a clash between the "older Ritschlianism" and the theology of Wilhelm Herrmann (which Drews and Achelis seem not to have fully understood). Cf. on this point Christoph Schwöbel, 'Einleitung' to *B–R Br.* 18.

[78] Karl Barth, 'Antwort an D. Achelis und D. Drews', *Zeitschrift für Theologie und Kirche*, 19 (1909), 479–86.

[79] Achelis, 'Noch einmal', 408.

than in the deepest depths of human consciousness, something Schleiermacher termed the 'affections'. Doctrine is simply the result of an attempt to set forth the content of the Christian's religious affections in speech. True objectivity, Barth wanted to say, is found in the Christ who gives Himself to be known in the depths of the human soul. Any other objectivity—and especially that of a doctrinal norm—would be a false objectivity. The problem is that the transition from the experience of revelation to conceptual clarification of that experience is a most difficult one. Barth cited Schleiermacher: 'stepping forth in thought and word is everywhere the corruptible; the innermost which lies back of thought and word is that which is in agreement with itself, the identical, but that can never be communicated externally as such.'[80] There is an objective and normative element in Christian religious experience but it is an element over which human beings have no control. If there is such a thing as a safeguard against subjectivism (and Barth seems to have assumed that there is), it lies in the power of God alone. On the human side, every attempt to give adequate verbal expression to the content of revelation must finally fail. As Barth put it, 'the normative, objective, eternal lies only in the "affection" of this inner experience. Everything which is set forth in thoughts and words belongs itself once again to the relativizing stream of history and is, as that which passes away, only a parable.'[81]

It is at this point that the issue is really joined. The objective revelation is experienced by each individual for herself, in the depths of her being. Each individual must decide for herself as to the contents of her religious "affections". And that means that the only thing that is finally normative in practice is the faith judgement of the individual. The value of any piece of tradition or contemporary life-expression for engendering or confirming or strengthening faith—broken and corruptible as all such words and concepts are—must be decided by the individual.

In Drews's criticisms however, Barth sensed a retreat to the orthodox notion of authoritative tradition—something which called forth as much invective from him as it would have from his teacher, Herrmann. Barth agreed with Drews that Christ alone has normative authority. But he understood Drews to be

---

[80] Barth, 'Antwort', 482.   [81] Ibid. 484.

saying that Christ is presented to us in the form of some 'tradition of the historical person Jesus'.[82] Barth felt that Drews had completely set aside Schleiermacher's starting-point in the inner life of the individual in order to start with an approved tradition about the historical Jesus. He rightly saw in Drews a representative of the 'older Ritschlian direction'[83]—typified by Kattenbusch and Kaftan—which had left the door open to a return to the orthodox notion of faith as assent to doctrine by its elevation of certain traditions about Jesus to the level of normativity. Barth's response to Drews makes clear, if anything does, the extent to which the older Ritschlianism was no longer a live option for him by the time he was ready to move into the pastorate.

In mid-August 1909, Barth finally left Marburg to begin work as a *Hilfsprediger* in the German-speaking Reformed Church in Geneva. The pastor of this church was Adolf Keller, who later became a well-known ecumenist. Barth's stay in Geneva would last two years.

Of Barth's various writings in this period, there is one especially which merits attention here. It was first given in the form of a lecture to pastors at Neuchatel on 5 October 1910. The subject was the problem of the relation of faith and history. It was later revised—in light of Ernst Troeltsch's famous lecture on 'The Significance of the Historicity of Jesus for our Faith'—and published in the *Schweizerische theologische Zeitschrift* in 1912.[84]

There is nothing really original in this essay. The position which it stakes out is completely indebted to Wilhelm Herrmann. It begins with the assertion that the problem of showing the relation of faith and history has been *the* problem in the theology of the preceding forty years. It was the characteristic problem of the Ritschlian movement; it has the same status now amongst the theologians in the history of religions school. Ritschl's merit lay in overcoming the one-sidedness of the *Bewußtseinstheologie* of the later Schleiermacherians of the Erlangen school. He did so by insisting that the object of theology lies in a historical revelation. But the way in which he defined 'historical revelation' rested finally upon an 'arbitrary

---

[82] Ibid. 483.   [83] Ibid. 485.
[84] Karl Barth, 'Der christliche Glaube und die Geschichte', *Schweizerische theologische Zeitschrift*, 29 (1912), 1–18, 49–72.

selection of thoughts [*Gedanken*] from the New Testament and the Reformation'.[85] In that his position involved an identification of revelation with certain thoughts, it was exposed to erosion by a more radical historical criticism—a weakness which was exploited by the history of religions school. The theologians of the latter school wanted to do history for the sake of history. They had shown the impossibility of verifying revelation and miracle in history. Indeed, they had demonstrated thoroughly the limits of the historical method. The historian *qua* historian has no access to revelation and miracle. The historian works only with relative magnitudes, not absolutes. According to Barth, no objection could be raised against the employment of the method of the historians of religion. It corresponded completely to the demand for truthfulness which had been self-evident within the bounds of science since Kant. But he quickly added that in employing this method, the historians of religion had stepped completely outside the circle of peculiarly theological problems. 'Where there is no talk of a religious relationship to the object, of revelation and miracle, but rather only of scientific knowing, of causes and effects, there faith and the doctrine of faith (i.e. theology in the strictest sense) are not involved.'[86] The work of the historians of religion is not entirely irrelevant to theology, however. It can and has performed essential service to theological work as a 'profane propaedeutic'.[87] It has had the effect of clearing the ground of all false objectifications of the object of theology.[88] In other words, Troeltsch had overcome Ritschl and his more consistent pupils. Now the path was clear for seeing the proper relation between faith and history.

For Barth, the solution to the problem is relatively simple once the terms are properly defined. Faith, he says, is 'experience of God [*Gotteserlebnis*], an immediate awareness of the presence

[85] Karl Barth, 'Der christliche Glaube und die Geschichte', *Schweizerische theologische Zeitschrift*, 29 (1912), 3.

[86] Ibid. 4.   [87] Ibid. 5.

[88] A similar point is made by Herrmann in a review of Troeltsch's 1911 lecture on the historicity of Jesus. 'Genuine religious faith always lives only from that which is given to a person in the present. Absolute, objective security is an illusion which can only weaken faith. That the [historical] science of the real can overthrow this madness is a help to faith.' See Wilhelm Herrmann, 'Die Bedeutung der Geschichtlichkeit Jesu für den Glauben; Eine Besprechung des gleichnamigen Vortrags von Ernst Troeltsch', in idem, *Schriften zur Grundlegung der Theologie*, ii. 289.

and efficacy of the power of life'.[89] Such an experience is to be carefully contrasted with all knowing which proceeds in accordance with the generally valid laws which govern the three branches of knowledge described by Cohen's epistemology:

faith is the historical moment *par excellence*. It stands heterogeneously over against the cognitive apparatus which assesses validity in logic, ethics, and aesthetics. For here two problems intersect one another which lie on completely different planes . . . the problem of the I, of the individual person, of the individual life, and the problem of law-structured consciousness, human culture, and reason.[90]

Barth here follows Herrmann in accepting the validity of Cohen's epistemology. The net effect of such a move is to place "knowledge" of God outside the realm of cognitive activity. In the strictest sense, there is no such thing as knowledge of God (*Gotteserkenntnis*). There is only experience of God (*Gotteserlebnis*). This way of distinguishing faith from knowledge helps to explain why Troeltsch's historical method falls outside the boundary of the truly theological; it belongs to the realm of knowledge which falls under Cohen's epistemology. It does not come into contact with the real object of theology. Barth also follows Herrmann in seeing faith as 'the historical moment *par excellence*'. It is the experience of faith which marks the birth of the individual as an individual. 'Through the regulative, heuristic, limit-conceptual moment of faith (which from the beginning belongs to the problem of the individual, not to the problem of reason), the abstract possibility of culture-consciousness is actualized, transformed into concrete reality.'[91] Barth then, agreed with Paul Natorp that faith activates the culture-consciousness of the individual (though of course, he could not agree with Natorp's further assertion that faith has no object). How then is Christian faith distinguished from the experience of God generally (as life-giving power)? '*Christian* faith has its peculiarity in the fact that here, the passive–active experience of God is *somehow* historically conditioned and determined through the *personality of Jesus* which has been present within human society.'[92] The remainder of the essay is devoted to an attempt to explain the significance of this 'somehow'.

[89] Barth, 'Der christliche Glaube und die Geschichte', 5.
[91] Ibid.
[90] Ibid. 6.
[92] Ibid. 7.

Barth's initial answer to the question of how the personality of Jesus impacts on the believer in the present is that Scripture provides a passive medium: 'it is a matter of an undemonstrable but experienceable fact of human–personal–individual life which shines *through* the reports contained in the documents as though through a transparency'.[93] We can catch sight of the inner life of Jesus shining forth in the lives of his earliest witnesses. Through a kind of empathy, we can enter into the very soul of a biblical author. 'We see what he has seen, we experience what he has experienced, we believe henceforth not for the sake of what he says but because we ourselves have heard and understood that Christ is truly Saviour of the world.'[94] It is a question here of coming into contact with the piety of the writers, not their words. But Barth expands on this answer so as to shift the focus of attention back to the present. The writers of Scripture are not finally necessary. The personality of Jesus can be mediated by a whole string of witnesses. In fact, anyone who has experienced the efficacy of Christ can be a mediator of that experience to us. 'The historical Jesus becomes the resurrected living Christ in the congregation of Christ.'[95] In the final analysis, the problem of the relation of faith and history (where history is defined as that which took place two thousand years ago) is dismissed by Barth as having no fundamental significance. Such a problem exists only for those who, like Troeltsch, stand outside of the experience of faith. For them, faith and history must fall apart as two separated phenomena.[96] But for those who live in the experience of faith, the two are one: 'Christ outside of us = Christ in us, history = faith . . .'.[97] It is not surprising that Barth could finally say 'Christ's righteousness becomes my righteousness, Christ's piety becomes my piety. He becomes I.'[98] Barth would one day recoil in horror at words like these.

The theology which emerges from Barth's earliest published essays is thoroughly Herrmannian. It has turned away from the original impulses which emanated from Ritschl's theology in favour of a renewal of ideas which have their source in the early Schleiermacher. And it has leaned heavily upon Cohen's epistemology in an effort to overcome Troeltsch's historicism. Within a few very short years, Cohen's epistemology would suffer ship-

[93] Barth, 'Der christliche Glaube und die Geschichte', n. 3.   [94] Ibid. 67.
[95] Ibid. 66.   [96] Ibid. 65.   [97] Ibid. 64.   [98] Ibid. 63.

wreck because of the collapse of German culture at the end of the war. When it did, Barth would have to find a new way to overcome Troeltsch. For now, however, all of that was still in the future. For now, this theology could and did go its way with supreme confidence—confidence above all in the experience of God which was its ground and motor. As we shall see in the next chapter, however, other influential factors would very soon come into play which would prepare the ground for a break with the theology which Barth inherited from Herrmann.

2

Socialism and Religious Socialism in Safenwil

(JULY 1911–AUGUST 1915)

1. BEFORE THE STORM: LONGING FOR A NEW WORLD

(i) *The Move to Safenwil*

Before the outbreak of the First World War Karl Barth was a dedicated and convinced theological liberal. But the dramatic events of August 1914 were to change all of that. In an oft-cited retrospective written in 1957, Barth remembered:

One day in early August 1914 stands out in my personal memory as a black day. Ninety-three German intellectuals impressed public opinion by their proclamation in support of the war policy of Wilhelm II and his counsellors. Among these intellectuals I discovered to my horror almost all of my theological teachers whom I had greatly venerated. In despair over what this indicated about the signs of the time I suddenly realized that I could not any longer follow either their ethics and dogmatics or their understanding of the Bible and of history. For me at least, 19th-century theology no longer held any future.[1]

It was this bitter experience of the 'twilight of the gods'[2] which brought about Barth's break with the liberal theology he had espoused in the years prior to the war.

But if Barth's break with the theology of his teachers only occurred with the catastrophe of August 1914, it must also be said that the ethos of the liberal world had become alien to him at a much earlier point in time. To put it this way is not to suggest that Barth's break with liberalism actually occurred earlier

---

[1] Karl Barth, 'Evangelical Theology in the Nineteenth Century', in idem, *The Humanity of God*, trans. Thomas Wieser (Atlanta: John Knox Press, 1978), 14.

[2] Karl Barth to Wilhelm Spoendlin, 4 Jan. 1915, cited by Busch, *Karl Barth*, 81.

than he himself thought. It has been argued, for example, that Barth's socialist stance in politics prior to the war already had brought his liberal theology into a 'process of dissolution'; indeed, at certain points, his theology had been 'broken open'.[3] But that is to put the matter much too strongly. Barth not only could but did succeed in large measure in integrating his ethical-idealistic brand of socialism with his commitment to a liberal theological outlook. Without the catalyst which the outbreak of war (and the ethical failure of his teachers) provided, Barth might well have continued to promote his version of a socialized Herrmannianism for some time.[4] The thesis which holds that Barth's break with liberalism was already under way before August 1914 cannot be sustained.

Still, it remains true that Barth became increasingly alienated on a deeply personal level from the liberal world of his teachers during the three years prior to the outbreak of the war.[5] Expressed positively: if Barth's disappointment over the ethical failure of his theological teachers was the impetus which sent him in search of a *new theology*, his search for a *new world* had been set in motion much earlier. And, as will be shown, that difference in ethos did give rise to certain *material* deviations from the theology of his teachers which, while not yet constituting a break on the level of starting-point and method, did help to prepare the ground for it.

In July 1911, Barth was called to the small industrial village Safenwil to begin what would be a ten-year pastorate. It was sometime shortly after his arrival that he reached a turning-point in his understanding of the relation of the gospel to politics—as he himself testified in a speech given to a meeting of a workers' association in Küngoldingen on 1 February 1914. Barth noted

---

[3] Wilfried Härle, 'Der Aufruf der 93 Intellektuellen und Karl Barths Bruch mit der liberalen Theologie', *Zeitschrift für Theologie und Kirche*, 72 (1975), 220.

[4] This has been convincingly demonstrated by Ingrid Spieckermann. See Spieckermann, *Gotteserkenntnis*, 56–64. For a thorough critique of Härle's work, see Anzinger, *Glaube und kommunikative Praxis*, 104–6.

[5] At the end of his life, Barth recalled, 'One thing . . . is certain, that even before 1910 I was a stranger in my innermost being to the bourgeois world of Ritschl and his pupils.' As we shall show, the statement requires only a slight adjustment from 'before 1910' to 'by early 1911' to be correct. See Barth, 'Concluding Unscientific Postscript on Schleiermacher', in idem, *The Theology of Schleiermacher. Lectures at Göttingen, Winter Semester of 1923/24*, trans. Geoffrey Bromiley (Grand Rapids: Wm. B. Erdmans, 1982), 262.

that it was during his *Vikariat* in Geneva that he had had his first
direct encounter with the miserable living conditions of the
working classes. But in spite of his involvement in various kinds
of relief work, he tended initially to regard 'social misery as a
necessary fact of nature in the midst of which faith held forth a
strong but impractical hope'.[6] He was not yet able to see any
connection between the gospel and socialism. Barth suggested
that two influences especially moved him beyond this point of
view. One was the impact which Calvin's idea of a city of God
on earth had on his understanding of Jesus' message of the
Kingdom of God. The other influence was, in all probability, his
careful study of Werner Sombart's *Sozialismus und Soziale
Bewegung*. 'It was through S. that I became acquainted with
socialism and was driven to more exacting reflection and study of
the matter. Since that time, I have held socialist demands to be
an important part of the application of the gospel, though I also
believe that they cannot be realized without the gospel.'[7] It was
therefore sometime early in his Safenwil period that Barth first
came to believe that a close connection existed between the
gospel and socialism.

That Barth only came to this conclusion in the summer of
1911 helps to explain how he could have passed his student years
in Germany without experiencing any significant tension with
his beloved professors—all of whom were political conservatives.
Herrmann's concern for the working classes extended as far as a
desire to see the worst abuses of modern industrialization amelio-
rated but not much further. His analysis of social problems
focused upon individual relations; it made no effort to investigate
structural and institutional forms of evil. He certainly had no
interest in a radical change in the prevailing capitalist system

---

[6] Barth, 'Evangelium und Sozialismus' (original manuscript in Karl Barth-Archiv,
Basle, Switzerland). The citations which appear here are taken from Friedrich-Wilhelm
Marquardt, *Verwegenheiten: Theologische Stücke aus Berlin* (Munich: Chr. Kaiser Verlag,
1981), 473.

[7] Ibid. Although Barth does not identify who the 'S.' was through whom he became
closely acquainted with socialism, I think that Marquardt is probably correct in assuming
that it is Sombart. The only mistake made by Marquardt was his belief that Barth had
already read Sombart during his semester in Berlin in 1906. Barth's personal copy of
Sombart was not printed until 1908. See *B–Th. Br.* I. 199, n. 6. It is most likely that Barth
only read Sombart after his arrival in Safenwil, as he himself would later recall. See below,
n. 20.

which governed economic and social relationships.[8] Herrmann's views on what was called at the time the 'social question' were hardly unusual for a German professor of theology in that period. German ecclesiastical circles simply did not provide fertile soil for the development of the kind of Religious Socialism which, at that very moment, was becoming a vital force in Swiss Church life.[9]

Such Christian Socialism as could be found in Germany prior to the war was of a conservative bent. The Evangelical Social Congress provides a good case in point. Founded in 1890 by Adolf Stöcker (among others), the Evangelical Social Congress provided a yearly forum for bringing together theologians, politicians, historians, and economists to hear papers directed to the social question. The motivation for founding the Congress lay largely in the desire to win back to the churches those workers who had fallen under the baleful influence of socialism. In other words, a very strong motive lying behind interest in the social question in Germany was the desire to oppose socialism.[10]

In the years before his conversion to socialism, Barth certainly did not approve of such a defensive approach to the "social

[8] The most significant sources for Herrmann's views on socialism are to be found in the following: Wilhelm Herrmann, *Ethik*; 'Religion und Sozialdemokratie', in idem, *Gesammelte Schriften*, 463–89; and 'Die sittlichen Weisungen Jesu: Ihr Mißbrauch und ihr richtiger Gebrauch', in idem, *Schriften zur Grundlegung der Theologie*, i. 200–41. The last named essays were originally given as addresses to the Evangelical Social Congress in 1891 and 1903 respectively. 'Die sittlichen Weisungen Jesu' is available in English under the title 'The Moral Teachings of Jesus' in Adolf von Harnack and Wilhelm Herrmann, *Essays on the Social Gospel* (London: Williams & Norgate, 1907), 145–225. Friedrich Wilhelm Kantzenbach has tried to demonstrate a certain openness on the part of Herrmann towards socialism but his argument rests upon a most one-sided use of materials and fails therefore to convince. See Kantzenbach, 'Das Sozialismusproblem bei Wilhelm Herrmann', *Neue Zeitschrift für systematische Theologie*, 18 (1976), 22–43.

[9] See H.-H. Schrey, 'Religiöser Sozialismus', *Religion in Geschichte und Gegenwart* (3rd. edn.), vi. 182. 'In the German ecclesiastical circles which were defined by Lutheranism, the conditions were essentially unfavourable for a movement which was directed not only toward works of charity but toward the goal of reforming the whole of society. The strong bond linking Protestantism to the bourgeoisie, the close combination of throne and altar, the resentment against socialism due to its hostility toward the churches and degeneration of the Lutheran two kingdoms doctrine into a doctrine according to which politics and economics function absolutely in accordance with their own inner laws—all of these factors hindered the advance of the Religious Socialist movement.'

[10] See Klaus Erich Pollmann, 'Evangelisch-sozialer Kongress (ESK)', in *Theologische Realenzyklopädie*, x. 647. It is worth noting that the President of the Evangelical Social Congress from 1902 to 1912 (the period in which we are most interested) was none other than Adolf von Harnack.

question". But his thinking had not advanced to a point where Herrmann's individualistic approach to social problems would have caused him any great difficulty. That much is amply demonstrated by a speech he gave in January 1906 as a student in Bern to Zofingia—the student association of which he was a member.[11] Entitled, 'Zofingia and the Social Question', the speech is important for the light it sheds on Barth's political views in the semester preceding his departure for Germany.

The immediate occasion for the speech was provided by Barth's unhappiness with the very high dues which were expected of each active member of Zofingia. Barth noted that the high cost of being a member had the effect of preventing those coming from the lower classes from seeking membership. Thus, the gap between rich and poor which was at that time threatening to divide society into two armed camps was mirrored in Zofingia. Barth reminded fellow members that they were representatives of a privileged class. Whereas the vast majority of people their age were already having to earn their livelihood under sometimes oppressive conditions, students had the privilege of studying at their leisure the greatest and most beautiful ideas human beings have ever conceived. Barth suggested that members might one day have to give an account of how they used these privileges to those who had not received them.[12] He therefore offered two concrete suggestions for how Zofingia members might begin now, as students, to prepare themselves inwardly for the life of responsible service and leadership which they would one day have to assume. The first was that Zofingia should seek to create the possibility for greater class diversification in their membership by lowering their dues. The second was that Zofingia members should behave in public in a way that did not emphasize their privileges, thereby reinforcing class differences in the larger world.[13] That was it; that was the extent of the young Barth's wisdom on how to address the grave crises of the time. Hardly the stuff from which great social revolutions are born.

[11] For further information on "Zofingia", as well as on the prehistory of Barth's first public lecture, see the editors' introduction to 'Zofingia und Soziale Frage, 1906', in Karl Barth, *Vorträge und kleinere Arbeiten, 1905–1909*, ed. Hans-Anton Drewes and Hinrich Stoevesandt (Zürich: TVZ, 1992), 61–71.

[12] Ibid. 82.   [13] Ibid. 90.

And yet, on the boundaries of Barth's reflections there is also evidence of a realization that the usual approaches to the 'social question' would not suffice. He suggested that social action like Stöcker's in Germany—which had as its secondary goal, the preservation of 'throne and altar'—'is and remains an absurdity [*ein Unding*]'. It represented the attempt to put new wine in old wine-skins. Both Jesus' command to love the neighbour, as well as the Swiss democratic tradition, called for more than self-interested ameliorative efforts.[14] In spite of such comments however, Barth had nothing positive to offer. He clearly had no real idea how to address the social crises of the time. Conspicuous by its absence is any kind of a positive appraisal of the socialist movement; in fact, there are indications that Barth regarded the socialists as something of a threat.

All of that would change, however, in the summer of 1911. Barth's conversion in Safenwil to the socialist cause under the influence of Sombart brought him into a relationship of 'critical solidarity'[15] with the Religious Socialist movement which had swept the Swiss churches during his absence in Germany. Unlike the social movements in Germany, Swiss Religious Socialism took a very positive stance toward the *Sozialdemokratie*,[16] believing that a rapprochement between the message of the socialists and the gospel preached by the churches was not only desirable but demanded by the gospel itself.

The spark which gave birth to the Religious Socialist movement was a remarkable book written by a Zurich pastor, Herrmann Kutter (1863–1931). The book was entitled *They Must! An Open Word to Christian Society* and was published in the late autumn of 1903.[17] It was a prophetic book. Kutter had read deeply in the writings of Marx and contemporary Marxists. He saw in socialism a kind of secular 'parable of the Kingdom'—a demonstration in deeds as well as in words of a vision of a new world which bore clear witness to that Kingdom which Jesus had

---

[14] Ibid. 75–6.   [15] Anzinger, *Glaube und kommunikative Praxis*, 71 n. 108.

[16] "*Sozialdemokratie*" was the most common way of referring to the international socialist movement prior to the split into communist and reformist parties during the course of the First World War. For a very fine history of socialism in the period with which we are concerned, see Carl Schorske, *German Social Democracy, 1905–1917: The Development of the Great Schism* (Cambridge, Mass.: Harvard University Press, 1955).

[17] Hermann Kutter, *Sie Müssen! Ein offenes Wort an die christliche Gesellschaft* (Berlin: Hermann Walther Verlagsbuchhandlung, 1904).

proclaimed. Kutter set forth this thesis by means of a series of striking antitheses. Yes, the socialists were quite often atheists, but it was they who were leading the struggle of the living God against the false gods of this world while the churches were demonstrating by the peace which they had made with the existing powers that the God in whom they believed was a dead God, who accepted everything and changed nothing, no matter how great the evil. Yes, the socialists were quite often materialists, on a theoretical level at any rate. But the truth was that the socialists believed that the material conditions could be changed, thereby giving expression to a vital *spiritual* vision, whereas the Christians, in treating existing conditions as though they could not be changed, showed that they were deeply rooted in and dependent upon the prevailing material conditions—that their spirituality was in fact a thinly veiled *practical materialism*. Yes, the socialists were quite often guilty of failing to take sin seriously. But here again, that was true only on a theoretical level. If 'taking sin seriously' meant sitting idly by and doing nothing about the misery and suffering of this world as many Christians did, then it would be better to be an unbelieving socialist who—while not perhaps believing in sin—nevertheless showed what it would really mean to take sin seriously by struggling to overcome its worst effects. The churches had falsified the message of the One who had come to make all things new, turning the gospel into a harmless, inward spirituality. Socialism was nothing less than the 'hammer of God', calling the churches to repentance, to renunciation of the dead God of the bourgeois classes, and to a renewal of faith in the living God of the Bible.[18]

The impact of Kutter's book was tremendous. It was greeted with great enthusiasm by Leonhard Ragaz (1868–1945), the pastor of the Basle Münster. Ragaz had for some time been deeply interested in the social question; Kutter's book helped to move him beyond a commitment to reform to the belief that what was needed now was a completely new economic system. Ragaz was by nature an activist and in the autumn of 1906, he presided over a meeting in the home of Pastor Hans Bader (in Degersheim) at which the Religious Socialist movement received its first formal

---

[18] My formulation of Kutter's antitheses owes much to the fine summary of Kutter's book found in Andreas Lindt, *Leonhard Ragaz: Eine Studie zur Geschichte und Theologie des religiösen Sozialismus* (Zollikon: EVZ, 1957), 236.

organization. The first of what would be regular yearly conferences was planned for April of the following year. Ragaz
founded the journal *Neue Wege* in November to disseminate his
views. Such was the success of the movement that Barth would
later say:

> Every young Swiss pastor who was not asleep or living somehow
> behind the moon or for whatever reason errant, was at that time in the
> narrower or the wider sense a 'Religious Socialist'. We became—in
> negative things more certain to be sure than in the positive—power-
> fully *antibürgerlich*.[19]

The move to Safenwil had the effect of deepening Barth's
sense that the modern industrial world had entered a stage of crisis. He became deeply involved in the trade-union movement:

> when I moved to the industrial village of Safenwil, my interest in theol-
> ogy as such had to step back noticeably into second place . . . I became
> passionately involved with socialism and especially with the trade-union
> movement. . . . I had to read Sombart and Herkner, I had to read the
> Swiss trade-union newspaper and the *Textilarbeiter*.[20]

Barth's interest was not purely academic. He took the lead in his
village in seeking to force the local textile industry to unionize.

> In the class warfare which was concretely before my eyes in my parish,
> I was touched for the first time by the real problematic of real life. This
> had as its consequence that . . . my studies were now directed towards
> factory legislation, insurance, trade-union news, and so forth, and my
> soul was claimed by the powerful battles which my support for the
> workers aroused, locally and throughout the canton.[21]

Barth's contribution to the trade-union movement took the
form of addresses to the local *Arbeiterverein* in which he sought to
create in the workers a sense of their need for solidarity. The lectures had another point as well of course. They also attempted to
show that Christian faith was not at odds with a commitment to
the Social Democracy. The first of these lectures was given in
October 1911, just three months after his arrival. In December,

[19] Karl Barth, 'Rückblick', in *Das Wort sie sollen lassen stahn: Festschrift für D. Albert Schädelin* (Bern, 1950); reprinted in Koch (ed.), *Karl Barth: Offene Briefe*, 189.
[20] Barth, 'Concluding Unscientific Postscript on Schleiermacher', in idem, *The Theology of Schleiermacher*, 263.
[21] Barth, 'Autobiographische Skizze Karl Barths', *B–B Br.*, 306; ET *Karl Barth–Rudolf Bultmann Letters*, 154.

he gave a lecture with the title 'Jesus Christ and the Social Movement', which was printed in the local newspaper of the workers' association. The publication of the lecture drew a stinging response from Walter Hüssy (an owner of local textile factories) in an 'Open Letter' published in the *Zofinger Tagblatt*. Barth then responded with an 'Open Letter' of his own.[22] This early "socialist speech"[23] is important not only because it provides documentation of the rapidity of Barth's drift from the ethos prevailing in Marburg but also because it sheds some light on his understanding of socialism.

(ii) *'Jesus Christ and the Social Movement'*

I really believe that the social movement of the nineteenth and twentieth centuries is not only the greatest and most urgent word of God to the present, but also in particular a quite direct continuation of the spiritual power which . . . entered into history and life with Jesus.[24]

With these stirring words, Barth set forth the central thesis of his lecture. Even a brief glance at this thesis-statement already reveals a great deal. In good Herrmannian fashion, Barth maintained that a life-giving power had entered into history through the life and death of Jesus of Nazareth. What is surprising in a 'convinced Marburger' is the interpretation which he then gave to the nature and effects of that life-giving power. Gone was the concentration on the existential problem of the self which had preoccupied Herrmann during Barth's student years. In its place was a political and economic problem. The theological foundation was still Herrmannian, but the superstructure had undergone drastic renovation.

What is it that entered into history through the life and death of Jesus? It is not the Church. Barth rejected with contempt the position of those who became interested in the social question solely out of a desire to stem the tide of working-class defection from the Church to godless socialism. Nor is that which entered

---

[22] This exchange may be found in English translation in Hunsinger (ed.), *Karl Barth and Radical Politics*, 19–45.

[23] The phrase 'socialist speeches' refers to the title which Barth himself gave to a collection of some forty-three addresses which he gave during his Safenwil period. See the 'Vorwort' to Barth, *Vorträge und kleinere Arbeiten, 1905–1909*, p. viii.

[24] Karl Barth, 'Jesus Christ and the Social Movement', in Hunsinger (ed.), *Karl Barth and Radical Politics*, 20.

history through Jesus to be identified with a Christian world-view. 'One can have Christian ideas about God and the world or about man and his redemption, and still with all that be a complete heathen. And as an atheist, a materialist, and a Darwinist, one can be a genuine follower and disciple of Jesus.'[25] No, what entered history through Jesus was a way of life, a basic attitude, an ethos.

Barth described this way of life in four movements: Jesus wanted to help those who are least; to establish the Kingdom of God here upon this earth; to abolish self-seeking private property; and to make persons into comrades. In each case, Barth's goal was to demonstrate that Jesus wanted what the socialists now want. Thus, the inner connection joining Jesus Christ and the social movement would be made clear.

The kind of socialism which Barth thought compatible with the gospel was conditioned by ethical idealism. At the outset, he sought to distance himself from the behaviour of particular socialists. What he was interested in, he said, was not particular persons but the subject-matter itself. Christians of all people should know that we all fall short in our actions of the ideals which we preach.

When I talk about the social movement, I am not talking about what some or all Social Democrats are *doing*; I am talking about what they *want*. . . . What concerns us is what all these persons have in *common*, what is left over after everything personal and accidental, good or evil, is taken into account, what they all with their words and deeds *want*. What they want comes to a few very simple thoughts and motifs, which together amount to a historical phenomenon which is self-contained and independent of the behaviour of socialists and the tactics of the socialist parties . . .[26]

Still, this idealist reservation should not prevent us from seeing that Barth's understanding of what the socialists 'want' did not involve any softening of the offence which the movement constituted for many Christians. In fact, one of his principal sources of information as to what the socialists were trying to achieve was taken from the official programme of the Swiss Socialist Party.[27] What the socialists wanted, according to Barth, was to

[25] Ibid. 22.   [26] Ibid. 21.
[27] Karl Barth, 'Answer to the Open Letter of Mr W. Hüssy in Aarburg', in Hunsinger (ed.), *Karl Barth and Radical Politics.* 42. Barth's other principal source was Werner

set aside the capitalist system of production in favour of state ownership of the means of production.

Capitalism is the system of production which makes the proletariat into the proletariat, i.e., into a dependent wage earner whose existence is constantly insecure. The materials necessary for production (investment capital, factories, machines, raw materials) are the *private property* of one of the co-workers, namely, the boss, the factory owner. The other co-worker (the 'labourer') possesses nothing but the power of his work, which he furnishes to the factory owner, while the net profits of the common work are accounted as capital—as the factory owner's *private property*. Socialism declares it is unjust to pay the one co-worker for his production so disadvantageously, while the other pockets the full actual gain of the common production. . . . This system of production must therefore *fall*, especially its underlying principle: *private property*—not private property in general, but private property as a means of production. Just as the work is collective or common, so must its net profits be shared in common. . . . the state, the whole, must itself become the producer and therefore the owner of the means of production. This in the briefest of words is the anticapitalist theory of Social Democracy.[28]

Barth admitted that this system of economy was nowhere to be found in the Gospels. But then, neither was the capitalist system. Capitalism and socialism were both produced by modern conditions which Jesus could not possibly have foreseen. Nevertheless, Jesus' attitude towards this modern problem could be validly inferred from his attitude towards private property. According to Barth, Jesus everywhere steadfastly opposed 'unrighteous mammon'—the use of material goods for self-seeking purposes. Material goods were to be held only in trust, in service of the common good. They were not to be held as "possessions". If

Sombart's well-known book, *Sozialismus und Soziale Bewegung* (Jena, 1908). The title of Barth's lecture was, in fact, an adaptation of Sombart's title. I have not been able to find any evidence for the contention of Helmut Gollwitzer that Barth 'eagerly read the writings of Marxist theoreticians from Marx through Kautsky to Lenin'. See Gollwitzer, 'Kingdom of God and Socialism in the Theology of Karl Barth', in Hunsinger (ed.), *Karl Barth and Radical Politics*, 102. Such a contention also seems unlikely in light of the fact that when Barth's friend Thurneysen turned to him for a reading-list of socialist literature, Barth sent along to him what he had—which included the book by Sombart as well as works by Heinrich Herkner, Paul Pflüger, and Gottfried Traub. Karl Barth to Eduard Thurneysen, 10 May 1917 *B–Th. Br.* I. If Barth did study Marxist literature, it was sometime after 1917, and even then, there is no primary source evidence which would confirm such a hypothesis.

[28] Barth, 'Jesus Christ and the Social Movement', in Hunsinger (ed.), *Karl Barth and Radical Politics*, 29

that was Jesus' view, then it is not hard to guess where Jesus would have stood on the great question which was dividing the world at the turn of the twentieth century. Jesus would have wanted what the socialists wanted.

Barth was clearly not a Marxist. With Leonhard Ragaz,[29] he placed an enormous stress on the necessity of first creating new men and women in order then to create a new and just order.

Jesus by word and deed opposed that material misery *which ought not to be*. Indeed, He did so by instilling persons with the Spirit which transforms matter. To the paralytic in Capernaum, He said first: 'Your sins are forgiven!' And then: 'Stand up, take up your bed, and walk!' He worked from the internal to the external. He created new men and women in order to create a new world. In this direction the present day Social Democracy still has infinitely much to learn from Jesus. It must come to the insight that we first need men and women of the future to create the state of the future, and not the reverse. But regarding the goal, Social Democracy is at one with Jesus.[30]

The new world would not be brought about through the operation of laws inherent in the historical process, as was posited by Marxism. The new world would be the product of a new ethos. Barth was, as we shall see, ambivalent about the use of revolutionary means to bring about the new world. The new world could not be truly new if it depended for its existence on the instruments of unrighteousness at work in the old world. But these differences from Marxism lay primarily in the realm of tactics. With regard to the goal, Barth was very close to the Marxists indeed. Having made his idealist reservation, Barth could say, '*Real* socialism is real Christianity in our time.'[31]

The strong element of ethical idealism in this lecture showed clearly that Barth still stood firmly on the ground occupied by his teachers. The internal transformation of the individual still has priority in his thinking. But—and this is significant—if a change in the inward person has a noticeable priority, it is nevertheless true that for Barth it is of the essence of such a change that it seeks expression in external relations. And this conviction brought him self-consciously into conflict with at least one of his

[29] See Lindt, *Leonhard Ragaz*, 239–40.
[30] Barth, 'Jesus Christ and the Social Movement', in Hunsinger (ed.), *Karl Barth and Radical Politics*, 28.
[31] Ibid. 36.

teachers, Adolf von Harnack. Indeed, although Harnack's name is never mentioned in this lecture, much of what Barth said here constituted a sustained criticism of the views set forth in the Berlin professor's famous book, *What is Christianity?*

Harnack saw a basic tension in Jesus' understanding of the Kingdom of God between future expectation and present fulfilment. He tried to resolve this tension by distinguishing between the 'kernel' and the 'husk' in Jesus' message. The 'husk' consisted in those elements which Jesus simply took over from His contemporaries and from the Old Testament, while the 'kernel' consisted in His original contribution and insight. What Harnack had in mind in speaking of the received element in Jesus' message was the idea that the Kingdom of God means the reign of God over the whole of creaturely reality. Such a conception (which is found especially in the prophetic literature in the Old Testament) had political overtones. It saw the world as standing under the sway of the Evil One, but said that a day was coming when God would defeat the Devil and establish His own reign over the world. Harnack called this conception of the Kingdom an 'external' one, and said that it constituted the husk which must be stripped away if we are to find Jesus' real contribution. The kernel of Jesus' understanding held that the Kingdom is a present reality; something which has already been established in the hearts of his followers. The Kingdom of God is, properly speaking, something inward, not outward. It is the union of the soul with the fatherly God, experienced as a present reality and secure possession. 'True, the Kingdom of God is the rule of God; but it is the rule of the holy God in the hearts of individuals . . . It is not a question of angels and devils, thrones and principalities, but of God and the soul, the soul and its God.'[32]

Harnack's conception of the gospel of the Kingdom of God allowed for no externalization, other than individual works of charity (which he certainly encouraged). The gospel which Jesus proclaimed had nothing at all to say to questions of how to organize society politically or economically. ' "My Kingdom is not of this world"; it is no earthly kingdom that the Gospel establishes. These words . . . forbid all direct and formal interference of reli-

---

[32] Adolf von Harnack, *What is Christianity?*, trans. Thomas Bailey Saunders (New York: Harper Torchbooks, 1957), 56.

gion in worldly affairs.'[33] To those who felt that the only way
that justice might be achieved in this world is through political
struggle, Harnack answered, 'Then let us fight, let us struggle, let
us get justice for the oppressed . . . but do not let us expect the
Gospel to afford us any direct help . . . The Gospel is above all
questions of mundane development; it is concerned not with
material things, but with the souls of men.'[34]

That Barth had Harnack specifically in mind is evident from
the way in which he introduced his critique of individualistic
conceptions of religion. The central phrase in which he describes
the position he rejects is taken almost word for word from
Harnack's book.

It is . . . one of the current misunderstandings that religion is a means of
making the individual quiet, cheerful, and where possible blessed in the
midst of the anxieties of life. . . . Religion beforehand and afterward
remains a matter between God and the soul, the soul and God, and
only that. This attitude is found today especially among the Christians
of Germany, above all to the extent that they stand under the influence
of Luther. They then distinguish themselves without exception by a
complete failure to understand Social Democracy.[35]

For Barth, such individualism rested finally upon a false disjunction between spirit and matter. The Kingdom which Jesus proclaimed is indeed within us, as Harnack said. But it 'must obtain
dominion over the external—over actual life—otherwise it does
not deserve the name. The Kingdom is not *of* this world, but of
God. It is *in* this world, however, for *in* this world God's will is
to be done.'[36] Barth's final judgement on this position is as follows: 'perhaps nowhere else has Christianity fallen farther away
from the spirit of her Lord and Master than precisely in this estimation of the relation between spirit and matter, inner and outer,
heaven and earth.'[37] Strong words! particularly when it is clear
that it is one of Barth's most revered teachers who is in view!

What we see in this lecture is not in any sense a break with
liberalism. It is rather, a critique of liberalism carried out from
within the house of liberalism. Methodologically, Barth is still
heavily indebted to Herrmann. But it is notable that he has

---

[33] Ibid. 115.   [34] Ibid. 116.

[35] Barth, 'Jesus Christ and the Social Movement', in Hunsinger (ed.), *Karl Barth and Radical Politics*, 34.

[36] Ibid. 27.   [37] Ibid. 26.

departed from his teachers on a significant material question in dogmatics—that of the nature of the Kingdom of God. As we turn now to a consideration of the sermons of 1913, we shall find that deviations were occurring in other areas as well. Taken all together, such material disagreements do not yet constitute a break, but they do help to prepare the ground for it. They help to account for the ferocity of the explosion which occurred in Karl Barth in the weeks following the fateful events of August 1914.

(iii) *The Sermons of 1913*

In November 1913, five of the six members of the church session (*Kirchenpflege*) in Safenwil resigned to protest against Barth's '*Sozipredigten*'—his 'socialist sermons'.[38] There was even some talk of having Barth removed from his post, but nothing came of it.[39] The elections which followed gave Barth a session more favourably disposed to his concerns. Nevertheless, the Religious Socialist themes receded noticeably from his preaching during the first half of 1914. That means that the richest source of Religious Socialist sermons published to date is to be found in the sermons of 1913.

These sermons deserve far more attention than they have received thus far.[40] A close reading of them shows that many of the themes which are most commonly identified with Barth's later "dialectical theology" have already emerged in 1913, long before the outbreak of the war.

[38] Karl Barth to Martin Rade, 19 Jan. (Feb.?) 1914, *B–R Br.* 89.

[39] The final straw for Barth's opponents in Safenwil may well have been his eulogy of Aug. Bebel. The chairman of the German Social Democratic Party (SPD) died on 13 Aug. 1913. While acknowledging that Bebel had made 'mistakes and errors', Barth said that that which had been good and true in his life had constituted 'a voice of God, an announcement of the coming Kingdom of God'. Barth, sermon, 31 Aug. 1913, in idem, *Predigten 1913*, ed. Nelly Barth and Gerhard Sauter (Zurich: TVZ, 1976), 435. Barth acknowledged openly two weeks later that several people had found his remarks deeply offensive. Barth, sermon, 14 Sept. 1913, in idem, *Predigten 1913*, 470.

[40] The only in-depth study devoted to these sermons is that of Jochen Fähler, *Der Ausbruch des 1. Weltkrieges in Karl Barths Predigten, 1913–1915* (Bern: Peter Lang, 1979). Fähler's work is very limited in scope however, and does not mine these sermons to the extent it could have for information relevant to an understanding of Barth's development. Because these sermons have not yet been translated into English, I am going to cite them at length. To be properly introduced to Barth's theology before the war, one must *feel* the ethical passion and longing for a new world which permeates these sermons. But that is possible only where Barth is allowed to speak for himself.

Most striking perhaps is the prominence of the theme of the judgement and wrath of God. Most interpreters of Barth's development have assumed that the emergence of this theme came about only as a result of the outbreak of war and the ethical failure of his teachers in the face of the ideology of war. But the truth is that this theme is a dominant one in Barth's thinking at least as early as the beginning of 1913—and perhaps even earlier. And there can be no question that his way of handling this theme brought his theology into significant tension with the theology of his teachers.

The category of divine judgement had suffered something of an eclipse among the Ritschlian theologians. For Ritschl himself, the biblical language of the wrath of God was to be referred to a single event at the close of history. It is that final reaction of God to those who spurn his love to the very end which results in their annihilation. Here, in this instance of final impenitence alone, it is appropriate to liken God's action towards the sinner to the state's punishment of a criminal—but nowhere else. God's relation to living sinners should in no way be conceived of as that of a judge. The essence of God is love. Righteousness is simply the consistency with which God pursues His saving purposes with men and women. As such, it is scarcely distinguishable from grace. Certainly there is no tension or opposition between the love of God and the righteousness of God. For Ritschl, every legal or judicial interpretation of the relation between God and the sinner was to be set aside. And even in the case of final judgement, the wrath of God is to be seen as describing an activity of God, not something existing in God Himself. Such language, when applied directly to God, is an illegitimate anthropopathism.[41]

Similar views can be found in Wilhelm Herrmann. Herrmann could speak of judgement as a present experience but his interpretation of it made it clear that it entailed no external action on the part of God. The judgement which is experienced by the sinner is reduced to his/her own self-condemnation in the presence of divine revelation.[42]

---

[41] For a good summary of Ritschl's position on these questions, see Otto Ritschl, *Albrecht Ritschls Leben* (Freiburg: Akademische Verlagsbuchhandlung von J. C. B. Mohr, 1896), ii. 198–9.

[42] Wilhelm Herrmann, *Dogmatik*, para. 42, p. 70; ET *Systematic Theology*, 109.

In Barth's sermons however, a different note is struck. Barth did not hesitate to characterize the divine–human relationship as a "legal" relationship.

Where God's love is at work, there righteousness too must have its place, either in' that one exercises it or in that one experiences it himself to his harm. God's love cannot engender anything else but righteousness, either as gift or as punishment. . . . Amos showed powerfully what it means to have fellowship with God, to stand in a covenantal relationship with Him. It is something different from the relationship of an animal with its young. It is something different from the love of parents who find their highest good in always seeing their darlings satisfied. The relationship of God to His own is a legal relationship [*ein Rechtsverhältnis*]. It does not rest on whim and inclination, but rather on truth.[43]

Moreover, the fact that God judges evil is grounded by Barth finally in the character of God Himself. That God judges evil tells us something about God Himself; it is not just a description of a divine action abstracted from the divine being. This, of course, reintroduces the problem of the relation of love and justice in God but Barth was not inclined to explain the problem away. Where Ritschl and Herrmann were intent upon resolving the tension between the love and justice of God by reducing the latter to the former, Barth was content to allow the two to stand over against one another in a relation of contradiction:

from the Bible, we learn only one thing, namely that God is *holy* without limit and just; that He dwells in a light which no one can approach [1 Tim. 6: 16] and that He therefore must cast evil from Himself and judge it—not for a limited period of time but in all eternity. Therefore, His judgement is *eternal and definitive*. But the same holy and righteous God is at the same time boundless *love*. He does not want the death of the sinner. Rather, He wills that the sinner would turn back and live. He is the Father who has called all, all of us to be His children . . . There is nothing that can break His will to love. Therefore, His love too is *eternal and definitive*. The two things contradict each other, do they not? Yes, but only in our thoughts. We want to let this contradiction calmly stand. Jesus' life and His cross proclaim to us both: God's holiness and God's love. Both are equally great and equally strong and equally powerful and both exist in a deep unity. We cannot comprehend this unity, but we can lay hold of it. Through experience, we can reach the conviction that both are eternally true and valid. It is then that we suspend the question and simply obey.[44]

The passages here cited give some indication of the conclusions Barth was coming to as to the nature of divine judgement and its ground in the holiness of God. But they provide only a very partial glimpse into the pervasiveness of the theme of judgement in these sermons and they do nothing to explain the passion and eloquence with which Barth spoke about it. Now, why should Barth so suddenly, at this precise point in time, become a passionate preacher of repentance and judgement? The answer can only be that his political activities and readings in socialist and Religious Socialist literature were opening his eyes to the radicality of human sinfulness.

Is humanity not like a person with a fever, tossed here and there by the powers of self-seeking, greed, pride, and hatred? Are these not the powers which dictate the laws which govern our businesses, our political life, and our social life? And do we not all sense how these laws also govern our souls, how again and again we think and do those things which we know ought not to be? Which we know are not right? Oh, sometimes it's as though we were chained up somewhere in an underground prison, and again and again we are forced to listen to the rattling of our chains, saying to us, 'You wretched, imprisoned people, you will never be free. Evil rules you and you are evil!'[45]

To those who would say that human society is noble and good, that knowledge and progress are its chief characteristics, Barth responded with the claim that all the goodness and beauty found in people throughout history—the men of the Bible included—must appear as 'trivial' when compared with the burden of 'stupidity and perversion' by which such goodness is surrounded.

Or our *modern culture* of which many are so proud! It is true that we know and are able to do infinitely more than one could know and do in earlier times. The human spirit has made conquests in the last two centuries as never before. But would we not like to cry out here once again: Dead works! when we place alongside these accomplishments the fact that self-seeking and superficiality and uncertainty in the most important things are nowadays, in spite of everything, greater than ever? What use are technology and education to us when inwardly we are still the old barbarians? Dead works![46]

[44] Ibid. 50; sermon, 26 Jan. 1913.   [45] Ibid. 68; sermon, 23 Feb. 1913.
[46] Ibid. 125; sermon, 21 Mar. 1913.

Barth had by this time assumed a critical stance towards ideas of the continual progress of human civilization—though he had not abandoned it entirely. He observed that belief in that light which shines in the darkness is much more difficult than belief in the darkness itself. Belief in the light is not an easy decision; it has the character of a 'dare' or a 'leap'.[47]

The prominence of the category of divine judgement in these sermons is undoubtedly a reflection of the anger which Barth himself felt at the spectre of people who refused even to consider the possibility that a more just social order might be found.

It is not only 'we', that is to say, our souls, our inner and personal life which must become light. Rather, the world must become light; everything around us must become light. We must not separate the two from one another. Unbelief is hidden in this separation . . . You may not say and think: I do want the light to apply to me personally and will strive to be subject to the will of God even in the small things. But what does it matter to me whether self-interest and stupidity and animal instincts rule outside, in the world of commerce, in public morality, in politics great and small? Let it be so! so long as I save my soul in this evil world. To speak or think that way is to speak or think in large measure as one who does not know God. Where do you get the right to set yourself apart in this way, as if God's actions were directed to you alone? . . . No, you may *not* do that. The misery of the world is *your* misery, its darkness is *your* darkness. . . . We must acquire for ourselves that holy sense of solidarity which bears the suffering of the world in its heart, not in order to sigh and shake our heads over it, but rather to take it in hand so that it will be otherwise.[48]

In the face of such apathy, Barth insisted that it was impossible to remain non-partisan in the great battle which was being waged. It was nothing less than a battle between the Kingdom of God and the Kingdom of evil. In his Easter sermon, he hammered away at this idea.

The message of Easter leads us to the boundary between two worlds. And on this boundary, a battle is raging. Two gigantic kingdoms are engaged in a war with one another. The night strives against the morning, the palpable-visible strives against the spirit, appearance against truth, the world against God. But we cannot and we may not be mere spectators of this battle of which Easter speaks. We have to become partisan on one side or the other.[49]

---

[47] Barth, sermon, 23 Feb. 1913, in idem, *Predigten 1913*, 70.
[48] Ibid. 72; sermon, 23 Feb. 1913.   [49] Ibid. 143; sermon, 23 Mar. 1913.

Although the outcome of this war was decided in principle in the crucifixion of Jesus, it has yet to be consummated. And as long as it continues, men and women will be confronted with a decision: whose side will they be on? To the extent that anyone is tempted to think that nothing can be done about the injustices of the present world-order, he/she acts as though the world will be victorious over God.

Barth clearly wanted to inflame the passions of his listeners. He wanted to bring them to a decision. He wanted them to shake off their lethargy and get angry. In a sermon on the cleansing of the Temple, he noted that Schleiermacher had been offended by the thought that Jesus could have been moved to wrath and that His anger could have brought Him to an act of violence. 'The Jesus of the cleansing of the Temple was no friend of his.' Against such a tendency, Barth said:

we do *ourselves* harm when we sullenly pass over this story in our New Testaments; something important is lost in *our* Christianity, in our character, when we do not acknowledge this feature in the picture of Jesus; we rob *ourselves* of a piece of the truth of God when we content ourselves with raising objections when confronted by the attributes which Jesus brings to expression here. Yes, Jesus did get *angry* when confronted by the gold trade in the forecourt of the Temple. But then, should a man or woman of God never get angry? Wrath is just as much a human emotion as joy and love. There is an unsuitable wrath just as there is an unsuitable joy and an unsuitable love. But not all wrath is wrong. Everything depends on when and how such emotion arises in us . . . There are people who are incapable of getting angry, who are always able only to laugh or shrug their shoulders, who are not disturbed by even the grossest injustice. Jesus was not one of them, and we have to make clear to ourselves that that is an excellence in Him, not a failing . . .[50]

Jesus' anger was justified because it was rooted in a higher conception of justice than the one by which men and women were accustomed to order their affairs. What took place in the Temple was, in its way, a revolution against the existing order.

Anyone for whom the customary is the highest ideal would have to be shocked by Him. Nowadays, He would be described in the newspapers as an evil agitator and disturber of the peace. The fact is that he broke through the human order and that is revolution, whether one wishes to

[50] Ibid. 28–9; sermon, 19 Jan. 1913.

call it that or not. But is it all that bad when human order is broken? If it is so decayed and rotten as it obviously was in this case? No, in that case, we should not grieve but rejoice. . . . There is a divine Law which is higher than all written law. When this divine law breaks through against the customary order, is it not then lamentable to complain as though something horrible has happened? There in the Temple, Jesus ignored the customary order with the fullness of the power of the Messiah. Who was the rebel, He who, with divine justification, rebuked an entire people? Or was it not this people, together with their laws, who were the rebels? Before this manifestation, our little objections must fall away. Yes, Jesus carried out a revolution—when the divine appears in human form, there must always be a revolution against human order. Let us be drawn into this struggle, my friends. This fight has to be carried out in great things and in small. Oh, if only we would awaken and want to *become* fighters![51]

Barth wanted his hearers to join him in 'declaring war' on the existing 'relationships' which governed social, political, and economic life.[52] The picture of Barth which emerges from these sermons is that of a man at war with the world around him—and this already in 1913!

A second element usually associated with Barth's later dialectical theology (and closely related to the theme of divine judgement) emerges with clarity in these sermons: namely, criticism of religion. Here too, Barth was brought into tension with the views of his teacher, Wilhelm Herrmann. Herrmann saw religion in almost wholly positive terms. Religion for him (as we saw in the previous chapter) is the ability of the individual to see the working of God in the events of her life. Such working, though it may be *perceived* by the individual as judgement, is not judgement in reality. God's actions towards men and women are continuously gracious. When the individual comes to understand that God really acts towards her as a Father and not a judge, then real faith has come into being. By contrast, Barth now saw religion as a much more ambiguous affair.

In a sermon on Amos 5:21–4, Barth spoke of a struggle of God against that religion which fails to see that real, genuine worship consists in letting 'justice flow down like waters and righteousness like an ever-flowing stream'. Without this commitment to

---

[51] Barth, sermon, 19 Jan. 1913, in idem, *Predigten 1913*, 38.
[52] Ibid. 313; sermon, 22 June 1913.

action on behalf of the cause of a more just world, religion is nothing more than 'dreadful lies'.[53] Where the command to let justice flow down like waters is not heard, there a chasm opens up between God and the worship of God.[54] There the prophet who speaks for God must announce, 'I hate, I despise your feasts, and I take no delight in your solemn assemblies. Even though you offer me your burnt offerings and cereal offerings, I will not accept them.' Barth suggested that if a modern-day Amos were to appear in the Switzerland of 1913, he would no doubt have much the same message to preach. God, he would say, wants nothing to do with your Christianity because you are a people who do not exercise love and truth. No doubt the people would react (as they did to Barth himself) with incomprehension and astonishment. They would point to their many works of charity and say 'things are not so bad'. And the modern-day Amos would answer, 'You allow the most notorious injustices to take their course in your midst, you so-called Christians. You give alcoholism free rein . . . You allow the exploitation of children barely out of school for the sake of profits and merely shrug your shoulders about it as you do about so many other things. Do you really think that your so-called religion has any value at all?'[55]

In another sermon, Barth spoke of religion as being like the colour that is painted over wood or stone. Outwardly, the wood or stone is pretty but underneath everything remains the same. In the same way, religion is very often simply a façade of belief which conceals the greatest unbelief. The respect of the religious for God is merely external; inwardly, they respect the world and its powers more.[56]

There can be little doubt that Barth saw himself in the role of the modern-day Amos.

A prophet is, in all things, precisely the *opposite* of that which most people expect from a pastor these days and of that which most pastors have really been. . . . Of a pastor people think: he is our employee. We have chosen him and we pay him and therefore it is the first responsibility of his office to strive to get along with everyone, to be nice to everyone and give offence to no one. The prophet is the employee of God. For him, it is a matter of indifference what people think of him and what they do to him. He cannot be comfortable with those to whom he is

---

[53] Ibid. 217; sermon, 4 May 1913.
[54] Ibid. 213, 220.
[55] Ibid. 216.
[56] Ibid. 152; sermon, 23 Mar. 1913.

sent. He knows that if he does his duty, they will be shocked by him
and indignant. Of a pastor, people expect above all that he preserve and
care for the old customs . . . The prophet is the representative of the
unaccustomed . . . he says: Either–Or![57]

This was surely a piece of self-description.

A third theme to emerge in these sermons—which also provided a hint of things to come—was that of the "wholly otherness" of God. "Wholly otherness" here refers above all to the
moral chasm which separates God from the human race.

> Whoever reads the Bible rightly cannot come away with the thought: I
> am now sufficiently pious and sufficiently worthy . . . She feels herself
> placed in the light of a truth in which our small and great untruthful-
> ness and pseudo-holiness and conceits are mercilessly unmasked. There
> the eternal antithesis between God and humankind appears to her
> openly and undeniably. . . . God is still wholly other and the true life is
> still wholly other than you now imagine for yourself![58]

Closely connected with this theme of the wholly otherness of
God is the attempt to make a critical distinction between the
Holy Spirit and the spirit of the times (the *Zeitgeist*). In his sermon on Pentecost Sunday, Barth noted that thirty years earlier
the *Zeitgeist* had been captured in watchwords like 'freedom' and
'progress'. But though such words could still be heard they were
no longer capable of commanding allegiance. The problem with
the *Zeitgeist* is that its power and validity are too short-lived. It
cannot possibly be identified with the Holy Spirit. Still Barth was
under no illusions as to the very real power of this spirit.
'Nowadays we see things this way; nowadays we don't believe
that any longer; nowadays we do it that way! There is a bewil-
dering enchantment concealed in this "nowadays".' It was that
enchanting power which made the spirit of the times so dangerous. 'God save us from the *Zeitgeist*.'[59]

[57] Barth, sermon, 4 May 1913, in idem, *Predigten 1913*, 209.

[58] Ibid. 252; sermon, 25 May 1913; cf. also ibid. 167–8; sermon, 13 Apr. 1913.

[59] Ibid. 225; sermon, 11 May 1913. Closer attention to this sermon might have altered
Herbert Anzinger's judgement that Barth's pre-war theology was everywhere governed
by a "*Fortschrittsoptimismus sozialistischer Provenienz*"—the optimistic belief that culture
would still develop under the guidance of socialism in the direction of a kingdom of
righteousness which would correspond to the coming Kingdom of God. Occasional notes
of hope can indeed be found, but they are already more than balanced by a realistic
appraisal of the obstacles standing in the way of such progress. See Anzinger, *Glaube und
kommunikative Praxis*, 90–1.

A fourth and final theme which ought to be considered here is that of the Kingdom of God and its relation to the history of this world. Barth's understanding of the Kingdom of God was, broadly speaking, Herrmannian. The Kingdom is not a second world to be laid alongside this one. It is this world—but this world made new. With Herrmann, he could say that God alone can bring this renewal.[60] Everything that humans are able to accomplish can only be transitory and the transitory is never more than a parable of the Kingdom.[61] Taken with strict seriousness, this would mean that human attainments—even those of the socialists—ought never to be identified with the Kingdom. But the distinction between the divine working and human working is never simple in practice. For Barth also believed that God carries out His work through forces and powers resident in human history. Human beings must be open to the coming of the Kingdom; they must work for it. In that they do so, the old world gradually gives way to the new.

And yet, here again, Barth's Religious Socialism gave to these received ideas a new twist. The coming of the Kingdom for Barth meant a revolution. The house in which men and women live—in other words, the entire network of social, commercial, and political relationships—would have to be torn down. Not one stone would be left standing on another. If God were to become master of this house, it would have to be rebuilt from the ground up. God will not be satisfied with works of charity and Christian unions and a welfare state. All of these things are earthly.[62] God does not want charity; He wants righteousness.

Barth's talk of 'revolution' should not mislead us: he was no advocate of armed insurrection. On the contrary; he rejected every attempt to bring about the Kingdom through the weapons of unrighteousness.

Just as little as one can surrender hope in the victory of the divine order over all corrupt and defective human order can one assail human orders in an arbitrary and short-sighted way. The world must slowly grow into this transformation. And God Himself it is who completes this transformation. He wants to lead humanity through the defective and perish-

---

[60] Herrmann, *Dogmatik*, para. 16., pp. 22–3; ET *Systematic Theology*, 43–4.

[61] Barth, sermon, 28 Dec. 1913, in idem, *Predigten, 1913*, 686. Barth is here quoting a line from Goethe's *Faust*, II: 'Everything transitory is only a parable.'

[62] Barth, sermon, 9 Mar. 1913, in idem, *Predigten 1913*, 101.

able to the perfect and eternal. We humans can only wait, standing at
the ready, until the call of God comes to us, to take the matter in hand.
And this call comes to us when we see that it is possible to replace the
old with the new by means of the 'weapons of righteousness' [Rom. 6:
13; 2 Cor. 6: 7], i.e. with a clean conscience and pure hands. So long as
that is not possible for us, so long as we have to do evil to fight evil, so
long is our struggle against evil—however well intended—a rebellion
against God.[63]

Barth could not give his approval to Christian participation in
revolutionary activities. The Kingdom would not come this way.
He fully expected that God would bring His Kingdom to earth
through the ethical striving of the truly converted.

On the other hand, even if Christians ought not to participate
in revolutions, this did not mean for Barth that God was not at
work in and through them. If the Kingdom could not be fully
realized by revolutionary means, it was none the less possible that
the Kingdom announced itself (in a provisional sort of way)
through civil disorders. It could well be the case that God's gracious purposes would only be realized through judgement. If
even Christians resisted the coming of the Kingdom, then it most
certainly would come in judgement. Like Kutter, Barth saw civil
conflicts, strikes, and civil unrest as an expression of the divine
displeasure. Such conflicts were seen as the judgement of God on
the sinfulness of a people who refused to change.

But judgement too cannot be the last word of God. Judgement too
must be a means and the way of His grace. When God judges and punishes, He is at the same time the Creator who calls new life into existence. Catastrophes and violent storms must serve the coming of His
Kingdom.[64]

Barth had not completely given up hope in a progress of the
human race. In fact, he spoke at times of the march of socialism
as unstoppable. But he now saw it as possible (and perhaps even
probable) that progress might only be made by fits and starts,
through 'catastrophes and violent storms'. Such storms could well
serve to awaken the people of God to the need of the hour, to
the desire to obey God and establish justice. As such, they were
to be seen as a means of grace.

[63] Barth, sermon, 2 Mar. 1913, in idem, *Predigten 1913*, 79–80.
[64] Ibid. 93; sermon, 9 Mar. 1913.

In this last year before the outbreak of the war, Barth saw clearly that the human race stood on the edge of catastrophe. He could observe for example that men and women who strive after the truth must see that 'we are proceeding towards an abyss; that there is infinitely much that is rotten and poisonous in our lives; . . . that certain things and relationships in the world are a disgrace for humanity; . . . that we are standing in a crisis like a sick man.'[65] He had not given up hope though, that the catastrophe might still be averted. He saw evidence that the threat of war had diminished in the 'declaration of war on war' issued by a gathering of the Socialist International in the Basle Münster in November 1912, as well as in a peace conference between members of the German and French parliaments which met in Bern in the summer of 1913.[66]

In concluding this treatment of the sermons of 1913, it should be pointed out that our interest here has been solely in those elements which brought Barth into a certain tension with the theology of his teachers. For the sake of a more balanced picture, it has to be noted that there is a tremendous amount of material here which demonstrates clearly that Barth was still thoroughly "liberal" in his basic theological orientation. Revelation was still understood in Herrmannian fashion. The primary subjective *locus* of revelation for Barth was still the conscience of the individual. On its objective side, revelation was closely identified with history.[67] In his soteriology, Barth still moved along lines first laid down by Albrecht Ritschl. He was extremely hesitant to affirm a bodily resurrection of Jesus. Resurrection for him meant the victory of Jesus over death and that victory was construed as the calm acceptance with which Jesus proceeded towards death at the hands of His enemies. Death held no fears for Him. And so Barth could say, 'It is wonderful to say and yet it is so: Jesus was

[65] Ibid. 91, 94.

[66] Ibid. 478; sermon, 21 Sept. 1913. Jochen Fähler has pointed out that the results of the meeting of the International Socialist Congress in Basle had not been so promising as Barth thought. The Congress was unable to come up with a unified strategy for stopping a war, should one break out. A general strike on an international level was proposed, but not accepted. The plan 'crashed on the rocks of a national veto which provided for support of national interests by the workers in the case of a defensive war. In the distinction between a justified defensive war and an unjustified war of aggression (which was to be opposed), the collapse of socialism in 1914 was adumbrated'. See Fähler, *Der Ausbruch des 1. Weltkrieges in Karl Barths Predigten*, 14.

[67] Barth, sermon, 13 Apr. 1913, in idem, *Predigten 1913*, 167–8.

resurrected before He died, long before.'[68] In sum, although nothing which has emerged in Barth's thought to this point adds up to a break with the theology of his teachers, the ground for such a break has been amply prepared.[69] And the source of the movement which has occurred can only be Barth's socialist engagement.

(iv) *'Belief in a Personal God'*

Barth's interest in academic theology did not suffer a complete eclipse during the early years in Safenwil. Ample evidence for this may be found in a lecture entitled 'Belief in a Personal God' which he gave on 19 May 1913 to the Pastors' Association in Canton Aargau.[70] The problem to which Barth devoted his attention in this lecture was how to relate the concepts "personality" and "absoluteness" when applied to God. The importance of this lecture from the point of view of the question of Barth's development lies first of all in the fact that it demonstrates an early affinity on Barth's part for dialectical thinking.[71] And secondly, it betrays a hint of the kind of analogical thinking which would later be referred to by Barth as the *analogia fidei* (the "analogy of faith").

Barth's argument in this essay is easily outlined. Religious experience has the character of an encounter between two persons (an I and a Thou[72]) which awakens absolute confidence in

[68] Barth, sermon, 29 June 1913, in idem, *Predigten 1913*, 324; cf. ibid. 146; sermon, 23 Mar. 1913.

[69] Cornelis van der Kooi is not wrong in his view that 'Until the summer of 1914, Barth proved admirably able to integrate his socialist opinions into a framework of thought oriented to Herrmann.' But he fails to see any points of conflict between Barth and Herrmann in the details. See van der Kooi, *Anfängliche Theologie: Der Denkweg des jungen Karl Barths* (Munich: Chr. Kaiser Verlag, 1987), 60. Similarly, Ingrid Spieckermann focuses her attention entirely on the fact that Barth's starting-point in religious experience remained unchanged prior to 1914, and she thereby overlooks significant development in material details. See Spieckermann, *Gotteserkenntnis*, 33. The same judgement must finally be made of the work of Herbert Anzinger, though his highly nuanced treatment of Barth's pre-war theology is the best to appear to date. Anzinger passes too quickly over the sermons, finding little in them which would alter the picture found in the published essays. This has to be considered a weakness. See Anzinger, *Glaube und kommunikative Praxis*, 90–1.

[70] Karl Barth, 'Der Glaube an den persönlichen Gott', *Zeitschrift für Theologie und Kirche*, 24 (1914), 21–32, 65–95.

[71] Beintker, *Die Dialektik in der 'dialektischen Theologie' Karl Barths*, 105–9.

[72] Barth, 'Der Glaube an den persönlichen Gott', 67.

the human subject. Both elements—the personal nature of the encounter and the experience of the Other as the Power over all things (which alone can ground the absolute confidence which results from the encounter)—belong to an authentic concept of God. Therefore, both "personality" and "absoluteness" are predicates of God which are demanded by religious experience. A concept of God which fails to give equal weight to these two elements will not do justice to the God who is known in religious experience. But it is impossible to synthesize the two concepts on the level of thought. The application of the predicate "personality" to an Absolute Subject will dissolve the element of absoluteness. "Personality" as we know it on a human, psychological level entails growth and change through the struggle (and often, failure) to accomplish tasks. Such a thought cannot be applied to an Absolute Subject without eroding absoluteness by finite restrictions. By the same token, the application of the concept of "absoluteness" to a Personal Subject will dissolve the element of personality. The element of striving and not yet having arrived which is proper to personality as we know it would be eliminated. Barth's conclusion was that every attempt at a unifying formula was to be rejected. He followed David Friedrich Strauss in ridiculing one such formula—that of an 'Absolute Personality'—as 'nonsense'.[73] So, given that both absoluteness and personality belong with equal fitness to that concept of God which arises necessarily out of religious experience, and given that these two elements cannot be thought together, the only solution is to allow them to stand alongside each other in open contradiction, each bearing valid witness to the truth.[74] Michael Beintker is quite right to see in this the same structural form of dialectical thinking which would later characterize Barth's second

[73] Ibid. 80.

[74] Ibid. 85. Barth's solution to this problem may not have been new. Herrmann took the same position in his posthumously published lectures on dogmatics. See Herrmann, *Dogmatik*, para. 37, pp. 61–2; ET *Systematic Theology*, 97–8. Although these lectures come from the year 1915/16, it is probable that he took the same position when Barth heard them in an earlier form in 1908. The probability rests upon the fact that Herrmann had already shown himself to be willing to allow such dialectical tensions to go unreconciled in other areas—such as the tension between divine omnipotence and human freedom—before the appearance of Barth's essay. See Herrmann, 'Der Widerspruch im religiösen Denken und seine Bedeutung für das Leben der Religion', *Zeitschrift für Theologie und Kirche*, 21 (1911), 1–16.

commentary on Romans—though it would disappear in the intervening period.[75]

The problem of analogy surfaces in Barth's consideration of the relation of human personality to divine personality. He rejected the thought that an analogy exists between human personality and the thought of God which would justify the attempt to understand the being and nature of God by a process of abstraction from what is known of human personality. The concept of God, as we have seen, entails a tension-filled relationship between absoluteness and personality. There is no such tension on the human level. In any case, the attempt to build up a concept of God by a process of abstraction from human personality would provide confirmation of Ludwig Feuerbach's belief that the concept of God was the result of the projection of human characteristics (stripped of all limitations) on to a transcendent (non-existent) being. But the truth is that the source of our concept of God does not lie in speculative abstraction. It lies in religious experience.

A concept of God which results from projecting human self-awareness into the realm of the transcendent cannot reach the reality of God, let alone describe it exhaustively. The concept of God proper to religion cannot be something projected from out of ourselves but rather only a reflection of a fact which has been created in us. This fact is the *life from God* which is given to us through our *connection with history*. This experience of being inwardly conditioned by history is *religious experience*. In it we have God and on the basis of it we can speak of God.[76]

Barth makes it quite clear that although a form of analogical thinking which takes human nature as its starting-point is to be excluded (because God is not like us), there yet remains the possibility that our concept of God can 'reflect' (analogically?) the inner content of a fact that is given to us. The possibility of an analogy which begins on the divine side, with God (or the life which is given in religious experience) as the archetype, is thereby left open. Hans Urs von Balthasar was right to see in this the emergence of an analogical thinking of the same structural form as the later *analogia fidei*.[77] Yet it is of the utmost importance to notice the great difference between this use of analogy

[75] Beintker, *Die Dialektik in der 'dialektischen Theologie' Karl Barths*, 109.
[76] Barth, 'Der Glaube an den persönlichen Gott', 89.
[77] Von Balthasar, *Karl Barth*, 226.

and all later uses.[78] Theological speech is here being made to conform to religious experience. That is to say, the *Urdatum* of the analogy is the content which is given in religious experience. And that which is given in religious experience is assumed by Barth to ground and justify speech about God. The fundamental theological axiom which makes this procedure possible is the assumption that 'we have God'. Because God is present immediately to the human subject in religious experience, talk of God that is appropriate to the divine reality is possible. It is precisely at this point of the assumption of a 'God in us' that Barth would soon have to rebel. Indeed, seen negatively, the fundamental axiom of Barth's later theology would be the contrary statement: 'We do *not* have God.' The significance of this for an estimation of Barth's development lies in the fact that the presence of a form of analogical thinking in this essay is no evidence of a continuity in Barth's development between the theology of his liberal period and what came later. When analogy (and dialectic for that matter) re-emerged later, they did so on the basis of radically different material considerations. Barth's *break* with his early theology lies here: in the abandonment of the liberal axiom of a 'God in us' in favour of new conception of the speaking of God which was better calculated to protect the sovereign freedom of the divine Subject in the process of revelation.

(v) *On the Eve of Armageddon*

The growing dissatisfaction Barth felt with the world as it is and the intense longing for a new world found poignant expression in the last days before the outbreak of the war in a review of the previous year's numbers of *Die Hilfe*. The editor of *Die Hilfe* was Friedrich Naumann (1860-1919), a man of enormous influence in the German churches. Naumann had begun his career as a liberal with a social conscience, working in the Inner Mission Movement in Hamburg. There was a time, early on in his career, when he held views similar to those which would later give rise

---

[78] Herbert Anzinger also sounds a cautionary note on this point. 'The truth in this [von Balthasar's] contention is that it is indeed Barth's intention in this essay to ward off the conception of a natural knowledge of God which is given to human beings simply by virtue of their createdness. Nevertheless, it seems to me that Barth's *bewußtseinstheologischen* and *kulturidealistischen* premises ultimately undermine this intention.' Anzinger, *Glaube und kommunikative Praxis*, 58 n. 88.

to the Swiss Religious Socialist Movement. It was during that phase that he founded *Die Hilfe* in 1890. But all of that had been in the spring of his career. Around 1895/6 he became convinced that a healthy economy could only be founded upon a secure and powerful national state. In the pages of *Die Hilfe* he wrote, 'Of what use to us is the best social policy when the Cossacks are coming? Whoever wishes to concern himself with domestic issues must first secure people, Fatherland, and borders; he must be concerned with national power. Here is the weakest point in the Social Democracy. We need a socialism which is capable of ruling . . . Such a socialism must be German-national.'[79] A trip to Palestine about that time convinced him that Jesus could not possibly have had a social programme; Palestine was simply too poor and desolate. He came to see attempts to bring Christian ethics to bear on political decision-making as utopian and impractical. Naumann became an ardent supporter of the German military build-up between 1905 and 1914. Barth's review, it should be noted, was written for *Die Christliche Welt* at the invitation of Martin Rade—who was Naumann's brother-in-law.

Barth acknowledged at the outset that *Die Hilfe* had performed a great service over the years, fighting for practical social progress, for unemployment insurance, trade unions, land and housing reforms. But he noted sadly the growth of a pragmatic spirit in its editor over the years. Naumann had reached a point where he could no longer see the relevance of Christianity for everyday political life. That involvement in politics will necessarily require an openness to compromise, Barth took to be self-evident. To say that political activity imposes concessions and compromises is to do no more than to describe the provisionality and imperfection of life generally.

But a politics which raises the necessary concessions and compromises to the dignity of generally valid ultimate ideas is very different from a politics which, to be sure, also makes concessions and compromises for the sake of immediate goals ('I do not do that which I will but rather, that which I hate, that I do'), but in doing so, constantly makes it known: these are provisionalities for which we do not for a minute have any enthusiasm and to which we do not allow ourselves to be

[79] Cited by Karl Kupisch, *Zwischen Idealismus und Massendemokratie: Eine Geschichte der evangelischen Kirche in Deutschland von 1815–1945* (Berlin: Lettner Verlag, 1955).

tied, because we believe in something greater. It is one thing to become accustomed to the world of relativities, finally becoming completely satisfied and . . . at home in them, as those who have no hope. It is another thing altogether, in the midst of this world of relativities, to be incessantly disquieted and full of longing, fundamentally revolutionary *vis-à-vis* that which exists, longing after the better which will come, after the absolute goal of a human community of life beyond all temporal necessities.[80]

Barth said that he had sought for this faith, for this unrest and longing in *Die Hilfe*, but in vain. In spite of his zeal for reform, Naumann knew nothing about overcoming the deeper causes of evil in society.

But there was, according to Barth, a political option on the contemporary horizon which did embody that faith. The Social Democracy distinguished itself from all other kinds of politics 'by the fact that here, the Absolute, God, is taken with seriousness politically'. Barth noted that *Die Hilfe* showed great understanding for the 'industrial-democratic element' in the Social Democracy, the 'entire reform apparatus in the social democratic programme'.

But precisely over against that which has given the Social Democracy its uncanny greatness, it knows of nothing better to do than . . . to shake its head over their ideals which are 'alien to reality', 'Utopia', 'fantasy', 'outmoded Marxist dogma', or even 'agitation talk'—that is the repertoire of their polemic against the left.[81]

For Barth, it was impossible that a Christian should ever think of making a final peace with the world as it is. Christian hope makes a person an alien in a world governed by sinful human beings and sinful social and political relationships. To take God seriously in the political realm means the refusal to acquiesce in existing possibilities. It means revolutionary unrest: constantly being urged forward by the longing for something better than anything offered by this world. This revolutionary unrest is the "religious" element in socialism.

Barth noted with dismay the enthusiasm with which Naumann had, during the past year, greeted signs that the reformist majority in the SDP were steering the party on a path

---

[80] Karl Barth, '*Die Hilfe* 1913', *Die Christliche Welt*, 28 (15 Aug. 1914), 776.
[81] Ibid. 778.

that would bring it back into the mainstream of German politics. Chief among these signs was the willingness of party chairman August Bebel to support the military appropriations bill which had been passed by the Reichstag in the summer of 1913 (an act which Naumann referred to as Bebel's 'last will and testament'). Barth still clung in these last days of July 1914 to the hope that such compromises as had occurred did not signify a fundamental departure from the traditional programme of the party, as Naumann seemed to suggest.

But even if Naumann is historically and practically right in the end, if the Social Democracy should be transformed into a radical reform party on the soil of capitalism and nationalism as *Die Hilfe* so much expects— we do not believe it—then that would be for us at most a new disappointment, as the politics of *Die Hilfe* is finally a disappointment for us, not, however, a proof that a politics which simply capitulates before certain alleged realities is the only possible, the correct politics. We should expect more from God.[82]

Unfortunately, as events were quickly to prove, Naumann understood August Bebel and the SDP better than Barth did. On 4 August, German troops entered Belgium. On that same day, Socialist representatives in the Reichstag voted unanimously to grant Chancellor Bethmann-Hollweg a credit of 5 million marks to support the war effort. Naumann was right. The Socialists did capitulate and became that 'new disappointment' of which Barth had written. But the "religious" element in socialism would remain true in Barth's view regardless of what particular socialists did. For that reason, Barth could happily join the Swiss Socialist Party on 26 January 1915 *after* his disappointment in the failure of the SPD in August 1914. For him, there was still something in the socialist vision of a human community that has overcome class warfare and national animosities which bore significant witness to the New Testament vision of the Kingdom of God.

The person who wrote the review of *Die Hilfe* in July 1914 was a person who could not feel at home in the world as it is. And yet, precisely as an alien in this world he was a joyful partisan on its behalf. He felt no inclination to abandon this world to its own devices. It was this world which must come under the rule of God if that other world was to be realized. This world

---

[82] Karl Barth, '*Die Hilfe* 1913', *Die Christliche Welt*, 28 (15 Aug., 1914), 776.

was worth fighting for. With the crushing disappointments in the months that followed, Barth was thrust irrevocably into the opposition. He became an outsider. It might be argued that the events which took place in that year marked him for the rest of his life. In all of his many and varied activities in the years that followed, he would always—in some measure—swim against the stream.

2. THE CRISIS OF AUGUST 1914 IN LETTERS AND SERMONS

In the first weeks after the outbreak of the war, Barth heard and read nothing of the reactions of German theologians. The chaos of the opening days of the war produced delays in the postal service. As a result, he received his copies of the first three issues of *Die Christliche Welt* which were published after the invasion of Belgium only towards the end of the month. When he finally read them, he fired off an angry letter to his former mentor, Martin Rade.

Barth noted at the outset that everything which was now written in *Die Christliche Welt* proceeded from the presupposition that Germany was right in the war. He did not wish to enter into the question of whether that presupposition was correct—though he left little doubt that he regarded the causes of the war to lie in sinful actions on both sides. What astonished him, however, was not so much the presupposition as the religious justification given for it.

You hold that presupposition to be necessary as the foundation for what you call 'godly preparedness for war'. And that is still worse than the presupposition itself. For me, the saddest thing in these sad times is to see how in all of Germany now, love for the Fatherland, delight in war, and Christian faith are brought together in hopeless confusion . . . That is the disappointment for us . . . that we have to see the *Chr. W.*, in this decisive hour, cease to be *Christian*, but rather simply place itself on the same level with *this* world.[83]

Barth regarded it as a 'scandal' that the contributors to *Die Christliche Welt* had tried to enlist God on their side in this sinful

---

[83] Karl Barth to Martin Rade, 31 Aug. 1914, *B–R Br.* 96.

situation—as if the Germans, together with their great cannons, were now acting as 'God's proxies'. God simply could not be 'drawn into the matter in this way'.[84] God's will could not be identified with the practical (and wholly sinful) necessities of the moment, for that was to make Him responsible for the actions of sinful human beings. Barth said that he would not accuse German Christians of having a different religion from the Swiss, but the insinuation was there none the less.[85]

In response, Rade made the suggestion that Barth allow his letter to be printed in Leonhard Ragaz' journal *Neue Wege*, together with an answer from his own pen. Barth saw little merit in this suggestion. He did think that a public airing of the issues would serve a good purpose—*if* it took place in a journal which was sure to be read by both sides in the debate (German and Swiss). He suggested either the *Zeitschrift für Theologie und Kirche* or *Die Christliche Welt*. To publish the exchange in a Swiss journal like *Neue Wege*, however—a journal which was scarcely read in Germany—would mean that it was directed in a one-sided way to the Swiss. Instead of a truly public debate, the exchange would serve only the purpose of giving Rade an opportunity to explain himself (and the Germans) to Swiss readers. But he also allowed that he would not block publication in Ragaz' journal if other alternatives proved to be impossible. And so the debate was indeed published in Switzerland.

Judging by the letters exchanged with Rade over the first two months of the war, there can be little doubt as to the general accuracy of Barth's later interpretation of the impact of these events on his theological development. To be sure, his later recollection that it was the publication of a manifesto by ninety-three German intellectuals (emphatically rejecting any German responsibility for the war) which deserved special credit for moving him to break with the theology of his teachers is misleading in one important respect.[86] It makes it appear that the break occurred more or less overnight and that is not the case. Barth was also wrong in placing the appearance of the manifesto in question in early August. It appeared on 3 October. Still, there can be little question that the appearance of that particular document had a special significance for Barth in that he found

[84] Karl Barth to Martin Rade, 31 Aug. 1914, *B–R Br.* 97.   [85] Ibid.
[86] See above, Ch. 2 n. 1.

Wilhelm Herrmann's signature on it. After its appearance, Barth wrote to Herrmann to express his dismay. The significant feature of this letter lies in its reference to the central category which Barth had been taught to prize highly by Herrmann.

Especially with you, Herr Professor (and through you with the great masters—Luther, Kant, and Schleiermacher), we learned to acknowledge "experience" as the constitutive principle of knowing and doing in the domain of religion. In your school it became clear to us what it means to "experience" God in Jesus. Now however, in answer to our doubts, an "experience" which is completely new to us is held out to us by German Christians, an allegedly religious war "experience"; i.e. the fact that German Christians "experience" their war as a holy war is supposed to bring us to silence, if not demand reverence from us. Where do you stand in relation to this argument and to the war theology which lies behind it?[87]

It is clear from the drift of Barth's questions that his primary difficulty at this point in time had to do with what he saw as a manipulation of religious experience to legitimate the most sinful and catastrophic of human actions. At this point, he still shared with Herrmann the belief that it is ultimately religious experience which provides the ground for theology; he simply disagreed as to how that experience should be interpreted. In the long run however, the question which the German *Kriegstheologie* raised for Barth was much more profound. If religious experience could give rise to such divergent and even contradictory conclusions, perhaps it could no longer be relied upon to provide an adequate ground and starting-point for theology. Although Barth did not arrive at that conclusion for some time, his relation to Marburg had already become severely attenuated. As he

[87] Karl Barth to Wilhelm Herrmann, 4 Nov. 1914, *B–R Br.* 115. In Martin Rade's published response to Barth's open letter, he had argued that the Swiss, as neutrals, would have great difficulty understanding the German people because they lacked the one essential prerequisite: the experience of war. Above all, Rade had in mind the 'overwhelming' experience of solidarity in the face of a common enemy. Rade did not say that God had willed the war. But he did say that God was the 'only possible ground and author' of the heartfelt unity experienced by the German people during the first days of the war. Martin Rade to Karl Barth, 5 Sept. [Oct.] 1914, *B–R Br.* 110. In fairness to Rade, it has to be said that his performance during the early months of the war was on the whole quite balanced. Barth himself came quickly to that realization: 'you . . . stand closer to us than any other representative of German Christianity.' Karl Barth to Martin Rade, 23 Nov. 1914, *B–R Br.* 120. Still, even in the case of Rade, Barth felt that a deep chasm stood between their respective positions.

expressed it in a letter to Rade, 'Something of the deep respect which I felt within myself for the German character is forever destroyed . . . because I see how your philosophy and your Christianity breaks into pieces in this war psychosis.'[88] And to Herrmann, 'Our relationship to you has become a mixture, a mixture of great gratitude and complete antithesis.'[89] As I say, this did not yet mean a break for Barth with his own most fundamental theological presuppositions. But on a deeply personal level, he was now an outsider.

All of Barth's thoughts during the first months of the war circled around a single, exceedingly difficult question: what was the significance of the war from a theological perspective? What did it all mean? Where did it stand in relation to the will of God? Truly, it was a knotty problem. On the one hand, Barth was deeply convinced that God stood unalterably opposed to war. The God who revealed Himself in Jesus of Nazareth was a God of peace, mercy, and love. Could such a God have willed this catastrophic war? That would make Him a liar, a God who spoke two languages and demanded of His people two contradictory ways of being in the world.[90] No, the war had its source in race hatred, unlimited economic competition, greed, pride, fear, insecurity, threats—in a word, in human sinfulness. Those were the sources on both sides of the conflict.

But now someone will say: yes, the war is horrible, but yet it is of God if it is a matter of a just cause. For God helps those who are in the right. Yes, in this way people seek to excuse themselves. . . . What then do just and unjust mean? As far back as one can think, self-seeking and pride on both sides have been the cause in every war. . . . That is very clear in the present war. One cannot speak of a just cause on either side. The great powers which now stand opposed to one another in the war have for decades feared one another and threatened one another with ever stronger armaments. Who led the way? Who feared the most? Who threatened the others the most strongly? . . . One will finally only be able to say: among the peoples of Europe at the end of

[88] Karl Barth to Martin Rade, 1 October 1914, *B–R Br.* 101.

[89] Karl Barth to Wilhelm Herrmann, 4 Nov. 1914, *B–R Br.* 114. Cf. also Barth's comment to Thurneysen, 'Marburg and German culture are losing something in my eyes through this collapse, and indeed, for ever.' Karl Barth to Eduard Thurneysen, 4 Sept. 1914, *B–Th. Br.* I. 10.

[90] Karl Barth, sermon, 27 Dec. 1914, in idem, *Predigten 1914*, ed. by Ursula and Jochen Fähler (Zurich: TVZ, 1974), 629.

the nineteenth and the beginning of the twentieth centuries, there was an immense ambition, a jealousy and a pride without equal and with all of that, they made the air too close for one another, and therefore they armed themselves against one another to the point of insanity, and therefore this world war finally had to erupt. Of a just cause on either side there can honestly be no talk . . . All of these things are completely alien to the innermost being of God. And if they nevertheless take place, then there is only one explanation for it: the innermost being of God is also completely alien to humankind.[91]

On the other hand, Barth was equally convinced that in some mysterious way, everything which comes to pass in this world happens in accordance with the plan of God:

God is our gracious, loving Father who very certainly so directs all things as is good for us. . . . the will of this our Father has to be effective absolutely and unconditionally . . . Who then is this God to whom we have to look in order to become free and strong? He is the infinite power who rules over all things and in all things. In Him and through Him everything that is exists and is held together. He gives to all things their life and movement. There is no particle which would be without Him and there was and will be no second in which He does not govern and rule. No power of nature can be against Him, and no human heart can set itself free from him.[92]

What then? If God stood opposed to this war and yet allowed it to be, what purpose did it serve in the unfolding of the divine plan for this world? The initial answer given in Barth's sermons was that the war represented the terrible judgement of God on the peoples of Europe.

Barth was inclined to see in the coming of the war the appearance of that horseman of the apocalypse with the power to take peace from the earth—in other words, he was inclined to see in the war an adumbration of that final judgement of the world spoken of in the Revelation of John (Rev. 6:4).[93] Never before had death and destruction been administered in such an orderly, technical, and business-like fashion. The 'signs of the times' seemed clearly to suggest: 'This is a *Gotteszeit* as never before. A time of judgement without equal.'[94]

And yet, judgement was not Barth's final word. If this was a time of judgement without equal, it was also—and 'precisely for

---

[91] Ibid. 463–5; sermon, 6 Sept. 1914.   [92] Ibid. 413–14; sermon, 9 Aug. 1914.
[93] Ibid. 430–42; sermon, 23 Aug. 1914.   [94] Ibid. 433; sermon, 23 Aug. 1914.

that reason'—'a very special time of grace.'[95] 'His present horrible judgement is an act of grace.'[96] The purpose of God's No of judgement is to set the human race back on the right path, the path that leads to righteousness.

Judgement! That means that God now wants to say to us once again that we are wrong, that He is not satisfied with us. He says it to us in that He interrupts our customary being and doing in so unheard-of a fashion, in that He places in the midst of our life a fact so hard and pitiless that we pay attention to it and have to become still before Him. . . . This is the way God punishes us, my friends. He flashes no lightning from heaven. He simply allows us to continue until one day we have gone so far that we punish ourselves through our own doing.[97]

Barth was deeply convinced that the judgement of God serves the graciousness of God; that the present time of judgement was only a stage in the dealing of God with the world which would serve the coming of His Kingdom. God, he insisted, 'holds the end in His hand'.

Nothing can finally endure from all the powers in the world which are hostile and contrary to the divine: affliction, hunger, error, lies, and destruction, everything vile and tragic is only a stage. Beyond them leads the sure way of God until finally the Son of Man comes in His power and glory . . . There is something remarkable and at bottom again and again incomprehensible about the fact that the way to complete divine sovereignty must pass through such evil, sin, and suffering . . . Who is able to penetrate the plans of God?[98]

There are two characteristics of Barth's theology during this first year of the war which merit special emphasis. The first has already emerged with clarity in the foregoing account. If ever Barth was inclined in his life directly to identify the actions of God with the negativities of history, this was the time. Here we have a "theology of crisis" in the strictest sense.[99] The Word of

[95] Barth, sermon, 23 Aug. 1914, in idem, *Predigten 1914*, 433.
[96] Ibid. 442.　　　[97] Ibid. 438, 440.　　　[98] Ibid. 404, 406; sermon, 2 Aug. 1914.
[99] The significance of this observation lies in the fact that what was later (in the early 1920s) called the "theology of crisis" was in fact misnamed—at least where Barth himself was concerned! As we shall see, it was an apt description for the theology of two of his closest colleagues of that period, Friedrich Gogarten and Rudolf Bultmann—a fact which alerts us in advance to the lack of real unity amongst these friends from the earliest days of their theological collaboration. On this point, see Werner Ruschke, *Entstehung und Ausführung der Diastasentheologie in Karl Barths zweitem "Römerbrief"* (Neukirchen-Vluyn: Neukirchener Verlag, 1987), 150.

God has been made a virtual reflex of societal conditions—in this case, of wholly negative conditions. The war is God's judgement. No further qualification is made. Barth saw no need at this point to question his ability to read the ways of God directly off the face of history. To that extent, his theology during this period immediately after the outbreak of the war is still built on the old "liberal" assumptions.

The second characteristic is perhaps more surprising. No one can read Barth's sermons in this period without being struck by the almost complete absence of any note of despair or pessimism. Sadness and grief most certainly abound! But Barth displays an unbroken confidence in the ability of God to bring His gracious purposes to fruition. However apocalyptic he was inclined to become when he looked at the human condition in the cruel light of the war, his belief in God remained firm. If anything, the overriding note heard in these sermons is one of optimism; not that optimism which depends for its existence upon a belief in the goodness of the human race, but an optimism born of a deeply personal, existential conviction that God is in control of the events which take place in this world.

3. THE SPLIT IN THE RELIGIOUS SOCIALIST MOVEMENT AND BARTH'S BREAK WITH LIBERALISM

Religious Socialism was never a unified movement. From its early days in 1906, it had known only a loose form of organization. Institutionalization was a thing feared by both of its leading lights, Herrmann Kutter and Leonhard Ragaz. The movement was held together more by personal connections than by anything else. It promoted its ideas and concerns through conferences and journals but it is characteristic that the journals were the organs not so much of the conferences as of the opinions of the editors; so, for example, *Neue Wege* bore the strong stamp of Ragaz, its founder and editor, and the *Freie Schweizer Arbeiter* was the voice of its editors, Gustav Benz and Otto Lautenburg.[100]

---

[100] That a man like Gustav Benz could play a role in Religious Socialism shows just how diverse the movement was. Benz was a socially minded, politically liberal pastor in Basle, who vehemently rejected the Social Democracy. As founder of the 'Evangelisch-sozialen Arbeiterverein', his pastoral work was combined with a strong interest in trade

From the beginning, tension had existed between Kutter, the movement's prophet, and Ragaz, its leading activist. As was pointed out earlier, that the Religious Socialist movement existed at all owed a great deal to Kutter's book, *Sie Müssen*. But Kutter himself wanted little to do with politics. From his point of view, it was senseless to try to 'Christianize' the Social Democracy. He was convinced that only Christians could understand the Christian message, and was therefore opposed to conferences which brought together 'unbelieving socialists' and pastors to see what they could contribute to each other.[101] Thus, Kutter had little direct involvement in the movement he had done so much to spawn. He continued to have a great impact on it through his writings and his personal relations—and extensive correspondence—with its leaders. On the other hand, his lack of involvement often gave him the freedom to be more radical than would have been possible had he been involved in a dialogue between Christians and socialists. For him, it was the Social Democracy as it was—in all of its godlessness—which God was using as an instrument to awaken the churches. It was their radicality which made them the 'hammer of God'. Hence, he could prefer the radicalism of a Karl Kautsky over the revisionism of an Eduard Bernstein.[102] 'They must'—i.e. the socialist must, in order to serve God's purposes, be as radical as possible. But in the meantime, 'we pastors'[103] must give ourselves over to a different kind of work. Pastors help to create the conditions for the new society by proclaiming the living God and bringing Christians to a life of immediacy with this God.

Although he had derived a great deal of inspiration from *Sie Müssen*, Ragaz saw in Kutter's refusal to be involved in politics (as a matter of principle) an ethical quietism. Like Kutter, Ragaz had studied the Marxist writings in depth. He found that he could not accept their central dogmas. His was a socialism grounded in ethical idealism. He rejected the principle of historical dialectic; the way to true socialism did not lie through the unfolding of a dialectic movement inherent in the historical

unions. See Max Geiger and Andreas Lindt (eds.), *Hermann Kutter in seinen Briefen, 1883–1931* (Munich: Chr. Kaiser Verlag, 1983), 261 n. 5.

[101] Hermann Kutter to Leonhard Ragaz, 11 Apr. 1907, in Geiger and Lindt (eds.), *Hermann Kutter in seinen Briefen*, 241–2.

[102] Lindt, *Leonhard Ragaz*, 234.

[103] Herrmann Kutter, *Wir Pfarrer* (Leipzig: H. Haessel Verlag, 1907).

process. A true socialism would only be brought about by ethical willing, by engagement in the practical task of creating a social ethos of brotherhood and solidarity out of which the will of the people would eventually express itself in the demand for a new order—an order seen by Ragaz as involving new economic structures, but also much more. He envisioned a new society infused by a new ethical spirit. Given his emphasis on ethical preconditions, it is not surprising that he rejected any tendency in contemporary Marxism toward the use of force to bring about the new society. The new world could not be created by using the tools of this one. Ragaz therefore gave himself increasingly to concrete involvement in the party, for it was only through direct involvement that one could hope to correct what was mistaken in Marxism and to underscore the importance of its Messianic vision.[104] Thus, from Kutter's point of view, Ragaz was engaged in a fruitless attempt to Christianize the socialists, an attempt whose chief danger lay in compromising what was truly "essential"—the proclamation of the living God and His Kingdom. From Ragaz' point of view, Kutter was hopelessly quietistic.

With the outbreak of the war, the already existing tensions became an open crisis.[105] Ragaz was of the opinion that in this time of peril, Swiss Christians should stand together as one in condemning the war. He called upon the Religious Socialists to make a united, open declaration of their opposition to the war and a commitment to working with the Socialist International and various pacifist organizations to bring about an end to hostilities. Towards that end, Ragaz called for a conference to meet in Bern on 12 November, to discuss such a declaration and a programme for action. Others were less certain of the wisdom of this plan. Gustav Benz declared that he would not take part in such a conference; it was, he said, a time for being silent and listening for the voice of God, not for precipitous action. The Ragaz forces went ahead with the conference, the result of which was a manifesto which declared that this was no time for remaining silent; what was needed was a public witness against the war. The manifesto called for an observance in the Swiss

---

[104] Ragaz joined the party in October 1913, roughly a year and a half before Barth took that step.

[105] The sketch which follows owes much to the fine account given by Markus Mattmüller, *Leonhard Ragaz und der religiöse Sozialismus* (Zollikon: EVZ, 1968), ii, ch. 5.

churches on Christmas Day to witness to the irreconcilability of
the message of Christmas with the war.

The publication of the manifesto provided the occasion for the
first serious disruption within the Religious Socialist movement.
Two wings formed within the movement. One wing formed
behind Kutter and Hans Bader, in support of the position of
Gustav Benz. The other wing, which promoted the manifesto,
was composed of Ragaz, Karl von Greyerz and the Religious
Socialists of French-speaking Switzerland.

As Markus Mattmüller has pointed out, the central question
lying behind the growing split was the attitude taken towards
Germany.[106] At the very outset of the war, Ragaz (like Barth)
had been favourably disposed to the German people. What put
him off was the *Kriegstheologie* of the German theologians. He
saw in their invocation of the divine in support of their cause an
appeal to Wotan, the ancient warrior-god of the heathen
Germanic tribes—certainly not the God revealed in Jesus Christ.
Ragaz decided very early on that the defeat of the German
national god was imperative, for the sake of the advance of the
Kingdom of God. His pacifist tendencies notwithstanding, Ragaz
became pro-Entente. For his part, Hermann Kutter was just as
decidedly pro-German. That was at least part of the reason he
and his friends wished to remain quiet. Kutter saw in German
culture (its idealism and its socialism) vastly superior points of
contact for the coming Kingdom of the spirit than could be
found in the materialism of the western powers.[107] In March
1915, Kutter would publish a small eight-page pamphlet in
which his opposition to Ragaz was clearly set forth.[108] He sought
to lay bare the danger with which he saw Religious Socialism to
be threatened. He called this danger a 'pharasaism of the Idea'.
One cannot simply postulate peace. Peace can only really come
through God's acting. The peace ideal of the Ragaz forces had
too much Idea in it and too little God. The pamphlet was
directed to the German public. Kutter expressed the hope that
the Germans would forgive those Swiss who had spoken out

---

[106] Mattmüller, *Leonhard Ragaz und der religiöse Sozialismus*, 212.
[107] Hermann Kutter Jr., *Hermann Kutters Lebenswerk* (Zurich: EVZ, 1965), 58.
[108] Hermann Kutter, *Ich kann mir nicht helfen . . ., Auch ein Wort an die deutschen Freunde der Religiös–sozialen* (Zurich: Orell Füssli, 1915).

against them; they would have done better to have remained quiet.

In the early months after the outbreak of the war, Barth tended to side with Ragaz, while Thurneysen favoured Kutter's point of view. It should be pointed out, however, that Barth's judgement in these matters remained unclouded by partisan politics. Already on 31 August, he devoted a sermon to the subject of the necessity of Swiss neutrality—a neutrality not just in the outward sense of refusing to join the battle in the field, but a true neutrality of the inner person. If the causes of this war lay in sinful actions and attitudes on both sides, as he steadfastly maintained, then taking sides was something that was absolutely forbidden for anyone seriously desiring the name of Christian. Unlike Ragaz, he saw clearly that the phenomena of a *Kriegstheologie* was not to be found in Germany alone; therefore, there was no reason to hope for a German defeat on this basis alone. Against Kutter, he did not believe that there was any reason to prefer German culture above all others. Did not France give us Calvin and Rousseau? Did not Russia give us Tolstoy?[109] He seemed to hope for a cessation of hostilities without a clear winner.[110] These considerations being left out of account then, Barth's preference for Ragaz was rooted in the concreteness of his plan of action in opposing the war. Kutter struck him initially as quietistic. But by February 1915, when Thurneysen advised

[109] Karl Barth, sermon, 31 Aug. 1914, in idem, *Predigten 1914*, 447. It is worth noting in this connection Barth's response to Thurneysen's lament on the occasion of Italy's entrance into the war in May 1915 on the side of the Entente Powers (Italy had originally belonged to the Triple Alliance but had declared neutrality in Aug. 1914). Thurneysen wrote, 'Today in Italy the dice are being cast, perhaps with respect to our fate too. For if Russia, England, France and Italy should become master over Germany, then that is something like a divine judgement on Europe because it would mean that the people of the best values and the best promise for the future would be crushed'. Eduard Thurneysen to Karl Barth, 20 May 1915, *B–Th. Br.* I. 44. Barth's response was this: 'I am disturbed . . . by what you wrote about Italy. Of course, this politics is an open villainy, but why it should distress us more deeply than Belgium [the violation of Belgian neutrality by the Germans] and the Lusitania is not clear to me. . . . Then too, the thought that Germany, with its best values and promise, would be lost—and we with them—if the other side should win, is alien to me. Why then?' Karl Barth to Eduard Thurneysen, 25 May 1914, *B–Th. Br.* I. 48.

[110] Ibid. 449. Barth foresaw the likelihood that if either side should win, the situation which emerged after the Franco-Prussian war of 1870–1 would repeat itself. The winning side would be haughty and proud, the losing side would thirst for revenge. Barth observed prophetically that if that happened, a new war would sooner or later become an inevitability.

that Barth take Kutter's orientation more seriously because Kutter's call for "waiting" was fundamentally more radical, Barth responded:

I am ready to learn much more from Kutter because he is indeed more radical than Ragaz. But as soon as Kutter wants to bring me into real opposition to Ragaz' standpoint, I cannot go along. I value in Ragaz his earnest desire to bring the religious orientation into connection with practical ethical goals . . . Ragaz may very often forfeit the religious depth when he cries every moment: see! here or there is the Kingdom of God!, but Kutter's fundamental and exclusive quietism appears to me to be just as much an impoverishment.[111]

Although still favouring Ragaz' response to the present crisis, this passage does bear witness to the fact that Barth's allegiance to his viewpoint was not complete. "Waiting" did not have to signify quietism; otherwise, Barth could not have said that Kutter was more radical. The strategy of "waiting" could rest on other grounds—namely, on the growing awareness that the hearing of the Word in the present situation was highly problematic. Barth had been inclined initially to follow Ragaz in identifying the voice of God with the negativities in the present historical moment. 'See! here is the Kingdom of God!' As time went by, he became increasingly aware that such a position was too uncritical.

On 8 March 1915, Barth again took up the quarrel between Ragaz and Kutter in a letter to Thurneysen. Noting that he now had a 'downright resentment' for this controversy, Barth pointed out that Kutter's constant negativity—exemplified by his tendency in the face of any plan, goal, act, etc. (whether ecclesiastical or political) to respond with '*That's* not it'—did not provide a way forward. Barth could agree with the negations up to a point. 'That's not it' simply meant that no human act or programme could be confused with God's Kingdom. With that, Barth was now in agreement. But the negations could not be allowed to make one impotent to act. Barth expressed his confidence that negations on the one side and affirmations on the other could not remain in an eternal, unreconciled antithesis, but must somehow be taken up into a higher unity.

---

[111] Karl Barth to Eduard Thurneysen, 5 Feb. 1915, *B–Th. Br.* I. 29.

Is it not better to give this dialectic between two emphases over to itself . . . instead of wanting to maintain them one-sidedly? Is it not better to strive after the point where Kutter's no and Ragaz' yes, Kutter's radical equanimity and Ragaz' energetic laying-hold of problems *a*, *b*, and *c* (that's it!) harmonize? I believe in the possibility of such a position even if I cannot yet immediately describe it.[112]

Barth was now ripe for a fundamental change of direction in his thinking.

The turning-point came sometime after April 1915. On 9 April, the close relations between the Rade and Barth families were permanently cemented by the marriage of Barth's younger brother Peter to Martin Rade's daughter Helene. On the way back from the wedding in Marburg, Barth and Thurneysen stopped off in Bad Boll (near Göppingen), where they spent five days speaking with Christoph Blumhardt. Blumhardt was a highly charismatic and prophetic figure. In him, the Pietism native to Württemberg had found a new social focus; his fervent proclamation of the coming Kingdom of God as a world-transforming power expressed itself in a very positive appreciation of the Social Democracy that was unique in Germany. He had joined the SPD in 1899 and was elected to serve as a deputy representing that party in the provincial parliament the following year. Although little or nothing is known today of the contents of Barth's conversation with Blumhardt, it is clear from a review which Barth wrote a year later just what it was that he found so compelling in him.

Blumhardt always begins right away with God's presence, might, and purpose: he starts out from God; he does not begin by climbing upwards to Him by means of contemplation and deliberation. God is the end, and because we already know Him as the beginning, we may await His consummating acts.[113]

During the course of the following summer, concrete evidence emerged that Barth had now adopted a new *Ansatz*—a new starting-point for theological reflection.

On 19 June, Barth wrote a letter to Rade in response to a recent devotional piece which the Marburger had printed in *Die Christliche Welt*. In it, he now argued that 'the *world*, understood

[112] Karl Barth to Eduard Thurneysen, 8 Mar. 1915, *B–Th. Br.* I. 33.
[113] Karl Barth, *Action in Waiting* (Rifton, NY: Plough Publishing House, 1969), 23–4.

as the totality of our life's conditions, is godless' and that Jesus
and His message stand over against it in a relation of antithesis as
a reality which is also complete in itself.[114] Christoph Schwöbel
has perceptively seen in this the first evidence of that 'sharp
antithesis which is characteristic of Barth's new theological starting-point'.[115] In Jesus, Barth said, a new world has broken into
this one, which radically calls into question everything human.
The central question of ethics—'What should we do?'—had
become exceedingly problematic, as Barth now saw all human
ethical striving as law, that is, as constructed on the grounds of
the old world that is passing away.[116]

This insight had a decided effect on Barth's stance *vis-à-vis* the
Kutter–Ragaz quarrel; it was to lead him to abandon his support
for Ragaz. In August, shortly after reading a published letter-
exchange between Ragaz and Emil Brunner, Barth wrote to his
friend Thurneysen.

I read his [Ragaz'] article thoroughly last night and find it very instruc-
tive, in the sense that he makes very clear what he is lacking *vis-à-vis*
Blumhardt and Kutter. . . . Decisive for me is . . . the starting-point.
Why plunge immediately into ethics ('what should we do?'), the old
question which avoids the real subject-matter, as if there were nothing
more pressing! Is it self-evident that 'we' 'represent' the Kingdom of
God? . . . Have we comprehended, experienced the Kingdom of God
in its radical seriousness? . . . Not a word of the "knowledge of God",
or "conversion", of "waiting" on the Kingdom of God, which is the a
priori of all "representing"!—In short, when I read this papal decision
of Ragaz', I am very happy to know Kutter. You really made him
accessible to me. That was an act![117]

Perhaps the most significant element in this passage is the note of
self-criticism. 'Is it self-evident that "we" represent the
Kingdom?' With this question, the fundamental axiom of
Herrmannian theology (the certainty given in religious experience) was now for the first time rendered dubious. Up to this
point in time, Barth had still operated on Herrmannian assumptions. He had identified the voice of God with the negative
experiences of history and he had done so with a good deal of

[114] Karl Barth to Martin Rade, 19 June 1915, *B–R Br.* 133.
[115] Christoph Schwöbel, 'Einleitung' to *B–R Br.* 34.
[116] Karl Barth to Martin Rade, 19 June 1915, *B–R Br.* 134.
[117] Karl Barth to Eduard Thurneysen, 6 Aug. 1915, *B–Th. Br.* I. 69–70.

self-confidence because, consciously or unconsciously, he still acted as though his own religious experience stood beyond all doubt. Given the certainty of religious experience, he had the right key in his hand for reading the ways of God off the face of history. He could not really be free of the axiom of religious experience until criticism turned inward; until he realized that the questionability of all things human when seen in the light of the otherness of God and His Kingdom had to apply to him and his friends as well as to their opponents. From now on, knowledge of God—the a priori of all true representation of the Kingdom—would be *the* central question in Karl Barth's new theology.[118] In principle, his break with liberalism was now complete. Though residual elements would endure for some time, requiring repeated attempts to make his new viewpoint consistent with itself, for all practical purposes, he had broken with Marburg theology for ever.

---

[118] This thesis has been admirably demonstrated by Ingrid Spieckermann. Spieckermann takes this letter to Thurneysen as the first clear signal of the emergence of Barth's new theology—and, therewith, of the break with the old. It is as useful a point of demarcation as any other. See Spieckermann, *Gotteserkenntnis*, 69–70.

PART I
Dialectical Theology in the Shadow of a Process Eschatology

(SAFENWIL,
AUGUST 1915–JANUARY 1920)

But now God has called a halt to the preceding development. Without regard for the Fall, He has allowed His creative, life-giving Word to be heard anew. Apart from the Law His power has become effective. Where it now finds receptivity, there a new world, nature and humanity, the Kingdom of freedom and peace in God, grows under the hard crust of the historical-psychological reality—a reality which for God is finished and therefore is coming to an end.

(Karl Barth, *Der Römerbrief, 1919*, 142)

3

The Righteousness of God

(SAFENWIL,
AUGUST 1915–NOVEMBER 1918)

I. THE NEW STARTING-POINT

Barth's new starting-point can best be described as critically realistic. To describe his starting-point as *realistic* is to point to the
new element in it as measured by the idealism of mainstream
nineteenth-century theology. In contrast, for example, to the
idealistic tendency of the Ritschlian school to treat God as a postulated source of the moral ought, Barth now regarded God as a
Reality which is complete and whole in itself apart from and
prior to the knowing activity of human individuals. He conceived of the relation of God to the world in terms of a fundamental *diastasis* (i.e. a relation in which the two members stand
over against each other with no possibility of a synthesis into a
higher form of being). This critical distinction between God and
the world found expression in a well-known formula as early as
November 1915: 'World remains world. But God is God.'[1] The
practical consequence of his realistic starting-point was that he
was now engaged in the (seemingly impossible) attempt to think
from a standpoint lying in God Himself (*'ein Denken von Gott*

---

[1] Karl Barth, 'Kriegszeit und Gottesreich', lecture given in Basle, Switzerland, 15 Nov.
1915; cited by Anzinger, *Glaube und kommunikative Praxis*, 120–2. It is clear from statements like the following that Barth was now engaged in a self-conscious effort to distance
himself from idealistic theology and religion. 'Of what concern to us is the God who was
once presented to us as the highest ideal of ethics?' 'The "Father in heaven" to whom He
[Jesus] points us is no ideality which lives from its antithesis; no formal, unreal magnitude
which in the final analysis belongs to this world . . . but rather, the Reality out of which
our entire world has fallen.' Furthermore, that God is our Creator and Origin is 'the only
positive thing . . . which we can say. All other speaking of God is a stammering; or else it
must—if it is to be valid—consist in loud negations'. (All citations taken from Anzinger.)

aus'[2]) and therefore, from a standpoint lying beyond this world, history, and human possibilities. The net effect was a significant reorientation of theology. Where nineteenth-century theology originated in a 'turn to the subject', Barth's course now clearly gave evidence of a 'turn to theological objectivism'.[3]

On the other hand, to describe Barth's realism as *critical* is to catch sight of the truly modern element in it. In no way did his realism represent a return to the somewhat naïve, metaphysically grounded realism of classical (medieval and post-Reformational) theology. Thomistic theology (to give just one prominent example) took its starting-point in the (uncritical) assumption of the existence of an "objectively real" empirical world which presents itself to the human knower to be known. On the basis of observations made of this world, it then asked after the first principles necessary to account for the order observed in it. Such a procedure was "uncritical" because it was not yet in a position to take seriously the role played by the human knower in constructing the "objects" of knowledge. It was also naïve in the extent to which it simply identified first principles with the living God spoken of in the biblical witness. Against such a procedure, Barth everywhere presupposed: 1. the validity of Kant's epistemology (where it touched upon knowledge of empirical reality), and 2. the success of Kant's critique of metaphysics. The "real" for Barth was not the world known empirically. The truly "real" is the wholly otherness of the *Self*-revealing God in comparison with whom the empirical world is mere shadow and appearance. Moreover, there is no epistemological way which leads from the empirical world to its divine source. The metaphysical way taken by classical realism would remain for ever closed to Barth. To that extent, Barth's brand of realism depended for its existence on the success of the critical element in idealism. Indeed, without idealism, it would have been unthinkable.

2. GOD IS GOD

The most immediate consequence of this new starting-point in thought was the fact that criticism of religion moved to the cen-

---

[2] The phrase was borrowed by Barth from Hermann Kutter. See Karl Barth, *Der Römerbrief (Erste Fassung) 1919*, ed. Hermann Schmidt (Zurich: TVZ, 1985), 71.

[3] Spieckermann, *Gotteserkenntnis*, 73.

tre of Barth's concerns. Religion now came to be seen as essentially profane, as belonging to the world of human possibilities resident in history and as such, hemmed in on all sides by error and confusion. Religion stands on this side of the great divide separating God from the world of men and women. Barth could still find positive value in religion, but his negative valuation tended to predominate. This emerges clearly in two addresses given in late 1915 and early 1916. 'Religion and Socialism' was a talk which Barth gave at a gathering of socialists in Baden on 7 December; 'The Righteousness of God' was given in Aarau on 16 January.

Barth was at great pains in 'Religion and Socialism' to distinguish "religion" from the object with which he was concerned as a pastor and theologian.

"Religion" is a very weak and ambiguous word. *Religion* is pious feeling [*Gefühl*] in individual men and women, together with the particular morality and the particular worship which proceeds from it. It is pious feeling in the purity and majesty which it attains here and there and at certain times, but also in the weakness and illusion and open error in which it is found again and again in each of us. The object [*Sache*] I am concerned with—and to which, to be sure, religion points—is something greater and clearer. It is not only a feeling, with all the weaknesses and uncertainties which surround all feelings. It is a *fact*. It is *the* fact which alone is worthy of the name. It is the only secure and certain reality there is, the fixed pole in the flood of appearances . . .[4]

The 'fact', the sure and certain reality above and beyond history, is, according to Barth, the Kingdom of God.

I have spoken of a *Kingdom* of God which is and which comes. I mean thereby simply that God is living, that God rules and will rule. There is a domain in which His lordship is already established, and there is another in which it has yet to be acknowledged. By that I mean simply . . . that everything made, artificial, untrue must give way to that which is original [*ursprünglich*]. That holy, sunny, majestic Being above us which greets us from afar, now as truth, now as beauty, now as love, is itself not made and artificial but rather the most original, the immediate for which we instinctively long. And so the Kingdom of God is simply the restoration of the original, immediate life which we have lost through a thousand dishonest human contrivances.[5]

---

[4] Karl Barth, 'Religion und Sozialismus', 1–2. Typescript in Karl Barth-Archiv, Basle, Switzerland.   [5] Ibid. 4.

Religion must not be confused with this great fact. 'What we call religion is only a *symptom*, a sign of this fact, one of its reflections in the very imperfect mirror of the human soul, human institutions, and experiments.'[6] Religion is not the only such symptom; indeed, nature and history abound with them. Nor is religion even the most important sign of the coming rule of God in the present. That honour belongs to socialism—at least in its ideal form, if not in its everyday reality. But of all symptoms and signs (of socialism as well as religion) it has to be said that they are only symptoms and signs; they are not the thing itself. Religion belongs to the realm of human striving, of that which is made by human hands, while the Kingdom is entirely original, uncreated. And like all things belonging to this world, religion is ambiguous in character. 'There is no human activity, there is no historical event, there are no personal virtues, which are simply free from impure, foolish, reprehensible, even fiendish elements.'[7]

On balance, Barth's description of religion in his Baden address was still positive. However broken and ambiguous the reality of religion might be, it could still be a sign of the coming of God's Kingdom. In his Aarau lecture a month later, the needle shifted in the direction of a more negative assessment.

'The Righteousness of God' is a meditation on two wills: the one, a will which is and always remains faithful to itself, free from all external bondage and from all caprice and vacillation; the other, a will 'which knows no binding and unshakeable order, but rather, a will which is grounded upon arbitrariness, whim, and self-seeking, a will without fidelity, divided and at odds with itself, a will without logic and coherence'.[8] The first will, the righteous will, is God's alone. The second, the unrighteous will, is human. According to Barth, everything about us stands under the sway of that second will. Its consequences are ever before our eyes: competition and war, class conflict, unrest and disorder. So pervasive are these manifestations that our reason would tell us that the unrighteous will which afflicts and oppresses us is the only will there is. Reason says that the human situation is unchangeable so we may as well make peace with it. But there is a voice within—the voice of conscience—which

---

[6] Karl Barth, 'Religion und Sozialismus', 2.   [7] Ibid. 3.

[8] Karl Barth, 'Die Gerechtigkeit Gottes', in idem, *Das Wort Gottes und die Theologie* (Munich: Chr. Kaiser, 1925), 6–7.

says no. It speaks of another will, a 'wholly other' will than the one we all know. What happens, Barth asks, when this voice is heard? We hear the voice of conscience but we do not let it speak to the end. We will not allow ourselves to be told that the righteous will is God's and can only come to us from God. Instead, we seek to silence the voice of conscience by creating a righteousness of our own. We erect great institutions of human righteousness in the form of morality, the state and its laws, and above all, in religion. But the truth is that all the human righteousness in the world cannot change our basic situation. Underneath the façade of righteousness, the human will remains unchanged. It remains unrighteous. Human righteousness is therefore built upon a lie. It is the attempt to create what cannot be created. If real righteousness is by definition *eternal* and unchanging, then it is God's alone. The human attempt to create it is, in reality, the attempt to be like God. It is the acceptance of the original lie: *Eritis sicut Deus!* Human righteousness, in whatever form it is found, is a Tower of Babel.

There is no more certain means of securing ourselves against the alarm cry of conscience than religion and Christianity. A wonderful feeling of security and safety sets in over against the unrighteousness whose power we sense all around us . . . It is a wonderful illusion if we are able to comfort ourselves with the thought that, in our Europe, next to capitalism, prostitution, housing speculation, alcoholism, tax fraud, and militarism, the Church's proclamation and ethics too, the "religious life", go their uninterrupted way. We are still Christians! Our people are still a Christian people! A wonderful illusion, but still an illusion, a self-deception! . . . What good is all the preaching, baptizing, confirming, bell-ringing, and organ-playing? . . . Will our relation to the righteousness of God be changed by all this? . . . Is not our religious righteousness too a product of our pride and our despair, a Tower of Babel, at which the Devil laughs more loudly than at all the others?[9]

Religion—and Barth is here speaking pre-eminently of Christianity—is at its heart, an exercise in self-delusion.

There is, however, a way to come into a right relation to the righteousness of God. According to Barth, this other way is entered not by doing, but by being still and listening to the message which conscience really wants to bring. What conscience would tell us if we would but listen is that the righteousness for

---

[9] Ibid. 12.

which we long God alone can bring. What we need to do above all is to give ourselves over to God to do His will.

> To do God's will means, however, to begin anew with God. God's will is not an improved continuation of *our* will. It stands over against our will as one that is wholly other. In the face of His will, there is nothing for our will but a radical re-creation. Not a reforming, but a re-creating and a becoming new.[10]

This is the way of faith, not of religion. It is the way of humility, not of pride. It is the way of repentance.

In these lectures, as Eberhard Jüngel has rightly observed, Barth had begun to work with 'fundamental distinctions and relations' which would recur in his later work in modified forms: first of all, in the sharp diastases of his second commentary on *Romans*, and then later in the fully elaborated form of the doctrine of analogy found in the *Church Dogmatics*.[11] Barth's theological development from this point on represented a more-or-less continuous unfolding of a single theme: God is God.[12] No further major breaks in his thought would take place. To be sure, Barth's development would not always proceed smoothly. The prominence given to the category of conscience in 'The Righteousness of God' gave forceful testimony to the fact that it would be some time yet before all such vestiges of his earlier world of thought had been eliminated. But it would be a mistake to assume on the basis of the continued presence of such elements that Barth had not yet broken successfully with liberalism. The crucial element which must decide this question is that of the framework of theological presuppositions within which such categories did their work. And the framework was provided by the sharp distinction we have just observed between God and humankind, between the righteousness of God and the unrighteousness of men and women. Even a statement as bold as 'conscience . . . remains the only place between heaven and earth where the righteousness of God is revealed'[13] is no argument against this. On the surface, such a statement may seem to give

---

[10] Barth, 'Die Gerechtigkeit Gottes', 15.

[11] Jüngel, 'Einführung in Leben und Werk Karl Barths', in idem, *Barth-Studien*, 33.

[12] Eberhard Busch, 'God is God: The Meaning of a Controversial Formula and the Fundamental Problem of Speaking about God', *Princeton Seminary Bulletin*, 7 (1986), 101–13.   [13] Barth, 'Die Gerechtigkeit Gottes', 5–6.

evidence of a kind of neutral zone in human being, untouched by the effects of human sinfulness; a *locus* of revelation within human subjectivity. And yet Barth went on to describe how the voice within is, again and again, crushed into oblivion so that it cannot do its work. Even the solution he suggests—that we become still and listen, and learn once again to acknowledge God as God—has about it the air of the impossible apart from some kind of action from God's side. However prominent the category of conscience may be in this early lecture, its functional value is so delimited by the framework in which it is set (i.e. the sharp antithesis between God and humankind) as to be rendered nearly void of further significance. Barth had no real interest in the question of the *locus* of revelation in human subjectivity from this point on.[14] On the contrary; he would do everything in His power to safeguard the distinction between an objectively real Self-revealing God and human consciousness. That concern is abundantly clear in *Romans* I.

3. THE THEOLOGY OF ROMANS I

(i) *Circumstances of Composition*

At the beginning of June 1916, Barth and his good friend, Eduard Thurneysen, decided that the time had come to rethink

[14] Stephen Webb's claim that Barth's appeal to conscience gives evidence that he was still at that point in time 'caught in the web of liberal theology in an attempt to ground religion in subjectivity' rests upon a highly selective reading of the essay in question and an all-too-narrow acquaintance with Barth's other writings (essays and letters) of this period. See Webb, *Re-figuring Theology*, 59. For Barth to have engaged in a "liberal" attempt to ground *religion* in subjectivity, he would (at the very least) have needed a positive interest in religion. But religion is treated in this essay as the contrary to the righteousness of God; an exercise in idolatry. Of a "liberal" attempt to ground religion in human subjectivity, there is not the slightest trace here. Had Webb concluded that Barth was seeking to ground *theology* in human subjectivity, that would have been more understandable; more understandable, but still wrong. For the attempt to ground theology in human subjectivity is the move made by idealistic theology, and Barth has clearly passed beyond idealism. 'The righteousness of God', Barth wrote, 'has been gradually transformed from the most certain fact into the highest of differing high ideals'. The tragedy is—as the war has clearly demonstrated—that the God of idealism is simply a mirror or projection of our own unrighteousness. This God, Barth concluded, 'is no God. He is an idol. He is dead.' In the face of such a God, we must become 'sceptics' and 'atheists'. See Barth, 'Die Gerechtigkeit Gottes', 10, 14. Barth's concept of God in this essay is realistic, thus demonstrating that the 'turn to objectivity' has already occurred. Against Webb's interpretation, see Jüngel, *Barth-Studien*, 33; Spieckermann, *Gotteserkenntnis*, 68–71; Anzinger, *Glaube und kommunikative Praxis*, 117–24.

the foundations of the theology they had inherited from their teachers in a more systematic fashion than heretofore. Barth devoted himself initially to an intensive reconsideration of the writings of Kant.[15] But by mid-July, Barth announced that he was now occupied with 'exegetical investigations' into Paul's letter to the Romans.[16] A week later, he reported in great excitement that he had discovered a guide to lead him through the exegetical thickets: 'J. T. Beck!! As an expositor of the Bible, he simply towers above the rest of the guild, even above Schlatter'. He added that he was now carefully recording the fruits of his studies in a notebook.[17]

In the months that followed, Barth filled notebook after notebook with his paraphrase of Romans. By the beginning of November, he had completed work on the first three chapters and began preparations for chapter 4.[18] The work was slowed for the next six months as the result of the appearance in Safenwil of Jakob Vetter, an evangelist who conducted revival-like meetings at the request of some of the members of Barth's congregation. Barth was horrified by the genetic-psychological description Vetter offered of the soul's journey to salvation (awakening, conversion, "sealing" in the Spirit, five stages in the soul's resistance to the Spirit, etc.), his appeal to the blood of Christ as a kind of medicine of the soul, and especially his constant reminder that the soul hangs suspended over the gaping abyss of hell. 'If *that* is Pietism, then we certainly no longer want to believe that the least point of contact exists between ourselves and the Pietists; they really are after something *completely* different than we are.'[19] Barth had good reason to be taken aback by this expression of Pietism; in addition to works by Beck, he was also being guided in his study of Romans by Pietistic writers such as Johannes Bengel, C. H. Rieger, and August Tholuck. The effect which Vetter's visit had on Barth was to motivate him to undertake an intensive study of Pietism, chiefly through the reading of biographies of David Spleiß, Ludwig Hofacker, August Tholuck, and

---

[15] Karl Barth to Eduard Thurneysen, 26 June 1916, *B–Th. Br.* I. 145.
[16] Karl Barth to Eduard Thurneysen, 19 July 1916, *B–Th. Br.* I. 146.
[17] Karl Barth to Eduard Thurneysen, 27 July 1916, *B–Th. Br.* I. 148.
[18] Karl Barth to Eduard Thurneysen, 7 Nov. 1916, *B–Th. Br.* I. 160.
[19] Karl Barth to Eduard Thurneysen, 20 Nov. 1916, *B–Th. Br.* I. 164.

the biblicist Gottfried Menken.[20] Work on *Romans* slowed to a crawl.

In March 1917, he completed his work on chapter 4 and turned his attention to the very difficult fifth chapter.[21] In July, he broke off his study of Pietism[22] to return to full-time work on Romans and was still at work on chapter 5 in September when the news came that his good friend Rudolf Pestalozzi (a Zurich businessman) had induced a publishing house in Bern to publish what had now become a "commentary" by offering a substantial subsidy to cover losses if the first run could not be sold.[23] The news spurred him on to a faster pace of writing. The writing of chapters 6 to 16 came a bit more easily and the first draft of the book was completed on 3 June 1918.[24]

There followed a period of intensive revision. The first chapters had been written a full two years before the last and it is understandable that in the meantime, Barth's perspective and concerns had become more clearly defined. He therefore set about the task of revising the opening chapters to make them more congruent with the concluding chapters. On 16 August, Barth sent the revised text to his publisher.[25]

The world had scarcely stood still during the two years Barth spent working on his commentary. In Germany, the initial enthusiasm for the war gave way by 1916 to a sense of resignation and horror as the death-toll mounted. In February 1917, revolution in Russia brought an end to the reign of the Czar. By April, the first major strikes were taking place in Germany to protest against food shortages and loss of real value in wages due to inflation. April also saw the entrance of America into the war.

In Switzerland too, the war had brought in its wake increasingly difficult living conditions. In August 1914, Switzerland had been dependent on foreign sources for two-fifths of its food and energy needs.[26] With the outbreak of the war, such sources dried

---

[20] See Busch, *Karl Barth und die Pietisten*, 45 ff.

[21] Karl Barth to Eduard Thurneysen, 18 Mar. 1917, *B–Th. Br.* I. 181.

[22] Karl Barth to Eduard Thurneysen, 17 July 1917, *B–Th. Br.* I. 215.

[23] Karl Barth to Eduard Thurneysen, 6 Sept. 1917, *B–Th. Br.* I. 227.

[24] Karl Barth to Eduard Thurneysen, 4 June 1918, *B–Th. Br.* I. 279.

[25] Hermann Schmidt, 'Vorwort des Herausgebers', in Karl Barth, *Der Römerbrief, 1919,* p. xiii.

[26] Jost, 'Bedrohung und Enge', 762.

up. The net effect was to drive up food and heating costs dramatically. The cost-of-living index more than doubled in the four-year period 1914–18. At the same time, the real value of wages earned by working-class people declined by 30 per cent. Conditions in the work-place deteriorated as the government allowed employers to lengthen work-days without requiring additional overtime pay.[27] In addition, the cost of mobilizing an army large enough to protect the borders against a possible disregard for Swiss neutrality had been enormous. The first-ever direct national tax was instituted in order to alleviate a national debt which tripled between 1913 and 1925.[28] Food rationing was instituted in 1917 and by June 1918, 692,000 people (out of a population of 3.8 million) were on the rolls of those entitled to emergency relief from the government.

It was in this context that the shock produced by the Bolshevik Revolution in Russia swept Switzerland in November of 1917. Extremists in the Swiss *Sozialdemokratische Partei* (SP) saw in the Russian experiment a model to be imitated in Europe as well, thereby adding to fears in the bourgeois classes that the Bolshevik Revolution might spread to Switzerland. Although such fears were largely unfounded (because Swiss socialists were committed in the main to attaining their goals through democratic means), it is nevertheless true that the demonstrations and local strikes which became increasingly frequent in the years 1917 and 1918 gave expression to a quite real class conflict.[29]

It was against this background that Barth was engaged in a revolution of his own—the writing of a new theology in the form of a biblical commentary. In addition to his heavy writing schedule, his preaching and catechetical responsibilities, he was also deeply involved in party affairs. On 8 June 1917, Barth served as a delegate to the SP Party Congress in Bern: a recognition of his contribution to shaping the goals and values of the local party chapter.[30]

[27] Christine Nöthiger-Strahm, *Der deutsch-schweizerische Protestantismus und der Landesstreik von 1918: Die Auseinandersetzung der Kirche mit der sozialen Frage zu Beginn des 20. Jahrhunderts* (Bern: Peter Lang, 1981), 54. (Hereafter cited as *Der Landesstreik*.)

[28] Jost, 'Bedrohung und Enge', 765.

[29] Nöthiger-Strahm, *Der Landesstreik*, 38–52.

[30] Karl Barth to Eduard Thurneysen, 8 June 1917, *B–Th. Br.* I. 207.

(ii) *Preliminary Observations*

It has often been observed that the second edition of Barth's commentary on *Romans* is a form of 'theological expressionism'.[31] Less common is the realization that the first edition was already written in what can only be described as an expressionistic style.[32] To be sure, there are differences between the two editions even on the level of style. The rich battery of explosive images found in the second edition are largely lacking in the first, as is the widespread use of paradox. In addition, the tone of the second edition is one of anger—which was not the case with the original (though it too was not lacking in pointed polemic). As Eduard Thurneysen remarked, after reading the first chapter of the second edition, 'It seems to me that you are writing this time not so much with the "joy of discovery" as with a certain wrath and not without a peculiar sense of terror. You do well to do so, even if everything becomes more enigmatic . . .'.[33] Such differences should not blind us, however to the artistic features of the first edition. It was (as reviewers were quick to point out) a book which everywhere gave evidence of the 'earnest, burning zeal' which 'surged' through its author;[34] a 'pneumatic-prophetic exegesis' redolent with an inexhaustible vividness;[35] a 'work of art . . . which reproduces the basic thoughts of that letter in the language of our time, indeed recast in the conceptual world of today';[36] a book which made rich use of 'irony'[37] to bring to nought its opponents; a book finally which one reviewer described as 'modern in grandiose one-sidedness, saturated with radical intellectual streams'.[38] One-sidedness, irony—in other

[31] Most influential, perhaps, in pointing in this direction was Hans Urs von Balthasar. Von Balthasar, *Karl Barth*, 90. See also Webb, *Re-figuring Theology*, 8–18.

[32] Stephen Webb's analysis of Barth's expressionism completely ignores the first edition of *Romans*.

[33] Eduard Thurneysen to Karl Barth, 28 Oct. 1920, *B–Th. Br.* I. 437.

[34] Philipp Bachmann, 'Der Römerbrief verdeutscht und vergegenwärtigt: Ein Wort zu K. Barths Römerbrief', *Neue kirchliche Zeitschrift*, 32 (1921), 518.

[35] Ibid.

[36] Adolf Jülicher, 'Ein Moderner Paulus-Ausleger', in Jürgen Moltmann (ed.), *Anfänge der dialektischen Theologie* (Munich: Chr. Kaiser Verlag, 1963), i. 88; ET James M. Robinson, *The Beginnings of Dialectic Theology* (Richmond: John Knox Press, 1968), 72.

[37] Wilhelm Loew, 'Noch einmal Barths Römerbrief', *Die Christliche Welt*, 34 (1920), 587.

[38] Ibid. 585.

words, the first edition already gave evidence of many of the stylistic features associated with the second edition.

To describe Barth's style as expressionistic is to call attention to the fact that many of the characteristic features in his writing were also found in expressionist literature; it is not to suggest that he was directly dependent upon any particular expressionist writer. His relationship to expressionism can only be accurately described as subterranean. But then again such direct dependency would not have been needed to justify describing Barth's work as expressionistic. Expressionism was scarcely a unified movement. The word has a wide range of application for the simple reason that expressionist painters and writers did not employ a single, uniform style to achieve their ends. If there was a common element, it lay in the belief that 'real reality' lay beneath the surface of the "reality" which presented itself to the senses; it was necessary to penetrate beyond the level of appearance to the truly real. Expressionists therefore sought to 'distort, extend and even fragment and shatter the surface of reality in order to uncover something even more real hidden beneath the surface'.[39] As we shall see, it was precisely this conviction that the truly real lies hidden beneath the surface of so-called reality which everywhere governed *Romans* I. In the light of this conviction, *Romans* I is rightly understood as an attempt to engage in a thoroughgoing criticism of the reality which lies ready to hand in an effort to create an open space for the emergence of the 'real reality' (i.e. God or the Kingdom of God). That this criticism did not finally prove radical enough in the view of the author (and had therefore to give way to the even greater radicality of *Romans* II) cannot be allowed to obscure the fact that criticism was already a central task of the first edition.

The targets of Barth's criticism in *Romans* I were many and varied. They fell into four major groups: 1. Liberalism–Pietism (i.e. historicism and psychologism—the stress on historical investigation or religious experience as the ground of theology); 2. Idealistic epistemology and ethics; 3. the "Positives" (churchly Christianity or "religion"); and 4. Religious Socialism (centred especially in the person of Leonhard Ragaz, though criticism of Hermann Kutter could also be found).

[39] Webb, *Re-figuring Theology*, 12.

If there is a common thread which joins these four (in the details, quite different) movements, it is the element of individualism. Barth's new theology represented an assault on a central feature of late nineteenth-century bourgeois culture: the understanding of the human individual as the creative subject of culture and history (and even of her own being and worth).[40] Against the divisive individualism which had given rise to class warfare and world war, Barth posited a divine "universalism":[41] the God who is complete and whole in Himself prior to all knowledge of Him stands over against the whole of so-called "reality" judging it, condemning all so that He might elect all. Barth's new theology was fundamentally anti-bourgeois in this sense: in stressing (as he did in *Romans* I) that God and the knowledge of God are never the secure possession of human beings (but must be received anew in each moment), Barth was at the same time attacking a religion which had assimilated itself to the needs of idealistically construed cultural development; a religion which prided itself on being the animating principle for that development. He was attacking a religion which provided bourgeois culture with perhaps its most crucial ideological support.

(iii) *Eschatology and History (Objective Soteriology)*

'World remains world but God is God.' One of Barth's central concerns in *Romans* I was to show how these two realities could be brought into relation with one another while maintaining and properly safeguarding the absolutely fundamental difference between them. To maintain the distinction was essential if he was to expound a truly realistic theology. Given the idealistic constructivist epistemology (whose general validity Barth continued to assume), the reality of the divine being and action could only be secured if it were distinguished from the outset (and kept distinct!) from the world known naturally by the human knower.

In this, his first major effort at explicating his new theology, Barth saw the problem and its solution as concentrated in the relation of eschatology to history. His attempt to resolve this

---

[40] Schellong, *Bürgertum und christliche Religion*, 96–115; see also Peter Eicher, *Bürgerliche Religion: Eine theologische Kritik* (Munich: Kösel-Verlag, 1983).

[41] Barth, *Der Römerbrief, 1919*, 117, 134–5.

problem found expression in two different—though complementary!—sets of images. The first is centred in a distinction
between 'so-called history' and 'real history'; the second in a
teleologically ordered conception of history as entailing a Fall
away from an original relationship of immediacy to God (the
'Origin') and the restoration of that relationship through an
'organically' construed process of 'return' to the Origin.[42]
Because the second set of images—and especially the central concept of an 'organic growth' of the Kingdom in history—are easily misinterpreted if they are not seen in the light of the
distinction between 'so-called history' and 'real history', we must
begin by examining these terms.

'So-called history' is the phenomenal history which is known
to us naturally through the empirical sciences of historical study,
psychology, and so on.[43] It is temporally structured history, that
is, history which is experienced as past, present, and future
through the observed (and deeply felt) fact that things and people
come into being and pass away.[44] Thus, 'so-called history' is
world history, the history of the world in which human beings
find themselves. It is a history which takes its rise in the Fall of
humankind away from its original relationship of immediacy to
and fellowship with God. With the Fall came death, and the history of this world is the history of alienation, ambiguity, and
death. 'The history of the world is the judgement of the
world.'[45] To be sure, this world is not lacking in reminders and
hints that a better world exists and will exist. Chief among them
is the presence of the Law, which is nothing less than a word of
God to men and women: 'the highpoint of *so-called* history'.[46]
The Law holds forth the promise of something better than the
sin and death which prevail in this world. But the Law cannot of
itself generate the capacity in human beings which would enable
them to fulfil its demands. A chasm exists between ethical ideal
and human life in that the Law remains unfulfilled by men and

---

[42] Herbert Anzinger rightly notes that although the 'conceptuality and imagery' here
employed are distinguishable, they are nevertheless 'structured in a unified way and to
that extent are merely two aspects of one and the same eschatology'. See Anzinger,
Glaube und kommunikative Praxis, 136. It will be difficult to improve on Anzinger's convincing and thorough interpretation of eschatology in *Romans* I. What follows is heavily
indebted to his analysis.

[43] Barth, *Der Römerbrief, 1919*, 64.   [44] Ibid. 86.   [45] Ibid. 48.
[46] Ibid. 76.

women. There is no one who does the Good. Therefore, the most essential characteristic of 'so-called history' is that it is the history of a rift—a split between ideal and life.[47]

But there is another history, a history of God; and there is another world, a world of God. In this history, the split between ideal and life is overcome and healed. The Law is fulfilled. The lost immediacy to God is restored. This is the 'real history' in whose light 'so-called history' is seen to be less than real, that is, mere appearance. The crucial interpretive question raised by Barth's reflections on eschatology in *Romans* I is this: how are these two histories (or alternatively, these two worlds) related?

An initial answer to this question is provided in the affirmation that the history of God's reconciling activity does not take place in some kind of transcendent realm but rather in the same space-time world in which we also live:

at *one* point in history, that which was intended, commanded, and prophesied by the Idea, by the Law, has taken place. . . . In the stream of so-called history, the new counter-element of the real history becomes visible. This event in which one movement is brought to an end and the beginning of a new movement is inaugurated consists in the fact that in 'the hiddenness of humanity' that transformation has occurred which the Law postulates but cannot produce.[48]

In Jesus Christ—above all in the cross—a 'turn' has taken place from the old aeon to the new aeon. 'The new world *has dawned.*'[49] And wherever men and women are found who say yes to the Yes which was spoken to them in Christ, where use is made of the 'new eyes and ears' which are given through the power of God, there 'the turn of worlds which took place in Christ continues.'[50] The Kingdom of God which has dawned in Christ continues on its way in the midst of our broken and sinful existence, achieving provisional victories here and there, establishing itself in a processive fashion.

Barth was at great pains throughout *Romans* I to insist that the new world is not a second world, standing next to and coming after the old world in some kind of temporal before-and-after sequence. Nor is it a purely transcendental world, without contact with this world. The new world is this world, but this world made new. And the process of renewal has already dawned in

---

[47] Ibid. 80, 85.   [48] Ibid. 85.   [49] Ibid. 86.   [50] Ibid. 21.

Christ. 'Real history' is present in, with, and under 'so-called history' as its 'hidden meaning and significance'.[51] 'Real history' and 'so-called history' interpenetrate one another—or more accurately, the former penetrates the latter.[52] 'Real history' is the hidden motor which drives 'so-called history' forward.[53]

Thus far, Barth's initial answer to the question of the relation of 'real history' to 'so-called history'. On this side of his reflections, the emphasis fell upon the *relation* of eschatology and history. The Kingdom of God ('real history') is present *in* history as we know it. But Barth was equally concerned to maintain and safeguard the *distinction* in the relation. He accomplished this above all through what may cautiously be called an *Urform* of the time–eternity dialectic which would come to dominate his reflections in the period of *Romans* II. The breakthrough in which 'real history' enters into 'so-called history' is interpreted by Barth as the irruption of the power of God from above, cutting through history 'longitudinally'[54]—or we might well say, perpendicularly.

In that God speaks His final Word, *the* Word, and in the measure in which it is heard, time is brought to a halt by eternity. In that time has been and is fulfilled in its deepest meaning, it is left behind . . . there the new world-time has dawned which is no longer time. There the eternal Now has appeared which fulfils time . . .[55]

In apparent contradiction to the earlier emphasis on the presence of the Kingdom in history, this passage suggests that there is another sense in which 'real history' does not belong to time as we know it. To be sure, 'it is not . . . timeless in the sense that it remains transcendent over against space-time reality.'[56] 'Real history' enters time as we know it, but it enters it without becoming subject to the law of coming into being and passing away which gives structure to our experience of time. 'Real history' is *in* history as we know it, but it is not *of* it; it is in history while remaining independent of it. It enters into history without

---

[51] Barth, *Der Römerbrief, 1919*, 67. Cf. 75: 'The meaning of history is God's meaning.'
[52] Ibid. 105: 'This is the faithfulness of God which is maintained in the new demonstration of His power . . . Time and the end of all times, so-called and real history, the world and the Kingdom of God, do not appear to Him one after the other, the second as the replacement and elimination of the first, but rather they are in one another [*sie sind ineinander*], the second as the fulfilment of the first (Matt. 5: 17–19).'
[53] Ibid. 308.   [54] Ibid. 67.   [55] Ibid. 86–7.
[56] Anzinger, *Glaube und kommunikative Praxis*, 141.

'spreading out' so to speak, along the horizon of chronologically successive time. And that can only mean that it enters time punctiliarly, without before or after. The breakthrough of the Kingdom into history takes place in the 'now-time'[57] or 'fulfilled time' in which time as we know it is brought to a standstill. Where Barth's initial response laid stress on the *presence* of the Kingdom in history, this further clarification emphasizes its absence. Taken together, these two answers to the question of the relation of 'real history' and 'so-called history' add up to a dialectical understanding. There is a real relation between these two realities in spite of the fundamental difference between them; and the relation, however real, does nothing to set aside the difference.

At times, Barth's desire to distinguish 'real history' and 'so-called history' could outweigh his desire to stress the relation. Here and there, a strong suggestion emerges that the 'turn' from the old aeon to the new aeon did not take place in history at all. It was a 'turn' which took place 'in heaven':

this aeon is not the last one. There is . . . not only a *jenseitige* truth, but also *jenseitige* events; a world history in heaven, an inner movement in God. What we call "history" and "events" are only a confused reflection of *jenseitiger* turns. One such *jenseitige* turn of the times is marked in our "history" by the *cross of Christ*.[58]

The 'turn' takes place in God, as a result of a divine decision. What happens in 'so-called history' is at best a reflection of that divine movement. And so Barth can say, for example:

The "historical Adam" as such is as inconsequential and unimportant as the "historical Jesus" as such! The fall of Adam and the death of Christ are important because of the general, comprehensive, *jenseitigen* turns in heaven, in the 'hiddenness of humanity' which have taken place here and there *behind* these unique historical events.[59]

But this talk of a 'turn in heaven' ought not to mislead us. Such turns do indeed make themselves felt in history as we know it. Barth's insistence on the *Ineinander* relation of eschatology and

---

[57] Barth, *Der Römerbrief, 1919*, 98.   [58] Ibid. 161.
[59] Ibid. 182. Cf. 189: 'Here as there [i.e. in Adam as in Christ], the human, individual, psychological, and historical is nothing more than the breaking-in point of the objective, cosmic power which stands behind it.'

history is in no way set aside by the apparent opposition of eternity and time.

With the breakthrough: Immanuel! God with us! which has taken place in now-time, in the messianic present, in the decisive turn of the aeons *in heaven*, a life process is also inaugurated *on earth*, on the historical-psychological side of our existence. We are no longer the same. We have been placed into the process which reaches from *Jenseits* into *Diesseits*.[60]

The 'turn in heaven' reaches into history and becomes visible there. 'The world has at *one* point become the world of God again.'[61] But—and this is the crucial point—the 'turn' becomes visible in a punctiliar way, at a *point* in time, without before and after. The *Ineinander* relation of eschatology and history is therefore not to be conceived of as a static, stable relation, but rather as a dynamic, living relation. 'Real history' is present in, with, and under 'so-called history'; to that extent the relation of the former to the latter is a continuous one. But the relation is also a dynamic one. It manifests itself in time in an actualistic way, in the form of 'breakthroughs'.

It is clear what Barth wanted to achieve with this dialectical relating of 'real history' and 'so-called history'. He wanted to put the movement and action of God in history beyond the reach of historical investigation. To say that an event has occurred in space and time which does not belong to space and time is to say that it is an event whose source lies outside the space-time continuum. This becomes especially clear when Barth speaks of this history of God as a 'hidden history'.[62] 'Real history' is a history which lies beyond the reach of historical study and investigation. It refers to an event which irrupts into history from without and is therefore not produced by forces operative on the surface of history. And so Barth says, 'The revelation in Christ is not a "historical" event, but rather the breakthrough of the power which *was* there and *will be* there; the disclosure of the never-resting, necessary, and real in the longitudinal cross-section of time.'[63] Again, all of this was done in the interests of theological realism. To place the 'real history' of the divine reconciling activity beyond the reach of the historian was at the same time to secure

[60] Barth, *Der Römerbrief, 1919*, 167.   [61] Ibid. 169.   [62] Ibid. 46.
[63] Ibid. 106.

the reality of God against the constructivist epistemology which governs all historical study.[64]

One final observation with respect to the distinction between 'so-called history' and 'real history': in the final analysis, this distinction serves as a circumlocution for two ways of being in the world which Barth refers to (in the language of Romans 5) as 'Adam' and 'Christ'.[65] 'Adam' and 'Christ' stand for two movements: a movement away from an original relationship of fellowship with God (Fall) and a counter-movement of return to the 'Origin' (reconciliation). These two movements are not to be conceived of as sequential, but rather as parallel and simultaneous.

[64] Hans Frei's interpretation of the relation of eschatology to history in *Romans* I reflects a weakness at this point. Concentrating his attention exclusively on Barth's talk of an 'organic growth' of the Kingdom, Frei interpreted the eschatology of *Romans* I as setting forth the idea of an 'immediate presence of God to history'. See Frei, 'The Doctrine of Revelation in the Thought of Karl Barth', 156. On this basis, he then advanced the thesis that Barth had not really broken with 'relationalism' in the first edition of *Romans*; he had merely shifted the *locus* of the relation from 'a subjective, experiential point to a more objective, cultural-historical one' (p. 131, cf. p. 167). To put it another way, Barth replaced the idea of an *Ineinanderstellung* of revelation and faith with the thought of an *Ineinanderstellung* of revelation and history (p. 146). And so Frei finally concluded that the break with liberalism which occurred in 1915 was followed by another break between the two editions of *Romans* which 'in some respects' was 'more thoroughgoing than the first break' (p. 89). '. . . the objectivity of his concept of revelation in the period of the first edition of *Der Römerbrief* still stood . . . largely on Schleiermacher's ground' (p. 172). Now, in part, this mistake in interpreting Barth's development in the period 1915–19 was rooted in Frei's failure to do justice to the overall framework within which the break with 'relationalism' took place—a point I mentioned earlier (see above, Ch. 1, n. 70). He could not see that what he was calling 'relationalism' in *Romans* I was of a very different kind than had been found in Barth's liberal period because it was understood realistically (as grounded in God) and not idealistically (as grounded in the human knower). But of even greater moment for Frei's misreading of Barth's development in this period was his lack of attention to the distinction (and relation) of 'real history' and 'so-called history', of eternity and time, as well as Barth's repeated insistence that the history of the 'organic growth' of the Kingdom is a *hidden* history. It is not finally possible to do justice to the eschatology of *Romans* I by speaking simply of an 'immediate presence of God to history'. We have to ask: *how* is God immediately present? Certainly, the 'real history' in which an immediate relationship to God has been recovered is continuously present in, with, and under history as we know it. But 'real history' only makes itself manifest in 'so-called history' in an actualistic fashion. That is the element which Frei overlooked. In fairness to Frei, it should be pointed out that the one-sided reading which he gave to the conception of the 'organic' was common among commentators on *Romans* I until fairly recently. As late as 1978, Eberhard Busch offered a similar analysis. See Busch, *Karl Barth und die Pietisten*, 75–8. A breakthrough to a more balanced, less one-sided interpretation occurred only in 1985 with Ingrid Spieckermann's careful analysis of the inadequacy of the organic model of explication for Barth's intention of speaking of a God–human relation which is grounded at every moment *von Gott aus*. See Spieckermann, *Gotteserkenntnis*, 85, 104–5.

[65] See Anzinger, *Glaube und kommunikative Praxis*, 142–6.

To put it this way is to suggest once again that the 'turn' which took place in Christ is not so much a historical 'turning-point' as it is a 'turn in heaven'.[66] The 'turn of aeons' is not something which had to await the appearance in history of the man Jesus of Nazareth in the years AD 1–30; it was something which was realized from the beginning of time, wherever the power which raised Jesus from the dead was active in creating faith. The prototypical example in the Old Testament of a person who already lived on the basis of the new reconciled life created by God in Christ was Abraham.[67] In addition, the two movements are not to be conceived as standing in a relationship of equilibrium or static opposition.[68] The first movement is an 'unreal reality' precisely because the second God-generated movement has already overcome it in principle. The turn of aeons has taken place (past tense).[69] In 'real history' it is a completed fact and in 'so-called history' it has made itself felt decisively in the cross of Christ.[70] To be sure, that does not prevent men and women from living as those who belong exclusively to the first movement. In and of ourselves 'we are all Adam'.[71] The two lines, Adam and Christ, cut through every individual existence in that every individual is confronted with the decision as to whether he/she will continue to live as 'Adam' or will live on the basis of the new presupposition created in Christ.[72] Wherever an individual determines herself for God in Christ, there time is 'fulfilled'. There the new divine 'unhistorical' possibility has been realized; time has been brought to a standstill by 'now-time'.[73] There the 'turn' which is

---

[66] Barth, *Der Römerbrief, 1919*, 164: 'behind the sacrificial death [of Christ] (which historically and psychologically considered was *not* unique) stands the unique new orientation in the "hiddenness of humanity", the turn of times in heaven, from which a real, radical renewal of things on earth is expected.'

[67] Ibid. 106–17.

[68] Ibid. 189: 'A way of God! Therefore, not a state, not a given, not a stable "reality"! Only in hell do such things exist. Where it is a question of God, there it is a matter of a movement which goes forwards, towards victorious decisions. The logical parallelism of the two worlds can only be erected in order that it may immediately be overcome. It may not be made into a system; it is only a momentary, passing truth.'

[69] Ibid. 87–8.   [70] Ibid. 225.   [71] Ibid. 187.   [72] Ibid. 198.

[73] Ibid. 87. Herbert Anzinger has rightly observed that Barth took up the notion of 'fulfilled time' again in CD I/2, but with a fundamental difference: whereas in *Romans* I, 'fulfilled time' is not limited to the time of Jesus Christ, in CD I/2, it is concentrated in the years AD 1–30. In my opinion, it is precisely the emergence of this 'Christological concentration' around 1936 which marks the opening of a final phase in Barth's theological development. Prior to 1936, every phase is marked by a concentration on the event of

a completed fact in Christ is actualized in the present and thereby continued.

We have already touched upon the second set of images employed by Barth in explicating his eschatology in *Romans* I; it remains now to clarify the significance of the key terms employed in the teleologically ordered model of Fall and return.

The Fall was a fall from a relationship of immediacy to the 'Origin' (*Ursprung*). Barth's use of the category '*Ursprung*' in *Romans* I is equivocal.[74] At times, it refers simply to God;[75] more often, it refers to the original, created relation of humankind (and the world) to God.[76] The presupposition of the Fall is creation. Barth's understanding of creation at that time was not yet that of a *creatio ex nihilo*, though it already tended in that direction.[77] The significance of this conception lies in the fact that Barth did not hold that the Creator and the creature were originally joined together ontologically, in a continuum of being. The vehicle of God's creative activity was everywhere understood by Barth to be the Word (the personal creative speech of God[78]); creation did not entail an emanation of the divine being. To be sure, the created relation of the creature to the Creator was one of 'immediacy'; a relation of intimate and life-giving fellowship between the Creator and the creature. But, intimacy did not entail for

revelation in the present, in the here and now, rather than on the ground of revelation in the there and then of AD 1–30. See Anzinger, *Glaube und kommunikative Praxis*, 142.

[74] The ambiguity in Barth's use of the term *Ursprung* is evidence of the fact that his use of it in *Romans* I was not influenced by neo-Kantianism—either in the form represented by Hermann Cohen or in that by Barth's philosopher brother Heinrich. In fact, Spieckermann has shown that Barth's use of the term at this point owes more to Hermann Kutter than to the neo-Kantians. See Spieckermann, *Gotteserkenntnis*, 92–5, 11–117; Anzinger, *Glaube und kommunikative Praxis*, 147–50.

[75] See e.g. Barth, *Der Römerbrief, 1919*, 20: 'The *Ursprung* . . . has once again opened His mouth.'

[76] Ibid. 65, 81, 169.

[77] Ibid. 300; cf. Barth, 'Unterweisung II 1917/18', in idem, *Konfirmandenunterricht, 1909–1921*, ed. Jürgen Fangmeier (Zurich: TVZ, 1987), 214. I say that Barth's view 'tended in the direction' of a *creatio ex nihilo* because he was also inclined to treat "nothing" as more or less synonymous with the "chaos" of Genesis 1. Taken with strict consistency, such a view would give rise to the thought of an original dualism between a creative principle and unformed matter. In the final analysis, Barth's conception is not fully and clearly worked out. What is clear however—given the prominence given to the spoken Word as the vehicle of God's creative activity—is that an emanationist understanding of creation is excluded.

[78] Barth's understanding of creation can also be deduced from his understanding of "new creation" since he saw the latter as an analogy of the former. Ibid. 114.

Barth the obliteration of the difference between divine being and creaturely being. In no way was the fundamental distinction of the Creator and the creature set aside. Most importantly, the created relation was understood by Barth as a *real* relation (grounded in and by God), and not as an idealistically postulated relation.[79] It was this original relation which was disrupted in the Fall.

The Fall was the consequence of Adam's desire for independence from God, for self-determination or autonomy.[80]

There is only *one* sin: the desire of human beings to be independent *vis-à-vis* God. Out of immediacy of being with God, the man fell . . . It was too little for him to simply be God's. He became interesting to himself. He transmitted properties and functions of God to himself. He wanted to be like God [Gen. 3,5]: a being unto himself, resting in himself and important for his own sake. . . . He became a knower, a superior being. He placed himself *next to* life, examining and observing. He began to analyse. He received evil, sharp, penetrating, and yet blind eyes. A view of himself, "knowledge of humankind", "experience", psychology, "historical" thinking—all of that is possible only *outside* of God.[81]

Whether 'Adam' was literally a historical figure as described in Genesis or not is a question Barth regarded as largely insignificant. 'Adam' for him is the name given to the point at which sin and death broke out in history.

It is a question here of world history in the pregnant sense: not of an individual, even if he were the first member of a series, but rather of the absolute disposition of a whole; not of a history among others, but rather of that which has occurred and will occur always and everywhere; of a *presupposition* of all occurrence which, to be sure, at *one* point in history first broke through and became knowable . . .[82]

In truth, all humans are 'Adam'. His spirit is the spirit of all men and women. His fate is their fate.[83] Human solidarity with the

---

[79] Hans Urs von Balthasar was wrong to see in the close connection of *Ursprung* with 'immediacy' in *Romans* I an idealistically postulated principle of *identity*, with a resulting pantheistic conception of the God–world relation. Such an interpretation rests upon a failure to take seriously the realistic doctrine of creation which is everywhere presupposed (and occasionally made explicit) in *Romans* I. See von Balthasar, *Karl Barth*, 71–5. Von Balthasar's misreading of the significance of Barth's talk of 'immediacy' was given wider currency in the English-speaking world through its promotion by Hans Frei. See Frei, 'The Doctrine of Revelation in the Thought of Karl Barth', 138. For a more adequate analysis of the concept of 'immediacy' in *Romans* I, see Anzinger, *Glaube und kommunikative Praxis*, 151.

[80] Barth, *Der Römerbrief, 1919*, 30.   [81] Ibid. 177–8.   [82] Ibid. 182.
[83] Ibid. 183; cf. 187.

progenitor of the race is simply a fact regarded by Barth as self-evident and not requiring further explanation.

With independence from God came death. Death was not merely the natural consequence of a loss of immediacy to the source of life, though it was that too. But the fact that the human race did not fall completely into non-being but remains suspended between life and annihilation is itself evidence of the fact that death as we experience it is a positive act of divine judgement (and of grace). Moreover, "death" is much more than a biological fact. The surrender of immediacy to God was at the same time the surrender of immediacy to the world and to other human beings. To stand over against the world as an observer, cool and analytical, is to treat the world and others as dead, as facts to be investigated. But to treat the world and people in this way is to 'be dead before death'.[84] The desire for autonomy results in heteronomy, enslavement to sin and death.[85]

At one point in history however, the mastery of sin and death was overcome and set aside. The history of the Fall suffered a 'reversal'.[86] In the cross of Christ, a new *presupposition* was created. How are we to understand this? Barth was adamant in his rejection of traditional penal substitution theories. Such views are too 'mechanical'. 'God is more spiritual than that!'[87] For Barth, reconciliation was constituted in Christ above all through His obedience. In Him, the chasm between ideal and life was closed. To be sure, He too carried within Himself the curse which had lain on the human race since Adam. He too was subjected to the fate of death which sin had brought into the world. But subjection to death did not entail for Him subjection to the *power* of sin which had first given rise to death.

His death was the definitive denial of this power on behalf of the human race, the manifest repeal of its order. For *this* death was the end—no, the completion of a human life in rediscovered immediacy to God. . . . As a child of the Father, His will surrendered to God's will, Jesus went into the darkness of death. In bringing His life to completion in this way, He introduces something new into the history of the world. In finishing His life in this way, He fundamentally overcomes the old. He dies, but in paying His tribute to the fate of death, He also dies to sin; He becomes for this power a dead, unreachable man . . .[88]

---

[84] Ibid. 181.   [85] Ibid. 272.   [86] Ibid. 218.   [87] Ibid. 193; cf. 194.
[88] Ibid. 225.

The cross of Christ meant nothing less than the 'death of death'. His death was the death of the old humanity which wanted to sin and had to sin. 'His death is therefore, so far from being a defeat, a victory; the reconciliation decided upon and accomplished in heaven; the power through which the grace of God has separated humankind from sin.'[89]

Barth's rather summary treatment of the work of Christ in *Romans* I provides little explanation for how Jesus' 'rediscovery' of a life of immediacy to God was possible under the conditions of fallen human existence. His clipped answer to the problem was quite simply: God was in Christ.[90] But what this meant in detail, he did not say. And perhaps he was not all that interested in the problem, so absorbed was he by the *background* of the reconciliation which took place in Christ, i.e. by the 'turn in heaven'. The 'turn in heaven'—that is the divine verdict on the obedience of the Christ;[91] a verdict which did not really wait for His historical appearing but was already operative from the beginning by way of anticipation and, in a real sense, made that obedience possible. Ultimately, Barth resolved the question of how the new world was created and inaugurated in Christ by appeal to the creative power of the Word as exemplified in the Genesis account of the first creation: '"God spoke: Let there be light! and there was light [Gen. 1: 3]."'[92]

What is clear is that the reconciliation achieved in and through Christ is understood by Barth to be a *cosmic* reconciliation. Barth's soteriology in *Romans* I is (as we suggested earlier) directed above all against religious individualism—and this marks a significant point of advance when measured by his earlier liberal theology. It is the entire world whose redemption is set in motion by the reconciliation achieved in Christ: 'world-redemption on the basis of world-reconciliation'.[93] The Kingdom of God has been 'planted' in history and nature; the righteousness of God which has appeared in Christ is like a 'germ cell' which, once established, will continue to grow until it reaches full matu-

---

[89] Barth, *Der Römerbrief, 1919*, 226.   [90] Ibid. 190.   [91] Ibid. 197–8.
[92] Ibid. 194.
[93] Ibid. 200. It is also worth noting that the distinction which is made in *Romans* I between reconciliation and redemption is one that would be abandoned in the second edition. In *Romans* II, reconciliation is collapsed into redemption (understood as a future event).

rity in the consummation of the Kingdom on earth.[94] At that point, the entire cosmos will be redeemed.

No category found in *Romans* I has received greater attention in the scholarly literature than that of the 'organic growth' of the Kingdom—with justification, for it was indeed central for Barth himself. But its significance is easily misconstrued.[95] To speak of the coming of the Kingdom as 'organic' meant above all two things for Barth.[96] First of all, it signified the universal character of the Kingdom. The Kingdom is an 'organism', whole and complete in itself. It is not a loose collection of individuals, but rather a totality, a unitary whole. '*Organismus gegen Monaden-wesen.*'[97]

We are not an external, accidental fellowship like the State or the Church . . . We are the inner, necessary fellowship which exists and is maintained by a higher will. We stand under grace. Through our reception into the 'body of Christ', we have been taken out of the disastrous situation of the individual before the Law. . . . Therefore, our fellowship does not present itself as an *aggregate*, a pile of sand; but rather, as an *organism*, whose individual parts *are* completed in it . . . and yet are *nothing*, nothing in and for themselves. [We] stand in the most living connection to one another conceivable.[98]

What is striking in this passage is the contrast drawn between the Church and the 'body of Christ'. The Church as a phenomenal, empirical reality is not to be identified with the 'body of Christ'. Christ's body is universal; it comprehends in principle all men and women (though not all have yet been incorporated into it).[99] The image of an 'organism' was meant to suggest that the Kingdom of God will ultimately embrace the whole of the

[94] Ibid. 24.

[95] The "organic" is a category Barth borrowed from J. T. Beck. In Barth's hands however, the category takes on a significance which had scarcely been envisioned by Beck. What Beck intended with the phrase 'organic growth' was a 'new nature principle', a cosmic and naturalistically conceived Christ-principle which transforms the world from within. Against such naturalism, Barth insisted that the history of God was a hidden 'absolutely not-given' history. Ibid. 136. The history of God is always grounded in the moment-by-moment, present action of God and never passes over into a 'nature principle'. For documentation of Beck's conception from his writings, see Spieckermann, *Gotteserkenntnis*, 103 n. 91.

[96] On this point, see Busch, *Karl Barth und die Pietisten*, 62; Anzinger, *Glaube und kommunikative Praxis*, 154–6.

[97] Barth, *Der Römerbrief, 1919*, 164.　　　　　　　　　　　　　　　　[98] Ibid. 476.

[99] The equation of the 'body of Christ' with the Kingdom of God and the 'new world' is clear: ibid. 254.

cosmos. 'There is no redeemed individual without a redeemed world.'[100] Viewed as an 'organism', the Kingdom is seen to be in opposition to the individualism, isolation, and fragmentation that characterize life under the hegemony of sin and death.

Second, Barth's choice of the phrase 'organic growth' to describe the coming of the Kingdom was designed deliberately to constitute a rejection of the notion that the Kingdom was a reality which could (even if only in part) be built by humans. 'The divine *grows organically*; therefore, it no longer needs *mechanical construction*.'[101] The Kingdom of God does not grow out of any possibilities existing in this world.

The Kingdom of God has come near. *That* is the ground on which we stand; not progress and development within hitherto existing possibilities, but rather the new life's possibility which has been created in Christ—the new creature in Him.[102]

To be sure, the Kingdom grows out of 'divine possibilities'[103] which Barth says can be found in every period, but it must be remembered that such 'possibilities' belong to a 'hidden history' of God standing back of phenomenal history. They do not belong to phenomenal history as such. And so Barth can say that the Kingdom represents a break with all movements and institutions created by human beings.

Judaism and Christianity and Idealism are not the New in the old world. Church and mission, personal ethics and morality, pacifism and Social Democracy do not represent the Kingdom of God but rather the old kingdom of humankind in new forms. There are no blessed possessors.[104]

The idea of the 'organic growth' of the Kingdom is completely misrepresented where it is identified with 'cultural-historical' development.[105] It is a *hidden* development which leaves traces in phenomenal history but is never simply identical with developments in phenomenal history. Thus, the concept of an 'organic growth' of the Kingdom is not only entirely compatible with the distinction between 'real history' and 'so-called history' but is only rightly comprehended in its light.

To summarize: in *Romans* I, Barth most certainly held to the

---

[100] Barth, *Der Römerbrief, 1919*, 228.   [101] Ibid. 90.   [102] Ibid. 164–5.
[103] Ibid. 68.   [104] Ibid. 42.
[105] Frei, 'The Doctrine of Revelation in the Thought of Karl Barth', 130–1.

idea of a gradual realization of the Kingdom of God in history. But the Kingdom does not grow out of possibilities lying ready to hand on the surface of history. 'The book is stamped by a process eschatology which clearly maintains *no* direct continuity between the Kingdom of God and the world but knows of a history of God which breaks through secretly out of the history of the death of this world.'[106] The Kingdom comes through a series of actualistically conceived 'breakthroughs' of 'real history' into phenomenal 'so-called history'; 'breakthroughs' whose interconnection and continuity are guaranteed by their rootedness in the teleology of 'real history'.

(iv) *Knowledge of God in Faith (Subjective Soteriology)*

Faith takes its rise, according to Barth, in baptism. Baptism 'is the objective, creative Word of God' which 'not only *signifies* but *is* the new creation'.[107] 'Through baptism God speaks the redeeming Word through which the objective truth of His grace is disclosed to us.'[108] This Word is an *effective* Word; through it, the individual is incorporated into Christ. We are only saying the same thing in another way when we say that the Word which God speaks in baptism is the Word which justifies—that is, which makes the righteousness of God effective in the individual. In this phase of his development, Barth was inclined to understand justification in effective terms. To be sure, such an understanding did not exclude forensic elements. Barth could, for example, speak of justification as an act in which God 'denies to the whole sinful development of this [fallen] individual its existence. He no longer recognizes it as real before Him. Forgiven! Covered! Nothing! He no longer views him/her as a member of the fallen world.'[109]

He also saw justification as entailing 'acquittal'[110]—the abolition of guilt.[111] But such elements were not primary for him. 'God *can* declare sin as nothing because He abolishes its presupposition . . .'[112] To be justified is to be 'organically incorporated into the living growth of divine righteousness'.[113] 'Our faith is

[106] Michael Beintker, 'Der Römerbrief von 1919', in Gerhard Sauter (ed.), *Verkündigung und Forschung: Beihefte zu 'Evangelische Theologie'*, 2 (1985), 24.
[107] Barth, *Der Römerbrief, 1919*, 212.   [108] Ibid. 213.   [109] Ibid. 116.
[110] Ibid. 194.   [111] Ibid. 117.   [112] Ibid. 116.
[113] Ibid. 113.

God's act in us. . . . God has planted a seed in us which must grow.'[114] Once again, the thought of an 'organic growth' emerges—this time, an organic growth of the individual in faith, knowledge of God and righteousness.

But here too, Barth's talk of 'organic growth' is placed under an eschatological reservation. The transformation through which men and women are made new creatures is a transformation which occurs 'in the hiddenness of men and women'.[115] Barth's use of this phrase (drawn from Romans 2: 16) was not intended to indicate a dimension of human being which would provide a point-of-contact for the relation to God (as, for example, was the case with Schleiermacher's talk of 'feeling'). It was not a circumlocution for a 'religious a priori'.[116] It was intended simply to direct attention away from any alleged capacity within human beings for a knowledge or experience of God. It was meant to lay stress on the objective character of a transformation that only occurs from without, in the sovereign freedom of the divine decision.

Grace is no "*Erlebnis*", no "*Erfahrung*". That is a prejudice of Pietism and a modern theology which, strangely enough, reads with Pietistic glasses. Grace obviously will not be without experiences; but grace is primarily the divine presupposition, the new order under which we are placed, the altered world-context into which our lives are inserted.[117]

The Spirit who creates faith is not a secure possession over which human beings can exercise control. 'One does not *have* the Spirit of God; rather, He has *us*.'[118] And that means that faith too is not a secure possession. 'You know that faith is something which one cannot *have*, but can only acquire anew, can only receive again and again as a gift . . .'[119] At every moment, the human individual stands anew under the 'crisis'[120] of the judgement of God with the question of her election (or reprobation) hanging in the

---

[114] Barth, *Der Römerbrief, 1919*, 147.

[115] Ibid. 66, 78, 81, 110, 340, 377, 384, 514, 518, 520.

[116] On this point, see Anzinger, *Glaube und kommunikative Praxis*, 170.

[117] Barth, *Der Römerbrief, 1919*, 206–7; cf. 149: 'It is not a matter of a movement of one's own spirit, but rather of the intuition of objective divine facts which is no psychological process, even though it has a psychological side.'

[118] Ibid. 307; cf. 337. Thus, as Werner Ruschke rightly remarks: 'The "having" of the Spirit of God is to be understood only actualistically, not ontologically.' Ruschke, *Entstehung und Ausführung der Diastasentheologie*, 187.

[119] Barth, *Der Römerbrief, 1919*, 449.   [120] Ibid. 441.

balance.[121] Thus, it is not the case that the 'seed' takes on a life of its own once it has been 'planted'; it does not grow to maturity without continuous divine intervention. The image of the 'seed' can only mislead if it is taken in that sense. Faith does not belong to the possibilities resident in the old aeon; it is much rather, a divine possibility and as such the contradiction of all existing possibilities. Barth was only underscoring this point when he suggested that faith is an event which takes place in the 'now-time' of revelation.[122] He was suggesting that faith is an event without 'before' or 'after'; without preconditions in the old aeon (in time as we know it) and without ongoing effects which pass over into human control.

Is there then no relation between the person we are 'in time' and the person we are 'in Christ'; between the old creature and the new creature? Barth's answer is certainly yes, there is a relation; it is the person who exists in time who is made new but the transformation may scarcely be observable. In our actual existence, it may well be that 'we still stand more strongly in the No than in the Yes, more strongly in the opposition than in the position, more strongly in destruction than in construction'.[123] We still stand within the 'zone of influence of the spirit of Adam';[124] indeed, we are 'in Adam' as well as 'in Christ'.[125] Nevertheless, Barth's expectation was that 'traces' of the new creature will become visible in the life of the believer who exists in time.[126] The 'turn' from the old humanity to the new is already complete 'in Christ'[127] and it is realized here and now in the form of

---

[121] Barth's doctrine of election in *Romans* I constituted the rejection of the thought of two fixed groups of individuals, one belonging to the "elect" and the other to the "reprobate". Election and reprobation were both conceived actualistically as the highly provisional status of the human individual before God, which depends finally on the question of whether genuine faith is present. Since faith is itself variable, it was always possible to lose one's election and regain it repeatedly. See ibid. 384.

[122] Ibid. 87.   [123] Ibid. 216.   [124] Ibid. 217.   [125] Ibid. 236.

[126] Ibid. 217: 'We do not *build* on our experience when we are conscious of ourselves as being people who are dead to sin . . . But we are not *without* such experience . . . We recognize in our lives the traces of our growth in the power of the new world, and these traces confirm to us that we are not deceived with regard to the direction we are being led in the conflict between the old and the new; that the reality of grace under which we stand is reality and not a new Idealism. There is a *psychology of grace* . . . which can perform a good service; not in grounding us but in helping us to picture the movement in which we stand.'

[127] Ibid. 237: 'You are not only in Adam, but also in Christ. Yes, you are much more in Christ than in Adam . . .'

'breakthroughs' in which faith is created and nourished. Here again, the relation is not a stable, static one. Faith is not a stable reality. It consists above all in seeking and longing after God, a readiness for the speaking and acting of God.[128] As soon as it becomes an object of interest in its own right, as soon as it becomes objective to itself, it ceases to exist. Thus, the dialectic created by the distinction of 'real history' and 'so-called history' is mirrored here in a dialectical relation between the 'real humanity' and the 'unreal' phenomenal human being existing in time. 'Breakthroughs' do indeed occur in which the 'real humanity' overcomes the old, unreal humanity in an actualistic way.

Barth's concern in setting forth this dialectical soteriology is clear: he wanted to place faith beyond the reach of psychological investigation. To do so was to safeguard his realistic starting-point in the Self-positing God who objectively places humankind in relation to Himself.

Thus far, we have considered Barth's treatment of soteriology from the standpoint of the dialectical relation of the new humanity to the old. There remains one more crucial element of his soteriology to be considered: the knowledge of God. The renewal of the individual is understood by Barth to be a process which takes place primarily on the 'spiritual–intellectual side of human being' and only secondarily on the 'psychological side'.[129]

Our *Sache* is our knowledge of God [*Erkenntnis Gottes*] which is realized in Christ; in which God does not become objective to us, but rather comes close to us, immediately and creatively; in which we not only see, but *are seen*, not only understand, but *are understood*; not only comprehend, but *are grasped*.[130]

Nowhere is the distance separating the theology of *Romans* I from Barth's pre-war theology more apparent than in his treatment of the knowledge of God. In Barth's liberal period, it will be recalled, knowledge (*Erkenntnis*) had been restricted to the "objects" generated by the laws governing each of the branches of human cognitive activity. Religious experience (*Gotteserlebnis*) had been appealed to in order to explain how cognitive, culture-creating activity is set in motion in the existing individual (i.e. how the transition from the ideal epistemological subject to the

---

[128] Barth, *Der Römerbrief, 1919*, 49, 63.   [129] Ibid. 21.   [130] Ibid. 19.

existing human knower takes place).[131] *Gotteserkenntnis* in the strict sense of the term was finally seen to be an impossibility. In *Romans* I, however, a dramatic shift was registered. Barth's concern now was precisely 'knowledge of God in the strictest sense'.[132]

How was such a shift possible? How could Barth now speak of knowledge of God as not only possible but real? What made the difference was above all the shift from an idealistic to a critically realistic starting-point. Conspicuous in the passage cited at the outset of this section is the realistic element: the human knower is herself seen, understood, grasped, laid hold of—*from without*. That is the characteristic element in Barth's treatment of the knowledge of God in *Romans* I: the thought that the human cognitive apparatus can be laid hold of from without and reoriented, redirected. Without being fundamentally altered in its basic functions and laws, the cognitive apparatus is grasped in its entirety and placed in a new framework. The human knower is made a participant in God's knowledge of Himself.[133] The possibility of the knowledge of God is thus grounded in Himself (i.e. possibility is grounded in Reality) and not in the possibilities established by the functions of human consciousness.

True knowledge of God is participatory, personal knowledge. Barth distinguished carefully between a merely external *Kenntnis* of God (such as can be acquired above all through the Law) and a relationally construed *Erkenntnis* of God. The step from one to the other is "absolute" because true knowledge of God can only be given by God Himself.[134] There is no bridge which leads from the former to the latter. True knowledge of God is a knowledge in which 'our logic' is renewed by being brought into conformity with the 'logic of God'. 'Our logic' refers to the exercise of the human cognitive apparatus in engendering "objects" of knowledge. The world known in this way is the old world which is passing away. But there is another world, a world which is '*engendered* out of the Truth itself in constant opposition

---

[131] See above, Ch. 1, Sect. 6.   [132] Barth, *Der Römerbrief, 1919*, 22.

[133] Ibid. 158: 'For it is the *love of God* which turns toward us through the gift of the Spirit . . . Not as "feeling" [*Gefühl*]. There may well be no "feeling" present in us. . . . Rather, as the re-acquired knowledge of God with which God immediately knows Himself . . .'

[134] Ibid. 65; cf. 79, 83, 129.

to the "reality" of the present, corruptible world which is not engendered out of the Truth itself'.[135] The 'logic of God' is the 'logic of reconciliation', and thinking which is conformed to it is based upon an acknowledgement of the divine Yes spoken to us in Christ.[136] 'Our logic' is restored to the 'logic of God' by a 'ceaseless, forward spiralling, wrestling, and striving to *think* the thoughts of God' after Him.[137]

In light of the foregoing affirmations, it is now possible to achieve a final clarification with regard to Barth's use of the category 'immediacy' in *Romans* I. The category was borrowed from Hermann Kutter's 1902 book, *Das Unmittelbare* ('The Immediate') but in Barth's hands, it underwent significant modification.[138] Whereas Kutter saw the original life of immediacy to God as an essentially non-rational (and even irrational) experience, for Barth it was a wholly rational, interpersonal experience. For Kutter, the Fall meant a lapse from direct experiencing into thinking as such. On his view, *all* thinking is the thinking of the observer, the spectator who stands over against the object (or subject) to be known at a distance. The only kind of knowledge Kutter acknowledged was that described by Kant: knowledge that is governed by the subject–object split. Thus, Kutter had not broken free of the assumption widespread amongst liberals that God is experienced but not known. For Barth however, the Fall was a fall from a participatory rationality (in which thinking is centred in the Other[139]) into a non-participatory, "objective", distanced, analytical rationality in which thinking is centred in the constructive activity of the human knower, and people and things are regarded as simply objects to be known. Barth probably had Kutter in mind when he pointedly observed that 'anti-intellectualism is a sign of

---

[135] Barth, *Der Römerbrief, 1919*, 471.   [136] Ibid. 170.

[137] Ibid. 471; cf. Barth, 'Unterweisung II, 1917/18', in idem, *Konfirmandenunterricht*, 214: 'We can really only think-after [*nach-denken*] what God has already thought.'

[138] For detailed analysis of the relation of Barth's theology in *Romans* I to the theology of Hermann Kutter, see above all Ingrid Spieckermann, *Gotteserkenntnis*, 82–5, 92–6; then also Anzinger, *Glaube und kommunikative Praxis*, 150–1, 188.

[139] To speak of a 'rationality centred in the Other' is to refer to the fact that '*God* is the primary Subject of the knowledge of God realized in Christ; *His* creative immediate efficacy is the realization of this knowledge. Human knowledge of God can therefore, from the outset, be nothing other than the willing inclusion in this divine creative knowledge; can only be the knowledge which is inherent in the immediate being-known which occurs through such willing.' Spieckermann, *Gotteserkenntnis*, 89–90.

intellectual embarrassment.'[140] The 'return to immediacy' for him meant a return to a situation in which Person communicates with person. God speaks; human beings hear.[141] Such communication is said to be 'immediate' because it is direct; i.e. it is not mediated by the "objects" known through the neo-Kantian constructivist epistemology. God is present to the human knower immediately and creatively, laying hold of the knowing apparatus and redirecting it. As Herbert Anzinger rightly notes, 'The perspective has changed . . . by 180 degrees. Faith is no longer to be understood as the reception of God into consciousness, but rather as the taking of consciousness into the region governed by God.'[142] Finally, 'directness' was not intended by Barth to suggest loss of distinction between the knower and the Known (or, much rather, between the Knower and the known). 'Above all, in speaking of an immediate unity of God and humankind, Barth did not mean identity in the sense of an indifferent realization in one another.'[143] The Holy Spirit has us; we do not have the Holy Spirit.[144] Although certain of Barth's phrases in *Romans* I can be taken to suggest something like a Protestant mysticism, such a conclusion is clearly against Barth's intention.[145]

How then is the knowledge of God concretely realized in the actually existing individual? Crucial to Barth's overall conception is the thought that the knowledge of God is 'realized in Christ'.[146] It is in Christ that God was definitively present, making Himself known. More specifically, the objective ground of the knowledge of God lies in the conjunction of the cross and resurrection of Christ. That the cross was the divine act of reconciliation was declared in the resurrection. It is in the light that streams forth from the resurrection that the real meaning and significance of the cross is made known.[147] Thus, revelation is concentrated objectively in the resurrection. But the resurrection is a meta-historical event; it is not accessible to historical and psychological investigation because its source does not belong to the forces operative on the surface of history. How does the light

---

[140] Barth, *Der Römerbrief, 1919*, 470.

[141] Cf. Barth, 'Unterweisung II, 1917/18', in idem, *Konfirmandenunterricht*, 217.

[142] Anzinger, *Glaube und kommunikative Praxis*, 183.   [143] Ibid. 184.

[144] Ibid. 307.

[145] Ibid. 159: 'The Holy Spirit in us is no subjective experience shrouded in mystical darkness, but rather the objective truth which has disclosed itself to us.'

[146] Ibid. 19.   [147] Ibid. 215.

which streams forth from the resurrection reach its goal? How do men and women become participants in the knowledge which is made real (and therefore possible) in this way? Barth can speak of the rise of knowledge in the individual in terms which hint of things to come in *Romans* II: as a 'dare' which 'can neither be explained nor justified historically and psychologically. It explains and justifies itself.'[148] More typical however is the thought that in and through baptism, God creates in us the faith which responds to the knowledge objectively revealed in Christ.

Now there are certainly weaknesses in Barth's conception of the knowledge of God. Barth's sketch of Christology in *Romans* I is extremely thin—which means that the objective content to which human minds are to conform in faith is left rather vague. Equally problematic was Barth's tendency at this time to leave the neo-Kantian epistemology largely unchallenged. The affirmation that God lays hold of the human cognitive apparatus and reorients it introduced an element of realism which would eventually drive Barth away from Cohen's conception back in the direction of a more classically Kantian epistemology. Finally, Barth did not set forth a doctrine of analogy which could make clear *how* it comes about that 'our logic' is made to conform to 'divine logic'. He simply affirmed the fact *that* such conformity is made possible on the basis of the realistically construed divine speaking. Barth was only at the beginning of a way which would lead ultimately to the theory of knowledge advanced in *Church Dogmatics* II/1. His way between *Romans* I and the *Church Dogmatics* would scarcely be a straightforward, linear one. It was a way strewn with curves and side-alleys. But already, the starting-point and framework of the later position are in place.

(v) *Dialectics in Romans* I

In his insightful analysis of dialectic in the early theology of Barth, Michael Beintker made a fundamental distinction between two types of dialectic.[149] To consider this distinction briefly will help to bring greater clarity into our interpretation of Barth's

---

[148] Ibid. 170.

[149] Beintker, *Die Dialektik in der 'dialektischen Theologie' Karl Barths*, 38–9. Beintker is here modifying a distinction originally coined by Henning Schröer between 'supplementary' and 'complementary paradoxes'.

explanation of the relation of eschatology to history on the one hand and the new creature to the old creature on the other. The first type of dialectic distinguished by Beintker is one he calls a 'supplementary dialectic'. In a dialectic of this type one member of a pair predominates in value and potency over the other. As a consequence of this 'imbalance' the predominant member is able to overcome the other. At some point, the stronger member takes up the weaker into itself with the result that the weaker member is either cancelled out altogether or is perhaps taken up into the other in a higher synthesis. In either case, an initial situation of simple opposition gives way to reconciliation. Thus, a 'supplementary dialectic' is one that admits of a certain progress. The second type is called a 'complementary dialectic'. Here, the two members stand over against each other in a relation of open contradiction or antithesis. No reconciliation or synthesis between the two is admitted; therefore, such movement as exists has the character of a ceaseless to-ing and fro-ing between the two without any real progress.

In *Romans* I, both the *realdialektische* relationship between 'real history' and 'so-called history' as well as the *realdialektische* relationship between 'real humanity' (in Christ) and the 'unreal humanity' (in Adam) are of the supplementary type. In both cases, what is in view is a relationship in which 'real reality' overcomes 'unreal reality'.

To be sure, only in Christ is the death of Adam a completed fact. In Christ, the righteousness of God has asserted itself decisively in history, triumphing over the spirit of Adam. The power of sin and death proved powerless in the face of the perfect obedience of Christ to the Father. For Him, Adam is no more; he has been slain and set aside. There is no equilibrium in the relationship of Adam to Christ. There is rather an irreversible movement from here to there, from death to life. Barth illustrates this movement by means of an appeal to a time–eternity dialectic in which eternity enters into history without being overcome by it, taking time up into itself, fulfilling it.[150] Thus, in *Romans* I, Barth did not treat eternity as the antithesis of time (as he would in

---

[150] Cf. Anzinger, *Glaube und kommunikative Praxis*, 156: 'Instead of a growth of the Christ organism in time, one must speak rather of a growth of time in the Christ organism.'

Romans II). Here 'syntheses' of eternity and time are regarded as not only possible but actual.

In 'real history' the 'turn' from Adam to Christ has already taken place (past tense). But in phenomenal 'so-called history' it must repeatedly take place (present tense). However true it may be that *in Christ* all things have been made new, it is nevertheless the case that men and women must continually '*become* what they are in Christ' moment by moment through actualistic 'breakthroughs' of the righteousness and knowledge of God into their temporal fallen existence. Where this occurs, the 'turn' from Adam to Christ is realized anew in the form of a provisional synthesis in which the old creature is (for the moment) taken up into and overcome by the new creature. Eternity enters once again into time, absorbing it and bringing it to a standstill—which is to say, the enslavement to the law of sin and death which governs temporal existence is momentarily broken. Again, these 'breakthroughs' are actualistic in character and therefore they do not give rise to a finished, stable condition. But there is a continuity between these 'moments' because they are grounded in and made possible by the completed 'turn' in Christ. 'So-called history' too is the scene of a dialectical way (a 'process dialectic') whose progress is guaranteed by the fact that the 'breakthroughs' which occur from time to time are not isolated, unrelated episodes but are grounded in the teleology of 'real history'.

In addition to these two forms of *Realdialektik*, one may rightly speak of a dialectical *Denkform* which corresponds to and is demanded by the real 'process dialectic'. Here again, it is Michael Beintker who has shown the way.

Dynamic, growth, movement, and process are the characteristic features of *Romans* I. Dialectic is here shown to be the *Denkform* which accords with *becoming*. Thinking cannot become fixed, desiring to adhere to a definite, once-and-for-all attained position. For in that case, one *moment* of the movement would have been grasped, comparable to a photograph which reduces the whole course of a movement to a single image and thereby "freezes" the movement. The *whole* of the movement falls from view. Precisely for that reason, everything depends upon finding a suitable way to express the *becoming* of the new world of God.[151]

---

[151] Beintker, *Die Dialektik in der 'dialektischen Theologie' Karl Barths*, 112–13.

The 'dialectic of becoming' as the principle *Denkform* of *Romans* I would quickly give way to a *Denkform* governed by an altogether different kind of dialectic: a dialectic in which the contradiction or antithesis of two magnitudes is steadfastly maintained in order to bear witness to a truth lying beyond both of them.[152] But before that would happen, Barth's eschatology would have to undergo a considerable radicalization.

(vi) *Critique of Idealistic Ethics*

If Barth's ethics had been wholly commensurate with his new starting-point, he would have replaced idealistic morality with a realistically conceived and actualistically realized 'command of God'. Certainly, the starting-point and framework for just such an ethic can be found in *Romans* I. But at this stage of Barth's development, the 'command of God' had a very narrow range of application. It was concerned largely with interpersonal relations. But there were also large regions of human experience in which Barth treated the 'command of God' as something which would not or could not be lived out. Virtually the whole of political life fell into this category. In such tragic cases, the Christian in search of guidance was referred by Barth to idealistic morality. In spite of offering (as we shall see) a rather rigorous critique of idealistic morality, he had no wish at this point simply to set it aside. This was undoubtedly because he was concerned above all to obviate every attempt to 'Christianize' political options and he probably did not see how such an aim could be realized if he were to introduce a divine command ethic into the realm of politics. He lacked a doctrine of analogy which might have made it clear how

---

[152] Ibid. 115. Herbert Anzinger has objected to Beintker's talk of a dialectical *Denkform* in *Romans* I on the grounds that its presupposition (a 'linear process eschatology') is lacking. Ultimately, Anzinger's objection seems to rest upon the thought that because the new aeon and the old aeon stand in an *Ineinander* relation, Christians simply stand on the boundary between both worlds (in the midst of the turn) and, therefore, no real progress is possible. Anzinger, *Glaube und kommunikative Praxis*, 246–7 (esp. n. 26). Such a reading seems to me to be the result of a failure to take seriously the teleology of 'real history'. In 'real history', the turn has taken place; there is no equilibrium in the relation of Christ to Adam. It is on this basis that Barth can say, 'You are much more in Christ than in Adam.' Barth, *Der Römerbrief, 1919*, 237. The process through which the truth of our existence is realized in history is, to be sure, not an unbroken linear one. But that is no argument against the existence of a largely hidden process, grounded in the teleology of 'real history'.

human action could 'correspond' to divine action without setting aside the distinction between them. In any case, the largely negative character of his eschatological starting-point simply did not offer sufficient ethical guidance to make a realistic 'divine command' ethic fully effective at this stage. The result is that Barth worked throughout *Romans* I with two fundamentally incompatible ethical programmes. In what follows, the attempt will be made, first, to sketch Barth's critique of idealistic ethics against the background of his understanding of the nature of sin; then to consider briefly the partial emergence of a realistic 'divine command' ethic. In the next section, we will consider the tragic realm of politics in which idealistic ethics still prevails.[153]

It will be recalled that sin and death came into the world as a result of the human desire for independence (autonomy) *vis-à-vis* God. The desire for independence was itself motivated by a longing for freedom, but the freedom achieved was in fact the very opposite of real freedom.[154] It was much rather a form of imprisonment and slavery. Adam had been created in a relation of immediacy to God, the world, and to other human beings. In his desire for autonomy, Adam stepped out of the original relation in which he had his being in God and took up a detached position over against Him, resting entirely in himself. He became a fully independent 'subject' for whom God could only be an 'object'. As a direct consequence of this action, he also distanced himself from the world and other human beings. He stood over against the world (which he now saw as a 'gigantic, overwhelming object'[155]) in the stance of the one who would acquire dominance over it through analytical reason. He cut himself off from all other persons, regarding them with suspicion as possible threats to his 'freedom'. For Barth, this move represented the loss of real freedom, for real freedom is (in Herbert Anzinger's phrase) 'communicative';[156] in other words, it is the capacity to limit oneself freely for the sake of granting freedom to another.[157] The truly free subject is the subject who is free *for* others, who lives in and through others. From a truly free being

---

[153] In this section too, I am heavily indebted to the work of Herbert Anzinger. See Anzinger, *Glaube und kommunikative Praxis*, 195–236.

[154] Barth, *Der Römerbrief, 1919*, 243.   [155] Ibid. 180.

[156] Anzinger, *Glaube und kommunikative Praxis*, 198–210.

[157] Barth, *Der Römerbrief, 1919*, 533.

whose subjectivity was structured through interpersonal 'communicative' relations, Adam became an 'individual': a subjective centre constituted *by* the self *for* the self, a subjectivity structured through self-relatedness and, therefore, a 'subjectivity imprisoned in itself'.[158] As a consequence, the human being of this aeon is 'an I, a limited subjectivity, an individual thrown back on himself, resting in himself and precisely for that reason, a sinful human being . . . the I which is only I, the human for himself, without God.'[159]

It is quite clear throughout Barth's analysis of sin that the target he had in view was the "modern" (idealistic) conception of consciousness as structured by the autonomous generation (and realization) of tasks. Where for the theologians of the Ritschlian school (as well as for neo-Kantian philosophy) the development of the "free" (which is to say, autonomous) personality is synonymous with the creation of an ethical agent, for Barth the desire for autonomy is the original sin. The quest for autonomy is the source of individualism, disorganization, and chaos in society.

Obviously, such a critique has political overtones. To place the conception of a self-constituted, self-centred, and self-relating subjectivity under the sign: Sin! was at the same time to strip the bourgeois preoccupation with self-realization through acquisition of money and power of any possible ideological justification. Barth's analysis of sin also constituted a critique of political liberalism, to the extent that liberalism made the freedom of the individual an end in itself. To be sure, the thoroughgoing criticism of individualism which emerged in the pages of *Romans* I did not constitute a blanket rejection of liberalism. It is not to be understood as the expression of a preference for collectivism, for example. No, for Barth, the solution to the chaos and disorganization created by liberal individualism is not the absolute state, but rather a grounding of the individual in the creative, life-giving power of God which raised Jesus from the dead.[160] 'Outside of the creative, living unity and truth of God, liberalism is sin.'[161] But grounded

---

[158] Ibid. 274.   [159] Ibid. 271.

[160] The state—whether the absolute state or a constitutional democracy—is said by Barth to be a 'merely' accidental, external arrangement. By contrast, the Christian fellowship is built on an inner relationship of love in freedom. See ibid. 476.

[161] Ibid. 242–3.

in that relation the individual is truly free; she is liberated from the 'supposed freedom' of Adam (which is no freedom at all) for a life in and for the other. 'The subjectivity of the individual is not eliminated through its incorporation in the Christ-organism; on the contrary, here for the first time, the individual comes into her own. She is liberated from the necessity of having to circle only around herself; she loses her self-relatedness.'[162]

It is against the background of his analysis of the nature of sin as centred in individualism that Barth advanced his critique of idealistic morality. The focus of the critique is the situation which arises when the individual has employed the Kantian categorical imperative to generate a norm (or norms) to govern her behaviour. When a norm so generated stands over against the self-constituting and self-relating individual, it cannot be understood in any other way than as an external demand which must be fulfilled by the individual (i.e. it must and will be understood as *law*). In that the individual responds to the "Law" as an individual—and there is no other way for her to respond to it—and tries to fulfil its demands, she only strengthens her self-constituting, self-relating orientation. She digs herself in deeper, making her sin more sinful. Thus, for the sinner who stands outside the 'body of Christ', the idealistic generation of the "Law" cannot help but further the process of individualizing.

Idealistic morality can only postulate the good; it cannot bring it to life.[163] Idealism is powerless to engender the 'new spirit' in and through which the will of God is done 'organically'; joyfully and freely and not out of obligation, as a response to "Law". Ultimately, idealistic morality crashes on the rocks of the fact that the good cannot be done by the sinner (i.e. by the individual *qua* individual). 'God's will cannot and will not be fulfilled in the individual.'[164] 'The individual is not the subject who can obey the imperatives of morality. God cannot be glorified in a merely "personal" life.'[165]

---

[162] Anzinger, *Glaube und kommunikative Praxis*, 192.

[163] Barth, *Der Römerbrief, 1919*, 81: 'Broken is the bridge, torn is the unity, insoluble is the contradiction. No *Ursprungsphilosophie* will succeed in bringing the righteousness of God to *life*, and no moral theology will finally be able to elevate the righteousness of men and women to the level of the *ideal*. All striving on both sides founders on the question of *reality*: the idea remains "only" idea and life remains "only" life.'

[164] Ibid. 265.   [165] Ibid. 272.

The good can be 'done' only by the one who lives a life of complete immediacy to God. And even to put it this way is already to betray Barth's intentions to some extent. The individual who is grounded in Christ does not so much 'do' the good as willingly allow it to be done in and through her. In other words, the individual does not do the good as an individual but as a member of the 'body of Christ'. The subject who 'does' the good is, in the first instance, Christ, then the 'body of Christ' (the Christian fellowship), and then and only then, the individual as a free participant in that body.[166] The good is realized through the objectively real divine action which grounds the Christian fellowship.

What then of ethics in the life of the Christian? How does her situation differ from that of the person 'under the Law'? Under the conditions of the new aeon, the question to which ethics seeks to provide an answer ('what should I do?') does not even arise. The new aeon is constituted by the restoration of a life of immediacy to God. And immediacy to God has as its consequence that human action flows naturally ('organically') from divine action. The individual who lives in immediacy to God does not have to ask what the good is; she simply does the good naturally as the outflow of the divine working in her. It follows that ethics only becomes possible and necessary under the conditions of the old aeon. To the extent that the Christian treats right action as a problem (as a question to be answered, a set of principles to be created)—to the extent, in other words, that she engages in *ethics*—to that extent she is only placing herself under the "Law" once again and cutting herself off from Christ. For she is, in that case, once again assuming an external relation to a "Law" whose demand must be fulfilled by her as an individual.

'What should I do?' Answer: Above all, don't ask that question any more! Every word of this question is ambiguous and misleading. For it abolishes freedom once again, placing itself *next to* the creative power of the good under which we are placed in Christ . . . We have to abide in the 'body of Christ' (Rom. 7: 4), in the power of the resurrection inaugurated in Him in which all moral ought proceeds organically out of

---

[166] Ibid. 475: 'It is not the *individual* who thinks, believes, and acts on her account and at her risk; rather, the "body of Christ" thinks, believes, and acts in her and through her, in the measure in which it can do so in this moment.'

the new 'being in the Spirit' (Rom. 8: 5–9), in which the good is not something *problematic*, but rather only something which *occurs*.[167]

Hence: 'On the basis of the ultimate viewpoint which we must adopt *in Christ*, there are *no ethics*'.[168]

Certainly, all of this sounds more than a bit utopian. How can the Christian *not* treat right action as a problem? How can she *not* engage in ethics? It is all well and good to say that in the Kingdom of God, the question of right action will no longer arise. But Barth also says that we do not yet live in the Kingdom of God. We live 'between the times'; between the time of the inauguration of the Kingdom and the time of its consummation. We live in history, and in history our relation to the creative divine source of the good is not a stable one. We belong not only to Christ, but also to Adam. We are members not only of the new aeon but also of the old. Under these conditions, the good will not be *wholly* natural to us. Our relation to the source of the good is an actualistic one; it is a relation which must be realized anew in each new moment and in each new ethical situation. Given that this is so, there must surely be times when the situation is most unclear; when the good that we would like to do does not simply arise organically within us and we are left in the deepest perplexity. Surely we need some guidance if we are going to be able to know what the good is. And even in those times when the good seems more clear to us, surely we need some standard if only to ensure to ourselves that we are not deceived in thinking that our action is immediately one with the divine action.

Barth was not at all blind to the need for such guidance; indeed, virtually all of his ethical reflections had as their goal a clarification of precisely this situation. Upon closer examination we find that Barth had an ethic after all, though he preferred not to call it that. He preferred to call it (following Romans 12: 1) 'Christian exhortation'. He reserved the term "ethics" for an idealistic morality which sought to generate universally valid laws to govern human behaviour. 'Exhortation', by contrast, is directed only to Christian brothers and sisters in whom the good (the 'will of God') is an effective power.

---

[167] Barth, *Der Römerbrief, 1919*, 263–4.   [168] Ibid. 524.

Outside of Christ, Christian exhortation has no meaning. . . . Directed
to men and women for whom the presuppositions of [Romans] chapters 5–8 have yet to become actual, and even directed to us in so far as
those presuppositions have yet to become actual, Christian exhortation
cannot work otherwise than as a strange form of the *Law* through
which no divine righteousness can arise but only the painful situation
described in 7: 7–13 and 14–25. Strange on the one hand because
"Christian ideals" pressed upon the "world" require of men and
women what they cannot achieve and, on the other hand, do *not*
require much that is important and interesting to the "world", passing
by its most urgent questions and needs in silence . . .[169]

'Christian exhortation' is not altogether lacking in 'norms', but
it derives its norms from the new being in Christ (rather than
through the application of the categorical imperative) and it does
so only in the immediacy of a concrete ethical situation. It seeks
to describe in human words an objectively real, God-given
'command of the moment'.[170] The 'command of the moment' is
recognized by the 'renewed mind' through a prayerful following
of 'the real divine development of things . . . *behind* the curtain of
time'.[171] That is to say, the will of God cannot be simply read off
the surface of history, but must be discovered at work beneath
the surface, so to speak. Still, the command of God is a command of the *moment*; it is wholly and completely *zeitgemäß*. Far
from being an abstract ethical principle, it is directed to a highly
concrete situation. Christian exhortation seeks to describe a
moment in the divine movement. Its principles are 'reflexive',[172]
i.e. not given but engendered in a concrete situation through the
objective working of the divine.

Is there a consistency to the will of God or is it simply capri-
cious and decisionistic in character? A close examination of
Romans I shows that Barth did indeed think that the will of God
follows a particular trajectory from moment to moment; it has a
definite *Tendenz*. And because the will of God has a definite tendency, Christian 'norms' which seek to mirror that will in a concrete situation will also be characterized by that tendency. So, for
example, God is at work in the world liberating men and women
from their self-relatedness and creating a community of fellowship and freedom.[173] A Christian action which is rooted and

[169] Ibid. 464.   [170] Ibid. 485.   [171] Ibid. 486.
[172] Anzinger, *Glaube und kommunikative Praxis*, 205.   [173] Ibid. 205–6.

grounded in the action of God will show itself to be so by its efficacy in producing fellowship and freedom. Or again, God is not

a God of the powerful *and* the lowly, but rather, one-sidedly, a God of the lowly . . . The movement of the Kingdom of God within social and cultural antitheses . . . is fundamentally and one-sidedly a movement from below. Those who participate in it must . . . desire to stand below, where everything depends upon God. I can be a Jew to the Jews and a Greek to the Greeks, but I cannot be a lord to the lords . . . Where idols are erected, I may not be present.[174]

A truly Christian action which is rooted and grounded in the action of God will show itself to be so by placing itself on the side of the 'lowly' and against the powerful.

Now admittedly, such descriptions of the 'will of God' offer only the most vague guidance for shaping conduct in the moment. Such vagueness was—in part, at least—deliberate. Barth's concern here was to avoid providing any grounds for the 'Christianizing' (absolutizing) of the 'norms' of Christian action. Christian exhortation cannot be turned into a new Law without ceasing to be Christian exhortation. Barth wanted to force his readers to look away from ideals to a realistically conceived and actualistically realized will of God.

Beyond the difficulties produced by such calculated vagueness, however, there are quite simply 'confused situations' which Barth believed are forced upon the Christian whether she wills or not; situations in which 'the power is not in you' to do the good, and all of the options open entail involvement in some sort of sin. As we shall now see, virtually the whole of political life fell for Barth under the heading of the 'confused situation'. At such times Barth believed it was necessary to fall back upon the 'ethics of the confused situation'[175] (i.e. the Kantian categorical imperative) for guidance. Even as Barth wrote these words, he had a specific 'confused situation' in mind: the political confusion created in the wake of the Bolshevik Revolution in Russia. What was a Christian to do when the only options seemed to be the continued support of an unjust (though legally constituted) state on the one hand and an equally unjust revolution on the other?

---

[174] Barth, *Der Römerbrief, 1919*, 490.   [175] Ibid. 495.

(vii) *Political Action and Christian Hope*

Barth's commentary on Romans 13: 1–7 was one of the very few sections in the latter half of the original manuscript to undergo extensive revision in the summer of 1918. The first draft had been written from the perspective of one who was still committed (however tenuously) to Religious Socialism. But sometime in June 1918, Barth made the decision to engage in a fundamental *Auseinandersetzung* with Leonhard Ragaz and Religious Socialism.[176] The stimulus which provoked him to this decision was probably an article published by Ragaz in *Neue Wege* in May in which the Zürcher made a more-or-less direct identification between the political struggle for democracy and freedom on the one hand and the struggle for the Kingdom of God on the other.[177] All of Barth's efforts in this section are directed finally to the goal of opposing every such identification. With the publication of this virulent attack on Ragaz in the pages of *Romans* I, Barth's break with Religious Socialism was complete.

Barth began his consideration of the Christian's responsibilities in the political sphere with a theological analysis of the state. Since the Fall, the righteousness of God no longer immediately directs the earthly relations of humankind. The course of the world in the old aeon is governed by a God-alienated will. The present state has taken the place of the 'state of God' which will one day be renewed in Christ. The state depends for its existence on the methods of the old aeon (i.e. the threat or actual use of repressive force); therefore it is evil.

Its name is "power", for its pure power and compulsive character stand in marked and acknowledged antithesis to the righteousness and freedom of the state of God. If the evil God-alienated will of humankind

---

[176] That Barth had Ragaz in mind throughout his discussion of Rom. 13: 1–7 is clear—in spite of the fact that he nowhere mentions him by name. In May 1920, after reading an article by Ragaz in which he called for Switzerland to join the League of Nations, Barth wrote to Thurneysen, 'It is a frightening proof of the fact that I did not unjustly saw him up in Romans 13 and that in a second edition there can be no deletions out of personal pity.' Karl Barth to Eduard Thurneysen, 3 May 1920, *B–Th. Br.* I. 386–7. There can be no doubt that Rom. 13: 1–7 constituted a definitive reckoning with Ragaz and Religious Socialism and *not* an *Auseinandersetzung* with Leninism as has been suggested by Friedrich-Wilhelm Marquardt. See Marquardt, *Theologie und Sozialismus*, 126–41.

[177] Anzinger, *Glaube und kommunikative Praxis*, 220–2.

has power on earth, then all power (call it what you will) . . . can only be *evil*. The power-state of the present is diametrically opposed to the intentions of God; it is evil in itself.[178]

Moreover, '*all* politics as the struggle for power, as the devilish art of winning elections, is *fundamentally* dirty'.[179] Not even the most noble intentions of the bearer of power can alter the essential *Widergöttlichkeit* of exercising power, even if that bearer should be named August Bebel.

Of course, the state could not exist apart from the permission of God. The state is in fact the instrument of God for punishing evil; it is a manifestation of the wrath of God. But such an instrumental use of the state does nothing to alter its essentially evil character: 'in accordance with the divine arrangement, injustice, caprice, and brutality from above must . . . hold in check injustice, caprice, and brutality from below'.[180] In other words, the state overcomes evil with evil.

Because the state belongs to the old aeon, it can be of no ultimate concern to the Christian. The Christian does not belong to the state. 'You *have* no "Fatherland"; you are *seeking* it (Heb. 11: 13–16).' The Christian's task cannot be to maintain or even improve the state. The state is unimprovable; the goal is 'to *replace* it'.[181] How? by armed insurrection? No. Barth is harshly realistic on this point. Revolution cannot possibly achieve the goal it sets for itself. It too wants to make all things new, but in making use of the unrighteous methods of the old aeon, it can (if successful) only succeed in replacing one state with another state—which is to say, one unjust order with another unjust order. In truth, only that 'order' can truly replace the state which is of a wholly different character; an 'order' which is rooted and grounded in mutual freedom and love. But that means that 'true socialism' is realized only in the 'state of God'; a 'state' which grows 'organically' out of the holy unrest which God has planted in the hearts of men and women; a 'state' which will only arrive when that unrest attains a kind of critical mass throughout the world, becoming a veritable flood which will sweep away every obstacle from its path.[182]

Out of your absolutely *jenseitig*-oriented expectation for the future, you

[178] Barth, *Der Römerbrief, 1919*, 501.   [179] Ibid. 502.   [180] Ibid.
[181] Ibid. 504.   [182] Ibid. 508.

must create the confidence and patience to concentrate yourselves strictly on the war of the spirit against the flesh (Rom. 8: 13), on the *absolute* revolution of God, and abandon the entire field of the penultimate to the process of dissolution into which it has fallen; without lifting a finger to maintain that which exists but also without mixing yourselves up in its destruction as such.[183]

The consummation which the Christian expects is not the result of a gradual ascent of humanity through political action, but rather the unveiling of a new creation. Politics belongs to the realm of the penultimate, a realm stamped and determined by the struggle for power. 'Never will the struggle for the decision between the old world and the new be fought out in the political arena . . .'.[184] At most, political struggles can become the occasion for the struggle between spirit and flesh. But the two struggles must not be confused. 'Your state and your revolution are in heaven, "in the hiddenness of men and women" (Rom. 2: 16)'.[185] And so Barth admonishes: 'Do not anticipate the divine world-revolution individually, but rather create its presupposition.'[186]

The Christian's contribution to creating the presupposition of the coming 'state of God' consists above all in denying to the present state the one thing it needs most for its survival: religious legitimation. In Barth's view, this is real revolutionary radicalism: not a violent rebellion which at best replaces one power-state with another, but the steadfast refusal to grant that the state has any God-given 'right' to exist. Truly revolutionary praxis consists in 'starving the state religiously'[187] and thereby subverting it, negating it. '[Christianity] does not compete with the state, it negates it: its presupposition and its essence. It is *more* than Leninism!'[188]

---

[183] Ibid. 506. [184] Ibid. [185] Ibid. 507. [186] Ibid. 516. [187] Ibid. 508.

[188] Ibid. 506. Barth's understanding of the 'absolute revolution' of God had a secular analogue in the revolutionary politics of the time, but it was not in Leninism as Friedrich-Wilhelm Marquardt has suggested. See Marquardt, *Theologie und Sozialismus*, 126–41. Barth had no counterpart for Lenin's concept of an intermediate stage between capitalism and true socialism (the so-called 'dictatorship of the proletariat') for the simple reason that for him, a state which is established by political revolution still belongs to the old aeon. A much more apt structural parallel to Barth's vision of a 'divine world-revolution' can be found in the understanding of revolution advanced by Rosa Luxemburg, the chief theoretician of left-wing German socialism and a powerful critic of Lenin's concept of a 'dictatorship of the proletariat'. On this point, see Anzinger, *Glaube und kommunikative Praxis*, 227–8.

'Starving the state religiously' does not mean, however, that the Christian is to withdraw altogether from political life. Ascetic withdrawal cannot create the presupposition for the coming of the Kingdom; it serves merely to preserve the political *status quo*; to undergird and strengthen the forces of reaction which would preserve the existing state. And that means that the Kingdom of God is as ill-served by the 'clericalization' of life as it is by its opposite (the identification of a particular political programme as the politics of God).[189] That the state exists at all is the result of the sinfulness of humankind generally, Christian as well as non-Christian. Through ascetic withdrawal the Christian only makes herself even more responsible for the existence of the state. Therefore, it is impossible *not* to be implicated in the guilt which accrues to all political activity. In the face of the tragic fact that—under the conditions of the old aeon—it is impossible to avoid responsibility for the inherent sinfulness of political life, the Christian should simply 'sin boldly' and be actively involved in politics.

In so far as you go *your* way and remain steadfastly at *your* work [of creating the presupposition for the coming of the Kingdom], you do not need to give a thought to your necessary complicity in political events . . . In that case, your sins are forgiven—even your political sins.[190]

What then should the Christian do in the face of the burning question of the day: 'subjection' to the state or revolution against it? Barth was unwilling to exclude either alternative as a matter of Christian principle. Either might be called for, depending to a large extent on the circumstances of the moment. But for the answer to that question, the Christian must fall back on 'the ethics of the confused situation' (i.e. idealistic morality). The New Testament has nothing to say on the subject.[191] The New Testament witnesses to the fulfilment of the Law by Christ; it has nothing to say in the way of setting forth a new "Law". When "ethics" has been consulted, Barth is convinced that 'it will scarcely be possible to place yourselves anywhere else than on the most extreme left. . . . That as Christians, you are to have nothing to do with monarchy, capitalism, militarism, patriotism, and liberalism is so self-evident that I scarcely need to say it.'[192]

---

[189] Barth, *Der Römerbrief, 1919*, 517.   [190] Ibid. 510.   [191] Ibid. 495.
[192] Ibid. 508–9.

Does that mean then that the Christian should join the revolution? Not at all. Barth clearly had a great deal of sympathy with the revolutionaries. Their goals were in large measure his goals as well. He could well understand the limits of human endurance which made it exceedingly hard to avoid exchanging blow for blow with an unjust state. Sometimes the power is simply not there which would make it possible to live at peace with all men and women.[193] But he could not get around his conviction that revolution could not achieve the goals it sets for itself. In the final analysis, Barth clearly favoured doing the work of the Kingdom within the existing state. The best alternative under the circumstances is to live within the state, taking part in its life (paying taxes, engaging in party activity, even serving in the military), but as one who does not belong to it, as one for whom the state is already doomed to pass out of existence.[194]

But whichever choice is made will involve the Christian necessarily—and therefore, tragically—in sin. It is impossible to place oneself once again under the "Law" (i.e. to engage in "ethics") without setting oneself outside Christ. The chasm separating the Kingdom of God from the world, the ultimate from the penultimate, Christian hope from "ethics", is absolute. Barth's conclusion: the one thing the Christian must not do under any circumstances is to seek to justify her decision for either 'subjection' or revolution 'religiously', by appeal to divine authority.

It is at this point that Barth pressed home his critique of Ragaz. If all political action necessarily involves the Christian in sin, then it will not be possible to identify any political cause with the cause of God. To those like Ragaz who wanted to invoke divine authority for their political goals, Barth said:

You want now to overcome evil with evil. You step forth now as the people of God competing next to the peoples of the world. . . . The watchword 'God with us!' is a desired and useful weapon on the political battlefield. The figure of the military chaplain is never lacking in the picture of war . . . But all the lustre and weight of a "Christian politics" cannot deceive us with respect to the fact that precisely as such, it bears

---

[193] Ibid. 513.

[194] Ibid. 519–20. It is extremely misleading to speak of Barth's position here as 'anarchistic' as Friedrich-Wilhelm Marquardt does. See Marquardt, *Theologie und Sozialismus*, 133. No anarchist would have agreed, as Barth clearly did, that military service is an obligation that the state has a right to impose on its citizens.

the worm in itself. God is not in it, precisely *when* and *because* we want to have Him in it. In that we want to conquer with Him, evil with evil, we betray Him. In that His people step forward, competing *next to* the peoples of this world, they cease to be *His* people. . . . *Our* work, the asking after God, the struggle 'in the hiddenness of men and women' (Rom. 2: 16), the work in heaven, remains undone.[195]

If the Christian engages in political activity as one who places no 'positive'[196] (i.e. religious) valuation on it and therefore continues to devote her attention to creating the inward presupposition for the coming of the Kingdom, she will be forgiven for her political sins. But if the Christian should seek to justify her action as a "Christian" duty, there then remains no forgiveness for her. Therefore, whatever her "ethics" tell her to do, she must do:

> *but not one step further!* Civil initiative and civil obedience, but *no* combination of throne and altar, *no* Christian patriotism, *no* spirit of democratic crusade. Strike and general strike and street-fighting if it must be, but *no* religious justification and glorification of it! Military service as a soldier or officer but under *no* circumstances as military chaplain! Social-democratic, but *not* Religious Socialist! The betrayal of the gospel does *not* belong to your political obligations.[197]

In the final analysis, Barth's critique of the Religious Socialist movement was that it was engaged in a kind of 'self-divinization'. Religious Socialism rested on the supposition of a relation of continuity between divine action and human action.[198] Thus (in Barth's view), Ragaz saw the Religious Socialist movement as itself the subject whose ethical labours would bring about the Kingdom of God on earth.[199] To that extent, he had not really broken free from the bourgeois (and idealistic) self-understanding according to which the human being is the subject of history.[200] Against such a tendency, Barth wanted to stress that God and

---

[195] Barth, *Der Römerbrief, 1919*, 513–14.   [196] Ibid. 519.   [197] Ibid. 520–1.

[198] Anzinger, *Glaube und kommunikative Praxis*, 224.

[199] In the aftermath of the anti-democratic Bolshevik revolution, Ragaz felt himself forced to re-evaluate his once high evaluation of the role played by the Social Democracy in the coming of the Kingdom. '*At one time*, it was our way to recognize . . . the truth of the Kingdom of God in the Social Democracy and to endure and accept whatever was alien and false in it (even though with pain); *now* our way is to represent alone the Kingdom of God . . . Socialism must be *Religious Socialism* . . .' Ragaz, 'Neue Wege VIII: Unser Sozialismus', *Neue Wege*, 11 (1917), 612; cited by Anzinger, *Glaube und kommunikative Praxis*, 223 n. 168. It is understandable that Barth would see a kind of self-divinization at work in such a statement.

[200] Schellong, *Bürgertum und christliche Religion*, 99, 103.

God alone is the subject who brings the Kingdom and, as such, the subject of history as well. Whatever human beings may do in helping to prepare the conditions for the coming of the Kingdom has no more significance than the presence of a doctor at a delivery has for the being and existence of a child.

It has to be said that Barth's reflections on ethics belong to the weakest sections of *Romans* I. His concern to reject every *direct* identification of the will of God with any political movement or programme was laudable and necessary. To stress the distinction of the Kingdom of God from every earthly approximation of it is the only adequate safeguard against turning Christian theology into ideology. But Barth's polemical concerns had resulted in a very definite one-sidedness. In emphasizing the critical distance separating political action from the struggle for the Kingdom of God, he failed to address adequately the question of their relation. Indeed, there can be no relation where social ethics is seen as belonging to a realm in which sin is necessary and unavoidable. Where that occurs, the struggle for the Kingdom will inevitably be focused on the 'inner person', with no necessary implications for external, social behaviour. Christian hope, in that case, will have nothing to contribute to the shaping of political ethics. Certainly, Barth scarcely intended such a result. This was a person who had once excoriated Adolf von Harnack for driving a wedge between the gospel and politics. But in spite of himself, his polemical concerns had brought him to a similar point. Rather than appeal to the ethical implications of Christian hope in the Kingdom in attempting to adjudicate between conflicting ethical options in a 'confused situation', Barth abandoned the entire field to idealistic morality—so afraid was he of attempts to 'Christianize' political options.

On the other hand, in his conception of a divine 'command of the moment', the basis of the ethics he would advance at the end of the 1920s was already adumbrated. What would have to happen in the meantime for that ethic to emerge fully is that Barth would have to exchange his largely critical, negative starting-point in eschatology for a more positive starting-point in Christology. With a well-developed Christology, Barth would have a much larger and well-defined content to draw upon in his attempt to formulate the 'divine command' in specific regions of human existence. He would also have to develop a doctrine of analogy which would enable him to show clearly how divine being and action can and should give rise to a corresponding being and action on the human level without setting aside the distinction between them. In the process, the field of ethics would lose a good deal of its tragic character.

(viii) *Barth's Later Critique of Romans* I

In the second, revised version of his commentary, Barth went to great lengths to distance himself from the organological conceptuality[201] which had stood at the centre of his reflections in the first edition. In no fewer than nine passages,[202] he spoke disparagingly of his tendency to establish 'a continuous connection between God's being and our own'.[203] There can be no doubt that the language of an 'organic growth' *could*—if taken literally—suggest something of an 'organically growing divine being and having in humanity',[204] but as our analysis has shown, such a position was really never intended. Equally problematic is Barth's later reading of the doctrine of justification in *Romans* I as 'Osiandrian'.[205] It is quite true (as we have seen) that Barth's view of justification at that time stressed the effective over the forensic. In *Romans* II, such an understanding would give way to a strictly forensic view. But already in *Romans* I 'efficacy' was placed under an eschatological reservation; it was an efficacy which was regarded as belonging in every moment to the sovereign and free action of God. In no way was the power of God thought to pass over into a sphere where it could be laid hold of by a human recipient and used or applied. To call such a view 'Osiandrian' is to do the first edition a grave injustice.[206] The question which begs for an answer here is: why did Barth

---

[201] The phrase 'organological conceptuality' is Anzinger's. See Anzinger, *Glaube und kommunikative Praxis*, 246. The phrase refers to the second model of eschatology employed by Barth in *Romans* I—and does so with less danger of creating confusion than would the simple adjective "organic".

[202] A complete listing of the passages in the second edition in which criticism is advanced against the first edition can be found in Nico T. Bakker, *In der Krisis der Offenbarung: Karl Barths Hermeneutik dargestellt an seiner Römerbrief-Auslegung* (Neukirchen-Vluyn: Neukirchener Verlag, 1974), 45–8.

[203] Barth, *Der Römerbrief, 1922*, 279.   [204] Ibid. 223.

[205] Karl Barth to Eduard Thurneysen, 3 Dec. 1920, *B–Th. Br.* I. 448.

[206] For a similar conclusion, see Anzinger, *Glaube und kommunikative Praxis*, 245 n. 21.

attribute to himself in retrospect positions he had never maintained?

In all likelihood, the answer to the question is tied to the history of the reception of the first edition.[207] It did not take long for misreadings to surface in the reviews. Already in Emil Brunner's review (which was the first to appear in print), Brunner attributed to Barth the notion that there is a 'part of our souls which is not imprisoned in the temporal and finite, but has remained an undisturbed reservoir for the voice of God, undistorted by "culture" and adaptation to the world of our mere human knowing'.[208] Of course, Brunner's talk of a 'divine reservoir in us'[209] represented a serious misreading of Barth's intentions, but it has to be said that Barth deserved a good deal of the blame for it, owing to his lavish (at times incautious) use of the 'organic' and 'seed' metaphors.[210] Later reviews tended to confirm Brunner's misreading. Philipp Bachmann noted that the 'religious relationship of a human being to God . . . appears to him [Barth] with particular emphasis under the viewpoint of the *immanence* of God in the human soul'.[211] Carl Mennicke, after protesting against what he saw as an 'abstract' and 'heteronomous' God-concept in Barth, concluded that Barth's own work offered sufficient proof of the impossibility of such a starting-point. Barth everywhere proceeded in practice on the basis of an autonomous 'experience' of God—albeit, one which he had tried to place beyond the limits of psychological analysis.[212] No doubt, the awareness that he had contributed to such misunderstandings made Barth more than a little self-critical.

Be that as it may, the motivation which led Barth finally to

[207] When the decision was finally made in Oct. 1920 to revise the commentary thoroughly rather than allow it to be reprinted, Barth wrote to Thurneysen, '. . . better this delay than that the first edition . . . should continue to give occasion for misunderstandings and errors.' Karl Barth to Eduard Thurneysen, 27 Oct. 1920, *B–Th. Br.* I. 435–6.

[208] Emil Brunner, '*Der Römerbrief* von Karl Barth: Eine zeitgemäß-unmoderne Paraphrase', in Moltmann (ed.), *Anfänge der dialektischen Theologie*, 81; ET Robinson, *The Beginnings of Dialectic Theology*, 65.

[209] Ibid. 84; ET 68.

[210] That both Barth and Thurneysen saw Brunner's interpretation as resting on a misunderstanding is clear from their exchange of letters on the subject. See Karl Barth to Eduard Thurneysen, 1 Dec. 1918, *B–Th. Br.* I. 304–5; Eduard Thurneysen to Karl Barth, 8 Dec. 1918, *B–Th. Br.* I. 306–7.

[211] Bachmann, 'Der Römerbrief verdeutscht und vergegenwärtigt', 520.

[212] Carl Mennicke, 'Auseinandersetzung mit Karl Barth', *Blätter für Religiösen Sozialismus*, 1 (1920), 7.

attribute to himself positions which he had not maintained seems clear: he wanted to consign *Romans* I to oblivion and to force the public to concentrate its attention solely on the second edition. What we see emerging in Barth's critique of *Romans* I is a tendency to exaggerate the distance which separated the second edition from the first in order to acquire an independent reading for the revised version.[213] Of course, the recognition that such a tendency was at work has important consequences for interpreting Barth's development. Any attempt to assess rightly the degree of movement and advance which has taken place between one phase and the next will have to bear in mind the fact that Barth was not always a reliable guide for interpreting his earlier works—particularly those which he wished his readers to leave behind.

4. SUMMARY

The first edition of *Romans* represented Barth's first major effort at an explication of his new theology. The fundamental intention which guided him throughout was to set forth an eschatologically conditioned theological realism which would overcome every attempt to ground theology in the human subject (whether idealistic, pietistic, or Religious Socialist). He wanted to speak of a knowledge of God which is grounded in itself alone. He wanted to place God's reconciling activity in Christ beyond the reach of historical investigation, and faith beyond the reach of psychological investigation—all in the interests of theological realism.

The central category by means of which he explicated this intention was that of the 'organic' presence or immediacy of God to human knowing (or alternatively, of the new aeon to the old). The immediate presence of God, Barth clearly wanted to say, is never the secure possession of the human subject. Human beings do not 'have' God; at best, they are 'had' by Him. The relation of God to human beings is actualistic in character, constantly

---

[213] Barth's tendency to exaggerate the difference between *Romans* I and *Romans* II was given classic expression in the preface to the second edition where he claimed that the revision had been so thorough that 'no stone has been left standing on another'. Barth, *Der Römerbrief, 1922*, p. vi.

needing to be made real 'from above'. Thus, only from God's side is the relation real and possible. From the human side, it is a continual need.[214] Unfortunately, the organological conceptuality was scarcely well suited for safeguarding Barth's theological intention. It was susceptible to misunderstanding, as reviews of *Romans* I made clear. It all too easily connoted the existence of a continuous relation of God to humankind which could be taken to justify the attempt to ground theology in human subjectivity after all. But that was far from Barth's intention. Thus, the organological conceptuality was doomed from the outset to the very quick abandonment it experienced in 1920.

[214] Spieckermann, *Gotteserkenntnis*, 105.

4

Theology in a Revolutionary Age

(SAFENWIL,
NOVEMBER 1918–JANUARY 1920)

1. SOCIAL-POLITICAL FACTORS IN BARTH'S FURTHER DEVELOPMENT?

In the period of twenty-three months between November 1918 and October 1920, Barth's theology underwent a further development in that his process eschatology gradually gave way to the consistent eschatology which would stamp the second edition of his commentary on *Romans*. The question to be addressed in this chapter is this: to what extent, if any, did the turbulent social-political developments which took place in this period influence Barth's theological development? The question was first raised in a striking way by Friedrich-Wilhelm Marquardt's thesis that disappointment over the outcome of the Russian Revolution produced in Barth a 'sensational anti-revolutionary turn'[1] which resulted in a radicalization of his critique of *all* that exists (the revolutionary and not just the reactionary).[2] This move in turn expressed itself theologically in a kind of divine 'transcendentalism' which radically distinguished God from the world.[3] The notion of an 'anti-revolutionary turn', it must be said at the outset, is deeply problematic. It rests, above all, upon a failure to see the extent to which a *diastasis* in the God–world relation is already at work in *Romans* I. Barth's critique of existing orders and relations in *Romans* I was already universal in scope. In addition, there was no affirmation of the revolutionary option in the first edition. It is therefore not surprising that there is far more consistency in Barth's interpretation of Romans 13 in the two editions than Marquardt allows. But the larger question raised by

---

[1] Marquardt, *Theologie und Sozialismus*, 142.   [2] Ibid. 144.   [3] Ibid. 149–59.

the second half of Marquardt's thesis is an important one and needs to be addressed. In what follows we will be asking about the impact on Barth's further development of not only the unfolding of the Russian Revolution but of all the social and political developments of the period.

2. THE SWISS LANDESSTREIK OF NOVEMBER 1918

The end of the war in November 1918 brought in its wake tremendous political uncertainty and chaos in the countries of central Europe. The six-month period from November 1918 to May 1919 saw the establishment of the Weimar Republic in Germany, the brutal repression of the Sparticist *coup* in Berlin, and the failed attempts to establish Soviet republics in Munich and Budapest. Switzerland was not immune to such forces, though there they tended to be less revolutionary in character.

Swiss socialism was unique in kind. Although the Swiss Social-democratic Party (SP) belonged to the First and Second Internationals, its commitment to Marxist agendas was decisively moderated by the peculiarities of Swiss political history. Already the first party programme of 1870 made it clear that the conditions prevailing in Switzerland were different from those in other central European countries. It was a programme which, among other things, 'affirmed the state and its democratic institutions of referendum and initiative'.[4] Again, the second revised programme of 1888, while calling for the nationalization of trade, industry, transportation, and agriculture, made it clear that such objectives were to be achieved by democratic means, through legislation. The stated goal of the party was not the improvement of the lot of the wage-earner alone; such a goal was dismissed as too parochial. The goal, according to an appeal of January 1889, was the creation of a society of economically and politically free men and women.[5] A third revision of the party programme in 1904 again sought to adapt Marxist theory to the Swiss situation; the result was scarcely an affirmation of Marxist orthodoxy.[6]

During the war, however, the socialist movement experienced a certain radicalization. This had less to do with the influence of

---

[4] Nöthinger-Strahm, *Der Landesstreik*, 25.   [5] Ibid. 24–7.   [6] Ibid. 27.

emigrants like Lenin and Trotsky than it did with changed conditions within Switzerland itself.[7] In the first days of the war the national parliament voted to give to the *Bundesrat* (i.e. the council of seven presidents of Switzerland) 'unrestricted power for the undertaking of such measures as are required for the maintenance of the security, integrity, and neutrality of Switzerland'.[8] Such broad-based powers quickly became the tool of repression in the face of a perceived internal threat from workers and socialist agitators. In the course of the war such factory legislation as existed was largely suspended by the government in the interests of increasing productivity. Twelve-hour work-days were not uncommon for adults; child labour was widespread. The government's response to demonstrations by workers in the streets of Swiss cities was to further restrict rights to public assembly and to employ the army to disperse crowds. The deepening conflict between government and workers produced its first fatalities in November 1917, when intervention by troops in a celebration of the Bolshevik Revolution by left-wing socialists in Zurich produced a small riot. As the result of these developments the SP became increasingly critical of government policy and finally confrontational (through its advocacy of the refusal of military service).

In January 1918, in the midst of growing civil unrest over unjust social conditions, the Swiss national parliament drafted a bill which would have made all persons between the ages of 14 and 60 eligible for immediate conscription into various forms of civil service (to be decided upon by the state). In view of this further encroachment on civil liberties, the SP joined together with leaders of various trade unions to form a committee of ten members to decide upon a common response—the so-called 'Olten Action Committee'. In July, the Committee succeeded in calling together a Swiss Workers' Congress which gave the Committee the authority to call for a mass strike (including the closing-down of trains and newspapers) should the government prove unwilling to address grievances. In the autumn local strikes in Zurich were met with a decision by the government to send troops into that city. The Olten Action Committee appealed to the government to remove the troops but to no avail. On 10

---

[7] Nöthinger-Strahm, *Der Landesstreik*, 33.   [8] Ibid. 46.

November, the Committee called for a nationwide mass strike to begin on the 12th and to last until the government agreed to a nine-point list of demands which included such items as the immediate election of a new national parliament (based on a new system of proportional representation which had been accepted in October), the introduction of a forty-eight hour working week, the introduction of a national old-age and disability-insurance programme, and the right of women to vote. In response, the government refused all demands and called for an immediate cessation of the strike. The strike proceeded for the most part without bloodshed, though the atmosphere in the cities was extremely tense.

On 14 November the strike action ended by decision of the Action Committee—in spite of the fact that the government had remained steadfast in its refusal to accede to any demands. The Committee's members no doubt realized that their control over striking workers was tenuous at best and feared outbreaks of violence. Throughout the episode their actions clearly showed that they had no intention of overthrowing the government. The strike was intended to protest against an unjust economic situation and to pressure the government into legislating new economic and social programmes to alleviate the plight of workers. In spite of the tendency of government and middle-class citizens to suspect Bolshevik influence in the events, and in spite of left-wing hopes that something more than a mere protest might be in the offing, the strike was non-revolutionary in intention and conduct.[9]

In the immediate context of these events, however, it is understandable that tremendous uncertainty prevailed as to the meaning and eventual outcome of the strike action. The possibility that control of the action might pass from the organizers to more extreme groups could not be excluded. Under the circumstances, it is not surprising that the events of November 1918 were followed by Karl Barth and Eduard Thurneysen with hope and a certain amount of trepidation. In late October Thurneysen wrote to his friend,

So where does the journey go from here? Towards world Bolshevism? Only one thing is clear to me: we must think of the Kingdom of God

---

[9] Ibid. 50.

consistently as "other" and keep our hope pure from all democratic and other "preliminary stages".[10]

With that Barth certainly would have agreed. But the maintenance of the critical distinction between the unfolding of contemporary events and the movement of the Kingdom did not mean that some inner connection between the two worlds might not exist.

As the strike unfolded, however, Barth found it exceedingly difficult to see the hoped for inner connection between the two worlds.

If only we had turned to the Bible *sooner*, so that we might now have firm ground under our feet! Now one broods alternately over the newspaper and the New Testament and sees precious little of the organic connection between the two worlds, of which one ought now to be able to give clear and powerful testimony. Or is it any different for you?[11]

Thurneysen's answer was given the following Sunday in a sermon in which he tried to interpret for his parishioners the 'deeper meaning' of the *Landesstreik* and the revolutionary changes which were then under way in Germany and Russia. Thurneysen made it clear that there was indeed an organic connection between the movement of God and the revolutionary events in Switzerland, Germany, and Russia. The root cause of the turbulence of the times, he suggested, lay in a longing for a new world which had been implanted by God in the hearts of working-class men and women. This was not at all to say that the motives of those then engaged in revolutionary activities were wholly pure.

It is true that this crying of poor, tormented, unfortunate men and women often expresses itself in a stormy and unruly way. It is mixed up with a good deal of human passion and avarice. Such men and women would often like most to shatter the old world and bring in the new by force. They forget that power itself is something that should be left behind in the old house; something which has no place in the new time which we would like to see come.[12]

[10] Eduard Thurneysen to Karl Barth, 30 Oct. 1918, *B–Th. Br.* I. 299.

[11] Karl Barth to Eduard Thurneysen, 11 Nov. 1918, *B–Th. Br.* I. 300.

[12] Eduard Thurneysen, 'Die neue Zeit' (Sermon, 17 Nov. 1918), in idem, *Die neue Zeit: Predigten, 1913–1930*, ed. Wolfgang Gern (Neukirchen-Vluyn: Neukirchener Verlag, 1982), 77.

But regardless of the motives and the questionability of methods employed here and there, the root of the transformation now altering the face of Europe lay in the longing for a wholly new world—a longing which had its source in God. Given the mixed motives of the revolutionaries and the intransigence of the ruling classes, the final outcome of the changes then under way was scarcely certain. But the task of Christians was to hear the call of God in the cry of the tormented and to ready themselves for service and sacrifice in the struggle against injustice.

Thurneysen was careful throughout not to identify the strike itself (or any other revolutionary events) with the will of God, though he made it clear that he stood in solidarity with the striking workers. On the whole, the sermon was very moderate in tone, though it was not received that way by bourgeois critics. News of his 'inflammatory address'[13] spread quickly, and Thurneysen found himself denounced locally as a 'Bolshevik pastor'.[14]

It is clear from the letters exchanged between the two Aargau pastors that the events of November had filled them with great hopes. The 'saddest thing of all', Thurneysen wrote, would be to see all the uprising for which they had been waiting 'remain without "fruits of righteousness" [Heb. 12:11]'.[15] That such hopes were to be disappointed on all fronts is clear. But it is equally clear that neither Barth nor Thurneysen could have been altogether surprised by the turn which events would take in the succeeding months. For years Barth had been saying that the new world could not be built by the methods of the old. That point had been forcefully reiterated in *Romans* I and was prominent in Thurneysen's sermon as well. It is scarcely conceivable that the disappointments which came their way would have had sufficient 'shock-value' to set them in motion. And, as we shall now see, Barth's political writings of 1919 gave clear evidence that throughout that politically decisive year he was a consistent opponent of the Bolshevization of Swiss socialism.

---

[13] Eduard Thurneysen to Karl Barth, 21 Nov. 1918, *B–Th. Br.* I. 303.
[14] Eduard Thurneysen to Karl Barth, 13 Jan. 1919, *B–Th. Br.* I. 309.
[15] Eduard Thurneysen to Karl Barth, 14 Nov. 1918, *B–Th. Br.* I. 301–2.

3. POLITICAL WRITINGS OF 1919

The year 1919 was a fateful one in the history of Swiss socialism. For much of the year a heated battle was waged over the future direction of the party, centred on the question of whether to seek admission to the Third International, which was founded in Moscow in March.[16] In early February a party frustrated by the apparent failure of the *Landesstreik* and seeking more radical solutions voted to sever its relation to the old Second International at an extraordinary Congress in Bern. In mid-July the executive committee of the party voted overwhelmingly (120 to 10) to join the Third (Communist) International. The move was opposed by a small number of influential socialists who saw in it an exchange of a democratic platform for a platform dedicated to establishing a 'dictatorship of the proletariat' through civil war—but to no avail. An extraordinary Party Congress meeting on 16–17 August in Basle voted 318 to 147 for entrance into the Communist International. Final approval of the proposal, however, rested with party membership as a whole which was to be balloted in early September. Throughout the month of August a flood of pamphlets and newspaper articles appeared warning members of the consequences of the Bolshevization of the party. In a surprising turn of events, the party membership voted against the leadership and rejected the proposal by a margin of 14,612 to 8,722. For the moment, the Swiss socialist movement stood alone, without international connections.

In April of the following year, however, the executive committee proposed that the party reconsider the question with the proviso that joining be made conditional upon a recognition by the Third International of the freedom of the Swiss party to determine the tactics appropriate to its situation. The hopes of the committee were dashed, however, when the hard-liners in Moscow set forth a list of twenty-one conditions of their own for acceptance—which included the exclusion of all 'reformists' from the party, the reorganization of the party along centrist lines, the renaming of the party as the 'Communist Party', and

---

[16] For a fine summary of the crisis in Swiss socialism in 1919 and the subsequent departure of the radical left to form the Communist Party of Switzerland, see Mattmüller, *Leonhard Ragaz und der religiöse Sozialismus*, ii. 502–34.

'unqualified support of all Soviet republics in their battle against counter-revolutionary forces'.[17] Recognizing that to accede to such demands would mean the split of the Swiss party and a serious weakening of their ability to attract new members, a significant number in the executive now felt they had no choice but to oppose entry into the Third International. When the party met in Bern in December 1920 for a final decision on the issue, the proposal was rejected by a vote of 350 to 213. At that point 209 delegates marched out of the hall and reconvened in the Hotel Dupont to found the Communist Party of Switzerland.[18]

From the outset of this controversy, Barth's sympathies lay with those who wanted to remain faithful to the traditional (democratic) platform of Swiss socialism. In February, at the extraordinary Congress which dissolved the party's relation to the Second International, Fritz Platten (the Party Secretary and a close friend of Lenin's) sought to convince the delegates that the time had come to commit the party programmatically to the Leninist conception of a 'dictatorship of the proletariat'. On 11 February an article appeared in the *Neuer Freier Aargauer* by Jacques Schmid (one of the most outspoken opponents of Platten's position at the Party Congress) which was greeted by Barth and Thurneysen with enthusiastic approval.[19]

Schmid's principal argument against a dictatorship of the proletariat was that it could not work.

Let us suppose that we did set loose a violent *coup* in Switzerland . . . what would come from it? A violent collision of progressive and reactionary forces. A bloodbath whose end would be some kind of dictatorship. Let us now suppose that we were victorious, what would we have achieved? A permanent active and passive resistance by a large part of our population. Resistance would absorb our powers until we were either at our end or made the necessary concessions . . .[20]

Platten's programme would simply replace the 'militarism of the bourgeoisie under which the whole world suffered and was half destroyed' in the course of the world war with the 'militarism of the proletariat. . . . But that is not progress.' Schmid conceded

[17] Ibid. 530.   [18] Ibid. 531.
[19] Karl Barth to Eduard Thurneysen, 12 Feb. 1919, *B–Th. Br.* I. 318; Eduard Thurneysen to Karl Barth, 14 Feb. 1919, *B–Th. Br.* I. 319.
[20] Jacques Schmid, 'Am Scheideweg', *Neuer Freier Aargauer: Sozialdemokratisches Tagblatt*, 11 Feb. 1919, 1.

that in Russia, conditions were sufficiently different to justify a temporary dictatorship.

> In Russia, where a reactionary dictatorship has governed for centuries, democracy can only be achieved through the powerful suppression of the old state, i.e. through the rule of the people. There a dictatorship must prevail until the people can be trained for democracy. We in Switzerland, however, have democracy. We only have to train our working people to use their rights to their advantage.[21]

Whatever differences might exist between Russia and Switzerland, however, Schmid made it clear that he did not believe that a true socialist state could be achieved through the method of violent revolution.

A few days after Schmid's article had appeared, Barth gave a lecture to the local workers' association in which he described the Russian Revolution 'as an attempt which had to be made but was not to be imitated'. He thought it unlikely that violent revolution of the kind then under way in Russia would achieve the socialist goal of a classless society; it would result rather in the exclusive rule of the proletariat. He concluded: 'The acknowledged shortcomings of democracy are not improved by its abolition.'[22]

In July the defeat of a moderate Social-democratic candidate by a bourgeois candidate in a cantonal *Regierungsrat* election moved Barth to write an open letter to the Aargau bourgeoisie which was printed on the front page of the *Neuer Freier Aargauer*. Barth saw the election as a missed opportunity on the part of the bourgeoisie to help slow the stampede of the Social Democracy towards Bolshevism. The election of a moderate would have demonstrated a willingness on the part of the bourgeois to work together to find solutions to the social and economic crisis confronting Swiss citizens. It would have strengthened the case of moderates in the SP that democratic methods would work if given time.

> There are still many in the Social Democracy who would like to avoid the threatening development towards the left. But they cannot be expected to stem the tide alone. . . . Is it really necessary that things fol-

[21] Jacques Schmid, 'Am Scheideweg', *Neuer Freier Aargauer: Sozialdemokratisches Tagblatt*, 11 Feb. 1919, 1.
[22] Cited by Busch, *Karl Barth*, 106.

low the same course with us that they are following in Russia and Germany; that the socialist movement is not taken seriously for so long until the day comes that it denies its roots and becomes a disastrous conflagration?[23]

In August, with the Party Congress in Basle looming on the horizon, Barth wrote an impassioned appeal to delegates to reject the proposed entrance into the Communist International. Of all Barth's published political writings in this period, this article—which appeared once again on the front page of the *Neuer Freier Aargauer*—offers the fullest insight into Barth's appraisal of Bolshevism. It bears the title 'That Which Must Not Be Allowed to Happen'.

Barth's critique could scarcely have been more pointed. Bolshevism, he said, was a 'brilliant deception'; it was not true socialism. 'The revolution envisioned by socialism is no more and no less than a conversion of the entire world, a conversion of the whole of humanity. Less is nothing.'[24] Such a conversion could only come about where the knowledge of the kind of change needed was sufficiently widespread—in other words, where a democratic consensus had been achieved. In Russia however, according to all the reports he had heard, the masses had not yet matured in the knowledge needed for a true socialism to arise. In the absence of the proper conditions, the Russian Revolution offered little more than 'bold, great words and promises and petit-bourgeois deeds'. The Russian Revolution had brought many changes but in the most important sense, it had left everything as it was. Bolshevism was filled with a thirst for revenge. It had conquered evil with evil.

Precisely for this reason, Bolshevism belongs to the old and not to the new being for which humanity longs. Whoever has understood the new which must come in its essence cannot make common cause with the Bolsheviks . . . Socialism may not simply become the counterpart of capitalism, the proletariat an all-too similar successor of the bourgeoisie, the class struggle a mere fight of one beast against another. If the Social Democracy should want to return to the opponent in kind, then it will become one with it. It may then become the trump of judgement and

[23] Barth, 'Ein Wort an das aargauische Bürgertum!', *Neuer Freier Aargauer: Sozialdemokratisches Tagblatt*, 10 July 1919, 1.

[24] Karl Barth, 'Das was nicht geschehen soll', *Neuer Freier Aargauer: Sozialdemokratisches Tagblatt*, 15 August 1919, 1.

the executioner's sword on the side of Bolshevism but it will *betray* the spirit from which it lives and lose its birth-right.[25]

Barth concluded: 'Bolshevism has no future. In the knowledge of that which *does have* a future, we cannot become Bolshevists.'

It should be noted that Barth also had some critical words for developments in Germany. The Weimar Republic represented, in his view, a 'watered-down' version of socialism.[26] Barth did not attempt to justify or explain this judgement here—no doubt because his criticism of Weimar was shared by most Swiss socialists of the time. In all likelihood, his criticism of Weimar was centred in the belief that the Weimar government had been formed by 'revisionists' who had surrendered the socialist goal of a complete alteration of social and economic relations in favour of the adoption of a modified, state capitalism. Thus Barth held that Bolshevism was committed (in theory at least) to the right goal but had become bourgeois in its methods. His disagreement with Weimar on the other hand centred on the question of goals. In both cases, a betrayal of true socialism had taken place. For the sake of a true socialism, the Swiss should not follow either example.

It would be extremely misleading to speak of Barth's critique of Bolshevism as arising out of a 'utopian-anarchistic' perspective.[27] The arguments employed in this article were drawn from an arsenal common to traditionalists in the party. The stress on the idea that only those changes are truly revolutionary which entail an improvement of life for all members of society (and not just for the working classes) represented a return to party goals established in 1889. It was classical *Swiss* socialism (embodied in the party platforms of 1870, 1888, and 1904)[28] to which Karl Barth gave voice, and not utopian anarchism.

In December 1920 Barth would serve for the second time as a delegate to a Party Congress; this time, at the Congress which made the definitive break with the Communist International. Barth cast his vote against entrance and watched—more with fascination than with sadness, it has to be said—as the Bolshevik

---

[25] Karl Barth, 'Das was nicht geschehen soll', *Neuer Freier Aargauer: Sozialdemokratisches Tagblatt*, 15 August 1919, 1.

[26] Ibid.   [27] Marquardt, *Theologie und Sozialismus*, 133.

[28] See above, Ch. 4, Sect. 2.

minority marched out of the hall to found the Communist Party of Switzerland.[29]

4. THE TAMBACH LECTURE (25 SEPTEMBER 1919)

The beginnings of the Weimar Republic did not bode well for its success. The Republic was born on 9 November 1918. On that day the Kaiser abdicated the throne and Chancellor Max von Baden turned to Friedrich Ebert, the Chairman of the SPD, with the request that he form a new government. That afternoon Philipp Scheidemann (the second-ranking member of the party) declared the birth of the Republic. From its inception the Republic was plagued with opposition—initially from former comrades on the extreme left. During the course of the war, the leadership of the SPD had been deeply split over the issue of the renewal of war credits with the result that a significant number left to form a new party, the Independent Socialist Party (USPD). In addition, those on the extreme left had banded themselves together to form the so-called 'Spartacus Union', under the leadership of Rosa Luxemburg and Karl Liebknecht. It was this group that was feared most by Ebert and his colleagues. Ebert was determined that a Bolshevik-style revolution should not take place in Germany; hence he made the fateful decision (on the same day he assumed office) to give the commander-in-chief of the Supreme Army Command, General Wilhelm Groener, authority for maintaining order. Thus were the fortunes of the fledgeling Republic entrusted to a group of arch-conservative nationalists possessed of little reason to want it to succeed and whose continued support in the future could scarcely be counted upon should another alternative present itself.[30]

Ebert's fears of an attempted *coup* were well founded. On the night of 5 January the Spartacists (now calling themselves the Communist Party) launched an attempt to seize the reins of power by capturing the centre of Berlin. Within days the rebellion had been crushed. Its leaders, Karl Liebknecht and Rosa Luxemburg, were arrested on the 15th by army officers and

---

[29] Karl Barth to Eduard Thurneysen, 11 December 1920, *B–Th. Br.* I. 454.
[30] Gordon A. Craig, *Germany: 1866–1945* (Oxford: Oxford University Press, 1981), 396, 402–14.

summarily executed without benefit of a trial. Further Spartacist uprisings during February and March in Bremen, Cuxhaven, and Wilhelmshaven were suppressed just as forcibly. The mopping-up concluded in May with the conquest of Munich (where the Bavarian Republic established by Independent Socialists in November had given way to a Soviet Republic in April).

In the days and months which followed the collapse of the monarchy and the abortive German Revolution, there were not a few pastors and theologians in Germany who were looking for something new in the Church's life, something which could address the radically new situation in which the German people now found themselves. In the spring of 1919, a new journal was founded under the direction of Otto Herpel, a pastor in Hessen, and Georg Flemmig, a teacher and school rector in Schlüchtern.[31] The journal was called *Der Christliche Demokrat: Wochenblatt für das evangelische Haus* and its first number was published on 6 April. A society was also created to support the new endeavour: the 'Vereinigung der Freunde des Christlichen Demokraten'. At its first meeting it was decided to plan a gathering for later that autumn in Tambach, a small village in Thuringia. The political views of the members of this circle were fairly diverse but they were united by an interest in Religious Socialism. Given the fact that Religious Socialism was older and more established in Switzerland, it was quite natural that the planners of the conference would turn to the Swiss for speakers.

Barth was not the first choice as speaker. He was not widely known in German church circles at this time. His commentary on Romans having received little notice, those who did know of him thought of him as a follower of Ragaz. He received an invitation but decided in August not to attend. At the last minute however, Ragaz (who was to speak) decided to stay at home and devote all his energies to opposing the proposed entry of the SP into the Communist International. In late August or early September Barth was asked to take his place. A more unsuitable choice for a speaker at a Religious Socialist Conference could scarcely have been found. The people gathered at Tambach had come to hear an explanation of Religious Socialism; what they received was a sustained assault on its foundational principles.

[31] A full account of the events leading up to the Tambach Conference may be found in Marquardt, *Der Christ in der Gesellschaft, 1919–1979*, 7–24.

'The Christian in Society' was a title that was given to Barth by the planners of the conference. He immediately disarmed it of the potential that its framers no doubt saw in it. The 'Christian' in society is Christ, not ourselves. 'Christ is that in us which we are not; which is rather, Christ in us.'[32] But is Christ in us? And is He in today's society? 'We hesitate to answer do we not, and we know why we hesitate.' Christ and society appear to stand in a relation of complete and total antithesis.

The Christian—in society! How these two magnitudes fall apart! How abstractly do they stand over against one another! How strange, almost fantastic, do the great syntheses of the Epistle to the Colossians seem to us today![33]

Why should that be so? Barth's answer pointed in two directions. First, from the side of the divine, God is a living God, a Reality complete in itself and not something which can be taken in hand (a set of principles perhaps) for the renewal of society.

The divine is something whole, complete in itself, completely new and different *vis-à-vis* the world. It will not allow itself to be applied, pasted on, and accommodated. It will not allow itself to be divided and distributed precisely because it is more than religion. It will not allow itself to be employed; it wants to tear down and build up. It is whole and entire or it is not at all. Where then does the world of God have windows towards our society?[34]

God will not be used for human purposes. Every attempt to do so is doomed to failure from the outset, for God will be everything or He will be nothing. Seen in that light, all easily executed combinations like 'Christian-social', 'evangelical-social', and 'religious-social' are an ill-advised attempt to secularize Christ (to take the great divine thing in human hands) and therefore represent a betrayal of Him.[35] That is one side of the problem.

On the other side is society. Society may be full of cracks within but outwardly it too is a 'whole, complete in itself—without a window towards the Kingdom of heaven'.[36] Social life, seen in terms of the economic and political relationships which govern it, proceeds according to its own inner laws. What has the extraordinary revolutionary period taught us, Barth asked, if

---

[32] Karl Barth, 'Der Christ in der Gesellschaft', in idem, *Das Wort Gottes und die Theologie*, 34.
[33] Ibid. 35.   [34] Ibid. 36.   [35] Ibid. 35–6.   [36] Ibid. 38.

not that no matter how much the political landscape has changed, things continue much as they were? The attempt to bring society to Christ has been no more successful than the attempt to bring Christ to society.

Humanly speaking, then, it is impossible to renew society in Christ. What were Christians to do? What was their role in society? Barth made it clear that he could not and would not take the way out of the dilemma which had once been adopted by Friedrich Naumann. Naumann's later development did at least take seriously the fact that God cannot simply be 'applied' to society. But Naumann's solution had been to give in to a radicalized version of the Lutheran "two kingdoms" doctrine—the belief that the gospel has to do only with the inner life of the Christian and has little or no relevance to the problem of how society should be structured politically, economically, and so on. In Barth's view, such a 'clericalization' of the gospel would inevitably result in the betrayal of society.[37]

But Barth did have an answer to the question he had posed: where does the world of God have an opening towards society? God would not be God if the matter rested with the antithesis in which the world of God stands over against this world. There must be a way from there to here, since clearly there is no way from here to there. Everything which he had said up to this point rested upon a presupposition: namely, that in the resurrection of Jesus from the dead the history of God has cut through the history of this world at a single point, 'perpendicularly from above'.[38] The movement whose power and significance has been unveiled in the resurrection of Jesus is a divine movement. The wholly other, eternal life of God has been revealed.[39] That the resurrection was 'bodily' means that the profane world has been addressed at the very point of its subjection to the powers of death and destruction.[40] When we know this, we can no longer live as if the laws which govern social relationships have an independent validity and significance. They have already been set aside in principle. In the light of the resurrection, we can no

---

[37] Karl Barth, 'Der Christ in der Gesellschaft', in idem, *Das Wort Gottes und die Theologie*, 38.

[38] Ibid. 40.   [39] Ibid. 43.

[40] Barth describes the resurrection as the 'appearance in our bodiliness of a bodiliness which is ordered in a way *totaliter aliter* to that to which we are accustomed—more we cannot say'. Ibid. 66.

longer live under the illusion that we can overcome the world but we also know that God can and will. We live in hope of the coming Kingdom.

To the question then, what is the Christian to do in society? Barth's answer is: 'there is nothing else to do but to follow attentively the movement of *God*.'[41] To follow the movement of God means in the first instance an affirmation of the world as it is. God wishes to be known as Creator of the world and not just as its Redeemer. 'Genuine eschatology casts light backwards as well as forwards.'[42] The new thing from above is also the most original which has been forgotten and overwhelmed. In spite of the veil which now lies over the world as it is, it is possible to 'look through' existing relations, to find in them traces or analogies of original, created relations. Barth was quick to point out how easy it is, in trying to look through the world to see the Creator, to see only the creature. 'Everything transitory is *only* a parable.'[43] And the parable is not the thing itself. The result of confusing the parable with the Reality to which it points is a false affirmation of the world. But the recognition that everything existing can contain analogies to the divine means that the world is not simply to be rejected or abandoned. Flight from the world (or, alternatively, from history) is not permissible.

To follow the movement of God means, secondly, to see and understand the movement of the wholly gracious judgement of God in the present aeon. The divine movement whose significance was disclosed in the raising of Jesus from the dead continues on its way in the present as the 'hidden transcendental meaning and motor' which cuts through (again, 'perpendicularly from above'[44]) contemporary movements of protest such as the youth movement, expressionism, and above all, the Social Democracy.[45] The task of the Christian in society is to comprehend such contemporary movements in God, to seek the *hidden* meaning which lies beneath the surface. Here again, such movements are at best parables. Even where our socializing, reforming, democratizing, and rebelling intends the most fundamental and comprehensive changes possible, they still fall short of the meaning of the Kingdom of God. Here too, it is necessary to

[41] Ibid. 69.   [42] Ibid. 51.   [43] Ibid. 55.   [44] Ibid. 40.
[45] Ibid. 46, 64.

'look through' such movements to find the movement of God hidden within.

Thus, both our yes to the world and our no are born from the Yes and the No of God and point to them. But neither our yes nor our no is identical with the divine Yes and No. And that means that 'neither our rest nor our unrest in the world, as necessary as both are, can be ultimate viewpoints'.[46] Neither the affirmation of the world nor the denial of it can be allowed to become themes in their own right. But if both affirmation of the world and criticism of it are possibilities open to the Christian, then how is the Christian to know what to do in this politically explosive year of 1919? What does Barth's own attentive following of the movement of God tell him? His answer was clear: the Christian should become a responsible 'comrade *within* the *Social Democracy*, in which the problem of opposition against that which exists is posed in *our* time; in which the parable of the Kingdom of God is given'.[47] Such a step might mean involvement in 'unconditional declarations of war'. But it might also mean involvement in 'patient reform work'. Neither could be excluded in principle since neither affirmation of the world nor denial of it provided an ultimate viewpoint.

Coming as it did *after* the split between the Communist Party and the Majority Socialists in Germany, Barth's ringing declaration that the Social Democracy was *the* parable of the Kingdom of God could only be construed as a vote of confidence in the Weimar Republic—a highly qualified vote of confidence, no doubt, but a vote of confidence all the same. Barth could scarcely have been unaware of how such a statement would be taken by his audience. And, in all likelihood, he intended that his comments be understood in this way.[48] However 'watered down' the socialism represented by the Weimar government, it would seem that Barth regarded it as the best hope for Germany in the present. To be sure, a parable is not the thing itself. Affirmation did not exclude criticism. But Barth had chosen deliberately to keep such criticisms as he had to himself and in acknowledging the

---

[46] Karl Barth, 'Der Christ in der Gesellschaft', in idem, *Das Wort Gottes und die Theologie*, 65.

[47] Ibid. 64.

[48] Certainly, he regarded the Spartacist revolution as an attempt to put new wine in old wineskins. Karl Barth to Eduard Thurneysen, 12 Feb. 1919, *B–Th. Br.* I. 318.

possibility that 'patient reform work' might be called for, he had extended an olive branch to the 'reformists'. The Tambach lecture shows Barth at this crucial juncture in the political history of Germany to be a *Vernunftrepublikaner* of the left-wing variety.

Judged from the standpoint of its significance for an understanding of Barth's theological development, the Tambach lecture showed that Barth's thought was in transition, though he had clearly not yet departed from the conception of eschatology which had governed *Romans* I. In spite of the fact that talk of an 'organic connection' between the world of God and our world had disappeared, the conception to which it testified remained. Barth could still say, for example, that 'It is precisely the wholly otherness of God . . . which drives us with compelling power to be on the look-out on our side for a root-like, principled, original connection of our life with that wholly other Life.'[49] He could still speak of 'our soul awakening to an awareness of its immediacy to God'. 'This awakening of the soul is the movement in which we stand, the movement of the history of God or of the knowledge of God, the movement in life to Life.'[50] He could still insist that the Kingdom of God wills to 'break forth' out of this world.[51] In spite of the pronounced emphasis on the diastatic relation of God and the world, knowledge of God had yet to become problematic in the way it would in the phase of *Romans* II. And so he could assert with an almost undialectical sense of assurance: 'We do know God'.[52]

What *is* new is the greater emphasis on the notion of analogy, which testifies to the fact that Barth's realism is by now making itself felt in a more consistent way in his ethics. Gone is the appeal to idealistic ethics in the 'confused situation'. In its place is the suggestion that certain events and movements stand in a clear analogical relation to the movement of the Kingdom of God. Such a relation has its ground in the divine action; there is no way which leads from here to there, no 'continuity which leads from the analogies into the divine reality'.[53] The movement

---

[49] Barth, 'Der Christ in der Gesellschaft', 43.   [50] Ibid. 44–5.

[51] Ibid. 63. Barth's rejection of the thought of an 'objective, developmentally conceived transition' from analogies of the Kingdom to the thing itself (p. 66) in no way entails a turning-against 'the eschatology of the hidden growth of the Kingdom' as Michael Beintker has argued. See Beintker, *Die Dialektik in der 'dialektischen Theologie' Karl Barths*, 118.

[52] Ibid. 49.   [53] Ibid. 66.

always proceeds 'from above to below, never the reverse'.[54] Therefore, our yes to the world should conform to the divine Yes; our no to the divine No. Although the conception of analogy which emerges here is still rudimentary, it has in it some of the essential features of the later *analogia fidei*. Such progress as has occurred in Barth's ethics, however, only made them more consistent with the theological perspective advanced in *Romans* I. The shift to the thoroughgoing eschatology which would govern *Romans* II still lay in the future.[55]

5. CONCLUSION

It would be foolish to suggest that the political developments of 1918 and 1919 had no influence whatsoever on the theological development which occurred between the two editions of *Romans*. Barth's frustration at his inability to discern an organic connection between the world of God and the events of November 1918 has been noted. That the events of November did not produce much in the way of 'fruits of righteousness' had to be disappointing to him. And yet the evidence which has emerged in the preceding pages argues against overestimating the significance of political events on Barth's abandonment of the organological model. Barth never gave any indication that he expected much from explosions like the Russian Revolution; in fact, just the opposite is the case. He believed that the masses in Russia were not ready for revolutionary changes, and that in such a situation, the so-called 'revolutionary deeds' of the Bolsheviks were in fact only a 'petit-bourgeois' rebellion—a mere exchange of government personnel and not the kind of

[54] Barth, 'Der Christ in der Gesellschaft', 67.

[55] The view that Barth's emphasis in this lecture on the wholly otherness of God and His Kingdom marks a decisive step away from the theology of *Romans* I has always found adherents. Hans Frei and George Hunsinger see in such an emphasis the 'beginning of Barth's break' with the organological model of eschatology. See Hunsinger, *Karl Barth and Radical Politics*, 210–11; cf. Frei, 'The Doctrine of Revelation in the Thought of Karl Barth', 497. In fact, however, a stress on wholly otherness or *diastasis* cannot of itself be made the decisive criterion for establishing the shift between *Romans* I and II since such a stress was contained from the outset in the divine realism which governed the first edition. What is decisive is the model used to explicate that wholly otherness; the shift is from a process eschatology to a consistent (i.e. radically futurist) eschatology. But that shift has yet to occur.

radical change for which he was looking. Most decisive is the fact that even after coming to the conclusion that Bolshevism had no future, he could still present a theology at Tambach that was stamped by the eschatology of *Romans* I. No, the political upheavals of 1918 and 1919 and their consequences were at most *a* contributing factor in leading to Barth's further development. More decisive was his reaction to reviews of his commentary (which showed him how easily his organological model of eschatology could be misunderstood) and the influence (as we shall now see) of Franz Overbeck, Heinrich Barth, and Søren Kierkegaard.

PART II

Dialectical Theology in the Shadow of a Consistent Eschatology

(SAFENWIL AND GÖTTINGEN, JANUARY 1920—MAY 1924)

It was because of the external and internal situation of those years that the divine No of judgement . . . had to be expressed more loudly and, in any case, heard more clearly, than the gracious Yes that we now thought ourselves to hear from the end—the real end—of all things and wanted to bring to expression. The subject-matter could, in the antithetical *form* in which it was initially presented, be brought without injustice into connection with the spiritual shattering which European men and women experienced as a result of the World War; being passionately greeted by some as an expression of the spirit of the time and just as powerfully rejected by others who were less open to this spirit, as a 'post-war phenomenon'. Furthermore, this impression was not so bad and could, with time, be corrected. What was dangerous was the subject-matter itself. Precisely because we were more consistent and proceeded more purely than our predecessors, we were well on the way to just as systematic a reduction of the eternity of God to the denominator of post-temporality—the eternally future—as the Reformers had to that of pre-temporality and the neo-Protestants to that of supra-temporality. In that we sought to free ourselves from those earlier one-sidednesses . . . we came upon the best way of making ourselves guilty of a new one-sidedness . . . And so it came about that we did not know how to speak of the post-temporality of God in such a way as to make clear what we really meant: that we wished to speak of God and not somehow of the general concept of the limit and the crisis.

(Karl Barth, *Kirchliche Dogmatik*, II/1, 715–16)

5

Shift to a Consistent Eschatology

(SAFENWIL,
JANUARY 1920–OCTOBER 1920)

I. THE FUNDAMENTAL PROBLEM ADDRESSED IN ROMANS II AND ITS SOLUTION

The fundamental problem being addressed by Barth throughout the phase of *Romans* II can be expressed in a variety of equally valid ways. The problem was this: how can God make Himself known to human beings without ceasing—at any point in the process of Self-communication—to be the *Subject* of revelation? That the knowledge of God given in revelation was a problem at all was, in Barth's view, because of two factors: the limits of human knowing on the one side, and divine election on the other. The way in which Barth conceived of the first half of this problem throughout this phase reflected his view that human knowledge is possible only where there is "intuitable" empirical data.[1] If God is to be known by humans, God must somehow make Himself to be "objective" to the human knower; He must place Himself within the range of "objects" which can be intuited by human beings. But how could God become an "object" of human intuition without making Himself subject to the control (the disposition, the management) of the human knowing apparatus? How could God be known by human beings without ceasing to be God, to be the master of the relation between God

[1] As will be indicated in this chapter, this understanding represented an important deviation from neo-Kantian epistemology—a turn in the direction of a more classically Kantian view. Whether Barth himself was fully conscious of this deviation or not is impossible to determine. At no point during this phase did he give himself over to the task of sustained and rigorous *philosophical* reflection upon problems of epistemology. The shift which occurred in his philosophical *point of view*—it was never more than that—was the consequence of his concentration on the *theological* problem of the knowledge of God.

and humankind? How can 'God be God'—not only before revelation, but during and after it?[2] That is one side of the problem.
The other side is constituted by the fact of divine election.[3] God
is only known by human beings living in history where and
when He chooses to be known; where and when the resistance
of sinful human beings against the knowledge of God is overcome by a sovereign and gracious act of God. Seen from both
angles, the problem is finally the same. It is the problem of *the
divine Subjectivity in revelation.*

Strictly speaking, this was not a new problem in this phase. It
had been implicit in Barth's turn to the 'wholly otherness' of
God (theological objectivism) from 1915 on. But there was a
precision now in the way it was formulated which had been
lacking in the phase of *Romans* I. The misreadings to which the
first edition had been subjected had taught Barth how easily a
knowledge of God which took its starting-point in God could be
transformed—in the process of knowing—into a thinking from a
starting-point in the human knower (Osiandrianism). Barth's
intention was still the same, but now the model of explication
was different. Barth abandoned the process eschatology of
Romans I in favour of a radically futurist 'consistent' eschatology
according to which the Kingdom of God is understood as that
which brings about 'the dissolution of all things, the cessation of
all becoming, the passing away of this world's time'.[4] '*Ein Denken
von Gott aus*' became—in the phase of *Romans* II—'*ein Denken
von Eschatologie aus*'. Thus, that which is most fundamental in the
shift which occurred between the two editions of *Romans* was
the exchange of one model of eschatology for another.

To put it this way is also to suggest that the common practice
of reserving the phrase "dialectical theology" for speaking of
Barth's theology in the phase of *Romans* II is misleading in the
extreme. Barth's theology was already dialectical in the phase of
Romans I (though certainly the fundamental contours of the
dialectics in question would be altered as a result of the shift in
eschatology). Michael Beintker is therefore both right and wrong

---

[2] Cf. in relation to this formulation of the problem Eberhard Busch, *Karl Barth und die
Pietisten*, 93.

[3] On this point, see esp. Barth's 1920 address to the Aarau Student Conference,
'Biblische Fragen, Einsichten und Ausblicke', in idem, *Das Wort Gottes und die Theologie*,
74.

[4] Ibid. 88.

when he says: 'Under the sign of eschatology, an everywhere tangible de-historicization of the salvation event was carried out in *Romans* II . . . Herein lies the real break between the two commentaries on *Romans*, which is also the reason why *Romans* I cannot be assigned to Barth's dialectical theology.'[5] Beintker is right to this extent: the change in eschatological models is what is truly fundamental to the shift between the two books. But if that is the case, why should the basic terminology used to describe the two phases in question not give immediate and clear expression to that judgement? Surely, the practice of reserving the term "dialectical theology" for the phase of *Romans* II only perpetuates the long-standing misreading of *Romans* I; worse still (because it has implications for how we speak of Barth's theology after the phase of *Romans* II) it privileges the dialectics of *Romans* II as though they alone are worthy of the name. In my judgement, the terminology employed to depict the various phases of Barth's development should seek to capture that which is most characteristic of the phase in question, as measured by the other phases.

Hence, the phases of *Romans* I and *Romans* II will be most accurately described by employing the terminology chosen here: 'dialectical theology in the shadow of a process eschatology' and 'dialectical theology in the shadow of a consistent eschatology'. In both phases the basic intention is the same: to speak of a presence of God (revelation, the Kingdom of God, the new humanity, etc.) *in* history in such a way as to make it clear that these realities are not *of* history.

2. THEOLOGY OF CRISIS OR THE CRISIS OF THEOLOGY?

It did not take long for critics of Barth's second commentary on Romans to dismiss it as a typical production of the period of crisis following the end of the war. On the surface, such a judgement is readily understandable. The category of "crisis" plays a very large role in *Romans* II—in sharp contrast to the preceding volume where it appeared only once.[6] Nevertheless, the

---

[5] Beintker, *Die Dialektik in der 'dialektischen Theologie' Karl Barths*, 44.

[6] Barth, *Der Römerbrief, 1919*, 441. It is important to note, however, that though the note of crisis is exceedingly rare in *Romans* I, the single use of the term makes it clear that it bears the same force and significance as it does in the second edition. Barth speaks in

depiction of the theology of the second edition of *Romans* as a 'theology of crisis' was arrived at much too quickly; it rests upon a superficial reading of the book.

The post-war period was indeed a time of pronounced cultural crisis in Germany. As devastating as the war had been in human and material terms (1.8 million Germans dead, 4 million wounded, the economy in ruins), the spiritual crisis produced by the loss of the war was even more shattering. For the vast majority of Germans, the war had not been viewed simply in military terms but as a clash of two distinct and—for the popular imagination—mutually exclusive world-views: the materialism of the democratic West versus the spirituality and historical mission of monarchical Germany. This was no new ideology, developed for the sake of its propaganda value during the war. Nineteenth-century textbooks of German history had taught students an elaborate historical mythology according to which (in one of its leading examples) human history had seen a succession of four great cultures: the Jewish, the Greek, the Roman, and the German.

Because of their virtues, excellences, and piety the German peoples became the 'vessel destined by God for the pure conservation of His truth. For the Jews and Greeks and Romans were enfeebled by their material nature (sensuality) and vices' . . . The picture of the German arose which, through mildness, earnestness, inwardness, depth, and devout nature, distinguished itself from the Western way of thinking which is characterized by critical reason, an analytic temperament, the tendency to tear down, the passion for destruction.[7]

Given the historical mission of the German people, it was inconceivable to most that Germany would lose the war. And so it was precisely this national conviction of a God-given destiny which

made the defeat a spiritual problem of the first rank, which exceeded its immediate political consequences. For its acknowledgement meant at

---

Romans I of the 'crisis . . . in which all men and women of all classes stand again and again before God'. "Crisis" is here used to describe the situation of all men and women when placed under the judgement of God. "Crisis" is thus descriptive of a *permanent* and *universal* feature of the human condition and *not* a temporary and provisional judgement of God on a particular culture.

[7] Klaus Scholder, 'Neuere deutsche Geschichte und protestantische Theologie: Aspekte und Fragen', *Evangelische Theologie*, 23 (1963), 529. Scholder is here quoting from a textbook of history by Friedrich Kohlrausch, *Kurze Darstellung der deutschen Geschichte*, 1822. The book was widely used in German schools in the 19th c. and by the 1890s was in its 15th edition.

the same time the acknowledgement of the superiority of "Western thinking" over German ideology; its revision in favour of an approximation of the old humanistic-natural law traditions of the West. The older generation of bourgeois-liberals, men like Ernst Troeltsch, Friedrich Meinecke, Hugo Preuß, Max Weber, Friedrich Naumann, and not least Thomas Mann, were ready to go this bitter way.[8]

But many in the younger generation were not. They came to view the war as only a 'stage in the epoch of world-historical transformation . . . Its loss was only a sign that the "German idea" was not yet pure, had not yet been worked out radically enough.'[9] It is easy to see with hindsight where such ideas led. From whatever political direction one viewed post-war realities, however, it was clear to all that German culture had entered a stage of crisis.

In light of these observations, it is logical to ask to what extent (if any) Karl Barth's shift from the process eschatological model which had stamped *Romans* I to the consistent eschatology of *Romans* II was a reflex of the cultural crisis through which German-speaking peoples were then passing. The question is a complex one and must be handled with care. Certainly, language like that of "crisis" would not have been chosen and given the prominence it was in *Romans* II had it not enjoyed a wide degree of usage in the culture of the time. And there can be little doubt that there were many at the time who heard in Barth's talk of "crisis" a direct reference to the cultural crisis through which Europe was then passing; and in his talk of divine judgement a direct criticism of contemporary political and cultural forms. But when it is remembered that Barth displayed a marked tendency throughout his life to use borrowed categories in a way that was entirely peculiar to himself (and which often contradicted the intentions of those who originally coined them), we will be

---

[8] Ibid. 516. Progressive liberals like Troeltsch had hoped before the war for some kind of synthesis of Western democratic ways with the more authoritarian parliamentary monarchicalism of Germany (a so-called German *Sonderweg*). It was only during the revolution of 1918/19 that Troeltsch became an unqualified supporter of parliamentary democracy. Cf. Wolfgang J. Mommsen, 'Deutschland und Westeuropa: Krise und Neuorientierung der Deutschen in Übergang vom Kaiserreich zur Weimarer Republik', in Horst Renz and Friedrich Wilhelm Graf (eds.), *Umstrittene Moderne: Die Zukunft der Neuzeit im Urteil der Epoche Ernst Troeltschs* (Gütersloh: Gütersloher Verlagshaus Gerd Mohn, 1987), 120.

[9] Ibid.

warned against a too hasty identification of the crisis which Barth's theology had in view at this time with the then contemporary cultural crisis.

A close examination of central texts in *Romans* II reveals a careful attempt to subject the term "crisis" to a searching *theological* criticism; to strip it of every hint of historical particularity (as a term descriptive of contemporary cultural conditions) in order then to employ it to speak of the result of the dialectic of judgement and grace disclosed and made real in the event of revelation. In so far as an individual recognizes in the cross of Christ the word of divine judgement, she is placed in crisis. She knows herself to be judged, rejected, reprobate. But to precisely the extent that she understands this word of judgement *in the light of the resurrection of Christ*, she knows herself also to be elect. She knows herself to be placed in the dialectic of reprobation and election, of judgement and grace. Such a crisis is not realized once and for all time in a single event in the life of an individual. It is realized anew with each fresh hearing of the Word of God in the cross and resurrection of Christ. It is thus a permanent crisis. Barth employs the 'permanent dialectic of time and eternity' in *Romans* II in order to bear witness to this theological dialectic.

The crisis of which Barth speaks in *Romans* II is not only permanent; it is also universal in scope. It is not to be limited to the experience of the individual. The whole of creaturely reality is placed in crisis by the Self-revelation of God in the cross and the resurrection. God Himself is the 'absolute crisis . . . for the world of humankind, time, and things'.[10] Because God is the absolute crisis of *all* creaturely reality, no particular event or historical situation may be directly identified with the Word of God.[11]

Thus, although Barth took more than a passing interest in the crisis of European culture, this was not the crisis which he had in mind in *Romans* II. And really, this should not be surprising. He

---

[10] Barth, *Der Römerbrief, 1922*, 51.

[11] For a more thorough discussion of the use of the category "crisis" in *Romans* II, see Ruschke, *Entstehung und Ausführung der Diastasentheologie*, 192–204. Ruschke's conclusion is worth noting: 'God reveals Himself in Jesus Christ as crisis for humankind—and indeed, not as one crisis alongside others, but rather as the one crisis from which the whole of human life experiences a critical transvaluation. Crisis in *Romans* II comprehends the knowledge of the diastasis in Jesus Christ as well as the knowledge of the overcoming of the diastasis through Jesus Christ. Crisis for Barth in *Romans* II is thus a strictly Christological category!' (p. 194). The point here is that "crisis" is used by Barth to describe a theological subject-matter, and not a cultural state of affairs.

was, after all, Swiss; he could not be traumatized by the defeat of Germany in the way German theologians were. Besides, as we have already seen, from the earliest days of the war, Barth argued for a position of inward neutrality. He was not a supporter of the German cause.[12] Because that was so, he was largely immunized against shock generated by German defeat. In truth, the contemporary cultural crisis remained on the periphery of Barth's reflections; it was not central. From the earliest days of their association, this distinguished him from a fellow-traveller like Friedrich Gogarten, though this difference was rarely, if ever, appreciated by contemporary onlookers.

For Gogarten, the cultural crisis had a special significance. In his famous essay, 'Zwischen den Zeiten', whose title was to provide the name for the journal of dialectical theology just two years later, Gogarten wrote to the Friends of the *Christliche Welt*:

Today, we see your world passing away. As to that which concerns this decline ['Untergang'], we can be as tranquil about it as if we had seen something perish to which we were not at all bound. . . . We do not wish to lift a finger to stop [this dissolution]. What would we be stopping in that case? And how should we do it? All these things have for some time been destroyed. . . . You may not demand from us that we stem this decline. . . . We are only happy about this decline for one does not like to live among corpses.[13]

The use of the word *Untergang* was a deliberate allusion to the dark, pessimistic brooding of Oswald Spengler in his *Der Untergang des Abendlandes* ('The Decline of the West').[14] Gogarten confirmed this when he went on to say, 'Therefore, we rejoice in Spengler's book. It proves, whether it is correct in the details or not, that the hour is here when this fine, intelligent culture discovers out of its intelligence, the worm in itself and when the trust in development and culture receives the death-blow. . . . Today is the hour of decline.'[15]

---

[12] See above, Ch. 2, sect. 3.

[13] Friedrich Gogarten, 'Zwischen den Zeiten', in Jürgen Moltmann (ed.), *Anfänge der dialektischen Theologie* (Munich: Chr. Kaiser Verlag, 1963), ii. 96–7; ET 'Between the Times', in Robinson (ed.), *The Beginnings of Dialectic Theology*, 278–9.

[14] Oswald Spengler, *Der Untergang des Abendlandes: Umrisse einer Morphologie der Weltgeschichte*, i. *Gestalt und Wirklichkeit* (Munich: C. H. Beck'sche Verlagsbuchhandlung, 1918).

[15] Gogarten, 'Zwischen den Zeiten', 98–9; ET 'Between the Times', 280.

In Barth's writings, there was no jubilation over the end of an epoch. In fact, he was not at all convinced that the previous cultural epoch had come to an end. Significantly, he felt nothing but antipathy for Spengler's book.[16] Nor was he at all inclined to pronounce an absolute, definitive word of judgement on culture. As he had noted at Tambach, neither culture-affirmation *nor culture-denial* can be absolute viewpoints.[17] Neither are to be directly identified with the Word of God. God's No of judgement is not to be confused with the human no to theology and culture which occurs in times of crisis. Where such confusion occurs, the result is an ideological binding of the Word of God which (though negative in character) is no less dangerous than the positive ideological binding of the Word which occurred throughout European theology in August 1914.[18] A critique of culture can at best have a parabolic significance; it can bear witness to the judgement of God. But the two are not to be identified.

If ever Barth had been tempted to advance a "theology of crisis", it had been in the period of approximately twelve months between August 1914 and August 1915.[19] During that period,

---

[16] Karl Barth to Eduard Thurneysen, 4 July 1920, *B–Th. Br.* I. 404: 'In Basle, I also read the introduction to Spengler's *Untergang des Abendlandes*—with displeasure and antipathy for this quick, insolent speaking about everything and everyone.' See also Barth's locus on "Providence" in the Göttingen Dogmatics, where he rues the fact that the category of fate has recently been brought back into theology by way of Spengler. Barth, '*Unterricht in der christlichen Religion*', ii. 251.

[17] See above, Ch. 4 n. 46.

[18] The categories 'positive ideological binding' and 'negative ideological binding' have been borrowed from Klaus Scholder. Scholder's judgement on the relation of Barth and Gogarten as "theologians of crisis" is worth quoting *in extenso*. 'But the question is whether, in this struggle against every ideological binding of the Word of God, a new ideology, namely the ideology of crisis, has not come in through the back door, so to speak. The question is appropriate in special measure for Gogarten. That fundamental principle of dialectical theology, that the Word of God in the freedom of its judging and redeeming power, means the crisis of all cultures and ideologies—this principle is under no circumstances reversible. That means: the Word of God as the Word of judgement and grace can be inferred from no historical situation, be it experienced as ever so deeply critical. It is God's Word alone which can effect the crisis. And in view of this crisis, all crises of world history are equally important or unimportant, equally significant or insignificant. Where this relation is reversed, there talk of the Word of God as the crisis of culture becomes an ideology. There the positive ideological bindings of the Word of God—Christian culture, Christian state, Christian morality, etc.—are only replaced by a negative ideological binding; in the place of the absolute Yes steps the absolute No. The essay "Zwischen den Zeiten" proclaims this absolute No.' Scholder, 'Neuere deutsche Geschichte und protestantische Theologie', 520.

[19] This point has been cogently argued by Ruschke, *Entstehung und Ausführung der*

Barth's sermons showed that he regarded the war as itself the Word of divine judgement—a form of negative natural theology. But with the recognition that he and Thurneysen (as Religious Socialists) did not 'represent' the Kingdom with their opposition to prevailing tendencies and developments,[20] he was never again inclined to see in his own criticism of theology and culture a mediation of the judgement of God. For the Barth of both the first and second editions of *Romans*, human criticism can have, at best, a parabolic significance. It can point beyond itself to the criticism which God has brought against creaturely reality in the event of the cross (though it must immediately be added that it can do so only for those who have already recognized the divine criticism of creaturely reality in the cross). But human criticism does not mediate divine criticism.[21] And that means that it can never be absolutized.

Barth's theology in the phase of *Romans* II was not a "theology *of* crisis"—that is, it did not see in the crises of the time a mediation of the Word of divine judgement. Rather it was a theology *to* and *for* a time of crisis in this specific sense: it was a theology which sought to redirect the attention of his readers from the

Diastasentheologie, 198–204. Ruschke analyses Barth's references to the Great War in *Romans* II and concludes that whereas Barth had been inclined in late 1914 to see the war as itself a revelation of the divine Word of judgement, in 1922 he treated the war under the heading of *Hinweis*—a "witness" to the revelation of judgement. See esp. p. 202.

[20] See above, Ch. 2 n. 116.

[21] The distinction employed here between the two figures 'mediation' and 'parable' has been drawn from Hartmut Ruddies' fascinating essay on Barth's relationship to so-called "Culture Protestantism". Ruddies argues (convincingly) that Barth was not opposed to "Culture Protestantism" *per se*. Rather, he was opposed to a specific form of it; viz. the kind of "mediating theology" which was expressed in an Ernst Troeltsch. Ruddies holds that Barth saw in attempts at mediation like Troeltsch's the assimilation and adaptation of the gospel to the demands of already existing cultural forms. But the rejection of such a "theology of mediation" did not mean that theology had no cultural task whatsoever. Theology in every age has the responsibility of finding and affirming parabolic patterns and structures in culture and society. In this way, theology shows its contemporary relevance (that it is a word directed to this hour and not to some other). See Hartmut Ruddies, 'Karl Barth im Kulturprotestantismus: Eine theologische Problemanzeige', in Dietrich Korsch and H. Ruddies (eds.), *Wahrheit und Versöhnung: Theologische und philosophische Beiträge zur Gotteslehre* (Gütersloh: Gütersloher Verlagshaus Gerd Mohn, 1989), 193–231. The only point I would add is that the source of Barth's difference from Troeltsch lay in his Reformed understanding of the priority of gospel over law—an understanding which (as Michael Beintker has shown) had already established itself in the crisis-motif which was so prominent in the phase of *Romans* II. See Beintker, 'Krisis und Gnade: Zur theologischen Deutung der Dialektik beim frühen Barth', *Evangelische Theologie*, 46 (1986), 442–56.

crises of the present to *the* crisis in whose light alone one might try to make sense of contemporary events. The political and cultural crises of 1918–20 cannot be made the source of the shift which took place between the two editions of *Romans*. For the influences which helped to produce Barth's new consistent eschatology, we shall have to look elsewhere.

3. FACTORS CONTRIBUTING TO BARTH'S FURTHER DEVELOPMENT (1919–1920)

In an oft-cited passage from the Preface to the second edition of *Romans*, Barth spoke of four factors which had led to 'further movement and a change of fronts'. Listed in the order in which Barth gave them, they are: 1. further study of Paul; 2. encounter with the posthumous writings of Franz Overbeck; 3. 'better instruction concerning the real orientation of the thought of Plato and Kant which I owe to the writings of my brother, Heinrich Barth; and increased attention to that which is to be gained for understanding the New Testament from Kierkegaard and Dostoevsky, in whose case the tips given to me by Eduard Thurneysen have been particularly illuminating'; and 4. the reception which the first edition found in reviews.[22] Careful study of all the possible influences on Barth's development in this phase (political, cultural, and theological) has convinced me that Barth understood himself quite well at this point; these are indeed the factors which contributed most to his abandonment of the eschatology of *Romans* I in favour of a more consistent eschatology. The most interesting question raised by this list is that of the relative weight to be assigned to each factor. In the English-speaking world especially, the prevailing assumption has long been that Søren Kierkegaard was the dominant influence leading to the changes introduced into the second edition.[23] European researchers were divided on the question until fairly

---

[22] Barth, *Der Römerbrief, 1922*, p. vii.

[23] T. F. Torrance's conclusion was typical: 'Theologically and philosophically it was undoubtedly Kierkegaard who had the greatest impact upon him [Barth], far greater than the actual mentioning of his name, in the *Romans*, for example, indicates.' Torrance, *Karl Barth: An Introduction to his Early Theology, 1910–1931*, 44.

recently.[24] A significant group of scholars working in the field of "early Barth" research have concluded that Kierkegaard's contribution, while not insignificant, was of much more limited value than was once thought.[25] Michael Beintker believes that the order in which Barth presented his influences was not accidental; the ordering was intended to attribute a priority of importance to the influence of Plato and Kant (as mediated by Heinrich Barth) over that of Kierkegaard.[26] Whether Beintker is right about Barth's intentions or not, the substantive point is correct: the influence of Heinrich Barth and Franz Overbeck was more important than that of the Danish philosopher. Kierkegaard's role was limited to strengthening Barth's commitment to certain modes of thought whose real origin lay in the influence of the distinctive form of neo-Kantianism elaborated by Barth's philosopher brother Heinrich in the years immediately following the war, and to providing him with a number of categories which (once they had been transformed for Barth's strictly theological purposes!) could be employed in clarifying a point of view which would, for the most part, have been complete without them. In what follows, the influences which led to the consistent eschatology of the second *Romans* will be treated in the

---

[24] Among those who questioned the predominance of Kierkegaard's influence were Henri Bouillard, *Karl Barth*, i. *Genèse et évolution de la théologie dialectique* (Aubier: Editions Montaigne, 1957), 107; and Gerhard Sauter, 'Die "dialektische Theologie" und das Problem der Dialektik in der Theologie', in idem, *Erwartung und Erfahrung: Predigten, Vorträge und Aufsätze* (Munich: Chr. Kaiser Verlag, 1972), 126. Those who wished to maintain the traditional view included Bakker, *In der Krisis der Offenbarung*, 94–100; and Jüngel, 'Von der Dialektik zur Analogie', in idem, *Barth-Studien*, 127–79.

[25] See e.g. Busch, *Karl Barth und die Pietisten*, 83; Spieckermann, *Gotteserkenntnis*, 109 ff.; Ruschke, *Entstehung und Ausführung der Diastasentheologie*, 111–47; and Beintker, *Die Dialektik in der 'dialektischen Theologie' Karl Barths*, 222–38.

[26] Beintker, *Die Dialektik in der 'dialektischen Theologie' Karl Barths*, 231. It should be noted that when Barth returned, just six years later, to the subject of the stimuli which provoked him to the revision of the first edition, his ordering of his influences was precisely the same. But significantly, he now added that he only became acquainted with Kierkegaard at that time '*in gewisser Auswahl*'—i.e. selectively. 'The greeting of more than one of these people who were hungry for reality caught me by surprise, and caused me to raise the question of the biblical meaning of the Kingdom of God a second time, stimulated by the posthumous publications of Overbeck; by a Kant who was understood in a new way from the side of Plato (with the help of my youngest brother who is a *Privatdozent* in philosophy in Basle); [and] by Kierkegaard and Dostoevsky, who were understood initially by means of a certain selection.' See Barth, 'Autobiographische Skizzen Karl Barths aus den Fakultätsalben der Ev.-Theol. Fakultät in Münster (1927)', in *B–B Br.* 308.

chronological order in which they made their impression upon Barth's mind, seeking to assess their importance as we go.

(i) *Heinrich Barth (1890–1965)*

Like his older brothers Karl and Peter, Heinrich ('Heiner') Barth was educated at the University of Bern, where he completed his doctoral studies in philosophy in 1913. And like his brothers, he too made his way to Marburg during the course of his studies, where he became a committed (albeit critical) follower of the Marburg neo-Kantianism of Hermann Cohen and Paul Natorp. His 1913 dissertation, 'Descartes' Begründung der Erkenntnis', showed his strong attachment to that school, but also his intention to move beyond it at a crucial point: the status of the Cohenian category of the *Ursprung* ('Origin').[27]

For Cohen, of course, human cognition was not understood to represent external reality; rather, "reality" is itself the product of the knowing process. The primary usage of the category of the *Ursprung* in Cohen's hands was that of stressing that 'pure thinking autonomously generates knowledge and being from its own inner resources. Thought needs nothing in the way of fuel for its dynamism, nor does it require any pre-existing matter as raw material for its creations.'[28] Thus, human thinking is rooted and grounded in itself, in the structure of human subjectivity. In his dissertation Heinrich Barth traced the historical roots of this grounding of human knowing back to the modern turn to the subject which took place in Descartes. The problem with the Cartesian *cogito*, in his view, is that it is incapable of grounding itself. What was required was a more original grounding of the subject and its objects in a non-given, absolutely superior, objective Reality which is 'fundamentally removed from the psychological sphere; indeed, from the given reality generally'.[29] It was in the turn to this wholly transcendent Reality—a Reality which Barth as a Christian philosopher did not hesitate to name 'God'—that philosophy would truly become "critical". For only the concept of God was capable of grounding the objectivity and

---

[27] Heinrich Barth, *Descartes' Begründung der Erkenntnis* (Bern: Akademische Buchhandlung von Max Drechsel, 1913).

[28] Fisher, *Revelatory Positivism?*, 41.

[29] Barth, *Descartes' Begründung der Erkenntnis*, 80.

power which belong to the concept of pure knowing. What Barth had done, in effect, was to take Cohen's category of the *Ursprung* and project its properties and functions on to an objectively real divine being.[30]

It should be noted that the anchoring of knowledge in a non-given, transcendent Reality also meant that Barth's version of neo-Kantianism was free of the positivistic tendencies which surrounded the Marburg school. Simon Fisher was not wrong to see in Cohen's epistemology an attempt to provide a philosophical grounding for the (then current) view of science in accordance with which 'scientific knowing . . . begins with basic mathematical-type principles which need to be posited before any research can commence.'[31] Cohen's understanding of the *Ursprung* was thus adapted to and modelled upon a positivistically conceived science. But Fisher would have done well to pay attention to Heinrich Barth's own explanation of his critical appropriation of Marburg neo-Kantianism. Had he done so, he would have been in a position to see just how far Karl Barth—who stood at this point under the influence of Heinrich—was from positivism.

I received my foundational academic instruction in the years before the First World War in the so-called 'Marburg school'. . . . This school, in which the transcendental idealism of Kant was renewed, is brought by contemporary philosophers into a close unity with the scientific-theoretical positivism of that time and is understood as its outgrowth. Nothing was further from my mind, however, than interpreting the critical idealism of this school positivistically. Rather . . . I saw the philosophy which was taught at that time in Marburg . . . in a perspective which allowed it to be seen in its continuity with the great metaphysical tradition of the West.[32]

[30] What Fisher writes of Karl Barth would have been more correct if it had been written of Heinrich Barth instead. 'If . . . through some strange and unforeseen theological pressures, originary thought was once more attributed to the divine mind, the neo-Kantian philosophy would start to resemble neo-Platonism. This, analogous to that ancient intellectual movement which began to turn Platonic Ideas into divine thoughts, increasingly challenged the methodological monism of Cohen and Natorp.' Fisher, *Revelatory Positivism?*, 62. Fisher was wrong, however, to think that this move only took place in the chaos of the post-war period; it had already been initiated by Heinrich Barth in the pre-war period. Wrong too was his assumption that Karl Barth's move was adequately described in this way, for as we shall soon show, Karl's use of the category of the *Ursprung* was controlled by a theological understanding which was not shared by his brother.

[31] Ibid. 40.

[32] Heinrich Barth, 'Grundzüge einer Philosophie der Existenz in ihrer Beziehung zur Glaubenswahrheit', *Theologische Zeitschrift*, 9 (1953), 101.

Already, before the war, Heinrich Barth was stressing the non-givenness of the Reality which grounds knowledge. And it was this element of non-givenness which made his thinking alien to all forms of positivism. In the years immediately following the war, Barth would make this element of non-givenness central to his thinking and give to it a critical function which aroused tremendous interest in his older brother Karl.

The writings which are of principal concern for us here are two: a lecture given by Heinrich at the Aarau Student Conference in March 1919 entitled 'Gotteserkenntnis';[33] and his *Antrittsvorlesung* given at the University of Basle in November 1920 on the theme 'Das Problem des Ursprungs in der platonischen Philosophie'.[34] Karl was present for both of these lectures and his letters to Thurneysen show that he was deeply stimulated by them.

'Gotteserkenntnis' was certainly intended as a word 'to the situation'. Presented barely four months after the war's end, when as yet the outcome of the revolutionary developments of the time were still uncertain, it called the attention of its hearers forcibly to the 'catastrophe' of the times—the collapse of the political and social structures of the West. And yet, Barth observed that those who would seek to find in such upheaval the promise of that last judgement in which good will finally be separated from evil are bound to be disappointed. The 'decisions' for which many long will not be found in the events themselves; 'they are made in us, they are made in God—and we would like to understand the former in the latter.'[35] Barth also noted that philosophy had an important role to play in addressing the situation—precisely by 'maintaining its distance from the movements of the day' and keeping itself 'pure' because it is borne not only by life but by the truth.[36]

Clearly Barth had not been affected by the cultural crisis in the same way as his German counterparts, who at that very moment were in the process of throwing over systems of thought like that taught by the Marburg school because of their alleged remoteness

---

[33] Heinrich Barth, 'Gotteserkenntnis', in Moltmann (ed.), *Anfänge der dialektischen Theologie*, i. 221–55.

[34] Heinrich Barth, *Das Problem des Ursprungs in der platonischen Philosophie* (Munich: Chr. Kaiser Verlag, 1921).

[35] Barth, 'Gotteserkenntnis', 222.   [36] Ibid. 224.

from life.[37] An unrepentant Barth declared: 'You will find the foundations of the standpoint represented here in Plato, in the Christian world of thought, in Kant and Fichte, and in the Marburg school.'[38]

Barth's talk of a 'continuity with the great metaphysical tradition of the West' might easily suggest that what was at stake was some kind of philosophical repristination. But that was not the case. What was intended was a critical rethinking of that tradition, purging it of its tendency to see the 'world of the spirit' by means of an 'analogy' to the 'natural world'.[39] The problem with classical metaphysics, in Barth's view, was that it believed that the 'spiritual world' was simply a 'higher, supernatural counter-world or world behind' the natural world. But such a 'world' was merely the counter-pole of the natural world. Rather than escaping from the natural world, such a conception of the 'spiritual world' still belonged to it.

So long as they [the classical metaphysicians] spoke in some way of the 'thing-in-itself' ['substances' and 'essences'], they were still speaking of things, even where they thought themselves to be representing thereby a higher, spiritual world. Things cannot be subordinated to one another. They stand alongside of one another as having equal value, even where there the spiritual and here the material world is meant. The metaphysical world towers above and surrounds the physical, but in that it defines itself over against the physical world, it limits itself and reveals its limitations.[40]

What was needed was to move beyond the metaphysical absolute of all natural theologies to an even more radically transcendent conception of God.

True freedom can not yet be grounded in a merely opposing kingdom, so long as a higher, spiritual something *can be compared at all* with the something of this world. A radical overcoming of nature alone can

---

[37] Barth, 'Grundzüge einer Philosophie der Existenz', 102: 'I went another way than most of my friends from my student days. The Germans, shaken by defeat in the first war, allowed the philosophy which they too had hitherto revered to sink into the abyss of their despair. Phenomenology became the preferred philosophy of the post-war period. As a Swiss, I had no compelling reason to participate in the politically-conditioned "revolution" which at that time was convulsively under way in Germany. So I remained true to classical philosophy, which at that time was best represented in the Marburg school; to be sure, not without drawing this standpoint out to reach conclusions which on the surface have little to do with the starting-point.'

[38] Barth, 'Gotteserkenntnis', 225.   [39] Ibid. 232.   [40] Ibid.

liberate us from its spell. *A fundamental negation must take place if the divine is to be recognized in its purity.*[41]

Barth had no intention of setting aside the neo-Kantian epistemology. Like Cohen and Natorp, he held that human knowing is productive, generating its contents in accordance with laws inherent in the categories of human understanding. The step which he took beyond neo-Kantianism was that of projecting the *Ursprung* (i.e. the standpoint outside of every given content generated by the cognitive apparatus of the human knower) into the realm of the Idea: a realm which was 'fundamentally withdrawn from the world'.[42] In so doing, he was using Plato to correct Kant (and the neo-Kantians). But he was also using Kant to correct Plato, in that he made the Idea to be formal in character.[43] The *Ursprung*, in Barth's hands, was thereby made to be a logical principle, a presupposition of all knowing. What was gained from this process of reciprocal correction was a standpoint from which to subject not only every given content of knowledge but also the human subject itself to radical criticism. 'An orientation to the *Ursprung* means continuous breaking with that which has become.'[44] 'Logic and science are true to the *Ursprung* in that they subject the givenness of contents to a radical negation in order to erect them anew in accordance with their own laws.'[45] From this standpoint, 'modern Cartesianism and psychologism in the grounding of knowledge has been overcome'.[46]

The God-concept which emerges from 'Gotteserkenntnis' is primarily that of a transcendentally deduced, logical principle. In and of itself, the *Ursprung* was purely formal in character; it was an '*Erkenntnisprinzip der kritischen Negation*'.[47] Where it was dressed out with certain ontological characteristics such as "Personality", there the philosopher Barth was no longer standing solely upon the soil of his critical idealism. He had had recourse to the idea of revelation. He noted that the consciousness which men and women have of the *Ursprung* is not to be had through 'living and moving in God' but rather 'in Christ'. The way of Christ which led from suffering and death to resur-

---

[41] Barth, 'Gotteserkenntnis', 234 (emphasis mine).   [42] Ibid. 240.
[43] Beintker, *Die Dialektik in der 'dialektischen Theologie' Karl Barths*, 228.
[44] Barth, 'Gotteserkenntnis', 239.   [45] Ibid. 238.
[46] Beintker, *Die Dialektik in der 'dialektischen Theologie' Karl Barths*, 228.
[47] Barth, 'Gotteserkenntnis', 236.

rection was a clear reminder for Barth that the truth of human existence is not to be found in the contradictions in which we find ourselves, nor in the dialectic of the presence and absence of God. The resurrection testifies to the truth we have forgotten: that *the* truth of human existence is that our Origin lies in God and that the decision which men and women were seeking in the revolutionary events of the time had already been made in God.[48] Clearly, even for Heinrich, God was more than the *Ursprung*, but his central concern was to argue that God cannot be properly conceived apart from the help provided by an *Ursprungsphilosophie*.

The relationship of the two Barth brothers had never been close, and never would be. Leaving aside the sibling rivalry which is natural for two such gifted people, it was their perception of the demands placed upon them by their differing disciplines which threatened from time to time to lead them into open conflict. Even in the years 1919–20, when their thinking was moving so obviously on parallel tracks and their collaboration was at its height, Karl could still complain from time to time about Heinrich's tendency to scrutinize his every move, subjecting him to criticism from the side of philosophy. 'I enclose a letter of warning from Heiner. . . . Is there something here I do not understand or have we reached a point with the philosophical police where we must hear their warning without obeying it?'[49] It is clear, however, that Karl had a good deal of respect for the work of his brother. Heinrich's God-concept may have been largely formal, but that in itself was a virtue to the extent that it constituted a forceful rejection of all natural knowing of God.[50]

Some two weeks after hearing the Aarau lecture, Karl wrote to Thurneysen, 'Heiner's lecture has become for me an impetus to keep much more powerfully in view the *totaliter aliter* of the Kingdom of God.'[51] It was above all the critical potential contained in Heinrich's *Ursprungsphilosophie* (and the sharp diastasis which it embodied) that attracted Karl. His own use of the category of the *Ursprung* in *Romans* II is a testimony to this influence. For the Barth of the second edition, God is 'not a *Ding an sich*,

[48] Ibid. 247.
[49] Karl Barth to Eduard Thurneysen, 28 Dec. 1920, *B–Th. Br.* I. 456.
[50] Ruschke, *Entstehung und Ausführung der Diastasentheologie*, 141.
[51] Karl Barth to Eduard Thurneysen, 13 Apr. 1919, in *B–Th. Br.* I. 325.

not a metaphysical essence alongside of other essences, not a second something, an other, an outsider, next to that which would be without Him, but rather the Eternal, the pure *Ursprung* of everything that is'.[52] Moreover, Heinrich's stress on the simultaneity of the negation and grounding (grounding through negation!) which the *Ursprung* means for the whole of reality became decisive for Karl's elaboration of the crisis motif in the second edition.[53] And from this crisis motif flowed the dialectical structure of the God–human relation in *Romans* II. The God–human relation is dialectical in character because it is actualized in the crisis in which God creates the new humanity by negating the old.

It is in the light of the foregoing analysis of the relationship of Karl and Heinrich Barth during this phase of Karl's development that a well-known (and often misunderstood!) passage from the preface to the second edition of *Romans* must be construed.

If I have a "system", it consists in that which Kierkegaard has called the 'infinite qualitative distinction' between time and eternity ... 'God is in heaven and you are on earth'. The relationship of *this* God to *this* human, the relationship of *this* human to *this* God is for me the theme of the Bible and the sum of philosophy in one. The philosophers call this crisis of human knowing the *Ursprung*. The Bible sees at the same crossroads Jesus Christ.[54]

A superficial reading of this passage might easily suggest that there is little or nothing that is truly essential to the theologian which cannot also be known by philosophers. But when it is kept in mind precisely *who* this philosopher was who spoke of the *Ursprung* as the crisis of human knowing, then we will be warned against concluding too much from this passage. It was clearly the critical idealism of Heinrich Barth which was in view here. Karl was not offering a theoretical reflection on the relation of theology and philosophy.[55] He was speaking in highly con-

---

[52] Barth, *Der Römerbrief, 1922*, 52.

[53] By the time he presented his inaugural address at the University of Basle in Nov. 1920, Heinrich too was speaking the language of "crisis". Barth, *Das Problem des Ursprungs*, 21: '*Jenseits* [the "other world" or the "next world"] means the crisis of *Diesseits* ["this world"], for the original, living Word which dwells in it is effective and sharper than any two-edged sword. For thought and ethical convictions, it has critical significance.'

[54] Barth, *Der Römerbrief, 1922*, p. xiii.

[55] See Ruschke, *Entstehung und Ausführung der Diastasentheologie*, 140.

crete terms about how he understood his own theology to be related to a particular philosophy. He was offering a quiet testimony to the importance of his brother's work for his own efforts.

Still, the differences in thought between the two brothers should not be overlooked. In *Romans* II Karl Barth employed a number of philosophical categories from a wide variety of sources because he found them helpful for bearing witness to a theological reality he was seeking to describe. His use of these terms was inevitably idiosyncratic, entailing adaptation and transformation of philosophical categories for theological purposes. And so it was with respect to his use of the category of the *Ursprung*: to speak of God in terms of the category of the *Ursprung* was helpful for pointing to *the* crisis which the being and existence of God means for the whole of reality. But Barth's conception of God in *Romans* II was not that of a "pure subject"; such a conception could not be adequate for describing his understanding of the Self-revealing God. As will be shown in the next chapter, his understanding of revelation was already that of an at least *functionally* Trinitarian event, even though he had not as yet reflected upon the problem of the immanent Trinity.[56] The God of *Romans* II may well perform all of the critical functions of Heinrich Barth's *Ursprung*, but the *Ursprung* is not God. It was the negative, critical potential which Karl was happy to exploit in this philosophical category. But the category could only be employed 'improperly' to set forth his positive theological vision.[57]

Finally, a most crucial difference between Karl Barth's critical theology and Heinrich Barth's critical philosophy lay here: in *Romans* II, Barth would make much in his doctrine of revelation of the idea that the "Unintuitable" (i.e. God, revelation, the resurrection) must become "intuitable" if it is to be known by

---

[56] Cf. in support of this point Spieckermann, *Gotteserkenntnis*, 132; and Ruschke, *Entstehung und Ausführung der Diastasentheologie*, 38.

[57] Werner Ruschke has rightly observed that those critics who have complained about Barth's failure to use "clean" (i.e. consistently defined) philosophical categories have themselves failed to realize that his use of them was governed by a theological subject-matter which required constant adaptation and alteration of their original meaning. This in itself is forceful testimony to the fact that *Romans* II was meant to be theology, not philosophy disguising itself as theology. See Ruschke, *Entstehung und Ausführung der Diastasentheologie*, 145–6.

human beings. And that could only occur where human beings have intuitions of objectively real empirical data. Such a view constituted a movement away from the thoroughgoing constructivist epistemology of the neo-Kantians (which had dismissed the Kantian category of "intuition"). And that meant that the theology of revelation set forth in *Romans* II was more Kantian than it was neo-Kantian. Without the element of intuition (which had been seen by Cohen as evidence of residual realism in Kant's philosophy), a critically realistic theology in the form Barth was now developing would have been impossible.

(ii) *Franz Overbeck (1837–1905)*

Franz Overbeck was one of the true outsiders of the nineteenth century. By calling, he was a Professor of New Testament and Early Church History in Basle from 1870 to 1897. Inwardly, he was an atheist, a man whose historical studies had led to the loss of faith. Already in 1873 his programmatic manifesto, *Über die Christlichkeit unserer heutigen Theologie*, announced his fundamental thesis that the whole of Church history was the history of a falling-away from the true essence of original Christianity, which consisted in an eschatologically conditioned, world-denying piety. To the extent that Christianity had, from the patristic period on, entered fully into the world and culture, it was a denial of that original faith. To be sure, Overbeck also believed that such a process was both inevitable and necessary; such sympathy as he felt for the religious zeal of the early Christians was tempered by the conviction that the presuppositions underlying it could no longer be sustained in the modern world. Still, historical honesty demanded the recognition that modern theology especially was 'unchristian'. It represented the destruction of genuine Christianity. In his later years, Overbeck made it his aim to carry out a 'profane' study of the history of Christianity in the hope that, by exposing the fundamental opposition between genuine Christianity and modern culture, modern men and women would at last be able to free themselves from the Christian religion.[58]

---

[58] See Niklaus Peter, *Im Schatten der Modernität: Franz Overbecks Weg zur 'Christlichkeit unserer heutigen Theologie'* (Stuttgart: J. B. Metzler Verlag, 1992); Niklaus Peter, 'Franz Overbeck', in Bernd Lutz (ed.), *Metzler Philosophen-Lexikon: Dreihundert biographisch-*

It was the posthumous publication of a loose collection of Overbeck's notes under the title *Christentum und Kultur* which brought him forcibly to Barth's attention.[59] In early January 1920 Barth announced to Thurneysen, 'Our Melchizedek is probably—Overbeck. Perhaps I will write something about him in the *Neue Werke.*'[60] The promised essay was probably finished by 19 February, though it did not appear until mid-June. Entitled 'Unfinished Questions to Today's Theology',[61] it was nothing less than a manifesto, a declaration of the fundamental impossibility of theology as conceived by modern men and women.

Barth's reading of Overbeck was certainly tendentious.[62] He found in him that which served his purposes and where concepts and categories did not serve his purposes, they were altered and transformed so that they might be made useful. Our interest here, however, is not so much whether Barth got Overbeck right, but rather to see what his reception of him can tell us about Barth's own development. To make that clear, however, we must begin with Overbeck.

The first "chapter" of *Christentum und Kultur* (written in May 1904)[63] contained some reasonably coherent (though somewhat disconnectedly presented) reflections on the philosophy of history. Central to Overbeck's musings was the problem of whether and how it was really possible to gain access to "history" at all. The history which is treated by historians begins with

werkgeschichtliche Portraits von den Vorsokratikern bis zu den Neuen Philosophen (Stuttgart: J. B. Metzler Verlag, 1989), 584–9; and Rudolf Brändle and Ekkehard Stegemann (eds.), *Franz Overbecks unerledigte Anfragen an das Christentum* (Munich: Chr. Kaiser Verlag, 1988).

[59] Franz Overbeck, *Christentum und Kultur. Gedanken und Anmerkungen zur modernen Theologie*, ed. by Carl Albrecht Bernoulli (Basle: Benno Schwabe & Co., 1919). Overbeck had the intention of writing a work against modern theology and for this purpose had gathered together a huge collection of notes (some 20,000 pieces in all)—excerpts from Church Fathers, bibliographical notes, comments on works, ancient and contemporary, etc. When he saw that he would not live long enough to complete the work, he gave his collection of notes to his good friend, Bernoulli, with the request that Bernoulli write the book for him. In the event, Bernoulli only published a selection of the notes under Overbeck's name. The information here provided was supplied to me by Niklaus Peter in a letter dated 3 Sept. 1993.

[60] Karl Barth to Eduard Thurneysen, 5 Jan. 1920, *B–Th. Br.* I. 364.

[61] Barth, 'Unerledigte Anfragen an die heutige Theologie', in idem, *Die Theologie und die Kirche*, 1–25; ET 'Unsettled Questions for Theology Today', in *Theology and Church*, 55–73.

[62] Eberhard Jüngel describes Barth's reading as resting upon a 'grotesque misunderstanding'. See Jüngel, 'Die theologischen Anfänge', in idem, *Barth-Studien*, 63.

[63] Overbeck, *Christentum und Kultur*, 18.

"tradition"—those artifacts (monuments and writings) which are the product of historical persons, events, and forces which lie in a region behind the artifacts. Historical writing begins with criticism of the artifacts, to test their reliability. But the execution of this task in modern times has resulted in the attempt to penetrate to the "primal history" (*Urgeschichte*) which lies behind the artifacts. And that is a step which Overbeck regarded as ultimately impossible.

Urgeschichtliche problems are in constant danger of being driven into a light in which all cats are grey. They are therefore only accessible to researchers who are capable of seeing in this light—that is, to researchers with "cats' eyes", who can find their way in the dark. . . . The veil which lies over every tradition is, in the case of *Urgeschichte*, intensified to the point of impenetrability.[64]

The statement that only those possessed of 'cats' eyes' can find their way in the darkness of this primal region is meant ironically. In point of fact, Overbeck was convinced that no one is possessed of this ability.

The real source of the darkness which lies over the primal region has to do with the fact that it deals with real life, with living things in their originating "essences", and not with artifacts. *Urgeschichte* is 'originating history' and 'originating history is, in the history of every living thing, of life generally, incomparable'.[65] In the history of every living organism, there is a moment in which the boundaries which set that entity apart from the world and make it to be an individual are eroded. 'In this moment, *Ur-* or *Entstehungsgeschichte* is distinguished from history. Thus arises the similarity of this moment with death and the ease with which history, in the commonly accepted sense of the word, gives the appearance of a history of decay.'[66] Overbeck's point is quite simply that every entity, every newly founded movement, as soon as it enters into relationship with other entities and movements, undergoes change and development. But that also means that it ceases to be what it was originally. If later developments are judged by the standard of what the thing was originally ("essentially"), all development has to be considered a falling-away from that essence.[67] And that moment in which the

[64] Overbeck, *Christentum und Kultur*, 20.   [65] Ibid. 21.   [66] Ibid.
[67] Ibid. 6.

transition occurs from being in and for itself to being in and for others—that moment which Overbeck likens to death—is not itself a temporal moment in the ordinary sense of the term, for there is never a moment when entities and movements are not already 'in history'. Thus, *Urgeschichte* belongs to 'pre-historical time', which is to be carefully distinguished from 'historical time'.[68] It is for this reason that 'originating history' is said to be 'incomparable'. 'Originating history' cannot be evaluated by the normal historical principles of analogy, criticism, and correlation. 'For Overbeck, *Urgeschichte* is a historical category which describes the impenetrable conditions of the possibility of that history which can be investigated. *Urgeschichte* is history in its origination.'[69]

The conclusion which Overbeck wanted to draw from these reflections is that an unbridgeable chasm exists between *Urchristentum* and all subsequent periods of Church history. A unity of author and book exists so long as the book is being written. Once written, however, a book takes on a life of its own. It enters into 'history as commonly understood' and the author disappears from view. 'Therefore, every "Introduction to the New Testament" is practically hopeless. *Urchristentum* still lives for us in books, but only in books, so that we know almost nothing of the men who wrote them. Let us therefore be under no illusions!'[70] Overbeck's reflections were thus intended as a fundamental criticism of the assumptions underlying the historical studies of such luminaries of the time as Adolf von Harnack (whose work was subjected to derision and scorn throughout this unusual book).

Now it is clear from the foregoing that the term *Urgeschichte*, as Overbeck employed it, was a *geschichtsphilosophische* category.[71] It served the purpose of demonstrating the hermeneutical limits governing every historical enquiry. *Urgeschichte* is history, but a special kind of history which underlies and conditions the history treated by historians. The one thing *Urgeschichte* is not is unhistorical or timeless. It was not intended to be an eschatological concept. But that was, in fact, the sense Barth wanted to give to the term.

In Barth's hands, *Urgeschichte* was made to be synonymous with

---

[68] Ibid. 21.   [69] Ruschke, *Entstehung und Ausführung der Diastasentheologie*, 39.
[70] Overbeck, *Christentum und Kultur*, 23.
[71] Ruschke, *Entstehung und Ausführung der Diastasentheologie*, 39.

protology: the unhistorical, unknown, and (humanly speaking) unknowable origin of the world and humanity.[72] Thus was the term translated by him into a theological category. At the other end of history lay for Barth an equally unhistorical, equally unknowable moment: death. 'Death,' Overbeck had written, 'is the moment in our individual life in which the latter enters into that same sphere of the unknown in which everything is found already in our lifetime, that sphere which lies beyond the world known to us . . .'[73] Here again, a theological transmutation took place. 'That same sphere' into which we are translated by death was made to refer once again to the unknown world from which we have come. Protology and eschatology were thus made to be identical in content. They are the 'last things' about which 'we really can know nothing at all'.[74]

That which lies *between* these "last things" is the *world*; our world, the given world, the comprehensible world. That which is "historical" or can become "historical" is *eo ipso* also *of this world*. For "historical" means "subjected to time" (p. 242). Whatever is subjected to time however, is bounded, relativized, declared to be by the "last things", of which we are now aware, whether we want to or not.[75]

With this radically dehistoricized conception of protology/eschatology providing a critical foundation, Barth then proceeded to draw three lessons for contemporary theology. First, Christianity, in so far as it is a historical phenomenon, subjected to time, is a contradiction of its true essence. That which is historical is of this world and, like all things belonging to this world, stands under the sign of death. Only that which belongs to the 'history *before* history' (*Urgeschichte*) is true Christianity.[76] Overbeck 'places us inexorably before the dilemma: if Christianity, then not history; if history, then not Christianity! "Historical" Christianity, i.e. Christianity subjected to time, is something absurd (p. 242).'[77] Taken in context, Overbeck meant by this statement simply that the earliest Christians expected the

---

[72] Barth, 'Unerledigte Anfragen', in idem, *Die Theologie und die Kirche*, 5; ET 'Unsettled Questions', in *Theology and Church*, 58.

[73] Overbeck, *Christentum und Kultur*, 297.

[74] Barth, 'Unerledigte Anfragen', in idem, *Die Theologie und die Kirche*, 6; ET 'Unsettled Questions', in *Theology and Church*, 58.

[75] Ibid.; ET 59. (The page number in this quotation, as in the quotations which follow, refers to Overbeck's text.)

[76] Ibid. 10; ET 62.   [77] Ibid. 9; ET 61.

immediate end of the world and that the continued existence of Christianity in time is, judged from the standpoint of that expectation, something absurd. But of course, Overbeck thought that expectation equally absurd. Barth has turned Overbeck's judgement on its head, making the thoroughgoing eschatological character of earliest Christianity to be its chief virtue. When Barth judges the history of Christianity in the light of that standard, his conclusion is: the history of the Church is the history of degeneration and decay.[78]

Second, because modern Christianity seeks above all things to establish itself in the world, to make itself a force alongside and supportive of other movements in modern culture rather than fundamentally opposing those movements, it is unchristian. And because the contemporary world takes modern Christianity to be representative of Christianity, it can no longer understand true Christianity.[79]

Third, the challenge laid at the feet of theology by Overbeck is ultimately that of whether theology is possible at all. Were theology to be responsible to its true calling, it would itself become eschatology; that is to say it would speak of that unknown and unknowable world of God. Such a theology would not speak on the basis of 'historical Christianity' but out of ' "the heart of the matter itself, the unhistorical Christianity" (pp. 9–10)'. It would speak '*sub specie aeterni*; i.e. on the basis of a standpoint which knows nothing . . . of time'.[80] It would itself be a 'piece of the "last things" '.[81] The question with which Barth left his readers was, is such a venture even possible? Barth himself gave no firm answer to the question. He noted merely that 'theology cannot be re-established otherwise than by an act of daring'[82] and that 'for the time being, it is necessary really to begin wilderness wanderings'.[83]

With these reflections, Barth's theology had taken a new turn, a turn to that consistent eschatology which would provide the perspective which would govern *Romans* II. 'A Christianity which is not eschatology, completely and without remainder, has absolutely nothing to do with *Christ*.'[84] However wilful Barth's reading of Overbeck may have been, the discovery of

---

[78] Ibid. 12; ET 63.　　　[79] Ibid. 13–18; ET 64–8.　　　[80] Ibid. 24; ET 72.
[81] Ibid. 25; ET 73.　　　[82] Ibid. 23; ET 72.　　　[83] Ibid. 24; ET 73.
[84] Barth, *Der Römerbrief, 1922*, 298.

Overbeck's posthumously published writings must be seen as the decisive impetus leading to the elaboration of his new model of eschatology. Under the influence of Overbeck, Barth would develop a rich battery of vivid images with which to set forth his revised eschatological perspective: *Todeslinie* (the 'line of death' which separates the historical world from the world of God); *Todesweisheit* (the true knowledge of God which is disclosed in the cross); *Futurum resurrectionis* (employed to suggest that salvation belongs wholly to the future, not to the present); and *Hohlraum* ('empty place'—a way of speaking of genuine faith as the product of an encounter with revelation).

As was the case with Barth's appropriation of the *Ursprungsphilsophie*, so also here: the critical corrections to which Barth subjected Overbeck are of great importance—not only for an understanding of Barth's theology but also for an accurate assessment of Barth's place in the cultural upheaval which swept through the German intellectual world in the post-war period. It is most significant that Barth did not make Overbeck's hermeneutical reflections on the impossibility of coming to know an author through her text to be one of the 'unfinished questions' needing to be addressed by the theology of that time. The truth is that Barth did not embrace Overbeck's scepticism on that point. As he roundly stated in the preface to the second edition of *Romans*, he did not doubt the capacity of historical-critical science to tell us much, indeed very much, about the historical world behind the text (the writer and his audience).[85] Barth's criticism was not directed to historical-critical study as such, for he himself wanted to see historical study as the first step in any truly theological exegesis of the Bible. His criticism was directed instead to the historicist assumptions of the guild of New Testament scholars, in accordance with which the meaning of the text was reduced to its historical sense.[86] Therefore, it is a serious mistake to conclude:

[85] Barth, *Der Römerbrief, 1922*, p. x: 'My complaint with regard to them [i.e. contemporary commentaries] is not directed towards historical criticism, whose justification and necessity I once again expressly acknowledge . . .'.

[86] I have made the case for this thesis *in extenso* elsewhere and will not repeat it here. See Bruce L. McCormack, 'Historical Criticism and Dogmatic Interest in Karl Barth's Theological Exegesis of the New Testament', in Mark S. Burrows and Paul Rorem (eds.), *Biblical Hermeneutics in Historical Perspective* (Grand Rapids: Wm. B. Eerdmans, 1991), 322–38.

Barth stands alongside both New Critical and current deconstructive critics of the Bible in maintaining that all literary creations, the Bible included, are primarily works of art, not by-products of history—as such, they possess a life of their own, a life relatively independent from the cultural and authorial milieus that produced them. Possessing semantic autonomy, the 'literary work exists, in a sense, outside of history, in a kind of aesthetic preserve' where the text's surplus of meaning escapes the finite conditions that gave rise to it in the first place.[87]

Had the author of these words sought an early forerunner of these schools of hermeneutical theory in Franz Overbeck, he would have been on more solid ground. As it is, his depiction of Barth's hermeneutics fails to grasp what was at stake for Barth in the relation of history to eschatology.

This observation leads quite naturally to a much more important point. Barth's dehistoricization of eschatology cannot rightly be interpreted as a manifestation of the 'anti-historical revolution' which took place in Germany after the war without some fairly weighty qualifications.[88] In the first place, the dehistoricization of eschatology did not entail for Barth the abandonment of history as it did for many of the figures associated with the 'anti-historical revolution' (Oswald Spengler, Stefan George, etc.). Barth was not '*anti*-historical'. What Barth's dehistoricized eschatology was seeking to accomplish was simply to bear witness to a Creator/creature distinction in terms sufficiently radical so that the confusion of revelation with history which could still arise on the basis of a misreading of *Romans* I could now be excluded. As stated above (in Sect. 1), the fundamental intention which had governed *Romans* I had not changed. Barth was still seeking to find a way to speak of a revelation *in* history, but not *of* history. But now, his emphasis fell so heavily upon the second half of this proposition that revelation seemed not to enter into history at all. The time–eternity dialectic generated by his dehistoricized eschatology cast such a heavy shadow over the whole of *Romans* II that readers from that day to this have come away with the impression that revelation cannot even come into contact with

[87] Mark I. Wallace, 'Karl Barth's Hermeneutic: A Way beyond the Impasse', *Journal of Religion*, 68 (1988), 403.

[88] This is the thesis argued by the Leipzig historian, Kurt Nowak. See Nowak, 'Die "antihistorische Revolution": Symptome und Folgen der Krise historischer Weltorientierung nach dem ersten Weltkrieg in Deutschland', in Renz and Graf (eds.), *Umstrittene Moderne*, 133–71.

history, that revelation exists only in a realm outside of history, a realm which has no contact with history. Such a reading is indeed understandable and it does lend itself to viewing its author as animated by an 'anti-historical' tendency. In the next chapter, however, it will be shown that this common reading of *Romans* II is wrong. *Romans* II sets forth a clear and coherent theological epistemology. The Barth of *Romans* II did indeed believe that revelation could at least 'encounter' history. Knowledge of God as conceived in this book is a real possibility, a possibility which is realized *by grace* in the real flesh-and-blood men and women who live *in* history.[89]

In the second place, Barth's attitude towards history was not rooted in the collapse of idealism which Kurt Nowak makes to be responsible for the unleashing of a widespread fear of relativism in German intellectual circles—a fear which in turn provided the impetus for the 'anti-historical revolution'.[90] On the contrary: the roots of Barth's attitude towards history lay in the critique of historicism advanced by his neo-Kantian teachers in Marburg[91]—a critique which he continued to maintain after the

---

[89] The basic structure of Barth's theological epistemology in *Romans* II is already adumbrated in his lecture to the Aarau Student Conference in March 1920—a lecture which he himself would later judge to be the 'first document' of the "turn" between *Romans* I and *Romans* II. There he flatly asserted: 'We are within and not without, . . . within the knowledge of God, within the knowledge of the last things of which the Bible speaks.' That is the presupposition from which we come. But all men and women have 'forgotten' this, their 'Origin'; they have turned themselves against it. Where then do we see the knowledge of God disclosed once again to rebellious men and women? In the death of death which takes place in the cross. 'Out of *death* comes life! From thence comes the knowledge of God, as of the Father, the Origin, the Maker of heaven and earth.' See Barth, 'Biblische Fragen, Einsichten und Ausblicke', in idem, *Das Wort Gottes und die Theologie*, 71, 89. For his assessment of his own development, see 'Autobiographische Skizzen Karl Barths', in *B–B. Br.*, 308.

[90] According to Nowak, the relativism inherent in historicism had never posed a serious threat to German intellectuals so long as they remained committed to idealism, for idealism seemed to afford a secure anchor outside the flux of history in the certitudes of "pure knowledge", universally applicable ethical judgements, etc. But by 1880, the inroads made by naturalism and positivism in the natural sciences especially had already begun to call idealism into question for some. With the collapse of idealism after the war, the long-repressed threat of relativism could no longer be ignored. The result was the 'anti-historical revolution' of the 1920s. See Nowak, 'Die "antihistorische Revolution" ', 134–5.

[91] Karl Barth to Eduard Thurneysen, 1 Jan. 1916, *B–Th. Br.* I. 121: 'My Advent sermons caused me to realize just how frightfully indifferent historical questions have become for me. Of course, that is nothing new for me. Under the influence of Herrmann, I already conceived of criticism only as a means to freedom *vis-à-vis* the tradition; not however, as a constitutive factor of a new liberal tradition, as Wernle and

war for the quite simple reason that, for him, idealism had not "collapsed". As we have tried to argue, Barth's critically realistic theology was built on a foundation laid by idealism, and that would always be the case.

Now these qualifications are not intended to suggest that the intellectual movements of the time had *no* impact on Barth's thinking. On a subterranean level, there was undoubtedly *some* connection between Barth's theology and the figures and movements associated with the 'anti-historical revolution'. But the attempt to specify precisely what that connection was seems invariably to overlook some one aspect of differentiation which makes comparisons difficult. This much can be said with certainty: the massive impact which *Romans* II had on theology in post-war Germany would be impossible to explain apart from the anti-historical mood of many thinking people. It is not surprising that many of Barth's earliest adherents misunderstood him as badly as his critics had—which also helps to explain why not a few of them eventually found their way into the NSDAP.

(iii) *Søren Kierkegaard (1813–1855)*

It is difficult to know precisely which of Kierkegaard's writings Barth read and when he read them. What can be known with certainty is that he read an abridged edition of Kierkegaard's *Journals*, *Training in Christianity*, and *The Moment*.[92] Whether he actually read *Either–Or*, *Sickness unto Death*, or *Fear and Trembling* is difficult to know; the purposes for which Barth makes use of such language in *Romans* II are sufficiently different from the intentions of Kierkegaard as to make it impossible to know whether he was acquainted with much more than the titles of

company would clearly like to have it.' It should be pointed out that indifference to historical questions is not at all the same thing as an 'anti-historical' attitude; nor does the rejection of a new liberal theology rooted in historical science entail the rejection of historical science.

[92] These are books which Barth had in his own library. The list that follows provides the bibliographical data of the editions which he possessed. Søren Kierkegaard, *Buch des Richters. Seine Tagebücher 1833–1855 in Auswahl*, trans. H. Gottsched (Jena/Leipzig, 1905); *Einübung im Christentum*, trans. H. Gottsched, in *Gesammelte Werke*, vol. ix (Jena, 1912); and *Der Moment (1855)*, trans. Chr. Schrempf, *Gesammelte Werke*, vol. xiii (Jena, 1909). (I have put together this list on the basis of the data provided by the editors of the Karl Barth *Gesamtausgabe*, in footnotes on allusions made by Barth to Kierkegaard in his letters and early lectures.)

these books. Beyond that, the concepts and phrases he derived from Kierkegaard can all be accounted for on the basis of the books which can be confirmed.[93] There is no good reason to think that he read the *Philosophical Fragments* or *Concluding Unscientific Postscript*—at least not in this period before the publication of *Romans* II.

As for the question of when he read these works, in the last years of his life Barth would recall that he was preoccupied with Kierkegaard as early as 1919.[94] But that is probably too early. The likelihood is that he only began to give serious attention to Kierkegaard in the spring and summer of 1920. His earliest allusion to Kierkegaard (so far as can be determined on the basis of already published materials) is to be found in a letter to Thurneysen from June 1919, in which he speaks offhandedly of 'Kierkegaard's protest against *Weltkirchlichkeit*' in the context of an announcement that he is reading works by Tertullian.[95] The earliest evidence that he has actually read something of Kierkegaard's is found in a brief quotation which appears in Barth's Aarau lecture in March 1920.[96] On 7 June, he noted in a letter to Thurneysen that he was reading Kierkegaard regularly. 'The writing often begins with small private morning devotions from Kierkegaard.'[97] Two weeks later he reported that he had devoted an entire evening to Kierkegaard's *The Moment*.[98] No further mention of actual readings in Kierkegaard's writings is to be found, though *very* occasionally he is alluded to by name. My

---

[93] Virtually all of the concepts and phrases which assumed an importance in *Romans* II can be found in *Training in Christianity*: Christ as 'the paradox' (pp. 20, 25, 57); the problem of 'contemporaneity' with Christ (pp. 56–60); the 'infinite qualitative distinction' (p. 124); the incarnation as the divine 'incognito' (p. 112); and the impossibility of 'direct communication' (pp. 121–8). All page references here are to the second edition of the text Barth had before him. See Søren Kierkegaard, *Einübung in Christentum* (2nd, revised edn.; Jena: Eugen Diederichs, 1924). From the *Journals* came the language of the 'corrective' and 'a bit of spice' in the food. See Barth, *Vorträge und kleinere Arbeiten, 1922–1925*, ed. Holger Finze (Zurich: TVZ, 1990), 68 n. 15. The editors refer us here to Barth's copy of *Das Buch des Richters*, 99–100.

[94] Karl Barth, 'Dank und Reverenz', *Evangelische Theologie*, 7 (1963), 339. Barth's exact words are: 'around 1919'.

[95] Karl Barth to Eduard Thurneysen, 28 June 1919, *B–Th. Br.* I. 336.

[96] Barth, 'Biblische Fragen, Einsichten und Ausblicke', in idem, *Das Wort Gottes und die Theologie*, 91. (I have been unable to locate the source of this quotation in Kierkegaard's writings.)

[97] Karl Barth to Eduard Thurneysen, 7 June 1920, *B–Th. Br.* I. 395. ('The writing' to which he refers is a collection of unpublished notes on 2 Cor.)

[98] Karl Barth to Eduard Thurneysen, 24 June 1920, *B–Th. Br.* I. 400.

own suspicion is that Barth's reception of Kierkegaard in this period was, to some extent at least, mediated to him by his friend Thurneysen (as was unquestionably the case with Dostoevsky). Certainly, that is the impression made by the reference to the influence of Kierkegaard in the preface to the second edition.[99]

It is beyond question that Kierkegaardian language and concepts play a significant role in *Romans* II. But what does such usage tell us about the degree of Kierkegaard's influence on Barth? The truth is, as Michael Beintker has recently pointed out, that most of the conceptual building-blocks needed to produce the characteristic shape of dialectic in *Romans* II were already in place *before* the encounter with Kierkegaard, through Barth's reception of his brother Heinrich's *Ursprungsphilosophie*. The diastasis motif, giving rise as it does in Heinrich Barth's philosophy to the idea that the *Ursprung* grounds human knowledge precisely by negating its prior attainments, goes a long way in explaining the predominance in the second *Romans* of those 'complementary dialectics' in which two members stand over against one another in a relation of contradiction or antithesis. The reception of Kierkegaard thus fell on already prepared soil.[100]

Even more decisive, however, for the question of Kierkegaard's influence on Barth is the fact that the problem for the sake of which Kierkegaard devised many of the concepts appropriated by Barth was not shared by the latter. Kierkegaard's central aim was to safeguard the reality of the thinking individual human being who exists in time against absorption into the Hegelian Absolute. In the place of the Hegelian dialectic of Spirit (in which the antithesis of finite and infinite is overcome in a higher synthesis), Kierkegaard substituted a "dialectic of existence" whose goal was to establish the authentic existence of the individual.[101] Theologically, the problem of existence was understood as that of how a person *becomes* a Christian (it being understood that on Hegelian soil, a person does not really need to "become" a Christian—she only needs to be made conscious of the relation of essential unity with God in which she stands by virtue of being a finite creature). And so, Kierkegaard's primary

---

[99] See above, Ch. 5, Sect. 3.

[100] Beintker, *Die Dialektik in der 'dialektischen Theologie' Karl Barths*, 233.

[101] Ibid. 234.

theological orientation was towards the problem of how revelation is subjectively appropriated by the individual.

Barth's central problem, however, was that of the divine subjectivity in revelation (see above, Sect. 1). He was understandably allergic to preoccupation with the problem of how human beings appropriate revelation; the question of the so-called *ordo salutis* was consistently treated by him with disdain because it threatened constantly to turn theology into anthropology. His concentration on God as the Subject of revelation was designed to secure the objectivity of revelation. To the extent that he turned his attention to the anthropological side of the salvation-event, his problem was to reflect upon the relation of the 'new humanity' (an eschatological reality) to the 'old humanity' (the sinner living in time, in history).

The significance of this rather dramatic difference in starting-point and orientation can be considered in several directions. First, Barth did not have quite the same aversion to 'syntheses' which Kierkegaard had. Indeed, the influence of his brother's category of the *Ursprung* led him to refer to creation and fall in terms of an original 'synthesis' of God and humanity out of which both thesis and antithesis take their rise and to which they will eventually return.[102] Thus, 'in clear distinction to Kierkegaard', Barth could 'bring the moment of synthesis as the protological/eschatological presupposition of the diastasis powerfully into play'.[103]

Second, Barth could—again under the guidance of his brother—make extensive use of the Platonic doctrine of *anamnesis* (memory). What occurs in the revelation-event is an awakening to an original relation long forgotten. For the anti-Hegelian Kierkegaard, such an idea was anathema.

Third, Barth was never committed to a truly Kierkegaardian 'dialectic of existence'. From the very beginning, this set him apart from three men who would very soon be numbered amongst his closest theological allies: Friedrich Gogarten, Rudolf Bultmann, and Emil Brunner. During the phase of *Romans* II, Barth could indeed speak of a certain 'dialectic of life' (or some

---

[102] This understanding was already a central theme of Barth's Tambach lecture (Sept. 1919). See Barth, 'Der Christ in der Gesellschaft', in idem, *Das Wort Gottes und die Theologie*, 51.

[103] Beintker, *Die Dialektik in der 'dialektischen Theologie' Karl Barths*, 234.

similar phrase[104]), but it is of the utmost importance to under-stand what he meant by the phrase and what significance he attached to it. To speak of life as "dialectical" is to refer to the fact that life in this world is characterized by contradictions: joy and sorrow, love and hate, birth and death, war and peace, etc. To see life in this way is naturally to raise the question of whether and how the contradictions can be overcome. But—and this is crucial for understanding the theological significance which Barth attached to this dialectic—to raise these questions is not yet to raise the question of God; the question to which God's revelation alone provides the answer. The question of God—where it is really *God* that we are seeking and not the false answers by which we seek to stifle and evade the question of God[105]—can only be raised where God makes Himself known. *Seen in the light of revelation*, the "dialectic of life" can be under-stood in its true theological significance—as the consequence of *the* contradiction in which we stand *vis-à-vis* God and from which God alone can deliver us. Where this is seen, then we may also understand that the dialectic of our yes and no to God is itself rooted in the dialectic of God's Yes (election) and No (reprobation) to us.[106] But the "dialectic of life" has no capacity in itself to bear witness to God and the recognition of the contra-dictions of life can in no way be construed as a precondition on the human side for the revelation-event. The "dialectic of life" has no theological significance whatsoever until it is brought into relation to the dialectic of judgement and grace which is actual-ized in revelation.[107] Already in the phase of *Romans* II, Barth understands the gospel to have a priority over law (even where he has yet to use the phrase). And that is what made his recep-tion of Kierkegaard to be different than that of Gogarten, Bultmann, and Brunner.[108]

---

[104] Karl Barth to Eduard Thurneysen, 7 Oct. 1922 in *Karl Barth–Eduard Thurneysen: Briefwechsel*, ii. *1921–1930* (Hereafter '*B–Th. Br.* II'), ed. Eduard Thurneysen (Zurich: TVZ, 1976), 103.

[105] Barth, 'Biblische Fragen, Einsichten und Ausblicke', in idem, *Das Wort Gottes und die Theologie*, 73–4.

[106] Ibid. 74–5.

[107] Ibid. 94: 'The resurrection is the *sovereignty of God*. . . . The truth gives up its alien, aloof, transcendent position *vis-à-vis* reality. It "plays" once again upon earth, as Prov. 8 puts it, as the living dialectic of all world-reality, in that it places the world's supposed answers in question and answers its real questions.'

[108] I am here opposing the thesis advanced by Eberhard Jüngel in his learned essay on

These reflections have not been intended to minimize the very real contribution which Kierkegaard made to the theology of *Romans* II. From Kierkegaard, Barth learned above all a style of communication ('indirect communication') and an attitude (the attitude of the critic of Christianity as a religion). And the Kierkegaardian understanding of the paradoxicality of the incarnation certainly provided Barth with ample ammunition for stressing the incomprehensibility of a revelation which can take place only as a divine possibility and never as a human possibility. But we overestimate Kierkegaard's importance if we wish to see in him the decisive influence on Barth's thought in this phase.

Having examined the influences which helped to bring about the shift in Barth's thought which occurred in the spring of 1920, the stage is now set for a close analysis of leading themes in the theology of *Romans* II.

dialectic in Barth's thought. See Jüngel, 'Von der Dialektik zur Analogie', in idem, *Barth-Studien*, 127–79. Jüngel believes that Barth's development in the twenties is best understood by seeing it against the background of his engagement with Kierkegaard. According to Jüngel, Kierkegaard's "dialectic of existence" provided a kind of inheritance in the face of which all the dialectical theologians (Barth, Brunner, Bultmann, and Gogarten) had to take a position. Does one interpret the divine–human relation from the side of humankind and therefore, *with* Kierkegaard, on the basis of the dialectic of finite and infinite which Kierkegaard saw as constituting the basic structure of human existence? If so (according to Jüngel), the divine–human relation must itself be seen as thoroughly dialectical. Or does one interpret the divine–human relation from the side of God and therefore, *against* Kierkegaard? If the latter is the case, then the divine–human relation will be seen as an undialectical relation. With the so-called 'turn to analogy', Barth decided for the latter option and at this point 'left his own school' (p. 178). The other dialectical theologians never deviated from the path originally taken and thus, a break-up of these one-time comrades became inevitable. What is striking here is that Barth is clearly seen as having at one time—during his so-called 'dialectical period'—adopted the first option. Jüngel's thesis has a number of flaws, two of which will be mentioned here. First, while it is quite true that the other dialectical theologians were inclined to take as their starting-point an analysis of existence in order then to see revelation as the solution to the "dialectic of existence", Barth never did so. Barth never saw the "dialectic of existence" disclosed by philosophical analysis as identical with the truly fundamental problem of human life in this world; at most, such a dialectic is a symptom of a deeper-lying problem (viz. sin) which is only recognized when the answer to it is given in revelation. Second, as we shall demonstrate throughout the remainder of this book, Barth would always see the *relation* of God to humankind as dialectical; indeed, the motor which would drive his 'analogy of faith' was the dialectical movement in which God takes up a creaturely magnitude in order to bear witness to Himself in and through it.

6

Clearing the Ground: The Theology of Romans II

(SAFENWIL,
OCTOBER 1920–OCTOBER 1921)

1. CIRCUMSTANCES OF COMPOSITION

It was not until late October 1920 that Barth made the decision to rewrite his commentary. The occasion was a visit by Friedrich Gogarten, whose acquaintance Barth had made at Tambach the previous autumn. After the departure of this new friend, Barth wrote with some excitement to Thurneysen,

And now a strange and frightening bit of news: after Gogarten . . . left, *Romans* began suddenly to shed its skin. That is, I suddenly realized that it cannot possibly be simply reprinted in its present form, but must be reformed in head and members. I am sending you a sample with this letter. Please compare it with the unskinned version and tell me *without delay* how it looks to you.[1]

The book (some 521 pages in the German text) was completed after just eleven months of feverish activity. Barth wrote as a man possessed, staggering 'between desk, dinner table, and bed like a drunken man'.[2] Needless to say, his pastoral responsibilities suffered during this time. This problem was eased considerably for five weeks in May and June 1921 when his good friend Fritz Lieb stepped in to act as pastor in his place. In the midst of all this chaos, Barth's wife Nelly gave birth to their fourth child, Robert Matthias, on 17 April.

Barth had good reason for working at an insane pace throughout the hot summer of 1921. On 31 January he had received a

---

[1] Karl Barth to Eduard Thurneysen, 27 Oct. 1920, *B–Th. Br.* I. 435.
[2] Karl Barth to Eduard Thurneysen, 3 Aug. 1921, *B–Th. Br.* I. 508.

letter from Johann Adam Heilmann, the pastor of the Reformed Church in Göttingen. For decades, the Reformed churches of Lower Saxony had been negotiating with the Prussian *Ministerium* (the body which governed the German universities) to gain permission to establish an honorary professorship in Reformed theology in Göttingen. With the support of some American Presbyterians who would provide the funds for founding a chair, the *Ministerium* had granted the needed permission. Heilmann was the moderator of the committee delegated with the responsibility of finding a professor to occupy this new post. As a consequence of a very strong recommendation from E. F. K. Müller (who held a similar professorship at the University of Erlangen), Heilmann was writing to find out if Barth would submit his name for consideration.

Barth was filled with misgivings. He had no earned doctorate; he lacked the training necessary to take up teaching responsibilities at a university level. He was also given pause by the fact that in more than one respect, he had felt himself recently to be moving 'rapidly towards Lutheranism' and wondered to what extent the occupant of such a chair would be bound by 'its Reformed stamp'.[3] A final consideration was Heilmann's request that if Barth were to come, he would cease 'agitation for my political convictions'.[4] Even after he agreed to allow his name to be put forward, he found himself hoping that someone else would be chosen. In May, as the time for a decision in Göttingen drew near, Barth wrote to Thurneysen, 'I see it coming with a sense of fatalism, more dejected than ever. And yet after conversations with Gogarten and the Pestalozzis, I also see that it is impossible to decline. It is a great catastrophe. As to what I am supposed to *say* there for three or six or eight hours, week in and week out, I dare not even think.'[5] His worst fears were realized when on 12 May the decision was made in Göttingen in favour of Barth's nomination. With the requirement of giving university lectures now looming on the horizon, the pressure to finish the revision of *Romans* was enormous.

His work was given further impetus by the intensity of his conviction that the idols erected by modern theology in its "lib-

[3] Karl Barth to Martin Rade, 31 Jan. 1921, *B–R Br.* 154.   [4] Ibid.
[5] Karl Barth to Eduard Thurneysen, 4 May 1921, *B–Th. Br.* I. 483.

eral" form were now ripe for toppling.[6] Barth's Tambach lecture
had had the effect in Germany of making him an overnight sensation. Now the first edition of his *Romans* was being read
widely, above all by theological students. After interviewing in
Göttingen in the spring of 1921, Barth stopped off in Erlangen to
consult with E. F. K. Müller. Shortly thereafter, Müller published
an account of the stir caused by the news of Barth's visit.

Seldom has a book had such a decisive impact upon theological students. . . . When at the end of the winter semester 1920/1, it became
known that Barth was to spend a few hours at my house on the next
day, no less than twenty-eight people appeared without invitation—and
this at a time when the majority of the students had already departed.
There is a Barth-*Gemeinde* among our theological youth, especially
among those students, male and female, who have breathed the modern
spirit and are seeking something deeper.[7]

The news of such developments and the rapid shift in fortunes
which they represented might have left the average person
speechless. But then, this was no time to be at a loss for words.
Romans II had to be completed quickly.

2. PRELIMINARY OBSERVATIONS

The frequent depiction of the rhetorical style of *Romans* II as
expressionistic is correct as far as it goes, but it does not tell the
whole story. Certainly, it is not the expressionistic qualities of the
rhetoric of the second edition which sets that work off from its
predecessor.[8] What makes the style of *Romans* II distinctive is the
tone of anger with which it is written; its proclivity for 'indirect
communication' (i.e. a Kierkegaardian form of communication
which seeks not so much to convince the reader of an argument
as it does to clear away obstacles to the Spirit's work of making
her to be a witness to the truth); and paradoxical forms of

[6] Already in the spring of 1920, after a meeting with Adolf von Harnack in Basle,
Barth observed: 'It is clear that the idols are tottering. Harnack gave the impression of a
broken man . . .'. Karl Barth to Eduard Thurneysen, 20 Apr. 1920, *B–Th. Br.* I. 380.

[7] E. F. K. Müller, 'Karl Barth's Römerbrief', *Reformierte Kirchenzeitung; Organ des
reformierten Bundes für Deutschland*, 71 (1921), 103; cited by Ralph Crimmann, *Karl Barths
frühe Publikationen und ihre Rezeption* (Bern: Peter Lang, 1981), 46–7.

[8] See above, Ch. 3, Sect. 3.ii.

expression (e.g. 'through faith, we are what *we* are *not*'[9]). Above all, the second edition is radical in its one-sidedness.

In later years, Barth himself would criticize the theology which he wrote in this phase for its 'powerful one-sidednesses'[10] and the 'almost catastrophic opposition of God and the world, God and humanity, God and the Church'[11] which it set forth. 'How things were cleared away there and almost only cleared away!'[12] But as Werner Ruschke has rightly observed: 'One-sidednesses are not falsehoods!'[13] It is significant that even in his most repentant moments, Barth never said that the diastasis motif which governed *Romans* II was simply wrong; it was rather—like all heresies worth their salt—a half-truth.

Were we right or were we wrong? We were certainly right! One only needs to read the *Glaubenslehren* of Troeltsch and Stephan! One only needs to read a dogmatics like that of Lüdemann, which in its way is of such high quality, or that of Seeberg! If those were not blind alleys! . . . Not a further modification within the received way of formulating questions . . . but precisely this radical turn was undoubtedly long over-due at that time. . . . Therefore, it could not be a question later and it cannot be a question today of disowning that turn or reversing it. It was a matter later and it is a matter today of a "retraction". But a *genuine* retraction does not in the least consist in a later retreat, but rather in a new beginning and attack in which what was said before is still said, but now is said better.[14]

As we shall seek to demonstrate throughout the remainder of this book, Barth never turned away from the starting-point which was embodied in the diastasis motif. The diastasis certainly had to be reformulated—in terms other than those provided by a consistent eschatology. But the 'wholly otherness' of God would remain a permanent feature of Barth's thought. The thesis to be argued here is that the gains made in *Romans* II are everywhere presupposed throughout the *Church Dogmatics*; that the continu-

[9] Karl Barth, *Der Römerbrief, 1922*, 125.
[10] Barth, 'Vorwort zum Nachdruck dieses Buches', in idem, *Der Römerbrief, 1919*, 7.
[11] Karl Barth, 'Reformierte Theologie in der Schweiz', in the Theological Faculty of the University of Amsterdam (ed.), *Ex auditu verbi: Festschrift für G. C. Berkouwer* (Kampen: Kok, 1965), 29.
[12] Karl Barth, *Die Menschlichkeit Gottes* (Theologische Studien, 48; Zurich: EVZ, 1956), 8.
[13] Ruschke, *Entstehung und Ausführung der Diastasentheologie*, 6.
[14] Barth, *Die Menschlichkeit Gottes*, 6

ity in theological perspective between these two great works so greatly outweighs the discontinuity that those who wish to read the dogmatics without the benefit of the lens provided by *Romans* II will understand everything in the wrong light.

Still, the fact remains that the theology of *Romans* II is one-sided, and sometimes extremely so. But the truth is that it was deliberately so. The work of clearing away debris (*Aufräumungsarbeit*) was almost the sole purpose of the second edition and the small works which belong to the phase which it defined.[15] What Barth was seeking to offer in these years was not so much a new theology as it was a 'corrective'[16]—though he certainly was also offering a new theology in inchoate form. It is important to bear in mind Barth's purpose for if we fail to do so, we will all too easily misunderstand the book. In the face of all the critical negations, we will all too easily miss the highly *positive* element in it. We will miss the quite coherent theological epistemology which is set forth in it and read it as an essay in theological scepticism—as many of Barth's contemporaries did and as many readers continue to do today.[17]

3. KNOWLEDGE OF GOD AND ESCHATOLOGY

Barth's theological epistemology in *Romans* II stands everywhere in the long shadow cast by Immanuel Kant. As we have already indicated, he took for granted the validity of Kant's epistemology as set forth in the First Critique, as well as the success of his attack on metaphysics. Barth's thinking (not just in this phase but

---

[15] A point also made by Beintker, 'Krisis und Gnade', 448.

[16] Karl Barth, 'Not und Verheißung der christlichen Verkündigung', in idem, *Das Wort Gottes und die Theologie*, 100.

[17] Stephen Webb provides an excellent example. Webb holds that in *Romans* II, 'Barth did not write about God but reenacts the religious situation by displaying a theology under an impossible pressure, a discourse deprived of its subject-matter.' Likening Barth's perspective to the 'epistemological nihilism' of Robert Wiene's film *Das Cabinet des Dr. Caligari* (Berlin, 1920), Webb concludes that what Barth offers in *Romans* II is 'antitheology'. And when (later) Barth failed to maintain his 'ironical' standpoint ('A theology suspended in the air of doubt and anxiety is going to be tempted to land somewhere'), 'his vision of the failure of our knowledge of God was turned into still one more positive theological program'. See Webb, *Re-figuring Theology*, pp. viii, 16, 149, 149, and 18 (in order of the citations presented here). *Romans* II as 'anti-theology'? The *Church Dogmatics* as just another 'positive theological program'? The remainder of this book will constitute the refutation of such claims.

in all phases of his development) was strictly "anti-metaphysical" in character. Since the meaning of such a claim is not self-evident, it would be helpful to say a word about it here at the outset.

"Metaphysics", as Barth understood it, refers to the classical attempt to provide an account for the order which a human subject observes in the world about her. Extrapolating from observed phenomena, she posits the existence of a First Cause or a First Principle. It is the rejection of this *order of knowing* which is in view when we speak of Barth as "anti-metaphysical". It is important to clarify this now, for just three years later (in his Göttingen lectures on dogmatics), Barth would not hesitate to reflect upon theological themes which the nineteenth-century mind had been accustomed to regarding as "metaphysical": the ancient Church doctrines of the immanent Trinity, the anhypo-static-enhypostatic Christology, the being and attributes of God, etc. To the vast majority of nineteenth-century theologians, these themes were "metaphysical" because they referred to alleged realities which lay beyond the limits of human knowing and therefore could only be accessed by means of the metaphysical way of knowing or by speculation. Barth was in agreement with the nineteenth-century theologians to this extent: if one were to be in a position to address the questions which arise in these regions of discourse, it would *not* be possible on the basis of the metaphysical way of knowing. The ground of the possibility would have to be sought elsewhere: in his view, in God's Self-revelation in Jesus Christ. So to speak of Barth as "anti-metaphysical" refers to his attitude towards a particular *way* of knowing (the path taken); it does not entail the bracketing-off of particular regions of discourse from discussion in an a priori fashion. Indeed, Barth would always be convinced that an anti-metaphysical stance in theology was thoroughly compatible with the consideration of the themes just enumerated.

The significance of Barth's anti-metaphysical attitude for an understanding of *Romans* II is this: Barth had been convinced for some time that the way taken by a person who seeks to know God will, to a large extent, determine the kind of God one arrives at, or even whether what is arrived at is God at all. In *Romans* II, he took great pains to show that what was typically understood as God in the theology of his time was, in reality, the

'No-God' of this world. Seen within the range of possible conceptions arising naturally out of human capacities for knowledge, what is understood under the name "God":

is always only a something in contrast to another something, a pole in opposition to a counter-pole, a magnitude next to other magnitudes, a yes in relation to a no; not, however, *the* Either which has already overcome the Or, not *the* Yes which lies beyond yes and no, not the power of the reversal from death to life. . . . For the God who is a something in contrast to something else, a pole over against a counter-pole, yes against no, the God who is not the completely free, unique, superior, victorious God, is the no-God, the God of this world.[18]

More than any other human possibility, Barth argues, it is religion which is responsible for creating the dualism of the here and the beyond.[19] But God is not 'the beyond'. God is not the 'elongation of nature into a super-nature or a behind-nature (metaphysics)'.[20] The being of God lies beyond what we naturally think of as the here (*Diesseits*) and the beyond (*Jenseits*).[21] 'God is not accidental, conditioned, bound to the opposition of here and there, but rather the *pure* negation, and therefore the *beyond* of the "here" and the "beyond". . .'.[22] God stands beyond all this-worldly polarities, contrasts, or dualisms, whether they be nature and spirit, materiality and ideality, body and soul, or finite and infinite.[23] God is not the Infinite! The Infinite is only a projection; it is the finite, stripped of all its limitations and projected on to a higher being. But because it is a projection, it always remains *inseparably bound* to the finite as its antithesis, its mirror opposite. It is not the absolutely free and creative Origin of all things. God is the Eternal, not the Infinite;[24] the Origin, not the First Cause set next to and in a series with other causes;[25] the Creator of all things, visible *and* invisible.[26] 'God stands over against humankind as Origin, not as Cause. . . . The human individual in his existence and being is always *created*; not somehow only conditioned but rather, together with everything which conditions and can condition him (and even if it should be called

---

[18] Barth, *Der Römerbrief, 1922*, 213.   [19] Ibid.   [20] Ibid. 164.
[21] Ibid. 271.   [22] Ibid. 118.
[23] Ibid. 146. Cf. 28: 'The antitheses *within* this divinized world (nature and culture, materialism and idealism, capitalism and socialism, secularism and ecclesiasticism, imperialism and democracy, among others) are not as serious as they give themselves out to be. They are antitheses *within* the world for which there is no paradox, no No, no eternity.'
[24] Ibid. 273.   [25] Ibid. 342.   [26] Ibid. 346.

"God") *created.*'[27] In other words, everything which can only
condition us is still only a created reality like unto ourselves and
therefore, to the extent that it is called "God", is only the No-
God of this world. In following Barth's relentless pursual of this
theme, it becomes clear that his purpose is to locate God beyond
the realm of any and every conceptuality readily available to us,
whether through a *via negativa* or a *via eminentiae* or a *via causali-
tatis.* The being of God lies on the far side of the 'line of death'
which separates the world of time, things, and people, together
with every conceptuality bound to it, from the eternal.[28]

Who or what then is this God who lies on the far side of the
'line of death'? He is the One who dwells in light inaccessible.[29]
He is the God who is Unknown[30] and, humanly speaking,
unknowable.

God is always beyond the grasp of humankind; new, distant, strange,
superior, never in our horizon, never in our possession. Whoever says
God says *miracle.* . . . as certainly as a human has no organ for the miracle, just as certainly all human experiencing and understanding cease
precisely there where—in God—the miracle begins. In so far as on the
human side, an affirmation and understanding of God comes about . . .
the impossible, the miracle, the paradox occurs.[31]

In this passage, the fundamental problem raised by Barth's reflections in *Romans* II makes its presence felt: how can the God who
is described as Unknown and unknowable become known? That
Barth was convinced that an affirmation and understanding of
God can and does come about is clear. But how is this possible?

The short answer is that God can only be known through
God. Knowledge of God is possible only as a divine possibility
(miracle!) and never as a human possibility. The human who possesses no organ for the miracle, no capacity in herself for the
knowledge of God, must somehow be made a participant in
God's knowledge of Himself. This is what Barth calls 'the impossible possibility of faith'[32]—a possibility whose source lies in God
alone. But is this really a solution or only a refined statement of
the problem? What does it mean? How does knowledge of God
come about in concrete terms?

God is the God whom we do not know, the Unknown God

<hr />

[27] Barth, *Der Römerbrief, 1922*, 342.   [28] Ibid. 95.   [29] Ibid. 11.
[30] Ibid. 11, 21.   [31] Ibid. 96.   [32] Ibid. 114.

who, if we are to know Him, must make Himself kno
must do so in such a way that He remains God even
cisely *in*—His revelation. This means for Barth that Go
"give" Himself to be known in such a way that He becomes (in
the sense of "is transformed into") something directly given to
our perception; something which we are then able to take into
our secure possession. It matters not at all whether such a direct
given be a historical magnitude or a psychological given. For
both historicism and pyschologism,[33] God is known directly. If
this were what was meant by God becoming knowable to us,
God would cease to be God.[34] He would pass over into our
world, becoming identical with some creaturely reality known to
us. But no; that God is *God* means that God is God not only
before He reveals Himself, but *as* He reveals Himself and *after*
He reveals Himself. Therefore, whatever 'becoming knowable' means, it does not mean becoming identical with any magnitude in this world—even if that entity should be named Jesus
Christ.

If God cannot be known directly, as both historicism and
psychologism in their varying ways suggested, then the only
possibility remaining is that He must be known *indirectly*, by
means of a medium. Furthermore, if in the process of God's Self-
revelation, He is not be transformed into the medium, this means
that at every point in the revelation process, the revelation must
remain distinct from its medium. To change the metaphor,
Barth's favourite way of describing this in *Romans* II—drawing
upon the term employed in Kant's epistemology—is to say, the
Unintuitable (*das Unanschauliche*, God) must become intuitable;
yet in such a way that no change in the Unintuitable is
involved.[35] So, in order that God remain distinct from the
medium of revelation, He *veils* Himself in the medium. He hides
Himself and remains hidden in the medium of revelation. Where
does He do this? What is the medium? A provisional answer
is: in Jesus Christ 'God reveals Himself relentlessly as the hidden,
only indirectly to be known God. Here He veils Himself

[33] These two targets of Barth's criticism are attacked separately but at times are cou-
pled together. This occurs with increasing frequency during the course of the 1920s,
becoming a shorthand for all that Barth opposes. Ibid. 260.
[34] Ibid. 261.
[35] In Barth's paradoxical expression: Revelation 'does not become intuitable next to
other intuitable objects; it becomes intuitable as the Unintuitable'. Ibid. 67.

definitively in order to be revealed only to faith.'[36] Here again the distinction must be observed: the medium of revelation is not the revelation. Jesus of Nazareth, a historical figure, standing on the plane of history, is *not* the revelation. He is the medium of revelation.[37]

But even now, we have not yet said all that needs to be said. Mediums can be of various kinds. It is conceivable that a medium could function as a medium solely by virtue of its existence as such and our innate capacity to 'see through it', so to speak. It is also conceivable that a medium of revelation, having no capacity in itself to be such, might be granted such a capacity by grace, through a past revelation-event, so that where once it had no capacity to be a bearer of revelation, it has now acquired such a capacity through the use which God has made of it in bearing witness to Himself in the past. Both of these understandings are roundly rejected by Barth. It would be more accurate to Barth's intentions to say that Jesus of Nazareth, standing on the plane of history, is not even the medium of revelation. As a historical figure, Jesus is the veil of revelation—the definitive veil to be sure, but no more than that. 'Precisely in that it is the revelation of the righteousness of God, the revelation in Jesus is at the same time the strongest veiling and making unknown of God thinkable. In Jesus, God becomes truly mystery, making Himself known as the Unknown . . .'[38] If the veil is to *become* a medium, that is if the veil—without ceasing for a moment to be a veil—is to be lifted so that light can shine through it, then an act of God is required: 'the becoming intuitable of the Unintuitable is again and again *God's* act, the act of His faithfulness or (which is the same thing) the act of faith. In so far as this act occurs . . . We stand here and now already in the reflected splendour of the coming things'.[39] Revelation thus has the character of an event. That the veil is made transparent for faith, that it truly becomes a medium, requires an act of God. God is the Subject of revelation and must always remain so.

---

[36] Barth, *Der Römerbrief, 1922*, 353.

[37] Cf. Ruschke, *Entstehung und Ausführung der Diastasentheologie*, 41: 'For this reason, Barth's theology knows of no Jesuology; rather it is decidedly Christology. Christ is the wholly other in Jesus, the revelation of God in Jesus, the "truth from beyond the grave", the "arrow from the other shore".'

[38] Barth, *Der Römerbrief, 1922*, 73.   [39] Ibid. 80.

[Handwritten marginal notes:]

Barth & Saussure are quite close: the medium or sign is arbitrary, not essentially linked, totally other from the signified; where S. and Derrida lose the plot is the leap then to saying so 'meaning' doesn't exist is the leap to saying there is nothing transcendent; on the contrary I think is the biggest proof of the utter transcendence of meaning or at least the possibility of it, language's not the meaning, the revelation, it is merely the medium of it, the meaning itself is truly & totally hidden in language, not part of it, it is ...

That the *Deus absconditus as such* is in Jesus Christ the *Deus revelatus*, that
is the content of the epistle to the Romans. Let it be well understood:
the content of Romans, of theology, of God's Word in a human
mouth, can only be that it is *this Subject* (the *Deus absconditus*) which has
this predicate (the *Deus revelatus*). . . . The other thing however: that
this Subject (the *Deus absconditus*) has *this predicate* (the *Deus revelatus*) . . .
that is not found in Romans, *that* is neither said nor written, but truly is
also not "done", because *that* cannot be the object of human striving at
all. If that enters in, then it is not a human being but God who has spoken and acted; then the miracle has occurred.[40]

Thus far, the provisional answer given by Barth to the problem of how God is known. But Barth was not fully satisfied by
this answer. He seems to have been haunted by the fear that his
readers might once again turn the veil into a medium which
functions as such, under its own steam, thus failing to preserve
the critical distance separating revelation and medium. So he
made his answer more specific and he did so by bringing into
play the dialectic of time and eternity.

In the strictest sense, revelation in *Romans* II is the resurrection
of Jesus Christ and only the resurrection. 'The resurrection is the
revelation, the disclosure of Jesus as the Christ, the appearance of
God and the knowledge of God in Him, the commencement of
the necessity of giving God the glory and of reckoning in Jesus
with the Unknown and the Unintuitable.'[41] But herein a problem seems to arise, for the resurrection is said by Barth to be the
'"unhistorical" event *par excellence*'.[42] 'The resurrection of Christ
from the dead is *revelation* and *intuition* of the unintuitable grace
of God (historically on the margin of the unhistorical and unhis-
torically on the margin of the historical).'[43] 'Whatever is or can
be "historical" is *eo ipso* also *of this world*. For "historical" means
"subjected to time". But whatever is subjected to time is limited,
relativized, manifest as "world" by the "last things" . . . '[44] But if
the resurrection is an "unhistorical" event, if it is an event which
takes place somehow outside time, how can it be known and
understood by those living in time?

What Barth most certainly did *not* intend was for any of
these statements to be taken literally; they were to be understood

[40] Ibid. 408.   [41] Ibid. 6.   [42] Ibid. 185.   [43] Ibid. 204.
[44] Barth, 'Unerledigte Anfragen an die heutige Theologie', in idem, *Die Theologie und
die Kirche*, 6; ET 'Unsettled Questions for Theology Today', in *Theology and Church*, 59.

paradoxically, as statements which point beyond themselves to the truth. For Barth, the resurrection of Jesus Christ was a 'bodily, corporeal, personal'[45] event. How could Jesus be raised *bodily* otherwise than "in" history? The only possible answer is: He could not. What we are seeing here is Barth's use of the time–eternity dialectic to drive home the point once and for all that revelation is *in* history, but it is not *of* history.

The resurrection from the dead is an absolutely unique event; unique in the sense that the forces operative on the surface of history cannot produce something like a resurrection. It is an "unhistorical" event in this specific sense: it does not belong to the realm of time because it is not produced by historical causation. The step from the historical to the "unhistorical" is the step from the corruptible to the incorruptible, from the old world to the new world. A deep chasm, a 'glacial crevasse', a 'polar region', a 'desert zone' separates them.[46] All of these metaphors are chosen by Barth to communicate the same thing: that the barrier region separating time from eternity, history from eschatology, humanity from God is impassable—impassable that is, *from this side*. From the side of God, however, all things are possible.

In this name [Jesus Christ], two worlds encounter and separate from one another, two planes intersect, one known and the other unknown. The known plane is that created by God, fallen from its original unity with God and therefore, the world of the "flesh" in need of redemption, the world of humankind, of time and of things, our world. This known plane is intersected by another unknown plane, the world of the Father, the world of the original creation and the final redemption. But this relation between us and God, between this world and the world of God, wants to be known. The seeing of the line of intersection is not self-evident. The point of the line of intersection—where it is to be seen and is seen—is *Jesus*, Jesus of Nazareth, the "historical" Jesus . . . That point of the line of intersection itself, however, like the entire unknown plane whose presence it announces, has no extension on the plane known to us. The emanation or much rather, the astonishing bomb-craters [*Einschlagstrichter*] and empty spaces [*Hohlräume*] through which it makes itself noticeable within the realm of historical intuitability are, even if they are called the "life of Jesus", not the other world which in Jesus comes into contact with our world. And in so far as this,

---

[45] Barth, *Der Römerbrief, 1922*, 183.   [46] Ibid. 25.

our world, is touched in Jesus by another world, it ceases to be directly intuitable as history, time, or thing.[47]

Here Barth speaks of an intersection, of a relation between the new world of God (eschatology) and the old world of fallen humanity (history). There can be no question as to his conviction that this relation is a real one; that the intersection of which he speaks really did take place. His point, however, is that it is a pure event; an event without before or after—which is to say, lacking any prior *conditions* which might be said to have produced the event and lacking as well any ongoing *effects* which might be said to be a continuing presence of that which produced the event. *That* is what Barth means in speaking of the resurrection as "unhistorical". It is in this light that the following well-known passage is to be understood.

In the resurrection, the new world of the Holy Spirit touches the old world of the flesh. But it touches it as a tangent touches the circle, without touching it and precisely in that it does *not* touch it, touches it as its boundary, as *new* world.[48]

A paradoxical statement, to be sure: the new world touches the old world without touching it. What can this mean? It means that the new world touches the old world at a single point, without extension along the line of historical time.

What Barth has achieved with this explanation of the relation of God to the world is that he has rendered the knowledge of God an insuperable problem from the human side. If the resurrection, as the point of intersection of God and the world, is completely lacking in spatial and temporal extension, then it is unintuitable to us; it lies beyond the reach of our knowing apparatus.

It is at this point that we arrive at Barth's final solution to the problem of the knowledge of God. His solution is that the unintuitable, unhistorical event of the resurrection *becomes, by an act of God's grace, intuitable in the event of the cross.* We see the Resurrected in the Crucified.[49] While, as a general answer, it is true to say that Jesus of Nazareth is the *locus* of revelation, Barth was not really interested in *Romans II* in the incarnation as such. He saw too many potential problems arising from treating the

[47] Ibid. 5.   [48] Ibid. 6.   [49] Ibid. 132.

solution to the problem of the knowledge of God in this way. So he restricted his focus to a single event (thereby underscoring the event-character of revelation): the event of the cross. Ultimately, the event of the cross and it alone is the place where the Unintuitable becomes intuitable. God becomes intuitable only *sub specie mortis*.[50] In faith, 'the death [of Christ] becomes the only (the only!) parable of the Kingdom of God'.[51]

The life of Christ, His resurrection in which faith has its source, becomes intuitable in His *oboedientia passiva*, in His death on the cross: solely, alone, and exclusively in His death on the cross. The doctrine of the *munus triplex* is a darkening and weakening of the concentrated New Testament conception. There is no second or third *something* which could step forth somehow independently *next to* this sole, alone, and exclusive meaning of Christ; neither the personality of Jesus nor the Christ-idea, neither His Sermon on the Mount nor His healing of the sick, neither His trust in God nor His love for His brethren, neither His call to repentance nor His message of forgiveness, neither His struggle against traditional religion nor His call to discipleship in poverty, neither the social nor the individual, neither the immediate nor the eschatological side of His gospel. However, all these things do radiate light in *the* light which proceeds from His death.[52]

Seen in the light which shines in and through the cross, the life of Christ too can take on parabolic significance. So too, can the law, and a myriad of other movements and figures.

But it must be remembered that the resurrection alone *is* the revelation. The light which shines in and through the event of the cross is borrowed light. The meaning of the cross is not self-evident; it has no power in itself to be self-interpreting. It does not communicate directly, in spite of its intuitability.

Direct communication and the receptivity for it occur in those rare but nevertheless possible cases which crop up, where one person dies for another; a mother during childbirth, a man from occupational exhaustion, a doctor or missionary in service, a soldier on the battlefield. Certainly, the death of Jesus as a historically effective event and as the object of such experiences ("martyrdom") also belongs to this series of directly communicating self-sacrifices.[53]

As an event on the plane of history, the passion of Christ is like any other event; it has no parabolic significance whatsoever. It

---

[50] Barth, *Der Römerbrief, 1922*, 137. [51] Ibid. 182. [52] Ibid. 136.
[53] Ibid. 138; cf. 263.

only *becomes* the parable of the Kingdom of God in the event of revelation; as a result of being seen in the light which shines forth from the resurrection.

What is the meaning of the cross when seen in the light of the resurrection? Christ is:

at the end of his way, a purely negative entity. By no means is He a genius, by no means a bearer of manifest or hidden psychic powers, by no means a hero, a leader, a poet or thinker. Precisely in this negation ('My God, my God, why have you abandoned me?'), precisely in the fact that He *sacrifices* every ingenious, psychic, heroic, aesthetic, philosophical—every thinkable human possibility whatsoever to an impossible *more*, an unintuitable *Other*, precisely therein is He the fulfiller of those possibilities of human development which, in the Law and the prophets, point most sublimely beyond themselves. *Therefore* God has raised Him, *therein* He becomes known as the Christ, *thereby* He becomes the light of the last things which illuminates all things and all people. We see in Him God's faithfulness really in the depths of hell. . . . Jesus is the Christ precisely because in Him the faithfulness of God appears in its final hiddenness, in its deepest mystery. All of that is not self-evident and never will be.[54]

Paradoxically, in Jesus' death in God-abandonment on the cross, God is fully present, faithful even unto hell. It is here, in the wholly negative experience of this one human being, that God gives Himself to be known. It is this experience above all which is the veil of God—the veil which must be lifted if God is to be known. Where the veil is lifted—or better, made to be *transparent*, for Jesus' death in God-abandonment never ceases to be a veil—where this occurs, there God is known. In the dialectic of veiling and unveiling which occurs in the cross and the resurrection, Barth sees the actualization of a relationship of correspondence between the hidden God and the death of this man in God-abandonment. God is revealed as the God who shows His faithfulness to the human race in the negation of every last temporal possibility up to and including death itself. Where the veil is lifted by God's gracious decision and act, where the light which shines forth from the resurrection makes clear the meaning of this man's death, there the event of the cross does indeed become *the* parable of the Kingdom. That the event of the cross can become *the* parable of the Kingdom means that in

[54] Ibid. 72.

and through it is revealed the fact that the Kingdom of God is realized only through the negation of all human, historical, temporal possibilities. The Kingdom of God lies on the other side of the 'line of death' which separates eschatology from history, time from eternity.

But this raises a further problem and here Barth's solution is advanced one final step. It is not at all questionable, Barth remarks, that the light *shines* in the darkness. What is questionable is whether there is anyone to see it.[55] Up to this point, we have dealt with what Barth would later call the 'objective possibility of revelation'. Now we must concern ourselves with the 'subjective possibility of revelation'.[56] Who is the subject by whom the revelation of God is known? Is there such a subject?

The subject of the knowledge of God is the new creature. But are we ever, at any point *in time*, new creatures? On the surface, Barth's answer to this question seems simple and straightforward. 'We are sinners and we remain sinners. Whoever says humanity, says unredeemed humanity.'[57] The only person we know is the person of unrighteousness.[58] The new creature is the unintuitable eschatological reality which lies beyond all continuity with the psychologically intuitable human subject.[59] That means that in so far as we are people living in this world, the world of time, we are not and cannot be new creatures.

The truth that *we are* new creatures exists for us always and everywhere only in its starting-point. And this starting-point means for us the end of all intuitability and intelligibility. Only at the end of the old creature can the beginning of the new become intuitable for us.[60]

Barth does allow that 'We are not only what we are; we are through faith what *we* are *not*.'[61] But that does not seem to help at all when he quickly adds, 'In every moment we must be suspect to ourselves whenever we reckon that we believe.'[62] The subject of the predicate "faith" is the new creature. '*I am not* this subject . . .'[63] If then, we are in faith what we are not, yet cannot have faith, are we ever what we are not? It would seem that our situation is hopeless and that knowledge of God has finally

<hr>

[55] Barth, *Der Römerbrief*, 1922, 370.
[56] Karl Barth, '*Unterricht in der christlichen Religion*', i. *Prolegomena*, 205, 207; ET *The Göttingen Dogmatics*, i. 167–8.
[57] Barth, *Der Römerbrief*, 1922, 59.   [58] Ibid. 127.   [59] Ibid. 134.
[60] Ibid. 126.   [61] Ibid. 125.   [62] Ibid. 126.   [63] Ibid. 125.

turned out to be a frank impossibility. But that would be a conclusion too hastily drawn.

Just as Barth's concern in the problem of revelation on its
objective side was that revelation not be made a predicate of history, so his concern here on the subjective side is that faith not
be made a predicate of the person living in time. Barth was trying to strip away any possibility of making faith to be a psychological given. But he did not want to deny that faith "exists" in a
highly actualistic sense, in the moment of revelation. Faith, like
revelation, is an event, without before or after.

in so far as with the unintuitable, impossible *object* of knowledge which
steps forth in the intuitability of the way of death taken by Jesus, a just
as unintuitable, impossible *subject* of knowledge (lying beyond the line
which divides and unites death and life) is posited . . . we *are* new creatures.[64]

The 'are' here is to be understood in an actualistic sense.

The determination of the new subject, the predication "we are—new
creatures!" is and remains therefore dialectically grounded, indirect,
through faith alone . . . not for a moment may this dialectical presupposition harden and petrify into a direct given.[65]

To put the matter another way, though the distance which
separates the old creature (the person living in time) from the
new creature (the eschatological subject) is safeguarded, there can
be no doubt that Barth was convinced that a relation between
the two is established in the moment of revelation. That relation
must be established again and again and therefore, we can always
only begin again at the beginning. But it really is established in
the moment of revelation. The circle is closed. We do indeed
know God:

the identification of the old with the new creature must first be accomplished in every temporal moment . . . In this respect too, a human
being stands on the *threshold*, on the threshold of the Kingdom of God
. . . But he *stands* on the threshold, hoping; and because hoping, he is
never completely without a provisional presence of that for which he
hopes.[66]

Walking in newness of life, Barth says in another passage, has
no more historical extension next to other events than does the

[64] Ibid. 185–6.   [65] Ibid. 141.   [66] Ibid. 159.

resurrection of Jesus from the dead. And yet, he adds: 'This eternal future of my "walking in newness of life" . . . projects into [*hineinragt*] my "living further in sin" .'[67]

There can be no question that the dominant tone of *Romans* II is determined by Barth's consistent eschatology. Because that is so, it is quite easy to miss the notes of a 'provisional' non-temporal presence of the Kingdom, an actualistic projection of the world to come into this world. But they are there.

Soteriology for Barth in *Romans* II is the subjective side of the problem of revelation. It is by means of an appeal to the power of the Holy Spirit that Barth finally makes clear how something that is unintuitable can become intuitable and how we who live in time can perceive in the intuitable passion of Christ the unintuitable revelation of God.

> Grace is the power of obedience because and in so far as it is the power of the resurrection, the power of knowledge in which we recognize ourselves as the subject of the *Futurum resurrectionis*, the power by means of which we dare to reckon with our being as the being of the new creature . . .[68]

It is the power of the resurrection which makes possible our knowing. Though always remaining unintuitable, the resurrection has a power—it is really the power of the Holy Spirit[69]—to cast its light on the event of the cross in such a way as to create understanding. *We are, in effect, grasped from the other side, from the side of the "unhistorical" resurrection, through this one* locus *in human history, the passion of Christ.* In that this occurs, the key is turned in the lock.

> The *power* of the resurrection is, however, the knowledge of this new man in which we know God, or much rather, become known by Him. . . . The power of the resurrection *is* the key, *is* the opening door, is the step over the threshold.[70]

That is Barth's doctrine of revelation in *Romans* II.

Earlier we noted that on the objective side, the event of revelation establishes a correspondence between the wholly negative

---

[67] Barth, *Der Römerbrief, 1922*, 175.   [68] Ibid. 192–3.

[69] Ibid. 134: 'The "Holy Spirit" is the work of God in faith, the creative and redemptive power of the Kingdom of God which, coming close by, touches a person and her world in faith and brings about a response, the way a glass rings when lightly touched.'

[70] Ibid. 187.

experience of the cross and the hidden God who gives Himself to be known in it. Now on the subjective side we see another correspondence which again is wholly negative in character: a correspondence between ourselves and Christ.

We are "related" to Christ intuitably, temporally understood, in so far as our existence as an existence in tribulation is—clearly without our co-operation—a parable, an analogy of His death. . . . Our *intuitable* kinship with Him (which becomes knowable to us in the mirror of His death on the cross as such) . . . is in itself identical with the fact of the incurable problematic of human existence generally.[71]

Thus an analogy exists between Christ's sufferings and our sufferings. In the parable of His death, we see ourselves as related to Him.[72]

Back in the 1960s, Tjarko Stadtland made the suggestion that in constructing an analogy between the questionability and suffering which humans bear about with them on the one hand, and the death of Christ in God-abandonment on the other, Barth had made a place for a '*negative* natural theology'.[73] Indeed, Stadtland could go so far as to say that the *analogia entis* (which Barth would later call 'the invention of the Antichrist'[74]) has found a place in Barth's early dialectical theology. But that is to turn the clear direction of Barth's thinking on its head.

We have already seen that Barth insisted that the 'way of death' of Jesus (His way to the cross) cannot be rightly understood apart from revelation. That by itself would make an analogy of being impossible, for such an analogy (by definition) would seek to construe the significance of Christ's death on the basis of a *general* understanding of human questionability and suffering. But Barth's view goes even further to cut the ground out from under an analogy of being. 'On the basis of a general understanding' would mean that an understanding of *human* questionability and suffering at least—if not Christ's—is accessible to anyone in the public arena, so long as she is armed with the proper tools of analysis (let us say, an existential or phenomenological analysis of human existence). But to that possibility as well, Barth said no. The questionability of human existence is

---

[71] Ibid. 176.   [72] Ibid. 265.

[73] Tjarko Stadtland, *Eschatologie und Geschichte in der Theologie des jungen Karl Barth* (Neukirchen-Vluyn: Neukirchener Verlag, 1966), 116.

[74] Barth, *KD* I/1, p. viii; ET *CD* I/1, p. xiii.

known only in revelation. It is not the suffering produced by this or that problem in human life, however great. The 'problematic of human existence generally' of which Barth speaks is the absence of God, and not just any god, but the God who alone is truly *God*. Of the absence of *this* God, we know nothing until God reveals Himself as the Unknown God. The crisis of which Barth speaks is the crisis which is brought about by revelation. It is the crisis in which we recognize ourselves as sinners and understand for the first time that we do not know God, that what we have thought of as God (whether as present or absent) is the No-God of this world. In that God reveals Himself as the Unknown God,[75] we see our true distress. Christ's death is the *Erkenntnisprinzip* (the criterion of knowledge) of our dying,[76] not vice versa. It is not just any death but the death of *this* man on a cross which tells us what death really is—but only in so far as the death of this man is seen in light which shines forth from the resurrection in the power of the Holy Spirit! 'That life comes from death and what death means, *this* death tells us.'[77] When seen from the vantage point of the cross, a human being is able to stand before God not in any attribute of her own but rather 'in the *divine* attribute in which Christ stood before God in the hour when His "religious consciousness" was the consciousness of His God-abandonment'.[78] *Vom Kreuz aus gesehen!*[79]

   Therefore, both terms of the analogy in question—our tribulation and the death of Christ—are understood in their proper significance only in the light of revelation. Where then are there grounds for a negative natural theology? There are none. There is no *analogia entis* here. There is no grounding of theology in existential or phenomenological analysis. What is striking here is the *direction* in which the analogy set forth by Barth proceeds. The analogy works 'from above to below', never in the reverse direction. Our existence in tribulation is analogically related to His death in God-abandonment; but His death is not analogous to our own. The meaning of this compressed formulation is this: we never comprehend the true significance of our tribulation until we see it as an analogy of Jesus' death in God-abandonment (which itself is only understood in the power of the Holy Spirit). Thus, the analogy is established 'from above' by means of a

---

[75] Barth, *Der Römerbrief, 1922*, 65.   [76] Ibid. 137.   [77] Ibid. 216.
[78] Ibid.   [79] Ibid.

divine act. That His death is not analogous to our own (the second half of the formulation) means that we cannot comprehend the true meaning and significance of His death in God-abandonment by taking our starting-point in a general understanding of death and suffering. Starting 'from below', there is no true analogy between our death and His. Therefore, if there is to be an analogy between His death and ours, the order of knowing must proceed from 'above to below'; it cannot be reversed.

In spite of the highly *negative* character of the analogy in question, the structural similarities to Barth's later 'analogy of faith' are unmistakable. Small wonder then that Ingrid Spieckermann refers to Barth's 'analogy of the cross' as the *Urgestalt* of the analogy of faith.[80] Like the analogy of faith, the analogy of the cross is a highly christocentric, actualistic analogy given in the moment of revelation, without preconditions or ongoing effects, working from above to below. The major difference between them is one of focus (the analogy of the cross concentrates on the relation of revelation to the event of the cross, the analogy of faith on the relation of revelation to human language) and content (the analogy of the cross has in view a highly negative content).

In spite of the fact that it has almost always been overlooked, the clear lines of a theory of how God is known are discernible in *Romans* II. It is primitive in comparison with Barth's later reflections on the analogy of faith, but it stands in a decided continuity with that later development. Whether the analogy of the cross can be regarded as an entirely successful theory of the knowledge of God is another question. Suffice it to say here that although it is a clear and coherent theory, it lacks sufficient attention to its ground in God Himself. How is it possible that God can take up a creaturely medium and bear witness to Himself in and through it without ceasing to be God? What is the condition of the possibility of revelation in God Himself? Answers to those questions would not be forthcoming until Barth devoted Himself

---

[80] Spieckermann, *Gotteserkenntnis*, 143. Spieckermann's discovery of what she calls the 'analogy of the cross' constitutes a major breakthrough in research on the second edition of *Romans*—a remarkable achievement after sixty-three years of scholarly reflection on this book, and one which has not yet attracted the attention it so richly deserves. Not one of the previous writers who has devoted a major essay or book to the problem of revelation in this phase has seen this analogy. Spieckermann deserves credit for penetrating the veil of scholarly opinion and recapturing a vital theme of *Romans* II.

to reflecting on the problems of an immanent Trinity and the incarnation; a task which he would only first take up three years later in Göttingen. Still, the doctrine of revelation as it was set forth in *Romans* II was already *functionally* Trinitarian. There are three distinguishable moments in the revelation process: revelation in itself, so to speak (the resurrection); revelation making itself "objective" in a medium (the veiling and unveiling of revelation in the event of the cross); and revelation creating a subject capable of receiving it (the actualization of the new humanity in time by the power of the Holy Spirit). Expressed in Trinitarian form: God reveals Himself in Jesus Christ by the power of the Holy Spirit. This is not yet a Trinity of being, but it is headed in that direction.

4. THE SOURCE OF THE CHARGE OF SCEPTICISM IN ROMANS II

Among the earliest criticisms of *Romans* II the most common was that it was characterized by a thoroughgoing scepticism with regard to the possibility of a real knowledge of God. Of the many who made this charge, Paul Althaus ranks among the most significant.

In a 1923 essay devoted to an evaluation of Barth's theology, Althaus argued that Barth's emphasis on the diastasis of time and eternity leads to a complete and final devaluation of history.[81] 'The mutually exclusive antithesis between God and history rests in Barth on his purely sceptical-relativistic view of history. . . . Freedom is given to the materialistic, profane, "sceptical" world-view and its justification acknowledged. Nietzsche and Overbeck prepare the way for knowledge of God with their complete radicalism and scepticism.'[82] But does an understanding which is prepared for in this way lead to knowledge of the biblical God? Althaus' answer was no. Barth's concept of God is without content. It remains purely formal, lacking all features of a personal life.[83] Barth's God is finally only a limit-concept, boundary, threat, crisis, and death.[84] 'In the strictest sense, a "relationship"

---

[81] Paul Althaus, 'Theologie und Geschichte: Zur Auseinandersetzung mit der dialektischen Theologie', *Zeitschrift für systematische Theologie*, 1 (1923/4), 746.

[82] Ibid.   [83] Ibid. 754.   [84] Ibid. 743.

[between God and humankind] cannot be spoken of.'[85] In Althaus' view, Barth's fundamental error was that he failed to see that 'eternity and time stand not only in the relationship of dialectical tension but rather, at the same time, for the sake of unconditional responsibility, in the relationship of immanence.'[86] It was a serious error, he said, to forget the positive relationship of history to eternity which lies beyond the dialectical.[87] In a famous statement, Althaus warned: 'A theology which is nourished by scepticism, dies from it.'[88]

Althaus' critique ultimately rests upon a misunderstanding, but it is a misunderstanding which is not without foundation in Barth's thinking. The source of the problem lay in the time–eternity dialectic. "Eternity", as Barth was defining it in this phase, is essentially "timelessness"—the antithesis of time. As a result, the relation of time and eternity is itself a timeless relation. Barth summarized his position nicely in lectures given in the summer semester 1923 (which also belong to this phase).

Last *things*, as such, are not *last* things, however great and significant they may be. He only speaks of *last* things who would speak of the *end* of all things; of their end understood so absolutely, so fundamentally, of a Reality so radically superior to all things, that the existence of all things would be grounded in it, in it alone . . . The end of history [*Endgeschichte*] would have to be synonymous for him with the primal history [*Urgeschichte*]. The boundary of time of which he speaks would have to be the boundary of all and every time and thereby, necessarily, the *origin* of time. . . . Whoever clearly grasps this is removed from the temptation to confuse the end of history [*Endgeschichte*] with a termination of history [*Schlußgeschichte*], however impressive and wonderful it may be. Of the *real* end of history it may be said at any time: the end is near![89]

Eternity, on this view, is equally near to (and equally far from) every point in time. Eternity cannot become time without ceasing to be eternity. But—as Michael Beintker rightly points out—eternity can 'encounter' time.

Eternity cannot become time. But eternity can *encounter* time. . . . On the basis of the surrender of every chronological temporality, it

---

[85] Ibid. 747.   [86] Ibid. 748.   [87] Ibid. 749.   [88] Ibid. 753.
[89] Karl Barth, *Die Auferstehung der Toten* (Munich: Chr. Kaiser Verlag, 1924), 59, 60; ET *The Resurrection of the Dead*, trans. H. J. Stenning (London: Hodder and Stoughton Ltd., 1933), 110, 112.

becomes possible to qualify in actuality every moment in time to be the reflection of the lightning-like, illuminating Now of the eternal moment. . . . Every temporal moment can become a parable of the eternal moment . . . Thus, Barth developed in *Romans* II distinct features of an 'eschatology of the *hic et nunc*', in which all moments of our time and history can be thought of as being in the *same* nearness to the eschaton.[90]

Beintker is absolutely right in noting that Barth's eschatology in this phase (governed as it is by the time–eternity dialectic) would make the incarnation extremely problematic; not to mention the historicity of revelation. So Althaus was on to something with his critique. But it has to be noted that this obvious consequence of the time–eternity dialectic stands in decided tension with the epistemology/soteriology described in the previous section. Given the time–eternity dialectic, Barth should not have been able to say that revelation and the new humanity project themselves into time—but he did. Althaus allowed himself to be lulled to sleep by Barth's one-sidedness. He failed to see that Barth intended not only to negate every attempt to make the knowledge of God a human possibility, but also to establish the knowledge of God as a divine possibility.

Given the misunderstandings to which the time–eternity dialectic so easily gave rise, why did Barth use it? Leaving aside the obvious fact that it was extremely effective in negating all human possibilities, it also had a positive function to perform.[91] It was useful for bearing witness to a theological state of affairs.

---

[90] Beintker, *Die Dialektik in der 'dialektischen Theologie' Karl Barths*, 53–4. Beintker has learned to describe Barth's eschatology in this phase in terms of an 'eschatology of the *hic et nunc*' from Walter Kreck. See Kreck, *Die Zukunft des Gekommenen* (Munich: Chr. Kaiser Verlag, 1966), 40–50. Also of interest here is Rudolf Bultmann's review 'Karl Barth, *The Resurrection of the Dead*', in idem, *Faith and Understanding*, trans. Louise Pettibone Smith (Philadelphia: Fortress Press, 1987), 66–94. The amount of agreement expressed by Bultmann with Barth's eschatology of the *hic et nunc* cannot be missed. In a real sense, Bultmann was the heir to this perspective and remained faithful to it long after Barth had abandoned it. On Bultmann's eschatology, see Kreck, *Die Zukunft des Gekommenen*, 50–62.

[91] In the preface to the second edition of *Romans*, Barth pointed out that the time–eternity dialectic had positive significance for him. Had this claim been taken more seriously at the time, it might have prevented readers from being hypnotized by his one-sided emphasis on the negations. See Barth, *Der Römerbrief, 1922*, p. xiii: 'If I have a system, it is limited to a recognition of what Kierkegaard called the "infinite qualitative distinction" between time and eternity; keeping it in view—so far as possible—in its negative and positive significance.'

Eternity cannot become time without ceasing to be eternity, but eternity can encounter time.[92] So too, in the case of revelation, God (as the content of revelation) cannot become the medium in which He veils Himself without ceasing to be God. The critical distinction between revelation and the medium of revelation must be preserved. So it was the *structural similarity* between the time–eternity dialectic and the dialectic of veiling and unveiling which made the former a useful tool for bearing witness to the latter. But the time–eternity dialectic was *only* a witness to the latter. There are limits to the usefulness of this model of explication. It is clear from the foregoing analysis of Barth's epistemology that God can do things which eternity (treated as an abstract principle) cannot. God can raise Jesus from the dead bodily; He can create the knowledge of God and faith in the sinner living in time. Unlike eternity, which can only limit or bound time, God can realize new possibilities in time. In a very real sense, the inadequacy of the time–eternity dialectic for witnessing to *all* that Barth wanted to say rendered it outdated from the very moment it was first articulated.

Obviously, Barth could not have been fully aware of this as he wrote *Romans* II. He certainly intended that his eschatology be taken seriously. But the charge of theological scepticism made it clear that Barth's critics took the time–eternity dialectic with much greater seriousness than he himself did. In response to Althaus' lengthy critique, Barth wrote a postcard to the author in which he observed

how powerfully must we have spoken past one another: I with my book, in that you could finally see in it only dialectic (= negative apologetics!) and a bit of "majesty" and behind that, a great zero with the word "God" in the centre; and now you with your review, in that I have difficulty—because you have not entered into my real concern but have only criticized my apparatus—I have difficulty responding to your criticisms with anything other than the Pauline 'may it never be!' Expressed in German: 'You rang the wrong bell. The man you are seeking lives next door!'[93]

---

[92] Beintker too, makes this to be the 'positive function' of the time–eternity dialectic. See Beintker, *Die Dialektik in der 'dialektischen Theologie' Karl Barths*, 54.

[93] Karl Barth to Paul Althaus, undated postcard, postmarked sometime in 1924, copy in Karl Barth-Archiv, Basle, Switzerland.

The distinction made here by Barth between his 'real concerns' and his 'apparatus' (by which—given Althaus' critique—only the time–eternity dialectic could have been meant) is a testimony to the fact that he did not take his 'apparatus' with the seriousness that Althaus did. The time–eternity dialectic was not directly identical with the subject-matter to which he wished to bear witness. And because that was so, it could be dispensed with without any real loss.

5. DIALECTICS IN ROMANS II

It has already been made quite clear that the time–eternity dialectic is not the only dialectic at work in *Romans* II. The time–eternity dialectic was employed to bear witness to the dialectic of veiling and unveiling in revelation. However, there still remain other dialectics at work in the phase of *Romans* II to which some attention needs to be given. In what follows, I shall attempt to classify the various dialectics at work in this phase according to type (making use of Michael Beintker's distinction between 'supplementary' and 'complementary' dialectics). It should be observed that although this classification is similar to the one offered by Beintker, it does not follow him at every point.[94]

There are four distinguishable types of dialectic at work in the phase of *Romans* II. Variations of expression can occur within each of the following classes, but for all practical purposes, the uses reduce to four types.

(i) *The Adam–Christ dialectic*

The first type of dialectic finds its exemplification in the dialectic of Adam and Christ, the old world and the new. This dialectic must be considered from God's standpoint, *sub specie aeterni*. To do so is to view the problem on what Beintker (following Barth) calls the ontic level of 'real reality'[95] as opposed to the phenomenological level (how it appears to men and women living in history).[96]

---

[94] See above, Introd. Sect. 1.   [95] Barth, *Der Römerbrief, 1922*, 269.
[96] Beintker, *Die Dialektik in der 'dialektischen Theologie' Karl Barths*, 38.

The old world of Adam is the fallen world, the world of history, time, people, and things. It is the world between the "unhistorical" events of creation/fall and redemption. It is the world we know. The God who is truly God cannot vacillate in His dealings with such a world. The God who indifferently swings to and fro between good and evil, between sin and grace, is the No-God of this world.[97] God *must* reject such a world but in rejecting it, He can also elect it. What He cannot do is to 'change His mind', now electing and now rejecting, back and forth with no real progress. God rejects once and for all that He may elect once and for all. He kills in order to make alive.

Interestingly enough, it was this dialectic which Barth chose to call a 'genuine dialectic', one which 'consists in the overcoming of the first member by the second . . . the order is not reversible'.[98] There can be no equilibrium between Adam and Christ. The old world and the new world are not two worlds placed alongside one another, for:

the possibility of the one is always the impossibility of the other and the impossibility of the one, the possibility of the other. Considered under the viewpoint of the "first" world, the "second" ceases to be second, and from the standpoint of the "second", the "first" is no longer the first. . . . The second has its ground of being in the non-being of the first.[99]

A movement back and forth between two equal members is not a 'genuine movement'. Genuine movement consists only in the overcoming of the old world of Adam by the new world of Christ,[100] the eternal world in which all things are made new, the redeemed world in which the original but lost unity with God is restored. Therefore:

The dualism of Adam and Christ, of the old world and the new world, is not a metaphysical dualism but a dialectical one. It is throughout the dualism of a movement, of a complete knowledge, of a way *from* here *to* there. The entire situation would be misunderstood if somehow the conception of a duality swinging to and fro in equilibrium or the two parts of an hour-glass reversing at will were to arise. . . . For the crisis of death and resurrection, the crisis of faith, is the turn from the divine No to the divine Yes and never, at the same time, the reverse as well.[101]

---

[97] Barth, *Der Römerbrief, 1922*, 169.   [98] Ibid. 167.   [99] Ibid. 142.
[100] Ibid. 143.   [101] Ibid. 155.

The new world is no other than the old world which has been overcome in Christ. The emphasis here (in the Adam–Christ dialectic) is on the 'has been overcome'. The decision has been made. In the death and resurrection of Christ, Christ has been made the 'new subject, the I of the *coming* world'. He is the bearer, recipient, revealer of the divine '*verdict of justification*', of the "divine election".[102] The new creature, 'my unintuitable existential I'[103] is, in the first instance, Christ, in whom the turn from old world to new world, from old creature to new creature, has taken place. Hence Barth can say:

> You stand with me before completed facts. Our embarrassment applies only to their interpretation, not to their reality. The Spirit 'has set you free from the law of sin and death'. You, the existential you! The turn, the reversal which has taken place in Christ, is yours.[104]

The Spirit 'means Either–Or, but an already anticipated Either over against an already finished Or'.[105] Unlike Kierkegaard, who made the subject of the Either–Or to be the human subject, Barth applies the language of Either–Or primarily to God. And the decision has already fallen; the victory has already been won.

Considered from the standpoint of God (*sub specie aeterni*), the dialectic of Adam and Christ, of judgement and grace, is a dialectic in which grace has already won out. It is striking that this dialectic tends more in the direction of Hegel than Kierkegaard. It is not the Kierkegaardian type of dialectic—which is always to be held open, which is static in character, in which a synthesis can only be awaited. Rather, it is a dialectic in which a real synthesis has occurred. It is what Beintker has called a 'supplementary dialectic'.

There are, of course, important differences from Hegel. For Barth, the triumph of God's grace over judgement is an act of God's freedom. It is not necessary to God. It is the decision and act of a living Person; not an automatic turning of the dialectical machinery. Second, it is much clearer in Hegel than in Barth that the synthesis represents a real advance over the starting-point. For Barth, eschatology tends to be equated with protology. Redemption does not bring about any greater blessing than was enjoyed in the original, created relation. But these differences

---

[102] Barth, *Der Römerbrief, 1922*, 160.   [103] Ibid. 281.   [104] Ibid. 258.
[105] Ibid. 266.

aside, the Adam–Christ dialectic does lean in Hegel's direction rather than Kierkegaard's.

Considerable weight has been placed in the foregoing analysis upon God's standpoint. This dialectic is an eternal dialectic. The movement is a movement which has taken place "in eternity", not in time. That is to say, the turn which has occurred was accomplished by the raising of Jesus from the dead, which is an "unhistorical" event. But the fact that this dialectic is eternal does not mean that it is unreal. What has taken place in Christ is the 'real reality', not reality as it appears to us. But when we go on to ask: what is the relation of this dialectic to men and women living in time, a new dialectic surfaces—a dialectic of the Kierkegaardian type.

(ii) *The Dialectic of Veiling and Unveiling* (*Revelation and Soteriology*)

On the phenomenological level of perceived reality, we can always only await redemption. Left to our own devices, we know only the old world of Adam. As already noted, the time–eternity dialectic is used by Barth to prevent any illegitimate synthesis of God and humanity from the human side. What is in view here is a dialectic of the strictly-to-be-maintained opposition, a static dialectic.

But as we have seen, the use made by Barth of the time–eternity dialectic did not prevent revelation from occurring 'in time'—from the divine side. God does reveal Himself to us here and now, and in so doing, makes known to us the victory already won in Christ. Like the time–eternity dialectic used to bear witness to it, the dialectic of veiling and unveiling also belongs to the Kierkegaardian type. In revelation, God conceals Himself in a creaturely medium. Yet the coming-together of God and the creaturely medium in no way results in a *synthesis* of the two. The 'infinite qualitative difference' between God and the world is not set aside; it is preserved. And because it is, the unveiling which occurs in and through the veil remains the divine prerogative. God chooses where and when the veil becomes transparent and faith is created. Revelation and redemption are thus experienced without becoming the secure possession of the human individual. So whether the human being has become the 'recipient' of revelation or not, she must always, at every moment, begin again at the beginning. In eternity, one can say only that the decision has been made (past tense). In time, no matter how often the decision is made (present tense) from the divine side, in the most significant sense, it is still to be made (future tense). That is why, on the phenomenological level, we can always only await redemption.

(iii) *Dialectical Method*

The first two dialectics are "real dialectics"; each describes a dialectical relationship between two magnitudes or states of affairs which are objectively real prior to human knowledge of them. Barth's conviction however, is that human knowledge of dialectical relations will also be dialectical in character. Knowledge of God consists for human beings in a following-after and a thinking-after the movement of God in His Self-revelation. Hence, it can only be dialectical.

In the phase of *Romans* II, Barth bore witness to this *erkenntnis-theoretische Dialektik* by means of his oft-discussed "dialectical method". Interestingly enough, Barth devoted very little attention to the problem of method in *Romans* II. It was only under the impact of the discussion generated by the book and the demands placed upon him by his new academic post in Göttingen that Barth would turn to a closer reflection on the problem of method in the occasional lectures given in the autumn of 1922. Still, comments on dialectical thinking and method are not wholly lacking in *Romans* II.

In the preface to the second edition of *Romans*, Barth considered at some length the problem of how Scripture is to be interpreted. The primary point of this discussion is that the meaning of words and phrases in the biblical text is to be construed in the light of the *Sache* ('subject-matter') of which they speak. The goal is to uncover 'the Word in the words'.[106] Barth referred to this process as 'critical theology'.[107]

The uncovering of the Word or *Sache* in the words and the measuring of the text by it was not assumed to be an easy task. A materially faithful treatment of the text is achieved only by means of a 'dialectical movement which is as inexorable as it is elas-

---

[106] Barth, *Der Römerbrief, 1922*, p. xii.   [107] Ibid. p. xiii.

tic'.[108] What Barth had in view was a movement of thought which is dialectical because it involves a 'participation in the inner tension of the concepts which are presented more or less clearly by the text';[109] a devoting of oneself to an 'attentive thinking-after [*Nachdenken*]'[110] the concepts.

What then is the *Sache*, the theme, the cardinal question, in the light of which the words and phrases of Scripture are to be interpreted?

what do I mean when *I* call the inner dialectic of the subject-matter and its recognition in the wording of the text, the decisive factor in understanding and interpretation? . . . 'God is in heaven and you are on earth.' The relation of *this* God to *this* human being, the relation of *this* human being to *this* God, is for me the theme of the Bible and the sum of philosophy in one.[111]

The theme of the Bible is a *dialectical relation*; the relation of a holy God to a fallen creature and the crisis which results from such an encounter. Interpretation involves a critical thinking-after the movement in which this relationship is established and a measuring of the words of the scriptural text in the light of it.

The recognition that a distinction is to be made between the Word and the words—a distinction which gives rise to the necessity of uncovering the relation between the two—leads to a further, logically prior question. How can human language (or any creaturely reality, for that matter) become a bearer of divine revelation? Barth did not reflect upon this question extensively at this point in his development, but he did lay a foundation for later reflection. That human language can become a bearer of divine revelation is a divine possibility, not a human possibility. 'God's Word, heard by *human* ears, proclaimed by *human* lips, is only *God's* Word when the miracle occurs. Otherwise, it is a human word like any other.'[112] Barth left no doubt that he was convinced that this divine possibility can be and is realized in this world.

The Word is near to you! . . . It is ready to be taken seriously, ready to assert itself . . . ready to be heard by us and spoken by us—the Word which, because it is the Word of Christ, will never be heard, never be spoken. We ourselves wait to hear and to speak it. . . . Precisely this

[108] Ibid, pp. xi–xii.   [109] Ibid. p. xii.   [110] Ibid. p. xiii.   [111] Ibid.
[112] Ibid. 350–1.

Impossible as such is close to us, ready, possible. It presses itself upon us. It wants to break in; it is already present. It is more possible than anything which we hold to be possible. The light shines in the darkness.[113]

Both sides of the problem are stressed in this passage. As human possibility, the Word is never heard. But as the divine 'impossible possibility' it is indeed heard.

Beyond the fact that it is a miracle when God's Word is spoken by human lips, Barth reflected little at this time on *how* the miracle occurs and what the implications of such a miracle would be. He was more concerned with the mandate which is laid upon us in spite of our complete inadequacy.

We speak of the Spirit. But can one do that? No, one cannot do that; for we have many words for the many possibilities of our lives, but not a single word for this, the impossible possibility. Why then are we not silent about Him? We must also be silent about Him but He is compromised by our silence as well as by our speaking. He is served by silence for its own sake as little as by speaking. And the fact remains that He is the *Word* which wants to be proclaimed in our speaking as well as in our silence. Not being able to speak and not being able to fall silent, having to speak and having to fall silent—*vis-à-vis* the Spirit we are in an ultimate distress . . . and there is *no* clear way out of this distress. May we take heed that our speaking occurs in its time and our falling silent in its time in order at the same time to understand that if we hit the mark, it is *not we* who have hit it . . . [but] the Spirit Himself has then spoken or fallen silent.[114]

If we are incapable of speaking God's Word, and yet the demand to do so is still laid upon us by God, what are we to do? We are to await the miracle and in the meantime testify to the human impossibility and thereby, to the necessity that God step forward and speak. We do this concretely by always being ready to negate every position we take, to balance every affirmation with a negation.

[The prophet] will take up no standpoint without the secret intention of vacating it again as quickly as possible when the tactical goal . . . is attained. He will never build up without at the same time making preparations for tearing down. He will always be ready to do everything against the dangerous stability of his/her own word and for the freedom of God's Word.[115]

[113] Barth, *Der Römerbrief, 1922*, 364–5.   [114] Ibid. 256.   [115] Ibid. 321.

Can I then think even a single thought which would somehow be the expression of the Spirit who compels me? Is somehow a single one of my words *the* Word which I seek, which I would like to speak out of my great need and hope? Can I then speak otherwise than in such a way that one word must again overcome the other?[116]

'We cannot *comprehend* God otherwise than in the duality [*Zweiheit*]; in the dialectical duality in which one must become two so that two may truly be one.'[117] The idea that human beings ought never to speak of God without using two words or statements which stand in a tension with one another would become the central focus of Barth's programmatic address, 'The Word of God as the Task of Theology', delivered in the autumn of 1922. In *Romans* II, however, all of these reflections upon method remained on the periphery of his thinking. His attention was absorbed primarily by the first two dialectics discussed above—the "real dialectics".

(iv) *The 'Dialectic of Life'*

We have already discussed this class of dialectics in relation to Kierkegaard in the previous chapter.[118] Suffice it here to say that these dialectics constituted a distinct class or type in this phase of Barth's development.

In concluding this discussion of dialectics in the phase of *Romans* II, it is natural to ask which of them is the most important or fundamental. What is at stake in this question is the determination of what it is that makes Barth's theology to be "dialectical". From the beginning, it was undoubtedly the so-called "dialectical method" which most impressed contemporary observers and led quickly to the depiction of the theological movement which grew up around Barth and his friends as "dialectical theology".[119] And certainly, it was the method of pitting theological statement over against counter-statement which Hans Urs von Balthasar

---

[116] Ibid. 243.   [117] Ibid. 342.   [118] See above, Ch. 5, Sect. 3. iii.

[119] Barth would later recall that it was in the year 1922 that the movement centred on the journal *Zwischen den Zeiten* was labelled 'dialectical theology' by some unknown observer. See Barth, 'Abschied', *Zwischen den Zeiten*, 11 (1933), 536. In all likelihood, this occurred in the aftermath of Barth's much-discussed Elgersburg lecture, 'The Word of God as the Task of Theology' which, as we have noted, was devoted to the question of method.

had principally in view when he spoke of a 'turn from dialectic to analogy'.[120] In truth, however, the so-called "dialectical method" was the least important of the dialectics at work in this phase. It was never intended to do more than bear vivid witness to the human impossibility of "correct" speech about God. Much more fundamental were the "real dialectics" out of which Barth's preoccupation with "dialectical method" sprang.

But which of the "real dialectics" described in our classification was most basic or fundamental? Judged from the standpoint of that which gave Barth's theology in this phase its characteristic stamp (over against the shape of his theology in other phases), it is the time–eternity dialectic which has to be considered the most important. After all, it was the consistent eschatology of *Romans* II which set that book apart from its predecessor, as well as from all later efforts. However, judged from the standpoint of its enduring importance—from the standpoint of what made Barth's theology in all of its phases after the break with Herrmannian "liberalism" to be "dialectical theology"—it is the dialectic of veiling and unveiling in revelation which was the most important. And it is natural that it should be so. After all, the purpose of the time–eternity dialectic was to bear witness to the dialectical relation between God and humankind established in revelation. Given all of this, it should not be surprising that the dialectic of veiling and unveiling would continue to be constitutive of the overall shape of Barth's theology long after the abandonment of the time–eternity dialectic of *Romans* II (which occurred during the course of Barth's lectures on dogmatics in Göttingen in 1924–5). Indeed, the dialectical structuring of God's Self-revelation would remain a permanent feature of Barth's thought, leaving its stamp on all of the works of the 1920s and continuing on into the *Church Dogmatics*, where it finally found its home in the 'Doctrine of God'.[121]

6. THE EMERGENCE OF A CRITICALLY REALISTIC ETHIC IN ROMANS II

Earlier, it was shown that in spite of Barth's criticisms of idealistic ethics in *Romans* I, he had been unable at that time to break

---

[120] See above, Introd., n. 19.   [121] Barth, *KD* II/1, 266; ET *CD*, II/1, 236.

completely free of an appeal to the Kantian categorical imperative in 'confused situations'. In the first edition he had worked with two not entirely compatible ethical programmes: a realistically conceived 'divine command' ethic (in the realm of interpersonal relationships) and an idealistic ethic (in the realm of politics).[122] In *Romans* II that inconsistency was overcome. Barth everywhere provides a critical correction to idealistic ethics in that he makes the unintuitable Christ the standard by which human ethical activity is to be judged and measured, rather than Kant's universal law of reason.[123] What emerges is an 'ethic of *witness*'[124]—witness to the divine command contained in God's Self-revelation in Jesus Christ.

For the Barth of *Romans* II, ethics is grounded in Christology: in the forgiveness of sins realized in the cross and resurrection of Jesus Christ.[125] The full significance of this claim can only be comprehended against the background of the 'infinite qualitative distinction' between God and humankind. Human beings living in time are sinners. For the sinful human being, the achievement of the good is an impossibility. But the ethical problem goes much deeper than the mere fact that human beings are unable to achieve the good that they would like to accomplish; even their self-chosen ethical goals—in that they are self-chosen—are the product of their self-relating, sinful orientation. Hence: 'The will of God is wholly other and never identical with the will of human beings.'[126] All of the ethical goals which human beings set for themselves and the attempts to achieve these goals stand in the shadow of this judgement. Seen in this light, ethics cannot be concerned with the promulgation of 'this-worldly goals' (something which Barth calls 'the Lutheran misunderstanding'), but in the critical negation of all human goals and the proclamation of

---

[122] See above, Ch. 3, Sects. 3. vi, 3. vii.

[123] Ruschke, *Entstehung und Ausführung der Diastasentheologie*, 86.

[124] Ibid. 81.

[125] Barth, *Der Römerbrief, 1922*, 416. It should be noted that Barth's attempt to ground his ethics in Christology in *Romans* II does not in the least contradict my earlier insistence that the whole of his theology in this phase was grounded in eschatology (see above, Ch. 5, Sect. 1). For the highly concrete form of Barth's Christological concentration in this phase (centred as it was in the events of crucifixion and resurrection) was itself a function of Barth's eschatology.

[126] Ruschke, *Entstehung und Ausführung der Diastasentheologie*, 73.

the forgiveness of sins.[127] Ruschke is right to see in this movement of thought the priority of gospel over law.[128]

What Barth was seeking to do was to relocate completely the problem of ethics. No longer was the problem of ethics to be conceived in terms of the situation in which individuals who do not know God ask the question: what should *we* do? Ethics must concern itself first and foremost with what God has done in Christ, and secondly with the demand which a recognition of God's gracious action lays upon human beings. Such a vision of the ethical problem again gave vivid expression to Barth's fundamentally anti-bourgeois outlook. 'This ethic escapes from bourgeois utilitarian and goal-oriented thinking. The truth of ethics does not depend on whether it makes use of the reality which is ready to hand. The criterion of the truth of this ethic is solely its witness to the reconciling work of God in Jesus Christ.'[129]

Human ethical activity which takes place under these presuppositions is distinguished by Barth in two classes: 'primary ethical activity' and 'secondary ethical activity'. These two classes are distinguished in this way because the latter kind of activity must flow from the former; otherwise, it is not in the least "ethical". The 'primary ethical activity' of human beings is worship—and specifically, that worship which consists in the offering of one's "body" (i.e. one's 'sensible, intuitable, historical existence') to God as a living sacrifice (Romans 12: 2).[130] 'Sacrifice means *surrender*, the renunciation of the human in favour of the divine, an unconditionally made gift.'[131] Such an action does not simply happen, where and when a human being determines himself for it. The "sacrifice" here in view takes place as the 'acknowledgement of that being-placed-in-question and seizure which he experiences from the side of the unfathomable God'. But notice: 'A sacrifice is not a human activity in which the will of God is carried out, in the sense that the one sacrificing himself becomes an organ of God through his action. A sacrifice is much rather a *demonstration* to the glory of God; a demonstration which is demanded by God . . . but which, in itself, is a human action, as good or as bad as any other.'[132] Even on the level of this 'pri-

---

[127] Barth, *Der Römerbrief, 1922*, 416.
[128] Ruschke, *Entstehung und Ausführung der Diastasentheologie*, 73.
[129] Ibid. 81.   [130] Barth, *Der Römerbrief, 1922*, 416.   [131] Ibid.
[132] Ibid. 417.

mary ethical activity', Barth was careful to restrict the significance of human action to a 'demonstration', a witness, a parabolic action. In and of themselves, such actions are still performed by sinful human beings and, as such, are not directly identical with the performance of the good.

All 'secondary ethical activity' must 'be joined to this primary activity, proceed from it, receiving from this context its character as "living, holy, pleasing to God"—as good . . .'.[133] Here again, the fact that any human action is accepted by God as "good" does not mean that it is directly identical with the performance of the good. Barth's point is that there are certain actions which God is pleased to accept as "good"; but they are "good" not by virtue of what they are in themselves but only because they are made to be so by God's decision to accept them. God's gracious action can *qualify* a human action, can establish it as an effective witness, can make it to be good. So whether any human action really serves as a demonstration of God's glory 'must be left completely and totally up to *Him. He* accepts and rejects.'[134] One thing is certain: no human action will be acceptable to God which seeks to be anything more than a demonstration, witness, and parable; which does not consist in the surrender of all human power and right for the sake of proclaiming the mercy and freedom of God.[135] In so far as any human action seeks to be something positive in its own right, it is conformed to this world which is passing away and not to its transformation.[136]

But if not all actions are accepted by God as "good", how can human beings know which ones are likely to be accepted? Can human beings know the will of God? In itself, of course, the will of God is unintuitable. But where and when God makes Himself known through the dialectic of veiling and unveiling, there the will of God too is known. The Self-revelation of God is not only revelation; it is also command.

Grace is the power of obedience. . . . It is *the* indicative which has the significance of the absolute, the categorical imperative. And it is *the* imperative, *the* call, *the* command, *the* demand which one cannot *not* obey . . . It is *the* knowing which has the corresponding willing immediately *in itself* and not *next to* itself as something other, secondary, additional. As the knowing of that which God wills, it is identical with the willing of the divine will. For grace is the power of the resurrection.[137]

---

[133] Ibid.   [134] Ibid. 418.   [135] Ibid.   [136] Ibid. 421.   [137] Ibid. 188.

Thus, 'the problem of "ethics" is identical with the problem of "dogmatics" '.[138] All ethical activity consists in discerning the will of God and bearing witness to it. Given the actualism of Barth's understanding of revelation, it is not surprising that the will of God must necessarily be sought afresh in each new moment. The will of God is not a "given" in the sense of being reducible to a set of laws applicable to every conceivable situation. The will of God is not static. The will of God is something which must be made known anew, in each situation. It must be "given" in each new moment. Still, the fact that Barth grounds ethics in Christology means that the divinely willed *direction* of human activity can be known, even if the details of the way to be taken remain unknown apart from a fresh hearing of the Word of God.[139]

'Demonstrations' which conform to the will of God, which bear witness to it, are of two kinds according to Barth. There are first of all those 'positive possibilities' in which human action is negatively related to the forms of life in this world; in which a protest is raised against the error of identifying human goals and achievements with the will of God. The greatest of these 'positive possibilities' is love of the neighbour. How can love of the neighbour entail a protest against the forms of life in this world? It can do so only in that the love spoken of here is agape, not eros. Erotic love affirms the human being in her sinfulness; in what she is as a self-absorbed, self-relating, self-determining, sinful creature. Agape love by contrast loves in her what she is *not*, but what she will be by the grace of God. In putting it this way, Barth is suggesting that the action of the believer must *correspond* to the dialectic of God's action.[140] The love of God towards sinful human beings expresses itself in the crisis in which God rejects what we are and elects what we are not. 'In the praxis of neighbour love, the believer corresponds to the rejecting and electing activity of God.'[141] In that the one who has received grace responds to it by loving the '*other* in the other'[142] (i.e. the unintuitable subject which he is through divine election), 'an

138 Barth, *Der Römerbrief, 1922*, 417.
139 Ruschke, *Entstehung und Ausführung der Diastasentheologie*, 80.
140 Barth, *Der Römerbrief, 1922*, 437.
141 Beintker, *Die Dialektik in der 'dialektischen Theologie' Karl Barths*, 261.
142 Barth, *Der Römerbrief, 1922*, 439.

intuitable analogy of his own election'[143] is actualized. Michael Beintker is absolutely right to see in this analogy an early form of what Barth would later call an *analogia relationis*.[144]

There are secondly those 'negative possibilities' in which witness is borne to the coming world of God by leaving certain things undone. Such actions were seen by Barth as positively related to the coming world and as such, can witness to it. The believer should take up an attitude of fundamental distrust towards all things which are 'set on high'; those persons and orders which are pre-eminent in this world.[145] She will sense everywhere the threat of idolatry: above all, in the creative development of the world by science, technology, art, morality, and religion. She will do nothing to strengthen the ideals of human beings—whether they be 'personal or collective, ethnocentric or international'.[146] She will exercise 'a certain biased preference for the oppressed, those who have had a bad deal, the immature, the sorrowful, and those caught up in revolution'.[147] But she will also recognize how quickly the lowly things of this world can become the things 'set on high'; how quickly humility can be turned into pride, causes can become idols, and the role of the builder of towers of Babel can shift from the one who affirms culture to the one who rejects it.[148] 'From moment to moment, it must be asked *in concreto* which things are now the "high" things from which Christianity must turn away, and which the "lowly" towards which it must turn.'[149] Thus, the stance of the Christian in this world is in constant flux; it must not be allowed to harden into a stable yes or no to any person, group, or nation. As we shall see momentarily, 'the great negative possibility' is located by Barth in the Christian's unwillingness to lend her approval to a revolutionary political option.

Given the purpose for which *Romans* II was written, it is understandable that Barth would lay the greatest stress possible on 'primary ethical activity'; understandable too that his treatment of 'secondary ethical activity' would have a highly negative feel (focused as it was upon protest and criticism). In *Romans* II,

[143] Ibid. 437. [Emphasis is mine.]
[144] Beintker, *Die Dialektik in der 'dialektischen Theologie' Karl Barths*, 262: 'In this passage, the concretization of the *analogia proportionalitatis* as an analogy of relation is suggested.'
[145] Barth, *Der Römerbrief, 1922*, 446.   [146] Ibid. 447.   [147] Ibid. 448.
[148] Ibid. 449.   [149] Ibid. 448.

Barth had little incentive to provide positive descriptions of 'secondary ethical activities'. It must be added, however, that at this point in time, there was little Barth could have done to flesh out his ethics in a more positive fashion. The Christology in which he grounded his ethics was stripped down to the bare essentials of cross and resurrection. Such a Christology was sufficient only to provide the most general ethical guidance. In 1924 his Christology would be dramatically enlarged—thus making possible the much fuller and more positive presentation in his lectures on ethics in 1928/9.[150] Still, it must not be overlooked that the ethics of *Romans* II provided the foundation for all that came later. Barth would never go back upon his insistence that ethics must be grounded in Christology.

It should be pointed out in conclusion that Barth's critical correction of Kantian ethics did not entail a simple rejection. Barth remained convinced that Kant's categorical imperative had an important critical role to play.[151] Because of its universality and objective validity as a formal principle, the categorical imperative provided a useful tool for unmasking the arbitrariness of all limited and privatized human goals—even those adopted with the help of the categorical imperative itself! Moreover, its objective validity was a witness to the objective validity of the divine command.[152] But the Kantian ethic was only a witness to an ethic of divine command; it was not a substitute for it. Barth sought to transcend Kant by giving his purely formal ethical principle a Christological content.[153] 'Grace is . . . *the* indicative which has the significance of the absolute, the categorical imperative.'[154] What emerged was a critically realistic ethic commensurate with his critically realistic theology.

7. POLITICAL ACTION IN ROMANS II

'The great negative possibility' consists in the refusal of the Christian to grant her approval to the revolutionary option. In

[150] Karl Barth, *Ethik*, ed. Dietrich Braun (2 vols.; Zurich: TVZ, 1973, 1978); ET *Ethics*, trans. Geoffrey Bromiley (New York: Seabury Press, 1981).

[151] Barth, *Der Römerbrief, 1922*, 188, 277, 418, 452–4.   [152] Ibid. 452–3.

[153] Ruschke, *Entstehung und Ausführung der Diastasentheologie*, 87.

[154] Barth, *Der Römerbrief, 1922*, 188.

Romans II, Barth laid greater emphasis upon criticizing the principle of revolution than upon criticizing the principle of legitimation. Why did he do so? Because, in his view, the revolutionary stands much closer to the truth than does the reactionary: 'it is less likely that one will become a reactionary on the soil of *Romans*.'[155] The threat of hubris which surrounds revolution is great because Christianity has a decided preference for unrest, questioning, and rejection. 'For us, the reactionary is the small danger; his red brother, however, the greater danger.'[156]

As in *Romans* I, so too here: the state is regarded with deep distrust and suspicion. 'Should the existing order make any other impression on the one who is *seeking* the order of God than that of the embodied triumph of injustice . . .?'[157] The state owes its existence to the assumption of certain individuals that they are invested with 'higher rights' than their fellow men and women and are therefore justified in calling for obedience and sacrifice—as if their power were the power of God. But such a claim is a fiction. No human being has the right to be objectively in the right over against other human beings.[158] The existing order is—precisely in its existence—evil.

Where the evil of the existing order is recognized, revolution is born. The revolutionary would like to overthrow the old order, replacing it with "justice". But in that he does so, he too claims for himself that which no human being can claim. He treats the "right" as a thing which he can control: 'he forgets that he is not the One, the *Subject* of that freedom for which he thirsts; . . . not the *Christ* who stands over against the Grand Inquisitor but, on the contrary, always only the Grand Inquisitor who stands over against the Christ.'[159] The revolutionary aims at '*the* Revolution, which is the impossible possibility'. But instead, he carries out 'the *other* revolution . . . the possible possibility of dissatisfaction, hatred, insubordination, rebellion, and destruction'.[160] What is the Christian to do in the face of this 'possible possibility'? She is to witness to *the* Revolution, by her 'notdoing'; by not becoming angry, by not attacking and not destroying. She is to deprive the existing order of pathos, thereby starving it out of existence.[161] That is 'the great negative possibility'.

---

[155] Ibid. 461.   [156] Ibid. 462.   [157] Ibid.   [158] Ibid. 463.
[159] Ibid. 464.   [160] Ibid.   [161] Ibid. 467.

In the early 1970s, Friedrich-Wilhelm Marquardt caused a great stir with his thesis that between *Romans* I and *Romans* II, Barth underwent 'a sensational anti-revolutionary turn'.[162] Such a thesis represents a drastic overstatement of the significance of the changes which Barth introduced into his commentary on Romans 13: 1–7 in the second edition. At most, one could say that the cautious approval which he extended to the revolutionary option in *Romans* I (an approval which even then was denied every Christian justification!) has been replaced by an ethic of non-violence. But the presuppositions upon which both decisions were made were the same. His attitude towards the state had clearly not changed. And he still regarded revolution as the attempt to overcome evil with evil; to bring in the new world through the methods of the old. What had changed between *Romans* I and *Romans* II was the situation. The forces of reaction were now everywhere on the defensive; the revolutionary forces were, for the time being, in the ascendancy. In the new situation, a shift in accent is understandable. Where before, Barth directed his attention to challenging the legitimacy of the state, he was now preoccupied with challenging the 'titanism' of the revolutionary. But this hardly represented an anti-revolutionary turn. It still remained true that the revolutionary was closer to the truth than the reactionary.

8. THE CHURCH AS THE *LOCUS* OF JUDGEMENT: BARTH'S CRITIQUE OF RELIGION, THE CHURCH, AND DOCTRINE

Perhaps no aspect of Karl Barth's early thought has been more criticized and less understood than his critique of religion. It is not at all unusual to read that Barth was the sworn enemy of religious experience and the organized Church. Such a reading ignores a great deal of evidence to the contrary. Barth made it quite clear that there is no grace without the experience of grace.[163] His critique of religion was not directed against religion as such but against *Religion an sich*[164]—religion for its own sake.

To be sure, Barth's case against religion could scarcely have

---

[162] Marquardt, *Theologie und Sozialismus*, 142.
[163] Barth, *Der Römerbrief, 1922*, 212.
[164] Barth, 'Der Christ in der Gesellschaft', 47.

been stronger. Religion was viewed by him as a *human* possibility. As such, it belongs to the world of time. It is flesh, not
spirit.[165] Moreover, it is the final human possibility—the place
where sin finally shows itself to be what it is, namely, robbery of
God.

Feuerbach was most certainly correct: with the religious possibility—
no, still more—precisely *through* it, the passions of sin are given, awakened, and energized. It is . . . the secret possibility of possibilities. . . .
For all human pathos lives somehow and finally from the pathos of the
'Eritis sicut Deus!' which precisely in the religious possibility becomes
conscious, intuitable experience and event . . .[166]

In religion as nowhere else, humankind takes hold of that which
is rightfully God's and seeks to domesticate it. In religion, sin cel-
ebrates its final triumph.

Religion . . . does not lead a person out of the problematic of guilt and
fate but into it. It brings no solution to the problem of life. It makes it
rather into an absolutely insoluble puzzle. . . . Religion is not something to be enjoyed or celebrated. It must rather be borne as a heavy
yoke which cannot be removed. Religion is not something which one
can wish upon another or extol or recommend. It is a *misfortune* which
breaks in with fatal necessity on some people . . .[167]

Apart from God, religion is the most dangerous enemy a person
can have.[168] Religion all too easily lulls a person into the complacent belief that she has done all that needs to be done for the
sake of her justification.

If this is the reality of religion, would it not be wise to abandon
it altogether? To be rid of it once and for all? In Barth's view, the
very question displays a complete lack of understanding.

Why then no outbreak of antireligious polemic with the goal of pointing to another, better human possibility somewhere above that peak?
Why not go on with Marcion to the proclamation of a new God in
contrast to the old God of the Law; or with Lhotzky to a really tangible
playing-out of the 'Kingdom of God' against 'religion'; or with
Johannes Müller to a pointing-out of a way out of mediacy back into
the land of the immediacy which was lost, to be sure, but which can
here and now be located; or with Ragaz to the demand to emigrate
from the Church and theology, which has become hopeless, into the

[165] Barth, *Der Römerbrief, 1922*, 220.
[166] Ibid. 218.   [167] Ibid. 241.   [168] Ibid. 250.

better world of the laity? Answer: *impossible!* The radicalism of all these attempts is only apparent . . .[169]

Why is all antireligious polemic which is guided by the desire to abandon religion and the Church only pseudo-radicalism? Because it presupposes a superior vantage point from which to criticize religion and has not seen that the crisis which has broken out in religion applies to its own standpoint as well. The 'line of death' runs through *every* human possibility, not just through religion. True radicalism understands that the crisis of God's judgement rests on all human possibilities; and understanding this, it places itself in the one place where the crisis is most apparent and intense—in the sphere of religion. There, in the final human possibility which too only yields death and destruction, the promise of something better, of a life lying beyond all human possibilities, can arise. True radicalism does not rest satisfied with criticizing religion only then to go in search of a new opium of the people. True radicalism invites the crisis to fall *on itself.* It drinks the last drops of the religious possibility and in so doing, testifies to the negation of all human possibilities.[170]

But this apparently tragic view of the necessity of religion does not exhaust Barth's evaluation of it. Religion can have a positive function. The relation of religion to the gospel is not unambiguous. It is not self-evident that religion must be the enemy of the gospel.

All doctrine, all morality, every cultic practice of the Christian congregation relates itself to this message in so far as it is only a bomb-crater, in so far as it only wants to be a void in which the message presents itself. The Christian congregation knows no words, works, and things which are holy in themselves. It knows only words, works, and things which, as negations, point to the holy. If anything "Christian" be unrelated to the gospel, it is a human by-product, a dangerous religious remnant, a deplorable misunderstanding, in so far as it wanted to be content instead of void, convex instead of concave, positive instead of negative, the expression of a having and being instead of an expression of a doing without and of hope.[171]

Religion is not positive by wanting to be so. It is positive by negating itself.

---

[169] Barth, *Der Römerbrief, 1922*, 223.   [170] Ibid. 236.   [171] Ibid. 12.

It must be remembered that it is the *knowledge* of God itself which brings on the crisis of judgement. To say that religion, or the Church, is the *locus* of judgement is also to say that it is the *locus* of revelation. Although the emphasis in *Romans* II falls on the former and not the latter, the latter is also true. This means that religion arises in the first instance as the result of the experience of grace in revelation. But only in the first instance! Religion only becomes all the things criticized by Barth when it seeks to preserve itself, becoming something positive for itself. Here it would be helpful to consider Barth's idea of 'revelation impressions'.

The encounter of revelation with this world leaves in its wake its negative image; a copy, an impression, like a bomb-crater.[172] Whether that impression is called the law, circumcision, or simply religion is of no consequence. Barth does not make any distinction among them in *Romans* II. As to form, they all belong to the old world. But they *can* refer to a content lying beyond themselves.[173]

"The law" is the revelation given by God, but precisely given and completed; the impression left behind by divine revelation in time, in history, in the life of humankind; the holy cinders of a miracle which has occurred; the burned-out crater of divine speech; . . . the empty canal in which, at another time, under different circumstances for other people, the living water of faith, of reasonable perception, flowed; a canal which is formed by concepts, intuitions, and commandments . . .[174]

Religion takes its rise in such an encounter but it is perpetuated when people dwell in the canals, sitting on their banks waiting for the water to flow again. But revelation is free. It is not bound to those canals in which it once flowed.[175] To the extent that religion regards revelation as bound to those remnants of revelations past, it misunderstands its own significance. Its justification lies in pointing beyond itself to the revelation which gave rise to it.[176] But religion deceives itself and thinks itself necessary to God and instead of bearing witness, gives itself over to self-preservation. 'The combatants for God without God are like a wanderer who remains standing by the signpost instead of *going* in the direction indicated. The signpost has become meaningless . . .'[177]

---

[172] Ibid. 106.   [173] Ibid. 162.   [174] Ibid. 40.   [175] Ibid. 41.
[176] Ibid. 213, 236.   [177] Ibid. 49.

Religion ought to be a signpost. Instead it becomes the ultimate attempt at self-justification.

Barth's ecclesiology in this phase bears all the marks of the just-recited critique of religion, as well as its potential for more positive valuation. Here again, both sides of Barth's paradoxical assessment must be appreciated.

The antithesis of the Church and the gospel is infinite. 'The gospel is the abolition [*Aufhebung*] of the Church, just as the Church is the abolition of the gospel.'[178] But Barth could not go the way of a Richard Rothe (and a Leonhard Ragaz, who followed him) in thinking that the Church could one day be dispensed with. Nor could he go the way of the Pietists in the Free churches who thought they could escape the guilt of the Church. True radicalism exists only in a participation in the life of the Church which remains constantly aware of the guilt which accrues to such participation. From this it follows that our task is to proclaim the gospel within the Church 'in the full, burning awareness of the infinite antithesis of the gospel and the Church, not standing over against the Church as those who are disinterested, who have no solidarity with it; but rather, giving ourselves to it'.[179] That the Church is the *locus* of divine judgement is a positive thing when it has been fully understood. For judgement is a gracious act. The Church is the *locus* of judgement, but it is so only because it is first the *locus* of revelation.

In this phase, Barth laid tremendous stress on the fact that the Church belongs to the world. But the one-sidedness of his criticism should not prevent us from seeing that the Church also belongs to revelation. Already, the foundation has been laid for a much more positive valuation. At every moment "in time", the Church is the Church of Esau, not of Jacob. It is rejected, not elected. But in the miracle of the speaking and hearing of the Word of God, the Church of Esau becomes unintuitably the Church of Jacob.[180] Where and when the Church knows and considers that it is the Church of Esau, room is created for this miracle. The Church is the place where the appropriate distance *vis-à-vis* God can be created and preserved, so that God may speak and act.[181] Barth could even go so far as to regard the ordinances of the Church in a positive light. Baptism, for example, is

---

[178] Barth, *Der Römerbrief, 1922*, 317.   [179] Ibid. 318.
[180] Ibid. 327.   [181] Ibid. 362.

a holy thing, a bearer of the truth, a sacrament, and—as *witness* to that which lies beyond—a means of grace.[182] Clearly, the Barth of *Romans* II cannot be characterized as the enemy of the Church and religious experience without a great deal of qualification.

Still, the Church is the Church of Jacob only in the event in which God reveals Himself. The true Church is to be conceived actualistically, not as enduring through time. In that the Church *also* exists "in time", as an empirical entity with a history, it is always the Church of Esau.

Church history is "weak" in the absolute sense. It is so in virtue of the infinite qualitative distinction between God and humankind. As human, completely human history, it is also flesh. It is flesh even when it portrays itself as *"Heilsgeschichte"*. And all flesh is like grass. The grass has withered and the flower decayed. But the Word of our God remains eternal.[183]

There is in reality, no sacred history which exists alongside of or above profane history. There are no saints among sinners.[184] The history of the children of god is profane. It belongs 'under the sign: "the genuine ring was presumably—lost!"'[185]

Barth's attitude towards doctrine flows from his critique of religion and the Church. In so far as doctrine is only conceived of as a 'revelation-impression', it can bear effective witness to the revelation-event in which it originated. But to the extent that the Church's doctrines are viewed as something to be handed on, doctrine becomes one of the chief means through which the Church gives itself over to the task of preserving itself, rather than awaiting fresh revelation. It is in this light that his critical assessment of scientific doctrinal theology is to be understood. 'The saving message of Christ, the Word of God as "doctrine"?! Theology as science?! We think we know the question marks which are to be placed here.'[186]

According to Barth, theology can only be carried out as an act of daring. It is not an act next to other acts. It is the act in other acts which places them all in question.

There exists next to these ordinary, regular "bourgeois" possibilities of consideration (no, not *next to* them but rather . . . in them *all*!), the extraordinary, the irregular, the . . . revolutionary possibility of daring

---

[182] Ibid. 172.   [183] Ibid. 259.   [184] Ibid. 32.   [185] Ibid. 48.
[186] Ibid. 432.

that attack. This attack . . . is *Romans*, is the speaking of God, is theology. . . . Theology has to do with grace, with the "Absolute Moment", with the voracious dialectic of time and eternity before which all other sciences have made themselves more or less secure and which nevertheless threatens them all. . . . [Theology] owes its historical existence and its place in the *universitas litterarum* to its essence as ultimate *risk* which must necessarily be dared, as the extraordinary, irregular, revolutionary *attack*. . . . To be scientific means fidelity to the object. Fidelity to the object in theology is unconditional respect before the uniqueness of the theme which is here chosen: humanity in its ultimate distress and hope, humanity before God. Scientific theology is repentance, rethinking, "renewed thinking" . . . It is the question mark and the exclamation point on the most extreme margin of the university.[187]

Where the subject-matter of theology is understood to be doctrines which have been handed down, there theology has become like the other sciences: regular, bourgeois, secure, complacent.

However, it is clear that the foundation has already been laid for a more positive valuation of doctrine. Even now 'positive theological speech is possible'.[188] But Barth was primarily concerned at this stage to hammer home the idea that theology is possible only as divine possibility. It is important to point this out now because, as we shall see, when further development in Barth's thought did occur, it occurred first on the level of his attitude towards doctrine, the Church, and so on. Barth's development in the period 1923–4 can be seen as the attempt to make a place for theology as "doctrine" without surrendering the understanding reflected in the passage just cited; theology as repentance, as continuous rethinking. It is remarkable to see just how quickly Barth would turn the terminology employed in this passage upside down. From the description of theology as irregular and extraordinary, Barth would move to a preference for regular dogmatics. How this was possible without betraying the viewpoint of *Romans* II will be the subject of the next two chapters.

9. BARTH'S LATER CRITIQUE OF ROMANS II

Barth's later critique of *Romans* II was much more accurate and fair than the critique he brought against *Romans* I in the second

---

[187] Barth, *Der Römerbrief, 1922*, 514–15.
[188] Ruschke, *Entstehung und Ausführung der Diastasentheologie*, 37.

edition. The critique was centred upon the dialectic of time and eternity.

It was due to the external and internal situation of those years that the divine No of judgement . . . had to be expressed more loudly and, in any case, heard more clearly, than the gracious Yes that we now thought ourselves to hear from the end—the real end—of all things and wanted to bring to expression. The subject-matter could, in the anti-thetical *form* in which it was initially presented, be brought without injustice into connection with the spiritual shattering which European men and women experienced as a result of the World War; being pas-sionately greeted by some as an expression of the spirit of the time and just as powerfully rejected by others who were less open to this spirit, as a "post-war phenomenon". Furthermore, this impression was not so bad and could, with time, be corrected. What was dangerous was the subject-matter itself. Precisely because we were more consistent and proceeded more purely than our predecessors, we were well on the way to just as systematic a reduction of the eternity of God to the denominator of post-temporality—the eternally future—as the Reformers had to that of pre-temporality and the neo-Protestants to that of supra-temporality. In that we sought to free ourselves from those earlier one-sidednesses . . . we came upon the best way of making ourselves guilty of a new one-sidedness . . . And so it came about that we did not know how to speak of the post-temporality of God in such a way as to make clear what we really meant: that we wished to speak of God and not somehow of the general concept of the limit and the crisis.[189]

In *CD* II/1, Barth wanted to say as clearly as possible that the eternity of God involves all three: pre-temporality, supra-temporality, and post-temporality. He noted that there had been an irony in his one-sided stress on post-temporality in *Romans* II. In seeking to combat the supra-temporality of the neo-Protestants, he had ended with something very close to it. He had interpreted post-temporality as a future which 'never has "come" and never will "come".'[190] Eternity was treated as stand-ing equally close and equally far away from every moment in time.

One can see that I said things there which, for the sake of a correct understanding of Romans 13: 11 f., can certainly be said and must be said on the margins. One also sees, however, how I missed that which

---

[189] Barth, *KD* II/1, 715–16; ET *CD* II/1, 634–5.   [190] Ibid. 716; ET, 635.

peculiar to this passage: namely the *teleology* which it attributes to *time*, as it moves towards a real end . . .[191]

The *telos* of time is that "last hour" towards which the whole of history proceeds; the "last hour" which marks the real end of history.

Thus, the crucial correction which Barth brought against *Romans* II was the abandonment of its consistent eschatology and the time–eternity dialectic by which it was secured. As we shall see, this first took place during the course of Barth's lectures on dogmatics in Göttingen and Münster, in the period 1924–6. It will be the task of the next two chapters to describe how this came about.

[191] Barth, *KD* II/1, 716; ET, 635.

7

Honorary Professor of Reformed Theology

(GÖTTINGEN,
OCTOBER 1921–APRIL 1924)

I. THE SITUATION IN GERMANY

The Germany to which Barth went in October 1921 was a Germany in the throes of an economic catastrophe. Peace had been formally established on 28 June 1919, when the German government acceded to the terms of the Versailles Treaty. The Allies had rejected any further negotiation of the terms. Feeling that further military engagement was no longer a viable possibility, the Germans reluctantly signed the treaty. The terms were overwhelming. Germany was stripped of all her colonies, Alsace-Lorraine was returned to France, and West Prussia, Upper Silesia, and Posen were given to Poland, thereby splitting East Prussia geographically from the rest of Germany. The German military was reduced to 100,000 men and the Rhineland was occupied by Allied troops to ensure its permanent demilitarization. To this was added the notorious 'war guilt clause'. By signing, Germany was acknowledging sole responsibility for causing the war, and as a result, the further responsibility of compensating the Allied powers for all the losses and damages which they had suffered. The definition of reparations was even extended to include all pension payments to Allied combatants as well as obliging the Germans to pay all the costs of the Allied occupation of the Rhineland.[1]

A Reparations Commission was established by the Allies to determine the exact extent of the German financial obligation.

---

[1] Craig, *Germany: 1866–1945*, 436.

When the amount was finally determined in May 1921, it was set at a figure which was roughly equivalent to 12.5 billion dollars (or 750 billion marks at the then current rate of exchange).[2] This was a staggering amount, well beyond the German government's capacity to deal with adequately. The initial instalments were paid only by printing new marks, thus depreciating even further a mark whose value was already in rapid decline. Over the next two years, inflation reached nightmarish proportions.

In late 1922 the Germans fell behind on their obligation, and on 11 January 1923 French troops occupied the Ruhr and seized control of its factories and their inventories. Having lost a vital source of raw materials, the productivity of German industries declined dramatically. Unemployment increased throughout Germany.[3] With the repayment of war debts now rendered an impossibility, inflation raged out of control. By August food riots were common. Before inflation peaked in late 1923, one dollar was the equivalent of 4 trillion, 200 billion marks.

By the end of 1923, 133 printing-presses had 1,783 presses running day and night to print Reichsbank notes, which had to be transported to banks of issue in large straw crates carried by armies of porters. The effect of this upon the value of the mark, measured in relation to the dollar, was catastrophic. Even now, in an age in which inflation has become a household word, it is difficult to convey a sense of the meaning of this plunging decline in the worth of the one commodity that more than any other serves man as a means of rational measurement of his situation. For millions of Germans these figures created a lunatic world in which all the familiar landmarks assumed crazy new forms and all the old signposts became meaningless, in which the simplest of objects were invested by alchemy with monstrous value . . . the penny postage stamp costing as much as a Dahlem villa in 1890.[4]

Such were the circumstances which determined the course of daily existence during Barth's years in Göttingen.

2. LIFE IN GÖTTINGEN

Less than three weeks after his arrival in Göttingen, with very little time for preparation, Barth launched his teaching career with

---

[2] Craig, *Germany: 1866–1945*, 440.   [3] Ibid. 448.   [4] Ibid. 450–1.

two lecture courses: one, a course in historical theology devoted to the Heidelberg Catechism and the other, an exegetical course on the letter to the Ephesians.

Barth's honorary chair carried with it a particular responsibility. He was to teach 'introduction to the Reformed confession, Reformed doctrine and Reformed church life'.[5] At that time Barth had only the barest acquaintance with the Reformed tradition: 'I did not even possess the Reformed confessional writings, and had certainly never read them'.[6] Barth had studied Calvin's *Institutes* during his years in Geneva (1909–11) but he had read them through the lens provided by his Herrmannian theology; i.e. at that time he thought he could easily 'unite idealistic-romantic and Reformed theology'.[7] So now, as he approached his new responsibility, he felt grossly unprepared. Among his very first acts in Göttingen was the purchase of E. F. K. Müller's *Die Bekenntnisschriften der reformierten Kirche*, to this day the most complete collection of Reformed confessions ever compiled. Barth set to work immediately to correct his woeful lack of 'historical breadth'. For the first five semesters, his main course dealt with some aspect of the history of the Reformed theological tradition (from Zwingli through Schleiermacher). In this way, he was laying the foundation for his first venture into the field of dogmatics in the summer semester of 1924. It would be helpful here at the outset to provide an overview of the courses which Barth offered in Göttingen. All of the following are lecture courses. Barth did not at this time think himself sufficiently prepared to offer seminars.

Winter semester 1921/2:
    Exposition of the Heidelberg Catechism
    Exposition of Ephesians
Summer semester 1922:
    The Theology of Calvin
Winter semester 1922/3:
    The Theology of Zwingli
    Exposition of James

---

[5] Busch, *Karl Barth*, 128–9.
[6] Barth, 'Autobiographische Skizzen Karl Barths', *B–B Br.* 309.   [7] Ibid. 306.

Summer semester 1923:
  The Theology of the Reformed Confessions
  Exposition of 1 Corinthians 15[8]
Winter semester 1923/4:
  The Theology of Schleiermacher[9]
  Exposition of 1 John
Summer semester 1924:
  Instruction in the Christian Religion: Prolegomena to
  Dogmatics
  Exposition of Philippians[10]
Winter semester 1924/5:
  Instruction in the Christian Religion: Dogmatics I
  Exposition of Colossians
Summer semester 1925:
  Instruction in the Christian Religion: Dogmatics II
  Exposition of the Sermon on the Mount

In each case, the main lecture course was the theology course, consisting of three to four lecture-hours per week. The lectures devoted to theological exegesis of New Testament epistles or passages were secondary; each of them was a one-hour course.

Barth proved to be a quick learner. But the process was still a traumatic one. Barth's distress over the huge gaps in his learning dominated the many letters he wrote to Thurneysen during the first two years:

apart from the daily requirements, I have to build my own scholarly structure, achieve a 'thorough mastery' as they say, in something. How does one do it? Will they ever be able to say that of me? Or shall I always be this wandering gypsy among all the honourable scholars by whom I am surrounded, one who has only a couple of leaky kettles to call his own and, to compensate, occasionally sets a house on fire?[11]

Barth was astonished by the library at Göttingen—so many books written about the 'dear God'; so much to learn.

---

[8] These lectures were published in 1924. See Barth, *Die Auferstehung der Toten*.

[9] These lectures were published in the framework of the Karl Barth *Gesamtausgabe*. See Barth, *Die Theologie Schleiermachers: Vorlesung, Göttingen, Wintersemester 1923/24*, ed. Dietrich Ritschl (Zurich: TVZ, 1978).

[10] These lectures were repeated in Münster in the winter semester 1926/7 and then published. See Karl Barth, *Erklärung des Philipperbriefes* (Munich: Chr. Kaiser Verlag, 1928).

[11] Karl Barth to Eduard Thurneysen, 11 Dec. 1921, *B–Th. Br.* II. 20–1.

The cellar with all its galleries and corners in which books stand tightly pressed together and wait for someone to investigate them and for new writers of books is completely suited to awakening mystical awe before the science; and rather timidly, I ask myself in this terrible thousand-voiced loneliness, what it should mean that I have been cast into precisely *this* corner of hell.[12]

At the outset, his approach to teaching had to remain on a rather basic level. 'I am for the moment in a reproducing, ruminating stage and I don't say much more than what "stands written in the books".'[13]

Barth's lack of preparation was made even more painful to him by the presence on the faculty of two men who, though his age, had already acquired an immense erudition. These were Emanuel Hirsch and Erik Peterson. Hirsch was a rabid nationalist and, later, a member of the Nazi party and adviser to Reichsbishop Ludwig Müller.[14] Though two years Barth's junior, he had been called to the post of *Ordinarius* (full professor) in Church history at Göttingen in May 1921. Thus he began his teaching activity in Göttingen in precisely the same semester as did Barth. Hirsch had been a student of Karl Holl, the initiator of the Luther-renaissance, and was himself extremely well versed in Luther. By the time he arrived in Göttingen, he had already written an important book on Osiander as well as having done extensive studies in Fichte's philosophy. To these subjects, he added a mastery of Kierkegaard in the course of the twenties. The simultaneous arrival of Hirsch and Barth in Göttingen in the autumn of 1921 initiated a fascinating relationship between two quite different people, a relationship often cordial and just as often explosive.[15] For his part, Barth was overawed by Hirsch's learning:

this Hirsch really knows an awful lot. He expresses his opinion on Indian religious history, Islam, the relationships in inner Africa, old and new methods of missions, fairy-tale research, Homeric heroes, etc. with an expert knowledge which leaves me standing there with my mouth

---

[12] Karl Barth to Eduard Thurneysen, 6 Nov. 1921, *B–Th. Br.* II. 6.

[13] Karl Barth to Eduard Thurneysen, 27 Nov. 1921, *B–Th. Br.* II. 15.

[14] See Robert P. Erickson, *Theologians under Hitler: Gerhard Kittel, Paul Althaus and Emanuel Hirsch* (New Haven, Conn.: Yale University Press, 1985), 147–9.

[15] For further information on the details of this relationship, see Walter Buff, 'Karl Barth und Emanuel Hirsch: Anmerkungen zu einem Briefwechsel', in Hans Martin Müller (ed.), *Christliche Wahrheit und neuzeitliches Denken: Zu Emanuel Hirschs Leben und Werk* (Tübingen: Katzmann Verlag, 1984), 15–26.

hanging open. I barely had heard the names of most of these things, and that is not even the speciality of this contortionist.[16]

There can be no question that in the struggle to acquire 'historical breadth'—a struggle which Barth at times felt himself incapable of winning—Hirsch provided a strong incentive and a model by which Barth measured his progress:

now during vacation, even more than during the semester . . . I am much more conscious of my thorn in the flesh, my terrible theological ignorance, sharpened by my quite miserable memory which constantly wants to retain only *quite* decisive things . . . Oh, if only someone would give me time, time, time to do everything *right*, to read everything at my tempo (and not at Hirsch's!), to take everything apart and put it back together again! I am almost inclined to say to you, like the rich man in hell [Luke 16: 27 f.], that you should let no hour pass fruitlessly in your pastors' houses or be spent on the newspaper as I unfortunately did all too often in Safenwil. You, too, could one day become professors, and then with what rage will you regard each book that you did not read . . .![17]

In spite of this counsel, Barth sometimes found it necessary, during this period of intensive study, to get away from it and do something else, so that what he had read could be assimilated on some deeper level. But he also noted that to relax even for a minute is 'a blessed custom of the country preacher which, to be sure, works very poorly in the university and which the agile Hirsch does not give in to (for which reason he also rightly gets ahead)'.[18] Wolfgang Trillhaas's judgement, while an exaggeration, still contains a grain of truth: 'E. Hirsch probably deserves credit for the fact that Barth was not lost to prophecy or false edification.'[19]

Erik Peterson too exerted a similar influence on Barth, though not to the same degree as Hirsch. Peterson shared Barth's disdain

---

[16] Karl Barth to Eduard Thurneysen, 11 Dec. 1921, *B–Th. Br.* II. 23.

[17] Karl Barth to Eduard Thurneysen, 26 Mar. 1922, *B–Th. Br.* II. 59, 60–1.

[18] Karl Barth to Eduard Thurneysen, 18 Dec. 1922, *B–Th. Br.* II. 121.

[19] Wolfgang Trillhaas, *Aufgehobene Vergangenheit: Aus meinem Leben* (Göttingen: Vandenhoeck & Ruprecht, 1976), 97. See also 'Emanuel Hirsch in Göttingen', in Müller (ed.), *Christliche Wahrheit und neuzeitliches Denken*, 43: 'the confrontation with Hirsch had lifelong after-effects on Barth. It made visible to him positions which, for him, were unacceptable. But it also impressed on Barth, in a fundamental way, the obligation to be scientific. What would have become of the so-called dialectical theology without Barth's encounter with Hirsch?'

for much of modern theology. In him, Barth found a kindred spirit—a rarity in the Göttingen faculty. Peterson's knowledge of patristic theological literature was superlative. Trillhaas describes how students would go back and forth from Barth's lectures to Hirsch's and Peterson's, like messengers bearing the latest news of opinions expressed by each of the professors concerned.[20] In this way, Barth was repeatedly called upon for his opinion on the teachings of others, in many cases in connection with subjects about which he had only scant knowledge.

Adding to the stress of life in Göttingen were tensions which Barth experienced with colleagues in the field of systematic theology. In the beginning he was greeted with an outward show of civility by Carl Stange, one of the two senior theologians. Stange undoubtedly regarded Barth as something of a curiosity. He was himself an unrepentant liberal and emphatically Lutheran. But he did establish with Barth and Hirsch a biweekly theological discussion group, which met on Sunday evenings in his home. Guests at these discussions included Georg Wobbermin (the other senior theologian), Otto Piper (a *Privatdozent* in systematics), and Ernst Strasser (Inspector of the Lutheran *Stift* in Göttingen).[21] In spite of such efforts, relations between Stange and Barth quickly deteriorated. At the outset of the second semester, a quarrel broke out in the faculty as a result of the fact that Lutheran students were already beginning to attend Barth's lectures at the expense of those given at the same hour by the Lutheran theologians, Stange and Wobbermin. According to Barth's report, at least, Stange regarded the students' decision to hear an honorary(!) lecturer in Reformed theology as a disgrace to the faculty. 'The Reformed Church in Hanover has no more significance than a millennial sect!'[22]

An even greater source of discomfort than the petty jealousies of colleagues, however, was the political climate which prevailed in Göttingen. Pastor Heilmann's request that Barth refrain from open promulgation of his political opinions has already been noted. Even had the request not been made, Barth would have

---

[20] Trillhaas, *Aufgehobene Vergangenheit*, 97–8.

[21] Holger Finze, editor's introduction to 'Über Kirche', in Karl Barth, *Vorträge und kleinere Arbeiten, 1922–1925* (Zurich: TVZ, 1990), 1.

[22] Barth is here quoting Stange from memory. Karl Barth to Eduard Thurneysen, 17 May 1922, *B–Th. Br.* II. 77.

been inclined to keep a low profile. The fact that he was a foreigner—and what is worse, a Swiss! (to remain neutral in the war was seen by most Germans of the time as tantamount to siding with the enemy)—was something that his German hosts were not inclined to let him forget. On the day after the assassination of Walther Rathenau (the Jewish Reichsminister for Foreign Affairs) by a right-wing, anti-Semitic extremist, Barth was invited to a tea at the home of the New Testament scholar Walter Bauer. There Rathenau's murder was discussed openly by his colleagues and condoned.

The German professors are really as bad as their reputation ...
Eschatology on the one side and the zoological garden on the other are the only two viewpoints in terms of which one can consider these "creatures" of the dear God. When one is confronted with them, one loses all desire to take action against them as the Swiss Religious Socialists were accustomed to do, and we occasionally with them. ...
'Colleague Barth' sits off to one side, letting his attentiveness be known by an occasional 'Ah ja, Mhm-soo?' What is one supposed to say when someone proclaims, with a bang of the fist on the table, that a Jew is always without a Fatherland and does not belong in a German government? Especially when one is Swiss and therefore himself something like a Jew?[23]

During the Göttingen years, Barth was relatively inactive politically, with the exception of private conversations with students and political discussions at the open evenings which he held in his home. He did his best to avoid open confrontation with nationalist colleagues like Hirsch and Stange.

It is in the light of the political climate in Göttingen, I think, that Barth's comments on the centennial celebrations of Ritschl's birth are to be understood.

Is it really necessary, in order to be a proper professor of theology to be a sturdy, dry, insensitive lump who notices nothing, but *nothing*—like the blessed Ritschl, at whose grave we stood yesterday in top hats, in celebration of the one-hundredth anniversary of his birth, to dedicate a wreath to him, 'the founder of the fame of our Göttingen theological faculty'? I read some chapters in his biography in the afternoon, shuddering as I did so. Or will I in time become such a blockhead? Either

---

[23] Karl Barth to Eduard Thurneysen, 28 June 1922, *B–Th. Br.* II. 88–9.

explode one day or become a blockhead?! If you see a third possibility, tell me for my comfort.[24]

In his book on Ritschl, James Richmond has roundly criticized Barth's comments as 'tasteless'[25] and explained them on the basis of a personal reaction to the rough ride given to him by his colleagues.[26] Seen in the light of the political climate in Göttingen, however, Barth's comments take on an entirely different colour. It is significant that it was the reading of Ritschl's *biography* which triggered this eruption from Barth. Throughout his life Barth would regard Ritschl as the 'prototype of the national-liberal German bourgeois in the age of Bismarck';[27] the kind of person who 'notices nothing, but *nothing*' around him, like the later Ritschlians who were willing to condone the murder of Walther Rathenau. And that, I think, is the clue to the source of Barth's virulent attack upon Ritschl and his followers, from the 1920s on through to the end of his life. Barth had already learned as a student of Herrmann to be critical of Ritschl's theology. But the vehemence of his attitude towards Ritschl from the twenties on was closely tied to the strong feelings of contempt which the political views of Ritschlian colleagues evoked in him.

In spite of Barth's efforts to lie low, trouble had a way of finding him. The French occupation of the Ruhr on 11 January 1923 found Barth in a mood of deep sympathy with the plight of the German people. In Göttingen, inflation had already forced a number of students to leave school.

Really, one asks oneself sometimes whether it might not be more sensible to toss all this theological rubbish into the corner . . . and transform oneself into a social worker who would bring as many Swiss francs as possible into the country and then disperse them to the different organizations and institutions for distribution. . . . One watches [the value of the mark] almost breathlessly. But in the meantime, people hunger and freeze notoriously in the thousands; tuberculosis and strange hunger diseases get the upper hand; students have to quit in the middle of the semester and take up another calling because they do not have the means to go on. It is very bad.[28]

---

[24] Karl Barth to Eduard Thurneysen, 26 Mar. 1922, *B–Th. Br.* II. 59–60.

[25] Richmond, *Ritschl: A Reappraisal*, 35. [26] See above, Ch. 1, n. 41.

[27] Barth, *Die protestantische Theologie im 19. Jahrhundert*, 599; ET *Protestant Theology in the Nineteenth Century*, 656.

[28] Karl Barth to Eduard Thurneysen, 18 Dec. 1922, *B–Th. Br.* II. 122.

Coming as it did on the heels of these developments, it is under-standable that the French occupation would initially awaken in Barth anger and outrage:

the French invasion of the Ruhr region should be mentioned, an event which makes my blood boil with indignation each day as the newspa-per arrives. Slowly, I am beginning to perceive things as a German would. May I ask you to send me occasionally important articles out of the Swiss newspapers which deal with Germany? Here, I see only my (democratic) *Göttinger Zeitung* and have, for example, no idea how these events are judged in Switzerland, whether the French reasons for the occupation are seen to be justified and if so, why. So please help me with a political exposé and make it clear whether I have cursed some-what unreasonably the French fiends who have broken in upon us out of the clear blue sky, stealing and murdering when the measure was already full and one thought that things could not become worse.[29]

Barth could even declare—only half in jest—that 'I am in danger of becoming a national and war theologian'.[30]

In the early days of the occupation, an incident took place which forced Barth to make clear publicly that there were limits to his pro-German sympathies. The occasion was a Christmas greeting sent by eighteen Parisian theological students to their fellow students at nineteen German universities. Unfortunately, the greetings arrived at their destinations almost simultaneously with the French occupation. Some of the German students, notably those at Marburg, responded in like spirit. At Göttingen, however, the arrival of this greeting was the occasion for a coun-cil of war at which the professors also voiced their opinions. Bauer, Stange, and Hirsch spoke against a civil response while Piper and Barth—who was present for the discussion only at the urging of the minority—spoke for it.

The German professors are really true masters at justifying their brutali-ties on spiritual, ethical, and Christian grounds. . . . Hirsch was *bad*. He spoke of the *una sancta* (the German people) and naturally of 'con-science' . . . and 'heart', but threatened with a sweep of the hand to have no further 'fellowship' with any student who signed. The next day, I had a terrible scene with him in which the words 'Swiss! Foreigner! Agitator! Disturber of the peace!' flew around my head . . .[31]

[29] Karl Barth to Eduard Thurneysen, 23 Jan. 1923, *B–Th. Br.* II. 130.
[30] Karl Barth to Martin Rade, 18 Jan. 1923, *B–R Br.* 184.
[31] Karl Barth to Eduard Thurneysen, 23 Jan. 1923, *B–Th. Br.* II. 131.

The result of this confrontation was an agreement to send a response to Paris composed almost entirely by Barth. 'Because I myself am "furious" about the French, I could with all my heart compose a protasis that was agreeable to Hirsch and then in th apodosis point out to the kind French theologians the unity of Christendom that is based only on Romans 11: 32, but is really to be *based* on it.'[32] Two months later, Barth was still rankled by the incident. 'As a foreigner, I have laid down my arms and *still* provoke anger.'[33]

There is a sequel to this story which occurred on 19 July.[34] On that day, two of the French students who had had a hand in the Christmas greeting visited Otto Piper with the intention of speaking in his home to Göttingen students about the work in France of a 'Christian League of Reconciliation'. Word of the visit leaked out and on the afternoon of the discussion in Piper's home, signs appeared in shop windows declaring 'French in Göttingen!' Demonstrating students gathered outside Piper's house and demanded that the 'French agitators' be 'delivered up'. Deciding that further discussion was inadvisable, Piper suggested that his visitors beat a hasty retreat to the railway station. An angry mob followed Piper and the students to the station. Singing national songs, the crowd seized from the French students their second-class tickets and replaced them with fourth-class tickets. The following day articles appeared in a local newspaper accusing Piper of an 'act of national disgrace' and posing the ominous question: 'How long do they want to allow a man with these sentiments to be active at the Georgia Augusta [the University of Göttingen] as lecturer and teacher of academic youth?' An attempt to disrupt Piper's lecture that day by nationalist students was thwarted by university officials. The following day Piper's home was raided by police. He was brought to a hearing before a police court and placed under arrest for 'harbouring enemy spies'. Two days later he was released because the charges were untenable. As for Barth's role in the affair, he seems to have been happy to take Martin Rade's advice: 'As a Swiss, you must be as restrained as possible.'[35]

[32] Ibid.   [33] Karl Barth to Martin Rade, 1 Mar. 1923, *B–R Br.* 188.
[34] The account which follows is taken virtually verbatim from Christoph Schwöbel's editorial note to a letter sent by Martin Rade to Barth. See *B–R Br.* 190 n. 1.
[35] Martin Rade to Karl Barth, 24 July 1923, *B–R Br.* 192.

Barth's reluctance to become involved in politics in Göttingen is certainly understandable. As a *Gastarbeiter* his position was extremely precarious. That would change at a stroke in the autumn of 1925, for with his appointment to a regular university professorship in Münster would come German citizenship, voting rights, etc. But for now, political action had to be put on hold.

In spite of the unhappiness which surrounded many of Barth's activities in Göttingen, the progress he made in his academic work was nothing short of astonishing. It would be a serious error to approach the works produced in these years as those of just any theological dilettante; or worse, to view the dogmatics lectures which were the fruit of these years as a failed attempt. The thesis which will be defended here is that Barth's first lectures in dogmatics mark a distinct advance over against the theology of *Romans* II. What one recent interpreter has said of *Die christliche Dogmatik im Entwurf*—the lectures on prolegomena to dogmatics which Barth gave in Münster and published in 1927—might just as well have been said of the earlier Göttingen version of the same. 'The step from the second edition of the *Römerbrief* to the *Christliche Dogmatik* is greater by far than the step from the *Christliche Dogmatik* to the *Church Dogmatics*.'[36] As one of Barth's students at that time later wrote: 'if one concedes to Schleiermacher that his "Speeches" of 1799 could claim a privileged status *vis-à-vis* the later works, a status which never became obsolete or faded, the same must be said also of the earliest form of Barth's dogmatics.'[37] The importance of these years for the further development of Barth's theology can scarcely be exaggerated.

3. MODIFICATION AND ELABORATION OF THE PERSPECTIVES OF ROMANS II (1921–1922)

The most significant modifications to occur in Barth's theology over the first five semesters in Göttingen had to do with his atti-

[36] Michael Beintker, 'Die christliche Dogmatik', in Sauter (ed.), *Verkündigung und Forschung: Beihefte zu 'Evangelische Theologie'*, 2 (1985), 62.

[37] Wolfgang Trillhaas, 'Karl Barth in Göttingen', in Dietrich Rössler, Gottfried Vogt, and Friedrich Wintzer (eds.), *Fides et communicatio: Festschrift für Martin Doerne* (Göttingen: Vandenhoeck & Ruprecht, 1970), 368.

tude towards doctrine and Church. Barth's attitude towards doctrine became more positive and, largely as a consequence, the Church came to be seen by him as the *locus* of authority in theology (rather than simply the *locus* of judgement as in *Romans* II). In themselves, these modifications are of little significance. Certainly, they did not represent an abandonment of Barth's attempt to ground theology in eschatology (or a Christology which was itself grounded in eschatology). So they were modifications *within* the overarching perspective which had governed *Romans* II. But these modifications did help to prepare the ground for the more significant shift which will be treated in the next chapter.

Barth's first foray into classical Reformed theology consisted in a classroom analysis of the Heidelberg Catechism. Initially, his impression of the Heidelberger was not favourable.

For the last ten days without interruption, I have been studying the Heidelberger and its sources and the literature about it. Nothing of importance seems to have occurred in relation to this symbol either at the time of its composition or in recent times. It clearly represents the moment in time when the unrest of the Reformation turned into ecclesiastical complacency . . .[38]

After launching into the lectures a few days later, Barth reported,

The Heidelberg Catechism is a decidedly questionable work. Precisely the first question is not good at all. I criticized it for an hour to the students today in order then to show them in the second hour how it is fortunately blown sky-high by the answer. It seems that Peter [Barth's pastor brother] is using the Heidelberger in his catechetical instruction in Madiswil. I would not risk that but would prefer to go back to the Genevan Catechism or to that of Leo Jud of 1541.[39]

For his part, Thurneysen was in the throes of putting together his own confirmation instruction and finding it quite difficult. But he considered a return to any of the Reformation catechisms a mistake.

Is not each of their sentences and formulations of questions (and the form itself of militant question and "answer"!) a foolhardy seeking of handholds by which one pushes oneself upward between precipitous walls? If one separates this bold dialectic from these walls (as happened

---

[38] Karl Barth to Eduard Thurneysen, 6 Nov. 1921, *B–Th. Br.* II. 5–6.
[39] Karl Barth to Eduard Thurneysen, 18 Nov. 1921, *B–Th. Br.* II. 9.

in orthodoxy and happens ten times over in modern religious education) . . . it all becomes amazingly simple and the practice could be followed in any Gymnasium by any class. But![40]

Towards the end of the semester, Barth's opinion had moderated somewhat. He thought that a good construction could be
placed upon the Christology of questions 15–19.

The Anselmian satisfaction theory is probably in its way very good and
so, too, the strange Christology of questions 15–17 which is constructed
in an a priori fashion. One has to value all of this as *Aufräumungsarbeit*
and then, over against that, see question 18 with its supposed historical
positivity as only a mathematical point which has no extension, as the
truly excellent question 19 shows.[41]

The importance of this passage is that it shows clearly that the
slow emergence of a more positive attitude towards early
Reformed orthodoxy would not have been possible had Barth
not read these theologians 'as exemplary dialecticians. Through
them, Barth was able to illustrate what dialectic would mean in
any theology which is conformed to its subject-matter.'[42]
Clearly, what was at stake here was no simple repristination.
Barth exercised a great freedom in his interpretation of 'the old
orthodoxy'; he did not feel bound to simply reproduce 'what
stands in the text'.

I really stand in a remarkable relationship to these old texts.
Continually, I could call almost *everything* good *and* not good. After I
consider the historical context and the sense, I decide for the one or the
other in accordance with the goals for instruction. Certainly, it must be
possible to explain the *Tridentinum* as well with more heartfelt and comprehending participation . . .[43]

Barth's massive use of seventeenth-century theologies in his dogmatics lectures of 1924–5 will be completely misunderstood if
this is not constantly borne in mind.

Barth's lectures on Calvin's theology in the summer semester
of 1922 are significant for our purposes here, for in them we

---

[40] Eduard Thurneysen to Karl Barth, 2 Dec. 1921, *B–Th. Br.* II. 17.

[41] Karl Barth to Eduard Thurneysen, 11 Feb. 1922, *B–Th. Br.* II. 36–7.

[42] Wolfgang Trillhaas, 'Der Einbruch der Dialektischen Theologie in Göttingen und
Emanuel Hirsch', in Bernd Moeller (ed.), *Theologie in Göttingen* (Göttingen: Vandenhoeck
& Ruprecht, 1987), 372.

[43] Karl Barth to Eduard Thurneysen, 11 Feb. 1922, *B–Th. Br.* II. 37.

catch sight of the emergence of a carefully circumscribed affirmation of the Reformed Scripture-principle. Barth wrote these lectures under extreme duress. Very often the lecture presented on a given day was only finished late the night before. Under such circumstances, it is not surprising that the lectures provide vivid testimony to the learning process which was under way.

In his 'Introduction' to the lectures on Calvin, Barth registered an objection to Calvin's use of the distinction between profane history and *historia sacra*. To be sure, Barth saw the distinction as valid and necessary. But Calvin equated *historia sacra* with 'biblical history'. For Barth, *historia sacra* is the eschatological history of God which stands over against all history, biblical and profane. 'Biblical history too can only *proclaim* the "*historia sacra*", the history of *salvation*, the history of *God*. And, on the other hand, "*historia sacra*" is the hidden meaning and content of *all* history; it is *the* history which wants to speak in and above and beyond so-called profane history as well.'[44] Seen in this light, Calvin's equation of sacred history with biblical history is a 'mythologizing biblicism'.[45] Of course, none of this was new; it was thoroughly consistent with the perspective which governed *Romans* II.

By the end of the semester, however, Barth's critical attitude towards biblical *history* had been considerably supplemented by a positive appreciation of the authority of the biblical *text*. This was indeed a new element in his thinking.

The role of *Holy Scripture* in the Reformed Reformation was different from the role it played in the Lutheran Reformation. Its dignity was *fundamental* here in a way which it had never been in Lutheranism, in spite of all the respect which it enjoyed there. The introduction of the Reformation here always meant the same thing: the establishment of the Word of God contained in the Bible as the norm of faith and life. The Reformed Church is first of all a school where one learns; secondly an institution in which one is reared.[46]

Barth noted that the Reformed Scripture-principle is 'surrounded by ambiguity': namely, the temptation to elevate the words of the biblical witness to the status of a law, to understand humankind's relationship to the Bible legalistically. Still, the affirmation of the normativity of the biblical witness was necessary

---

[44] Karl Barth, *Die Theologie Calvins, 1922*, ed. Hans Scholl (Zurich: TVZ, 1993), 2.
[45] Ibid. 3.
[46] Ibid. 522.

for the sake of the Reformed character of the reformation desired.

Throughout these lectures, Barth wanted to see the principal difference between the Reformed and Lutheran Reformations as lying in the concern of the former with the problem of ethics; the problem of discerning the significance which the vertical relationship of God to humanity in Christ has on the horizontal plane of human relationships in time. It was this concern which, in Barth's view, made Reformed Christianity to be the 'second turn of the Reformation' (as distinguished from the 'first turn' which occurred with Luther's emphasis on justification by faith).[47]

The affirmation of the Scripture-principle was therefore seen by Barth as:

unavoidably connected with the attempt to *relate* eternity to time, to *relate* the forgiveness of sins to the life of sinful humanity, to *relate* spirit to existence in the flesh, to *relate* love, the incomparable, to a very ordinary obedience. . . . Where the *Reformed* attempt is dared, there the special significance of Holy Scripture is given in that the question of a *norm*, of a standard in accordance with which the relating must take place, the question of a *rule* of faith and life, of knowledge and action, is the primary question, the question of life. The relationship to time which is here the focal-point of concern makes a temporal *form* and *order* [of the relation] . . . indispensable.[48]

Reformed Christianity found its norm in the canonical Scriptures and in them alone.[49] It was the 'whole Bible', not selected portions of it, which was in view here.[50]

The indispensability of the Bible as the rule of faith and life was not understood by Barth at this time to exclude the possibility that God could speak elsewhere, in nature and history. He saw it as one of Calvin's virtues that he left room for a 'natural revelation'; but a natural revelation which was 'actualized' by reading 'the Word of God in nature and history' through the lens provided by the Bible.[51] But the right use of this 'lens' presup-

---

[47] Karl Barth, *Die Theologie Calvins, 1922*, 66, 89–90.   [48] Ibid. 523–4.
[49] Ibid. 524.   [50] Ibid. 529.
[51] Ibid. 217. It should be noted that this is not the same as an affirmation of "natural theology", a possibility which Barth consistently rejected. What decided whether a theology was "natural" or not was not the *locus* of revelation but the source (the power) by means of which revelation (in the Bible or in nature and history) was actualized. Since revelation in either *locus* is always the effect of God's gracious action alone, there was nothing "natural" about a theology which derived its material from either *locus*.

posed its right interpretation, which Barth regarded as impossible apart from the witness of the Holy Spirit.

Calvin never spoke of the inspiration of the Bible without, at the same time, asserting a counter-principle of the most subjective character. I am thinking here of the '*testimonium spiritus sancti internum*'; the voice of the truth which causes itself to be heard not only in the Bible but also in its believing reader or hearer, so that the process by means of which the content of the Bible becomes certain and authoritative for her does not in the least consist in a dictatorship of the letter of the Bible and a subjection of human reason beneath it, but rather . . . in a conversation of the truth with itself which, as the Holy Spirit in the biblical letter and as the Holy Spirit in the heart of the believing human, is first of all two [things], but in reality, is one . . .[52]

It is the necessity of penetrating through the witness of the human author to the mind of God which makes the authority of the Bible in Reformed Christianity to be something other than legalistic: 'God Himself must bear witness to the one who wants to hear the witness of the biblical writer . . .'.[53] With these caveats in place however, Barth was now willing to attribute a unique authority to the Bible as the rule of faith and life.

The break between the first and the second year of teaching in Göttingen was spent largely in preparing and delivering three special lectures: 'The Need and Promise of Christian Preaching' at Schulpforte on 25 July 1922; 'The Problem of Ethics Today' at Wiesbaden on 25 September; and 'The Word of God as the Task of Theology' at Elgersburg on 3 October. Of the three it is the last named which is of the greatest interest for our purposes here.

The lecture at Elgersburg was given to the 'Friends of the *Christliche Welt*'. The significance of this lecture lies in the fact that here, for the first time, Barth offered a programmatic reflection upon theological *method*. The structure of the lecture was provided by a threefold thesis: 'As theologians, we ought to speak of God. We are, however, human and as such cannot speak of God. We should recognize both our ought and our cannot and by that recognition give God the glory.'[54] Barth devoted one section each to the three parts of this thesis.

It was in the second of these sections that Barth took up the

[52] Ibid. 222–3. [53] Ibid. 525.
[54] Barth, 'Das Wort Gottes als Aufgabe der Theologie', in idem, *Das Wort Gottes und die Theologie*, 158.

problem of method. He noted that there were basically three ways in which theologians throughout the centuries have sought to speak of God: the dogmatic way, the critical way, and the dialectical way. To see this discussion in the proper light, it is of the utmost importance to remember that all three of these ways stand under the heading: 'We are, however, human and as such cannot speak of God.' All three ways end with the same insight: that human beings are incapable, in and of themselves, of speaking of God. This is true of the dialectical way no less than it is of the other two.

For to speak of God, if it were taken seriously, would mean to speak on the basis of revelation and faith. To speak of God would mean to speak God's Word, the Word which can only come from Him, the Word *that God becomes human*. We can say these four words but we have not yet thereby said the Word of God in which is truth. To say that, to say that *God* becomes *human* in such a way that it really is *God's* Word, that would be our theological task.[55]

To speak God's Word would mean to say these words *as God says them*. But clearly, that is humanly impossible. That is the critical reservation under which the whole of Barth's reflections on method stand.

The first way is the dogmatic way. This is the path taken by theological orthodoxy. Dogmatism assumes that there is a more-or-less direct relationship between its statements about God and the being of God. With the greatest naïvety and therefore, with the greatest confidence, dogmatism constructs positive statements about God. It begins with the thesis that God becomes human and derives from it the familiar (traditional) Christological, soteri-ological, and eschatological dogmas. Seldom is this way completely avoided, nor should it be. Even the most convinced liberal, when she desires to go beyond her customary psychologism and to speak of God (and not just of human piety), will inadvertently employ positive dogmatic formulations. The strength of the dogmatic way lies in its 'taste for objectivity'.

When the decisive insight is acquired that the theme of theology is not the divinization of humankind but rather the incarnation of God, where this insight flashes even only occasionally in a theologian, there he acquires a taste for the objective . . . Then the world in which he

---

[55] Barth, *Das Wort Gottes und die Theologie*, 166.

now finds himself—a world he has previously despised and doubted as "supranaturalistic"—gradually and almost effortlessly becomes meaningful to him.[56]

Barth did not desire simply to reject this way. He clearly saw it as vastly superior to all historicism and psychologism. But the dogmatic way, like all human ways, must ultimately fail. It cannot speak of God. Its greatest weakness lies in the fact that it does not recognize its inability.

To be sure, one cannot speak of God even in the most powerfully and vividly conceived supranaturalism. In this way, we can only bear witness that we would like to do so. The weakness of orthodoxy is not the so-called supranaturalistic content of the Bible and its dogmas. That is its strength. It is rather the fact that it—that we, in so far as there is a bit of the dogmatician in us all—do not get beyond placing this content (even if it were the word "God") over against ourselves and other people as a thing, an object, in a mythological-pragmatic fashion: there it is, believe it![57]

Dogmatism fails because it substitutes its statements for the divine speech which must take place if theology is to succeed in its task.

The second way is the critical way. Here one would speak of God by negating humanity. This is the way pursued by mysticism. But it is also, in a different way, the path chosen by idealism. According to this way, 'God is no this and that, no thing, no something, no *vis-à-vis*, no second; but rather, pure being, without quality, filling all things.'[58] It should be clear by now that the critical way was a way which Barth had often pursued in *Romans* II (in reliance on his brother Heinrich). It was the way taken where the goal was simply to clear the ground of errors. Barth acknowledged as much in his Elgersburg lecture when he said, 'We have all been found on this way and will never be able to resist frequenting it for a stretch now and then . . .'.[59] But it should also be clear by now that the critical way was not the only way taken, even in *Romans* II. God was never directly identified by Barth with the 'pure subject'.

The strength of the critical way lies at the point where the dogmatic way is weakest. 'Here something happens. Here we are not left standing with the instruction to believe. Here the human

---

[56] Ibid. 168.   [57] Ibid.   [58] Ibid. 169.   [59] Ibid.

is attacked in the most serious way.'[60] But here too the conclusion is the same: we cannot speak of God. The only thing we are certain of is that humanity is negated. But we must not forget that no negation which human beings are capable of carrying out is as great, as fundamental, as *the* Negation which is 'carried out by the positivity of God'.[61] Our negations do not bring about *the* Negation. Even Luther's and Kierkegaard's critiques of Christendom were unable to do that. 'Only where *God* (in that objectivity which orthodoxy knows only too well!) becomes human, stepping into our emptiness with His *fullness*, with His Yes into our no, only there is God spoken of.'[62]

The third way is the dialectical. In Barth's view, the dialectical way is 'far and away the best'.[63] The dialectician understands the relative adequacy of each of the other two ways and presupposes the great truths contained in each of them.

Here, from the outset, the positive unfolding of the thought of God on the one hand and the critique of humanity and of everything human on the other are both taken very seriously. But neither is allowed to occur independently but rather, under a constant looking-away to their common presupposition, to the living truth which itself is not to be named, which stands in the middle and gives to both—the affirmation and the negation—their proper meaning and significance for the first time.[64]

Still, the constant looking-away to the living truth offers no guarantee that human beings will be able to speak of God. Human beings are incapable of relating their affirmations and negations to the living truth in the centre for the simple reason that the living truth is nowhere directly given into human control. The only thing left to do in such circumstances is to bear witness to this state of affairs by constantly relating human affirmations to human negations, and vice versa. Barth continues:

That God (but really God!) becomes human (but really human!), that is constantly seen [by the dialectician] as that living truth, as the decisive content of a real speaking of God. But how should the necessary relation of both sides to this living centre be presented? The genuine dialectician knows that this centre is inconceivable and unintuitable. Therefore, she will give way to direct communication about it as seldom as possible, knowing that all direct communications *about it*—be

[60] Barth, *Das Wort Gottes und die Theologie*, 170.   [61] Ibid.   [62] Ibid. 171.
[63] Ibid.   [64] Ibid.

they positive or negative—are not communications *about it* but rather always *either* dogmatics *or* criticism. On this narrow ridge of rock one can only keep moving, not stand. Otherwise, one will fall either to the right or to the left, but one will certainly fall. The only thing left to do . . . is to relate both affirmation and negation to *one another*, to clarify the yes by the no and the no by the yes, without persisting for longer than a moment in a rigid yes *or* no . . .[65]

Since we have no direct access or control over God's Self-revelation (a revelation which is the absolutely necessary presupposition of all genuine speaking of God), we cannot speak of God. Humanly speaking, theology is an impossibility. Theology is possible only where God speaks when He is spoken of. In such a situation, what human beings *can do* is to testify to human inadequacy—as well as the necessity that God speak if theology is to succeed—by the continuous negation of every theological statement through the immediate affirmation of its opposite. This continual practice of pitting statement over against statement is what Barth means by "dialectical method".

Again, it cannot be emphasized enough that Barth's entire discussion of method stands under the sign of failure. Dialectical method is preferable only because it gives vivid testimony to the negative sign which stands outside the bracket in which all theology is undertaken; not because, in itself, it is more successful than dogmatism or criticism. All of Barth's efforts in this lecture are devoted to hammering home a single point. If theology is to be possible at all, it can only be possible as a divine possibility.

How does it come about that human speaking becomes in a necessary, in a compelling way, significant, capable of bearing witness? That is the problem which is posed in a particularly vivid way on the soil of the dialectical method, because here everything is done which can be done to make human language significant and capable of bearing witness. *Whenever* dialectical speaking has proved to be significant and capable of bearing witness . . . it was not on the basis of what the dialectician did or was able to do . . . but rather, because . . . the living truth in the centre, the reality of God asserted itself . . . But this possibility—the possibility that God *Himself* speaks when He is spoken of—does not lie on the dialectical way as such but there, where this way too *comes to an end.*[66]

Three points in the foregoing account should be underscored. First, the three ways described by Barth were not seen by him as

[65] Ibid. 171–2.　　[66] Ibid. 174.

mutually exclusive. Most theologians, he said, employ more than one of them. In point of fact, in his Göttingen lectures on dogmatics of 1924/5, Barth would employ all three methods from time to time. And even in the *Church Dogmatics*, he would employ both dogmatic and dialectical methods; only the critical method would fall largely into disuse. Thus the difference between the Göttingen Dogmatics and the *Church Dogmatics*, from the standpoint of method, is at most a shift in emphasis. In the Göttingen Dogmatics dialectical method is predominant. Later it is subordinated to dogmatic method (without ever being completely eliminated).

Second, all methodological reflection stands in the shadow of a negative sign. Karl Barth certainly had a method (or better, methods). But it must be understood that method for him was nothing more than an emergency measure adopted in the face of a disaster—not unlike *ad hoc* laws adopted in times of national catastrophe. "Method" is a human tool by means of which the attainment of human goals is made possible. But the goal of theology is to speak of God and success in this effort would mean speaking of God as God Himself would speak of Himself (i.e. it would mean speaking the Word of God). This is not a humanly attainable goal and no method in the world is going to make it so. Therefore the adoption of a method (even dialectical method) cannot be for the purpose of making theology possible. The selection of a method is made with a much more limited goal in mind: that of bearing formal witness to human inadequacy and divine adequacy. To that extent, dialectical method was an "anti-method";[67] *and Barth's later "dogmatic method" was no less so.*

Third, as stressed above, these reflections were not intended to say that theology was completely and utterly impossible. His point was simply that theology is humanly impossible. But there yet remains another ground for the possibility of theology. 'It could be . . . that the Word, the Word of God of which we will never speak, has put on our weakness and folly so that *our* word, *in* its weakness and folly, might become capable of becoming at least the veil and earthly vessel of the Word of God.'[68] The relation which is here established between the incarnation and the possibility of doing theology ought not to be missed. It is a

[67] Ruschke, *Entstehung und Ausführung der Diastasentheologie*, 67.
[68] Barth, 'Das Wort Gottes als Aufgabe der Theologie', 178.

theme which would assume an ever-increasing importance for Barth. God can indeed take up and use human words to bear witness to Himself, in spite of their inherent inadequacy. It is within this framework of understanding that the significance of the well-known conclusion to this lecture is to be appreciated. 'Can theology, should theology, proceed beyond the *prolegomena* to Christology? It could be that *everything* is said in the prolegomena.'[69] This rhetorical question has been read by many to mean that Barth intended to prohibit going beyond prolegomena to dogmatics proper.[70] Seen in context, however, Barth is simply reiterating the point made throughout this lecture: that the transition from prolegomena to Christology is possible only where God speaks. Thus the lecture ends with an affirmation that theology is indeed possible—as a divine possibility.

To conclude these reflections on Barth's Elgersburg lecture, it should be pointed out that one of the central defects of the von Balthasarian formula of a 'turn from dialectic to analogy' has now become clear.[71] Von Balthasar placed both of these things—dialectic and analogy—on the same plane of discourse. He treated them both as methods. Dialectical method was simply replaced by analogical method. In truth, however, while the dialectic in question is a method, analogy is not. Analogy belongs to a vastly different realm of discourse. Analogy—whether the analogy of the cross or the later analogy of faith—is a description of the result of a divine action. It is the description of a relation of correspondence between the divine Self-knowing and human knowledge of God which arises as a consequence of God's act of Self-revelation. Talk of analogy has to do with what God does;

---

[69] Ibid.

[70] In his 1956 dissertation, Hans Frei took Barth's rhetorical question to be a prohibition: we are not to go beyond prolegomena. Indeed, he thought that before Barth's adoption of analogy (which he, like so many others, associated with the Anselm book of 1931), Barth had to make such a prohibition because he lacked any basis for going further. See Frei, 'The Doctrine of Revelation in the Thought of Karl Barth', 134. Frei's misreading of this passage rested, to a certain extent, on something of an optical illusion. Frei knew only Barth's published works. Since, before writing Anselm, Barth had only published the prolegomena to his second cycle of dogmatics lectures (the *Christliche Dogmatik* of 1927), one could easily assume that that in itself was evidence of Barth's inability to go any further. Had Frei known of Barth's unpublished materials, he would have known that long before Anselm, Barth had already lectured on the entire corpus of dogmatics—twice! Moreover, he would have known that Barth's commitment to dialectical method in those years had not in the least restrained him from doing so.

[71] See above, Introd., Sect. 2.

talk of dialectic emerges here in the context of what human beings can do in light of the fact that they have no capacity for bringing about the Self-speaking of God. The difference between these two realms of discourse is fundamental.

4. THE SECOND ACADEMIC YEAR IN GÖTTINGEN (1922/3)

By the summer of 1922 the theological revolution which Barth and a few like-minded friends were attempting to carry out had reached a certain critical mass. In August Barth met with Thurneysen and Gogarten at the Bergli—the summer home of Rudolf Pestalozzi in Oberrieden (near Zurich)—to found a new theological journal which would provide an organ for disseminating their views. It was decided that the editor-in-chief should be Georg Merz, the director of Christian Kaiser Verlag in Munich. Barth, Thurneysen, and Gogarten would serve as co-editors. The first number of *Zwischen den Zeiten* ('Between the Times') was published in January 1923. During the eleven years of its existence, *Zwischen den Zeiten* set the agenda for progressive, anti-establishment theology. It was to theology, one might say, what Herwarth Walden's *Der Sturm* had been to expressionistic painting and Franz Pfemfert's *Die Aktion* to expressionistic literature in pre-war Berlin: journals whose very names breathed of discontent and rebellion.

From the beginning, Barth's relationship with Gogarten was a rocky one. Barth saw in his friend a degree of self-assurance which always made him wonder whether a new ideology might not be in the offing. His reservations were so strong that he probably would not have set sail on the new venture with Gogarten on board had it not been for Thurneysen, who spoke for his inclusion.[72] He was horrified by Gogarten's suggestion that the new journal be called 'The Word'.

'The Word' is, in my opinion, insufferably arrogant. Better to call it 'The Ship of Fools' than this sacred millstone, which accords all too well to Gogarten's intentions and usual behaviour. God knows, it will

---

[72] Karl Barth to Georg Merz, 14 Sept. 1922, *B–Th. Br.* II. 98.

never do in Germany that *we* should have the insolence to go marching out with 'The Word' on our lips.[73]

Beyond the personality differences which were obviously involved, there were substantive differences which were clearly recognized by Barth; differences which were focused in Gogarten's talk of 'orders of creation',[74] his undialectical use of the 'Lord Jesus' as the guarantor of his truth-claims,[75] and his lack of a real eschatology.[76] The immediate consequence of these theological differences was a division within the leadership of *Zwischen den Zeiten* over questions of strategy: 'Gogarten would like in general to see us occupy only the *front*-line trenches where mines are bursting constantly, but that is not the way to carry on a war.'[77]

In the midst of these new responsibilities, Barth continued to further his learning process in 1922 and 1923 with lecture courses on 'The Theology of Zwingli' and 'The Theology of the Reformed Confessions'. Zwingli turned out to be a major disappointment for Barth. He saw in this first-generation Reformer 'the very image of the familiar modern-Protestant theology with a few eggshells from the early Church thrown in'.[78] Barth fared much better with the course on the confessions. The fruit of these lectures is to be found in an address entitled 'Reformed Doctrine: Its Essence and Task', which was given at a regional gathering of the World Alliance of Reformed Churches in Emden on 17 September 1923.

Until the First World War, the World Alliance had had the character of a Presbyterian organization, i.e. the churches which had full membership came largely from the United States and Great Britain. In light of the failure of the churches in the Great War to stem the tide of nationalism, it is understandable that the member churches saw a wider alliance with Reformed bodies on the Continent as a first step toward greater ecumenical unity generally, and that they saw such a step as imperative for the sake of peace in Europe. It was this sentiment which had

73 Karl Barth to Eduard Thurneysen, 16 Oct. 1922, *B–Th. Br.* II. 110.
74 Karl Barth to Eduard Thurneysen, 28 Sept. 1922, *B–Th. Br.* II. 100.
75 Karl Barth to Eduard Thurneysen, 26 Feb. 1922, *B–Th. Br.* II. 47.
76 Eduard Thurneysen to Karl Barth, 23 Feb. 1923, *B–Th. Br.* II. 148.
77 Karl Barth to Eduard Thurneysen, 21 July 1924, *B–Th. Br.* II. 265.
78 Karl Barth to Eduard Thurneysen, 23 Jan. 1923, *B–Th. Br.* II. 132.

prevailed at a major Continental Conference of the World Alliance which had met at Zurich a few weeks before the Emden gathering.

Barth's decision to speak on the subject of 'Reformed Doctrine' was prompted by an account of the Zurich meeting which had appeared in the *Neue Zürcher Zeitung* on 3 August. The author of this news release was Adolf Keller, formerly the senior pastor of the German-speaking congregation in Geneva and Barth's mentor during the first year of his *Vikariat* in 1909/10. In his account, Keller had this to say.

It could not escape an attentive observer that fruitless theological discussion played a minimal role at this meeting. The Conference was imbued by a strong spiritual striving to comprehend as untheologically as possible and to cause to come to life the old truths of the Reformation in their religious significance for the present. And with this turning back to the old sacred inheritance there was, at the same time, a spirit of resolute determination to press forward and make practical test of the old truths in new relationships.[79]

It was Keller's tendency to see theological discussion as 'fruitless' and his celebration of the attempt to understand the old truths 'untheologically' which stirred Barth to a response. To the rising tide of conviction that doctrine was somehow less valuable and important than 'life', Barth wanted to argue:

if the talk which surrounds us today of the 'cultivation of a consciousness which is more strongly Reformed in character' should prove to be true, it must show itself in the willingness to go with earnestness and rigour the way which Luther *and* Calvin went, the way which leads from *thought* to action, and no other.[80]

To the call for practical tests of old truths, Barth responded that it was not at all clear that those who would be testing the old truths had any comprehension of what it was which was to be tested. Could it escape the notice of the 'sharp-eyed children of this world' that 'we have here a predicate without a subject?'[81] What is the 'sacred inheritance' of the Reformation? Barth noted that it would not be enough to be able to repeat certain doctrinal formulas of the early Reformed churches. Among critics, too,

---

[79] Cited by Barth, 'Reformierte Lehre, ihr Wesen und Aufgabe', in idem, *Das Wort Gottes und die Theologie*, 179.

[80] Ibid. 183.   [81] Ibid. 181.

there is a kind of repristination—a mouthing of old formulas without comprehension of the presuppositions which gave rise to them, so that one could then proceed quickly to the matter of critical testing. What disturbed Barth in the present situation was the (to his mind) almost total lack of appreciation for what he called the one presupposition of Reformed doctrine. Without the recovery of that presupposition no course of action— whether the writing of a new Statement of Faith or the adoption of one of the old Reformed standards—could produce "Reformed" doctrine. What was this presupposition, the whence of Reformed doctrine? Barth's answer was the Scripture-principle, which held that every doctrine must be measured against an unchangeable and impassible rule in which alone was truth: namely, the Word of God.[82] It was the Scriptures which the old Reformed theologians held to be the measure of truth and not any particular interpretation of them by pious men of the past, even though their names should be Calvin and Zwingli; the Scriptures as a whole (the canon), and not a particular doctrine drawn from them which would then provide a material principle from which the rest of the contents of dogmatics could be derived. Barth strenuously objected to the idea that the Scripture-principle was only a formal principle. 'That *God* witnesses to Himself in Holy Scripture was for our fathers not at all "only" form; it was not "form" at all, but rather, the most present, living, and complete content.'[83] For Barth, formal principle and material principle were one and the same—the Word of God standing behind Scripture which must witness to itself in Scripture if it is to be known. God can only be known through God: that is the point of the Scripture-principle. The Scripture-principle said simply that revelation means that *God* is speaking.[84] Unless God speaks, the Bible is a shut door before which we can only bow in fear and trembling. It was this presupposition—God is speaking—and the attitude of brokenness it implied which had to be recovered. Until it was recovered, any course of action would be a mistake. Given that Barth obviously thought that he understood the one presupposition of Reformed doctrine, it is not surprising that he had an opinion on the subject of a new confession. He was opposed to such a move. He was more

[82] Ibid. 193.   [83] Ibid. 194.   [84] Ibid.

inclined to hope for an agreement on the proper understanding of old Reformed norms of doctrine, amongst which his preference was for the Genevan Catechism of 1545.[85]

Throughout this lecture, Barth was seeking to establish the subordinate relationship of *every* confession (new and old) to Scripture. But where this subordination is observed and put into practice, it is then possible to go on to see that there is indeed such a thing as 'right doctrine'.

Doctrina is the Christian human word which has passed through the crisis, the merciless cleansing and purifying of the Word of God attested in the Scriptures. It remains human word; it does not itself become *verbum divinum*. But nevertheless, when this way is travelled, it is a legitimate, pure *praedicatio verbi divini*.[86]

What emerges in this lecture is a first, very tentative step beyond commitment to the Scripture-principle to the thought that the confessions too can bear an appropriate authority. A year later, in his Göttingen lectures on dogmatics, Barth would define the authority of the confession as wholly derivative, human authority—the authority of a secondary witness to revelation. For now, the critical negations are still the most prominent feature of his thought on the subject.

The Reformed churches knew nothing of a dogma in the strict, hierarchical sense. Doctrinal *authority* was in no sense for them Christian history; but rather, *Scripture* and *Spirit*, *both* of which stand beyond Christian history (the Scriptures too!). Being faithful to the fathers would have to mean conducting ourselves as they conducted themselves: allowing history to speak, but as a witness beyond history to revelation; . . . not confusing the authority which is given to the Church with the authority which grounds the Church . . .[87]

Despite all the caveats by which it is surrounded, there is present here a cautious affirmation that doctrine which has passed through the crisis of testing in the light of the Word of God can indeed witness beyond itself to revelation. Moreover, there is an acknowledgement of a relative authority which is given to the Church. And that was certainly a new element in Barth's thinking.

That none of these modifications amounted to a shift away from the eschatological perspective which governed *Romans* II is

---

[85] Barth, 'Reformierte Lehre, ihr Wesen und Aufgabe', 198–9.
[86] Ibid. 194.   [87] Ibid. 186.

also clear. Barth's lectures on 1 Corinthians 15 in the summer semester 1923 (published a year later under the title *Die Auferstehung der Toten*) showed that his commitment to a consistent eschatology had not waned.

An event of great importance took place in the autumn of 1923, for it was then that Barth first encountered the writings of Erich Przywara, a Polish Jesuit who specialized in Augustine studies. Throughout the course of the 1920s, Przywara was a frequent contributor to *Stimmen der Zeit*, a Catholic theological journal published in Freiburg. Because Przywara's contributions consisted in assessments of contemporary trends in theology, Karl Barth frequently found a place in them. The first of these occasions was greeted with not a little bit of enthusiasm by Eduard Thurneysen.

Acquire for yourself a copy of Number 11 of *Stimmen der Zeit*, August 1923, Herder Freiburg. There you will find a remarkable and extensive essay about us from the side of the Catholic partner. It is interesting because he makes the Catholic standpoint very clearly visible. Along the way, essential and penetrating remarks on Augustine occur. It is an expert who speaks there. We come off very well, even though our real concern has not been seen.[88]

The essay in question bears the title 'God in Us or above Us? (Immanence and Transcendence in Today's Spiritual Life)'.[89] That Barth and company 'came off well'—at least as compared with liberal Protestantism—is no exaggeration. In many respects Przywara was the most formidable opponent yet to have entered the lists against Barth. He shared much of Barth's assessment of the reigning theology; he had gone further in understanding Barth's concerns than any previous critic; and at at least one point where he raised a question, Barth would himself see a need for further clarification and advance in the coming months.

Przywara, like Barth, saw contemporary theology as having arrived at the end of an era. The period in which the history and psychology of religion had predominated was in its death throes. Decision was the word of the hour and the arena in which

---

[88] Eduard Thurneysen to Karl Barth, 30 Sept. 1923, *B–Th. Br.* II. 190. That Barth took his friend's advice and acquired a copy is beyond doubt. A heavily underlined copy can be found in the Karl Barth-Archiv in Basle.

[89] Erich Przywara, 'Gott in uns oder über uns? (Immanenz and Transzendenz im heutigen Geistesleben)', *Stimmen der Zeit*, 105 (1923), 343–62.

decision would have to be made was that of the concept of God. But, Przywara argued, the decision could only be made legitimately when Catholicism and Protestantism, each for its own part, reflected upon the concept of God native to it, and on that basis, carried out the necessary debate. There could be no easy syntheses on the order of Friedrich Heiler's 'evangelical Catholicity'; only a rigorous consideration of the historical roots of the doctrine of God proper to each tradition.[90] Given Barth's antipathy to "untheological" elements in the ecumenical movement, this had to be welcome news.

Przywara's argument can be summed up simply: only Catholicism has a concept of God in which transcendence and immanence each play their proper role. It is a concept which is neither objectivist nor subjectivist but allows both tendencies to come to full expression. The standard for measuring all Catholic understanding of God was, for Przywara, Augustine's 'God in us—god above us'.[91] Luther's God, on the other hand, was a wholly transcendent God—a God who alone is truly real and capable of effecting things in the created world.[92] Given this understanding of Luther, it is not surprising that Przywara greeted the Barth–Gogarten school as the 'rebirth of genuine Protestantism'. 'If Luther belongs to any group in present-day Protestantism, then he belongs to them and is their father.'[93] Far from being the fanatic subjectivist which Barth's liberal Protestant critics made him out to be, Przywara saw Barth as a one-sided objectivist; one in whom subjectivism and immanence cannot come to expression. For his part, Barth would certainly have felt that in being placed on the side of objectivism, someone had at last got him right (though he would not have been ready to accept the criticism that immanence does not come to expression in his theology).

To Barth's wholly other God, Przywara contrasted Augustine's God of the *'analogia entis'*[94]—a momentous phrase destined to play a large role in Barth's future debate with Catholicism. In Przywara's view, Barth has put:

in the place of the "analogy" between God and the creature, the pure "negation". If the *analogia entis* of the Catholic concept of God means

[90] Erich Przywara, 'Gott in uns oder über uns?', 343.   [91] Ibid. 344–5.
[92] Ibid. 347–8.   [93] Ibid. 350.   [94] Ibid. 344.

the mysterious tension of a "similar–dissimilar", corresponding to the tension of the 'God in us and above us', then in the Protestant concept of God, the "similarity" has been completely crossed out.[95]

The final consequence of Barth's one-sidedness is that he knows of no true unity of God with humankind. And that meant that, in Barth's hands, both the Incarnation and an ecclesiology which would help to explain the continuing presence of God in the world are rejected.[96]

This was indeed food for thought. Przywara's sketch of Barth could hardly be set aside as simply mistaken. His description of a one-sided conception of God as transcendent was accurate to a great degree (at least with regard to *Romans* II). The one defect in Przywara's account was his attribution to Barth of the way of 'pure negation'. In the list Przywara provided of his reading in Barth's works, the one conspicuous omission was 'The Word of God as the Task of Theology'.[97] Had he read it, he would have realized that the way of pure negation had been considered there under the heading 'the critical way', only to be set aside as less helpful than the 'dialectical way'. Nevertheless, Przywara's account reflected widespread reading and serious reflection.

One point especially looms large in Przywara's critique: the lack of an adequate doctrine of the Incarnation. That was a point to which Barth would almost immediately devote serious attention. It is hard to avoid the impression that Przywara's critique had pointed the way Barth needed to go for the sake of further clarification. This essay leads one to believe that if an overriding stimulus to Barth's future development were to be sought in the winter of 1923/4, then the first place to look would be his first encounter with Catholicism. Barth himself confirmed this impression in the foreword to the fourth edition of *Romans* in February 1924. There he spoke of the lack of understanding on the part of his Protestant reviewers and then added,

Several opinions from the Catholic side gave me more to think about. Their reviews have, at least in part, pushed me into an accurate under-standing of the matter which concerns us and above all, have done so on a level of theological discussion which I could not concede to many of my honourable reviewers on this side of the great divide. How is one to interpret this—to me, truly unexpected—encounter in certain

---

[95] Ibid. 350.   [96] Ibid. 355.   [97] Ibid.

common foundational principles? Erich Przywara, SJ, sees in our "school" (!), in contrast to that of Otto and Heiler, 'a genuine rebirth of Protestantism' . . .[98]

Especially striking is Barth's surprise at his discovery of shared 'foundational principles'. It is noteworthy that it was in this fore-word to the fourth edition that Barth announced, for the first time since the massive revision which had resulted in *Romans* II, that the book really needed once again to be revised 'in head and members'.[99]

One last event in the run-up to Barth's dogmatics lectures deserves mention. In November 1923 Barth carried out a public debate with Paul Tillich in the pages of *Theologische Blätter*. Tillich argued that the Christ-event was only rightly understood when interpreted symbolically, as the expression of a revelation which occurs elsewhere (in culture, history, and nature). He wondered whether Barth and Gogarten had not contradicted their own insistence on the non-immediacy of revelation when they went on to place so much emphasis on the once-and-for-allness of the revelation in Jesus. Was this not to single out and objectify revelation in a particular piece of history? The form of the question was more appropriate to Gogarten than to Barth, but nevertheless Barth's response is most interesting. Where he had spent so much time in the previous three years insisting upon the *distinction* of revelation and Christ's humanity, now he had to argue that in distinguishing them, we cannot *separate* them. Ultimately, the reason a separation of Christ and Jesus cannot be made (even as we rightly distinguish them) is that that which is revealed in Jesus is not an idea or principle (not 'the Unconditioned'), but a Person; a Person who, in His particular-ity, can freely choose to reveal Himself where and when He wishes—with all of the concreteness and particularity that implies. But there was also, in Barth's view, a second reason. In focusing his attention on this one piece of history to the exclu-sion of all others:

it is a matter of affirming that we are by no means intellectual monads wandering lost in space; by no means relying on ourselves in the author-ity of free speculation, in the ambiguity of our relation to God and its interpretation. We are *baptized Christians*. For us . . . 'there is', according

---

[98] Barth, *Der Römerbrief, 1922*, p. xxiv.   [99] Ibid. p. xxiii.

to the testimony of Scripture and the confession of the Church, a history which is qualified as *the* site of *the* salvation history . . .[100]

Barth's first response was not an appeal to the authority of the Church; there must be no misunderstanding on that point. But an appeal to the Church's authority as a second court of appeal was now not out of order.

What is "absurd" from the Christian or *theological* point of view is not at all what Tillich designates to be so—'the once and for all'—which [it] is rather our theological duty to affirm. What is "absurd" is all unreflecting, unclassical, disrespectful deviation from the formula of the Council of Chalcedon. For to hold quietly to this formula would *mutatis mutandis*, even today, give evidence of insight.[101]

Finally, accusing Tillich of opening the door to relativism, Barth concluded,

I do not wish to have anything to do with a Tower of Babel theology. We definitely do *not* want a theology free of presuppositions, in which each, according to his free, blissful, Protestant arbitrariness and inventions, would be turned loose to think and talk as his spirit suggested— even if this occurred under the banner of 'theonomy'! Not only God, not only Christianity, but the Church—by which I mean 'the one holy catholic Church' and to a lesser degree, also, the individual churches to which we belong—is the presupposition of theology.[102]

The evolution in Barth's esteem for the—at least secondary— authority of the Church is quite evident. Even more significant is the fact that Tillich had forced Barth point-blank to think further about the problem of the contingency of revelation; i.e. what it means to affirm that one piece of history has been qualified by revelation as '*the* site of *the* salvation history'. The stage was now set for a thorough reconsideration of the doctrine of the incarnation.

[100] Karl Barth, 'Von der Paradoxie der "positiven Paradoxes": Antworten und Fragen an Paul Tillich', in Moltmann (ed.), *Anfänge der dialektischen Theologie*, i. 185; ET 'The Paradoxical Nature of the "Positive Paradox": Answers and Questions to Paul Tillich', in Robinson (ed.), *The Beginnings of Dialectic Theology*, 151.
[101] Ibid. 186–7; ET 152.   [102] Ibid. 188; ET 154.

PART III

Dialectical Theology in the Shadow of an Anhypostatic-Enhypostatic Christology

(FIRST STAGE: PNEUMATOCENTRISM, 1924–1936)

If my work up to this point has been effective here and there as a marginal gloss and corrective and should continue to be effective in this way, that could not and cannot be my intention. I was and am a regular theologian at whose disposal stands not the Word of God but at best a 'doctrine of the Word of God'. I feel myself neither justified nor obligated to persist in the demeanour of the prophet, in the attitude of the breakthrough, in which some clearly perceived me for a moment and in which they now want to perceive me again and again, to their joy and comfort . . . I am not conscious of having ever done anything else than—old? new theology?—in any case, theology, whereas the Word of God spoke for Himself or did not speak when and where it pleased God. I went my way before and I went my way after *Romans* on the earth. That means for me concretely . . . that I had to engage and have engaged in Christian dogmatics, without being able to ask what will become of it.

(Karl Barth, *Die christliche Dogmatik im Entwurf*, 8)

8

The Göttingen Dogmatics

(GÖTTINGEN,
APRIL 1924–OCTOBER 1925)

I. SHIFT FROM AN ESCHATOLOGICAL TO A
CHRISTOLOGICAL GROUNDING OF THEOLOGY

In May 1924 Barth made a momentous discovery. During the
course of his first lectures in dogmatics, he came upon the anhypostatic-enhypostatic Christological dogma of the ancient
Church in a textbook of post-Reformation theology. He saw in
it an understanding of the incarnate being of the Mediator which
preserved that infinite qualitative distinction between God and
humankind which had been at the forefront of his concerns
throughout the previous phase. The central thrust of the ancient
dogma was that the Logos (the second Person of the Holy
Trinity) took to Himself human flesh (i.e. a human "nature",
complete, whole, and entire) and lived a human life in and
through it. The proximity to Barth's dialectic of veiling and
unveiling was obvious. In that God takes to God's Self a human
nature, God veils God's Self in a creaturely medium. He enters
'the divine incognito'—a situation of unrecognizability. Outwardly (and inwardly!), He is a human being like any other. But
the Subject of this human life—we may liken this to Kant's conception of an unintuitable, noumenal self—was at every point
the Second Person of the Trinity; a Subject who, because of the
veil of human flesh, remains unintuitable. Because of His unintu-
itability, God can only be known in Jesus where He condescends
to grant faith to the would-be human knower; where He unveils
Himself in and through the veil of human flesh.

With the adoption of the anhypostatic-enhypostatic model of
Christology, Barth had accomplished two things of fundamental

importance. First, the eschatological reservation which, in the phase of *Romans* II, had been safeguarded by the time–eternity dialectic, *was now built into the very structure of his Christology*. And that meant that the time–eternity dialectic could now gradually be dispensed with with no loss of the critical distance between God and humankind which that dialectic had once secured. Thus the shift from an eschatological to a Christological grounding of theology could take place with no weakening of the eschatological reservation. Theology in the shadow of an anhypostatic-enhypostatic Christology was as much a *critically* realistic theology as the previous theology in the shadow of a consistent eschatology had been. There was no relaxation here of Barth's fundamental radicalism. What is in view here is an advance along the same line which Barth had first entered in 1915; not a break with it. But second, and equally important, the incarnation could now be given its due. No longer did Barth need to reduce the 'site' of revelation to a single 'mathematical point'—the event of the cross. Now, the dialectic of veiling and unveiling on its objective side could comprehend the whole of the incarnate existence of the Mediator. That is the nature of the advance which occurred in this phase.

The distinction between Barth's theology in this phase and the next phase (to be described in the last chapter) is this: although the theoretical ground of Barth's theology in this phase was found in his Christology, his basic orientation (his existential focus, if you will) was towards the revelation-event which occurs *in the here and now* on the basis of God's Self-revelation in Christ. He did not try, as he would later, to read all of his doctrines off God's Self-revelation in Christ in the there and then of AD 1–30. In many cases, he tried to read his doctrines off the event in which revelation is received in the present. Thus, though the ground of his theology was now clearly Christological, his theology was largely pneumatocentric. This emerges (as we shall see) with the greatest clarity in his doctrine of election, which was centred in the concrete situation of the person who is addressed by revelation in the here and now. When the doctrine of election was later modified (after 1936), Barth's theology would undergo a final adjustment. It would become a Christologically grounded, christocentric theology.

2. PREPARATIONS FOR DOGMATICS

By November 1923 the inflation had reached its peak. The way out of the morass was found in the issue of a new mark, covered this time by mortgage bonds which were backed by the assets of industry and agriculture.[1] The next six years were characterized by relative stability, as the Weimar Republic made great strides under the direction of its Minister of Foreign Affairs, Gustav Stresemann, towards re-establishing itself on an equal footing with other European nations. The French exploitation of the Ruhr was ended by the Dawes Plan in the spring of 1924. Following that success, Stresemann succeeded in negotiating substantial reductions in the reparations payment schedule, as well as admission to the League of Nations. When Stresemann died on 3 October 1929, on the eve of world-wide depression, there were already warning signs that anti-democratic forces were gaining strength in Germany. But during the years 1924–9, there was—by Weimar standards—relative calm.

The cultural world too saw a shift in 1924—from the predominance of Expressionism to that of the '*Neue Sachlichkeit*' (the 'New Objectivity'). The ecstatic and abstract style of Expressionism gave way in the new political climate to a spirit of resignation, expressed in sobriety and cool realism. For all of their disgust at the prevalent cultural decadence and their disquiet and longing for renewal, the expressionists had still retained a vestige of optimism, the belief that through the protest of their abstract art things could be changed. The expressionists had seen themselves as agents of revolutionary change. The '*Neue Sachlichkeit*' represented a drastic loss of innocence. Optimism gave way to unrestrained pessimism. Revolutionary tendencies were renounced in favour of a sober coming-to-grips with reality as it is. The critique of the '*Neue Sachlichkeit*' by Marxist revisionist historians contains a good deal of truth. On this view, the '*Neue Sachlichkeit*' was the artistic expression of a 'reformist *Realpolitik*' which promoted fetishism (the passive acceptance of social reality as it is). The turn to a 'new objectivity' had everything to do with the recovery of a certain balance by the reigning capitalist

---

[1] Craig, *Germany, 1866–1945*, 467.

forces.[2] It is not surprising then that many artists who may be categorized as belonging to this movement later became National Socialist realists. But it has to be added that disillusioned left-wing artists turned to realism as well (revisionist historians reserve the term 'Verism' for the art of people like Max Beckmann and Otto Dix), so that in terms of style alone it is not possible to say what political position was being represented. The subject-matter treated was a crucial indicator obviously.

Barth's style had been in the process of change since *Romans* II. It would be tempting to see this change as part and parcel of a shift in cultural mood.[3] But there are a number of problems with this assessment, not least of which is that Barth displayed little interest at this time in contemporary art. In addition, Barth's style had already undergone some change from the moment of his entrance into the academic field. His shift to a calm and measured academic style in 1924 was therefore a continuation of a tendency of several years' standing. Most importantly, however, Barth was not in the least seized by a spirit of resignation in the face of seemingly unchangeable social realities, as were many of his contemporaries. His starting-point in the wholly other God remained as constant as ever it had been from 1915 on. Belief in a God who can change the situation (any situation!) did not incline him to suddenly—in the post-inflationary calm—come to grips with the "given" social reality. His critical posture towards the "given" remained unchanged. If one were to seek a closer explanation of Barth's growing distance from the expressionistic style of *Romans*, the first place to look would be his concern in late 1923 that a school was forming behind him. Already there were signs that the thought-forms and categories of *Romans* II were being reduced to slogans by a number of well-meaning pastors.[4] Barth was deeply concerned not to form a school, because a school would mean the domestication of the criticism which he had hoped to carry out. With the threat of a school forming behind him looming clearly on the horizon, it was time for

---

[2] Jost Hermand, 'Unity within Diversity? The History of the Concept "*Neue Sachlichkeit*"', in Keith Bullivant (ed.), *Culture and Society in the Weimar Republic* (Manchester: Manchester University Press, 1977), 174.

[3] Stephen Webb provides an excellent illustration of a scholar who is unable to resist this temptation. See Webb, *Re-figuring Theology*, 150–3.

[4] Eduard Thurneysen to Karl Barth, 22 Nov. 1923, *B–Th. Br.* II. 200; Karl Barth to Eduard Thurneysen, 4 Mar. 1924, 234.

something new. Thus it was the internal theological situation, more than anything else, which accounts for Barth's shift in style. In this, as in the simultaneous emergence of interest in the theological wealth of the Church's past, Barth remained the 'outsider', a man given to swimming against the stream.

In the midst of the winter semester 1923/4, Barth announced his intention to lecture on 'Prolegomena to Dogmatics' in the spring. The proposal was met with resistance from his Lutheran colleagues. On 27 December, Barth reported that Carl Stange had made a motion at a faculty meeting that Barth be required to announce his lectures as 'Prolegomena to *Reformed* Dogmatics'. According to Barth's account, Stange's expressed goal was to have this adjective entered into the *Testatbücher* of the students who attended his lectures, so that Lutheran consistories would be alerted to the fact that Lutheran students were hearing Reformed dogmatics. His hope was that the consistories would compel Lutheran students to hear Lutheran dogmatics (i.e. the lectures given by Stange and Wobbermin).[5] Barth objected strenuously on the grounds that Reformed dogmatics are as ecumenical as any other, and therefore do not require the adjective 'Reformed'. This objection was met by the argument that his teaching mandate required him to teach Reformed dogmatics. In the end, Barth contented himself with asking if he could announce his lectures under the title given by Calvin to his great work: '*Unterricht in der christlichen Religion*'. He took some solace in the fact that Stange's great predecessor, Albrecht Ritschl, had also published a small dogmatics with this title. This lent to the title a certain ecumenical character, whatever his colleagues might think. Though Barth was still not happy, this was the title agreed upon.

But the title was a small consideration when compared to the *content* of this dogmatics.

Much more interesting and burning is naturally the question of what should happen in this dogmatics . . . It pursues me into my dreams. At any rate, the insertion of the word "prolegomena" is very much in place in that it must "somehow" deal with the determination of the *object*, of the *concept* of it, and the *method* which results from it. The

---

[5] Karl Barth to Eduard Thurneysen, 27 Dec. 1923, *B–Th. Br.* II. 213.

guiding principle must be not to *want* too much and not to *do* too little, so as not to fall into any speculative or barbarically orthodox hole. Yes, good heavens, now the dog must take to the water, Eduard . . . If only we had remained silent at that time when we were so close to becoming harmless and orderly disciples of Wernle; or later . . . when we were thinking of settling down at Kutter's table; or still later, when we . . . began with pale faces to proclaim the wisdom of death and the void. None of that involved as yet a dogmatics, with consideration of concept and method. On the contrary; how we would have laughed at such possibilities at that time. But the trouble is that we have never been *silent* and now we are in for it . . .[6]

Barth dreaded the moment which would inevitably come, when he would have to stand up and give an account of himself. It reminded him of that moment in the dentist's chair, when the machinery had begun to whirr and one knew that the drill would very soon put in an appearance.[7]

Barth's distress at the prospect of lecturing on dogmatics can scarcely be exaggerated. The fullest insight into his thinking on the subject of the preferable procedure in and organization of a dogmatics emerges in a remarkable letter-exchange with Emil Brunner in January. The occasion for the exchange was Brunner's appointment as an *extraordinarius* Professor for theology at the University of Zurich. Brunner too, was in the position of offering his first lectures in dogmatics during the summer semester of 1924. Like Barth, he too was in a panic as to how to proceed. So he wrote to Barth for advice—a commodity which Barth had little of at the moment.

Brunner's letter began by listing the possible approaches to dogmatics which he had been able to recall from the history of dogmatics.[8] His own preference would have been to write dogmatics in connection with some confessional document(s). This would have been the most honest approach since it would make clear his conviction that dogmatics is not presuppositionless; that the dogmatician approaches his work on the basis of a quite definite faith. Given that the Swiss cantonal churches had dissociated

---

[6] Karl Barth to Eduard Thurneysen, 5 Feb. 1924, *B–Th. Br.* II. 222.

[7] Karl Barth to Eduard Thurneysen, 20 Apr. 1924, *B–Th. Br.* II. 243.

[8] Emil Brunner to Karl Barth, 23 Jan. 1924, original in Karl Barth-Archiv, Basle, Switzerland, 1.

themselves from every confessional standard in the nineteenth century, however, this preferred way was seen by Brunner as impossible. It would be laughable, he said, for a Swiss to suddenly appeal to the authority of a confession (even if only on a secondary level) as the starting-point for dogmatics. What then? Brunner noted that he saw three other possibilities: a biblical theology in the style of a J. T. Beck or J. C. K. von Hofmann; a history and sociology of religions approach; and speculative theology (which knows in advance where it will end, namely with Christian results). He then discussed the advantages and disadvantages of each. He himself was inclined for the present to take up a fifth alternative which had been proposed to him by a Hungarian professor of theology: dogmatics in connection with Calvin's *Institutes*.[9] Brunner concluded with an appeal for advice.

Barth responded on 26 January. To his mind, the 'table of possibilities' had the following form.

1. "Loci" in connection with the *Römerbrief* (Melanchthon!).
2. Biblical theology à la Beck.
3. Speculative [theology] à la Biedermann.
4. Scholastic [theology] (in the place of Petrus Lombardus: Calvin's *Institutio*, therefore, like your Hungarian authority, or the Genevan Catechism of 1545).
5. "Prophetic", i.e. to be Calvin himself, to pound the table, and under constant check 1. by the Bible and 2. by the early Church and Reformation, to go one's own self-chosen way.
6. Confessional: the material in dogmatics is, in this case, "dogma". If the degenerate modern Reformed Church gives us nothing of the kind, then we clearly stand again at the *beginning* of the Reformed Reformation. We have to ask what dogma was *before* the confessions and would come therefore to the Apostles' Creed. Confessions to be used *heuristically*. The authority of Scripture as the *origin* of all this stuff, naturally.
7. The clear nonsense: Schleiermacher and everything which creeps and flies after him.[10]

Barth's preferences among this range of possible approaches are not surprising, given his work to this point on Calvin and the Reformed Confessions, but it is important to note them as a

---

[9] Ibid. 3.
[10] Karl Barth to Emil Brunner, 26 Jan. 1924, copy in Karl Barth-Archiv, Basle, Switzerland, 1–2.

benchmark against which to measure his later progress—that is, what he in fact achieved in the Göttingen Dogmatics.

Naturally, only 1, 4, 5, and 6 come into consideration. No. 1 would be tempting, but I would like to take the bull by the horns more powerfully. For a long time, No. 4 appeared to me to be the only possibility. For the moment, I am inclined to a combination of No. 5 and No. 6...[11]

For some time then, Barth had been in favour of an approach which he labelled "scholastic"—i.e. the construction of dogmatics as a kind of "Sentence Commentary", with the exception that Peter Lombard's *Sentences* would be replaced by Calvin's *Institutes* or the Genevan Catechism of 1545. For the moment however, he was vacillating between the 'prophetic' and the 'confessional' (in which case, the Apostles' Creed would have provided the basic text). Clearly, Barth's thinking was still very much in flux and would continue to be so for the next several months.

The spring vacation of 1924 was spent in frantic preparation, consisting above all in an intensive programme of reading. Barth's reading began with the Apologies of Justin, Aristides, Tertullian, and Athenagorus; the *Octavian* of Minucius Felix; Origen's *Contra Celsum*; Gregory of Nyssa's *Logos Catechetikos*; and Augustine's *Enchiridion*.[12] On 20 April, Barth reported that he was now reading hundreds and hundreds of pages pell-mell. His reading list now included Karl Heim, Thomas Aquinas, D. F. Strauss, Alexander Schweizer, Wilhelm Herrmann, and F. A. B. Nitsch. For Barth, this was a 'time of sighing, an evil time'.[13]

It was somewhere about this time that Barth made a helpful discovery which would show him the way out of his dilemma: Heinrich Heppe's old textbook of Reformed dogmatics.[14]

I shall never forget the spring vacation of 1924. I sat in my study in Göttingen, faced with the task of giving lectures on dogmatics for the first time. Not for a long time could anyone have been as plagued as I was at that time by the question, could I do it? And how? My biblical and historical studies to date had driven me more and more from the good society of contemporary and, as I saw with greater clarity, of

---

[11] Karl Barth to Emil Brunner, 26 Jan. 1924, 2.
[12] Karl Barth to Eduard Thurneysen, 4 Mar. 1924, *B–Th. Br.* II. 236.
[13] Karl Barth to Eduard Thurneysen, 20 Apr. 1924, *B–Th. Br.* II. 243.
[14] Heinrich Heppe, *Die Dogmatik der evangelisch-reformierten Kirche* (Elberfeld, 1861). (This was the edition used by Barth.)

almost the whole of modern theology. I saw myself, so to speak, without a teacher; alone in the wide open spaces. . . . It was at that time that, along with the parallel Lutheran work of H. Schmid, Heppe's volume, which today is newly edited, fell into my hands; out of date, dusty, unattractive, almost like a table of logarithms, dreary to read, rigid and remarkable on almost every page I opened; in form and content corresponding rather exactly to that which I, like so many others, had described to myself decades ago as the 'old orthodoxy'. Well, I had the grace not to be slack. I read, I studied, I reflected, and found that I was rewarded by the discovery that I found myself, here at any rate, in an atmosphere in which the way through the Reformers to Holy Scripture was more meaningful and natural than in the atmosphere of the theological literature which had been stamped by Schleiermacher and Ritschl . . .[15]

The strong attraction which Barth felt to the dogmatics of post-Reformation orthodox theologians was rooted above in its strongly ecclesial character. The dogmatics of these old theologians not only took up and preserved 'the great concerns of the Reformation'; they did so while attempting 'a worthy continuation of the doctrinal constructions of the early Church' and maintaining 'continuity with the ecclesiastical science of the Middle Ages'. And so, Barth observed, 'I found myself visibly in the realm of the *Church*'.[16]

Behind Barth's praise for the ecclesial character of orthodox dogmatics lay a hermeneutical problem of considerable proportions. Barth noted that numerous attempts had been made in the modern era to return to the Bible by way of the Reformers. Such attempts, carried out as they were by theologians on the right as well as on the left, had only resulted in confusion. In the midst of this welter of conflicting opinion, Barth advocated the use of an ecclesial hermeneutic.

I did and still do maintain that it is a good thing not to proceed too hastily with the popular "breakthrough" to a biblical-Reformational theology, but rather, to linger at length at the station called "orthodoxy". The "breakthrough" has all too often meant that one has merely broken through once again to a new mixture of Enlightenment and Pietism! It can only succeed where one has learned beforehand to read

[15] Karl Barth, 'Zum Geleit', in Heinrich Heppe, *Die Dogmatik der evangelisch-reformierten Kirche,* ed. Ernst Bizer (Neukirchen: Buchhandlung des Erziehungsvereins Neukirchen, Kreis Moers, 1935), p. iii.
[16] Ibid. p. iv.

the Reformers as teachers of the *Church* . . . Precisely that, however, one can and must learn from the old orthodox theologians.[17]

What Barth was suggesting is that, if one desires to receive guidance from the *Church* (and specifically, from the voice of the Church in the past), the best place to begin is not with the Reformers, but with the theologians and confessions which came after them. To be sure, the reflections of these later theologians were derivative. But it was necessary that the insights of theological geniuses like Luther and Calvin be submitted to the Church for critical testing and approval—necessary, that is, for the sake of the ecclesial character of the Reformation.[18] In Barth's view, it is the Church's responsibility to point the way out of the confusion. And the Church has, from the beginning, taken up this responsibility through its communal and public confession. The writings of the orthodox theologians are to be seen as the fruit of extensive reflection upon those confessions which constituted the Church's response to the reforming activities of Luther, Zwingli, and Calvin. Seen in this light, it is understandable that Barth would have seen the orthodox as the 'first station' to pass through on the way to a biblical-Reformational theology.

Beyond their churchly character, it was the "scientific" character of the old orthodox dogmatics which Barth found most impressive.

I found myself . . . in the realm of a Church *science* which was respectable in its way. I had occasion to marvel at the long, peaceful breathing, at the prudence, the solidity, the strict relation to the object, the superior style and methods, reliable in themselves, with which this "orthodoxy" worked. I had occasion to be astonished at the wealth of problems and the beauty (*pulchritudo*) of their trains of thought. I saw in these old fellows that it can be worthwhile to reflect upon the smallest point with the greatest power of Christian presupposition, and precisely for the sake of the much-appealed-to "life", to take the truth-question with complete seriousness all along the line.[19]

It should be emphasized however, that it was also clear to Barth that 'a return to this orthodoxy (in order to stand still with them and to do things the same way!)'[20] was impossible. He

---

[17] Ibid. p. v.   [18] Cf. *KD* I/1, 296; *CD* I/1, 279.

[19] Barth, 'Zum Geleit', in Heppe, *Die Dogmatik der evangelisch-reformierten Kirche*, pp. iii–iv.

[20] Ibid. p. iv.

could not share all of its presuppositions; nor could he make its method his own.

Initially Barth employed a number of textbooks as sources of post-Reformation orthodoxy: works by Alexander Schweizer, C. E. Luthardt, Karl von Hase, and Hermann Bavinck in addition to Heinrich Schmid's *Dogmatik der evangelisch-lutherischen Kirche* and the textbook by Heppe.[21] By the second semester, however, Heppe and Schmid had become his 'constant companions'. Indeed, Heppe quickly became his foundational text.

The treatment of the Göttingen Dogmatics which follows will obviously have to be quite selective. It will not be possible to treat each and every doctrine; nor will it be possible in the case of those doctrines which are considered, to treat them exhaustively. The criterion of selection will be a genetic one. I will treat only those doctrines in which advances occurred which fuelled Barth's development as a whole. In addition to the prolegomena sections which touch upon the nature of the dogmatic task (the determination of its object and method), the three *loci* to be treated are: Trinity, Christology, and election. A closer theological analysis of the Göttingen Dogmatics will be undertaken in the sequel to the present work.

It is of the utmost importance to bear in mind in what follows that the Göttingen Dogmatics were never revised by their author with a view to publication. They are the document of a very rapid evolution in Barth's thought. As such, they set forth points of view at the outset which are almost immediately qualified and set aside by the emergence of a new perspective.

3. DEUS DIXIT

The first prolegomena lecture was given on 2 May. Barth began with a very tight and concise definition of dogmatics which was then elaborated through the course of the first two paragraphs,

---

[21] The editions employed by Barth were as follows: Alexander Schweizer, *Die Glaubenslehre der evangelisch-reformierten Kirche* (2 vols.; Zurich, 1844 and 1847); C. E. Luthardt, *Kompendium der Dogmatik* (Leipzig, 1873); Karl von Hase, *Hutterus Redivivus* (Leipzig, 1862); Hermann Bavinck, *Gereformeerde Dogmatiek* (4 vols.; Kampen, 1906–11); and Heinrich Schmid, *Dogmatik der evangelisch-lutherischen Kirche* (4th edn.; Frankfurt am Main/Erlangen, 1858). (Each of these titles is still to be found in Barth's personal library in the Karl Barth-Archiv, Basle, Switzerland.)

under the heading 'Introduction'. The brief definition is this: dogmatics is 'scientific reflection on the Word of God'.[22] Three aspects of this definition require amplification: the object of theology (the Word of God), the status of dogmatics in relation to the object (reflection), and the meaning of the word 'scientific'.

Dogmatics, Barth wrote, occurs only in a highly concrete situation. The word about God spoken by the theologian must, if it is to be a word about *God*, occur in a definite relation to the Word of God, to a 'giving-Himself-to-be-known from the side of God'.[23] Revelation, in its strictest, most proper and original sense, is defined here as a speaking by God, '*Deus dixit*'.[24] It is in this context that Barth first developed his well-known doctrine of the 'threefold form' of the Word of God.[25]

The Word of God is first of all that speaking of God which is identical with God; identical, because it is a speaking by God. Barth calls this form of the Word "revelation". As revelation, the Word of God does not continue. Revelation in itself is an eternal happening. Barth could even say, it has 'never happened'. 'It is what it is *in* time, but as the *boundary* of all time, it is as far from us as heaven from earth.'[26] It is quite clear that such a statement still stands under the impress of the eschatological perspective which had governed *Romans* II. But Barth continues. If the Word of God is to be known, it must be received by us in the present. It must, in some form, continue. The Word of God in its second form is Holy Scripture. Holy Scripture is the witness of the prophets which was engendered by their encounter with the '*Deus dixit*', by the speaking of God to them. As the testimony of the prophets and apostles, Holy Scripture is a piece of history and as such does not continue. It is a piece of the past and is as far from us as all things are which belong to the past. The third form of the Word of God is Christian preaching, and as preaching the Word of God does continue. It reaches us in the present. It is the present form of the Word. Preaching which is based upon the testimony of the apostles and prophets is God's Word, to the extent that the '*Deus dixit*' makes itself known

[22] Barth, '*Unterricht in der christlichen Religion*', i. *Prolegomena*, 3; ET *The Göttingen Dogmatics*, 3.

[23] Ibid. 16; ET 12.

[24] The phrase '*Deus dixit*' was taken by Barth from the Dutch neo-Calvinist, Hermann Bavinck. See ibid. 18; ET 14.

[25] Ibid. 19, 46; ET 14, 47.   [26] Ibid. 20; ET 15.

through it. Barth thus carefully distinguished between three forms of the Word: the Word in its eternal form, the Word in its historical form, and the Word in its present form.

Although, in this discussion of the distinction of the three forms, Barth placed considerable stress upon the *distance* of the first two forms from those of us who come later in time, the accent shifted to *nearness* when Barth discussed the unity of the three forms. He treated the problem of the unity and differentiation of the three forms in terms of the language developed by the early Church for treating the problem of the Trinity.

'*Verbum domini manet in aeternum.*' It is no other in that it is now the first, now the second, now the third; and always, whenever it is one of the three, it is also, in some sense, the other two. The Word of God upon which dogmatics reflects is . . . one in *three*, three in *one*: revelation, Scripture, preaching . . . not to be confused, not to be separated. *One* Word of God, *one* authority, *one* truth, *one* power—and yet, not one but three addresses. *Three* addresses . . . and yet, not three Words of God, authorities, truths, and powers, but rather, one. The Scripture is not the revelation, but rather *proceeds from* the revelation. Preaching is neither revelation nor Scripture, but rather *proceeds from* both. But Scripture is the Word of God no less than revelation, and preaching no less than Scripture. . . . no "*prius*" or "*posterius*" therefore; no "*maius*" or "*minus*"; the Word of God in the same glory, the first, the second, the third: '*unitas in trinitate*' and '*trinitas in unitate*'.[27]

Barth's reflections up to this point do not represent a serious advance over against *Romans* II. The eschatology of the *hic et nunc* presides over everything that has been said here.

But Barth was not able to be satisfied with an 'eternal revelation'. The contingency of revelation, he quickly realized, is not a second thing, to be laid alongside of revelation in itself; it belongs to revelation. So, on 15 May, he observed:

The '*Deus dixit*' designates a *hic et nunc*. Or much rather, *illic et tunc*; for it is better to say immediately that the annoying '*there* in Palestine' and '*at that time* in the years 1–30' is not in the least to be gotten around, if one really wants to think the Christian thought of revelation. . . . The contingency with which the Church perceived in this and that writing the witness of revelation, and *in the* witness, the revelation itself, is not an accident. This contingency belongs to the *essence* of revelation. '*Deus dixit*' designates a special, once and for all, contingent happening . . .[28]

[27] Ibid. 19; ET 14–15.   [28] Ibid. 70; ET 59.

The accent has clearly shifted. Where, just a few days before, Barth had said that Revelation, in itself, is an eternal event, he now made the contingent side of the event to be essential to it. Now Barth wanted to identify the '*Deus dixit*' with the 'divine nature in Christ'.[29] Not a Subject who stands outside of history is the Subject of the '*Deus dixit*', but a Subject in history. With this subtle but momentous shift of accent, '*Deus dixit*' comes to mean primarily 'God has spoken' in AD 1–30—and on this basis alone 'God continues to speak'.

In conjunction with this stress on the contingency of revelation, a new element emerged. It will be recalled that an *Urgestalt* of the *analogia fidei* was already at work in *Romans* II, namely the 'analogy of the cross'. For some time now, Barth had been moving towards an understanding of positive exemplifications of analogy. With the adoption of the concept of the Word in three forms, this tendency had attained a new level of clarity. Just as the incarnation entails a 'qualified history',[30] so too the problem of Scripture and preaching as the Word of God entailed for Barth the affirmation of *qualified words*[31]—words qualified by their relation to the Word in the event of revelation to be bearers of that revelation. Citing Heinrich Bullinger's statement in the Second Helvetic Confession—'The preaching of the Word of God is the Word of God'[32]—Barth asked:

Should one not at least gather from this confident assertion the *question* whether there might not be words which (although they are human words, mere words like all others) are, at the same time, more than that; namely, for the sake of the knowledge out of which they arise, are communication of truth from one person to another? Becoming human is, therefore, not yet humanisation, and Protestantism meant originally: to believe in the becoming-human of the Logos precisely in spoken human *words* . . .[33]

God's act of taking up a creaturely reality and revealing Himself in and through it was no longer restricted to the event of the cross, and not even to the incarnation. God was now seen by Barth as taking up human language, and bearing witness to

---

[29] Barth, '*Unterricht in der christlichen Religion*', i. *Prolegomena*, 74; ET 62.
[30] Ibid. 72; ET 60.   [31] Ibid. 38–41; 31–3.
[32] *Second Helvetic Confession*, ch. 1, para. 4.
[33] Barth, '*Unterricht in der christlichen Religion*', i. *Prolegomena*, 40; ET *The Göttingen Dogmatics*, 32–3.

Himself in and through it. The result of such a divine action is that human words are qualified to be bearers of revelation. The complete inadequacy of human language for revelation is not set aside in the least. But in that the Word of God conceals Himself in human words, a relation of correspondence is established, an analogy between the Word and the words. What we see emerging here is the first tentative articulation of the *analogia fidei* in the strict sense in which Barth would later employ the term.

A close corollary of this new, positive conception of analogy is the stress which Barth now laid upon the intrinsically verbal character of revelation. Against those who wished to associate revelation with an experience of the holy or the irrational, Barth said,

> The procedure of the Self-revealing God is a *dicere*; its content is *word*. Certainly, Word of *God*, to be taken on the lips of no human being and repeated, standing over against all words which *we* speak in fundamental differentiation; but not thing, matter, nature, but rather, *word*, *Logos*, a communication of *spirit*, revelation of *reason*, and our being addressed by God is, in the most pregnant sense, *knowledge*, appropriation of the *Word*, a thinking after of the *thoughts* of God . . . No modern anti-intellectualism and anti-moralism may cause us here to put life, the irrational, the holy, etc. in place of the Word, and experience, shaking, becoming overwhelmed, and other such things in the place of knowledge. . . . Its content is truth; therefore, it comes to us in the form which corresponds to truth. Not in the form of an ambiguous being but rather in the form of the *Word* which wants to be *known* as bearer of the truth, gives itself to be known . . . It is for this reason that the testimony of the prophets and apostles comes to us in the form of *words*, and it is for this reason that permission and demand come to us—not to babble, not to mime, not to make music, but rather—to *speak* of God.[34]

There can be little question but that Barth's reference to 'the holy' had in view Rudolf Otto's book by that name.[35]

Having looked carefully at Barth's understanding of the object of theology, we may now turn to the second aspect of his brief

---

[34] Ibid. 74–5; ET 62–3.

[35] At the same point in the *Church Dogmatics*, Barth made this explicit. 'Whatever "the holy" of Rudolf Otto may be, it certainly cannot be understood as the Word of God, for it is the numinous, and the numinous is the irrational, and the irrational can no longer be distinguished from an absolutized natural force. But everything depends upon this differentiation if we are to understand the concept of the Word of God." See Barth, *KD* I/1, 140; ET *CD* I/1, 135.

definition, the reflection itself. According to Barth, dogmatics exists for the sake of preaching. That preaching, a fully human act, becomes the Word of God is not at all self-evident, and it does not lie within the power of the dogmatician to make it so. Nevertheless, it is the task of the dogmatician to criticize and correct preaching in the light of the Word of God; to call attention to the Word of God *in* preaching; to bring it to expression and then to apply it in criticism of preaching.[36] Preaching is, therefore, both the starting-point and the goal of dogmatics.[37] As starting-point, it is the raw material of dogmatic reflection.[38] The initial question of the dogmatician is, to what extent is the address occurring in Christian preaching one with the address occurring through the prophets and apostles, and one with the revelation which brought forth the prophetic-apostolic *kerygma*?[39] To what extent is it the Word of God? Dogmatics thus takes its rise at the point where the reality which is (ostensibly) hidden in Christian speech is sought for. Dogmatics addresses itself to the question of '*right* preaching'; i.e. of '*pure* doctrine'.[40]

Preaching as the Word of God proceeds from a double origin in revelation and Scripture. This means that the reflection in which dogmatics is engaged entails a return to revelation and Scripture, by which preaching is then criticized and corrected.[41] The double origin is very important. It means that it will not be sufficient merely to appeal to Scripture. Not even the repetition of the words of Scripture would be the Word of God. Nor is it possible to appeal directly to revelation, apart from Scripture. The first would be a mere historical report, the second, a product of the human imagination.[42] The Word of God is present where there is a correlation of Spirit and Scripture; where revelation attests itself in and through Scripture. In the light of a fresh hearing of the Word of God given in this way, the dogmatician seeks to articulate the viewpoints which necessarily arise from it in the form of dogmas. The dogmas are then offered to the Church as modest guides for a preaching which sees the necessity of stepping forth with the claim of being the Word of God. Again, it

[36] Barth, '*Unterricht in der christlichen Religion*', i. *Prolegomena*, 23; ET *The Göttingen Dogmatics*, 17–18.
[37] Ibid. 28; ET 23.   [38] Ibid. 29; ET 24.   [39] Ibid. 30; ET 24.
[40] Ibid. 37; ET 30.   [41] Ibid. 47; ET 37.   [42] Ibid. 46; ET 37.

does not lie in the power of the dogmatician to make preaching to be the Word of God. Only God can make preaching to be the Word by testifying to Himself through it. But this recognition ought not to lead to the conclusion that it does not matter what is said from the pulpit. It does matter. Dogmatics assists preaching by offering guidance as to what ought to be said and what ought to be left unsaid if no obstacle is to be placed in the way of the Self-speaking of God.[43] Dogmatics helps preaching to create a free space for the Word to unveil itself in the words.

In broad strokes, this is the dogmatic method which Barth would continue to advocate in his 1931 book on Anselm and in *Church Dogmatics* I/1 and I/2. The only modification which would occur in the meantime is that the preaching which is here made to be the starting-point and goal of dogmatics would be further concretized. In *Church Dogmatics* I/1 the proclamation which dogmatics is to test critically is 'that form of yesterday's proclamation in which the latter has already been tested, criticized and corrected, i.e. the results of the history of dogmatics itself'.[44] It is the dogmas of the Church which ultimately require critical testing. In putting it this way, Barth will suggest that the critical testing which takes place today is part of a history of such critical testing whose fruit has found expression in the dogmas of the Church. Thus it is dogmas which will become the starting-point (or raw material) and goal of dogmatics. Such modifications, however, do not fundamentally alter the basic understanding which is already set forth here in the Göttingen Prolegomena; they merely provide further concretization.

The final aspect of Barth's definition of dogmatics still to be considered is set forth in the adjective "scientific". Here, in continuity with his long-standing view, Barth defined "scientific" as '*Sachlichkeit*, the most exact adaptation of knowing and of knowledge to the peculiarity of its object'.[45] Barth elaborated the significance of this definition against the background of the method just described. The return from preaching to Scripture and revelation must be *planmäßig* ('orderly' or 'methodical'). There is a more free dogmatics, a dogmatics which is carried out under the immediate inspiration of one or two particular viewpoints. Barth

---

[43] Ibid. 36; ET 29.   [44] *KD* I/1, 80; ET *CD* I/1, 78.
[45] Barth, '*Unterricht in der christlichen Religion*', i. *Prolegomena*, 10; ET *The Göttingen Dogmatics*, 8.

calls this more free, often more chaotic style 'irregular dogmatics'. Irregular dogmatics are not to be despised. Such efforts have
often produced rewarding results, and historically 'regular dogmatics' has grown out of irregular attempts. In the long run,
however, regular, scientific dogmatics must be undertaken to
give backbone to the irregular: 'the will to complete work will
be better here than resting content with work only half done;
however true it may be that much half-way done or one-quarter
done work is actually more fruitful in terms of its inner value
than much that is fully done.'[46] In these words, a new tendency
announces itself which we have not seen before: the urge to
completeness, to comprehensiveness.

It may be recalled that Barth had already employed the distinction between the "regular" and the "irregular" in *Romans* II,
with what appeared to be drastically different results. In *Romans*
Barth had referred to the sciences as 'ordinary, regular, bourgeois
possibilities of consideration' in comparison with which theology
is the 'extraordinary, irregular . . . revolutionary' act of daring
which places all human possibilities, including theology itself,
under the attack of God.[47] In speaking now of theology as a science, had Barth gone the comfortable way of bourgeois consideration? There are many who have thought so, but the answer is
no. What Barth had learned in the meantime—and since the
Elgersburg lecture—was to see the dogmatic way in the light of
the presuppositions of the dialectical way. That is to say, the act
of daring on the part of the theologian to speak of God—an act
to which dialectical thinking gives such vivid testimony—was
now seen by Barth as providing the indispensable presupposition
and context for dogmatic thinking as well.

It was now dogmatics, and not just theology generally, which
Barth called an act of daring. Dogmatics entails risk; it is life-
threatening. Consider the situation! The Word of God comes to
those who are entirely inadequate for it, and it comes with the
command that it be taken up and spoken in human words. We
have been commanded to do a task and have been condemned
thereby, for none of us is able (in and of ourselves) to fulfil it.
The sword of Damocles hangs over the head of every dogmati-

---

[46] Barth, '*Unterricht in der christlichen Religion*', i. *Prolegomena*, 48; ET 39.
[47] Barth, *Der Römerbrief, 1922*, 514.

cian in every moment.[48] In comparison with the fear engendered by this demand, the threat posed to the Church by modern unbelief is trivial. 'Do not fear those who kill the body but are unable to kill the soul; fear the One who can cast body and soul into hell (Matt. 10: 28).'[49] The world, Barth observed, knows nothing of real doubt, of truly destructive criticism.[50] The dogmatician, in obedience to the command, seeks *the* dogma, but all she finds are dogma*s*—at best approximations of *the* dogma.[51] Hence every attempt falls under judgement, the attack of God. Every attempt requires critical correction. Why is this so? Because the object of dogmatics is God Himself; *Deus dixit*— God speaking in person. And that means that the object of *this* science is not given over into human hands. Human beings have no power of disposal over it. It is this which makes dogmatics an impossible task (humanly speaking!). In Barth's view, any definition of dogmatics which failed to grasp this—which substituted for the true object of dogmatics one which lies within the grasp of humans (say, historical magnitudes or the content of psychological experience)—would indeed be a bourgeois, self-satisfied, and self-satisfying science. For such a view, dogmatics is the easiest thing in the world. The last thing it is is life-threatening. What Barth has done is to remove dogmatic thinking from the compartment to which he had assigned it in *Romans* II—the compartment of 'bourgeois science'—and to transfer it to the place previously occupied by dialectical thinking alone. The definition of dogmatic method which he now advocated is no longer the one he had once set aside at Elgersburg. He has redefined it. Dialectical method and dogmatic method are both alike in this: both stand under the sign of failure. To put it another way, Barth's dogmatic method presupposes *an initial dialectical moment of negation* in which God's judgement is invited to fall on all previous efforts (including our own). Dogmatic method, so understood, preserves the concern resident in dialectical method—namely to strip human beings of every last vestige of self-confidence. In this way Barth's radicalism was not dampened in the least by his 'turn to dogmatics'.

One further point with enormous relevance for a sound

understanding of Barth's development: it is because dogmatic method and dialectical method operate under the same presupposition (i.e. the judgement of God) that they could coexist throughout the remainder of the twenties and on into the *Church Dogmatics*. Whatever Barth might say in his *formal* considerations of method, *in practice* he would always use both methods. Moreover, dialectical method would never simply disappear. It would appear in the *Church Dogmatics*, as a rule, at precisely those points at which it had already been employed in the Göttingen Dogmatics—above all, in the doctrine of God.[52] With the redefinition of dogmatic thinking, the decision as to which method to employ could be made solely on the basis of the intrinsic demands of the subject-matter in question. Seen in this light, it should be clear that we will never arrive at a sound understanding of Barth's development by focusing merely on the presence or absence of dialectical thinking. The presence or absence of dialectical thinking, in itself, establishes little or nothing with regard to the nature of that development.

4. AUTHORITY IN THE CHURCH

Barth returned to a treatment of methodological issues in the closing paragraphs of his prolegomena lectures, and it would aid clarity if we were to jump ahead for a moment to consider those points which amplify the understanding already provided. We will return to a more chronological procedure in the next section.

Up to this point, we have seen that dogmatics consisted for Barth in critically testing the content of preaching in the light of its double origin in Revelation and Scripture. Preaching was thus seen to be the starting-point and raw material of dogmatics. In para. 9, 'Authority', we learn of the hermeneutical difficulties which surround the attempt to return to revelation and Scripture. 'No one reads the Bible directly. We all read it through a set of glasses, whether we want to or not . . .'.[53] In

---

[52] For a thorough demonstration of this claim, see Terry L. Cross, 'The Use of Dialectic in Karl Barth's Doctrine of God as Found in the *Church Dogmatics*, II/1', Ph.D. dissertation (Princeton Theological Seminary, 1991).

[53] Barth, '*Unterricht in der christlichen Religion*', i. *Prolegomena*, 279; ET *The Göttingen Dogmatics*, 229.

view of the welter of conflicting voices which compete for our attention in our attempts to hear the Word of God in Scripture, Barth advocated for the first time an ecclesial hermeneutic. The return to Scripture, he said, should be carried out within the Church and under the guidance of the Church. To be sure, the authority of the Church is not equal to that of Scripture. It is a historical, relative, and formal authority.[54] But it is authority none the less. The Church's authority forms what Barth called the 'condition of the objective possibility of the mediation of revelation'.[55] The Church should and does condition our hearing of the Word of God.

Barth named three classes of 'authoritative factors' by means of which the Church exercises its relative authority. The Church exercises its authority first by determining the circumference and form in which the witness of the prophets and apostles comes to us.[56] Both the extent of the canon (which writings are to be included) and the determination of an authoritative text (a *textus receptus*![57]) of the Bible are questions which the Church is responsible to decide. The second authoritative factor is 'the interpretation which has been given to the witness of revelation by particular teachers of the Church and by general ecclesiastical doctrinal decisions'.[58] The Church has the obligation to tell its theologians and preachers precisely which Church Fathers and which confessions are to be heard in the attempt to interpret Scripture. The third authoritative factor is 'the external and internal situation of the historical moment'.[59] The Church must have an authoritative word to speak to the present situation in all of its concreteness, a command of the hour, a word which comprehends the meaning of every individual historical moment. The meaning of the situation is not to be found on the surface of events, however. It is hidden beneath the surface but is revealed to those who really perceive the Word in Scripture.[60] It is, therefore, not the historical moment *qua* history which is authoritative. The Word of God alone remains authoritative. But if the Word of God is to come to us, it must speak to us in our

---

[54] Ibid. 299; ET 245.   [55] Ibid. 278; ET 228.   [56] Ibid. 283; ET 232.
[57] It should be noted that Barth backed off from advocating a *textus receptus* in the *Church Dogmatics*. See *KD* 672–3; ET *CD* I/2, 602–3.
[58] Barth, '*Unterricht in der christlichen Religion*', i. *Prolegomena*, 288; ET *The Göttingen Dogmatics*, 237.
[59] Ibid. 296; ET 242–3.   [60] Ibid. 297–8; ET 244.

situation. The Church has an obligation to give a relatively authoritative interpretation of the significance of the Word for the present hour. Barth subsumed this third factor under the heading of the 'teaching office' of the Church.

It is impossible, Barth noted in conclusion, for the Scriptures to come to us as the Word of God unless there be an authoritative canon and text, Fathers and dogmas, and teaching office.[61] These factors form the 'empty canals'[62] through which the Word comes to us. When it is recalled that in *Romans* II, it was precisely the 'empty canals' of revelation past which the Church was supposed *not* to abide in, the distance which separates *Romans* II from the Göttingen Dogmatics is clearly seen. But we would not be justified in seeing in this shift the emergence of a spirit of repristination.

Barth was quite careful to subordinate the authority of the Church to the authority of Scripture. To do so is to place a limitation on the limit which the Church constitutes for its people. It is to acknowledge a Norm by which all relative norms are themselves measured and therefore, it means a 'crisis of the crisis'[63] which the Church places us in. This phrase—'a crisis of the crisis'—is indeed remarkable. 'Crisis' in *Romans* II had referred to the divine judgement to which all things are subjected by revelation. Here, there is no retreat from that position. But it also remains true that human beings can do nothing, in and of themselves, to bring about *the* crisis of revelation. What human beings can do, as they await the crisis brought by revelation, is to bear witness to their need by submitting themselves to the provisional and relative crisis of judgement by the Church. They do this in that they allow themselves to be guided by the Church's confessions, etc., in their attempts to hear the Word of God in Scripture. But if they know what they are doing, they will do all of this under constant recognition of the need for the divine crisis to fall upon the relative crisis. The need to test critically the Church's message is not to be lost to sight.

Thus, dogmatic thinking, as Barth was now defining it, begins with a moment of relative crisis (which is the only kind human beings have at their disposal); a moment in which the dogmatician submits his/her opinions to the searching criticism of the

---

[61] Barth, '*Unterricht in der christlichen Religion*', i. *Prolegomena*, 299; ET 245.
[62] Ibid. 300; ET 245.   [63] Ibid.; ET 246.

authority of the Church. If the matter rested there, the result could only be repristination. But it does not rest there. It only begins there.

When Barth turned finally to a formal consideration of method in para. 13, he defined dogmatic method in terms of dialectical method. Why did he do that? In a very real sense, dialectical method had become superfluous. He had already (in the preceding paragraphs) fully elaborated a dogmatic method before he ever turned to a formal consideration of "method". And he had done so without reference to the much-discussed dialectical method. If now, in para. 13, he once again advocated dialectical method, it was because he could still see valid uses for that method. And he could see no difficulty in defining dogmatic method as dialectical because the presuppositions of his dogmatic method were precisely the same as those governing his previous advocacy of dialectical method. The crucial point to observe here, however, is that Barth had set forth two distinct methods in the prolegomena lectures, not one. And in the actual execution of his dogmatics, it is the dogmatic method which predominated, not the dialectical method.

In concluding this treatment of method in the Göttingen Dogmatics, it would be most illuminating to cast a glance back at the 'table of possibilities' which Barth had outlined in his letter to Brunner in January 1924 and to ask: which of these possibilities did Barth finally employ? Which predominated? A complete justification of the answer which will be put forward here can only be given in the sequel to the present work. But we may at least adumbrate here the answer which will be fully demonstrated there. It will be recalled that, in January, Barth had said that he inclined towards a combination of the "prophetic" and the "confessional"—which would have made the Apostles' Creed the foundational text of his lectures. What Barth finally accomplished in the Göttingen Dogmatics, however, is best understood as a combination of the "scholastic" and the "*loci*" approaches. The Göttingen Dogmatics is above all a "Sentence Commentary"; a "Sentence Commentary" not on Lombard's *Sentences*, however, nor even on Calvin's *Institutes* or the Genevan Catechism of 1545, but rather on Heinrich Heppe's textbook on Reformed dogmatics.

There is a telling statement in Barth's treatment of angelology in para. 21 which makes quite clear how he himself conceived his procedure by that point. Barth is explaining to his students the direction which his course of lectures would now take as he turns his attention to the doctrine of humanity.

But before we can approach our . . . next task, a heavy beam is placed in our way in the form of the doctrine of *angels* and *demons*—at least if we wish to follow the primer of the old dogmatics as we have done until now—and we will not be able to avoid taking some kind of position on the subject, though the old Adam would certainly like to induce us all to do so.[64]

By his own testimony, Barth has been faithfully following a 'primer of the old dogmatics'. Now it must be said that to comment on a basic text is not slavishly to adopt the positions taken there. Barth demonstrated throughout his dogmatics lectures a willingness to correct the tradition. On the other hand, a "Sentence Commentary" is not a *summa*. It is not simply a spinning-out of one's own thread. It is rather a school exercise, a first product demonstrating the coming of age of a theologian. It is a theology written as a commentary on a wealth of problems and questions bequeathed to it by theologians of the past. It is thus bound to a particular text. Barth's Göttingen Dogmatics amply display this trait, which is characteristic of the medieval tradition of commentaries on the *Sentences*. In each *locus*, Barth offered his own position in connection with an exposition of relevant material found in the textbooks by Heppe and Schmid. Defined carefully in this way, it is a "scholastic" dogmatics which Barth taught in Göttingen.

5. THE DOCTRINE OF THE TRINITY

In para. 5 of the prolegomena, Barth took up the doctrine of the Trinity for the first time. The reason he took it up here, in the prolegomena, was to provide an answer to the question: 'Who is the Subject of revelation?' In raising this question he was also, at the same time, seeking to set forth a well-ordered reflection on the *ground* of the possibility of revelation. That is to say, given his particular conception of revelation as *Self*-revelation, he was now

---

[64] Barth, '*Unterricht in der christlichen Religion*', ii. 310.

confronted with the necessity of developing an understanding of the immanent Trinity which would *ontically* ground the possibility of a revelation so understood.

The first notice that Barth gave that he was preoccupied with the problem of the immanent Trinity was in a letter to Thurneysen on 20 April. 'With the incarnation, it is best to proceed cautiously, so that one may not run headlong into the exclusive "Jesus Christ"-pit of the Lutherans. . . . A Trinity of *being*, not just an economic Trinity! At all costs, the doctrine of the Trinity! If I could just get the right key in my hand there, then everything would come out right . . .'[65] The concern which surfaced here in the reference to the 'exclusive "Jesus Christ"-pit of the Lutherans' is clear. Barth was concerned to oppose a concept of revelation which was guilty of a deification of the creature—even if the creature in question was named Jesus of Nazareth. God alone is the content of revelation. It is in this light that the significance of the following striking statement is to be understood: 'Dogmatics and the preaching which follows it will, in my opinion, again have to dare to be less christocentric and, in return, somewhat more faithful to the subject-matter . . .'[66] Less christocentricity here means the resolute refusal to historicize revelation. Revelation is *Self*-revelation; it is God alone and God in His entirety or it is no revelation. This is the same basic concern which had also animated Barth in *Romans* II. But now he saw clearly that only a doctrine of the Trinity could ground this view of revelation.

Barth began his lectures on the Trinity by once again rehearsing his conception of revelation. 'The content of revelation is God alone, wholly God, God Himself.'[67] Barth noted that such a definition entailed a delimitation on four sides. First, in saying that the content of revelation is *God*, Barth was rejecting any view which would make a distinction between a 'formal and a material principle in the concept of revelation'; i.e. between 'a content-less *speaking* or Self-revealing of God *in and for itself*' and a 'particular, concrete *content* of this speaking of God which would then somehow consist in the communication of His love,

[65] Karl Barth to Eduard Thurneysen, 20 Apr. 1924, *B–Th. Br.* II. 245.
[66] Barth, '*Unterricht in der christlichen Religion*', i. *Prolegomena*, 110; ET *The Göttingen Dogmatics*, 91.
[67] Ibid. 105; ET 87.

His will to fellowship, the forgiveness of sins, and the like . . .
Whoever thinks of the *"Deus dixit"* as *empty* does not know it at
all . . .'[68] With these words, Barth was announcing his rejection
of every idealistic derivation of the doctrine of the Trinity on the
basis of an a priori analysis of 'pure subjectivity' (as occurred, for
example, in Hegel). The concept of the Word of God must
never be treated, in idealistic fashion, as purely formal (i.e. empty
of content). In and for itself, the Word of God is already the fullness of content. Therefore, the content of the Word of God in
and for itself is identical with the content of the Word of God
addressed to human beings. The revealing Subject may not be
distinguished from the revealed object.[69] And this, as we shall
see, meant that there can be no distinction in content between
the immanent Trinity and the economic Trinity. Second, in saying that the content of revelation is God alone, Barth was rejecting any confusion of revelation with the medium in which it
veils itself.

Just as no thing, no contingent magnitude, no historical fact as such is
the *dicens*, so also none of these things is the *dictum*, the content of revelation. . . . God alone is the Subject but also the *content* of revelation—
even in the humanity of Christ. The historical Jesus as such is . . . the
creature of the triune God; a creature, so that the Reformed could
emphasize and expressly state that the rule *'finitum non est capax infiniti'*
also applied to this creature.[70]

For Barth, to say that both the Subject and the content of the
revelation in Jesus of Nazareth was God entails the affirmation
that 'the *Person* of the God-man was exclusively the Word, the
Logos of God'.[71] Third, in saying that the content of revelation
is *wholly* God, Barth was rejecting any view which would seek to
quantify revelation, making God partly hidden and partly
revealed (as occurs in all traditional natural theologies). 'Either
God speaks, or He does not speak. But He does not speak more
or less, partially, in quantities, here a little and there a little. That
is a contradiction in terms, an anthropomorphism, a fundamental
naturalization of revelation . . .'[72] If God is present in revelation,
then He is present with the totality of His being; otherwise, we

---

[68] Barth, *'Unterricht in der christlichen Religion'*, i. *Prolegomena*, 107; ET 88–9.
[69] Ibid. 116; ET 95.   [70] Ibid. 108; ET 89–90.   [71] Ibid. 109; ET 90.
[72] Ibid. 111; ET 92.

do not have to do with the revelation of *God*. The hiddenness of
God may not be made to refer to what God is 'in Himself', in
distinction from what He is revealed to be 'for us'. If God is
revealed, then it is God in the entirety of His being which is
revealed. The hiddenness of God may rightly refer only to the
concealment of the whole being of God in a creaturely veil.
Fourth, in saying that the content of revelation is God *Himself*,
Barth was rejecting any view which would seek to establish a
continuity between revelation and human thinking and feeling.
What a human being does in response to God's Self-speaking can
stand in a relation of analogy to what God is doing, but the
actions must be held apart dialectically. 'The human does something corresponding, parallel, analogical, in his sphere of existence to that which God does in His. His reasoning activity
receives, more strongly or weakly, a certain theoretical and practical orientation . . . But all of this can only be the shadow of
revelation . . .'[73] Here again, the basic structure of the *analogia
fidei* emerges with clarity.

With these four delimitations in place, Barth turned on 26
May to the task of showing how the doctrine of the Trinity provides the necessary presupposition and ground of his doctrine of
revelation. It is of the utmost importance to observe that Barth
took as his starting-point—at least, as regards to what we might
call 'the order of discovery'—the primitive Christian confession
'Jesus is Lord' (i.e. a historical starting-point). His starting-point
was not speculative; nor was his derivation of the doctrine of the
Trinity the fruit of a merely logical or grammatical analysis of the
relation of subject, predicate, and object. Against Hegel's speculative understanding of the Trinity, Barth noted that he understood the doctrine of the Trinity as the problem of the
'unsublate-able [*unaufhebbaren*] subjectivity of God'.[74] *Un*sublate-
able: if revelation has as its content God Himself, God alone and
God in His entirety, then the event of revelation cannot entail a
change in the being of God, whether by addition or
diminution.[75] There is no evolution in God from a lower to a
higher state of consciousness; no synthesis in which God could
conceivably attain a higher level of existence.

But how can this be? How can God become a Subject in time

---

[73] Ibid. 114; ET 94.   [74] Ibid. 120; ET 98.   [75] Ibid. 146, 150; ET 119, 122.

without involving Himself in a change? Barth's answer was twofold. First, God remains the Subject even *in* the earthly form of a revealed object. Where Hegel identified the divine subjectivity with the human subjectivity in and through which it unfolds, Barth maintained the dialectical opposition between them. God is Subject *in* the earthly form; God does not become the earthly form. But second, and more importantly, Barth held that God as a Subject in time corresponds completely to God as a Subject in eternity. In revelation, God corresponds to Himself.[76] The immanent Trinity is thus identical in content with the economic Trinity.[77] Barth insisted on a doctrine of the immanent Trinity, a Trinity of *being*, because only in this way was it possible for him to show that the Subject of revelation in Jesus Christ was truly God. The Subject of revelation is not a second *next to* God, but a second *in* God, and, therefore, fully God.[78]

The difference between Barth's doctrine and Hegel's should be clear. This is not an idealistic doctrine of the Trinity, for it does not understand the subjectivity of God as the ideal projection of human subjectivity. It is a critically realistic doctrine of the Trinity which begins, in a posteriori fashion, with the fact of the divine Self-revelation (and the witness to it of the primitive Church) and asks, what must be true of God if God has done this? What must God be in eternity if He can reveal Himself in time without ceasing to be God? Barth's derivation of the Trinity is thus the fruit of an analysis of a *concrete* act of a *concretely existing* Subject.[79]

Barth began his derivation of the doctrine of the Trinity by asking, what did it mean for primitive Christians to affirm that 'Jesus is *Lord*'. The term "Lord", he noted, is a translation of the Old Testament name for God. How could it come about that Jesus could be called God? Initially, Barth thought, this must have been because the earliest Christians heard in the voice of Jesus the voice of an Other. Who is this Other to whom Jesus

---

[76] Barth, '*Unterricht in der christlichen Religion*', i. *Prolegomena*, 117; ET 96.
[77] Ibid. 123; ET 101.   [78] Ibid. 150; ET 122.
[79] I mention all of this because of Wolfhart Pannenberg's fascinating, but misguided, thesis that 'Barth took over Hegel's derivation of the doctrine of the Trinity from the concept of the subjectivity of God.' See Pannenberg, 'Die Subjektivität Gottes und die Trinitätslehre: Ein Beitrag zur Beziehung zwischen Karl Barth und der Philosophie Hegels', in idem, *Grundfragen systematischer Theologie* (Göttingen: Vandenhoeck & Ruprecht, 1980), ii. 104.

rendered obedience, even unto death; and who then raised Him from the dead, exalted Him, and gave Him the name which is above every name? Who is the One who has such power over Jesus and gives to Him such power? The answer of the early Christians was that He is "the Father", the One who exists on a plane wholly transcending the contradiction in which Jesus finds Himself in dying on the cross. The One whom Jesus proclaimed is *'free*, where we are imprisoned'.[80] He lives and moves and has His being *above* the contradiction in which we find ourselves. To describe the God who was proclaimed by Jesus, the early Church came perforce to employ expressions like 'maker of heaven and earth', for He is the Origin of all things finite. But He was all of these things as the Father of Jesus Christ.

It is not as though Jesus only subsequently gave and attached the name "Father" to the Creator of all things, the Unconditioned, the Limit, the critical negation of the given, the Origin, the *"a se ipso existenti"*, who was already known. No, Jesus *reveals*, He first *shows* the Father and, with Him, everything the Father is and does. *No one* comes to the Father except through *Him* [John 14: 6]. Therefore, first (and I mean fundamentally: first!), the knowledge of the eternal Father *in the Son*; *then* and *therein* the knowledge of what that means: the Lord at the beginning and end of our contradiction, the Creator of heaven and earth . . .[81]

That God is the Father means, therefore, first and foremost, that He is the Father of the Son and only on that basis, the Father of all of created reality.[82] On this basis, it will be right to see in the Father the '*"principium"* (which is not to be confused with *"causa"*) *"in deitate"*', the '*"fons deitatis"*'.[83]

The use of language like *'principium'* and *'fons deitatis'*, it should be pointed out, does not bring Barth's doctrine into close proximity to Hegel's; it is not the result of a projection of the autonomous human subject on to an equally autonomous First Person of the Trinity.[84] For, at this point in time at least, when the foundations of Barth's doctrine of the Trinity were being laid, he had no difficulties in affirming the existence of *three*

---

[80] Ibid. 136; ET 112.
[81] Ibid. 137–8; ET 112–13.
[82] Ibid. 138; ET 113.
[83] Ibid. 139; ET 114.
[84] See Pannenberg, 'Die Subjektivität Gottes und die Trinitätslehre', in idem, *Grundfragen systematischer Theologie*, ii. 100.

divine Subjects.[85] The subjectivity of the Father is thus misunderstood if it is interpreted in terms of the modern concept of the autonomous subject. If there is a historical antecedent to Barth's view, as it is expressed here, it is to be found in the Council of Toledo of 675 and Augustine.[86]

Barth then returned a second time to the situation of primitive Christianity. What did it mean to say that *'Jesus* is Lord'? It meant, first of all, that He reveals the Father. But the Father is God. No one can reveal God but God Himself. Therefore, if Jesus Christ reveals the Father, He Himself must be God and, in accordance with Barth's formula, 'wholly God'.[87] The explanation of this must not set aside the rule *'Finitum non capax infiniti'*.[88] It remains as true as ever that the humanity of Jesus is not to be directly identified with the revelation. That Jesus Christ is God means that God is the revealing Subject in the human Jesus.

To know the Lord, not only as the *Whence* of revelation, but also seeing Him, hearing Him, touching Him *in* the revelation, clearly means: knowing Him not only above, but rather, *in* the contradiction of our existence; there, where *we* are. Miracle of miracles, God is *there* too. He is *so* much the eternal Lord that the limits stretched out before *us* do *not* exist for Him; that He, the *Victor* over the contradiction is *with us!*[89]

'His eternity *above* time becomes an eternity *in* time . . .'[90] So God is not just the first and the last, the wholly transcendent Maker of heaven and earth who lives and moves and has His being above the contradiction of our existence. He also has His being in the contradiction of our existence. With this affirmation Barth had, in principle, broken through the time–eternity dialectic of *Romans* II.

The word "Son" means, for Barth, that God is not only the Father who exists above the contradiction. God is also the Son who exists in the contradiction and overcomes it from within. And given Barth's stipulation that the One who does all of this can only be God if He is not changed in the process, it follows that the Son is not the Son merely because He does this work.

---

[85] Barth, *'Unterricht in der christlichen Religion'*, i. *Prolegomena*, 121–2; ET *The Göttingen Dogmatics*, 100.

[86] For the sources referred to here, see ibid. 139 n. 42; ET 114 n. 46.

[87] Ibid. 143; ET 117.   [88] Ibid. 144; ET 117.   [89] Ibid.; ET 118.

[90] Ibid. 138; ET 113.

'He is not what He is, the Son, because and in that He does this
"*opus ad extra*". . . . He is what He is as the Son of the Father
who sends Him into the world. But the sending of the Son by
the Father into time is to be distinguished from the *eternal* relationship between them which grounds it.'[91] However true it
may be that the immanent Trinity and the economic Trinity are
identical in content, the distinction between them is nevertheless
valid and necessary. It is the eternal relation of Father and Son—a
relation which the ancient Church described in terms of its doctrine of the '*generatio*' or '*filiatio*'[92]—which is the ground or condition of the possibility of the incarnation, the sending of the Son
into time. Thus, what the Son is in time corresponds perfectly to
what He is in eternity. The Son too is wholly God; God a second time, God in a second Person or Subject.

Finally, Barth returned a third time to the situation of primitive Christianity. What did it mean that men and women were
able to make the confession 'Jesus is Lord'? How was such a faith
possible? Barth's answer was to point to the witness of Paul: 'No
one can say "Jesus is Lord" except by the Holy Spirit' (1 Cor. 12:
3).[93] To the person who is lost in sin, who is incapable in and of
herself to know God, God's revelation comes: 'to me, to the person I am, the Lord who is *above* and *in* the world gives Himself
to be known as *my* Lord . . .'.[94] We know God because God
bestows upon us the gift of faith. 'God *Himself* is the content of
revelation, even in our *perception* of His Word, even in our *being*
addressed, even in the *reception* of His gift.'[95] That God is present
to us, in our time, that He represents Himself to us and us to
Himself, means that God exists in a third *hypostasis*, as a third
"Person". As was the case with the Son, Barth seemed to want to
ground the outward work of the Holy Spirit in time in His eternal relations with Father and Son, though here his efforts were a
bit more tentative—perhaps as a result of the press of time. The
'outpouring of the Spirit, the mission of the Spirit in *time* must
be distinguished from the eternal relationship in God Himself . . .
As God is Father and Son from eternity and in eternity, as the
Father generates the Son, as the Son is generated by the Father,
so too is He from eternity and in eternity Spirit . . .'.[96] Following
the Western Church, Barth saw the mode of origination of the

[91] Ibid. 146–7; ET 120.   [92] Ibid. 147; ET 120.   [93] Ibid. 153; ET 125.
[94] Ibid.   [95] Ibid. 155; ET 126.   [96] Ibid. 156; ET 128.

Holy Spirit in terms of the *filioque*: the Spirit "proceeds" from both the Father and the Son.[97] Though Barth did not explicitly use the language of "grounding" in this context, the drift of the argument suggests that that is what he had in view.

Given the fact that Barth was having to learn this subject-matter on his feet, it is astonishing how far he has come. Certainly, the treatment of the doctrine of the Trinity in the *Church Dogmatics* was much more rigorous and elaborate. And he would abandon the talk of three Subjects or Persons. But what was said here quite clearly laid the foundation for what was to come.

One final comment on the significance of what Barth has achieved in these lectures on the Trinity. For late-nineteenth-century theologians of the Ritschlian school, a speaking of God's being *in se* was evidence of an illegitimate, metaphysical speculation. We have seen how Barth's anti-metaphysical attitude was basic to his achievement in *Romans* II. Had he now suffered a regression into metaphysical speculation? No; just the opposite is the case. Barth's concern was to stress that God *in se* is not to be conceived as a second, higher being of God behind the being of God in revelation. Against all forms of Sabellianism, ancient and modern, Barth held that the Trinity is not 'only an arrangement, a condescendence, an economy, a mode of revelation for the sake of humankind alone. And therefore, the three divine Persons, *hypostases*, *prosopa*, are not only masks, ways of appearing, modes of subsistence, behind which God's essence is hidden as something other, higher, as the real and one being of God.'[98] Since God's being *in se* is not a second, hidden being behind God's being in revelation, no metaphysical speculation is required to penetrate it. Thus, far from involving Himself in metaphysical speculation, Barth's identification of the economic and immanent Trinities has strictly anti-metaphysical significance. He was seeking to show that it is possible to speak of the being of God *in se* on the basis of revelation alone.

6. THE INCARNATION OF GOD

After treating the doctrine of the Trinity, Barth moved on in para. 6 of the prolegomena to a consideration of Christology—

---

[97] Barth, '*Unterricht in der christlichen Religion*', i. *Prolegomena*, 157–60; ET 128–30.
[98] Ibid. 123; ET 101.

again, from the standpoint of its relevance for a proper concept of revelation. Where the doctrine of the Trinity dealt with the content of revelation, the doctrine of the incarnation was addressed to the problem of the 'objective possibility of revelation'.[99] In other words, how is it possible that God's revelation encounters human beings living in history? Does it indeed come all the way to where we are? If so, how? That was the problem Barth now wished to address. It should be noted that Barth turned to the problem of the possibility of revelation only after he had already treated its reality—its 'essence' in para. 3 (*'Deus dixit'*) and its content or Subject in para. 5 (the doctrine of the Trinity).[100] 'The problem of the possibility of revelation can only be seriously raised and treated where its *reality* is known. The possibility of revelation can, as a matter of principle, only be constructed a posteriori. All reflection on how God *can* reveal Himself, is really only a thinking-after of the fact that God *has* revealed Himself.'[101]

Before turning to Barth's interpretation of the incarnation, it should be noted that in presupposing the Self-revelation of God in Jesus Christ, Barth was placing the orthodox Christology of the fifth century on an entirely new foundation. The strict delimitation of revelation to 'Self-revelation' is, as Wolfhart Pannenberg has rightly observed, a modern innovation. Here a point of contact with Hegel is not to be denied.[102] Of course, to say that the conception is modern is not to disqualify it from consideration as the best-possible analysis of the conception implied in and presupposed by the primitive Christian confession. Still, Self-revelation is a modern conception. Therefore, however orthodox his formulations turn out to be—and here they are most certainly orthodox, not neo-orthodox (whatever

[99] Ibid. 172; ET 140. [100] Ibid. 163; ET 133.
[101] Ibid. 173, 185; ET 141, 151.
[102] See W. Pannenberg (ed.), *Revelation as History* (New York: The Macmillan Company, 1968), 4: 'The new stress is the exclusive use of the concept "revelation" to mean the self-disclosure of God, without any imparting of supernatural truths. This innovation can be classed as a legacy of German idealism.' Pannenberg is right to note Barth's indebtedness to Hegel and his right-wing followers like Philipp Marheineke. The only correction I would offer is that, at the point where Barth seeks to give content to the notion of 'Self-revelation', he does not begin speculatively, with an a priori construction, but rather, with an a posteriori reflection on what God has shown Himself to be in Jesus Christ. That is the crucial difference between an idealistic conception of 'Self-revelation' and a critically realistic one.

that might mean)—they are not the fruit of a repristination of the
ancient modes of consideration. These formulations are to be
understood as the consequence of the requirements resident in
Barth's conception of revelation. This is true even where Barth
affirms the dogma of the Virgin Birth. The Virgin Birth is a conclusion, not a starting-point; and it is affirmed not on the
grounds of the biblicist's commitment to the infallibility of
the infancy narratives found in Matthew and Luke, but rather on
the grounds of the logic of an anhypostatic-enhypostatic conception which was itself necessitated by Barth's wholly modern conception of Self-revelation. With this qualification in place, we
may turn to Barth's treatment of the incarnation.

The Subject of the incarnation has already been established in
the doctrine of the Trinity. It is the eternal Son, the second
Person of the Trinity, who becomes human. Ultimately, of
course, 'the *whole* Trinity is the Subject of revelation, of the
incarnation: the Father as the *"fons actionis"*, the Son as its
"medium" and the Spirit, by whom the conception of the Son in
the Virgin is accomplished, as its *"terminus"*. But the result is not
the incarnate Trinity but the incarnate *Logos*.'[103]

Revelation in the form of incarnation was necessary, in Barth's
view, because of the Fall. 'Revelation, or more precisely, incarnation . . . takes place as a result of the *Fall* and for the sake of its
reversal; for the redemption of humankind from evil, guilt and its
punishment.'[104] Prior to the Fall, revelation to the paradisiacal
human was direct and immediate. It is only as a consequence of
the Fall that revelation must be "objective"; i.e. that it must
occur in and through the veil of human flesh. At an earlier point
in his lectures, Barth appeared to provide a second ground for
the necessity of the incarnation. In addressing the question, why
incarnation in a human rather than in a star, a stone, or an animal? Barth suggested that it is in the encounter with another
human that we learn of a subject who will not make herself
objective to us apart from an act of volition—who will not be
objective without remaining subject. Kierkegaard was right,
Barth said. 'The subjective is the objective.'[105] But it is clear that

---

[103] Barth, '*Unterricht in der christlichen Religion*', i. *Prolegomena*, 189; ET *The Göttingen Dogmatics*, 154.
[104] Ibid. 190; ET 155.
[105] Ibid. 168; ET, 137. Barth's source for this idea is Soren Kierkegaard, *Philosophische*

Barth did not intend to set forth here an independent, second ground of the necessity of the incarnation. Already in the context of his lectures on the Trinity, Barth had noted,

I regard it as an absolutely intolerable situation when the grounding of the fundamental Christian doctrine is, even for a moment, thought to be dependent upon whether natural, spiritual, and religious analogies are correct . . . intolerable because the doctrine of revelation is no longer the doctrine of *this* subject-matter in the moment when its legitimation is sought elsewhere than *in this subject-matter itself*. . . . To speak of revelation means strictly and exclusively: to speak *on the basis of* revelation. The ontic and the noetic ground are one in this subject-matter.[106]

That a human subject remains subject in making herself objective to another is at most a parable of divine Self-revelation; a parable which can function as such only where God is already known. Barth was not grounding theology in an I–Thou philosophy (with an appeal to Kierkegaard).

The incarnation consists in the assumption of a human nature by the eternal Son. The '*assumptio*' did not entail any alteration in the divine nature of the Son. What it meant was that, without surrendering anything proper to Himself as divine, the Son took on a '*human* mode of existence'.[107] The *kenosis* of the Son was thus understood by Barth to be a positive rather than a negative act; a *kenosis* by addition, not by subtraction. 'Not the deity as such, the divine, the being which is common to the Father, Son and Spirit, became human; but rather, the *Son*, although naturally without ceasing to be what He is, and therefore in and with the whole of His divinity.'[108] Likewise, the human nature assumed is not altered through its assumption. The union of the Logos with the human nature was understood by Barth to entail no divinization of the human. What is in view is a 'unity in differentiation', 'a strictly dialectical union',[109] which in no way sets aside the qualitative distinction between divine nature and human nature.

It is at this point that Barth introduced the ancient dogma of the *anhypostasia* and *enhypostasia* of the human nature of Christ.

Broken/Abschließende unwissenschaftliche Nachschrift, ed. and trans. H. Gottsched and Chr. Schrempf (Jena: Eugen Diederichs, 1910), ii. 265–323. Clearly, by this point in time, Barth had read in this work.

[106] Ibid. 131, 133; ET, 107, 109.   [107] Ibid. 192; ET 156.
[108] Ibid. 192–3; ET 156.   [109] Ibid. 170; ET 139.

The sources from which Barth had learned of this theolo-
goumenon were Heppe and Schmid. The first notice that Barth
had given of this discovery was on 23 May, in the context of his
lectures on the Trinity.[110] Now he made full use of it.

> This individual in which the human nature is embodied has never
> existed as such. The humanity of Christ (although it is body *and* soul,
> although it is *Individuum*) is nothing subsistent or real in itself. It did
> not, for example, exist *before* its union with the Logos . . . *The human
> nature of Christ has no personality of its own*; it is *anhypostatos* . . . Or, posi-
> tively expressed, it is *enhypostatos*; *it has personality*, subsistence, reality,
> *only in its union with the Logos of God*.[111]

The net effect of this teaching is the rejection of every form of
adoptionism. It is not as though the Logos chose to inhabit at
some point an already existing human being. Rather, a human
nature which had not previously existed was created especially
for this Subject (the Logos) to be His own. Thus, there was not a
moment when this human nature did not have its being and existence grounded in the Person of the Logos.

The affirmation of the Virgin Birth was a consequence of this
'never a moment'. That the God-man was 'conceived by the
Holy Spirit' and 'born of the Virgin Mary' means that it was the
Spirit who formed a human nature from the 'substance' of the
Virgin, sanctified it from the taint of original sin, and united it in
the Virgin's womb to the eternal Son. 'The Person of the Son
must be conceived by the Person of the Spirit so that a new
humanity may arise.'[112] The continuity of historical, sinful
humanity is thus broken and the continuity with original, paradisiacal humanity is restored.[113]

The relevance of this Christology for Barth's conception of
revelation ought to be clear. The anhypostatic-enhypostatic
model was well suited for clarifying what was at stake in speaking
of revelation as revelation in concealment, as indirect communication. For the Subject of this revelation is the Person of the
Logos who has veiled Himself in human flesh. Barth could still
affirm the principle which he first enunciated in *Romans* II: in
revelation, it is the *deus absconditus* who is, without ceasing to be
the hidden, the *deus revelatus*.[114] 'The incarnation of God in any

---

[110] Barth, '*Unterricht in der christlichen Religion*', i. *Prolegomena*, 109; ET 90.
[111] Ibid. 193; ET 157.   [112] Ibid. 201; ET 164.   [113] Ibid. 199; ET 162.
[114] Ibid. 166; ET 136.

case means: the revelation of God in its *hiddenness* and therefore, the radical de-divinization of the world, of nature, of history, the complete divine incognito, the communion of God with humankind exclusively by means of *indirect* communication . . .'[115] On the other hand, Barth was now able quite calmly to assert that 'Christian revelation and Christian faith are historical.'[116] To be sure, revelation is *in* history in such a way as to be withdrawn from all direct intuitability. And so Barth still employed the term *Urgeschichte* to describe the relation of revelation to history. But now the meaning of the term had moderated. Now it was equated with 'pre-history', rather than with 'unhistorical' (and thereby came closer to Overbeck's original intentions). The hiddenness of God is a hiddenness in history, because the Subject in whom the humanity of Jesus is made real and exists is a Subject in history.

Now there are a number of questions left unanswered by Barth's treatment of the incarnation in para. 6, most crucial of which is that of the precise nature of the *'unio personalis'*. What Barth had offered to this point made the differentiation of God and humankind in the union quite clear. But the union itself was left unexplained. However, Barth had only been treating the subject from the standpoint of its relevance to the problem of revelation. In the summer semester of 1925, he returned to the subject, this time from the standpoint of its relevance to the problem of reconciliation. In para. 28, 'Christ Jesus: His Person', Barth reflected further on the nature of the hypostatic union by means of a running debate with classical Lutheran Christology.

For classical Lutheranism, the hypostatic union of the Logos with a human nature entailed a communication of the attributes of the divine nature to the human nature of Christ. On this basis, it became possible to affirm that the human Jesus participated in the divine attributes of omnipresence, omnipotence, etc. This was the Lutheran doctrine of the ubiquity of Christ's human nature: if the Logos continued to fill heaven and earth subsequent to the hypostatic union, then the human nature of Christ must also have done so, since the human nature is present wherever the divine nature is present. Thus, the Lutherans were less interested in the hypostatic union than they were in the

[115] Ibid. 177; ET 144.   [116] Ibid. 182; ET 148.

'communion of natures' which they saw to be the consequence of the hypostatic union. They 'wanted to *experience* immediately the divine triumph over the antithesis of God and human-kind',[117] and to this end they made the divine nature to be directly given in the human nature. The result was that the over-coming of the contradiction was sought in the human nature as such.

In Barth's view, this position rested upon the failure to distin-guish adequately between "person" and "nature". It was not the divine nature (that which is shared by all of the members of the Godhead) which was made flesh. It is the second Person of the Trinity who was made flesh.[118] For their part, the Reformed too could affirm a *communio naturarum*. But this was not the cen-tre of their interest. 'Reformed orthodoxy depicted . . . that *Unio* [*hypostatica*] as an *immediate* union, as the genuine sense of the union of God and humanity in Christ, and moved the other *unio*, the *unio* between the divine *nature* and the human [nature] into the background, as a *mediate* union . . .'[119] Thus, the union of the natures is an indirect union, mediated through the Person in whom both natures are grounded.

This view carried with it two very important implications. First, that the hypostatic union of the Logos with the human nature was understood to be *immediate* meant that all the attrib-utes and operations which are proper to the human nature are rightly attributed to the Logos. Barth here cited with approval the early seventeenth-century Reformed theologian, Amandus Polanus. 'Whatever is predicated of Christ is affirmed of His whole—i.e. undivided—Person, truly and really [*vere et realiter*].'[120] The predication of human attributes and operations to the second Person of the Trinity is therefore not to be taken as merely verbal but rather as a real predication. Against Zwingli's tendency to reduce the affirmation 'Christ has suffered' to a mere figure of speech (on the assumption that because divine nature cannot suffer, the suffering can only properly be attributed to the human nature),[121] Barth held: 'That which acts is clearly the *Person*. The nature can only act as the nature of the *Person*. Here however, the One who acts can only be *God*, even though in the human nature. . . . Therefore, *unio personalis* or *hypostatica*, whereby, under *persona* or hypostasis is exclusively to be understood: the Person of the *Logos*.'[122] The predication of the attributes of both natures to the Person of the union is therefore understood by Barth to be 'direct and undialectical'.[123]

But second, that the union of the natures was understood to be indirect, mediated through the Person of the union, meant that the antithesis between God and humankind is preserved—even in the union. Barth further radicalized the Reformed notion of a mediate union of the natures by actualizing the hypostatic union. According to Barth, on Reformed soil:

One seeks and finds the essence and the power of this union not in the *having-been*-united [*Gleichgesetztheit*] of the two magnitudes divine and human nature, but rather . . . in the *being*-united [*Gleichsetzung*]; not in the *having-become* but in the *becoming* of the God-man; in the *act* whose bearer and executor is the divine Person, not the divine nature in itself and as such. . . . Hence, the sharp differentiation and superordination of the *unio hypostatica vis-à-vis* the *communio naturarum*.[124]

The hypostatic union was therefore understood by Barth not to have taken place in a single moment, in the conception perhaps, but as taking place, moment by moment, in that the Logos continuously wills to assume the human nature. The effect of this view is to place the *communio naturarum* in a very pale light.[125] Does this mean that the antithesis between God and humankind is not overcome? No; it simply means that it is not overcome *in the human nature*, as the Lutherans would have it through their interpretation of the *communio naturarum*. The antithesis is overcome in the *Person of the union*, through the real predication to Him of the sin, guilt, and punishment of humankind. 'The Son of God . . . enters, with His incarnation, into the *broken* covenant between God and humankind; He steps under the *wrath*, under the *judgement*, under the *punishment* of God. He takes to Himself, not merely in appearance, but really, the *reatus ex culpa in poenam*.'[126] And in suffering this punishment, He overcomes the antithesis. But the overcoming of the antithesis in the Person of the Logos in no way sets aside the antithesis on the level of the

---

[122] Ibid. 36.   [123] Ibid. 47–8.   [124] Ibid. 40.   [125] Ibid. 38.
[126] Ibid. 34.

relationship of the natures. Divine attributes and operations cannot be predicated of the human nature. Though Barth does not offer a thorough explanation of why this should be, the reason seems clear enough: attributes and operations may only properly be predicated of persons or subjects. But there is no human subject here to whom divine attributes and operations might be attributed. The only Subject here is the second Person of the Trinity. It is therefore to Him and Him alone that the properties of deity may be attributed. And so, however true it may be—on the basis of the fact that the Son of God takes to Himself human nature, suffering, etc.—that God is capable of the human, the relation cannot be reversed. The Reformed principle '*finitum non capax infiniti*' remains in force.[127]

Barth's conclusion was that reconciliation consists in the fact that 'the faithfulness of God triumphs in the Person of Christ over the unsublated antithesis of God and humankind'.[128] In other words, without setting aside or removing the antithesis, the Son of God takes it to Himself and in taking it to Himself without being overcome by it, He triumphs over it.

This has not been meant to be anything like an exhaustive treatment of Barth's doctrine of the incarnation. But what has been presented is sufficient for establishing the nature of the advance which occurred in Barth's thinking in 1924. Barth's adoption of the anhypostatic-enhypostatic Christology marked a watershed in his development. Its significance for his development lay, first of all, in the fact that the dialectic of veiling and unveiling had now been localized in the incarnation as a whole, and not just in the event of the cross. Second, he could now affirm the presence of the second Person of the Trinity in history, as a Subject who enters fully into the contradiction of human existence and overcomes it, without fear of historicizing revelation. The eternal Son is present in history indirectly, never becoming directly identical with the veil of human flesh in which He conceals Himself (since divine attributes are not properly predicated of the human nature). Third, the Adam–Christ dialectic was no longer seen as an eternal dialectic as in *Romans* II. It is a dialectic which is rooted and grounded in history. The turn from Adam to Christ has taken place. It is no accident that

---

[127] Karl Barth *Gesamtausgabe*, 46.   [128] Ibid. 56.

once Barth had brought revelation fully and completely into history, he was now able to distinguish more carefully between reconciliation (as a historical event) and redemption (as an eschatological event).[129] Reconciliation was no longer absorbed into a future redemption which never arrives. Fourth, he could now appeal to the incarnation as the ground and prototype of the *analogia fidei*. The ability of God to take up a creaturely medium like human language and bear witness to Himself in and through it is demonstrated principally in the fact that He has taken up a human nature and lived a human life in and through it.

With the adoption of the anhypostatic-enhypostatic model of Christology, Barth's theology had moved into a new phase. The anhypostatic-enhypostatic model had supplanted the time—eternity dialectic as the central parable for expressing the *Realdialektik* of God's veiling and unveiling.

7. FOOTNOTE TO BARTH'S CHRISTOLOGY: THE DEBATE WITH ERIK PETERSON

In July 1925 Erik Peterson published a highly critical assessment of dialectical theology, and in particular of Barth's 1922 Elgersburg lecture, 'The Word of God as the Task of Theology'. Bultmann too received some rough handling in this essay, which was published in pamphlet form under the title 'What is Theology?'[130] Initially, a common response by both Barth and Bultmann had been envisioned. As a result of some miscommunication between them, the joint effort was not realized. Each wrote an independent response. The two essays then appeared back to back in the first number of *Zwischen den Zeiten* in 1926.[131]

---

[129] Barth divided the material in the Göttingen Dogmatics into seven chapters. The first three belong to the prolegomena volume. The remaining four were (in order): the doctrine of God, the doctrine of humanity, the doctrine of reconciliation, and the doctrine of redemption.

[130] Erik Peterson, 'Was ist Theologie?', in idem, *Theologische Traktate*, 11–43.

[131] Karl Barth 'Kirche und Theologie', in idem, *Die Theologie und die Kirche*, 302–28; ET 'Church and Theology', in idem, *Theology and Church*, 286–305; Rudolf Bultmann, 'Das Wesen der dialektischen Methode', *Zwischen den Zeiten*, 4 (1926), 40–59; ET 'The Question of "Dialectical" Theology: A Discussion with Erik Peterson', in Robinson (ed.), *The Beginnings of Dialectic Theology*, 257–74.

Barth's response to Peterson has become an important stop in recent interpretations of his development, thanks largely to the importance assigned to it by Eberhard Jüngel.[132] In fact, however, none of the concepts brought forth by Barth in his response were new. He easily drew upon concepts he had already developed three months earlier, in para. 28 of his dogmatics lectures. It is therefore a misreading of the situation to say that Barth was 'alarmed' by Peterson's attack.[133] Nor was he 'considerably influenced' by it.[134] The truth is that Barth found it a 'bad'[135] piece and he thought that it was probably written on a whim.[136]

Not for some time have I read something which so excited and angered me as this glittering and, in every respect, impudent pamphlet, by which we all are placed once again in the same corner with Herrmann. In this case, we would probably have to put ourselves there.[137]

The focal-point of Peterson's critique of Barth was the thesis advanced in the Elgersburg lecture: we ought, as theologians, to speak of God; we are, however, human beings, and as such cannot speak of God; we ought to recognize both our ought and our cannot and thereby give God the glory. For Peterson, the seriousness of the situation described in this thesis was only apparent. It is the seriousness of one who takes seriously only his own speaking of God, but not God Himself.

Theology, according to Peterson, is possible only on the basis of a threefold presupposition: the existence of revelation, faith, and obedience. That revelation *is* means that God has become a human being.

Only under the presupposition that God has become a human being and has thereby made possible for us a participation in the *scientia divina*, only under this presupposition is it meaningful to speak in theology of a real, even if only analogical, knowledge of God.[138]

This means further that theology is only a real possibility if revelation contains within itself a relative knowability.

---

[132] Jüngel, 'Von der Dialektik zur Analogie', in idem, *Barth-Studien*. See above, Introd., Sect. 1.

[133] Ibid. 133.   [134] Ibid. 134.

[135] Karl Barth to Rudolf Bultmann, 11 Aug. 1925 in *B–B Br.* 50.

[136] Karl Barth to Rudolf Bultmann, 26 Oct. 1925, *B–B Br.* 57.

[137] Karl Barth to Rudolf Bultmann, 25 Sept. 1925, *B–B Br.* 53.

[138] Peterson, 'Was ist Theologie?', in idem, *Theologische Traktate*, 16.

The Göttingen Dogmatics 369

If, on the other hand, revelation is a paradox, then there is no theology. . . . if revelation is a paradox, there is also no revelation. For a revelation which cannot be known to a certain extent is no revelation.[139]

In view of the fact that God has spoken in Jesus Christ, the theologian can only respond in the obedience of faith, if she wishes her theology to be taken seriously as theology. To say, as Barth does, that we cannot speak of God, is to be disobedient in the face of the fact of revelation. But then, Peterson added, disobedience belongs to the essence of all dialectical thinking.[140] Dialectical thinking treats revelation as a sort of timeless, abstract, dialectical possibility in which God provides the synthesis of our thesis and antithesis.[141] To deny or ignore the concrete reality of revelation is to be disobedient. Dialectic can succeed only in constant self-annulment. Theology understood as dialectic can never arrive at valid theological statements. It can only make known its own questioning and its questions are necessarily left open.[142] Thus, dialectical theology answers the question 'What is theology?' with the curt response 'there is theology only in that there is no theology'.[143] In Peterson's judgement, a theology which understands itself in this way is no theology.

Barth was not in the least shaken by Peterson's critique of dialectic. Peterson's treatment of dialectic struck him as a caricature, a 'bogeyman with which one frightens children'.[144] He was not willing to surrender his claim that theology, as a human enterprise, must be dialectical in character. He reiterated his argument at Elgersburg. Humanly speaking, theology is impossible. It is possible only on the basis of the divine Self-speaking, an event over which humans have no control.

The revelation of which theology speaks is not dialectical; it is no paradox. That does not even need to be said. But when *theology* begins, when we humans *think*, *speak*, and *write* . . . on the basis of revelation, then dialectic—i.e. a forming of principally incomplete thoughts and statements, in which every answer is once again a question, and which all together point beyond themselves towards fulfilment in the inexpressible reality of the *divine* speaking—is the actual form of our doing and acting . . .[145]

[139] Ibid. 18.   [140] Ibid. 14.   [141] Ibid. 17.   [142] Ibid. 16.
[143] Ibid. 11.
[144] Barth, 'Kirche und Theologie', 322; ET 'Church and Theology', 302.
[145] Ibid. 319; ET, 299.

There was certainly a new element in this explanation as measured by Barth's theology in the phase of *Romans* II (to which the Elgersburg lecture belongs). Barth now says that 'the revelation of which theology speaks is not dialectical; it is no paradox.' That did indeed represent an advance. As a result of the modification which occurred in Barth's understanding of Christology in 1924, he could no longer affirm in a one-sided fashion that Christ is the Paradox.[146] But did such an advance entail the elimination of the dialectic in the relation of God and humankind?

Jüngel would like to see in Barth's affirmation of an undialectical, non-paradoxical revelation a turning-point in Barth's development. He is certainly right to sense that something important is announced in this affirmation (though the turning-point would have to be located in May 1924 rather than in the summer of 1925), but he is right for all the wrong reasons. Jüngel holds that Barth's talk of an 'inner dialectic of the *Sache*' in the preface to *Romans* II marks the beginning of his dialectical phase and that that phase came to an end at the point where Barth no longer maintained a 'dialectic in the being to be known'.[147] But the truth is that Barth still held that the relation of God and humankind is dialectical—even and precisely in the God-man. The antithesis of divine nature and human nature is not set aside through its overcoming in the Person of the Logos. Seen in that light, Barth still held to a dialectic 'in the being to be known' (i.e. in the God-man) and continued to do so after the debate with Peterson.[148] So what significance does the affirmation of an undialectical, non-paradoxical revelation carry? In para. 28, Barth had noted: 'The *Unio personalis* in the God-man'—by which meant the Logos—'stands above [*über*], not in the dialectic of God and humankind'.[149] It can only be this that Barth has in view in affirming an undialectical revelation. He means simply that *in itself*, revelation is undialectical. The Person of the Logos is not dialectically structured. But the being of the Mediator (the

---

[146] Barth, *Der Römerbrief, 1922*, 5–6.

[147] Jüngel, 'Von der Dialektik zur Analogie', in idem, *Barth-Studien*, 143.

[148] In the 1927 Prolegomena, Barth still maintained a dialectic in the being to be known. See Barth, *Die christliche Dogmatik im Entwurf*, 301: '. . . the unity [of divine nature and human nature] must be understood as strictly dialectical unity . . .' Jüngel has clearly given Barth's affirmation of an undialectical revelation in the response to Peterson more freight than it can bear.

[149] Barth, 'Unterricht in der christlichen Religion', para. 28, p. 48.

Person of the Logos in His two natures) *is* dialectically structured. In that the Logos reveals Himself in and through the veil
of human flesh without becoming directly identical with it, there
is a dialectic in the being to be known.

Barth's 'turn' in 1924 did not consist in a simple and straightforward abandonment of a dialectic in the being to be known. It
consisted in his thoroughly Reformed reception of the anhypostatic-enhypostatic model of Christology, in accordance with
which it had become possible to recognize an 'undialectical point
of unity'[150] in the Person of the Logos who triumphs over the
antithesis of God and humankind without eliminating it. This
understanding—however sharp the language used to express it—
remained foundational for all of Barth's later reflections on
Christology. He never went back on his basic insight that the
presence of God in the veil of creaturely flesh is a presence in a
reality that is different from God.[151] To that extent, the 'inner
dialectic of the *Sache*' would always be preserved.

8. THE DOCTRINE OF ELECTION

The location of Barth's doctrine of election was classically
Reformed. He treated election in para. 18 in his doctrine of
God, as the first of God's works. But the execution revealed a
considerable innovation.

Barth saw the doctrine as a necessary consequence arising out
of an analysis of the situation of revelation. God's revelation is a
revelation in concealment. Confronted with such a revelation a
twofold possibility arises: the possibility of faith on the one side
and unbelief on the other. Either a person will know and understand what is hidden in the veil or she will not. Either way, the
ground of the decision which is made here is not to be found on
the human side. The ground lies solely and exclusively on the
side of God, in the eternal decision which God makes with
respect to each person who stands in that concrete situation.[152]

---

[150] Ibid. 50.

[151] Cf. Barth, *KD* IV/1, 195; ET *CD* IV/1, 178 where Barth says that the form of revelation—i.e. the humanity of Jesus—does not correspond to revelation, but 'contradicts'
it.

[152] Barth, '*Unterricht in der christlichen Religion*', ii. 166; ET *The Göttingen Dogmatics*, i.
440.

That a person who confronts the revelation hidden in a veil should see only the veil and nothing more requires little or no explanation. In itself, the veil is a wall, an utterly opaque barrier between the hidden God and the human observer. Nothing special needs to happen to a person for her to be completely unable to see and hear what there is to be seen and heard here. Such a response is only natural. What requires explanation is the response of faith. Given the impossibility of the situation, faith can only be explained in terms of the divine willing. Faith is awakened and effected by means of an irresistible work of the Holy Spirit. But if faith is the effect of a concrete divine act, then logically, the absence of faith is the result of the divine non-willing. The absence of faith means that God has done nothing, that He has simply passed by the person in question. Thus, election on the one side and reprobation on the other are rooted and grounded in the decision which God makes in this highly concrete situation.

The innovation which Barth introduced into the Reformed doctrine of predestination consisted in his rejection of the classical division of the human race into two groups (the elect and the reprobate) whose numbers were fixed and determined from eternity-past by God's decree. Predestination, for Barth, is not a decision by means of which God determined all of His actions towards particular men and women before time began. It is not a completed act. Barth was quite happy to speak of predestination with the tradition as eternal, unconditional, and double. But "eternal" for him was not synonymous with pre-temporality. It was by reducing eternity to pre-temporality that Reformed orthodoxy risked confusing God with fate or, at least, making Him 'the prisoner of His own gracious or ungracious decision':

predestination, precisely as eternal predestination, is the divine decision in *act*, the divine *deciding* with respect to men and women in which God is and remains free *vis-à-vis* every person in every moment of time, continuing with him from decision to decision. God's eternity means 'my times stand in *Your* hands'. It is not a petrified eternity but rather *His living* eternity, the eternity of His will, the eternity in which He is Lord.[153]

Predestination is that ever-present activity of God by which He determines in every event of revelation who the hearers of that

---

[153] Barth, '*Unterricht in der christlichen Religion*', ii. 184; ET 454.

revelation will be. It is a description of an ongoing, never completed act; the living reality of the divine deciding and acting in each new moment. What this means is that God is free to elect or reject a particular individual at different times in her life. In the concrete situation of revelation, a person who formerly saw and heard nothing of revelation in its concealed form may now do so. But it may also happen that a person who formerly did see and hear revelation, now experiences nothing. Having experienced election, she now experiences rejection.

Now obviously, such a view raises serious questions with regard to personal assurance of election and salvation. With respect to this problem, Barth observed that human certainty is always relative at best. Absolute certainty exists in God alone. Human certainty is well founded, however, to the extent that it looks away from itself to the source whence it comes. It consists above all in looking to the revelation of God in Christ as the basis for faith. Barth could also appeal to the fact that there is no symmetry between election and rejection. Election and rejection are not 'equally true and real'.[154] Election is the goal even of rejection.[155] But that is a description only of what happens in revelation: the believer hears the Yes of God spoken to her in the No which a revelation *in concealment* constitutes for her. It is not to be taken as an affirmation of universal election, as though one could maintain with certainty that election is the end of all the ways of God. Barth emphatically rejected the doctrine of apocatastasis as 'enthusiastic metaphysics'.[156] So assurance of election is something which can only be received moment by moment by people living in time. More than that cannot be said—and in Barth's view, should not be said.

Barth's understanding of election at this time was thus theocentric and actualistic. It was theocentric in that his concern was everywhere to turn attention away from predestinated human beings to the predestinating God. It was actualistic in that it was the description of a concrete event in time, not of a fixed and unchangeable reality. What is missing in this account, as judged by the standards of Barth's later, mature doctrine of election (in *CD* II/2), is any serious reflection on the fact that election is 'in Christ'. Certainly, Barth could and did affirm even now that the

---

[154] Ibid. 192; ET 460.   [155] Ibid. 193; ET 461.   [156] Ibid. 211; ET 475.

basis of the election of individuals was to be found 'in Christ'. But such a thought had no constitutive significance for his doctrine as a whole. His attention was wholly absorbed by the concrete situation of revelation in the present moment.

9. THE END OF BARTH'S TEACHING ACTIVITIES IN GÖTTINGEN

On 22 July 1925 Barth received word from Berlin that he had been appointed as Professor of Dogmatics and New Testament Exegesis in Münster. After all of the difficulties he had experienced because of his honorary status in Göttingen, this promotion must have been all the more gratifying in that the post was originally envisaged for an *extraordinarius* (the equivalent of a senior lecturer or associate professor). Two days later, he was treated to a torchlight procession through the darkened streets of Göttingen by the entire student body of the theological faculty, complete with police protection, a speech by Barth, and cheers for their beloved 'Georgia Augusta'. On 25 October Barth departed for Münster in Westphalia.

9

Professor of Dogmatics and New Testament Exegesis in Münster

(OCTOBER 1925–MARCH 1930)

I. PRELIMINARY CONSIDERATIONS

It is customary in treatments of Barth's development to devote a good deal of attention to the revised version of his prolegomena lectures which was published in 1927 under the title *Die christliche Dogmatik im Entwurf*. And certainly this was justified as long as the earlier Göttingen version was not available. In truth, however, *Die christliche Dogmatik im Entwurf* added little that was decisively new. The fundamental decisions which had governed the Göttingen Prolegomena were maintained. And even on a material level, though there is certainly expansion and clarification at some important points, Michael Beintker is undoubtedly right in his suggestion that Barth had the Göttingen material constantly before him as he wrote this book.[1] It should be noted that Barth himself judged the revision of the Göttingen material to be similar in scope to that once carried out in the rewriting of *Romans*—'almost no stone has been left standing on the other'.[2] But that is clearly an exaggeration. The truth is that a synchronic comparison, section by section, of *all three versions* of the prolegomena (the Göttingen and Münster versions together with *Church Dogmatics* I/1 and I/2) makes evident the extent to which the fundamental dogmatic decisions which control even *Church Dogmatics* I/1 and I/2 were already made in 1924/5 in Göttingen.

For this reason, I shall not be giving independent attention to *Die christliche Dogmatik im Entwurf*. I shall treat in this chapter

---

[1] Michael Beintker, 'Unterricht in der christlichen Religion', in Sauter (ed.), *Verkündigung und Forschung*, 2 (1985), 46.

[2] Karl Barth to Eduard Thurneysen, 8 Nov. 1926, *B–Th. Br.* II. 441.

only those events and works that will help to explain the decisions made by Barth, which will be described in the next chapter.

2. A CHALLENGING CONVERSATION PARTNER: ROMAN CATHOLICISM

In late October 1925 Barth joined the relatively small Protestant theological faculty at the University of Münster in Westphalia. Münster was a predominantly Catholic city. Priests and nuns on the streets were a constant reminder to Barth that he was no longer in that stronghold of Lutheranism, Göttingen. The change of location was highly symbolic in its way, for Barth was increasingly coming to regard Catholicism as his major opponent, rather than liberal Protestantism. During the years in Münster, Barth gradually withdrew from further public exchanges with neo-Protestant theologians. The evaluations of his theology which were published in the pages of *Die Christliche Welt* and other Protestant journals convinced him that his critics were more interested in explaining away his theology through social-psychological analysis than they were in engaging his theological concerns.[3] He now expected little stimulation for further reflection from that quarter.

Barth found a more challenging conversation partner in Roman Catholicism. This undoubtedly had a lot to do with the fact that Barth had a burning interest in material dogmatic questions. With liberal Protestantism having given itself over to the study of history and philosophy of religion, there was no one else to whom Barth could turn at that time, if he wished to discuss dogmatics.

Barth's understanding of Catholicism was deepened in a couple of ways. Starting probably in early 1927, Barth became a reg-

---

[3] In a letter printed in *Die Christliche Welt*, Otto Ritschl explained the origins of Barth's theology in terms of Swiss neutrality during the war. He argued that the coercion of a people into passivity, when that people is capable of 'great deeds', and the inability to do anything about the suffering of a neighbouring people, lead naturally to the kind of 'deep pessimism' one finds in Barth's theology. Ritschl, 'Vierundzwanzigsten Brief', *Die Christliche Welt*, 41 (1927), 844. For more detailed analysis of Barth's relations with liberal theologians in this period, see Wilhelm Neuser, *Karl Barth in Münster, 1925–1930* (Theologische Studien, 130; (Zurich: TVZ, 1985), 23–37).

ular member of a theological circle composed largely of lay Catholics.[4] The circle even met in Barth's home on occasion. Other members included Dr Bernhard Rosenmüller (an instructor in philosophy of religion in the Münster philosophy faculty) and his wife; Dr G. Hasenkamp (the editor of the *Münsterischen Anzeiger*) and his wife; and the Catholic student pastor Dr Robert Grosche. There were also occasional visitors such as the Catholic philosopher of religion, Theodore Steinbüchel (from Gießen). The first evidence that we have that Barth had joined the circle was in a letter to Thurneysen.

> Last Monday, I had a very good evening with the Catholic philosopher of religion Steinbüchel from Gießen, and his colleague here in Münster, concerning reason and revelation, Trinity, Christology, and Church; a far-ranging conversation of the kind that one could not have with a Protestant theologian. . . . One could honestly and joyfully give them one's hand and sense already something of the *Una Sancta*.[5]

By 1928 the circle had become a regular theological "institute", meeting every month or two.[6] Papers were presented and discussed on topics such as the idea of appropriations in the doctrine of the Trinity, sin and grace, and the essence of evil. The other members of the circle introduced Barth to two nineteenth-century Catholics with whom he had previously been unacquainted: J. A. Möhler, the founder of the 'Tübingen school' of Catholic theology, and Matthias Scheeben. As a Christmas present in 1928, Barth sent Thurneysen the four volumes of Scheeben's *Handbuch der katholischen Dogmatik*, which he referred to as 'the standard work of modern German Catholic dogmatics'.[7]

In addition to the stimulus provided by this new circle, Barth acquired some first-hand information on the Catholic roots of Protestant dogmas through two of his seminar studies. Barth had not yet felt competent to undertake seminars at Göttingen. They were a new component of his teaching activities in Münster. The complete list of Barth's course offerings in Münster is as follows:

---

[4] For a more complete description of this circle, see Neuser, *Karl Barth in Münster*, 37–40.

[5] Karl Barth to Eduard Thurneysen, 4 Feb. 1927, *B–Th. Br.* II. 460.

[6] Neuser, *Karl Barth in Münster*, 38.

[7] Karl Barth to Eduard Thurneysen, 21 Dec. 1928, *B–Th. Br.* II. 637.

Winter semester 1925/6:
   Lectures: Eschatology (completion of the Göttingen Dogmatics); Exposition of John's Gospel
   Seminar: Calvin's *Institutes*
Summer semester 1926:
   Lecture: History of Protestant Theology since Schleiermacher
   Seminar: Anselm's *Cur Deus homo?*
Winter semester 1926/7:
   Lectures: Prolegomena to Dogmatics (i.e. *Die christliche Dogmatik im Entwurf*); Exposition of Philippians
   Seminar: Schleiermacher's *Glaubenslehre*
Summer semester 1927:
   Lectures: Dogmatics I; Exposition of Colossians
   Seminar: Readings from Luther's and Calvin's Commentaries on Galatians
Winter semester 1927/8:
   Lecture: Dogmatics II
   No seminar
Summer semester 1928:
   Lecture: Ethics I
   Seminar: Albrecht Ritschl
Winter semester 1928/9:
   Lectures: Ethics II; Exposition of James
   Seminar: Thomas Aquinas' *Summa Theologiae* I
Summer semester 1929:
   (Free semester)
Winter semester 1929/30:
   Lecture: History of Protestant Theology since Schleiermacher
   Seminar: The Reformation Doctrine of Justification

Noteworthy in this context is that in the summer semester of 1926, Barth led his students through Anselm's *Cur Deus homo?*—a seminar which he would repeat in Bonn in the summer semester of 1930. And in the winter semester of 1928/9, the topic of his seminar was the first part of Thomas Aquinas' *Summa Theologiae*.

During the Münster years, Barth gave a number of special lectures which reflected his ongoing concern with Catholicism. Among them, two especially merit attention here because they make clear wherein Barth found Catholicism attractive and wherein he felt compelled to register an emphatic protest. The first is a lecture delivered to the Catholic Centre Party at the University of Münster on 11 July 1927. The theme is 'The Concept of the Church'.[8]

In this lecture Barth had a single thesis to defend with two parts: when Catholics and Protestants think of the Church they are thinking of the *same* reality, but each side thinks of this reality very differently. First then, it is the same reality. Discussion is made all too easy, Barth said, by the assumption that the opponent is kneeling before some kind of strange idol. If that were the case, the division would not be at all painful. But it is not true, and therefore the pain of the division is quite real. That the reality in view is the same for both sides is shown by the basic definition of the Church which is common to Protestantism and Catholicism. Both sides affirm that the Church is one, holy, Catholic, and apostolic. And both sides are capable of making the same affirmations with regard to the meaning of these four characteristics. Barth takes this so far as to include an affirmation of an apostolic authority based on Matthew 16: 'there is no fundamental need to become excited over the well-known application of the "Thou art Peter" to Peter's Church in Rome. Over this, we do not need to quarrel.'[9]

And yet—and here the dialectic turns—there are two decisively different ways of viewing this reality. There is a difference of framework, a difference in the horizon of interpretation, which turns on the answer given to one question. And the answer given to that question makes all the difference in the world as to how the same affirmations made of the one reality are, in fact, understood. The question is the nature of grace. For Protestantism, the decisive element in understanding grace is that the Church (and therefore the individual in the Church) does not 'possess the slightest mastery over grace'[10] as humans do over other realities which are perceived, known, and experienced. The Church is the instrument of God's grace. It is this as a visible, historical entity. But the Church has no more control over the grace which brings her into existence moment by moment than do the individuals which comprise her. Grace is the claim of God on humankind. This relation cannot be reversed. If it is,

[8] Karl Barth, 'Der Begriff der Kirche', in idem, *Die Theologie und die Kirche*, 285–301; ET 'The Concept of the Church', in *Theology and Church*, 272–85.
[9] Ibid. 292–3; ET 278.   [10] Ibid. 295; ET 280.

grace is no longer grace. The Church, therefore, has no claim on God.

The splendour of the Church can consist only in its hearing in poverty the Word of the eternally rich God, and making that Word heard by men and women. The Church does not control that Word as earthly things can be controlled. Nor does the Church possess the Word as material or intellectual goods are normally possessed. . . . Nor does the Church take the Word for granted, as it would count on something which was not a gift.[11]

This means concretely that the four characteristics of unity, holiness, catholicity, and apostolicity are not at the disposal of the Church. They remain properties of God's act as, moment by moment, He brings the Church into existence. They are not the properties of a statically existing historical entity.

Throughout this brief address, Barth made it clear that in his view, to take the Catholic conversation partner seriously means to look him in the eye, to see him in all his strangeness and difference, and to see that he is just as shocked by us as we are by him. It is of the utmost importance for assessing Barth's attitude towards Catholicism to see that polemic was not, for him, a sign of contempt; just the opposite is the case. It was a sign of the deepest respect. It was respect for the conversation partner *as she is*, in all the difference that entails. Disrespectful would be an attitude which suggested that the other's diversity had no significance either because the dispute was just a wrangle over words or because belief is less important than peaceful, unthinking coexistence. It is also disrespectful to regard the other in complete detachment, as though the division were so cemented in place as to render further discussion fruitless in advance, as though the other's diversity no longer places a claim upon one's self. Respect, therefore, has to entail an open and frank acknowledgement of the (from one's own point of view) *hetero*-doxy of the conversation partner.

A second, more substantive lecture was delivered before Protestant audiences in Bremen on 9 March 1928, in Osnabrück on 15 March, and finally, in Düsseldorf on 10 April. Its title was

---

[11] Karl Barth, 'Der Begriff der Kirche', in idem, *Die Theologie und die Kirche*, 298; ET 282.

'Roman Catholicism: A Question to the Protestant Church'.[12] The fundamental question which Roman Catholicism posed to the Protestant Church, Barth argued, was the extent to which the Protestant Church was really a church. Protestantism had originally meant reformation, not revolution. It had sought neither the destruction of the Church nor its transformation into something wholly different. The Reformers wanted rather to rebuild the Church, to purify it of elements which had come to encumber and conceal its true substance. That the true substance of the Church was contained in Catholicism was never in question. Protestantism meant simply a new and better comprehension of the one substance of the Church.

But this original understanding of the meaning of 'Protestantism' has subsequently been supplanted.

A preference for a different interpretation of Protestantism assumes that in the meantime, in the eighteenth century or at the turn from the eighteenth to the nineteenth, a kind of second reformation occurred, for which the way had fortunately been prepared by the Humanists and the left-wing Anabaptists of the sixteenth century itself. Thus a second, new Protestantism has appeared on the scene as the true Protestantism. Its character would consist not so much in the *restoration* of the one substance of the Church as it would in its *surrender*.[13]

What then is this true substance which makes a church to be a true Church of God? What is the substance which neo-Protestantism threatened to relinquish entirely? According to Barth it is the understanding that the Church is the house of God. It is *God's* presence which makes the Church to be the Church. God is the Subject of the Church, not its object. Where this relation is reversed, where God is made to be the object and human beings the subject of the Church, there the substance has been lost. The Church has ceased to be the Church.

Where neo-Protestantism threatened to surrender completely the substance of the Church, Catholicism preserved it. In Catholicism, 'the substance may be distorted and perverted, but it is not lost!'[14] Catholicism constitutes a forceful question to the

---

[12] Karl Barth, 'Der römische Katholizismus als Frage an die protestantische Kirche', in idem, *Die Theologie und die Kirche*, 329–63; ET 'Roman Catholicism: A Question to the Protestant Church', in *Theology and Church*, 297–333.

[13] Ibid. 337; ET 313.   [14] Ibid. 339; ET 315.

Protestant Church as to what the latter has done with the substance because Catholicism's

dogma, its ritual of worship, its general attitude, in spite of all to which
we may object, does hold before the eyes of men and women something of that which the Reformation reformed, restored, brought into
clear light and improved, rebuilt and made valid—that *without* which
the whole Reformation would have been purposeless. . . . Catholicism
becomes this question to us because in its presuppositions for the
Church, in spite of all contradictions, it is closer to the Reformers than
is the Church of the Reformation insofar as it has actually and finally
become the new Protestantism.[15]

Roman Catholicism stands closer to the Reformers than does
neo-Protestantism! 'We cannot deny that we feel more at home
in the world of Catholicism and among its believers than in a
world and among believers where the reality about which the
Reformation centred has become an unknown or almost
unknown entity.'[16] So as to leave no one in the dark as to the
meaning of this statement, Barth added in a footnote,

If I today became convinced that the interpretation of the Reformation
on the line taken by Schleiermacher–Ritschl–Troeltsch (or even by
Seeberg or Holl) was correct, that Luther and Calvin really intended
such an outcome of their labours, I could not become a Catholic
tomorrow, but I should have to withdraw from the evangelical Church.
And if I were forced to make a choice between the two evils, I should,
in fact, prefer the Catholic.[17]

What was it about contemporary Catholicism which convinced Barth that the substance had been preserved there? As the
notes to this lecture make clear, Barth had been carrying out
careful studies of the Roman Catechism, the Roman mass and
the theology presupposed in it, and had been reading Bernhard
Bartmann's *Lehrbuch der Dogmatik* and Karl Adam's *Das Wesen des
Katholicismus*. He mentioned with great appreciation Adam's
statement that God is 'the real I of the Church'.[18] He appealed to
the theology reflected in the *Gloria*, in which it is confessed:
'Thou who sittest at the right hand of the Father, have mercy
upon us. For Thou alone art holy, Thou alone art Lord, Thou

---

[15] Karl Barth, '*Der römische Katholizismus*', 338; ET 314.   [16] Ibid.
[17] Ibid. 338–9 n. 3; ET 314 n. 1.   [18] Ibid. 339 n. 4; ET 314 n. 2.

alone art highly exalted, Jesus Christ!'[19] Perhaps even more important than these is the fact that the Trinitarian and Christological doctrines of the ancient Church have been preserved in contemporary Catholicism.[20] The presence of these doctrines is a good indicator that the substance has been preserved; the absence of them would signify the loss of the substance. Of course, Barth was not blind to the degree to which the divine Subject of the Church threatened to be replaced in Catholicism by human surrogates who were all too directly identified with the One whom they represented.[21] But this did not keep him from acknowledging that Catholicism intended otherwise, as the quote from Karl Adam demonstrated.

Barth's conversation with Catholicism reached a climax of sorts with his invitation to Erich Przywara to give an address in Münster in February 1929. The lecture was entitled 'The Catholic Church-Principle' and was later printed in *Zwischen den Zeiten*.[22] Barth arranged that Przywara would participate with him in leading his seminar on Thomas on the morning following the special lecture. There was also time for an intense debate in the privacy of Barth's home. After Przywara had departed, Barth wrote to Thurneysen in excitement.

Erich Przywara, SJ, gave a two-hour-long lecture on the Church which, considered from the point of view of its skilled craftsmanship, was simply a dainty morsel, a masterpiece. He then shone in my seminar, once again for two hours, answering our carefully prepared questions. And finally, he "overwhelmed" me here for two evenings' worth, just as, according to his doctrine, the dear God overwhelms people with grace (at least within the Catholic Church) so that the formula 'God in–above humankind from God's side' is, at one and the same time, the motto of his existence as well as the dissolution of all Protestant and modernist, transcendentalist and immanentist stupidities and constraints in the peace of the *analogia entis*.[23]

Two phrases in Barth's account deserve special mention, for they give an indication of what he found compelling in Przywara's brand of Catholicism as well as the point at which he would have

---

[19] Ibid. 339; ET 315.   [20] Ibid. 340; ET 316.
[21] Ibid. 339; ET 314–15.
[22] Erich Przywara, 'Das katholische Kirchenprinzip', *Zwischen den Zeiten*, 7 (1929), 277–302.
[23] Karl Barth to Eduard Thurneysen, 9 Feb. 1929, *B–Th. Br.* II. 652.

to demur. The first of these is 'God in–above humankind from God's side'. The first half of the this formula was not new. Przywara had introduced it in his 1923 article considered above.[24] But the stress on 'from God's side' was new—to Barth, at any rate. Here was a man who intended to speak *von Gott her*, just as much as Barth did. Or so it seemed to Barth. The second phrase is 'in the peace of the *analogia entis*', and in it Barth's reason for eventually rejecting Przywara's 'God in and above us' was announced. We shall return to that in a moment.

That Barth understood Przywara to be striving for a concept of God consistent with a right doctrine of the Word (*von Gott her*) is clear from the continuation of his account to Thurneysen.

Yes, Eduard, what was that? And what is the meaning of this Catholicism which, in spite of all our [400th anniversary] celebrations of the Reformation, so alertly puts in an appearance? Was that an angel of the Antichrist or a chosen instrument of the Lord? The Grand Inquisitor or really a disciple of the 'apostle of the peoples'? Or both at the same time or neither . . .? Obviously, this possibility too exists: there are people like us who . . . no longer burn [people] as was done 400 years ago, but simply *laugh* down from an ultimate height; like us in that *they too* do so with a calling upon *God* (with all Kutterish emphasis!), in the name of the Church, with the Bible under one arm, knowing as we do (and perhaps much better) of death and the devil, time and eternity, with the real human being of today in mind. Is it the most cunning world which laughs there or is there something in it of the laughter of the One who dwells in heaven? Is it perhaps fitting that in this year in which we celebrate the 200th anniversary of Lessing's birth, we turn our attention for a change to the parable of the three rings?[25]

It is that burning question which forms the necessary horizon for comprehending the significance of a series of lectures delivered by Barth later that month in Dortmund. The lectures bear the title 'Fate and Idea in Theology'[26] and are devoted to the problem of the relation of philosophy and theology. But when this essay is read in the light of the situation-in-life in which it was written, it is hard to avoid the impression that Erich

---

[24] See above, Chapter 7, Sect. 4.

[25] Karl Barth to Eduard Thurneysen, 9 Feb. 1929, *B–Th. Br.* II. 654–5.

[26] Karl Barth, 'Schicksal und Idee in der Theologie', in idem, *Theologische Fragen und Antworten* (2nd edn.; Zurich: TVZ, 1986), 54–92; ET 'Fate and Idea in Theology', in *The Way of Theology in Karl Barth: Essays and Comments*, ed. H. Martin Rumscheidt, trans. George Hunsinger (Allison Park, Pa.: Pickwick Publications, 1986), 25–61.

Przywara is the silent conversation partner throughout. It is here that Barth discussed the concept of an *analogia entis* for the first time in print, and the understanding of it which unfolds here would remain characteristic of Barthian polemics in the future. That Barth took the phase over from Przywara is beyond doubt. Although Przywara had not himself coined the term, it is most unlikely that Barth had any acquaintance with its history.[27]

'Fate and Idea' takes the form of a discussion of two fundamentally different orientations in theology, each of which corresponds to a basic orientation in philosophy. These two orientations are realism and idealism. Barth was concerned to argue that neither of these orientations may be excluded from theology. Each represents a valid concern which any good theology will have to take seriously.

The valid concern represented by realism is, in the first instance, its insistence that God is real. God has an objective existence apart from and prior to human knowledge of it. We cannot avoid ascribing "being" to God and the minute we do, we have entered into the way of the realist. But realism means more than the simple affirmation that God exists. It also has something to say about how this God is known. For the realist, knowledge of God begins with a knowledge of directly experienced reality. Here too Barth saw a valid concern. From the days of *Romans* II on, Barth's doctrine of revelation had laid great stress on the fact that God could not be known unless He gave Himself to us in objects of this world. In so far as the givenness of the media of revelation (the humanity of Christ, the Bible, preaching) play a strong role in Barth's doctrine of revelation, realistic elements are prominent in his thought.

But at this point, questions arise. In what sense does directly experienced reality play a role in the knowledge of God? Wherein is the possibility of knowing God grounded? In the classical realism of Thomas, that possibility is grounded in a way that Barth found impossible on the basis of a genuine doctrine of the Word of God.

'God is'—what else could that mean than that God participates in being? Certainly, the next statement which is immediately added is that

---

[27] The term derives from the late scholasticism of the 15th c. See on this point J. Teran-Dutari, 'Die Geschichte des Terminus "*Analogia entis*" und das Werk Erich Przywaras', in *Philosophisches Jahrbuch der Görres-Gesellschaft*, 77 (1970), 163–79.

He is Himself being, the Origin and Perfection of all that exists. And the first statement, together with its corollary, is founded in turn (in its classical form, as conceived by Thomas Aquinas) upon a third statement (which can just as well be thought of as their consequence): that everything existing as such participates in God. In that everything existing is conceived as creature, it exists in a relation of the greatest dissimilarity to the Creator. Yet, in that it too has being, it exists in a relation of the greatest similarity to the Creator (*analogia entis*).[28]

As Barth understands him, Thomas grounds the possibility of our knowledge of God in that *similitudo Dei* which is ours (and the world's) by virtue of our (and its) createdness. On the basis of this analogy, knowledge of God can be simply 'read off of the given'.[29] But a God whose being is understood in this way becomes indistinguishable from a hidden feature of the world. The great danger of realism in its pure form is that God becomes indistinguishable from fate: *Deus sive natura*. And the *Deus sive natura* is not the God who reveals Himself in His Word.[30]

From Barth's point of view, to ground the possibility of the knowledge of God in an analogy which is built into the world as created renders revelation superfluous. Revelation can, at most, be a confirmation and strengthening of what is already known in another way. But that is to misunderstand revelation. Revelation tells us something new, something we could not have told ourselves without it.[31]

Realism has a valid concern, but its role in theology is strictly delimited by a genuine doctrine of the Word of God. God is real, yes; God is *the* Reality compared with which all that we are accustomed to think of as real takes on an aspect of unreality. Moreover, directly experienced reality does play a role in revelation. But the media of revelation do not function to provide revelation by virtue of some intrinsic capacity, built into them with their creation. Nor is such a capacity given to them subsequently *per infusionem*. The media of revelation function as such by virtue of a gracious act of God.

Truly, the reality which is given to us in the Church and in the Bible can always be everything else but *similitudo Dei* ... God not only unveils Himself but also veils Himself in revelation because it is revela-

---

[28] Barth, 'Schicksal und Idee', in idem, *Theologische Fragen und Antworten*, 62; ET 'Fate and Idea', in *The Way of Theology in Karl Barth*, 33.
[29] Ibid.; ET 33.   [30] Ibid. 72; ET 42.   [31] Ibid. 69; ET 39.

tion and not revealedness. Therefore, only with this proviso can we think and speak realistically in a theology of the Word of God—only under the presupposition that the act-character of the reality of God on which Thomas laid so much stress is brought into play in a way completely different from the way in which Thomas appeared to do . . . the *similitudo Dei* must be given to us in every moment as something new from heaven.[32]

Whereas realism in theology begins with an almost naïve confidence that that which is experienced directly can lead us to a knowledge of God, idealism begins with doubt about the reliability of the way taken by the realist. Instead of orienting itself first to the question of reality, idealism orients itself first to the question of truth, a truth which is superior to the given and calls it into question. Idealism is *critical* thinking, thinking which has become aware of itself. It seeks a non-given, non-objective, unconditional truth which provides the necessary ontic and noetic presupposition of the given, the objective, and the conditional. In so far as it puts in an appearance in theology, idealism puts great stress on the non-objectivity (the Subjecthood) of God, God's hiddenness and otherness.

Where one tries to think the thought of God seriously, there one must distinguish between the givenness of God and the givenness of all other being, and indeed, distinguish so fundamentally that the being of God in relation to all other being is candidly attributed non-givenness and to that extent, non-being.[33]

Idealism, like realism, has a valid concern which has to be heard in theology.

In that it reminds us of God's non-objectivity and therefore of the inadequacy of all human thinking and speaking of God, idealism guards the object of theology from confusion with all other objects. Idealism directs theological thinking and speaking to the God who, only in His genuine otherness [*Jenseitigkeit*], is really God. A theology which has really been purified of idealism could be nothing other than a pagan monstrosity.[34]

Yet idealism has its inherent dangers as well; dangers which are all the more serious in that idealism (in Barth's view) stands closer to the truth. The fact that the idealist starts with the non-givenness of the truth means that greater stress is placed on

---

[32] Ibid. 70; ET 40–1.   [33] Ibid. 74; ET 44.   [34] Ibid. 77; ET 47.

the dissimilarity of God to the world than on similarity. Barth here cited the formula of the Fourth Lateran Council (a formula frequently appealed to by Przywara!) as an example of typically idealistic thinking in theology: *similitudo Dei* and *major dissimilitudo*.[35] The danger resident in such formulations (precisely because they are so near to the truth) is that idealism will all too easily be thought of as a more suitable way to God than realism. But idealism is no more able to provide a way to God than its counterpart. The accessibility of God to us is our accessibility to Him. Idealism within the bounds of theology ought to have a purely critical function: to remind us that the truth is not identical with the given (i.e. to break through naïve realism). If it seeks to do more, it forgets that it has no criterion at its disposal by which it can lay hands on the truth. The criterion of truth has to be given with revelation—again and again and again. Where idealism fails to perform its critical function, where it all too positively treats its access to the world of ideas as if it were access to God Himself, there God has become indistinguishable from the Idea: *Deus sive ratio*. But 'the equation *Deus sive ratio* is just as intolerable for theology as the equation *Deus sive natura*.'[36] The *Deus sive ratio* is the Idea and the Idea is not the God who reveals Himself in His Word.

If 'Fate and Idea' is read as a response to Przywara, then it seems clear that Barth was posing two questions to him. First, he was asking Przywara if he did not see that the *analogia entis* finds its home more naturally among the realists than among the idealists. Barth could not have been unaware of the fact that Przywara's doctrine of analogy was developed in the closest possible connection to the formula of the Fourth Lateran Council and that his patron saint was Augustine, a man whom Barth referred to in this lecture as '*the* great idealist among the theologians'.[37] In correlating the *analogia entis* more closely with the *similitudo Dei* of the realists than with the *major dissimilitudo* of the idealists, I do not think that Barth was misinterpreting or misrepresenting Przywara as many scholars have alleged[38]—not at this

---

[35] Barth, 'Schicksal und Idee', in idem, *Theologische Fragen und Antworten*, 77; ET 46.
[36] Ibid. 81; ET 50.   [37] Ibid. 75; ET 45.
[38] See von Balthasar, *Karl Barth*, 269; Eberhard Jüngel, *God as the Mystery of the World* (Grand Rapids: Wm. B. Eerdmans, 1983), 282; and Beintker, *Die Dialektik in der 'dialektischen Theologie' Karl Barths*, 246–51.

stage in their dialogue at least. In all likelihood, he was simply indicating that the phrase *analogia entis* carries more freight than Przywara personally would allow. Barth saw in this phrase the ill-advised attempt to order both God and humankind into a higher concept, namely "being"; to make both God and humankind simply differing exemplifications of being in order then to ascend from a knowledge of creaturely being to a knowledge of God (natural theology). So Barth was asking Przywara if his own doctrine of analogy did not take him willy-nilly in the direction of Thomas's realism and away from Augustine's idealism. Second, Barth was asking Przywara if he did not see that the transcendence of God is something different from the self-transcendence of created and finite spirits which expresses itself in concepts like the Unconditioned, etc.[39] And if he did see that, did he also understand that the way to this God was not a 'general way . . . open and accessible at all times to everyone'?[40] Did he see that the knowledge of God is actualized strictly and solely by an act of God?[41] In sum, did Przywara see the necessity (on the basis of Christian revelation) of what we have been calling a "critically realistic" theology?

'Fate and Idea' was irenic in tone. It raised questions while studiously avoiding accusations.

In the question as to whether a particular theology has a mere concept of God or the living God as its object, one could see the first criterion for an answer in whether we understand our own relativity and therefore whether we have the necessary patience *vis-à-vis* other theologians . . .[42]

Before the year was out, however, the irenic tone had faded. Barth became increasingly convinced in the months which followed this lecture that he had been right in his initial suspicions concerning the *analogia entis*. In part, this was the result of further study. Barth was granted a free semester in the summer of 1929 which he planned to use in preparing volumes II and III of *Die christliche Dogmatik im Entwurf* for publication. As things turned out, he used the time for extensive reading, above all in Augustine and Luther.[43] The fruit of this reading is to be found

---

[39] Barth, 'Schicksal und Idee', in idem, *Theologische Fragen und Antworten*, 79; ET 'Fate and Idea', in *The Way of Theology in Karl Barth*, 49.

[40] Ibid. 78; ET 47.   [41] Ibid. 80; ET 49.   [42] Ibid. 90; ET 58.

[43] Karl Barth to Eduard Thurneysen, 29 Apr. 1929, *B–Th. Br.* II. 660.

in a lecture given on 9 October in Elberfeld with the title 'The Holy Spirit and the Christian Life'.[44] In these lectures, his rejection of Przywara's *analogia entis* became rather more definitive. Barth himself said of 'The Holy Ghost and the Christian Life':

> It is implicitly and explicitly the most anti-Catholic piece I have ever written. But there are also many other anti's contained therein; e.g., two footnotes against E. Hirsch! The extremely angry antithesis in which I find myself precisely in relation to his theology has once again become clear to me in a very lively way, remarkably through my preoccupation with Augustine. I believe that as long as we do not root Augustinianism completely out of the doctrine of grace, we will never have a Protestant theology.[45]

The angry mood in which Barth found himself at the end of 1929, however, had much less to do with Hirsch (and Augustine and Przywara for that matter) than this comment would seem to indicate. The real source of his anger and frustration was, as we shall see in the next section, the growing tensions within the circle of dialectical theologians.

In 'The Holy Ghost and the Christian Life', Barth answered the questions he had posed to Przywara. He had read in the meantime Przywara's 1926 book on the philosophy of religion.[46] For Barth, it was now clear: the element of continuity in the divine–human relation is rooted by all Catholic theology, following Augustine, in creation itself. This is the Catholic meaning of *analogia entis*. Against this, Barth held that the fact of creation establishes only a Creator–creature distinction and therefore discontinuity. Continuity in the relation to God is a 'second miracle of the love of God'.

If creaturehood is to be understood strictly as a reality desired and posited by God in distinction from His own reality, as the miracle of a reality which has place and existence next to His own reality by virtue of His love, then the continuity between God and the creature too, the true *analogia entis* in virtue of which He, the uncreated Spirit can be

---

[44] Karl Barth, 'Der heilige Geist und das christliche Leben', in Karl Barth and Heinrich Barth, *Zur Lehre vom heiligen Geist*, Beiheft 1 of *Zwischen den Zeiten* (Munich: Chr. Kaiser Verlag, 1930), 39–105; ET *The Holy Ghost and the Christian Life*, trans. R. Birch Hoyle (London: Frederick Muller Ltd., 1938).

[45] Karl Barth to Paul Althaus, 14 Sept. 1929, copy in Karl Barth-Archiv, Basle, Switzerland.

[46] Erich Przywara, *Religionsphilosophie katholischer Theologie* (Munich: Druck und Verlag von R. Oldenbourg, 1926).

revealed to the created spirit, cannot belong to the creature as such but only to the Creator *in His relating* to the creature. It cannot be understood as an original endowment of the creature, but rather only as a second miracle of the love of *God*; as incomprehensible, unmerited, divine *gift*. The human as creature is not in a place from which he can establish and survey his relation to God (for example, in a scheme of a unity of similarity and dissimilarity) and, on that basis, understand himself as 'open upwards', and therefore he is not able to attribute his knowing to a revealedness of God proper to him as such.[47]

The phrase 'open upwards' is Przywara's. In a footnote to this phrase, Barth said that the creature is not to be thought of as 'open upwards'—'even when this "open upwards" is interpreted as "*von Gott her*" (E. Przywara, pp. 22, 67). The necessary scruple already urged against Augustine would have to be pressed in still greater measure against Thomas Aquinas.'[48]

Barth had not finally been satisfied that Przywara's talk of '*von Gott her*' had been sufficient to remove his *analogia entis* from the sphere of Thomas's realistic reflections. His understanding of the *analogia entis* would not undergo any significant modification from this point on.

3. THE BREAK-UP OF THE DIALECTICAL THEOLOGIANS

Of growing concern to Barth during the years in Münster were relations among the dialectical theologians. Barth watched the further development of Gogarten and Bultmann at first with uneasiness and then with disapproval. Even Barth's relationship with Georg Merz began to deteriorate and both Barth and Thurneysen began to worry about the future of *Zwischen den Zeiten*. The journal would not be laid to rest until 1933, when each of the editors (with the exception of Gogarten) wrote a farewell address to explain to readers why they could no longer collaborate. Yet it is true, as Wilhelm Neuser has observed, that when Barth moved from Münster to Bonn in 1930, 'the theological split between these former comrades-in-arms was already an accomplished fact.'[49]

---

[47] Barth, 'Der heilige Geist und das christliche Leben', in Barth and Barth, *Zur Lehre vom heiligen Geist*, 43–4; ET *The Holy Ghost and the Christian Life*, 14–15.
[48] Ibid. 44 n. 16; ET 15 n. 1.   [49] Neuser, *Karl Barth in Münster*, 6.

Seen in general terms, Barth's concern with Gogarten and Bultmann was very much bound up with his growing realization that his own Reformed starting-point had to bring him into conflict with their Lutheranism. This was not a petty struggle over institutional identity; the issues were substantive. At first, both sides would have liked to believe that what united them was of greater importance than confessional differences. But eventually it became clear that these differences did exist and that they were having a considerable impact on how major issues were construed. This was only a gradually dawning recognition and when it came into the open, it was not pleasant for any of those involved.

Barth and Thurneysen first caught sight of the Lutheran in Gogarten in relation to his handling of the problem of the relationship between revelation and history. That there was such a relationship, Barth could no longer contest. But in Barth's view, it was an indirect relation; a relation which is actualized by the divine Subject and always remains under His control. Barth continued to be adamantly opposed to the Lutheran *"est"* as he had first put it in his 1923 lecture at Elgersburg.[50] In Luther's insistence on the literal force of the "is" in the words of institution ('This is My body'), Barth saw the opening of a door to every *direct* identification of revelation and history. It was this *est* which he and Thurneysen began to perceive in Gogarten in the summer of 1926.

This evening, I suddenly comprehended much of Gogarten's hidden doctrine. Above all, it became very clear to me that with Gogarten, it is once again a question of a clear grasping after the *est*, of nothing else! Sometimes, the most dangerous identifications of God with history have passed virtually unnoticed.[51]

Barth was at that time working on his first attempt at a history of nineteenth-century theology.

What the Germans in general want has become very clear to me these days in my preoccupation with [Philipp] Marheinecke, behind whom stands Hegel and behind Hegel doubtless—Luther? That God in us, we in God thinking, which lies beyond what *we* call "dialectical" thinking.

---

[50] Barth, 'Das Wort Gottes als Aufgabe der Theologie', in idem. *Das Wort Gottes und die Theologie*, 178.

[51] Eduard Thurneysen to Karl Barth, 10 June 1926, *B–Th. Br.* II. 422.

Something of that is also haunting Bultmann and Gogarten, but in the details they are remarkably incomprehensible to me.[52]

In the autumn of that same year, Gogarten put the finishing touches on a major book, *I Believe in the Triune God*.[53] He sent the first half of his manuscript to Thurneysen.[54] In the middle of October, he made his way to Switzerland for two days of discussion with the Swiss pastor. Thurneysen sat in silence and listened as Gogarten explained what he wanted to say in his new book. Thurneysen's impression was that the problematic with which Gogarten was concerned represented a drastic narrowing of the field of theology. Gogarten's problem was the incarnation, but the incarnation in isolation from the doctrine of the Trinity and eschatology, and therefore with all attention directed to the humanity of Christ. 'Where is God? In heaven? Of what concern to me is God in *heaven*? In Christ, He is there for me, specifically in the One who has become human.'[55] Gogarten wanted to seek God in the humanity of Christ, but even that seemed to Thurneysen to be merely a stage on the way to his real goal. The real goal was to show that in virtue of the incarnation, we now have the possibility of encountering Christ not just in the human Jesus, but also in the neighbour. Gogarten wanted to unfold the doctrine of reconciliation in terms of an I–Thou philosophy. Christ Himself meets us in the neighbour (our thou) and sets us free from our self-centredness. Such, at any rate, was Thurneysen's interpretation of the matter. Thurneysen could only listen and send Gogarten on his way in peace.

The effect which Thurneysen's account of his 'I–Thou' encounter with Gogarten had on Barth was to move him to publish a lecture he had given on Feuerbach in his course on the nineteenth century. Barth did not want to confront Gogarten in public. He thought it best to place 'Feuerbach' alongside Gogarten's 'book of confessions of modern Protestantism'. 'If the book [Gogarten's] is good, then Feuerbach may speak as *testis veritatis for* it. If it is not good, then he may speak as a ghost *against*

---

[52] Karl Barth to Eduard Thurneysen, 15 June 1926, *B–Th. Br.* II. 424.

[53] Friedrich Gogarten, *Ich glaube an den dreieinigen Gott: Eine Untersuchung über Glauben und Geschichte* (Jena: Eugen Diederichs Verlag, 1926).

[54] Eduard Thurneysen to Karl Barth, 27 Sept. 1926, *B–Th. Br.* II. 433.

[55] Eduard Thurneysen to Karl Barth, 30 Oct. 1926, *B–Th. Br.* II. 439.

it. In any case, in this historical moment, he belongs on the stage; he who already knew something of the thou and I . . .'[56]

Barth's confidence in Bultmann also began to cool in 1926. It was in that year that Bultmann published his book on Jesus.[57] Barth had looked forward to the book and had expected great things from it. He was disappointed. As he explained two years later to Paul Althaus, his difficulties centred on Bultmann's less than complete break from the old tendency to regard the New Testament as a source of historical material.

The Jesus which he offers us is very beautiful, especially because He too was clearly already a dialectical theologian. But I absolutely cannot comprehend how or by what right one comes to carving precisely this Jesus out of the New Testament and setting Him up. I had expected that the radical criticism of Bultmann, which in itself is quite pleasing to me, would bring it about that New Testament science would henceforth look away from *all* other pictures of Jesus than the completely concrete one of the New Testament writers . . . My disappointment in Bultmann's book consisted in the fact that I saw it proceeding in the old way, with an uncontrolled mixture of the usual historical criticism and the new material criticism [*Sachkritik*]; in the way according to which the New Testament is read as historical source rather than as witness.[58]

Bultmann heard from a friend that Barth had expressed himself critically towards his Jesus book and he wrote on two occasions, asking for clarification. Barth remained silent. Finally, in a third letter, Bultmann acknowledged his belief that in his closer relationship to Gogarten than to Barth the old Lutheran–Calvinist antithesis was at work. He expressed the hope that this old controversy would not be renewed, however, because the elements which united them were of more decisive importance. In any case, he hoped that Barth's silence did not mean that Barth had given up on him.[59]

Barth was not at all inclined at this point in time to give up on Bultmann. Gogarten's book on the Trinity caused him far more difficulties than did Bultmann's book. Still, he had to acknow-

---

[56] Karl Barth to Eduard Thurneysen, 8 Nov. 1926, *B–Th. Br.* II. 442.

[57] Rudolf Bultmann, *Jesus (Die Unsterblichen)*, i. (Berlin, 1926).

[58] Karl Barth to Paul Althaus, 30 May 1928, copy in Karl Barth-Archiv, Basle, Switzerland.

[59] Rudolf Bultmann to Karl Barth, 21 Apr. 1927, *B–B Br.* 68.

ledge the truth of Bultmann's suspicion that confessional differences were at work in their disagreements. 'In some way, the old controversies between the Lutherans and the Reformed, which were never settled, do cause us difficulties on both sides and will perhaps come to a head in a great explosion *within Zwischen den Zeiten.*'[60] For the time being, however, he was content to let Bultmann and Gogarten forge ahead, to seek to clarify to themselves and others what they wanted. The time for explosions had not yet arrived and Barth did not want to see their disagreements made public.[61]

Barth's own development was by now causing considerable discomfort to the chief editor of *Zwischen den Zeiten*, Georg Merz. The friction which developed in Barth's friendship with Merz was a very sad episode. Unlike Gogarten, with whom Barth had never felt close,[62] Merz was a real friend. Fortunately, their friendship would survive the difficult years ahead.

Merz had first become acquainted with Barth at Tambach in September 1919. In the aftermath of that tumultuous meeting, he had read *Romans* I. He had seen in it a new Reformation and had viewed Barth as a young Luther.[63] The situation had begun to sour for him in the summer of 1924. That summer the Barth family had vacationed at Pany (in Graubünden) and Merz was among those who came for a visit.[64] What happened there is unclear. Apparently it had something to do with politics. Merz complained that Barth would not allow anyone around him to contradict his views. But it is clear that what later bothered Merz most was Barth's turn to dogmatics. Merz had a certain feeling of horror when confronted by the 'old theology'—namely theologoumena like the anhypostatic-enhypostatic Christology.[65] Merz had the impression that his hoped-for Reformation was stillborn and was already being replaced by the kind of medieval scholasticism to which post-Reformation theology had once had recourse.

[60] Karl Barth to Rudolf Bultmann, 28 Apr. 1927, *B–B Br.* 70.

[61] Karl Barth to Eduard Thurneysen, 15 May 1927, *B–Th. Br.* II. 500.

[62] Karl Barth to Rudolf Bultmann, 12 June 1928, *B–B Br.* 84.

[63] Eduard Thurneysen to Karl Barth, 6 Apr. 1927, *B–Th. Br.* II. 487. Thurneysen is reporting to Barth on the contents of a letter he had just received from Merz.

[64] The brief account of Merz' visit to Pany which follows is taken from a letter from Barth to Thurneysen in which he recounts a conversation which he had just had with Merz in Munich. Karl Barth to Eduard Thurneysen, 25 March 1927, *B–Th. Br.* II. 481.

[65] Karl Barth to Eduard Thurneysen, 26 Dec. 1926, *B–Th. Br.* II. 451; Eduard Thurneysen to Karl Barth, 29 Dec. 1926, ibid. 452.

The Reformed element in Barth was also a sticking point. In the early days of their friendship, nothing in Barth's theology could have warned Merz of the degree to which Barth would one day insist on carrying through a Reformed project. Once it did arise, Merz found it alienating. 'He no longer knows concretely where I stand; rather, he has only a general idea of the "Reformed" position I represent, with which he has no sympathy.'[66]

Merz was strongly opposed to the publication of Barth's prolegomena volume, *Die christliche Dogmatik im Entwurf.*[67] In response Barth wrote an impassioned *apologia* in the foreword. Without naming Merz explicitly, he gave voice to his friend's objections: that 'the spring of the "message of the Reformers" . . . has been followed all too quickly by a questionable scholastic autumn', and that the 'danger of orthodoxy' which had been hovering over his head for some time had now clearly befallen him.[68] Barth made it clear that what Merz wanted of him—that he should continue in the attitude of a prophet and not construct a new theology—rested on a fundamental misunderstanding. Human beings (whether prophets or theologians) stand with both feet on the earth. No one has control over the Word of God. God either speaks or He does not when He is spoken of. That is just as true for the prophet as it is for the theologian. Because that is the case, the prophet too can never escape being a theologian because he has, at best, a *doctrine* of the Word of God at his disposal. Even the marginal gloss and the corrective is a form of theology, an irregular form to be sure, but theology none the less. It does not lie in the power of any human being to bring about a Reformation. That decision rests with God alone. What a human being has to offer is always only a theology; whether regular or irregular is a secondary consideration.

In fairness to Merz, it has to be said that this understanding of theology represented a shift in Barth's outlook since the days when he had specifically said that he did not want to offer a new theology but only a marginal gloss and a corrective.[69] In those days Barth clearly could not unite the marginal gloss with dog-

---

[66] Karl Barth to Eduard Thurneysen, 7 Apr. 1927, *B–Th. Br.* II. 492.

[67] Karl Barth to Eduard Thurneysen, 26 Dec. 1926, *B–Th. Br.* II. 450.

[68] Barth, *Die christliche Dogmatik im Entwurf*, 7.

[69] Barth, 'Not und Verheißung der christlichen Verkündigung', in idem, *Das Wort Gottes und die Theologie*, 100.

matics. Subsequently, his view of dogmatics had changed. He had been able to define it in a way that did justice to his dialectical concerns. That was something that Merz had most certainly failed to understand. Merz need not have had any worries about a revival of scholasticism—not in the classical sense, at any rate.

During these years Barth watched the progress of Emil Brunner's theology from a carefully maintained distance. Brunner was widely acknowledged by most onlookers to be a dialectical theologian and he himself certainly saw the cause which Barth represented as being his own as well. The reticence which Barth displayed towards Brunner initially had to do more with personality differences than material objections. When *Zwischen den Zeiten* was founded in 1923, Barth advised caution in inviting Brunner to be a regular contributor.[70] He was troubled by the self-assurance with which Brunner carried out his attack on Schleiermacher in his book *Die Mystik und das Wort*. Brunner's ability to be so definite, so final, with regard to his judgement on Schleiermacher stemmed finally from his possession of the one key which would unlock all doors—his 'biblical-Reformation' faith.[71] Brunner had sent his manuscript to Barth in the autumn of 1923, so these reservations were expressed in letters to Thurneysen a full year before his review of the book made them public.[72] In the meantime, a serious material disagreement had surfaced.

Brunner was among those who visited Barth and Thurneysen at Pany during the summer vacation of 1924. The subject which the three discussed at length was Brunner's attempt to establish a propaedeutic or prolegomena to dogmatics which was based on a particular understanding of the relation of law and gospel. Brunner held that there was a knowledge of God which could be acquired in independence of revelation. This was a knowledge of God which was given through a knowledge of the law which is '*innata*, rational'. 'For knowledge of the law we need no revelation whatsoever . . .'[73] He had in mind a 'knowledge of God

[70] Karl Barth to Eduard Thurneysen, 16 Feb. 1923, *B–Th. Br.* II. 145.

[71] Karl Barth, 'Brunners Schleiermacherbuch', *Zwischen den Zeiten*, 2 (1924), 60.

[72] Karl Barth to Eduard Thurneysen, 31 Oct. 1923, *B–Th. Br.* II. 196; 30 Jan. 1924, ibid. 216.

[73] Emil Brunner to Karl Barth, undated, original in Karl Barth-Archiv, 2. Though undated, Brunner speaks as though Barth were still in Pany, which suggests a date sometime in the late summer of 1924.

through ideas, occurring autonomously, *semper et ubique*'.[74] Barth
told Brunner that this ordering of the relation of law and gospel
was Lutheran. That was enough to incite Brunner, upon return-
ing home, to study Calvin—especially *Institutes*, II. ix–xi on the
relation of the Old and New Testaments. Brunner reported his
findings to Barth. Calvin was no different from Luther in his
belief that knowledge of the law was innate. Calvin's departure
from Luther in his view of the relation of the Old and New
Testaments represented a loss to the Reformed position, not a
gain. Brunner saw in it a fatal transition from the careful delimitation of the *Deus dixit* to Jesus Christ to the orthodox doctrine
of inspiration, according to which the word of the Bible is made
synonymous with the Word of God.[75] For Brunner, a treatment
of the 'dialectic of law and gospel', wherein it is shown how
knowledge of the gospel is distinguished from knowledge of the
law, was the necessary propaedeutic to a dogmatics.[76]

The position for which Brunner argued at Pany and in the letter which followed his visit, could not have been unexpected to
Barth. Brunner had already expounded something like it in his
book on Schleiermacher.[77] There he explained that in knowing
the claim of God through the law, a person knows that he is
related to God—a relation which is, paradoxically, a relation of
the most inward participation in and the greatest distance to
God. 'The greatest proximity is at the same time the greatest distance. The more a person recognizes the law—which is his "spiritual life" and that upon which all spiritual creativity, all
humanity rests—the more he knows himself to be placed under
judgement.'[78] Thus, the net effect of this autonomous knowledge of the law is that a person knows himself to be placed under
judgement. This is not yet a knowledge of God which yields reconciliation. For that, one must be addressed by the Word. Still,
this knowledge of the law is preparatory to a hearing of the
Word. 'Grace . . . is not a result of the crisis, although it can
enter in only in the crisis, in "despair"—there, where the person
is at the end of his rope.'[79]

---

[74] Ibid.   [75] Ibid. 2.   [76] Ibid. 1.
[77] For this observation, I am indebted to Wilhelm Neuser, *Karl Barth in Münster*, 47–9.
[78] Emil Brunner, *Die Mystik und das Wort* (2nd edn.; Tübingen: J. C. B. Mohr, 1928),
298.
[79] Ibid. 298–9.

Years later, in 1934, Barth and Brunner would enter into a pamphet war—the famous 'Nein!' controversy—over precisely these issues. Even the argument over how Calvin was to be understood, which played a large role in the later controversy, is already adumbrated in 1924. Wilhelm Neuser's judgement that the controversy over the 'point of contact' in 1934 could have broken out any time after 1925 requires only a slight adjustment (from 1925 to 1924) to be absolutely correct. 'When Barth publicly hurled his "no!" against Brunner in the year 1934, an argument which had been going on for a long time merely came out into the open.'[80]

During the twenties, however, Barth was not at all inclined to take such differences of opinion as any great tragedy. He tended to play down such disagreements publicly in order to present a united front to the outside world. In his review of Brunner's Schleiermacher book, he did not even mention the issue of law and gospel at all. Neuser's assessment of the review is probably correct. 'One has the impression that Barth seeks to put Brunner's statements in order so that the justified concern of the book could not fall victim to a critique of Brunner's method.'[81] Barth saw the situation as being peaceful enough to allow everyone time to work out what they wanted in a clearer fashion. He contented himself with remarking to Thurneysen, 'I have a foreboding that Emil is rushing headlong into destruction with his "law and gospel", i.e. straight into the arms of Althaus and Holl. He should watch out.'[82] For a time, such patience seemed to be rewarded. Brunner's 1927 book, *The Mediator*, was praised by Barth,[83] probably in no small measure because of Brunner's adherence to the anhypostatic–enhypostatic model in Christology.

In the months which followed Barth's disappointment over Gogarten's book on the Trinity and Bultmann's *Jesus*, Barth lived up to his intentions to let the others go their way. He felt that an open argument between the leading figures of their movement could only add fuel to the fire of their opponents and cement their present division. If, on the other hand, they remained quiet, they would have time to come to some kind of resolution. If

[80] Neuser, 'Karl Barth in Münster', 49.   [81] Ibid. 47.
[82] Karl Barth to Eduard Thurneysen, 26 Nov. 1924, *B–Th. Br.* II. 293.
[83] Karl Barth to Eduard Thurneysen, 30 Dec. 1927, *B–Th. Br.* II. 555.

they could find none, there would be plenty of time for public debate later.

The publication of Barth's prolegomena in 1927 initiated a final phase in the relations of the dialectical theologians, a phase of clarification and, ultimately, of rupture. The first objections to the prolegomena came from Marburg. Bultmann's concern focused on the problem of the relation of philosophy to theology. He was quite ready to concede to Barth that philosophy could only be the *ancilla theologiae*—the handmaiden of theology, and not the mistress. If dogmatics should be enslaved to a system of philosophy, it would cease to be dogmatics. But if dogmatics ignores the help of philosophy, especially with respect to the investigation of the ontology underlying the concepts employed by dogmatics, then dogmatics would fall prey to an uncritically adopted, outmoded philosophy. Philosophy ignored does not go away; it surfaces as the mistress which is hidden in the old concepts which have been adopted. Having set out to remain free of philosophy, dogmatics would find itself in the end a handmaid. It was precisely this tendency which Bultmann thought he sensed in Barth's reappropriation of ancient dogmas.[84] The only way to ensure that dogmatics remains free is to *use* philosophy critically.

Bultmann certainly had a point, as Barth readily conceded. But what Bultmann was really calling on Barth to do was to abandon completely traditional concepts and to replace them with concepts which had been 'purified' by existential philosophy: 'because faith is the faith of a believer, i.e. of an existent person . . . dogmatics too can *only* speak in existential-ontological concepts.'[85] Bultmann here displayed a blind-spot of his own. In his conviction that dogmatics could make use of existentialist categories alone, Bultmann had, in fact, transgressed his own rule. He had made theology the servant of existentialist philosophy, for it was from that quarter that he derived the content of his leading theological concepts. It would be a while, however, before Barth would see this clearly. In his response, he defended his own position without subjecting Bultmann's to a searching criticism. In his defence, he said he was not sure he had the skill, the time, or the desire to find a new terminology. In any case, to set aside his current procedure would mean the abandonment of

---

[84] Rudolf Bultmann to Karl Barth, 8 June 1928, *B–B Br.* 81.
[85] Ibid. (Emphasis is mine).

the one task which he regarded as most important: to hear the voice of the Church and of the Bible.[86] But Barth gave no indication that he did not approve of Bultmann's own efforts to achieve a philosophically 'clean' terminology. Although he certainly had reservations, the full implications of Bultmann's approach were not yet clear to him.

Gogarten too had criticisms to make of Barth's prolegomena and he chose to make them public in a review.[87] Gogarten professed himself to be in complete agreement with the starting-point for theological reflection which Barth had insisted upon.[88] All questions in theology should be treated on the basis of God's self-revelation in Jesus Christ; the *Deus dixit* was the absolutely essential starting-point. To Gogarten's mind, however, Barth had not remained consistent with this starting-point. Barth frequently spoke as if he had a starting-point other than the one he had announced. Did not Barth often speak of God in a realm where He existed in and for Himself and, therefore, in isolation from the human being He had become in Jesus Christ? Was it not this 'God in isolation' which was Barth's secret starting-point?[89] Barth's starting-point then was not the revealed God, the 'God for us', but the as-yet-unrevealed God, God's being in itself and for itself.[90] For Gogarten, no talk of God was admissible which directed its attention to a realm above history. Even Barth's talk of *Urgeschichte* probably went too far.[91] Gogarten wanted to restrict all talk of God to the God who had become human. This restriction alone would bring Barth's theology into conformity with its announced starting-point. The source of Barth's inconsistency at this point lay in his refusal to think through and clarify in his own mind the concept of history.[92] Gogarten's criticism lay in the same direction as Bultmann's. Every concept employed in theology contains within it an understanding of God and an understanding of humanity (and with the latter, a particular understanding of history). By taking up traditional concepts in his discussion of the Trinity, for example, without having first critically examined their contents in the light of contemporary

---

[86] Karl Barth to Rudolf Bultmann, 12 June 1928, *B–B Br.* 84–6.

[87] Friedrich Gogarten, 'Karl Barths Dogmatik', *Theologische Rundschau*, NF 1 (1929), 60–80.

[88] Ibid. 70–80.   [89] Ibid. 72.   [90] Ibid. 72, 78.   [91] Ibid. 75.

[92] Ibid.

philosophy, Barth had committed himself to the understanding of God and humanity imbedded in them. This was the likely source of Barth's talk of a realm above history.

A similar problem arose for Gogarten on the side of Barth's understanding of humanity. Just as Barth's starting-point in reflecting upon God was the God in isolation from humanity, so his reflections on anthropology found their starting-point in the human in isolation from God. Gogarten found evidence for this assertion in the priority which Barth (apparently) gave to a phenomenological mode of consideration over the existential. For Gogarten, to construct an anthropology in this way is to forget the incarnation. The only proper starting-point for a truly theological anthropology is the human who is addressed by God's Word. If one thinks on the basis of a consideration of this human being, then one is, at the same time, taking seriously the fact that the Word became flesh.[93] Barth opened the door to such a starting-point when he set forth the thesis that God became human because 'only the human can *encounter* the human'.[94] But Barth chose not to go through this door. Behind this criticism lay Gogarten's conviction that only an I–Thou philosophy could help to make clear what is at stake in the situation of revelation, where a human being is addressed by another human being— though he did not make this clear in his review.

Gogarten's review was published in November 1928. Thurneysen greeted its arrival with the judgement that it was a bit 'dictatorial', but he retained the hope that somehow the various horns in their orchestra might still produce a common sound.[95] For his part, Barth remained silent. Certainly, the review did not prevent Barth from backing Gogarten as his successor at Münster that autumn, when he was called to succeed Otto Ritschl at Bonn, though his support was a bit half-hearted.[96]

Barth was thoroughly enjoying his free semester in the summer of 1929 and could even speak of himself as having entered an 'irenic phase',[97] when Emil Brunner's essay, 'The Other Task

---

[93] Friedrich Gogarten, 'Karl Barths Dogmatik', *Theologische Rundschau*, NF 1 (1929), 73.

[94] Ibid. 74.

[95] Eduard Thurneysen to Karl Barth, 15 Nov. 1928, *B–Th. Br.* II. 624.

[96] Karl Barth to Eduard Thurneysen, 16 Nov. 1929, *B–Th. Br.* II. 686.

[97] Karl Barth to Eduard Thurneysen, 30 May 1929, *B–Th. Br.* II. 662.

of Theology' appeared in *Zwischen den Zeiten*.[98] Brunner's essay represented not simply a criticism of this or that aspect of Barth's theology, but rather a far-reaching criticism of his entire procedure. To be sure, Brunner too saw the legitimacy of a truly dogmatic theology. But if dogmatic theology were pursued by itself, without attention to the 'other task' of theology, dangerous misunderstanding would arise. This 'other task' Brunner called 'eristic theology'.

'Eristic theology' was conceived by Brunner as polemical theology.[99] He disdained the word "apologetics" for two reasons. Because of the traditional connotations associated with "apologetics", the word easily suggested an attempt to defend the truth of the faith before the bar of reason. But it was precisely the 'axiom of reason'—the idea that reason is the final court of appeal in all questions of truth—which Brunner said had to be shattered, and it was the task of eristic theology to carry out the attack. Moreover, "apologetics" suggested a kind of Pharisaical attitude, according to which those under attack are a particular group of people standing outside the Church, rather than the "unbeliever" in us all. For both of these reasons, Brunner preferred the term 'eristics'.[100]

What then was eristics supposed to do, in concrete terms? The goal of eristic theology is to compel the "opponent" to abandon her "theoretical" attitude towards her existence and to begin to think existentially.[101] The "theoretical" attitude is the attitude of the spectator, of the person who is uninvolved, unconcerned. An "existential" attitude, by contrast, is one in which the person is passionately concerned about the problem of her own existence. For such a person, the problem of existence has become a life-or-death question of meaning. To compel this shift in attitude, eristics has to demonstrate to the "opponent" that a fundamental contradiction pervades her entire life, because she is not what she wants to be. The eristiker has to demonstrate further, that it is impossible for the individual to deliver herself from the contradiction. At the point at which a person sees the contradiction in her life and realizes the impossibility of helping herself, despair

---

[98] Emil Brunner, 'Die andere Aufgabe der Theologie', *Zwischen den Zeiten*, 7 (1929), 255–76.

[99] Ibid. 259.   [100] Ibid. 256, 258.   [101] Ibid. 261.

sets in. The "aesthetic"[102] or theoretical attitude has been left behind; an existential attitude has been adopted. She is now ready to hear the Word of God. Brunner trades heavily on Kierkegaardian concepts in this analysis and well he should; Kierkegaard was for him the greatest eristiker of all time and his description of the movement from the aesthetic to the existential reflects his adoption of Kierkegaard's dialectic of existence as the most appropriate way to describe how a person becomes a Christian.[103]

Brunner was quite confident that he could compel a person to adopt an existential attitude. He had seen it work hundreds of times.[104] And he was equally confident that this preparation would make a person more open to the approach of the Word. The latter confidence was rooted in his belief that to awaken a person to the contradiction of her existence was to awaken her to the question of God.[105] For when a person awakens to her own questionability, the only answer which will satisfy the longing which arises at that point is God. And even more basically, the contradiction in human existence is the question of God because the individual *already* knows God at some level of her being, and it is this knowledge which gives rise to the contradiction in the first place.

Brunner thus saw the question of God as intrinsic to human existence. 'Existence would not be a question if we did not participate in the truth of God. Only because we are in God, and know God, can we ask after Him.'[106] It is the 'grace of creation',[107] the *imago Dei*[108] in human beings, which makes it impossible that all knowledge of God has been eradicated by the Fall. 'The gospel does not turn to a person who knows nothing at all.'[109] The question of God arises in the first place because something of an original knowledge of God remains in the sinful creature. Of course this knowledge is, at the same time, not-knowledge. It is vitiated by sin. Hence arises the contradiction in human life. But knowledge remains, vitiated though it may be. This knowledge—or the question of God to which it gives rise—provides a 'point of contact'[110] in the human individual for

[102] Emil Brunner, 'Die andere Aufgabe der Theologie', *Zwischen den Zeiten*, 7 (1929), 265.
[103] Ibid. 266.   [104] Ibid. 272–3.   [105] Ibid. 262.   [106] Ibid. 263.
[107] Ibid. 264.   [108] Ibid. 263.   [109] Ibid. 262.   [110] Ibid.

the message of the gospel. It is the task of eristic theology to teach the "opponent" to understand the question which she is really asking. The first step towards this is to lay bare the illusory nature of the theoretical self-understanding which Brunner saw to be governing contemporary historical consciousness. To do so is to awaken men and women to a true understanding of their questionability so that they could then see that the question they are really asking is the question of God. Because the shattering of the illusory self-understanding of men and women is the first task of eristic theology, eristics is carried out on the soil of anthropology. Only there could it acquire an understanding of the precise contours of the self-understanding of contemporary men and women. Brunner thought that Gogarten's work in the area of anthropology marked him as *the* eristiker in contemporary theology.[111]

Brunner did not want to deny the importance of dogmatic theology, but he made it clear that, in his view, the need for eristic theology was more pressing. It was here that his criticism of Barth's prolegomena began in earnest. 'Let us not deceive ourselves: the cultivation of dogmatics for the sake of completely pure doctrine, as necessary as it is within the Church, is not even the most urgent need within the Church, to say nothing of the contemporary situation generally.'[112] To pursue dogmatics as Barth does, without treating eristics alongside of it as the initial exercise, places dogmatics in a very dangerous position. It gives the impression of detachment, of a view of faith and of truth which is not existential. Barth's dogmatics runs the risk of encouraging spectator theology, however much he himself may be existentially involved. 'It is questionable to me, for example, whether Barth has not, without wanting to, supported that theoretical misunderstanding through his transition from the eristics of *Romans* to the "presenting" style of the Dogmatics . . .'[113] Barth would only be in a position to guard against this misunderstanding if he were to take seriously the eristic task.

Barth himself knows how to speak to the real person. But the danger is great that his principles and attitude will entice others to speak no longer to the real person—and that always means to speak to today's men and women—and therefore, not to *speak* at all, but rather to

[111] Ibid. 260 n. 1.   [112] Ibid. 274.   [113] Ibid. 271.

declaim. Dogmatic theology has to fall prey to this danger when it does not have eristic theology next to it.[114]

The position which Brunner here developed represented a quite natural unfolding of his earlier reflections on the relation of law and gospel. The autonomous knowledge of God which he earlier defined in terms of a knowledge of the law, he now associated with the constitution of human beings in the image of God (the 'grace of creation'). His reassurances that he too knew well that faith was a creation of the Holy Spirit[115] could not but sound hollow when he went on to treat the 'point of contact' in men and women as a 'bridge to faith'.[116] In any case, his view that men and women are 'addressable' because there is no one who can avoid seeking God,[117] could not have placed him more at odds with Barth. For Barth, it is simply not true that all people, by nature, are seeking after God. No one seeks, by nature, after God. The question of God (if it is really the question of the God and Father of our Lord Jesus Christ) only first arises where God has made Himself known in the event of revelation. Far from being something in a person to which the Word is addressed, the question of God is awakened only by the address itself. That men and women have an awareness of the ambiguity of existence, or that they are often, as a result, *homo religiosus*, that they seek meaning, fulfilment, etc. is all to be granted. But so far from being identical with a seeking for God, all of these searches are just the opposite: they are attempts to avoid asking the question of *God*. The reality of the knowledge of God has to precede the question.

Barth's reaction was, however, quite calm. Thurneysen felt that Brunner's essay called for a response.[118] Barth was inclined to agree but thought it best that someone else undertake it. He suggested Karl Hartenstein, the director of the Basler Mission.[119] Hartenstein had already told Thurneysen of his disagreement with Brunner, and Barth thought that a response from one who had spent his life in missionary work would be a more credible

---

[114] Emil Brunner, 'Die andere Aufgabe der Theologie', *Zwischen den Zeiten*, 7 (1929), 274.

[115] Ibid. 259.   [116] Ibid. 273.   [117] Ibid. 267.

[118] Eduard Thurneysen to Karl Barth, 3 July 1929, *B–Th. Br.* II. 669.

[119] Karl Barth to Eduard Thurneysen, 9 July 1929, *B–Th. Br.* II. 672. As things turned out, Hartenstein did not write a response.

witness against Brunner's talk of a 'point of contact'. In any case, he seemed unwilling to allow any unpleasantness to disturb his idyllic summer.

The 'irenic phase' proved to be short-lived. During the autumn, Barth had too many demands on his time to devote much attention to his friends. He was busy preparing his response to Przywara and Augustinianism, 'The Holy Spirit and the Christian Life', which he delivered in early October. But Gogarten was not one to let sleeping dogs lie. He seemed determined to pressure Barth into a change of direction. In the last number of *Zwischen den Zeiten* for the year 1929, a new essay appeared from his pen. The title was 'The Problem of a Theological Anthropology'.[120] In it, Gogarten argued that the problem which most urgently thrusts itself upon theology in any age depends upon how men and women understand themselves in the period in question. Since the Middle Ages, a radical shift in human self-understanding had occurred. During the Middle Ages, humanity was understood to be the goal and centre of God's creative activity. The world of nature was seen as redolent with purpose, having been created by God in order to provide a theatre of His glory which could lead men and women to a knowledge of Himself and provide them with enjoyment and sustenance. With the rise of modernity, all of this changed. The human species was dislodged from its position as centre of the world and, as a result, the significance of humankind was no longer self-evident. According to the modern self-understanding, any significance which humanity has is not bestowed but created by human action. The concept of history had become the key to anthropology in modern times. The complete historicity of human life was affirmed. The modern person understands herself as the subject of history. History is a series of objectifications of the human spirit.[121]

Now Gogarten was not saying that he affirmed the modern self-understanding of men and women; far from it. But he did feel that this self-understanding posed the most decisive challenge which theology had to face. Gogarten saw the anthropological turn which theology had taken in Schleiermacher as the

---

[120] Friedrich Gogarten, 'Das Problem einer theologischen Anthropologie', *Zwischen den Zeiten*, 7 (1929), 493–511.

[121] Ibid. 503–4.

incorporation of the modern self-understanding into theology itself. Dialectical theology was right to want to free itself of this anthropology.

But Gogarten was also convinced that the anthropological turn had been unavoidable. If theology was really to speak to the concretely existing men and women of its day, it had to speak to them precisely at that point at which they sought to makes themselves free of God. In modern times, this meant addressing people at the point of their self-understanding as historical (creative) beings. It meant further that anthropology had to be at the centre of theological reflection.

I am convinced that one may not follow Schleiermacher on his way for even a single step . . . But today, one cannot avoid a very explicit discussion of the problem of anthropology. Yes, and more than that, I am of the opinion that it is not possible today to do real theology . . . in any other way than by placing the problem of anthropology in the centre of attention. Only when that happens will a theology be created which really achieves that which it is there for, namely to be an aid to the living and public proclamation of God's Word.[122]

Gogarten clearly understood the anthropologizing of theology in two senses. Anthropologizing could mean the incorporation of the modern self-understanding into theology as its most fundamental, constitutive element. This Gogarten rejected. But in so far as anthropologizing meant that in all its work, theology should be addressing itself to that hidden element in human consciousness which secured the individual from a hearing of the Word of God, Gogarten was in favour of it. Concretely, this meant for Gogarten that the first task of theology was to clarify its own concepts, to uncover and excise any alien elements in them which had been provided by the modern spirit. In order to do this, it must first illuminate and clarify the self-understanding of contemporary men and women. Gogarten's concern in all of this was clearly a practical one. Only where theology attacks men and women at the point of their deepest certainty and deepest need will it be able to proclaim the gospel in a way that will make it comprehensible.[123] The degree of agreement with Brunner's programme of eristics emerges quite clearly here.

---

[122] Friedrich Gogarten, 'Das Problem einer theologischen Anthropologie', *Zwischen den Zeiten*, 7 (1929), 505.

[123] Ibid. 510.

Of course, this programme for theology had to collide with Barth's own. Gogarten's starting-point was determined by the self-understanding of men and women and, to that extent, by the *Zeitgeist*. Theology, for him, was not (in the first instance, at least) a matter of reflection upon the Word of God, of trying to construct theology in such a way as to reflect in itself the way taken by the Word in addressing itself to human beings. There can be no question that Gogarten was stepping up the pressure being placed upon Barth to change his course. Barth could not, in the face of repeated challenges to his entire procedure, maintain his policy of peaceful coexistence with his friends. A decision was being thrust upon him. He could decide for a change or he could decide to follow resolutely the path he had already laid down for himself. If he chose to do the latter and rejected the appeals of Brunner and Gogarten, he could make his rejection public or he could make it in private. Those were the options before him. Brunner and Gogarten were campaigning for a public response.

In early January 1930 Barth heard a lecture in Münster given by Friedrich Karl Schumann, Professor of Theology in Gießen. The subject treated was apologetics. A few days later Barth was in Marburg to deliver a paper of his own, 'Philosophical and Theological Ethics'.[124] Discussion with Bultmann followed and Barth returned home, disturbed, frustrated, and at the limits of his endurance. He communicated his concern to Thurneysen.

My dear Eduard, a very bad business is brewing all along the line which I want under no circumstances to have any part of. Is it not true that gradually all of the people who apparently stood close to us want something which we . . . did not want and which stands in the closest possible connection with, if it is not identical to, that which we fought against from the very beginning . . .?[125]

Barth cited, as examples, Bultmann's 'theology of believing existence', which derived its legitimation from an existential philosophy; Gogarten's stress on historicity and anthropology; and Brunner and Schumann, in their belief that they were able to make unbelieving men and women 'unsure' of themselves. Barth could not see in any of these attempts anything other than a renewal of the relationship of theology to philosophy which had

[124] This paper was never published.
[125] Karl Barth to Eduard Thurneysen, 26 Jan. 1930, *B–Th. Br.* II. 700.

prevailed in the nineteenth century. The only difference was that the philosophy which now provided the 'untheological presupposition' upon which everything else was made to depend was a negative, existential philosophy.

I don't know. Maybe I am seeing things too passionately during the heat of the semester, but all the hairs on my head simply stand on end when I consider the entire household by which we are most closely surrounded, and I don't know whether it might not come one day to a great resistance and farewell article to Emil, Paul [Tillich], Friedrich, Rudolf, *e tutti quanti* . . .[126]

Time did not improve Barth's disposition. If anything, he had become even more unyielding and angry when he wrote to Bultmann ten days later. Barth spoke of their discussions together in Marburg and said:

What I heard from you ties in with a lecture by Schumann that I heard eight days earlier here in Münster, and also with the basically uncongenial article by Gogarten, and finally with Brunner's eristics, to form a pattern which I might have spotted earlier but which has only just struck me, slow as I am with concepts. From my standpoint, all of you, though your concerns differ from mine in different ways, represent a large-scale return to the fleshpots of Egypt. I mean that if I am not deceived, all of you—in a very new and very different way from that of the nineteenth century—are trying to understand faith as a human possibility, or, if you will, as grounded in a human possibility, and therefore you are once again surrendering theology to philosophy. I cannot as yet envisage what this formal and fundamental return to old paths— the forsaking of which is one of my most pressing concerns—means for the material content of theology. To see it clearly, I should have to know your dogmatic and ethical principles, both in detail and as a whole, far better than I do. . . . Where people play around with a natural theology within the framework of a preunderstanding that has not been attained theologically, the inevitable result is that they end up in rigidities and reactionary corners which are no better than the liberalisms of others. On the contrary, where this happens, I would rather be in hell with the Religious Socialists than land up in a heaven in which it will be one's lot to be condemned to a 'state of life' for all eternity, to have to gaze at a "Thou" that is foreordained by creation, and to have to maintain this condition for redemption.[127]

    [126] Karl Barth to Eduard Thurneysen, 26 Jan. 1930, *B–Th. Br.* II. 701.
    [127] Karl Barth to Rudolf Bultmann, 5 Feb. 1930, *B–B Br.* 100–2. Barth is referring at the end of the passage to Gogarten's favourite themes ('states of life', etc.).

Now those were fighting words! The explosion within *Zwischen den Zeiten* which Barth had foreseen as a possibility as early as April 1927 had become a reality.[128] The 'farewell article' of which Barth spoke in the letter to Thurneysen would not be written until the end of 1933. But the rift was already quite real. Peaceful coexistence had given way to cold war.

[128] Karl Barth to Rudolf Bultmann, 28 Apr. 1927, *B–B Br.* 70.

10

Fides quaerens intellectum

(BONN, MARCH 1930–JUNE 1935)

1. THE END OF THE WEIMAR REPUBLIC

The years 1929–31 saw the return of political and economic crises. Years later Barth would look back on these years and reproach himself for not taking the threat of National Socialism more seriously. 'I was thoroughly wrong at that time in not perceiving danger in National Socialism, which had already begun its ascent. From the very beginning, its ideas and methods and its leading figures all seemed to me to be quite absurd. I thought that the German people were simply too sensible to fall prey to that possibility.'[1] Barth's memory is correct. He did not take the threat posed by right-wing political fanaticism seriously until it was already well established.

During its brief history, the Weimar Republic saw fifteen different governments come and go.[2] The next-to-last was the so-called 'Great Coalition', put together by SPD Chancellor Hermann Müller in June 1928. The members of his cabinet were disunited from the outset. Each tended stubbornly to represent the interests of his own party so that the government never functioned as a true coalition.[3] It was certainly in no position to cope with a crisis.

Crisis was not long in coming. During the winter of 1928/9, the economy fell into a recession. By spring the number of unemployed seeking compensation had reached 1.5 million. The problem was exacerbated immeasurably by the stock-market crash of October 1929. The effects of the depression were felt around the world, but in Germany they were particularly devastating. The Müller cabinet resigned on 27 March 1930—just as

---

[1] Karl Barth, 'Zwischenzeit', *Kirchenblatt für die reformierte Schweiz*, 118 (1962), 38.
[2] Craig, *Germany, 1866–1945*, 509.   [3] Ibid. 524.

Karl Barth was arriving in Bonn. Three days later a new government was formed under Heinrich Brüning of the Catholic
Centre Party. It was also a new *kind* of government. Brüning was
convinced that a desperate situation called for extreme measures.
He proposed to address the fiscal crisis by raising taxes and
reducing government spending, in the hope of promoting sav-
ings and bringing down inflation.[4] He knew his plan would be
unpopular and would not receive the support of the parliament,
but that mattered little to him. He was prepared to enforce his
policy with or without parliamentary support. What that meant
in practice was that he was prepared to invoke Article 48 of the
Weimar constitution: an emergency-powers provision that gave
to the President (Paul von Hindenburg) the right to enact policy
by decree. And that is precisely what happened.

On 16 July parliament voted against Brüning's budget and the
Chancellor responded by promulgating his budget by emergency
decree (with the President's support). When the Reichstag
demanded that the decree be abrogated, Brüning dissolved the
Reichstag and called for new parliamentary elections on 14
September. In the meantime, his budget remained in force by
presidential decree.

It was a brash act. As Gordon Craig has pointed out, this was
hardly an auspicious time for an election.

There were dozens of politicians in Germany in 1930 who had the
gravest misgivings about holding elections in the middle of a deepening
depression, when people were bewildered and resentful and all too
ready to listen to radical tub-thumpers. . . . The election campaign itself
was bound to be so violent that it would jeopardize civil order, and the
Reichstag that resulted from it would almost certainly be less effective
and manageable than the present one, which still had two years to run.
Unless one were willing to abolish the Reichstag entirely—and not
even the military politicians had reached that point yet—new elections
might make the government's position intolerable.[5]

The days and nights before the election were indeed filled with
violence in the streets. The real beneficiaries were the extremists
of the left and the right. The Communists tallied 4,600,000 votes,
giving them 77 seats in the Reichstag. The Nazis, who had
received only 809,000 votes and 12 seats in parliament in the

---

[4] Ibid. 538.   [5] Ibid. 540.

1928 election, now received 6,400,000 votes and 112 seats, making them the second strongest party in Germany (behind the SPD).[6] The Nazis celebrated their victory with more violence in the streets.

Brüning had hoped for a parliament more amenable to his programme. What he got was a parliament rendered completely dysfunctional by the frequent walk-outs of Nazi representatives. The next two years saw one presidential decree after another, as unemployment rose to 5,615,000 by February 1931. Although technically the Republic endured until the constitution was set aside by Hitler, for all practical purposes the Republic came to an end in July 1930, when Heinrich Brüning invoked the emergency-powers act, thus setting aside parliamentary democracy in favour of government by presidential decree.

In all honesty it must be said that Karl Barth was quite slow to perceive the danger that threatened the Republic. He continued to support a socialist direction in politics.[7] But the fact that he could make light in January 1929 of having sung 'Deutschland, Deutschland über alles' with gusto at a celebration of Bismarck's achievements demonstrates that, at that time, he was still relatively unburdened by any warning signs that the Republic was in danger.[8]

When did Barth become more aware of the threat to the Republic? Although such an awareness probably dawned gradually, it seems likely that it was only in the aftermath of the September 1930 elections that he recognized what was happening. 'After moving to Germany, I imposed upon myself a political interlude which lasted nearly ten years. But early last year, in view of the fact that right-wing terror was gaining the upper hand, I thought it right to make it clear with whom I would like to be imprisoned and hanged.'[9] One would want to be cautious here until more evidence is available, but such testimony would seem to suggest that Barth's 'political awakening' occurred in early 1931.

---

[6] Craig, *Germany, 1866–1945*, 542.

[7] Barth voted socialist in the 1928 elections. Karl Barth to Eduard Thurneysen, 18 Aug. 1928, *B–Th. Br.* II. 607.

[8] See Neuser, *Karl Barth in Münster*, 64. Neuser is here citing from a letter from Barth to Emil Brunner dated 14 Jan. 1929.

[9] Karl Barth to Hans Asmussen, 14 Jan. 1932, copy in Karl Barth-Archiv, Basle, Switzerland. Barth is here explaining why he joined the SPD on 1 May 1931.

2. TEACHING ACTIVITIES IN BONN

Barth was officially called to Bonn on 26 October 1929.[10] He stayed on at Münster one more semester, during which he served as Dean of the Faculty. He arrived in Bonn in March 1930 and began teaching there in the second semester. Barth's appointment had an instant impact on the fortunes of the theological faculty. The number of students doubled immediately (from 170 to 340); and reached a peak of around 400 by 1933.[11] Barth's main lecture course was held in the second largest lecture hall in the university—a room which seated 322. Remarkably enough, given the number of theological students in Bonn at the time, Barth regularly succeeded in filling this lecture hall to capacity.[12]

Barth's seminars were by now so popular that he was forced to limit participation to thirty regular members and thirty auditors.[13] Students earned the right to participate through their performance on an examination which Barth would set in advance of the seminar in question. The topics chosen for the seminars during the first years in Bonn showed that Barth was still preoccupied with Catholicism and natural theology. The list of course offerings in Bonn (so far as I have been able to establish it[14]) is as follows.

Summer semester 1930:
    Lectures: Ethics I; Exposition of James
    Seminar: Anselm's *Cur Deus homo?*
Winter semester 1930/3:
    Lectures: Ethics II; Exposition of Philippians
    Seminar: The Reformation Doctrine of Sanctification
Summer semester 1931:
    Lecture: Prolegomena to Dogmatics (*Church Dogmatics* I/1)
    Seminar: Schleiermacher: Introduction to the *Glaubenslehre*
Winter semester 1931/2:
    Lecture: Prolegomena to Dogmatics (*Church Dogmatics* I/1)

---

[10] J. F. Gerhard Goeters, 'Karl Barth in Bonn, 1930–1935', *Evangelische Theologie*, 47 (1987), 139.
[11] Ibid. 140.   [12] Ibid. 141.   [13] Ibid.
[14] Unlike the lists provided for Barth's years in Göttingen and Münster, this one is incomplete. It has been culled from Eberhard Busch's biography. But Busch does not make mention of every lecture course and seminar taught.

Seminar: The Problem of Natural Theology
Summer semester 1932:
  Lecture: Prolegomena to Dogmatics (*Church Dogmatics* I/1)
  Seminar: Ritschl's *Unterricht in der christlichen Religion*
Winter semester 1932/3:
  Lectures: Theology of the Nineteenth Century I; Exercises in Sermon Preparation
  Seminar: Luther's Large Catechism
Summer semester 1933:
  Lectures: Theology of the Nineteenth Century II; Exposition of John's Gospel
Winter semester 1933/4:
  Lectures: Prolegomena to Dogmatics (*Church Dogmatics* I/2); The Sermon on the Mount
  Seminar: The Doctrine of Justification
Summer semester 1934:
  Lecture: Prolegomena to Dogmatics (*Church Dogmatics* I/2)
  Seminar: Theology of the Formula of Concord

One of the perks of Barth's new position in Bonn was a fund for visiting lecturers. Guests included Heinrich Scholz (from Münster), who spoke in his seminar on Anselm in the summer semester of 1930 on the *Proslogion*; Scholz again in December 1930, speaking on the question of whether it was possible to view evangelical theology as a science; and Erich Przywara in the seminar on natural theology in the winter semester 1931/2.

The growing tensions with the other dialectical theologians continued to preoccupy Barth during his first year in Bonn. In July 1930 he gave a special lecture in Frankfurt and Heidelberg entitled 'Theology and the Men and Women of Today'. Though Brunner was never cited by name, it is obvious that this lecture constituted Barth's public response to his call for an eristic theology. The definition of theology which Barth offered here already constituted a rejection of Brunner's programme. Theology, he said, is critical reflection on the Word of God which is heard in the Church. Because the Word, where it is heard, creates the Church, Barth could insist 'Theology is therefore a function of the Church.'[15] This affirmation carried with it a contrary: theo-

---

[15] Karl Barth, 'Die Theologie und der heutige Mensch', *Zwischen den Zeiten*, 8 (1930), 375.

logy is *not* reflection on the meaning of life. Theology has to return again and again to its starting-point in the Word, in the knowledge that we humans are not able to reflect on the final, deepest, most proper meaning of our existence because our existence has irretrievably lost its meaning. To begin with this knowledge is already to confess that theology belongs to the Church, for the Church is the place where every humanly contrived answer to the question of meaning has been seen to be unworthy of belief. 'Meaning is the truth which we find. The Word is the truth which gives itself to be found. That is the difference. . . . The truth and certainty of the Word of God is the place from which, with the Church itself, theology can only *proceed*—after which it can in no way *strive*.'[16] It is impossible not to see in this a response to one of Brunner's most cherished assumptions: namely, that a proper philosophical analysis of human existence would make it clear that all men and women are in some way striving after God. Barth's answer is that human existence has been so deprived of its true meaning that it cannot of itself yield the right question. It is not surprising then, that in the light of the Word, *all* the questions which men and women ask are seen to be an evasion of the question of God. In no way can an analysis of existence provide a *preambula fidei* or bridge to the Word. 'Certainty of God *precedes* self-certainty every time.'[17]

But theology as critical reflection on the Church's proclamation in the light of the Word is a most peculiar science. The criterion by which the Church measures is the Word, and the Word is something which cannot be reckoned with, humanly speaking. It cannot be brought into play by those who wish to judge themselves in its light. It can only be prayed for because it remains sovereignly free.[18] The truth of theology depends completely and absolutely on the Self-attestation of its criterion, and that means on the divine choice, predestination, the decision which falls upon it.[19] But what kind of science is this whose fundamental axiom is not given to it? At the heart of Christian theology properly understood is a scandal, a stumbling-block, namely the divine predestination.

How can modern men and women relate themselves to this science, given the fact that it contains a scandal at its

---

[16] Ibid. 375–6.   [17] Ibid. 378.   [18] Ibid.   [19] Ibid. 380.

starting-point? Barth outlines three responses which he rejects. The first is atheism. Atheism recognizes the scandal clearly and having recognized it, can only reject theology. The second response is that of traditional liberalism, which entails a redefining of the nature of theology so as to remove the offence. The third response is, for our purposes, the most interesting, for it is here that Barth would clearly like to locate his erstwhile fellow-travellers, Gogarten, Brunner, and Bultmann. Of all the responses given by modern men and women to the scandal of theology, this response is the most dangerous. For the attempt which is made here to domesticate the scandal and render it harmless is far more subtle than that of liberalism.[20] The scandal is recognized and pronounced good. But it is pronounced good from the standpoint of a secured position, on the basis of which use can be made of the scandal. Here, no less than with liberalism, there is no willingness to rest content with a Word which can only ground itself. An attempt is made to ground the possibility of faith in human life and thus to make it a human possibility. But where liberalism sought a kind of positive grounding, the new response seeks a negative grounding. Differences aside, both tendencies find their classical forerunner in Thomas.

Should there not be a metaphysic which shows that knowledge must necessarily be crowned by faith, the natural virtues by supernatural virtues, in order to be genuine knowledge and genuine virtue? Perhaps a negative metaphysic, an apparently very un-Thomistic metaphysic, not of the completion but rather of the perplexities of human knowing; an ontology of the hollow-space [*Hohlraum*] whose size corresponds precisely to that of faith and theology, and would, to that extent, point clearly to their truth? An 'eristic' theology which would have the task of making it clear to modern men and women, with fatherly sagacity, that they must necessarily entangle themselves in evil self-contradiction in that they think themselves able to help themselves without Christian faith? Or a doctrine of history whose truth would correspond precisely to that which the biblical presentation of the relation of God and humanity describes as reality? Or an anthropology whose innermost kernel would disclose itself as at least the photographic negative of Christology?[21]

---

[20] Karl Barth, 'Die Theologie und der heutige Mensch', *Zwischen den Zeiten*, 8 (1930), 392.

[21] Ibid. 394.

Barth was very concerned at the time of this address with a situation which he saw to be developing in the evangelical
churches in Germany. Everywhere, he noted, there were people
in the Church who, having grown weary of atheism and liberalism, were 'rediscovering their Catholic hearts.' By this, Barth
meant that from every corner and in every possible way, the cry
for natural theology was being heard with increasing intensity.
This development represented, to his mind, 'the most dangerous
possibility in a most dangerous moment'.[22]

In a less direct way, this lecture also constituted a response to
Brunner's criticism that Barth's style of theologizing in his prolegomena represented a de-existentializing of the concept of faith.
Brunner had suggested that Barth had shifted from an eristic theology in *Romans* to a 'presenting' style of dogmatic theology.
From the outset, this valuation rested on a misunderstanding.
Romans was not eristic theology, and could not be judged so simply because it was written in an expressionistic style which was
popular in those days. For it was not directed to the 'opponent'
of faith; it was directed (as was *Die christliche Dogmatik im
Entwurf*) to that person within the Church who was all too certain of her faith. But the major issue here was whether the style
of dogmatics alone, or the absence of an eristic theology alongside of it, meant a de-existentializing of faith. Barth's answer is
clear. Faith is the *risk* of obedience to a command which can be
secured by no grounding of human contrivance.[23] It is precisely
a proper understanding of the Word of God which can only be
grounded in itself by an act of sovereign freedom which ensures
that faith can only be ventured as an act of daring, and therefore
as existential in the highest degree. Brunner, by contrast, had
sought to secure the possibility of faith on the human side by
grounding it in an existential-philosophical analysis of human
existence. From Barth's point of view, it is Brunner who has de-
existentialized faith by trying to anchor its possibility on the
human side. Once the possibility of faith has been grounded in a
human capacity—even a God-given human capacity—all
remaining talk of decision, encounter, anxiety, etc. is just an
empty show.[24]

Throughout the tumultuous year 1930, Bultmann tried to

[22] Ibid. 395.   [23] Ibid. 393.   [24] Ibid. 393-4.

bring the "pillars" of dialectical theology together in Marburg for a frank, face-to-face airing of differences.[25] But the plan came to nothing. Gogarten elected not to come. Brunner's schedule conflicted to some extent with the dates proposed by Bultmann (for October), and in the end, given the difficulties which stood in the way, Barth decided to forgo the trip to Marburg as well.[26] The proposed summit meeting was never rescheduled.

In spite of the rift which was now obvious to all concerned, Barth continued to play his role on the editorial staff of *Zwischen den Zeiten*, and probably could have done so indefinitely had not the political situation changed so dramatically in January 1933. On the day after Hitler's seizure of power, Barth met with Albert Lempp, the owner of Christian Kaiser Verlag (which published *Zwischen den Zeiten*). He suggested that the time had come to lay the journal to rest. Lempp persuaded him to let things continue for the time being, but from that point on, the names of the editors no longer appeared on the title page. Each would be responsible only for his own work.[27] But when in the course of that summer, Barth saw in print Gogarten's affirmation of Wilhelm Stapel's dictum that the law of God is identical with the law of the German people, Barth had had enough. Gogarten had made common cause with the 'German Christians'. Was this not the logical conclusion of the direction he had been taking for many years? On 18 October 1933 Barth composed his 'Farewell' to *Zwischen den Zeiten*. In the current political situation, Barth thought it could only confuse people to allow them to see his articles alongside those of a person whose theology he regarded as a betrayal of the gospel.[28]

Aside from preoccupation with in-fighting amongst the dialectical theologians and anxiety over developments in the political sphere, Barth's major concern in the period stretching from the summer of 1930 to the following summer was the production of a book on Anselm. We must now undertake a close examination of the teachings in that book, and their significance for Barth's development.

[25] Rudolf Bultmann to Karl Barth, 16 Feb. 1930, *B–B Br.* 104.
[26] Rudolf Bultmann to Karl Barth, 2 Oct. 1930, *B–B Br.* 113; Karl Barth to Rudolf Bultmann, 3 Oct. 1930, ibid. 114–15.
[27] Busch, *Karl Barth*, 223–4.
[28] Karl Barth, 'Abschied', 539–40.

3. WHAT'S NEW IN *ANSELM*?

(i) *The Nature of the Problem*

It is a commonplace in the literature on Barth's development that through his study of Anselm, Barth was led to a new starting-point in thought; a thought-form so new that he was forced to abandon his original project in dogmatics (*Die christliche Dogmatik*) as a 'false start'[29] and begin again at the beginning with a new dogmatics, the *Church Dogmatics*. Barth himself deserves a good bit of responsibility for the elaboration of this view. In 1939 he was invited by *The Christian Century* to contribute an essay to their 'How My Mind Has Changed' series. There Barth wrote,

in these years I have had to rid myself of the last remnants of a philosophical, i.e. anthropological . . . foundation and exposition of Christian doctrine. The real document of this farewell is, in truth, not the much-read brochure *Nein!*, directed against Brunner in 1934, but rather the book about the evidence for God of Anselm of Canterbury which appeared in 1931. Among all my books I regard this as the one written with the greatest satisfaction. . . . For before, I had been at least partly hampered . . . by the eggshells of philosophical systematics.[30]

There can be no question that Barth's characterization of his development in terms of an overcoming of the 'eggshells of philosophical systematics' greatly influenced the seminal study of his theology written in 1951 by Hans Urs von Balthasar. Von Balthasar depicted Barth's development in the 1920s as a rather single-minded attempt to overcome every last vestige of grounding of theology in philosophy. The decisive turning-point was seen to have come with the study of Anselm.[31] As noted above, in the Introduction, von Balthasar characterized this shift as a 'turn from dialectic to analogy'. In accordance with this scheme, "dialectic" was seen as an attempt to ground theology philosophically by means of the categories provided by existentialism and phenomenology; "analogy" as an attempt to develop a "pure" theology, grounded in revelation alone.

Barth lent further encouragement to von Balthasar's thesis of a turn from dialectic to analogy in the preface to the second edition of *Fides quaerens intellectum* in 1958.

---

[29] Barth, *KD* III/4, p. viii; *CD* III/4, p. xii.
[30] Barth, *How I Changed my Mind*, 42–4.   [31] Von Balthasar, *Karl Barth*, 101–2.

Only a comparatively few commentators, for example Hans Urs von Balthasar, have noticed that my interest in Anselm was never a side-issue for me . . . most of them have completely failed to see that in this book on Anselm, one encounters if not *the* key, then certainly *a* very important key to understanding the movement of thought which has urged itself upon me more and more in the *Church Dogmatics* as the only one appropriate to theology.[32]

If Barth's self-evaluation in 1939 had given shape to von Balthasar's interpretation, then by 1958 von Balthasar's schema had further reinforced Barth's view. That the 'movement of thought' first announced in *Fides quaerens intellectum* came 'more and more', as Barth put it, to stamp the *Church Dogmatics*, is reflective of von Balthasar's judgement that the *analogia fidei* only gradually bore fruit in the *Church Dogmatics*.

Subsequent interpreters have, virtually without exception, followed von Balthasar in seeing the Anselm book as a kind of watershed in Barth's development. Michael Beintker's conclusion is representative of a host of scholars: 'in Barth's Anselm book, the transition from *Die christliche Dogmatik* to the positions of the *Church Dogmatics* is reflected. Here, a turn in the starting-point in thought [*Denkansatz*] becomes tangible, which allows us to fix the definitive departure from "dialectical theology" at *Fides quaerens intellectum.*'[33]

But how well does this picture accord with the facts? Is there really a new *Denkansatz* in the Anselm book such as would justify the conclusion that what Barth discovered in his study of Anselm forced him to abandon *Die christliche Dogmatik* and start over again? The answer which will be given here is negative. The book on Anselm does not give expression to a 'revolution'[34] in Barth's thought; there is no new starting-point to be found here. Moreover, the theological method set forth in this book is not essentially different from the dogmatic method which was first outlined in the Göttingen Prolegomena. Beintker is closer to the truth when he says, 'Barth's thinking in the 1920s steers

---

[32] Karl Barth, *Fides quaerens intellectum: Anselms Beweis der Existenz Gottes im Zusammenhang seines theologischen Programms*, ed. Eberhard Jüngel and Ingolf Ulrich Dalferth (Zurich: TVZ, 1981), 6; ET *Anselm: Fides quaerens intellectum, Anselm's Proof of the Existence of God in the Context of his Theological Scheme*, trans. Ian W. Robertson (London: SCM Press, 1960), 11.

[33] Beintker, *Die Dialektik in der 'dialektischen Theologie' Karl Barths*, 183.

[34] Frei, 'The Doctrine of Revelation in the Thought of Karl Barth', 194.

toward the programme of theological rationality unfolded in the
Anselm book almost as if directed to a goal'.[35]

(ii) *Anselm in Die christliche Dogmatik*

The immediate stimulus for Barth's book on Anselm was a special lecture given by his friend, Heinrich Scholz, in conjunction
with his seminar on Anselm's Christology. The lecture took
place on 11 July 1930. The subject chosen was the "ontological
proof" for the existence of God found in *Proslogion* 2–4. As a
result of this lecture, and the conversation which followed, Barth
decided to devote his attention to a new interpretation of those
pivotal chapters of the *Proslogion*.[36] He was thoroughly convinced
that what was offered there was not at all a "proof" in the usual
sense of the term. One could not rightly apprehend what "proving" meant to Anselm unless one saw chapters 2–4 of the
Proslogion in the context of his overall theological programme,
that is, the *way* to theological knowledge advocated by Anselm.

Before proceeding to a sketch of Barth's Anselm interpretation, it is important to note that this interpretation had been prepared for for some time. Barth first dealt with Anselm extensively
in the summer semester of 1926, in his first seminar on *Cur Deus
homo?* (the Bonn seminar was a repetition of the 1926 seminar).
The first fruit of that earlier study is to be found in *Die christliche
Dogmatik*, where Anselm's way of theological knowledge was
advocated as a helpful corrective to that of neo-Protestantism.[37]

The concern which controlled Barth's reflections in the section of *Die christliche Dogmatik* in which this comparison appears
was establishing the way of knowledge which leads to the reality
of God. Here, as everywhere in Barth's consideration of this
problem from *Romans* I on, the nature of the object to be known
determines the way taken in knowing. The Word of God which
constitutes the object of dogmatic thinking is no "object" in the
ordinary sense. The Word of God is the Subject who veils or
hides Himself in ordinary objects in order to make Himself
known. But in doing so, He is not transformed into those objects
which veil Him. He makes Himself objective in our world

---

[35] Beintker, *Die Dialektik in der 'dialektischen Theologie' Karl Barths*, 193.
[36] Barth, *Fides quaerens intellectum*, 1; ET *Anselm*, 7.
[37] Barth, *Die christliche Dogmatik im Entwurf*, 131–8.

without surrendering His non-objectivity,[38] His irreducible Subjecthood. To put it in terms of Cartesian epistemology,[39] God is never caught in the polarity of subject and object as are all ordinary objects of nature and history. On the other hand, the veils in which the Word gives Himself to be known *are* caught in that polarity, and are therefore subject to all the limitations imposed upon them by the ordinary processes of human knowing.

An object which was the content of my consciousness, whose knowledge rests in me just as much as in itself (as is, indeed, to be said of the 'world in nature and history')—I am as superior to such an object as it is to me. I have just as much power over it as it has over me. I dispose of it, as it disposes of me. In no way does its reality rest in itself; rather, it is reality only in the *correlation* of known object and knowing subject . . . To these objects, the Word of God does not belong. Its reality rests entirely in itself. Therefore, the knowledge of it does not rest just as much in me as in itself, but rather *only* in it. If I know God—and that is indeed what is at stake here—then *this* 'I know' must be distinguished most emphatically from all other 'I know'.[40]

Although it is true that the Word of God gives Himself to be known in objects which are caught in the subject–object polarity, yet He remains free of it and therefore in control of the knowing event. 'The reality of the Word of God rests absolutely in itself. We know it in that we are known in it.'[41]

If all this be true, what way of knowing is open to us? The only way is that way which begins in prayer. It is here that Anselm provided Barth with an example of the kind of theological method he was advocating. In his *Proslogion*, Anselm wants to understand (*intelligere*) the existence of God.[42] At the beginning of this attempt to understand stands the prayer of faith. The first chapter of the *Proslogion* takes the form of a prayer for illumination. Anselm understands that 'one can understand God only on the basis of faith'.[43] For this reason, his prayer concludes with the statement that he does not seek knowledge so that then, and on that basis, he can believe. Rather, his belief leads him to want to know. *Credo ut intelligam.*

---

[38] Barth, *Die christliche Dogmatik im Entwurf*, 129.
[39] Beintker, *Die Dialektik in der 'dialektischen Theologie' Karl Barths*, 190–1.
[40] Barth, *Die christliche Dogmatik im Entwurf*, 135–6.   [41] Ibid. 109.
[42] Ibid. 131.   [43] Ibid.

That Anselm has faith does not make the way to understanding easy. True, Anselm seeks understanding as one who is a believing Christian. He knows that God has created him and re-created him and given him every good thing. Yet, 'still I do not know You'.[44] God has hidden his face from Anselm and he is as one who is blind. But, Barth observed, it is important to note that Anselm's uncertainty is not absolute. It is the uncertainty of the believer who knows God and precisely because he does know Him, knows that he does not know Him. It is the uncertainty which has its source in a firm and certain knowledge that, in this relationship, God is the Lord. For knowledge of *this* God, he can only pray. 'Teach me to seek You and show Yourself to the one who seeks You.'[45]

The programme for theology which flows naturally from this state of affairs is one in which the theologian is placed in a situation of complete dependency. *Intelligere*, the attempt to attain to theological knowledge, is a human activity which occurs on the basis of a prior act of God. God must show Himself. The *reality* of the Word of God as event precedes and grounds the *possibility* of the knowledge of it.[46] 'Knowledge here means fundamentally acknowledgement [*An-erkenntnis*]. Thinking means thinking-after [*Nach-denken*] . . .'[47]

Of course, none of this was new. This tendency of thought had governed Barth's thinking since his break with Herrmannian liberalism in 1915. As Michael Beintker rightly observed, 'Barth's placing of the reality before the possibility is the consistent result of his struggle for a thinking "from God to us", or alternatively, a "viewing things from God's standpoint", which has stamped and motivated Barth's entire theological attitude since the days of *Romans* I.'[48]

The point of comparing Anselm with neo-Protestantism is to show how different is the neo-Protestant conception of the Word of God and the way to theological knowledge which derives from it. Neo-Protestant theology, Barth observed, thinks of the Word of God as something imparted, given over to human consciousness. Following Schleiermacher, it therefore sees theology as *Glaubenslehre*, as an unfolding of the contents of the human religious consciousness. Barth gave as an example of such

---

[44] Ibid. 132.   [45] Ibid. 133.   [46] Ibid. 304–8.   [47] Ibid. 136.
[48] Beintker, *Die Dialektik in der 'dialektischen Theologie' Karl Barths*, 190.

thinking his contemporary, Erich Schaeder. Schaeder understands the task of theology this way: 'The finite spirit or personal consciousness of the present moment is investigated by theology for its possession of divine spirit and the conditions of that possession.'[49] This vision of theology does not rest upon the conviction that revelation has ever to be given anew. Revelation has been given and is now the spiritual possession of the finite spirit. How different the attitude which derives from this understanding is from that of Anselm! 'For a reality in his consciousness, he [Anselm] would obviously not pray. He would rather confirm it, as do contemporary theologians, in order to make use of it.'[50] Where Anselm's *intelligere* is surrounded by uncertainty, neo-Protestant theology is characterized by an 'unheard of certainty'.[51]

There is one other significant point in *Die christliche Dogmatik* where Anselm's example is invoked.[52] It not only confirms the previous analysis but leads still further in the direction of the interpretation advanced in *Fides quaerens intellectum*. The passage in question appears in the context of a treatment of the reality of the incarnation. Here Barth raised the question as to whether he has constructed an a priori Christology. Has his Chalcedonian Christology been anything more than an attempt to deduce from the demands of his *concept* of revelation what the God-human must be like? Does his Christology amount to nothing more than the attempt to construct the objective possibility of revelation without reference to Jesus Christ, only then to find this possibility instantiated in the incarnation? Barth's answer is no. What he has constructed is not the possibility of revelation but the possibility of *thinking* about it. And this can only be done in an a posteriori fashion.[53] The possibility of thinking through the nature of the incarnation correctly is grounded in its reality. 'If the revelation was not real, if the incarnate Word was not on the horizon, attested by the prophets and apostles, proclaimed by the Church, if the task of thinking and speaking in accordance with the object was not placed before us, we would abstain from all constructing.'[54] It is only because God's address to humankind in

[49] Barth, *Die christliche Dogmatik im Entwurf*, 125. Barth is here citing Erich Schaeder, *Das Geistproblem der Theologie* (Leipzig/Erlangen, 1924), 2–3.

[50] Barth, *Die christliche Dogmatik im Entwurf*, 132.   [51] Ibid. 131.

[52] Ibid. 304–8.   [53] Ibid. 307.   [54] Ibid.

the concreteness of the incarnation has occurred that the obligation to understand it—to think it through to the end and in its
necessity—is placed upon us. "Necessity" here does not mean
the logical necessity of a proof. "Necessity" here means, given
that the incarnation is, how must we think about it?

> We raised the questions which human reason has to put to itself and
> answer once it has perceived the revelation which really has occurred . . .
> That does not mean: as if Christ were not there, as if we did not believe
> in Him. 'Credo ut intelligam' is the self-evident and not for a moment to
> be suspended presupposition of all the reflection which we exercise
> here. Rather, our knowing of Him on the basis of faith must once
> again begin at the beginning, with nothing, as if we had never given
> ourselves, as if the Church had never given itself, an account of what
> the revelation which has occurred and been perceived means, what
> possibilities of thought are prescribed for us by the revelation which has
> occurred and been perceived. . . . That is what "intelligere" or "ratio-
> nabiliter demonstrare" means in Anselm's sense.[55]

When this is done, Barth suggested, when we have thought
through the necessities given to thought by the reality of revelation, we will see that the Chalcedonian Christology is still the
most appropriate available.[56]

What is important for our purposes here is not the Christology
but the nature of theological thinking being advocated, and the
appeal to Anselm. Here, as in the previous passage we considered, it is quite clear that the reality of the Word of God must
precede and ground every attempt to think correctly about it.
But Barth has here added a further point. To "prove" in the
sense that Anselm meant it is not at all a "proof" as normally
understood. To "prove", to "demonstrate rationally", means simply to explicate the meaning of the object of faith as it is given to
us in the incarnation. To "prove" is to show how we must necessarily think about the event of revelation if our thinking is to
correspond to it. This explanation of Anselm's understanding of
"proof" has reference only to the Cur Deus homo? In Fides
quaerens intellectum, Barth would make extensive use of this
understanding in order to interpret Proslogion 2–4. But that
would only be a further application of the interpretation set forth
in Die christliche Dogmatik.

---

[55] Ibid. 305–6.   [56] Ibid. 308.

(iii) *Fides quaerens intellectum (1931)*

Barth's primary intention in writing *Fides quaerens intellectum* was to treat the 'problematic Anselm' of *Proslogion* 2–4 in a 'wholly other' way than had hitherto been attempted. He wanted to show that the so-called "ontological proof" set forth by Anselm was not a proof at all, in the ordinary sense of the term. The biting words with which he concluded his book bear this out.

> That Anselm's proof of the existence of God has repeatedly been called the "ontological" proof of God, that commentators have refused to see that it stands in another book than does the well-known doctrine of Descartes and Leibniz, that anyone could seriously think that it is even remotely affected by what Kant brought against these doctrines—all that is so much nonsense on which no more words ought to be wasted.[57]

It is of the utmost importance to keep Barth's motivation in mind. This is a book on Anselm. It is not a book on Barth's theology—however true it may be at the end of the day that it tells us more about Barth than it does about the eleventh-century theologian. Barth did not intend here to provide a full account of his own theological method. For that, we must look to *Church Dogmatics* I/1 and I/2, taken as a whole. It is true that much of his method emerges here, but it is not complete.

The importance of this observation lies in the fact that at the centre of attention in the Anselm book stands the question of what it means to "demonstrate rationally" in theology. By putting the spotlight on 'theological science' in this way, the book easily induces readers to lose sight of all the qualifications which keep this science from becoming 'an ordinary, bourgeois possibility of consideration', as Barth once defined sciences in general in *Romans* II.[58] To be sure, qualifying factors also appear in the Anselm book. But since no emphasis is placed upon them, they are all too easily lost to view. In order to see the matter in the proper light, it is helpful to read *Fides quaerens intellectum* in the light of *Church Dogmatics* I/1, para. 5. 4, 'The Speech of God as the Mystery of God'. There Barth emphatically reaffirms the dialectic of veiling and unveiling in revelation (which was and

---

[57] Barth, *Fides quaerens intellectum*, 174; ET *Anselm*, 171.
[58] Barth, *Der Römerbrief, 1922*, 514–15.

continued to be the root of his dialectical theology).[59] But even without the benefit of *Church Dogmatics* I/1, it is clear enough that the dialectic of veiling and unveiling is the unspoken—and at a few dramatic points, fully articulated—presupposition of the theological method set forth in the Anselm book. What follows is an attempt to read the Anselm book as an exercise in dialectical theology.

The consideration of what it means to "demonstrate rationally" falls into two parts, suggested by the subtitle of the Anselm book: 'Anselm's Proof of the Existence of God in the Context of his Theological Programme'. The first (and shorter) part is devoted to Anselm's theological method and the second to a close analysis of the proof in *Proslogion* 2–4. It is the section on method which is of the greatest interest for us here.

On the surface, Anselm's theological programme is deceptively simple. 'Faith seeking understanding' means to think-after [*Nachdenken*] that which has already been said in the *Credo* of the Church.[60] The task of theology is to reflect upon the meaning of the *Credo*; to ask—given that the *Credo* is true—*to what extent* is it true?[61] What is the meaning of a particular article of faith in the context of the *Credo* as a whole?[62] That is what Barth means by asking about the extent of its truth. '*Intelligere* comes into existence through thinking-after the *Credo* which has already been spoken and affirmed.'[63] And so Barth can say, 'In relation to the *Credo*, theological science, as the science of the *Credo*, can only have a positive character.'[64] But what is it that is being affirmed here? If theology consists merely in an interpretation of the Apostles' Creed, then it would indeed appear to be a most positive, bourgeois science. But perhaps the way of knowledge being described by Barth is more complex than such statements suggest. We must enquire further into the nature of this *intelligere*.

Intelligere means initially to reflect on what has been said in the *Credo*. But it means more than that. The *intelligere* is 'successful' when it achieves a *vera ratio*, that is, when the reason of the seeker (the noetic *ratio*) is brought into conformity with the inherent rationality of the object (the ontic *ratio*).[65] Does this

[59] Barth, *KD* I/1, 168–94; ET *CD* I/1, 162–86.
[60] Barth, *Fides quaerens intellectum*, 40; ET *Anselm*, 40.   [61] Ibid. 26–7; ET 27–8.
[62] Ibid. 54; ET 55.   [63] Ibid. 26; ET 37.   [64] Ibid. 25; ET 26.
[65] Ibid. 47; ET 47.

mean that human thought is to be conformed to the inherent rationality of the *Credo*? Yes and no; the situation is more complex than that. Barth further distinguishes in Anselm's ontic *ratio*, the *ratio fidei* of the *Credo* and, lying behind it, a second and ultimate *ratio*—the *ratio veritatis*. 'Strictly understood, the *ratio veritatis* is identical with the *ratio summae naturae*; that is, with the divine Word who is consubstantial to the Father.'[66] In the truest sense, the object with which conformity is sought is the *ratio veritatis*, the Word itself, which is related to the *ratio fidei* but is to be distinguished from it. What is sought is the conformity of noetic *ratio* (the thinking of the would-be knower) with the *ratio veritatis* which is hidden in the *Credo* (and the Bible).[67]

Now because the *ratio fidei* (the *Credo*) is not identical with the *ratio veritatis* (the Word), conformity with the *ratio veritatis* will not be a simple matter of reading and understanding the outward text of the Creed. Revealed truth has an 'inner text' which must be grasped if the outward text is to be rightly understood.[68] What is required is a special movement of thought which goes beyond mere reading.[69] The outward text has to be read in relation to the inner text. But the inner text is not readily accessible. If the reader is to penetrate through the outer text to the inner text, she must be grasped through the reading of the outer text from the other side.[70] It is not in mastering the object but in being mastered by it that the interpreter achieves a true comprehension of the ontic *ratio* of the object of faith, and the *intellectus* that is sought takes place.[71] That means that the attainment of the *ratio intellectus* that is in conformity with the *ratio veritatis* hidden in the *ratio fidei* depends upon a divine decision, and therefore upon grace. That means further that the way to be taken in knowing God begins in prayer and faith.

It is of the utmost importance to notice here that ontic *ratio* precedes and grounds noetic *ratio*.[72] The search for a true cognition of the object arises out of a faith which is really faith in this object. It is of the nature of faith, where it does exist, to desire knowledge: 'we cannot believe in this God without His becoming the Author of a *vera cognitio*—that is, faith in Him also demands knowledge of Him.'[73] Thus, ontic *ratio* stands at the

---

[66] Barth, *Fides quaerens intellectum*, 45; ET *Anselm*, 45.   [67] Ibid. 47; ET 47.
[68] Ibid. 41; ET 41.   [69] Ibid. 42; ET 42.   [70] Ibid. 41, 47; ET 41, 47.
[71] Ibid. 55; ET 55.   [72] Ibid. 53; ET 53.   [73] Ibid. 17; ET 17.

beginning and at the end of the *intellectus fidei*. It is that which is sought, but it is also that which gives rise to the search in the first place.

Now at this point an interpretive problem arises in our exposition of the Anselm book. It is most likely that we should distinguish between Anselm (as Barth understands him) and Barth's own theological viewpoint at one decisive point.[74] That point is the relation (and distinction!) of the *ratio veritatis* and the *ratio fidei*, of the Word and the Creed. We have said that the *Credo* is not identical with the Word for Anselm, and in the strictest sense, that is true. But Anselm tends to blur the distinction by treating the witnesses to past acts of revelation as though they themselves had become revealed truth. Anselm knows that the truth that Bible and Creed possess is a truth conferred upon them by Truth itself. To that extent, he preserves the distinction. But he tends to treat that conferral as a once-and-for-all act that is completed and finished. He tends to treat Bible and Creed as revealed-ness, a thing which Barth's doctrine of the threefold form of the Word of God (reaffirmed in *Church Dogmatics* I/1) will not allow him to do. For Barth, even the Bible as a witness to past revelation 'is not in itself and as such God's past revelation'.[75] For Anselm, on the other hand, although the divine decision in which noetic *ratio* is brought into conformity with the ontic *ratio* is a decision which must be made again and again, the divine decision in which the ontic *ratio* of the object to be known (the *ratio fidei* of the Creed) is brought into conformity with the *ratio veritatis* (the Word itself) is a decision which *has been made*. And that means that, for Anselm, the *ratio fidei* 'is, without question, identical with the *ratio veritatis* in the strict and proper sense'.[76] This confusion of the *ratio fidei* and the *ratio veritatis* is what causes Anselm's theology to have such a positive character. For where the two are identified, the conformity of noetic *ratio* to the *ratio fidei* is sufficient to guarantee conformity to the *ratio veritatis* as well.

[74] It should be emphasized that the contrast being drawn here is not between the 'historical Anselm' and Barth's view of him but rather between Barth's interpretation of Anselm and his own self-understanding. Thus, in what follows, 'Anselm' refers everywhere to Barth's interpretation of him. No attempt will be made to test the historical accuracy of Barth's reading of Anselm.

[75] *KD* I/1, 114; ET *CD* I/1, 111.

[76] Barth, *Fides quaerens intellectum*, 46; ET *Anselm*, 47.

On the other hand, it must be admitted that Barth nowhere simply pronounces Anselm's equation to have been a mistake. The reason for this is no doubt that he does not regard Anselm's mistake to be so serious as to disqualify him from consideration as a dialectical theologian. Regardless of whether the divine decision which granted to the *Credo* its share in the truth has been made or not, the decision as to whether the *ratio veritatis* will be recognized in the *ratio fidei* must still be made. 'Even here, decision enters into it, not as to whether it is *ratio veritatis* but whether it can be recognized as such. In the *Credo* and the Bible, it is hidden and must reveal itself in order to make itself known to us. It does this, however, only if and in so far as the Truth, God Himself, does it.'[77] Anselm was still a theologian of grace. He understood that the knowledge of God is dependent upon God's gracious decision. That is what made him attractive to Barth.

And yet we do not have to seek far for qualifications of Anselm's positivity.

We already know something of the dialectic in the concept *intelligere*. It is not self-evident that the *intelligere* is even to a certain extent an *intelligere* of the thing in itself. Even this qualified *intelligere* by which men and women are enabled to see something of the face of God must be prayed for, because all right seeking (that too is grace!) would be of no help whatsoever if God did not "show" Himself, if the encounter did not become real from His side and if the finding, the qualified *intelligere*, did not thereby become an event. . . . Everything depends not only upon the fact that God gives the grace to think *rightly* of Him, but rather also on the fact that God Himself is on the horizon of this thinking as *object*, "showing" Himself to the thinker, and thereby qualifying a "correct" thinking to be an *intelligere* of the thing in itself.[78]

A number of old themes emerge in this passage. First, knowledge of God is an event. The actualism of Barth's theory is preserved. Second, *intelligere* is a dialectical concept. Because God must "show" Himself to our thinking if it is really to be conformed to Him, our knowledge of God is dependent upon a dialectical movement on God's side (a *Realdialektik*). A thinking which depends in this way on a *Realdialektik* is itself a dialectically conditioned thinking. Thus, dialectic remains on the noetic level as well. Third, because the *intelligere* is qualified in an event, "cor-

---

[77] Barth, *Fides quaerens intellectum*, 46–7; ET *Anselm*, 47.
[78] Ibid. 38–9; ET 38–9.

rect" thinking which conforms to its object is not an enduring state of affairs. And that means theology remains (just as in the Göttingen Dogmatics) incomplete and broken, in constant need of correction.

In the light of the foregoing, it is not surprising that Barth can still say, 'All theological statements are inadequate for their object. . . . In the strictest sense, only God has a concept of God. All we have are concepts of objects which are not identical with God.'[79] All is not hopeless, of course. 'Just as everything which is not God would be nothing without God, but through God is something . . . so also, statements which really are only appropriate to objects which are not identical with God, are able to be true statements when applied to the inexpressible God, *per aliquam similitudinem aut imaginem* . . .'[80] Concepts which are inadequate in themselves for giving expression to God can be given a relative adequacy by God's grace. In that this happens, an analogy is actualized between the concept and its divine referent. On this basis, theological statements can indeed be relatively true statements. It follows from this that all theological statements have an 'interim' character. They constantly await better instruction.[81]

Such qualifications of theological positivity, however, stand on the periphery of Barth's reflections in the Anselm book. At the centre stands the highly positive theological task of asking after the meaning of the *Credo* which has been affirmed. And it is in this framework that Barth interprets the meaning of Anselm's "proof". To "prove" means to investigate the meaning of a particular article of faith *x* given that articles *a, b, c, d* and so on are assumed to be true.[82] Anselm is not seeking to prove *that* God exists. That much is already known on the basis of revelation. Anselm is asking what else we must say about the existence of God, given the truth of the *Credo*. The existence of God figures here as the unknown article *x* to be investigated. The formula with which Anselm reasons about the existence of God ('something beyond which nothing greater can be conceived') is not of his own contrivance. It is a revealed name in the form of a prohibition.[83] It forbids him to conceive of God in any way which would allow him to conceive of anything else that is greater. Anselm uses this 'rule of thought'[84] as a key by means of which

[79] Ibid. 28; ET 29.   [80] Ibid. 28–9; ET 29.   [81] Ibid. 30; ET 31.
[82] Ibid. 54; ET 55.   [83] Ibid. 77; ET 75.   [84] Ibid. 88; ET 87.

to explicate the meaning of God's existence. And that is what "proof" finally means, as Barth understands it: it means *explicatio*.[85]

Barth's book on Anselm is not a wholly reliable guide to his own theological method—regardless of what he might say on the subject later—unless it is read dialectically. To ask after the internal coherence of a particular doctrine *x* with the rest of the Creed is an operation which is placed in brackets by the fact that conformity to the *ratio fidei* offers no guarantee whatsoever that conformity will also be established with the *ratio veritatis*. It could be that the Creed will need to be corrected. But we will only be able to know that as a result of a fresh event of revelation—an event over which we have no control and for which we can only pray. Thus, the *intellectus fidei* stands radically under an eschatological reservation. It is what human beings can do, in the meantime, as they wait upon a fresh event of revelation. All of this must be said if the programme outlined in the book on Anselm is to agree in every detail with the one which is more fully elaborated in *Church Dogmatics* I/1 and I/2.

(iv) *Critical Evaluation of Proposed "New Elements" in the Anselm Book*

We turn now to our primary question. Is there anything in the Anselm book which is decisively new? Anything which would have compelled Barth to view *Die christliche Dogmatik* as a 'false start'? Certainly, the categories by means of which Barth sought to explicate the nature of theological rationality are new. But are the basic methodological decisions which underlie this programme really new? What follows is a brief survey of some of the answers given to the question of the new element in the Anselm book.

1. 'That the Truth makes itself *objective* for us without becoming ensnared in the network of the Cartesian subject–object polarity is the decisive discovery of Barth's Anselm book.'[86] This suggestion comes from Michael Beintker. The thought contained in this depiction of Barth's doctrine of revelation is, however, anything but new.

---

[85] Cf. Barth, *KD* I/2, 28–34; ET *CD* I/2, 25–31.
[86] Beintker, *Die Dialektik in der 'dialektischen Theologie' Karl Barths*, 191.

Beintker's thesis stands in the closest proximity to a further bit of analysis. He holds that the phase of *Romans* II was characterized by a Kantian/neo-Kantian stress on the non-objectivity of the Word. 'In the Anselm book, the imprisonment in transcendental thinking has been definitively overcome: the divine Truth has come to us and gives itself to us to be known.'[87] The emphasis now falls upon the knowability of the Word as a result of being made objective in the *Credo*.

There is some truth in Beintker's characterization of Barth's development. The phase of *Romans* II was stamped by an emphasis on the non-objectivity of the Word (though it is scarcely accurate to describe this in terms of 'imprisonment in transcendental thinking'). Even then, however, elements of objectivity were not excluded. The difficulty there was that these elements were constantly threatened by the time–eternity dialectic. But with the grounding of the knowability of God in the anhypostatic-enhypostatic Christology in 1924, God's ability to make Himself "objective" (without ceasing to be Subject) came to the fore. The step from this solution to the problem of the relation of revelation and history to a structurally similar solution to the problem of theological rationality was a very small one.

On the other hand, the stress on the objectivity of the Word did not mean a loss of respect for non-objectivity—not in 1924 or 1931. As Beintker himself says, in the Anselm book as well, Barth's conception of the objectivity of God in revelation is no ordinary conception. What is at stake here is a 'dialectic of objectivity and non-objectivity'.[88] But if that be true (and it is), then the distance separating *Romans* II from the Anselm book has been lessened considerably. For what is Beintker's dialectic of objectivity and non-objectivity if not the dialectic of *Anschaulichkeit* and *Unanschaulichkeit* of *Romans* II? To be sure, the dialectic of veiling and unveiling was rooted more firmly in history by Barth's new Christology in 1924, and that is an advance. But it is the same basic dialectic that is in view in both *Romans* and Anselm.

There is a further troubling feature in Beintker's analysis. In spite of his talk of a dialectic of objectivity and non-objectivity, he tends to place too much emphasis on the objectivity of the *Credo*, thus treating Anselm's identification of the *ratio veritatis* with the *ratio fidei* as though it represented Barth's view as well.[89] But to grant to the *Credo* such a status is impossible if the dialectic is retained. Beintker cannot have it both ways: he cannot admit that the dialectic is retained and then treat the objective knowability of the Word in the *Credo* as if the dialectic did not exist. But he does precisely that when he suggests, for example, that Barth 'executed a 180-degree turn' away from treating the knowledge of God as the 'impossible possibility' (as in *Romans* II).[90] If God must "show" Himself if He is to be known, if the veil must still be lifted according to the Anselm book, how can knowledge of God be any less of an 'impossible possibility' now? Where is the 180-degree turn? There is none.

2. 'With the turn to a position which can proceed from the objectivity and knowability of the Truth in the *ratio fidei*, the necessity for the thought-form of dialectic on the noetic plane falls away. Here logic takes the place of dialectic.'[91] This position too is Beintker's. He holds that with the Anselm book, Barth had reached a point where there is a 'clear primacy of the logical over the dialectical'[92] in his theological procedure.

There can be no question that logic plays a large role in the Anselm book (and in the *Church Dogmatics*). In that Barth speaks here of theology as the explication of the Creed, logic plays a large and indispensable role. Barth can even affirm in this context the necessity of using that logic which is based on the law of contradiction in seeking the meaning of the unknown article *x* of the Creed.[93]

But—and this is a rather large qualification—logic has its role to play in the realm of what *we* can and should do as theologians. What we do is always doomed to failure if God does not "show" Himself. And that means that the indispensable presupposition of the logical unfolding of the meaning of the Creed is the dialectic of veiling and unveiling. Beyond and above all our reflections stands dialectic. But if all we do is placed in brackets by the *Realdialektik* in which God veils or unveils Himself, then it will not do to speak simply of a 'clear primacy of logic over dialectic'. Seen in the proper light, dialectic retains its primacy over logic. Resolving the question of what is 'primary' will not be a simple

---

[89] Beintker, *Die Dialektik in der 'dialektischen Theologie' Karl Barths*, 186.
[90] Ibid. 195.   [91] Ibid. 188.   [92] Ibid. 187.
[93] Barth, *Fides quaerens intellectum*, 55; ET *Anselm*, 55.

task of weighing how often Barth employs logic and how often he employs dialectic. Seen in that way, of course, logic plays a larger role in the *Church Dogmatics* than does dialectic. But 'primacy' is not a question which can be resolved by means of a quantitative calculus. It is a question of which *conditions* the use of the other, which is more basic. From that point of view, dialectic remains primary and Karl Barth was still a dialectical theologian in the *Church Dogmatics*.

3. With the Anselm book, Barth turned 'from dialectic to analogy'. This is the thesis associated with the name of Hans Urs von Balthasar. We have already seen that analogy and dialectic coexisted throughout the 1920s. Analogy is not a new element in the Anselm book. Michael Beintker has recast this formula in a more cautious form, however, that merits consideration. From dialectic as the *leading* thought-form, Barth turned to analogy as the *leading* thought-form.[94] 'With *Fides quaerens intellectum*, the departure from dialectic as a leading thought-form decisive for the acquisition of theological statements can be attested.'[95]

The advantages of this formulation are obvious. It allows for the coexistence of dialectic and analogy before and after the Anselm book. It merely asserts that a shift of emphasis has occurred. There is, however, a major defect with this formulation as well. Its success depends on an alleged predominance of dialectical method for acquiring theological statements prior to 1931. But a close study of the Göttingen Dogmatics makes it clear that, even then, dialectical method was not predominant; dogmatic method was. Barth's analysis of theological topics typically began with the Confessions and early Protestant theologians which provided, at one and the same time, the raw material of dogmatics and a relatively authoritative guide in the effort to construct theological statements. Dialectical method was employed in those areas of investigation which invited such a method—most especially, the doctrine of God and Christology. And dialectical method continued to be employed in the *Church Dogmatics*, as a rule, in precisely those areas in which it was already employed in the Göttingen Dogmatics. Thus, talk of a 'turn' to analogy as a leading thought-form for the acquisition of theological statements would not be altogether incorrect—if it

---

[94] Beintker, *Die Dialektik in der 'dialektischen Theologie' Karl Barths*, 194.
[95] Ibid. 19.

were placed in 1924 rather than in 1931. Even then, however, such a formulation can scarcely be adequate for describing Barth's development in 1924, because it does not penetrate deeply enough. Barth's shifts in method were everywhere the function of material decisions in dogmatics.

4. In the Anselm book, Barth stressed for the first time that ontic necessity and rationality have an ontological priority over noetic necessity and rationality. This is the thesis of Eberhard Jüngel, T. F. Torrance, and Ingrid Spieckermann.[96] But here again, there is a problem. As Beintker has rightly pointed out, 'The *prae* and *prius* of the ontic before the noetic is based on the ontological precedence of reality *before* possibility in the theological attitude to the question of truth.'[97] The problem is that the ordering of the reality before possibility dates back to the days of *Romans* I.[98] To ground noetic *ratio* in ontic *ratio* is simply to explore in detail the implications of the priority of the reality of the Word over the possibility of knowledge of it for an understanding of theological rationality. Seen in this light, the elements stressed by these three scholars represent a significant clarification of Barth's method but not a change of method.

5. In *Fides quaerens intellectum*, Barth overcame every last remnant of the attempt to ground, support, or justify theology by means of existential philosophy. The source of this language is Barth himself, but it is of the utmost importance to see it in its original context. In the preface to *Church Dogmatics* I/1, written in 1932, Barth observed, 'I now think myself to have understood some things better (among which are certainly my own intentions), in that I have eliminated in this second version of the book everything I possibly could which might appear to seek a grounding, support or even only a justification of theology in existential philosophy.'[99] Regardless of how incautiously Barth might later have suggested that he had in fact provided a 'grounding , support or justification' of theology in existential philosophy, in 1932—at the point at which the revision of *Die christliche Dogmatik* actually occurred—Barth spoke only of the elimination

---

[96] Jüngel, 'Einführung in Leben und Werk Karl Barths', in idem, *Barth-Studien*, 48; Torrance, *Karl Barth: An Introduction to his Early Theology*, 182–3; Spieckermann, *Gotteserkenntnis*, 228–9.

[97] Beintker, *Die Dialektik in der 'dialektischen Theologie' Karl Barths*, 188.

[98] Ibid. 190.　　　[99] Barth, *KD* I/1, p. viii; ET *CD* I/1, p. xiii.

of elements which *might appear* to provide such a grounding, etc. And, as the context makes clear, such an appearance was contrary to his intentions at the time of writing *Die christliche Dogmatik*. This assessment of Barth's self-understanding in 1932 is also borne out by a close examination of the "retractions" which are to be found in *Church Dogmatics* I/1.

The most significant of these "retractions" is one that is advanced as a justification for an alteration of the arrangement of the earlier prolegomena. In *Die christliche Dogmatik*, at the outset of para. 5, 'The Word of God and the Human Individual as Preacher', Barth had announced a 'transition' in his 'mode of consideration'.[100] After having established a threefold form of the Word of God in para. 4 by means of a 'phenomenological' mode of analysis, he declared that he was now going on to an 'existential' analysis of the human as preacher and hearer of the Word in paras. 5 and 6. The reviews of *Die christliche Dogmatik* (above all, those by Theodore Siegfried and Friedrich Gogarten) had taught Barth how easily such language could be misunderstood. 'To my horror, T. Siegfried interpreted the passage as follows: "On this foundation (i.e. the existential thinking introduced) he proposes to build his dogmatics." '[101] It is very important to observe carefully Barth's reaction to Siegfried's analysis.

This was not really my intention. But I ought to have had the better judgement to see that to drag in those concepts at this point in relation to what I wanted to say there was a superfluous and dangerous game: superfluous because it was not in any case followed by any attempt to prove the doctrine of the Word of God by showing it to be posited by existential thinking or by advancing an existential philosophy as its background and justification: and dangerous because all that follows could be understood on the basis of that passage as if it were intended to provide an existential-philosophical grounding of theology . . .[102]

Barth here clearly says that in spite of all appearances to the contrary, he did *not* attempt to ground theology in existential philosophy.

There was a second point made in this context. At the end of paras. 5–7 of *Die christliche Dogmatik*, Barth had advanced a series of 'closer definitions' of the Word of God. The arrangement

---

[100] Barth, *Die christliche Dogmatik im Entwurf*, 69.
[101] Barth, *KD* I/1, 129; ET *CD* I/1, 125–6.   [102] Ibid. 129; ET 126.

made it appear that Barth was trying to derive his doctrine of the Word from an analysis of the concrete situation of the preacher or hearer of the Word of God.

An anthropology, albeit a Church anthropology, was thus being advanced as the supposed basis on which we know decisive statements about God's Word. In this regard, along with the general declaration that from now on, and especially in paras. 5–7, we should be concerned with existential thinking, I was paying homage to false gods. . . . If there is one thing the Word of God certainly is not, it is not a predicate of humanity, even of the human who receives it, and therefore, not of the human who speaks, hears and knows it in the sphere of the Church.[103]

Although this statement is much stronger, its effect is muted by Barth's belief that 'In fact, the more precise definitions were not at all deduced from the [existential] analysis. But I proceeded as though they could and should be.'[104] Barth remained as convinced as ever in *Church Dogmatics* I/1 that the concrete definitions of the Word which he had advanced in his earlier work were appropriate, but now he insisted that they had not been derived from an existential analysis of the situation of the preacher and hearer of the Word of God at all. They had their ground elsewhere, namely in the Word itself.[105] Thus, he could rectify the situation quite easily by simply dropping paras. 5 and 6 while retaining the precise definitions which had emerged from them.

On closer examination this "retraction" too turns out to be not much of a retraction. It concedes little in the way of real error. Basically, all that is granted is that at this point in *Die christliche Dogmatik*, Barth had been inconsistent with his basic intention. The damage was hardly fatal. No change in his understanding of the Word had resulted from dropping the offending paragraphs. If the 'mode of consideration' in these paragraphs had had any constitutive significance, it would be reasonable to expect such a change. But no change was forthcoming, because none was necessary.

One other "retraction" deserves mention, for it stands in close connection to the preceding. In *Die christliche Dogmatik*, Barth wrote, 'The hearing human is included in the concept of the Word of God just as much as the speaking God. He is "co-

---

[103] Barth, *KD* I/1, 130; ET *CD* I/1, 126–7. [104] Ibid. 130; ET 126.   [105] Ibid.

posited" in it, as Schleiermacher's God is in the feeling of absolute dependence.'[106] In *Church Dogmatics* I/1, Barth expressed astonishment that he could have said such a thing.[107] Barth's reconsideration here is based on the fact that the Word does not have to be addressed to human beings to be what it is. The Word is what it is essentially as a result of the free communication which exists between the members of the godhead. That the Word is *also* directed to human beings is a fact but not a necessity. Therefore, the human recipient of the Word is 'co-posited' in the event of revelation as an actual fact, but this co-positing is not necessary to the Word. If human beings hear the Word, this is God's free grace. The basis upon which this reconsideration was advanced was simply a variation on Barth's insistence (of long standing) that creation and revelation are not necessary to God. God is perfectly fulfilled within the intra-Trinitarian life apart from addressing Himself to an other.[108] Once again, the "retraction" proves on closer inspection to be of greater value in appearance than in reality.

Did Barth attempt to ground, support, and justify theology by means of existential philosophy? The answer must be no, though he did succumb to the temptation from time to time to seek corroboration, in that direction, of a doctrine of the Word which he steadfastly maintained was grounded in itself. Why then did Barth later exaggerate the defect in *Die christliche Dogmatik*? For an answer to that question, we must return, in the next section, to a genetic mode of analysis.

On the basis of this brief survey, it is clear that what is "new" in the Anselm book is at most a *relatively* more faithful unfolding of the dogmatic method which Barth had been employing since 1924. There is no new starting-point here, and no new thought-form.

4. WHY "CHURCH" DOGMATICS?

It has been customary in previous interpretations of Barth's development to associate Barth's need to rewrite *Die christliche*

---

[106] Barth, *Die christliche Dogmatik im Entwurf*, 148.
[107] Barth, *KD* I/1, 145; ET *CD* I/1, 140.
[108] Barth, '*Unterricht in der christlichen Religion*', ii. 226–35.

Dogmatik with the study of Anselm. It was Anselm who forced him to begin once again at the beginning, so that *Church Dogmatics* I/1 and I/2 were not so much a revision as a new book. We have noted that Barth himself bore a good bit of responsibility for this reading of the matter. It is the contention here, however, that *Church Dogmatics* I/1 and I/2 are indeed merely a revision of the 1927 work. Simply put, Barth exaggerated the difference between the two. Now if this contention be true, then it becomes more comprehensible why the importance of the Anselm book grew in Barth's mind over time. The exaggerated importance of *Fides quaerens intellectum* was a reflex, a by-product of the exaggerated difference between the two published versions of the prolegomena. The importance of the Anselm book was connected in Barth's mind with the newness of *Church Dogmatics* I/1.

But this assessment leaves us with a couple of residual problems. First, if the difference between *Die christliche Dogmatik* and *Church Dogmatics* I/1 and I/2 is not all that great (judged on the level of the 'movement of thought' governing each), why did Barth exaggerate the difference between the two? Second, why did he change the title from 'Christian' to 'Church' Dogmatics? When did he do so? What was his motivation? Was it his study of Anselm? If not, then what? Ordinarily, these two questions are treated as though they were synonymous. It is our belief that they should be distinguished.

First then, the matter of exaggeration. It must be observed at the outset that the tendency to exaggerate the newness of a new version of an old work has been seen before in Barth. We saw it already in Barth's tendency to exaggerate the defects in the first edition of his commentary on *Romans*. We saw it again in his assessment of the newness of *Die christliche Dogmatik* as over against the Göttingen Prolegomena. To some extent, this tendency alone would be a sufficient explanation, apart from any external forces which may have been pressing in on Barth. A tendency to exaggeration in matters of this nature was simply a personality quirk. Karl Barth was a man who lived in the immediate. Even where his ideas were not new, how he expressed himself on a given day always reflected the needs and concerns which forced themselves upon him at that moment. In his enthusiasm for his work, everything was new to him every day.

This alone would be enough to account for an exaggeration here and there.

In this case, however, there were indeed external pressures which help to account for Barth's tendency to want to see *Church Dogmatics* I/1 as a completely new book. In what follows, we will look briefly at the history of the revision of *Die christliche Dogmatik*. The goal is to understand how Barth came to over-emphasize the newness of *Church Dogmatics* I/1. It may be conceded at the outset that the study of Anselm was a contributing factor in the revision. But to call *Church Dogmatics* I/1 a 'revision' is already to delimit the importance of the Anselm book for Barth's development. Along the way, we will want to pay particular attention to any available evidence which would give us some indication of what Barth thought of the Anselm book—at the time he was writing it.

Barth had originally planned to publish volumes II and III of *Die christliche Dogmatik* by the end of 1929 and for this purpose he requested and received a sabbatical for the summer semester 1929.[109] He also thought of bringing out a slightly revised edition of the prolegomena in conjunction with the two new volumes. To that end, he began in early 1928 to enter marginal notes of citations from his readings in his personal copy of the prolegomena. Through this practice, he found that the prolegomena was becoming so enriched that, shortly before the onset of his free semester, he decided to use his free time just for reading. The publication of the three volumes would have to wait.

By early spring 1930, however, Barth realized that the prolegomena needed more than just material additions. Reviews of his book had taught him how easily he could be misunderstood and he now realized that some modifications in the text would have to be made. When Theodore Siegfried's *Das Wort und die Existenz* appeared in early 1930, Barth wrote to the author that his book 'will serve me as a warning, to express myself in a second revision more clearly and simply and thus be serviceable to the matter with which I am concerned'.[110] This letter was writ-

[109] For more detail on the history of this revision, see Gerhard Sauter and Hinrich Stoevesandt, 'Vorwort zur Neuausgabe', in Barth, *Die christliche Dogmatik im Entwurf*, pp. xi–xviii. The following presentation draws heavily on information found there.

[110] Karl Barth to Theodore Siegfried, 6 Mar. 1930; cited by Sauter and Stoevesandt, 'Vorwort zur Neuausgabe', p. xvi. The modification which resulted from Siegfried's misunderstanding was the first "retraction", treated in the previous section.

ten just prior to Barth's departure for Bonn. When it is recalled that the study of Anselm took place in the summer semester, it becomes clear that Barth's conviction that modifications in the prolegomena were necessary (if his intentions were to be clearly understood) *predated* the study of Anselm.

Barth began to write his book on Anselm during the summer vacation (July–October 1930)—thus further postponing the revision of the prolegomena. The book was originally intended to be a brief response to the theses on the *Proslogion* which Heinrich Scholz had presented in Barth's seminar, but as Barth wrote, the work grew in scope. By October, he had finished the first part. By January, he had nearly finished a first draft. In April 1931 he had to put the work aside in order to begin writing the lectures that became *Church Dogmatics* I/1. It was not until August 1931 that the Anselm book was finished.

What were Barth's thoughts about it as he wrote? Did he report any flashes of new insight, any moments of sudden clarity, or perhaps the discovery of a new starting-point in thought? The answer is that his comments on the work as it proceeded were all rather mundane. They touched mainly on his fear that his readers might find the book too difficult and even boring. Typical was a comment to Thurneysen: 'I sometimes fear that the book may afterwards be boring or, in any case, laborious to read, and may have interested me more than the people.'[111] Taken all in all, there is nothing in the letters to make one think that Barth has learned anything really illuminating. On that score, there is complete silence. Barth's reserve in this regard is matched by the preface to the first edition of the work.

I do not want to deny that I regard Anselm's Proof of the Existence of God in the Context of His Theological Programme to be an exemplary model of good, penetrating and orderly theology which at every point has instructed and edified me, though I could not and would not identify myself with its author . . . I look forward calmly to the suspicion which lies close to hand in this context, that I would like to have read this or that into the thinker of the eleventh century in order, cloaked by his shadow, to advance it in the twentieth. Who has eyes other than

---

[111] Karl Barth to Eduard Thurneysen, 9 Jan. 1931, copy in Karl Barth-Archiv, Basle, Switzerland. I must record my debt here to Frau Elisabeth Stoevesandt, who searched on my behalf through Barth's unpublished correspondence in the Barth-Archiv, to locate any references made by Barth to the Anselm book in the period in which he was writing it.

his own with which to read? With this reservation, I think I am able to say that I have brought forth nothing here than what I have read in Anselm.[112]

It would appear that Barth's major concern as he released the book was a hermeneutical one: would he be judged to have read his own programme into Anselm? How different this preface is from the second, written in 1958, which speaks of the influence which Anselm exercised on the 'movement of thought' which then stamped the *Church Dogmatics*! Most significant of all is Barth's desire to distance himself to some extent from Anselm. 'I could not and would not identify myself with its author.'

By the end of 1930 Barth had come up with a new conception for the overall plan of his dogmatics. He now saw it as divided into five volumes rather than three, with the ethics included as an integral part of dogmatics.[113] This view was no doubt influenced by the fact that he was at that time repeating his ethics lectures of 1928/9. This five-volume arrangement proved to be definitive; it would eventually govern his *Church Dogmatics*.

Incredibly, for some weeks into the summer semester of 1931, as Barth began to give *Church Dogmatics* I/1 in the form of lectures to his students, he was still operating under the illusion that he could finish the prolegomena in one semester as he had previously. By 29 May he thought he might have to continue working on it into the summer vacation in order to finish it.[114] By 4 June the full magnitude of what he was undertaking had dawned upon him.

I tremble only a little at the thought of the external size which already the first volume of the planned complete work will receive. If I live long enough and have the energy and, above all, the illumination to some day carry through the whole in this style, it will become an *opus* which in bulk will scarcely lag behind the *Theologia didactico-polemica* of the blessed Andreas Quenstedt, which I now also look into frequently. But it really is high time that at least 'in outline' a really thick Protestant dogmatics is written once again, next to the many brochure-like efforts.[115]

[112] Barth, *Fides quaerens intellectum*, 3; ET *Anselm*, 9.
[113] Karl Barth to Karl Stoevesandt, 12 Dec. 1930; cited by Sauter and Stoevesandt, 'Vorwort zur Neuausgabe', p. xvi.
[114] Sauter and Stoevesandt, 'Vorwort zur Neuausgabe', p. xvii.
[115] Karl Barth to Georg Merz, 4 June 1931; cited by Sauter and Stoevesandt, 'Vorwort zur Neuausgabe', p. xvii.

It would be three semesters before Barth finished what had been the first half of the previous prolegomena, and he would not be finished with the whole until 1938, some eleven years after the publication of *Die christliche Dogmatik*.

In looking back over the period of revision, the factors which contributed most to the final outcome were the reviews of *Die christliche Dogmatik*, the material additions which resulted from Barth's further readings, and the study of Anselm. These factors are sufficient to account for the revisions which actually took place, but the question still remains to be answered: why exaggerate the difference between the two versions of the prolegomena? Nothing we have seen so far gives us any indication as to what the solution to this problem might be.

The answer, in all probability, is tied to the dramatic change in the political situation in January 1933. Although Barth's break with his former colleagues was complete for all practical purposes by January 1930, it was not until late 1933 that he chose to make that fact public through his withdrawal from *Zwischen den Zeiten* and his public denunciation of Gogarten in the final number.[116] Until then, he was content to distance himself from his colleagues in more subtle ways. For example, in the preface to *Church Dogmatics* I/1, written in August 1932, Barth called attention to the independence of his own work, without offering any criticism of his friends.

Whether in agreement or opposition this book will be the better understood the more it is conceived, as I have already said in the preface to the first edition, as standing on its own, and the less it is conceived as representing a movement, tendency or school. In this sense, too, it aims to be a Church dogmatics. I may take it as well known that there exists between Eduard Thurneysen and myself a theological affinity which is of long standing and has always shown itself to be self-evident. Again, among theological colleagues, ministers, and non-theologians I know many men and women towards whom I am conscious of being wholeheartedly sympathetic in general outlook. But this does not constitute a school, and I certainly cannot think in this emphatic way of those who are commonly associated with me as leaders or adherents of the so-called "dialectical theology". It is only fair to them as well as to me that in its new form too, this book should not be hailed as the dogmatics of dialectical theology. The community in and

---

[116] See Barth, 'Abschied', 536–44.

for which I have written it is that of the Church and not a community of theological endeavour.[117]

With the change in the political situation (and above all, as a consequence of Gogarten's political activities in the summer of 1933), Barth could no longer allow the public to associate him with Gogarten. He had to provide a public demonstration of their estrangement. The tendency to exaggerate the defects in *Die christliche Dogmatik* only emerged after Barth's 'Farewell' to *Zwischen den Zeiten*. There is no trace of it in *Church Dogmatics* I/1, where Barth refers to *Die christliche Dogmatik* as simply the 'first edition' (rather than using pejorative language like 'false start'). The exaggeration of the distance between the two versions of the prolegomena was therefore a function of Barth's desire to distance himself publicly from the other dialectical theologians.

As for the change in title, dating it is a knotty problem indeed. It is rather astonishing that in all the letters exchanged between Barth and Albert Lempp (the publisher of Barth's works) in the period 1930–2, no mention is ever made of what so many consider a momentous event. The letters to Thurneysen as well are entirely silent on this point.[118] The decision was probably made and discussed in personal conversation with Lempp, but one might have expected that some mention of it would have been made in a letter somewhere. What this suggests is that at the time the decision was made, Barth probably regarded the change of title as a secondary consideration—a decision which had to be made for the sake of greater consistency but which he was far from regarding as revolutionary. In any case, Barth had ample reason as early as October 1929 to change the title. In his lecture at Elberfeld on 'The Holy Ghost and the Christian Life', he complained of a growing tendency to triumphalism in the German churches. He saw in such a tendency a fundamental failure to distinguish between *Holy* Spirit and human spirit. With this in mind, he observed:

Would it not be appropriate ... to proceed with greater caution in using the adjective "Christian" than has become customary in our

[117] Barth, *KD* I/1, p. x; ET *CD* I/1, pp. xiv–xv.
[118] Here again, I am grateful to Frau Elisabeth Stoevesandt, for carefully sifting through unpublished correspondence for hints as to Barth's motivation in altering the title.

victorious modern Christendom? What is meant by Christian world-view, Christian morality, Christian art? What are Christian personali-ties, Christian families, Christian circles, Christian parties and Christian newspapers, Christian societies, Christian institutions and endeavours? Who gives us permission to use this predicate so lavishly, especially when we have to know that the conferring of this adjective in its proper, serious sense is completely withdrawn from our authority? . . . Ought not a serious consideration of the office of the Holy Ghost in the forgiveness of sinners to have at least this small consequence, that some of these adjectives will flow from the mouth and from the pen with greater difficulty in the future?[119]

Could a person who could write these words continue for long to call his dogmatics "Christian"? One must at least acknowledge that with such a pronouncement the days of "Christian" dogmat-ics were numbered. Barth himself hinted that precisely this con-sideration lay behind his decision, in the preface to *Church Dogmatics* I/1. 'In substituting the word Church for Christian in the title, I have tried to set a good example of restraint in the lighthearted use of the great word "Christian", against which I have protested.'[120] Certainly, by the time he delivered the lecture 'Theology and the Men and Women of Today' in July 1930, Barth could calmly declare 'Theology . . . is a function of the Church'[121]—which was the material reason he gave for the change of title in the preface to *Church Dogmatics* I/1.[122] Thus, the reasons for which Barth would change the title were already well established in his outlook before he began work on the Anselm book.

5. DISMISSAL AND DEPARTURE FROM BONN

Barth's role in the German Church struggle in the period 1933–5 has been treated often, and need not be repeated here. In any case, there is little reason to think that any of the events which transpired in these years had any significant influence on the last major development, which will be described in the next chapter.

---

[119] Barth, 'Der heilige Geist und das christliche Leben', 92–3; ET *The Holy Ghost and the Christian Life*, 70.
[120] Barth, *KD* I/1, p. viii; ET *CD* I/1, p. xiii.
[121] Barth, 'Die Theologie und der heutige Mensch', 375.
[122] Barth, *KD* I/1, p. viii; ET *CD* I/1, p. xiii.

Suffice it to say that Barth was suspended from the exercise of his teaching duties in Bonn on 26 November 1934 for refusing to give an unqualified oath of loyalty to Adolf Hitler. On 22 June 1935 Barth was formally dismissed by the Minister of Cultural Affairs in Berlin. Two days later, he was offered a chair in theology in the city of his birth, Basle, Switzerland.[123] On 6 July the Barth family departed Bonn, bringing Barth's years of service in Germany to an end.[124]

[123] Busch, *Karl Barth*, 255–62.
[124] Goeters, 'Karl Barth in Bonn, 1930–1935', 150.

PART IV

Dialectical Theology in the Shadow of an Anhypostatic-Enhypostatic Christology

(SECOND STAGE: CHRISTOCENTRISM, 1936–)

Question: What do you yourself say about the development of your theology?

Answer: Yes I know, there are people who say there was a break in my theology between the *Römerbrief* and now. For me, there was never a break there! In the *Römerbrief* I drew back the bow, took aim at a definite target, and let the arrow fly and the subject-matter which was there in question changed in the process—and afterwards, appeared quite differently.

(Karl Barth, 'Brechen und Bauen: Diskussion mit Prof.
Karl Barth am 5 August 1947' in idem,
Der Götze wackelt, 112)

11

The Eternal Will of God in the
Election of Jesus Christ

(BASLE, JUNE 1935–OCTOBER 1936)

I. CHRISTOCENTRISM

"Christocentrism" means different things to different people.
Formally, it simply means that a Christology stands at the
approximate centre of a particular theology, giving to it its characteristic shape and content. That much is true of all so-called
"christocentric theologies". Materially, however, the meaning of
the term can differ widely for the simple reason that the doctrine
of Christ which is placed at the centre of theology differs from
one "christocentric" theologian to the next. Albrecht Ritschl and
Adolf von Harnack were certainly "christocentric" theologians.
At the centre of their theologies stood the historical figure, Jesus
of Nazareth—His unique relationship to God, His fidelity to His
calling, His teachings, and His works of love. From his earliest
student days on, Karl Barth had reacted against the historicism
which underlay this particular brand of "christocentrism". As late
as 1924 he ventured the opinion that 'dogmatics and the preaching which follows it must, in my opinion, dare once again to be
somewhat less christocentric',[1] and when he did so, it was precisely this form of "christocentrism" that he was protesting
against. Wilhelm Herrmann too had been a "christocentric" theologian, but the focal point for him had not been the 'historical
Jesus' who is the object of scientific historical study but rather the
'inner life' of Jesus which can only be seen and understood
by faith. All of this is to say that the customary description of
Barth's theology as "christocentric" has very little explanatory

---

[1] Barth, 'Unterricht in der christlichen Religion', i. Prolegomena, 110; ET The Göttingen
Dogmatics, 91.

value unless one goes on to define concretely what "christocentrism" meant in his case. In what sense was Barth's theology
"christocentric" and when did it become so?

In his 1939 contribution to the 'How my Mind Has Changed'
series, Barth provided the answer to the first half of our question:
'in these years I had to learn that Christian doctrine, if it is to
merit its name and if it is to build up the Christian Church in the
world as she must needs be built up, has to be exclusively and
conclusively the doctrine of Jesus Christ—of Jesus Christ as the
living Word of God spoken to us men and women. . . . I should
like to call it a Christological concentration . . .'.[2] "Christocentrism", in Barth's case then, refers to the attempt (which characterized his mature theology) to understand every doctrine from
a centre in God's Self-revelation in Jesus Christ; i.e. from a centre in God's act of veiling and unveiling in Christ (which Barth
understood in terms of a highly actualistic, a posteriori
Chalcedonianism). "Christocentrism", for him, was a methodological rule—not an a priori principle, but a rule which is
learned through encounter with the God who reveals Himself in
Christ—in accordance with which one presupposes a particular
understanding of God's Self-revelation in reflecting upon each
and every other doctrinal topic, and seeks to interpret those topics in the light of what is already known of Jesus Christ. Clearly,
this methodological commitment marks an advance over the
dogmatic method outlined in each of Barth's prolegomena
(including *CD* I/1 and I/2). It does not in the least set aside that
method; but at the point where Barth would seek to correct critically Christian proclamation in the light of a fresh hearing of the
Word of God, the "christocentrism" so described provides a further concretization of what Barth thought that criticism would
most likely entail. The practical consequence of the employment
of this rule—to give just two brief examples—is that there could
be no independent doctrine of creation and providence (i.e. a
doctrine of creation which is fleshed out without reference to the
covenantal purposes of God which ground God's creative activity); and no independent anthropology (independent, that is, of
reflection upon the true, restored humanity disclosed in Christ).
The questions which such an advance raises for a genetic study of

---

[2] Barth, *How I Changed my Mind*, 43.

Barth's development are: when did this modification first occur? And what brought it about?

The answer to be given here is that this final adjustment came about in the summer of 1936, under the impress of a lecture given by a Parisian pastor, Pierre Maury, on the subject of election. More than any other influence in Barth's life, it was Maury who deserves credit for opening the way to that form of "christocentrism" which became synonymous with the name of Karl Barth.

2. REFORMATION CELEBRATIONS IN GENEVA (1936)

The hectic pace of Barth's life was not lessened by exile from Germany. Although he could no longer play a leading role in the Church struggle there, he continued to exercise what influence he could through special lectures (in which he sought to awaken Christians in Switzerland and elsewhere to the dangers faced by Confessing Christians in Germany), as well as through letters.[3] In his lecture courses, he continued in the winter semester 1935/6 and the summer semester 1936 to work his way through the material which would constitute *Church Dogmatics* I/2.

In June 1936 he travelled to Geneva to take part in a meeting of the 'Congrès international de théologie calviniste' which was timed to coincide with the 400th anniversary of the arrival of the Reformation in that city. The theme of the conference was Calvin's doctrine of predestination. Barth would later provide a rather full report on the proceedings in *Church Dogmatics* II/2.[4] There he recounted how his brother Peter, an internationally known Calvin scholar, had presented a paper which sought to correct Calvin's doctrine in the direction of a purely actualistic (*aktuellen*[5]) understanding of election; i.e. a view which tied God's electing and rejecting activity exclusively to the event in which God reveals God's Self in and through the proclamation of the Church, that event in which it is decided—for the moment—who will truly hear the Word of God and who will not. The 'existentiality' of Peter Barth's view was loudly opposed by a number of scholars, who wished to maintain a more

---

[3] See Busch, *Karl Barth*, 271–6.
[4] Barth, *KD* II/2, 207–14; ET *CD* II/2, 188–94.   [5] Ibid. 209; ET 190.

traditional view of predestination in terms of a 'fixed', pre-temporal decree of God. In his account of the debate which ensued, Karl Barth made it clear that while he certainly preferred his brother's position to the traditional one, it too was encumbered by an insuperable defect. The purely actualistic understanding of election makes God's dealings with men and women appear as a 'mere game' with no definite goal. What was required was a critical correction in the actualistic view. 'If it is presupposed that predestination is identical with the election of Jesus Christ, *then* the thesis of an actualistic [*aktuell*] predestination is grounded in a way which makes it unobjectionable and which secures it from misunderstandings on the left hand and on the right hand.'[6] What is required is the presupposition that the content of the eternal will of God has been made known in Jesus Christ, and that the content of that will is grace. The covenantal dealings of God with humankind in history are grounded in the eternal decision in which God determines Himself in Jesus Christ to be gracious. Where this is presupposed, it is then understood that the acts of God take place against the background of a history which has a goal—namely that God may be merciful to all men and women. 'In this history, God's will is completely unambiguous.'[7]

What Karl neglected to say, in advancing this criticism of the view which Peter Barth had defended on that day in June 1936, was that the view which he had himself maintained right up to the moment in which he had arrived in Geneva was precisely the view defended by his brother.[8] Furthermore, he omitted to say that it was only as a result of his hearing of another paper there, a paper given by Pierre Maury, that he had been led to make the critical correction which, in *Church Dogmatics* II/2, he introduced against the view he had once held. No doubt, the oversight was unintentional. Barth later testified to the importance of Maury's paper for his own thinking on the subject of election.

Most of those present at the Calvinist Congress were hardly prepared to accept with their hearts, or even to register with their minds, what

---

[6] Barth, *KD* II/2, 210; ET *CD* II/2, 191. [7] Ibid. 211; ET 192.

[8] This is the view which Karl Barth set forth in his Göttingen Dogmatics. See above, Ch. 8, Sect. 8. It should be noted that as late as 1932, Barth could still make divine election synonymous with the calling of believers in time, without regard for the eternal ground of this action. See Barth, *KD* I/1, 49; ET *CD* I/1, 48.

Pierre Maury was saying to them then. There were but few who realized the implications of his thesis in the course of the years that followed . . . But I remember one person who read the text of that address with the greatest attention—myself! . . . One can certainly say that it was he who contributed decisively to giving my thoughts on this subject their fundamental direction.[9]

The title of Maury's Geneva address was 'Election and Faith'.[10] Its central thesis was at once simple and profound. The doctrine of election is not to be treated in abstraction from the concrete reality in which it is realized and made known, namely Jesus Christ. 'Outside of Christ, we know neither of the electing God, nor of His elect, nor of the act of election.'[11] It is in the cross of Christ, above all, that we learn that there is no election without rejection. 'One cannot speak of damnation as a decision of God otherwise than on the basis of the cross on Golgotha, but on this basis one must speak of it.'[12] If election is election in Christ, this means first of all that Christ has taken our rejection upon Himself. 'We do not suffer and will never suffer what Christ has innocently suffered.'[13] And if Christ has taken our rejection upon Himself and borne it away, this means that the purposes of God where men and women are concerned are positive. 'The cross on which Christ was damned, does not damn us. It makes us children of God.'[14] Reprobation is thus a moment on a way which God goes with His people; a way whose goal is election. If, in the cross, Christ is seen to have been the object of God's rejecting wrath, so in the resurrection, He is seen to be the object of God's electing love. All other men and women are elect for His sake, 'in Him'. Predestination, it turns out, is "double"—but not because it has in view two distinct categories of persons (the "elect" and the "reprobate"), but rather because it has a double content (election and rejection) which are both realized in Christ.[15]

What Maury had done was to call for a truly Christological grounding of election. Where Barth had been inclined in the Göttingen Dogmatics to derive an understanding of predestination from the situation of the recipient of revelation in the here

---

[9] Karl Barth, Foreword, in Pierre Maury, *Predestination and Other Papers*, trans. Edwin Hudson (London: SCM Press, 1960), 15–16.

[10] Pierre Maury, *Erwählung und Glaube* (Theologische Studien, 8; Zurich: EVZ, 1940).

[11] Ibid. 7. [12] Ibid. 12. [13] Ibid. 13. [14] Ibid. [15] Ibid. 17.

and now, Maury had relocated the doctrine by making Christ to be the object of God's predestinating activity.

3. GOD'S GRACIOUS ELECTION

It did not take long for the impact of Maury's address on Barth's thinking to be registered publicly. In late September 1936 Barth travelled to Debrecen, Hungary, to give lectures on the subject of 'God's Gracious Election'.[16] These lectures set forth the basic viewpoints which would govern the massive treatment of the theme of election in *Church Dogmatics* II/2.

Barth's central thesis in Debrecen was that God's gracious election can only be known and understood as it is revealed in Jesus Christ. It is not a necessity of thought.[17] That is to say, it is not a first principle by means of which the system of causes and effects observed in the world is itself grounded and conditioned. But neither is it to be posited as the ground of religious experience.[18] In saying this, Barth seems to have had in mind Calvin's tendency to make predestination the explanation for the everywhere observable fact that when the gospel is proclaimed, some believe and some do not.[19] But his rejection of this possibility also constituted a departure from his own procedure in para. 18 of the Göttingen Dogmatics. In contrast to these two possibilities which have again and again plagued Christian reflection on the doctrine of predestination, Barth wanted now to advocate a strictly Christological grounding of the doctrine.[20]

The chief effect of this decision is that the content of the doctrine of predestination can only be explicated in terms of Christology. The Subject of election is the eternal Son of God (together with the Father and the Holy Spirit).[21] He it is who chooses Himself for the human race, to be the bearer of our sin and all of its consequences. It follows that the object of the divine election is—in the first instance—the eternal Son in His human nature.[22] In Him, the full reality of the divine predestination in both of its aspects is realized. In both of its aspects: that means that Jesus Christ was elected to take our rejection upon

---

[16] Karl Barth, *Gottes Gnadenwahl* (Theologische Existenz heute, 47; Zurich: EVZ, 1936).
[17] Ibid. 11.   [18] Ibid. 12.   [19] Jean Calvin, *Institutes*, III. xxi. 1.
[20] Barth, *Gottes Gnadenwahl*, 16.   [21] Ibid. 46.   [22] Ibid.

Himself. We only rightly comprehend the divine reprobation when and where we see it realized in Him. 'There and only there!'[23] Jesus Christ experienced the outpouring of the divine wrath in our place. He made Himself to be the object of the divine reprobation. In that this has occurred, it is made clear that rejection is 'not a final but rather a penultimate word'.[24] 'The relation of election and rejection is not to be seen as a fixed juxtaposition. The two concepts describe a *way* which amounts to an immense change. The New Testament describes it as the transition from death to life.'[25] The goal of His rejection is the election of the human race. Our election is a reality in Him, not just a possibility.

The advance which has occurred over against the treatment of election in the Göttingen Dogmatics should be clear. No longer are election and reprobation treated as possibilities which are realized anew in each fresh revelation–event. The election of the human race has taken place in Jesus Christ—'there and then'. Let there be no misunderstanding: the actualism of Barth's doctrine of revelation has not been damped down in the least. But it is no longer the case that the election or rejection of the individual is decided moment by moment in the revelation–event. The election of the individual has already been decided in Jesus Christ. What is decided in the revelation–event is not whether the individual is elect or not, but whether she will respond to her election in faith and obedience; whether, in other words, she will live as one who is elect (and, therefore, on the basis of the truth of her existence) or as one who is reprobate (and, therefore, on the basis of a lie).

As a consequence of this stabilization of election in Jesus Christ, the dialectic of veiling and unveiling which continued to stand at the centre of Barth's doctrine of revelation was placed in a new framework of understanding. Where once the revelation–events described by Barth seemed to be discrete and occasional, without any definite relationship to one another, it is now clear that they are joined together as moments in a single, unified history. The way of God with His people is a way whose meaning is grounded in God's eternal will in Jesus Christ to be gracious. The dialectic of veiling and unveiling would henceforth be

---

[23] Ibid. 23.   [24] Ibid. 51–2.   [25] Ibid. 51.

understood by Barth to be a 'teleologically ordered dialectic'.[26] The relationship between veiling and unveiling is not a symmetrical, equivocal, and vacillating one. Veiling occurs for the purpose of unveiling. That this is so is guaranteed by the fact that rejection occurred for the purpose of election. The hint of divine arbitrariness which still surrounded the doctrine of predestination in the Göttingen Dogmatics has been swept away.

The modification which has here been introduced into Barth's doctrine of election was to have still other, far-reaching consequences for his theology as a whole. The doctrine of predestination was now seen by Barth to be a 'regulative principle' which 'stands at the beginning of and behind all Christian thinking'.[27] The significance of this statement will become clear if we consider more closely what it means to say that Jesus Christ is the Subject and object of God's gracious election. That Jesus Christ is the Subject and the object of election means that He is its ground. He is not merely the means to the execution of another will of God which lies hidden to view 'behind' the will of God disclosed in His Self-revelation in Jesus Christ. If it is true that God has opened His heart to the world in Jesus Christ, then there can be 'no higher will in God than His will to be gracious'.[28] Barth emphatically rejected the old Reformed understanding of election in terms of a *decretum absolutum*—i.e. a decree to elect a fixed number of men and women and to reject a fixed number of others—as a decree prior to the decree to send forth the eternal Son as Mediator.[29] But if there is no other will in God than His will to be gracious, then it will also not be possible to treat the doctrine of creation independently of the doctrine of reconciliation.[30] God's purposes in creating and sustaining the world are His redemptive purposes. And that means too that God's power, goodness, and wisdom in creation cannot be treated in abstraction from the mercy and righteousness of God. It is a speculative doctrine of God which would seek to establish the meaning of His power, goodness, and wisdom without reference to the goal which God has set for Himself in that gracious election of the human race which is the ground of all of His activities.[31]

Barth did not realize the full implications of these reflections

[26] Barth, *KD* II/1, 266; ET *CD* II/1, 236.   [27] Barth, *Gottes Gnadenwahl*, 35.
[28] Ibid. 8.   [29] Ibid. 17, 44.   [30] Ibid. 43.   [31] Ibid. 8.

all at once. In the winter semester 1936/7, which followed immediately on the heels of the Debrecen lectures, his lecture course was devoted to the last fifth of the material which would comprise *Church Dogmatics* I/2. Here his central problematic was that of norm and method in theology. The "Christological concentration" which has been described did not yet make itself felt in these sections—which should not be altogether surprising since the shift in question was not concerned so much with dogmatic theory as it was with the actual execution of dogmatic method in relation to particular doctrinal topics. The place where theory and practice first came together, i.e. the place where a Christologically grounded, christocentric theology first makes itself felt, is in *Church Dogmatics* II/1, in relation to the particular question of the being of God.

In his consideration of the being of God, Barth now advanced the thesis that 'God is who He is in the act of His revelation.'[32] It is not simply that the being of God is made known to human beings in revelation; it is rather that the being of God is itself established in the act of revelation. God's being is a 'being in act'.[33] The act of revelation which Barth had in view was no longer that series of revelation-events in which God gives Himself to be known to us here and now, but *the* act of revelation in which all of these subsequent revelation-events are grounded. The stabilization of election in Jesus Christ (i.e. the affirmation that the eternal will of God in which God determines His own being has as its content Jesus Christ) had the consequence of refocusing Barth's attention quite strictly on the act of revelation which took place 'there and then'. And thus, the treatment of the being of God as a 'being in act' was carried out by means of a Christological concentration which was far more consistent in its application than anything to be found hitherto in the Göttingen Dogmatics. The being of God, Barth now said, is to be understood in terms of the categories of event, act, and life; but not event, act, and life in general. The being of God is established in a most concrete and unique event. '*Actus purus* is not sufficient as a description of God. To it there must be added at least "*et singularis*".'[34] The singularity of the event in which God's being is established and determined is guaranteed by the

---

[32] Barth, *KD* II/1, 288; ET *CD* II/1, 257.   [33] Ibid. 293; ET 262.
[34] Ibid. 296; ET 264.

fact that it consists in the incarnation of the Word and the out-pouring of the Holy Spirit.[35] God's being is a being in this particular act. And—most decisively for our purposes here—God's being as a being in this particular act is not something new for God when it occurs in time. There is no being of God in eternity in which He is not already God in this act for the simple reason that this act of God's occurs as the result of His eternal decision. The divine election in eternity is, first and foremost, an act of Self-determination. It consists in God's determination to be God in a particular relation to humanity and in no other way.

As and before God seeks and creates fellowship with us, He wills and completes this fellowship in Himself. In Himself, He does not will to exist for Himself, to exist alone. On the contrary, He is Father, Son, and Spirit and therefore alive in His unique being with and for and in another. . . . Therefore what He seeks and creates between Himself and us is in fact nothing else but what He wills and completes and therefore is in Himself.[36]

A christocentric doctrine of election thus provides the ground for Barth's explication of the being of God in *Church Dogmatics* II/1.

We could go on here to consider at length the way in which Barth's consideration of the 'perfections' of God in *Church Dogmatics* II/1 was also controlled at every point by the Christological concentration we have already observed. But that is not necessary. What we have already seen is sufficient to establish the point being made here. With the material modification of his doctrine of election in 1936, Barth's theology had arrived at a new stage of consistency with itself. Henceforth, his theology would not only be Christologically grounded in theory but in practice as well. No doubt, a closer examination of the *Church Dogmatics* would reveal other significant alterations in the details of Barth's treatment of various doctrinal topics. But none could have the sweeping significance for the shape of his theology as a whole which the modification in his doctrine of election had.

---

[35] Barth, *KD* II/1, 300; ET *CD* II/1, 267.

[36] Ibid. 308–9; ET 275. The logical conclusion of the drift of thought contained in this passage is to be found in *Church Dogmatics* II/2, where Barth maintained: 'God is not *in abstracto* Father, Son and Holy Ghost, the triune God. He is so with a definite purpose and reference; in virtue of the love and freedom in which in the bosom of His triune being He has foreordained Himself from and to all eternity.' See *KD* II/2, 85; ET *CD* II/2, 79.

The distinctive form of "christocentrism" which would stamp all of the later volumes of the *Church Dogmatics* was the consequence of his call at Debrecen for a Christologically grounded doctrine of election.

CONCLUSION

Through all the phases of his development after the break with Herrmannian liberalism in 1915, Karl Barth was a critically realistic dialectical theologian. That is the red thread which runs through the whole of the development, making it to be a unified whole in spite of the differing models of explication employed from one phase to the next.

It is well known that Barth disdained the term "dialectical theology" as a piece of self-description. Given, above all, the tensions which existed between the members of the dialectical theology movement throughout the 1920s and their eventual break-up, Barth's reticence in this regard is understandable. For just this reason the adjectival phrase "critically realistic" has been employed throughout the present work in an effort to distinguish Barth's version of dialectical theology from all the alternative conceptions (for example, the dialectical theologies of a Rudolf Bultmann or a Paul Tillich).

It should be noted that the choice of the phrase "critically realistic" was not made out of a desire to establish a comparison between Barth's theology and those contemporary schools of philosophical reflection which have also found in the phrase something apt for describing their own epistemologies. No such comparison was intended, for it is doubtful that it can be made—for two reasons.

First, as the phrase has been used here, it describes a strictly theological epistemology. "Critical realism" here has the significance of a witness to the mystery of the divine action in revelation. To a large extent, this witness has a negative character. Like the Chalcedonian formula, it points out errors on the right hand and on the left without giving positive expression to the truth in the middle. And the reason is quite simply that the truth in the middle can only be expressed by God.

In an illuminating passage in *Church Dogmatics* I/1, Karl Barth discussed at length the impossibility of identifying the Word of God with either the secular form in which the divine content

veils itself or the divine content in absence of the secular form—
for both content and form belong to the event of the Word.
But here a problem immediately arises. The event of the
Word occurs only where a synthesis of content and form take
place, but this is a synthesis which no human being can bring
about:

it is a matter of hearing the whole, the real Word of God, and therefore, both the *unveiling* of God in His veiling as well as the *veiling* of
God in His unveiling. The secular form without the divine content is
not the Word of God and the divine content without the secular form
is also not the Word of God. We can neither stop at the secular form as
such nor can we fly off beyond this and try to enjoy the divine content
alone. The one would be realistic theology, the other idealistic theology, and both bad theology. . . . The coincidence of the two is clear to
God but not discernible by us. What is discernible by us is always form
without content or content without form. Our thinking can be realistic
or idealistic but it cannot be Christian. Obviously the concept of synthesis would be the least Christian of all, for it would mean no more
and no less than trying to achieve God's miraculous act ourselves. . . .
Faith means recognizing that synthesis cannot be attained and commit-
ting it to God and seeking and finding it in Him.[1]

In and of ourselves, our thinking in the face of the Word can
only be realistic or idealistic thinking. It will be thinking which is
concentrated either on the veil or on a content which has been
set apart from the veil. If we seek to go beyond these human
possibilities—if we seek to achieve a synthesis of the two—we
are seeking that which is beyond the realm of human possibility.
Where genuine synthesis of the secular form and the divine content has occurred, there human efforts have ceased. There the
miracle has occurred; God has acted. It is to bear witness to this
divine possibility which lies beyond the human possibilities of
realism and idealism that the term "critical realism" has been
employed in this book.

Second, as has been argued throughout this book, to the
extent that Barth concerned himself with philosophical epistemology at all, he was an idealist (and more specifically, a
Kantian). All of his efforts in theology may be considered, from
one point of view, as an attempt to overcome Kant by means of
Kant; not retreating behind him and seeking to go around him,

---

[1] Barth, *KD* I/1, 182; ET *CD* I/1, 175.

but going through him. The phrase "*critical* realism", as applied to Barth's theological epistemology, has the decided advantage over competing alternatives of pointing to the great debt which he owed to the Kantian tradition in philosophy.[2] But if all this be true, then it also means that Barth still had a very strong foot in the nineteenth century. Thus, comparisons with contemporary options in philosophical epistemology would very easily give rise to anachronistic readings of Barth's theology, with all of the distortion that entails. For this reason too, I have deliberately chosen not to seek to justify the use of the term by means of a comparison with those philosophers who make use of it today, but have allowed the exposition of the subject-matter under investigation to provide the justification.

One final observation: however critical Barth may have been of modern theology, it is of the utmost importance—if we are to have a more accurate understanding of the history of theology in the last two centuries—to see that dialectical theology in the form in which it was taught by Barth was a thoroughly *modern* option. It was, after all, only by presupposing the legitimacy of Kantian epistemology that he was enabled to envision the dialectic of veiling and unveiling in God's Self-revelation in the form he did. Moreover, as we have had occasion to see, many of the themes most commonly associated with his name—the rejection of natural theology and apologetics, the attack on historicism, etc.—were themes learned at the feet of the great nineteenth-century liberal theologian, Wilhelm Herrmann.

Perhaps the most pressing need in contemporary theology is a historical one. It is high time that we subject the dominant historiography of nineteenth- and twentieth-century theology to critical scrutiny. The pattern—liberal, neo-orthodox, post-liberal (and whatever other "posts" one might wish to thrown in)—is much too simplistic. It fails to grasp adequately the complex relationship of theology in the early half of the twentieth century— and, I would say, of theology in our day as well—to nineteenth-century antecedents and serves all too often as an ideological crutch to justify whatever theological programme a particular theologian would have advocated without its help. I personally would regard it as a most hopeful sign that theology

---

[2] Cf. Ingolf Ulrich Dalferth, 'Karl Barth's Eschatological Realism', in Sykes (ed.), *Karl Barth: Centenary Essays*, 14–45.

today is becoming self-critical, if the celebration of our "post-modernity" were restrained long enough to ask the crucial question: precisely what is this "modernity" that we think ourselves now to have transcended? What does it mean to be "modern" in the realm of theology? Rigorous and comprehensive study of Karl Barth's theology can no longer be avoided if an adequate answer to that question is to be given.

BIBLIOGRAPHY

PRIMARY LITERATURE

KARL BARTH

Books, Book-Length Lecture Series, and Collections (in chronological order)

Vorträge und kleinere Arbeiten, 1905–1909, ed. Hans Anton Drewes and Hinrich Stoevesandt (Zurich: TVZ, 1992).

Konfirmandenunterricht, 1909–1921, ed. Jürgen Fangmeier (Zurich: TVZ, 1987).

Predigten 1913, ed. Nelly Barth and Gerhard Sauter (Zurich: TVZ, 1976).

Predigten 1914, ed. Ursula and Jochen Fähler (Zurich: TVZ, 1974).

Der Römerbrief (Erste Fassung) 1919, ed. Hermann Schmidt (Zurich: TVZ, 1985).

Der Römerbrief, 1922 (Zurich: TVZ, 1940).

Die Theologie Calvins, 1922, ed. Hans Scholl (Zurich: TVZ, 1993).

Vorträge und kleinere Arbeiten, 1922–25, ed. Holger Finze (Zurich: TVZ, 1990).

Die Auferstehung der Toten (Munich: Chr. Kaiser Verlag, 1924). ET *The Resurrection of the Dead*. trans. H. J. Stenning (London: Hodder & Stoughton Ltd., 1933).

Die Theologie Schleiermachers: Vorlesung, Göttingen, Wintersemester 1923/24, ed. Dietrich Ritschl (Zurich: TVZ, 1978). ET *The Theology of Schleiermacher. Lectures at Göttingen, Winter Semester of 1923/24*, trans. Geoffrey Bromiley (Grand Rapids: Wm. B. Eerdmans, 1982).

Das Wort Gottes und Die Theologie (Munich: Chr. Kaiser Verlag, 1925).

'Unterricht in der christlichen Religion', i. *Prolegomena, 1924*, ed. Hannelotte Reiffen (Zurich: 1985). ET *The Göttingen Dogmatics: Instruction in the Christian Religion*, vol. i, trans. Geoffrey Bromiley (Grand Rapids: Wm. B. Eerdmans, 1991).

'Unterricht in der christlichen Religion', ii. *Die Lehre von Gott/Die Lehre vom Menschen, 1924/1925*, ed. Hinrich Stoevesandt (Zurich: TVZ, 1990). ET *The Göttingen Dogmatics*, vol. i. (contains the first third of the German edition).

'Unterricht in der christlichen Religion', para. 28 (lectures delivered in Göttingen, summer semester 1925). Typed manuscript copy in Karl Barth-Archiv, Basle, Switzerland.

Erklärung des Johannes-evangeliums 1–8: Vorlesung, Münster, Winter-semester 1925/26, ed. Walther Fürst (Zurich: TVZ, 1976).

Vom christlichen Leben (Munich: Chr. Kaiser Verlag, 1926).

Die christliche Dogmatik im Entwurf, ed. Gerhard Sauter (Zurich: TVZ, 1982).

Erklärung des Philipperbriefes (Munich: Chr. Kaiser Verlag, 1928). ET *The Epistle to the Philippians*, trans. J. W. Leitch (London: SCM Press, 1962).

Die Theologie und die Kirche (Munich: Chr. Kaiser Verlag, 1928). ET *Theology and Church*, trans. Louise Pettitbone Smith (London: SCM, 1962).

Ethik I: Vorlesung, Münster, Sommersemester 1928, ed. Dietrich Braun (Zurich: TVZ, 1973).

Ethik II: Vorlesung, Münster, Wintersemester 1928/29, ed. Dietrich Braun (Zurich: TVZ, 1978). ET *Ethics*, trans. Geoffrey Bromiley (New York: The Seabury Press, 1981). (Contains both *Ethik I* and *Ethik II*.)

Fides quaerens intellectum: Anselms Beweis der Existenz Gottes im Zusammenhang seines theologischen Programms, ed. Eberhard Jüngel and Ingolf Ulrich Dalferth (Zurich: TVZ, 1981). ET *Anselm: Fides quaerens intellectum*, trans. Ian W. Robertson (London: SCM Press, 1960). (Reprint edn.; Pittsburgh: The Pickwick Press, 1975.)

Die kirchliche Dogmatik (Munich: Chr. Kaiser, 1932, and Zürich: EVZ, 1938–65). ET *Church Dogmatics*, trans. Geoffrey Bromiley (Edinburgh: T. & T. Clark, 1956–69).

Die protestantische Theologie im 19. Jahrhundert (5th edn.; Zurich: TVZ, 1985). ET *Protestant Theology in the Nineteenth Century* (Valley Forge, Pa.: Judson Press, 1976).

Credo (Munich: Chr. Kaiser Verlag, 1935). ET *Credo*, trans. J. S. McNab (New York: Scribner, 1962).

Theologische Fragen und Antworten (2nd edn.; Zurich: TVZ, 1986).

Der Götze wackelt: Zeitkritische Aufsätze, Reden und Briefe von 1930 bis 1960, ed. Karl Kupisch (Berlin: Käthe Vogt Verlag, 1961).

Evangelical Theology: An Introduction, trans. Grover Foley (Grand Rapids: Wm. B. Eerdmans, 1963).

Shorter Articles, Essays, and Addresses

'Zofingia und Sociale Frage' (lecture delivered in Bern, 20 January 1906), in idem, *Vorträge und kleinere Arbeiten, 1905–1909*, ed. Hans Anton Drewes and Hinrich Stoevesandt (Zurich: TVZ, 1992).

'Moderne Theologie und Reichgottesarbeit', *Zeitschrift für Theologie und Kirche*, 19 (1909), 317–21.

'Antwort an D. Achelis und P. Drews', *Zeitschrift für Theologie und Kirche*, 19 (1909), 479–86.

'John Mott und die christliche Studentenbewegung', *Centralblatt des Schweizerischen Zofingervereins*, 51 (1910/11), 487–502.

'Jesus Christ und die soziale Bewegung' (lecture delivered to the Safenwiler Arbeiterverein, 17 December 1911). ET 'Jesus Christ and the Movement for Social Justice', in George Hunsinger (ed.), *Karl Barth and Radical Politics* (Philadelphia: Westminster Press, 1976), 19–37.

'Answer to the Open Letter of Mr. W. Hüssy in Aarburg', in George Hunsinger (ed.), *Karl Barth and Radical Politics*, 40–5.

'Der christliche Glaube und die Geschichte' (revised version of a lecture delivered to the German Pastors' Conference of Western Switzerland in Neuenburg, 5 October 1910), *Schweizerische Theologische Zeitschrift*, 29 (1912), 1–18, 49–72.

'Rezension von: Heim, Karl: "Das Gewissheitsproblem in systematischer Theologie bis zu Schleiermacher: Leipzig: Hinrichs, 1911"', *Schweizerische Theologische Zeitschrift*, 29 (1912), 262–7.

'Der Glaube an den persönlichen Gott' (lecture delivered to the Association of Pastors in the Aargau, 19 May 1913), *Zeitschrift für Theologie und Kirche*, 24 (1914), 21–32, 65–95.

'*Die Hilfe*, 1913', *Die Christliche Welt*, 28 (1914), 774–8.

'Gottes Vorhut' (sermon delivered in Safenwil, 14 February 1915), *Neue Wege: Blätter für religiöse Arbeit*, 9 (1915), 89–97.

'Friede', *Die Glocke: Monatliches Organ des Christlichen Vereins junger Männer*, 23 (June 1915), 55–6.

'Religion und Sozialismus' (lecture delivered to the Sozialistische Partei der Schweiz (SPS) in Baden, 7 December 1915). Copy in Karl Barth-Archiv, Basle, Switzerland.

'Die Gerechtigkeit Gottes' (lecture delivered to the Aarau Church Council, 16 January 1916), in idem, *Das Wort Gottes und die Theologie*, 5–17.

'Das Eine Notwendige' (sermon delivered to the Aarau Christian Student Conference, 13 March 1916), *Die XX. Christliche Studenten-Konferenz (Aarau, 1916)* (Bern: Franke, 1916), 5–15.

'Der Pfarrer, der es den Leuten recht macht: Eine religiös-soziale Predigt' (sermon delivered in Safenwil, 6 February 1916), *Die Christliche Welt*, 30/14 (6 April 1916), 262–7.

'Auf das Reich Gottes warten', *Der freie Schweizer Arbeiter*, 9/49 (15 September 1916), 1–3; 9/50 (22 September 1916), 2–3. ET *Action in Waiting* (Rifton, NY: Plough Publishing Company, 1969).

'Die neue Welt in der Bibel' (lecture delivered in Leutwil, 6 February 1917), in idem, *Das Wort Gottes und die Theologie*, 18–32.

'Religion und Leben' (lecture delivered in Safenwil, 9 October 1917), *Evangelische Theologie*, 11 (1951/2), 437–51.

'Ein Wort an das aargauische Bürgertum', *Neuer Freier Aargauer: Sozialdemokratisches Tagblatt*, 14/157 (10 July 1919), 1.

'Das was nicht geschehen soll', *Neuer Freier Aargauer: Sozialdemokratisches Tagblatt*, 14/188 (15 August 1919), 1–2.

'Vergangenheit und Zukunft', *Neuer Freier Aargauer: Sozialdemokratisches Tagblatt*, 14/204 (3 September 1919), 1–2; 14/205 (4 September 1919), 1–2. ET 'Past and Future', in James M. Robinson (ed.), *The Beginnings of Dialectic Theology* (Richmond: John Knox Press, 1968), 35–45.

'Der Christ in der Gesellschaft' (lecture delivered in Tambach, 25 September 1919), in idem, *Das Wort Gottes und die Theologie*, 33–69.

'Vom Rechthaben und Unrechthaben' (lecture delivered to a Sozialdemokratischen Volksversammlung in Suhr, 29 November 1919), *Das neue Werk: Der Christ im Volksstaat*, 1 (1920), 635–41.

'Biblische Fragen, Einsichten und Ausblicke' (lecture delivered at the 24th Aarau Student Christian Conference, 17 April 1920), in idem, *Das Wort Gottes und die Theologie*, 70–98.

'Unerledigte Anfragen an die heutige Theologie', in idem, *Die Theologie und Die Kirche*, 1–25. ET 'Unsettled Questions for Theology Today', in *Theology and Church*, 55–73.

'Grundfragen der christlichen Sozialethik: Auseinandersetzung mit Paul Althaus', *Das neue Werk*, 4 (1922), 461–72. ET 'Basic Problems of Christian Social Ethics: A Discussion with Paul Althaus', in Robinson (ed.), *The Beginnings of Dialectic Theology*, 46–57.

'Not und Verheißung der christlichen Verkündigung' (lecture delivered in Schulpforte, 25 July 1922), in idem, *Das Wort Gottes und die Theologie*, 99–124.

'Das Problem der Ethik in der Gegenwart' (lecture delivered in Wiesbaden, September 1922), in idem, *Das Wort Gottes und die Theologie*, 125–55.

'Das Wort Gottes als Aufgabe der Theologie' (lecture delivered in Elgersburg, 3 October 1922), in idem, *Das Wort Gottes und die Theologie*, 156–78.

'Ein Briefwechsel mit Adolf von Harnack', in idem, *Theologische Fragen und Antworten*, 7–31. ET 'Correspondence Between Adolf von Harnack and Karl Barth', in Robinson (ed.), *The Beginnings of Dialectic Theology*, 165–87.

'Ansatz und Absicht in Luthers Abendmahlslehre', in idem, *Die Theologie und die Kirche*, 26–75. ET *Theology and Church*, 74–111.

'Reformierte Lehre, ihr Wesen und ihre Aufgabe' (lecture delivered in Emden, 17 September 1923), in idem, *Das Wort Gottes und die Theologie*, 179–212.

'Die Kirche und die Offenbarung' (lecture delivered first in Lübeck, 30 November 1923), in idem, *Vorträge und kleinere Arbeiten, 1922–1925*, 307–48.

'Von der Paradoxie des "positiven Paradoxes": Antworten und Fragen an Paul Tillich', in Jürgen Moltmann (ed.), *Anfänge der dialektischen Theologie* (Munich: Chr. Kaiser Verlag, 1963), i. 175–89. ET 'The Paradoxical Nature of the "Positive Paradox": Answers and Questions to Paul Tillich', in Robinson (ed.), *The Beginnings of Dialectic Theology*, 142–54.

'Brunners Schleiermacherbuch', *Zwischen den Zeiten*, 2 (1924), 49–64.

'Menschenwort und Gotteswort in der christlichen Predigt' (lecture delivered first in Königsberg, 25 November 1924), *Zwischen den Zeiten*, 3 (1925), 119–40.

'Schleiermachers "Weihnachtsfeier"', in idem, *Die Theologie und die Kirche*, 106–35. ET 'Schleiermacher's Celebration of Christmas', in *Theology and Church*, 136–58.

'Sunt certi denique fines', *Zwischen den Zeiten*, 3 (1925), 113–16.

'Das Schriftprinzip der reformierten Kirche' (lecture delivered first in Basle, 20 April 1925), *Zwischen den Zeiten*, 3 (1925), 215–45.

'Die dogmatische Prinzipienlehre bei Wilhelm Herrmann' (lecture delivered first in Hanover, 13 May 1925), in idem, *Die Theologie und die Kirche*, 240–84. ET 'The Principles of Dogmatics According to Wilhelm Herrmann', in *Theology and Church*, 238–71.

'Wünschbarkeit und Möglichkeit eines allgemeinen reformierten Glaubensbekenntnisses' (lecture delivered first in Duisburg-Meiderich, 3 June 1925), in idem, *Die Theologie und die Kirche*, 76–105. ET 'The Desirability and Possibility of a Universal Reformed Creed', in *Theology and Church*, 112–35.

'Kirche und Theologie' (lecture delivered first in Göttingen, 7 October 1925), in idem, *Die Theologie und die Kirche*, 302–28. ET 'Church and Theology', in *Theology and Church*, 286–306.

'Die Kirche und die Kultur' (lecture delivered in Amsterdam, 1 June 1926), in idem, *Die Theologie und die Kirche*, 364–91. ET 'Church and Culture', in *Theology and Church*, 334–54.

'Ludwig Feuerbach' (fragment from lectures delivered summer semester 1926 on 'The History of Protestant Theology since Schleiermacher'), in idem, *Die Theologie und die Kirche*, 212–39. ET 'Ludwig Feuerbach', in *Theology and Church*, 217–37.

'Schleiermacher' (fragment from lectures delivered summer semester 1926 on 'The History of Protestant Theology since Schleiermacher'), in idem, *Die Theologie und die Kirche*, 136–89. ET 'Schleiermacher', in *Theology and Church*, 159–99.

'Das Halten der Gebote' (lecture delivered to the 30th Aarau Christian

Student Conference, 9 March 1927), *Zwischen den Zeiten*, 5 (1927), 206–27.

'Rechtfertigung und Heiligung' (lecture delivered first in Rudolstadt, 20–1 April 1927), *Zwischen den Zeiten*, 5 (1927), 281–309.

'Der Begriff der Kirche' (lecture delivered in Münster, 11 July 1927), in idem, *Die Theologie und die Kirche*, 285–301. ET 'The Concept of the Church', in *Theology and Church*, 272–85.

'Das Wort in der Theologie von Schleiermacher bis Ritschl' (lecture delivered in Elberfeld, 19 October 1927), in idem, *Die Theologie und die Kirche*, 190–211. ET 'The Word in Theology from Schleiermacher to Ritschl', in *Theology and Church*, 200–16.

'Der römische Katholizismus als Frage an die protestantische Kirche' (lecture delivered in Bremen, 9 March 1928), in idem, *Die Theologie und die Kirche*, 329–63. ET 'Roman Catholicism: A Question to the Protestant Church', in *Theology and Church*, 307–33.

'Karl Barth an Karl Heim, 12 June 1928', *Die Furche*, NF 14 (1928), 23–5.

'Schicksal und Idee in der Theologie' (lectures delivered in February–March 1929), in idem, *Theologische Fragen und Antworten*, 54–92. ET 'Fate and Idea in Theology', trans. George Hunsinger, in H. Martin Rumscheidt (ed.), *The Way of Theology in Karl Barth* (Allison Park, Pa.: Pickwick Publications, 1986), 25–61.

'Die Lehre von den Sakramenten', *Zwischen den Zeiten*, 7 (1929), 427–60.

'Der heilige Geist und das christliche Leben' (lecture delivered in Elberfeld, 9 October 1929), in Heinrich Barth and Karl Barth, *Zur Lehre vom heiligen Geist* (Munich: Chr. Kaiser Verlag), 1930, 39–105. ET *The Holy Ghost and the Christian Life*, trans. R. Birch Hoyle (London: Frederick Muller Ltd., 1938).

'Bemerkungen zu Hans Michael Müllers Lutherbuch', *Zwischen den Zeiten*, 7 (1929), 561–70.

'Maria' (sermon on Luke 1: 26–8, 1 December 1929), in Karl Barth and Eduard Thurneysen, *Die große Barmherzigkeit* (Munich: Chr. Kaiser Verlag, 1935), 106–15.

'Quosque tandem . . .?', *Zwischen den Zeiten*, 8 (1930), 1–6.

'Die Theologie und der heutige Mensch' (lecture delivered in July 1930), *Zwischen den Zeiten*, 8 (1930), 374–96.

'Zu Erik Petersons Übertritt zum römischen Katholizismus', *Theologische Blätter*, 10 (1931), 59–60.

'Die Not der evangelischen Kirche' (lecture delivered on 31 January 1931), in idem, *Der Götze wackelt*, 33–62.

'Die Arbeit als Problem der theologischen Ethik', *Theologische Blätter*, 10 (1931), 250–6.

'Verheißung, Zeit-Erfüllung', *Zwischen den Zeiten*, 9 (1931), 457–63.

'Fragen an das "Christentum"', in idem, *Theologischen Fragen und Antworten*, 93–9.

'Abschied', *Zwischen den Zeiten*, 11 (1933), 536–44.

Nein!: *Antwort an Emil Brunner* (Theologische Existenz heute, 14; Munich: Chr. Kaiser Verlag, 1934).

'Zum Geleit', in Heinrich Heppe, *Die Dogmatik der evangelisch-reformierten Kirche*, ed. Ernst Bizer (Neukirchen: Buchhandlung des Erziehungsvereins, 1935), pp. vii–x. ET 'Karl Barth's Foreword', in Heinrich Heppe, *Reformed Dogmatics*, trans. G. T. Thomson (London: Allen & Unwin, 1950; reprint edn., Grand Rapids: Baker Book House, 1978), pp. v–vii.

Gottes Gnadenwahl (Theologische Existenz heute, 47; Munich: Chr. Kaiser Verlag, 1936).

Die Menschlichkeit Gottes (Theologische Studien, 48; Zurich: EVZ, 1956).

'Evangelical Theology in the Nineteenth Century', in idem, *The Humanity of God*, trans. Thomas Wieser (Atlanta: John Knox Press, 1978).

Foreword, in Pierre Maury, *Predestination and Other Papers*, trans. Edwin Hudson (London: SCM Press, 1960).

'Dank und Reverenz', *Evangelische Theologie*, 7 (1963), 337–42.

Autobiographical Material

'Autobiographische Skizzen Karl Barths aus den Fakultätsalben der Ev.-Theo. Fakultät in Münster', in *Karl Barth–Rudolf Bultmann Briefwechsel, 1922–1966*, ed. Bernd Jaspert (Zurich: TVZ, 1971), 301–11. ET *Karl Barth–Rudolf Bultmann Letters, 1922–1966*, trans. Geoffrey Bromiley (Grand Rapids: Wm. B. Eerdmans, 1981), 150–7.

How I Changed my Mind (Edinburgh: The Saint Andrew Press, 1969).

'Die Neuorientierung der protestantischen Theologie in den letzten dreißig Jahren', *Kirchenblatt für die reformierte Schweiz*, 96 (1940), 98–101.

'Karl Barth', in *Schweizerköpfe der Gegenwart* (Zurich: Verlag 'Schweizerköpfe der Gegenwart', 1945), i. 117–21.

'Rückblick', in *Das Wort sie sollen lassen stahn: Festschrift für D. Albert Schädelin* (Bern, 1950); reprinted in Karl Barth, *Offene Briefe, 1945–68*, ed. Diether Koch (Zurich: TVZ, 1984).

'Zwischenzeit'. *Kirchenblatt für die reformierte Schweiz*, 118 (1962), 38–9.

'Ein Brief an den Jubilar' (to Fritz Lieb on his 70th birthday, 10 June 1962), *Evangelische Theologie*, 22 (1962), 282–5.

'Reformierte Theologie in der Schweiz', in The Theological Faculty of the University of Amsterdam, *Ex auditu verbi: Festschrift für G. C. Berkower* (Kampen: Kok, 1965), 27–36.

'Concluding Unscientific Postscript on Schleiermacher', trans. George Hunsinger, in Karl Barth, *The Theology of Schleiermacher*, 261–79.

Letzte Zeugnisse (Zurich: EVZ, 1969). ET *Final Testimonies*, trans. Geoffrey Bromiley (Grand Rapids: Wm. B. Eerdmans, 1977).

Collections of Letters

JASPERT, BERND (ed.), *Karl Barth–Rudolf Bultmann: Briefwechsel, 1922–1966* (Zurich: TVZ, 1971).

KOCH, DIETHER (ed.), *Karl Barth: Offene Briefe, 1945–68* (Zurich: TVZ, 1984).

SCHWÖBEL, CHRISTOPH (ed.), *Karl Barth–Martin Rade: Ein Briefwechsel* (Gütersloh: Gütersloher Verlagshaus Gerd Mohn, 1981).

STOEVESANDT, HINRICH (ed.), *Karl Barth–Kornelis Heiko Miskotte: Briefwechsel, 1924–1968* (Zurich: TVZ, 1991).

THURNEYSEN, EDUARD (ed.), *Karl Barth–Eduard Thurneysen: Briefwechsel*, i. *1913–1921* (Zurich: TVZ, 1973).

——, *Karl Barth–Eduard Thurneysen: Briefwechsel*, ii. *1921–1930* (Zurich: TVZ, 1974).

Single Letters

Karl Barth to Paul Althaus, postcard, 1924 (exact date not recorded). Copy in Karl Barth-Archiv, Basle, Switzerland.

Karl Barth to Paul Althaus, 30 May 1928. Copy in Karl Barth-Archiv, Basle, Switzerland.

Karl Barth to Paul Althaus, 14 September 1929. Copy in Karl Barth-Archiv, Basle, Switzerland.

Karl Barth to Hans Asmussen, 14 January 1932. Copy in Karl Barth-Archiv, Basle, Switzerland.

Karl Barth to Emil Brunner, 26 January 1924. Copy in Karl Barth-Archiv, Basle, Switzerland.

Karl Barth to Eduard Thurneysen, 9 January 1931. Copy in Karl Barth-Archiv, Basle, Switzerland.

Karl Barth in Collaboration with Eduard Thurneysen

Suchet Gott, so werdet ihr Leben! (2nd edn.; Munich: Chr. Kaiser Verlag, 1928).

Komm Schöpfer Geist!: Predigten (Munich: Chr. Kaiser Verlag, 1924).

RELATED SOURCES

ACHELIS, ERNST CHRISTIAN, 'Noch einmal: Moderne Theologie und Reichgottesarbeit', *Zeitschrift für Theologie und Kirche*, 19 (1909), 406–10.

ALBERS, A. 'Johannes Müller und Karl Barth; was sie uns heute sind', *Die Christliche Welt*, 35 (1921), 498–501.

ALTHAUS, PAUL, 'Theologie und Geschichte: Zur Auseinandersetzung mit der dialektischen Theologie', *Zeitschrift für systematische Theologie*, 1 (1923/4), 741–86.

——, 'Zur Lehre von der Sünde', *Zeitschrift für systematische Theologie*, 1 (1923/4), 314–34.

BACHMANN, PHILIPP, 'Der Römerbrief verdeutscht und vergegenwärtigt: Ein Wort zu K. Barths Römerbrief', *Neue kirchliche Zeitschrift*, 32 (1921), 517–47.

BARTH, HEINRICH, *Das Problem des Ursprungs in der platonischen Philosophie* (Munich: Chr. Kaiser Verlag, 1921).

——, 'Grundzüge einer Philosophie der Existenz in ihrer Beziehung zur Glaubenswahrheit', *Theologische Zeitschrift*, 9 (1953), 100–17.

——, 'Gotteserkenntnis', in J. Moltmann (ed.), *Anfänge der dialektischen Theologie* (Munich: Chr. Kaiser Verlag, 1963), i. 221–55.

BRUNNER, EMIL, *Erlebnis, Erkenntnis und Glaube* (1st edn.; Tübingen: J. C. B. Mohr, 1921).

——, *Die Mystik und das Wort* (Tübingen: J. C. B. Mohr, 1924).

——, letter to Karl Barth, 23 January 1924. Copy in Karl Barth-Archiv, Basle, Switzerland.

——, letter to Karl Barth, late summer(?) 1924. Copy in Karl Barth-Archiv, Basle, Switzerland.

——, 'Die andere Aufgabe der Theologie', *Zwischen den Zeiten*, 7 (1929), 255–76.

——, 'Die Frage nach dem "Anknüpfungspunkt" als Problem der Theologie', *Zwischen den Zeiten*, 10 (1932), 505–32.

——, 'Der Römerbrief von Karl Barth: Eine zeitgemäß unmoderne Paraphrase', in J. Moltmann (ed.), *Anfänge der dialektischen Theologie* (Munich: Chr. Kaiser Verlag, 1963), i. 78–87. ET '*The Epistle to the Romans* by Karl Barth: An Up-to-Date, Unmodern Paraphrase', in James M. Robinson (ed.), *The Beginnings of Dialectic Theology* (Richmond: John Knox Press, 1968), 63–71.

BULTMANN, RUDOLF, 'Die liberale Theologie und die jüngste theologische Bewegung', *Theologische Blätter*, 3 (1924), 73–86. ET 'Liberal Theology and the Latest Theological Movement', in idem, *Faith and Understanding*, 28–52.

——, 'Das Problem einer theologischen Exegese des Neuen Testaments', *Zwischen den Zeiten*, 3 (1925), 334–57. ET 'The Problem of a Theological Exegesis of the New Testament', in James M. Robinson (ed.), *The Beginnings of Dialectic Theology* (Richmond: John Knox Press, 1968), 236–56.

——, *Jesus and the Word* (New York: Scribners, 1958).

BULTMANN, RUDOLF, 'Karl Barth, *The Resurrection of the Dead*', in idem, *Faith and Understanding*, trans. Louise Pettitbone Smith (Philadelphia: Fortress Press, 1987), 66–94.

DIEM, HERMANN, 'Credo ut intelligam: Ein Wort zu Hans Michael Müllers Kritik an Karl Barths Dogmatik', *Zwischen den Zeiten*, 6 (1928), 517–28.

DREWS, PAUL, 'Zum dritten Mal: Moderne Theologie und Reichgottesarbeit', *Zeitschrift für Theologie und Kirche*, 19 (1909), 475–79.

ECKE, GUSTAV, *Die theologische Schule Albrecht Ritschls und die Evangelische Kirche der Gegenwart* (Berlin: Reuther & Reichard, 1897).

FOERSTER, ERICH, 'Marcionistisches Christentum'. *Die Christliche Welt*, 35 (1921), 809–27.

GEIGER, MAX, and LINDT, ANDREAS (eds.), *Hermann Kutter in seinen Briefen, 1883–1931* (Munich: Chr. Kaiser Verlag, 1983).

GOGARTEN, FRIEDRICH, 'Die Krisis unserer Kultur', *Die Christliche Welt* 34 (1920), 770–7, 786–91. ET 'The Crisis of Our Culture', in James M. Robinson (ed.), *The Beginnings of Dialectic Theology* (Richmond: John Knox Press, 1968), 283–300.

——, 'Zwischen den Zeiten', in Jürgen Moltman (ed.), *Anfänge der dialektischen Theologie* (Munich: Chr. Kaiser Verlag, 1963), ii. 95–101. ET 'Between the Times', in Robinson (ed.), *The Beginnings of Dialectic Theology*, 277–82.

——, *Ich glaube an den dreieinigen Gott: Eine Untersuchung über Glaube und Geschichte* (Jena: Eugen Diederichs Verlag, 1926).

——, 'Karl Barths Dogmatik', *Theologische Rundschau*, NF 1 (1929), 60–80.

——, 'Das Problem einer theologischen Anthropologie', *Zwischen den Zeiten*, 7 (1929), 493–511.

HARNACK, ADOLF VON, *What is Christianity?*, trans. Thomas Bailey Saunders (New York: Harper Torchbooks, 1957).

HARTMANN, HANS 'Zur inneren Lage des Christentums. Versuch einer Stellungnahme zum religiösen Sozialismus der "Schweizer"', *Die Christliche Welt*, 35 (1921), 84–88.

HERRMANN, WILHELM, 'Die Sittlichen Weisungen Jesu: Ihr Mißbrauch und ihr richtiger Gebrauch', in idem, *Schriften zur Grundlegung der Theologie*, i. 200–41. ET 'The Moral Teachings of Jesus', in Adolf von Harnack and Wilhelm Herrmann, *Essays on the Social Gospel* (London: Williams & Norgate, 1907), 145–225.

——, 'Der Widerspruch im religiösen Denken und seine Bedeutung für das Leben der Religion', *Zeitschrift für Theologie und Kirche*, 21 (1911), 1–16.

——, *Ethik* (5th edn.; Tübingen: J. C. B. Mohr, 1913).

——, 'Albrecht Ritschl, seine Größe und seine Schranke', in Karl Holl (ed.), *Festgabe von Fachgenossen und Freunden A. von Harnack zum siebzigsten Geburtstag dargebracht* (Tübingen: J. C. B. Mohr, 1921), 405–6.

——, 'Die Auffassung der Religion in Cohens und Natorps Ethik', in idem, *Gesammelte Schriften*, ed. Friedrich Wilhelm Schmidt (Tübingen: J. C. B. Mohr, 1923), 377–405.

——, 'Der evangelische Glaube und die Theologie Albrecht Ritschls', in idem, *Gesammelte Schriften*, 1–25.

——, 'Die Lage und Aufgabe der evangelischen Dogmatik in der Gegenwart', in idem, *Gesammelte Schriften*, 95–188.

——, 'Religion und Sozialdemokratie', in idem, *Gesammelte Schriften*, 463–89.

——, 'Der Streitpunkt in betreff des Glaubens', in idem, *Gesammelte Schriften*, 254–74.

——, 'Warum bedarf unser Glaube geschichtlicher Tatsachen?', in idem, *Gesammelte Schriften*, 214–38.

——, 'Zur theologischen Darstellung der christlichen Erfahrung', in idem, *Gesammelte Schriften*, 230–53.

——, *Dogmatik* (Gotha and Stuttgart: Verlag Friedrich Andres Perthes, 1925). ET *Systematic Theology*, trans. Nathaniel Micklem and Kenneth Sanders (London: Allen & Unwin, 1927).

——, 'Die Bedeutung der Geschichtlichkeit Jesu für den Glauben; Eine Besprechung des gleichnamigen Vortrags von Ernst Troeltsch', in idem, *Schriften zur Grundlegung der Theologie*, ed. Peter Fischer-Appelt (Munich: Chr. Kaiser Verlag, 1967), ii. 282–9.

——, 'Hermann Cohens Ethik (1907)', in idem, *Schriften zur Grundlegung der Theologie*, ii. 88–113.

——, 'Die Wirklichkeit Gottes', in idem, *Schriften zur Grundlegung der Theologie*, ii. 290–317.

——, *The Communion of the Christian with God*, trans. J. Sandys Stanyon and R. W. Stewart (Philadelphia: Fortress Press, 1971).

Hirsch, Emanuel, *Deutschlands Schicksal. Staat, Volk und Menschheit im Lichte einer ethischen Geschichtsansicht* (2nd edn.; Göttingen: Vandenhoeck & Ruprecht, 1922).

Jülicher, Adolf, 'Ein Moderner Paulus-Ausleger', in J. Moltmann (ed.), *Anfänge der dialektischen Theologie*, i. 87–98. ET 'A Modern Interpreter of Paul', in James M. Robinson (ed.), *The Beginnings of Dialectic Theology* (Richmond: John Knox Press, 1968), 72–81.

Kaftan, Julius, *Dogmatik* (7th and 8th improved edn.; Tübingen: J. C. B. Mohr, 1920).

Kant, Immanuel, *Critique of Pure Reason*, trans. Norman Kemp Smith (New York: St Martin's Press, 1965).

KATTENBUSCH, FERDINAND, *Von Schleiermacher zu Ritschl* (3rd fully revised edn., Gießen: J. Ricker'sche Verlagsbuchhandlung, 1903).

———, *Die deutsche evangelische Theologie seit Schleiermacher*, vol. ii (Gießen: Verlag von Alfred Töpelmann, 1934).

KUTTER, HERMANN, *Sie Müssen! Ein offenes Wort an die christliche Gesellschaft* (Berlin: Hermann Walther Verlagsbuchhandlung, 1904).

———, *Wir Pfarrer* (Leipzig: H. Haessel Verlag, 1907).

LOEW, WILHELM, 'Noch einmal Barths Römerbrief', *Die Christliche Welt*, 34 (1920), 585–7.

MAURY, PIERRE, *Erwählung und Glaube* (Theologische Studien, 8; Zurich: EVZ, 1940).

MENNICKE, CARL, 'Auseinandersetzung mit Karl Barth', *Blätter für Religiösen Sozialismus*, 1 (1920), 5–8.

MOLTMANN, JÜRGEN (ed.), *Anfänge der dialektischen Theologie* (2 vols.; Munich: Chr. Kaiser Verlag, 1963).

MÜLLER, HANS MICHAEL, 'Credo ut intelligam: Kritische Bemerkungen zu Karl Barths Dogmatik', *Theologische Blätter*, 7 (1928), 167–76.

OVERBECK, FRANZ, *Christentum und Kultur: Gedanken und Anmerkungen zur modernen Theologie*, ed. C. A. Bernoulli (Basle: Benno Schwabe & Co., 1919).

PETERSON, ERIK, 'Das Problem der Bibelauslegung im Pietismus des 18. Jahrhunderts', *Zeitschrift für systematische Theologie*, 1 (1923/4), 468–81.

———, 'Der Lobgesang der Engel und der mystische Lobpreis', *Zwischen den Zeiten*, 3 (1925), 141–53.

———, 'Briefwechsel mit Adolf von Harnack', in idem, *Theologische Traktate* (Munich: Kösel Verlag, 1951), 293–322.

———, 'Was ist Theologie?', in idem, *Theologische Traktate* (Munich: Kösel Verlag, 1951), 9–44.

PFISTER, OSKAR, *Die gegenwärtige Metamorphose der theologisch-kirchlichen Parteien in der Schweiz: Eine kritische Orientierung* (Zurich: Verlag von A. Frick, 1904).

PRZYWARA, ERICH, 'Gott in uns oder Gott über uns? (Immanenz und Transzendenz im heutigen Geistesleben)', *Stimmen der Zeit*, 105 (1923), 343–62.

———, 'Neue Religiosität?', *Stimmen der Zeit*, 109 (1925), 18–35.

———, 'Wesen des Katholizismus', *Stimmen der Zeit*, 108 (1925), 47–62.

———, 'Neue Theologie? Das Problem protestantischer Theologie', *Stimmen der Zeit*, 111 (1926), 348–60.

———, 'Das katholische Kirchenprinzip', *Zwischen den Zeiten*, 7 (1929), 277–302.

———, 'Problematik der Gegenwart', *Stimmen der Zeit*, 116 (1929), 99–115.

RAGAZ, LEONHARD, *Weltreich, Religion und Gottesherrschaft* (2 vols.; Erlenbach-Zürich: Rotapfel-Verlag, 1922).

RITSCHL, ALBRECHT, 'Theology and Metaphysics', in Philip Hefner (ed.), *Albrecht Ritschl: Three Essays* (Philadelphia: Fortress Press, 1972), 151–217.

RITSCHL, OTTO, *Albrecht Ritschls Leben* (2 vols.; Freiburg: J. C. B. Mohr, 1892 and 1896).

——, 'Vierundzwanzigster Brief', *Die Christliche Welt*, 41 (1927), 844–5.

——, 'Rezension über Barths *Christliche Dogmatik im Entwurf*', *Theologische Literaturzeitung*, 53 (1928), 217–28.

ROBINSON, JAMES M. (ed.), *The Beginnings of Dialectic Theology* (Richmond: John Knox Press, 1968).

SCHMID, JACQUES, 'Am Scheideweg', *Neuer Freier Aargauer: Sozialdemokratisches Tagblatt*, 14/34 (11 February 1919), 1–2.

SCHMIDT, HANS WILHELM, *Zeit und Ewigkeit: Die letzten Voraussetzungen der dialektischen Theologie* (Gütersloh: C. Bertelsmann, 1927).

THURNEYSEN, EDUARD, 'Die neue Zeit' (sermon delivered in Leutwil, 17 November 1918), in idem, *Die neue Zeit: Predigten, 1913–1930*, ed. Wolfgang Gern (Neukirchen-Vluyn: Neukirchener Verlag, 1982), 72–83.

——, *Dostojewski* (Munich: Chr. Kaiser Verlag, 1921). ET *Dostoevsky*, trans. Keith Crim (Richmond: John Knox Press, 1964).

——, 'Sozialismus und Christentum', *Zwischen den Zeiten*, 1 (1923), 58–80.

——, 'Schrift und Offenbarung', *Zwischen den Zeiten*, 2 (1924), 3–30.

——, 'Der Prologue zum Johannes-Evangelium', *Zwischen den Zeiten*, 3 (1925), 12–37.

——, *Christoph Blumhardt* (Munich: Chr. Kaiser Verlag, 1926).

——, *Das Wort Gottes und die Kirche* (Munich: Chr. Kaiser Verlag, 1927).

——, 'Zum religiös-sozialen Problem', *Zwischen den Zeiten*, 5 (1927), 513–22.

TILLICH, PAUL, 'What is Wrong with "Dialectic" Theology?', *Journal of Religion*, 15 (1935), 127–45.

——, *Systematic Theology*, vol. i. (Chicago: University of Chicago Press, 1951).

——, 'Critical and Positive Paradox: A Discussion with Karl Barth and Friedrich Gogarten', in James M. Robinson (ed.), *The Beginnings of Dialectic Theology* (Richmond: John Knox Press, 1968), 133–41.

——, 'Answer to Karl Barth', in Robinson (ed.), *The Beginnings of Dialectic Theology*, 155–8.

TRAUB, FRIEDRICH, 'Karl Barths Dogmatik', *Monatschrift für Pastoraltheologie*, 24 (1928), 77–87.

TROELTSCH, ERNST, 'Über historische und dogmatische Methode in der Theologie', in idem, *Gesammelte Schriften* (Tübingen: J. C. B. Mohr, 1913), ii. 729–53.

——, 'Half a Century of Theology: A Review', in *Ernst Troeltsch: Writings on Theology and Religion,* ed. Robert Morgan and Michael Pye (Atlanta: John Knox Press, 1977), 53–81.

——, 'The Significance of the Historical Existence of Jesus for Faith', in *Ernst Troeltsch: Writings on Theology and Religion,* ed. Morgan and Pye, 182–207.

SECONDARY LITERATURE

ANZINGER, HERBERT, *Glaube und kommunikative Praxis: Eine Studie zur "vordialektischen" Theologie Karl Barths* (Munich: Chr. Kaiser Verlag, 1991).

BAKKER, NICO T., *In der Krisis der Offenbarung: Karl Barths Hermeneutik, dargestellt an seiner Römerbrief-Auslegung* (Neukirchen-Vluyn: Neukirchener Verlag, 1974).

BALTHASAR, HANS URS VON, *Karl Barth: Darstellung und Deutung seiner Theologie* (4th edn.; Einsiedeln: Johannes Verlag, 1976).

BECK, LEWIS WHITE, 'Neokantianism', in Paul Edwards (ed.), *The Encyclopedia of Philosophy* (New York: the Macmillan Company and the Free Press, 1967), vol. v.

BECKMANN, JOACHIM, *Das Wort bleibt in Ewigkeit: Erlebte Kirchengeschichte* (Neukirchen-Vluyn: Neukirchener Verlag, 1986).

BEINTKER, MICHAEL, *Die Gottesfrage in der Theologie Wilhelm Herrmanns* (Berlin: Evangelische Verlagsanstalt, 1976).

——, 'Die christliche Dogmatik', in Gerhard Sauter (ed.), *Verkündigung und Forschung: Beihefte zur 'Evangelische Theologie',* 2 (Munich: Chr. Kaiser Verlag, 1985), 58–65.

——, 'Der Römerbrief von 1919', in Sauter (ed.), *Verkündigung und Forschung,* 2, 2–28.

——, 'Unterricht in der christlichen Religion', in Sauter (ed.), *Verkündigung und Forschung,* 2, 45–9.

——, 'Krisis und Gnade: Zur theologischen Deutung der Dialektik beim frühen Barth', *Evangelische Theologie,* 46 (1986), 442–56.

——, *Die Dialektik in der 'dialektischen Theologie' Karl Barths* (Munich: Chr. Kaiser Verlag, 1987).

BERKHOF, HENDIKUS, *Two Hundred Years of Theology* (Grand Rapids: Wm. B. Eerdmans, 1989).

BERKOUWER, G. C., *The Triumph of Grace in the Theology of Karl Barth,* trans. Harry R. Boer (Grand Rapids: Wm. B. Eerdmans, 1956).

BOUILLARD, HENRI, *Karl Barth*, i. *Genèse et évolution de la théologie dialectique* (Aubier: Editions Montagne, 1957).

BRÄNDLE, RUDOLF, and STEGEMANN, EKKEHARD (eds.), *Franz Overbecks unerledigte Anfragen an das Christentum* (Munich: Chr. Kaiser Verlag, 1988).

BRINKSCHMIDT, EGON, *Sören Kierkegaard und Karl Barth* (Neukirchen-Vluyn: Neukirchener Verlag, 1971).

BUFF, WALTER, 'Karl Barth und Emanuel Hirsch: Anmerkungen zu einem Briefwechsel', in Hans Martin Müller (ed.), *Christliche Wahrheit und neuzeitliches Denken: Zu Emanuel Hirschs Leben und Werk* (Tübingen: Katzmann Verlag, 1984).

BUSCH, EBERHARD, *Karl Barth: His Life from Letters and Autobiographical Texts* (Philadelphia: Fortress Press, 1976).

——, *Karl Barth und die Pietisten: Die Pietismuskritik des jungen Karl Barths und ihre Erwiderung* (Munich: Chr. Kaiser Verlag, 1978).

——, 'God is God: The Meaning of a Controversial Formula and the Fundamental Problem of Speaking about God', *The Princeton Seminary Bulletin*, 7 (1986), 101–13.

CRAIG, GORDON A., *Germany: 1866–1945* (Oxford: Oxford University Press, 1981).

CRIMMANN, RALPH P., *Karl Barths frühe Publikationen und ihre Rezeption* (Bern: Peter Lang, 1981).

CROSS, TERRY L., 'The Use of Dialectic in Karl Barth's Doctrine of God as Found in *Church Dogmatics*, II/1', Ph.D. dissertation (Princeton Theological Seminary, 1991).

DALFERTH, INGOLF U., 'Karl Barth's Eschatological Realism', in S. W. Sykes (ed.), *Karl Barth: Centenary Essays* (Cambridge: Cambridge University Press, 1989), 14–45.

DANNEMANN, ULRICH, *Theologie und Politik im Denken Karl Barths* (Munich and Mainz: Chr. Kaiser Verlag/Matthias-Grünewald Verlag, 1977).

——, 'Der unvollendete Abschied vom Bürgertum: Karl Barths Kritik des religiösen Sozialismus', in Günter Ewald (ed.), *Religiöser Sozialismus* (Stuttgart: Verlag W. Kohlhammer, 1977), 91–113.

——, ' "Den Gefangenen Befreiung!"—Impulse der religiös-sozialistischen Bewegung in der Theologie Karl Barths', in Martin Stöhr (ed.), *Theologische Ansätze im religiösen Sozialismus* (Frankfurt: Haag & Herchen Verlag, 1983).

DEHN, GÜNTHER, *Die alte Zeit, die vorigen Jahre: Lebenserinnerungen* (Munich: Chr. Kaiser Verlag, 1964).

DRESCHER, HANS-GEORG, 'Ernst Troeltsch's Intellectual Development', in John Powell Clayton (ed.), *Ernst Troeltsch and the Future of Theology* (Cambridge: Cambridge University Press, 1976), 3–32.

EICHER, PETER, *Bürgerliche Religion: Eine theologische Kritik* (Munich: Kösel-Verlag, 1983).

ERICKSON, ROBERT P., *Theologians under Hitler: Gerhard Kittel, Paul Althaus, and Emanuel Hirsch* (New Haven, Conn.: Yale University Press, 1985).

EVANG, MARTIN, *Rudolf Bultmann in seiner Frühzeit* (Tübingen: J. C. B. Mohr, 1988).

FÄHLER, JOCHEN, *Der Ausbruch des 1. Weltkrieges in Karl Barths Predigten, 1913–1915* (Bern: Peter Lang, 1979).

FISCHER-APPELT, PETER, 'Einleitung', in Wilhelm Herrmann, *Schriften zur Grundlegung der Theologie*, vol. i (1966).

FISHER, SIMON, *Revelatory Positivism? Barth's Earliest Theology and the Marburg School* (Oxford: Oxford University Press, 1988).

FREI, HANS, 'The Doctrine of Revelation in the Thought of Karl Barth, 1909 to 1922', Ph.D. dissertation (Yale University, 1956).

FREY, CHRISTOFER, *Die Theologie Karl Barths: Eine Einführung* (Frankfurt: Athenäum Verlag, 1988).

GAY, PETER, *Weimar Culture: The Outsider as Insider* (New York: Harper Torchbooks, 1968).

GESTRICH, CHRISTOPH, *Neuzeitliches Denken und die Spaltung der dialektischen Theologie: Zur Frage der natürlichen Theologie* (Tübingen: J. C. B. Mohr, 1977).

GOETERS, J. F. GERHARD, 'Karl Barth in Bonn, 1930–35', *Evangelische Theologie*, 47 (1987), 137–50.

GOLLWITZER, HELMUT, *Reich Gottes und Sozialismus bei Karl Barth* (Munich: Chr. Kaiser Verlag, 1972). ET (abridged) 'The Kingdom of God and Socialism', in George Hunsinger (ed.), *Karl Barth and Radical Politics* (Philadelphia: Westminster Press, 1976).

GRAF, FRIEDRICH WILHELM, ' "Der Götze wackelt"? Erste Überlegungen zu Karl Barths Liberalismus-Kritik', *Evangelische Theologie*, 46 (1986), 422–41.

——, ' "Kierkegaards junge Herren": Troeltschs Kritik der "geistigen Revolution" im frühen zwanzigsten Jahrhundert', in Horst Renz and Friedrich Wilhelm Graf (eds.), *Umstrittene Moderne: Die Zukunft der Neuzeit im Urteil der Epoche Ernst Troeltschs* (Gütersloh: Gütersloher Verlagshaus Gerd Mohn, 1987), 172–92.

——, 'Der Weimarer Barth—Ein linker Liberaler?', *Evangelische Theologie*, 47 (1987), 555–66.

GROLL, WILFRIED, *Ernst Troeltsch und Karl Barth—Kontinuität im Widerspruch* (Munich: Chr. Kaiser Verlag, 1976).

HÄRLE, WILFRIED, 'Der Anruf der 93 Intellektuellen und Karl Barths Bruch mit der liberalen Theologie', *Zeitschrift für Theologie und Kirche*, 72 (1975), 207–24.

HEPPE, HEINRICH, *Die Dogmatik der evangelisch-reformierten Kirche*: *Dargestellt und aus den Quellen belegt*, ed. Ernst Bizer (Neukirchen: Buchhandlung des Erziehungsverein Neukirchen, 1935). ET *Reformed Dogmatics*, trans. G. T. Thomson (London: Allen & Unwin, 1950; reprint edn., Grand Rapids: Baker Book House, 1978).

HERMAND, JOST, 'Unity Within Diversity? The History of the Concept "Neue Sachlichkeit" ', in Keith Bullivant (ed.), *Culture and Society in the Weimar Republic* (Manchester: Manchester University Press, 1977), 166–82.

HUBER, GERHARD, 'Heinrich Barths Philosophie', in idem, *Philosophie und christliche Existenz*: *Festschrift für Heinrich Barth* (Stuttgart/Basle: Verlag Helbing & Lichtenhahn, 1960), 199–249.

HUNSINGER, GEORGE, *How to Read Karl Barth*: *The Shape of his Theology* (New York: Oxford University Press, 1991).

—— (ed.), *Karl Barth and Radical Politics* (Philadelphia: Westminster Press, 1976).

JASPERT, BERND, 'Rudolf Bultmanns Wende von der liberalen zur dialektischen Theologie', in idem, *Rudolf Bultmanns Werk und Wirkung* (Darmstadt: Wissenschaftliche Buchgesellschaft, 1984), 25–43.

JOHNSON, ROGER, *The Origins of Demythologizing* (Leiden: E. J. Brill, 1974).

JOST, HANS ULRICH, 'Bedrohung und Enge (1914–45)', in Beatrix Mesmer (ed.), *Geschichte der Schweiz und der Schweizer* (Basle and Frankfurt: Helbing & Lichtenhahn, 1986), 731–819.

JOSUTTIS, MANFRED, *Die Gegenständlichkeit der Offenbarung*: *Karl Barths Anselmbuch und die Denkform seiner Theologie* (Bonn: H. Bouvier und Co. Verlag, 1965).

JÜNGEL, EBERHARD, *The Doctrine of the Trinity*: *God's Being is in Becoming* (Grand Rapids: Wm. B. Eerdmans, 1976).

——, 'Einführung in Leben und Werk Karl Barths', in idem, *Barth-Studien* (Zurich and Cologne: Benziger Verlag, and Gütersloh: Gütersloher Verlagshaus Gerd Mohn, 1982), 22–60.

——, 'Die theologischen Anfänge: Beobachtungen', in idem, *Barth-Studien*, 61–126.

——, 'Von der Dialektik zur Analogie: Die Schule Kierkegaards und der Einspruch Petersons', in idem, *Barth-Studien*, 127–79.

——, *God as the Mystery of the World*, trans. Darrell L. Guder (Grand Rapids: Wm. B. Eerdmans, 1983).

KANTZENBACH, FRIEDRICH WILHELM, 'Das Sozialismusproblem bei Wilhelm Herrmann', *Neue Zeitschrift für systematische Theologie*, 18 (1976), 22–43.

KOOI, CORNELIS VAN DER, *Anfängliche Theologie*: *Der Denkweg des jungen Karl Barth* (Munich: Chr. Kaiser Verlag, 1987).

KORSCH, DIETRICH, 'Christologie und Autonomie: Zu einem Interpretationsversuch der Theologie Karl Barths', *Evangelische Theologie*, 41 (1981), 142–70.

——, 'Fraglichkeit des Lebens: Karl Barth und Wilhelm Herrmann im Gespräch über Offenbarung und menschlichen Subjektivität', *Zeitschrift für dialektische Theologie*, 1 (1985), 33–51.

——, 'Intellectus fidei: Ontologischer Gottesbeweis und theologische Methode in Karl Barths Anselmbuch', in Dietrich Korsch and Hartmut Ruddies (eds.), *Wahrheit und Versöhnung: Theologische und philosophische Beiträge zur Gotteslehre* (Gütersloh: Gütersloher Verlagshaus Gerd Mohn, 1989), 125–46.

KRECK, WALTER, *Die Zukunft des Gekommenen* (Munich: Chr. Kaiser Verlag, 1966).

——, *Grundentscheidungen in Karl Barths Dogmatik* (Neukirchen-Vluyn: Neukirchener Verlag, 1978).

KUPISCH, KARL, *Zwischen Idealismus und Massendemokratie: Eine Geschichte der evangelischen Kirche in Deutschland von 1815–1945* (Berlin: Lettner Verlag, 1955).

KUTTER, HERMANN, JR., *Hermann Kutters Lebenswerk* (Zurich: EVZ, 1965).

LEHMANN, PAUL, 'Karl Barth, Theologian of Permanent Revolution', *Union Seminary Quarterly Review*, 28 (1972), 67–81.

LINDT, ANDREAS, *Leonhard Ragaz: Eine Studie zur Geschichte und Theologie des religiösen Sozialismus* (Zollikon: EVZ, 1957).

——, 'Karl Barth und der Sozialismus', *Reformatio*, 24 (1975), 394–404.

MACKEN, JOHN, *The Autonomy Theme in the "Church Dogmatics": Karl Barth and his Critics* (Cambridge: Cambridge University Press, 1990).

MARQUARDT, FRIEDRICH-WILHELM, *Der Christ in der Gesellschaft, 1919–1979: Geschichte, Analyse und aktuelle Bedeutung von Karl Barths Tambacher Vortrag* (Theologische Existenz heute, 206; Munich: Chr. Kaiser Verlag, 1980).

——, 'Erster Bericht über Karl Barths "Sozialistische Reden"', in idem, *Verwegenheiten: Theologische Stücke aus Berlin* (Munich: Chr. Kaiser Verlag, 1981), 470–88.

——, *Theologie und Sozialismus: Das Beispiel Karl Barths* (3rd edn.; Munich: Chr. Kaiser Verlag, 1985).

——, 'Der Actuar aus Barths Pfarreramt', in *Karl Barth: Der Störenfried?*, in Friedrich-Wilhelm Marquardt, Dieter Schellong, and Michael Weinrich (eds.), *Einwürfe*, 3 (Munich: Chr. Kaiser Verlag, 1986), 93–139.

——, 'Vom gepredigten Jesus zum gelehrten Christus', *Evangelische Theologie*, 46 (1986), 315–25.

MATTMÜLLER, MARKUS, *Leonhard Ragaz und der religiöse Sozialismus*, vol. ii (Zurich: EVZ, 1968).

MECHELS, EBERHARD, *Analogie bei Erich Przywara und Karl Barth: Das Verhältnis von Offenbarungstheologie und Metaphysik* (Neukirchen-Vluyn: Neukirchener Verlag, 1974).

MERZ, GEORG, 'Die Begegnung Karl Barths mit der deutschen Theologie', *Kerygma und Dogma*, 2 (1956), 157–75.

——, *Wege und Wandlungen: Erinnerungen aus der Zeit von 1892–1922* (Munich: Chr. Kaiser Verlag, 1961).

MOMMSEN, WOLFGANG J., 'Deutschland und Westeuropa: Krise und Neuorientierung der Deutschen im Übergang vom Kaiserreich zur Weimarer Republik', in Horst Renz and Friedrich Wilhelm Graf (eds.), *Umstritten Moderne: Die Zukunft der Neuzeit im Urteil der Epoche Ernst Troeltschs* (Gütersloh: Gütersloher Verlagshaus Gerd Mohn, 1987), 117–32.

MORGAN, ROBERT, 'Ernst Troeltsch and the Dialectical Theology', in John Powell Clayton (ed.), *Ernst Troeltsch and the Future of Theology* (Cambridge: Cambridge University Press, 1976), 33–77.

MORRISON, CHARLES CLAYTON, 'How their Minds Have Changed', *The Christian Century*, 56 (1939), 1194–8.

NEUSER, WILHELM, *Karl Barth in Münster, 1925–1930* (Theologische Studien, 130; Zurich: TVZ, 1985).

NÖTHIGER-STRAHM, CHRISTINE, *Der deutschschweizerische Protestantismus und der Landesstreik von 1918: Die Auseinandersetzung der Kirche mit der sozialen Frage zu Beginn des 20. Jahrhunderts* (Bern: Peter Lang, 1981).

NOWAK, KURT, 'Die "antihistorische Revolution": Symptome und Folgen der Krise historischer Weltorientierung nach dem Ersten Weltkrieg in Deutschland', in Horst Renz and Friedrich Wilhelm Graf (eds.), *Umstrittene Moderne: Die Zukunft der Neuzeit im Urteil der Epoche Ernst Troeltschs* (Gütersloh: Gütersloher Verlagshaus Gerd Mohn, 1987), 133–71.

PANNENBERG, WOLFHART, 'Introduction', in idem (ed.), *Revelation as History* (New York: The Macmillan Company, 1968), 3–21.

——, 'Die Subjektivität Gottes und die Trinitätslehre: Ein Beitrag zur Beziehung zwischen Karl Barth und der Philosophie Hegels', in idem, *Grundfragen systematischer Theologie: Gesammelte Aufsätze* (Göttingen: Vandenhoeck & Ruprecht, 1980), ii. 96–111.

PETER, NIKLAUS, 'Franz Overbeck', in Bernd Lutz (ed.), *Metzler Philosophen-Lexikon: Dreihundert biographisch-werkgeschichtliche Portraits von den Vorsokratikern bis zu den Neuen Philosophen* (Stuttgart: J. B. Metzler Verlag, 1989).

——, *Im Schatten der Modernität: Franz Overbecks Weg zur 'Christlichkeit unserer heutigen Theologie'* (Stuttgart: J. B. Metzler Verlag, 1992).

488 *Bibliography*

PÖHLMANN, HORST GEORG, *Analogia entis oder Analogia fidei? Die Frage der Analogie bei Karl Barth* (Göttingen: Vandenhoeck & Ruprecht, 1965).

POLLMANN, KLAUS ERICH, 'Evangelisch-sozialer Kongress (ESK)', in *Theologische Realenzyklopädie* (Berlin and New York: Walter de Gruyter, 1977), x. 647.

RAABE, PAUL (ed.), *The Era of German Expressionism* (Woodstock, NY: The Overlook Press, 1985).

RATHJE, JOHANNES, *Die Welt des freien Protestantismus: Ein Beitrag zur deutsch-evangelischen Geistesgeschichte, dargestellt an Leben und Werk von Martin Rade* (Stuttgart: Ehrenfried Klotz Verlag, 1952).

RENDTORFF, TRUTZ, 'Radikale Autonomie Gottes: Zum Verständnis der Theologie Karl Barths und ihrer Folgen', in idem, *Theorie des Christentums* (Gütersloh: Gütersloher Verlagshaus Gerd Mohn, 1972), 161–81.

—— (ed.), *Die Realisierung der Freiheit* (Gütersloh: Gütersloher Verlagshaus Gerd Mohn, 1975).

——, 'The Modern Age as a Chapter in the History of Christianity; or, The Legacy of Historical Consciousness in Present Theology', *Journal of Religion*, 65 (1985), 478–99.

——, 'Karl Barth und die Neuzeit: Fragen zur Barth-Forschung', *Evangelische Theologie*, 46 (1986), 298–314.

RICHMOND, JAMES, *Ritschl: A Reappraisal* (London: Collins, 1978).

ROBERTS, RICHARD, 'The Reception of the Theology of Karl Barth in the Anglo-Saxon World: History, Typology and Prospect', in Stephen W. Sykes (ed.), *Karl Barth: Centenary Essays* (Cambridge: Cambridge University Press, 1989), 115–71.

RUDDIES, HARTMUT, 'Karl Barth im Kulturprotestantismus: Eine theologische Problemanzeige', in Dietrich Korsch and Hartmut Ruddies (eds.), *Wahrheit und Versöhnung: Theologische und philosophische Beiträge zur Gotteslehre* (Gütersloh: Gütersloher Verlagshaus Gerd Mohn, 1989), 193–231.

——, 'Karl Barth und Ernst Troeltsch: Aspekte eines unterbliebenen Dialogs', in Horst Renz and Friedrich Wilhelm Graf (eds.), *Umstrittene Moderne: Die Zukunft der Neuzeit im Urteil der Epoche Ernst Troeltschs* (Gütersloh: Gütersloher Verlagshaus Gerd Mohn, 1987), 230–58.

——, 'Karl Barth und Martin Rade: Ein theologisch-politischer Briefwechsel', *Evangelische Theologie*, 44 (1984), 298–306.

——, 'Karl Barth und Wilhelm Herrmann: Aspekte aus den Anfängen der dialektischen Theologie' *Zeitschrift für dialektische Theologie*, 1 (1985), 52–89.

RUMSCHEIDT, H. MARTIN, *Revelation and Theology: An Analysis of the*

Barth–Harnack Correspondence of 1923 (Cambridge: Cambridge University Press, 1972).

RUPP, GEORGE, *Culture-Protestantism: German Liberal Theology at the Turn of the Twentieth Century* (Missoula, Mont.: Scholars Press, 1977).

RUSCHKE, WERNER, *Entstehung und Ausführung der Diastasentheologie in Karl Barths zweitem Römerbrief* (Neukirchen-Vluyn: Neukirchener Verlag, 1987).

SAUTER, GERHARD, 'Die "dialektische Theologie" und das Problem der Dialektik in der Theologie', in idem, *Erwartung und Erfahrung: Predigten, Vorträge und Aufsätze* (Munich: Chr. Kaiser Verlag, 1972), 108–46.

——, 'Weichenstellungen im Denken Karl Barths', *Evangelische Theologie*, 46 (1986), 476–88.

SCHELLONG, DIETER, *Bürgertum und christliche Religion* (Munich: Chr. Kaiser Verlag, 1975).

——, 'Barth Lesen', in *Karl Barth: Der Störenfried?*, in Friedrich-Wilhelm Marquardt, Dieter Schellong and Michael Weinrich (eds.), *Einwürfe*, 3 (Munich: Chr. Kaiser Verlag, 1986), 5–92.

SCHMID, HEINRICH, *Die Dogmatik der evangelisch-lutherischen Kirche: Dargestellt und aus den Quellen belegt*, ed. Horst Georg Pöhlmann (Gütersloh: Gütersloher Verlagshaus Gerd Mohn, 1983). ET *Doctrinal Theology of the Evangelical Lutheran Church*, trans. Charles A. Hay and Henry E. Jacobs (Minneapolis: Augsburg Publishing House, 1961).

SCHOLDER, KLAUS, 'Neuere deutsche Geschichte und protestantische Theologie: Aspekte und Fragen', *Evangelische Theologie*, 23 (1963), 510–36.

SCHORSKE, CARL E., *German Social Democracy, 1905–1917: The Development of the Great Schism* (Cambridge, Mass.: Harvard University Press, 1955).

SCHREY, H.-H., 'Religiöser Sozialismus', *Religion in Geschichte und Gegenwart*, 3rd edn. (Tübingen: J. C. B. Mohr (Paul Siebeck), 1957), vi. 182.

SHINER, LARRY, *The Secularization of History: An Introduction to the Theology of Friedrich Gogarten* (Nashville: Abingdon Press, 1966).

SMART, JAMES D., *The Divided Mind of Modern Theology: Karl Barth and Rudolf Bultmann, 1908–1933* (Philadelphia: Westminster Press, 1967).

SMITH, STEVEN G., *The Argument to the Other: Reason beyond Reason in the Thought of Karl Barth and Emmanuel Levinas* (Chico, Calif.: Scholars Press, 1983).

SPIECKERMANN, INGRID, *Gotteserkenntnis: Ein Beitrag zur Grundfrage der neuen Theologie Karl Barths* (Munich: Chr. Kaiser Verlag, 1985).

STADTLAND, TJARKO, *Eschatologie und Geschichte in der Theologie des jungen Karl Barth* (Neukirchen-Vluyn: Neukirchener Verlag, 1966).

STECK, K. G., and SCHELLONG, DIETER, *Karl Barth und die Neuzeit* (Munich: Chr. Kaiser Verlag, 1973).

STEPHAN, HORST, and SCHMIDT, MARTIN, *Geschichte der evangelischen Theologie in Deutschland seit dem Idealismus* (3rd edn.; Berlin: Walter de Gruyter, 1973).

SYKES, STEPHEN W. (ed.), *Karl Barth: Studies of his Theological Method* (Oxford: Oxford University Press, 1979).

TANNER, KLAUS, 'Antiliberale Harmonie: Zum politischen Grundkonsens in Theologie und Rechtswissenschaft der zwanziger Jahre', in Horst Renz and Friedrich Wilhelm (eds.), *Umstrittene Moderne: Die Zukunft der Neuzeit im Urteil der Epoche Ernst Troeltschs* (Gütersloh: Gütersloher Verlagshaus Gerd Mohn, 1987), 193–208.

TERAN-DUTARI, JULIO, 'Die Geschichte des Terminus "*Analogia Entis*" und das Werk Erich Pryzwaras', *Philosophisches Jahrbuch der Görres-Gesellschaft*, 77 (1970), 163–79.

THURNEYSEN, EDUARD, *Karl Barth: "Theologie und Sozialismus" in den Briefen seiner Frühzeit* (Zurich: TVZ, 1973).

TÖDT, HEINZ EDUARD, 'Karl Barth, der Liberalismus und der Nationalsozialismus', *Evangelische Theologie*, 46 (1986), 536–51.

TORRANCE, T. F., 'Theology of Karl Barth', *The Scotsman*, 14 April 1952.

——, *Karl Barth: An Introduction to his Early Theology, 1910–1931* (London: SCM Press, 1962).

TRACK, JOACHIM, 'Analogie', *Theologische Realenzyklopädie*, ii. 625–50.

TRILLHAAS, WOLFGANG, 'Karl Barth in Göttingen', in Dietrich Rössler, Gottfried Voigt and Friedrich Wintzer (eds.), *Fides et communicatio: Festschrift für Martin Doerne* (Göttingen: Vandenhoeck & Ruprecht, 1970), 362–75.

——, *Aufgehobene Vergangenheit: Aus meinem Leben* (Göttingen: Vandenhoeck & Ruprecht, 1976).

——, 'Emanuel Hirsch in Göttingen', in Hans Martin Müller (ed.), *Christliche Wahrheit und neuzeitliches Denken: zu Emanuel Hirschs Leben und Werk* (Tübingen: Katzmann Verlag, 1984), 220–39.

——, 'Der Einbruch der Dialektischen Theologie in Göttingen und Emanuel Hirsch', in Bernd Moeller (ed.), *Theologie in Göttingen* (Göttingen: Vandenhoeck & Ruprecht, 1987), 362–79.

ULLMANN, WOLFGANG, 'Karl Barths zweite Wende. Eine neuer Interpretationsvorschlag zu "Fides quaerens intellectum"', in Heidelore Köckert and Wolf Krötke (eds.), *Theologie als Christologie* (Berlin: Evangelische Verlagsanstalt, 1988), 71–89.

WALLACE, MARK I., 'Karl Barth's Hermeneutic: A Way beyond the Impasse?', *Journal of Religion*, 68 (1988), 396–410.

WARD, W. R., *Theology, Sociology and Politics: The German Protestant Social Conscience, 1890–1933* (Bern: Peter Lang, 1979).

WEBB, STEPHEN H., *Re-figuring Theology: The Rhetoric of Karl Barth* (Albany, NY: State University of New York Press, 1991).

WINZELER, PETER, *Widerstehende Theologie: Karl Barth, 1920–35* (Stuttgart: Alektor Verlag, 1982).

—— , 'Der Sozialismus Karl Barths in der neuesten Kritik', *Evangelische Theologie*, 48 (1988), 262–72.

Name Index

Subject Index